Dictionary of Literary Biography

72 *French Novelists, 1930-1960,* edited by Catharine Savage Brosman (1988)

73 *American Magazine Journalists, 1741-1850,* edited by Sam G. Riley (1988)

74 *American Short-Story Writers Before 1880,* edited by Bobby Ellen Kimbel, with the assistance of William E. Grant (1988)

75 *Contemporary German Fiction Writers, Second Series,* edited by Wolfgang D. Elfe and James Hardin (1988)

76 *Afro-American Writers, 1940-1955,* edited by Trudier Harris (1988)

77 *British Mystery Writers, 1920-1939,* edited by Bernard Benstock and Thomas F. Staley (1988)

78 *American Short-Story Writers, 1880-1910,* edited by Bobby Ellen Kimbel, with the assistance of William E. Grant (1988)

79 *American Magazine Journalists, 1850-1900,* edited by Sam G. Riley (1988)

80 *Restoration and Eighteenth-Century Dramatists, First Series,* edited by Paula R. Backscheider (1989)

81 *Austrian Fiction Writers, 1875-1913,* edited by James Hardin and Donald G. Daviau (1989)

82 *Chicano Writers, First Series,* edited by Francisco A. Lomelí and Carl R. Shirley (1989)

83 *French Novelists Since 1960,* edited by Catharine Savage Brosman (1989)

84 *Restoration and Eighteenth-Century Dramatists, Second Series,* edited by Paula R. Backscheider (1989)

85 *Austrian Fiction Writers After 1914,* edited by James Hardin and Donald G. Daviau (1989)

86 *American Short-Story Writers, 1910-1945, First Series,* edited by Bobby Ellen Kimbel (1989)

87 *British Mystery and Thriller Writers Since 1940, First Series,* edited by Bernard Benstock and Thomas F. Staley (1989)

88 *Canadian Writers, 1920-1959, Second Series,* edited by W. H. New (1989)

89 *Restoration and Eighteenth-Century Dramatists, Third Series,* edited by Paula R. Backscheider (1989)

90 *German Writers in the Age of Goethe, 1789-1832,* edited by James Hardin and Christoph E. Schweitzer (1989)

91 *American Magazine Journalists, 1900-1960, First Series,* edited by Sam G. Riley (1990)

92 *Canadian Writers, 1890-1920,* edited by W. H. New (1990)

93 *British Romantic Poets, 1789-1832, First Series,* edited by John R. Greenfield (1990)

94 *German Writers in the Age of Goethe: Sturm und Drang to Classicism,* edited by James Hardin and Christoph E. Schweitzer (1990)

95 *Eighteenth-Century British Poets, First Series,* edited by John Sitter (1990)

96 *British Romantic Poets, 1789-1832, Second Series,* edited by John R. Greenfield (1990)

97 *German Writers from the Enlightenment to Sturm und Drang, 1720-1764,* edited by James Hardin and Christoph E. Schweitzer (1990)

98 *Modern British Essayists, First Series,* edited by Robert Beum (1990)

99 *Canadian Writers Before 1890,* edited by W. H. New (1990)

100 *Modern British Essayists, Second Series,* edited by Robert Beum (1990)

101 *British Prose Writers, 1660-1800, First Series,* edited by Donald T. Siebert (1991)

102 *American Short-Story Writers, 1910-1945, Second Series,* edited by Bobby Ellen Kimbel (1991)

103 *American Literary Biographers, First Series,* edited by Steven Serafin (1991)

104 *British Prose Writers, 1660-1800, Second Series,* edited by Donald T. Siebert (1991)

105 *American Poets Since World War II, Second Series,* edited by R. S. Gwynn (1991)

106 *British Literary Publishing Houses, 1820-1880,* edited by Patricia J. Anderson and Jonathan Rose (1991)

107 *British Romantic Prose Writers, 1789-1832, First Series,* edited by John R. Greenfield (1991)

108 *Twentieth-Century Spanish Poets, First Series,* edited by Michael L. Perna (1991)

109 *Eighteenth-Century British Poets, Second Series,* edited by John Sitter (1991)

110 *British Romantic Prose Writers, 1789-1832, Second Series,* edited by John R. Greenfield (1991)

111 *American Literary Biographers, Second Series,* edited by Steven Serafin (1991)

112 *British Literary Publishing Houses, 1881-1965,* edited by Jonathan Rose and Patricia J. Anderson (1991)

113 *Modern Latin-American Fiction Writers, First Series,* edited by William Luis (1992)

114 *Twentieth-Century Italian Poets, First Series,* edited by Giovanna Wedel De Stasio, Glauco Cambon, and Antonio Illiano (1992)

115 *Medieval Philosophers,* edited by Jeremiah Hackett (1992)

116 *British Romantic Novelists, 1789-1832,* edited by Bradford K. Mudge (1992)

117 *Twentieth-Century Caribbean and Black African Writers, First Series,* edited by Bernth Lindfors and Reinhard Sander (1992)

118 *Twentieth-Century German Dramatists, 1889-1918,* edited by Wolfgang D. Elfe and James Hardin (1992)

119 *Nineteenth-Century French Fiction Writers: Romanticism and Realism, 1800-1860,* edited by Catharine Savage Brosman (1992)

120 *American Poets Since World War II, Third Series,* edited by R. S. Gwynn (1992)

121 *Seventeenth-Century British Nondramatic Poets, First Series,* edited by M. Thomas Hester (1992)

122 *Chicano Writers, Second Series,* edited by Francisco A. Lomelí and Carl R. Shirley (1992)

123 *Nineteenth-Century French Fiction Writers: Naturalism and Beyond, 1860-1900,* edited by Catharine Savage Brosman (1992)

124 *Twentieth-Century German Dramatists, 1919-1992,* edited by Wolfgang D. Elfe and James Hardin (1992)

125 *Twentieth-Century Caribbean and Black African Writers, Second Series,* edited by Bernth Lindfors and Reinhard Sander (1993)

126 *Seventeenth-Century British Nondramatic Poets, Second Series,* edited by M. Thomas Hester (1993)

127 *American Newspaper Publishers, 1950-1990,* edited by Perry J. Ashley (1993)

128 *Twentieth-Century Italian Poets, Second Series,* edited by Giovanna Wedel De Stasio, Glauco Cambon, and Antonio Illiano (1993)

129 *Nineteenth-Century German Writers, 1841-1900,* edited by James Hardin and Siegfried Mews (1993)

130 *American Short-Story Writers Since World War II,* edited by Patrick Meanor (1993)

131 *Seventeenth-Century British Nondramatic Poets, Third Series,* edited by M. Thomas Hester (1993)

132 *Sixteenth-Century British Nondramatic Writers, First Series,* edited by David A. Richardson (1993)

133 *Nineteenth-Century German Writers to 1840,* edited by James Hardin and Siegfried Mews (1993)

134 *Twentieth-Century Spanish Poets, Second Series,* edited by Jerry Phillips Winfield (1994)

135 *British Short-Fiction Writers, 1880-1914: The Realist Tradition,* edited by William B. Thesing (1994)

136 *Sixteenth-Century British Nondramatic Writers, Second Series,* edited by David A. Richardson (1994)

137 *American Magazine Journalists, 1900-1960, Second Series,* edited by Sam G. Riley (1994)

138 *German Writers and Works of the High Middle Ages: 1170-1280,* edited by James Hardin and Will Hasty (1994)

139 *British Short-Fiction Writers, 1945-1980,* edited by Dean Baldwin (1994)

140 *American Book-Collectors and Bibliographers, First Series,* edited by Joseph Rosenblum (1994)

141 *British Children's Writers, 1880-1914,* edited by Laura M. Zaidman (1994)

142 *Eighteenth-Century British Literary Biographers,* edited by Steven Serafin (1994)

143 *American Novelists Since World War II, Third Series,* edited by James R. Giles and Wanda H. Giles (1994)

144 *Nineteenth-Century British Literary Biographers,* edited by Steven Serafin (1994)

145 *Modern Latin-American Fiction Writers, Second Series,* edited by William Luis and Ann González (1994)

146 *Old and Middle English Literature,* edited by Jeffrey Helterman and Jerome Mitchell (1994)

147 *South Slavic Writers Before World War II,* edited by Vasa D. Mihailovich (1994)

148 *German Writers and Works of the Early Middle Ages: 800-1170,* edited by Will Hasty and James Hardin (1994)

149 *Late Nineteenth- and Early Twentieth-Century British Literary Biographers,* edited by Steven Serafin (1995)

150 *Early Modern Russian Writers, Late Seventeenth and Eighteenth Centuries,* edited by Marcus C. Levitt (1995)

151 *British Prose Writers of the Early Seventeenth Century,* edited by Clayton D. Lein (1995)

152 *American Novelists Since World War II, Fourth Series,* edited by James R. Giles and Wanda H. Giles (1995)

153 *Late-Victorian and Edwardian British Novelists, First Series,* edited by George M. Johnson (1995)

154 *The British Literary Book Trade, 1700-1820,* edited by James K. Bracken and Joel Silver (1995)

155 *Twentieth-Century British Literary Biographers,* edited by Steven Serafin (1995)

156 *British Short-Fiction Writers, 1880-1914: The Romantic Tradition,* edited by William F. Naufftus (1995)

157 *Twentieth-Century Caribbean and Black African Writers, Third Series,* edited by Bernth Lindfors and Reinhard Sander (1995)

158 *British Reform Writers, 1789-1832,* edited by Gary Kelly and Edd Applegate (1995)

159 *British Short-Fiction Writers, 1800-1880,* edited by John R. Greenfield (1996)

160 *British Children's Writers, 1914-1960,* edited by Donald R. Hettinga and Gary D. Schmidt (1996)

161 *British Children's Writers Since 1960, First Series,* edited by Caroline Hunt (1996)

162 *British Short-Fiction Writers, 1915-1945,* edited by John H. Rogers (1996)

163 *British Children's Writers, 1800-1880,* edited by Meena Khorana (1996)

164 *German Baroque Writers, 1580-1660,* edited by James Hardin (1996)

165 *American Poets Since World War II, Fourth Series,* edited by Joseph Conte (1996)

166 *British Travel Writers, 1837-1875,* edited by Barbara Brothers and Julia Gergits (1996)

167 *Sixteenth-Century British Nondramatic Writers, Third Series,* edited by David A. Richardson (1996)

168 *German Baroque Writers, 1661-1730,* edited by James Hardin (1996)

169 *American Poets Since World War II, Fifth Series,* edited by Joseph Conte (1996)

170 *The British Literary Book Trade, 1475-1700,* edited by James K. Bracken and Joel Silver (1996)

171 *Twentieth-Century American Sportswriters,* edited by Richard Orodenker (1996)

172 *Sixteenth-Century British Nondramatic Writers, Fourth Series,* edited by David A. Richardson (1996)

173 *American Novelists Since World War II, Fifth Series,* edited by James R. Giles and Wanda H. Giles (1996)

174 *British Travel Writers, 1876-1909,* edited by Barbara Brothers and Julia Gergits (1997)

175 *Native American Writers of the United States,* edited by Kenneth M. Roemer (1997)

176 *Ancient Greek Authors,* edited by Ward W. Briggs (1997)

177 *Italian Novelists Since World War II, 1945-1965,* edited by Augustus Pallotta (1997)

178 *British Fantasy and Science-Fiction Writers Before World War I,* edited by Darren Harris-Fain (1997)

179 *German Writers of the Renaissance and Reformation, 1280-1580,* edited by James Hardin and Max Reinhart (1997)

180 *Japanese Fiction Writers, 1868-1945,* edited by Van C. Gessel (1997)

181 *South Slavic Writers Since World War II,* edited by Vasa D. Mihailovich (1997)

182 *Japanese Fiction Writers Since World War II,* edited by Van C. Gessel (1997)

183 *American Travel Writers, 1776-1864,* edited by James J. Schramer and Donald Ross (1997)

184 *Nineteenth-Century British Book-Collectors and Bibliographers,* edited by William Baker and Kenneth Womack (1997)

185 *American Literary Journalists, 1945-1995, First Series,* edited by Arthur J. Kaul (1998)

186 *Nineteenth-Century American Western Writers,* edited by Robert L. Gale (1998)

187 *American Book Collectors and Bibliographers, Second Series,* edited by Joseph Rosenblum (1998)

188 *American Book and Magazine Illustrators to 1920,* edited by Steven E. Smith, Catherine A. Hastedt, and Donald H. Dyal (1998)

189 *American Travel Writers, 1850-1915,* edited by Donald Ross and James J. Schramer (1998)

190 *British Reform Writers, 1832-1914,* edited by Gary Kelly and Edd Applegate (1998)

191 *British Novelists Between the Wars,* edited by George M. Johnson (1998)

192 *French Dramatists, 1789-1914,* edited by Barbara T. Cooper (1998)

193 *American Poets Since World War II, Sixth Series,* edited by Joseph Conte (1998)

194 *British Novelists Since 1960, Second Series,* edited by Merritt Moseley (1998)

195 *British Travel Writers, 1910-1939,* edited by Barbara Brothers and Julia Gergits (1998)

196 *Italian Novelists Since World War II, 1965-1995,* edited by Augustus Pallotta (1999)

197 *Late-Victorian and Edwardian British Novelists, Second Series,* edited by George M. Johnson (1999)

198 *Russian Literature in the Age of Pushkin and Gogol: Prose,* edited by Christine A. Rydel (1999)

199 *Victorian Women Poets,* edited by William B. Thesing (1999)

200 *American Women Prose Writers to 1820,* edited by Carla J. Mulford, with Angela Vietto and Amy E. Winans (1999)

201 *Twentieth-Century British Book Collectors and Bibliographers,* edited by William Baker and Kenneth Womack (1999)

202 *Nineteenth-Century American Fiction Writers,* edited by Kent P. Ljungquist (1999)

203 *Medieval Japanese Writers,* edited by Steven D. Carter (1999)

204 *British Travel Writers, 1940-1997,* edited by Barbara Brothers and Julia M. Gergits (1999)

205 *Russian Literature in the Age of Pushkin and Gogol: Poetry and Drama,* edited by Christine A. Rydel (1999)

206 *Twentieth-Century American Western Writers, First Series,* edited by Richard H. Cracroft (1999)

207 *British Novelists Since 1960, Third Series,* edited by Merritt Moseley (1999)

208 *Literature of the French and Occitan Middle Ages: Eleventh to Fifteenth Centuries,* edited by Deborah Sinnreich-Levi and Ian S. Laurie (1999)

209 *Chicano Writers, Third Series,* edited by Francisco A. Lomelí and Carl R. Shirley (1999)

210 *Ernest Hemingway: A Documentary Volume,* edited by Robert W. Trogdon (1999)

211 *Ancient Roman Writers,* edited by Ward W. Briggs (1999)

212 *Twentieth-Century American Western Writers, Second Series,* edited by Richard H. Cracroft (1999)

213 *Pre-Nineteenth-Century British Book Collectors and Bibliographers,* edited by William Baker and Kenneth Womack (1999)

214 *Twentieth-Century Danish Writers,* edited by Marianne Stecher-Hansen (1999)

215 *Twentieth-Century Eastern European Writers, First Series,* edited by Steven Serafin (1999)

216 *British Poets of the Great War: Brooke, Rosenberg, Thomas. A Documentary Volume,* edited by Patrick Quinn (2000)

217 *Nineteenth-Century French Poets,* edited by Robert Beum (2000)

218 *American Short-Story Writers Since World War II, Second Series,* edited by Patrick Meanor and Gwen Crane (2000)

219 *F. Scott Fitzgerald's* The Great Gatsby: *A Documentary Volume,* edited by Matthew J. Bruccoli (2000)

220 *Twentieth-Century Eastern European Writers, Second Series,* edited by Steven Serafin (2000)

221 *American Women Prose Writers, 1870-1920,* edited by Sharon M. Harris, with the assistance of Heidi L. M. Jacobs and Jennifer Putzi (2000)

222 *H. L. Mencken: A Documentary Volume,* edited by Richard J. Schrader (2000)

223 *The American Renaissance in New England, Second Series,* edited by Wesley T. Mott (2000)

224 *Walt Whitman: A Documentary Volume,* edited by Joel Myerson (2000)

225 *South African Writers,* edited by Paul A. Scanlon (2000)

226 *American Hard-Boiled Crime Writers,* edited by George Parker Anderson and Julie B. Anderson (2000)

227 *American Novelists Since World War II, Sixth Series,* edited by James R. Giles and Wanda H. Giles (2000)

228 *Twentieth-Century American Dramatists, Second Series,* edited by Christopher J. Wheatley (2000)

229 *Thomas Wolfe: A Documentary Volume,* edited by Ted Mitchell (2001)

230 *Australian Literature, 1788-1914,* edited by Selina Samuels (2001)

231 *British Novelists Since 1960, Fourth Series,* edited by Merritt Moseley (2001)

232 *Twentieth-Century Eastern European Writers, Third Series,* edited by Steven Serafin (2001)

233 *British and Irish Dramatists Since World War II, Second Series,* edited by John Bull (2001)

234 *American Short-Story Writers Since World War II, Third Series,* edited by Patrick Meanor and Richard E. Lee (2001)

235 *The American Renaissance in New England, Third Series,* edited by Wesley T. Mott (2001)

236 *British Rhetoricians and Logicians, 1500-1660,* edited by Edward A. Malone (2001)

237 *The Beats: A Documentary Volume,* edited by Matt Theado (2001)

238 *Russian Novelists in the Age of Tolstoy and Dostoevsky,* edited by J. Alexander Ogden and Judith E. Kalb (2001)

239 *American Women Prose Writers: 1820-1870,* edited by Amy E. Hudock and Katharine Rodier (2001)

240 *Late Nineteenth- and Early Twentieth-Century British Women Poets,* edited by William B. Thesing (2001)

241 *American Sportswriters and Writers on Sport,* edited by Richard Orodenker (2001)

Documentary Series

1 *Sherwood Anderson, Willa Cather, John Dos Passos, Theodore Dreiser, F. Scott Fitzgerald, Ernest Hemingway, Sinclair Lewis,* edited by Margaret A. Van Antwerp (1982)

2 *James Gould Cozzens, James T. Farrell, William Faulkner, John O'Hara, John Steinbeck, Thomas Wolfe, Richard Wright,* edited by Margaret A. Van Antwerp (1982)

3 *Saul Bellow, Jack Kerouac, Norman Mailer, Vladimir Nabokov, John Updike, Kurt Vonnegut,* edited by Mary Bruccoli (1983)

4 *Tennessee Williams,* edited by Margaret A. Van Antwerp and Sally Johns (1984)

5 *American Transcendentalists,* edited by Joel Myerson (1988)

6 *Hardboiled Mystery Writers: Raymond Chandler, Dashiell Hammett, Ross Macdonald,* edited by Matthew J. Bruccoli and Richard Layman (1989)

7 *Modern American Poets: James Dickey, Robert Frost, Marianne Moore,* edited by Karen L. Rood (1989)

8 *The Black Aesthetic Movement,* edited by Jeffrey Louis Decker (1991)

9 *American Writers of the Vietnam War: W. D. Ehrhart, Larry Heinemann, Tim O'Brien, Walter McDonald, John M. Del Vecchio,* edited by Ronald Baughman (1991)

10 *The Bloomsbury Group,* edited by Edward L. Bishop (1992)

11 *American Proletarian Culture: The Twenties and The Thirties,* edited by Jon Christian Suggs (1993)

12 *Southern Women Writers: Flannery O'Connor, Katherine Anne Porter, Eudora Welty,* edited by Mary Ann Wimsatt and Karen L. Rood (1994)

13 *The House of Scribner, 1846-1904,* edited by John Delaney (1996)

14 *Four Women Writers for Children, 1868-1918,* edited by Caroline C. Hunt (1996)

15 *American Expatriate Writers: Paris in the Twenties,* edited by Matthew J. Bruccoli and Robert W. Trogdon (1997)

16 *The House of Scribner, 1905-1930,* edited by John Delaney (1997)

17 *The House of Scribner, 1931-1984,* edited by John Delaney (1998)

18 *British Poets of The Great War: Sassoon, Graves, Owen,* edited by Patrick Quinn (1999)

19 *James Dickey,* edited by Judith S. Baughman (1999)

See also DLB 210, 216, 219, 222, 224, 229, 237

Yearbooks

1980 edited by Karen L. Rood, Jean W. Ross, and Richard Ziegfeld (1981)

1981 edited by Karen L. Rood, Jean W. Ross, and Richard Ziegfeld (1982)

1982 edited by Richard Ziegfeld; associate editors: Jean W. Ross and Lynne C. Zeigler (1983)

1983 edited by Mary Bruccoli and Jean W. Ross; associate editor Richard Ziegfeld (1984)

1984 edited by Jean W. Ross (1985)

1985 edited by Jean W. Ross (1986)

1987 edited by J. M. Brook (1988)

1988 edited by J. M. Brook (1989)

1989 edited by J. M. Brook (1990)

1990 edited by James W. Hipp (1991)

1991 edited by James W. Hipp (1992)

1992 edited by James W. Hipp (1993)

1993 edited by James W. Hipp, contributing editor George Garrett (1994)

1994 edited by James W. Hipp, contributing editor George Garrett (1995)

1995 edited by James W. Hipp, contributing editor George Garrett (1996)

1996 edited by Samuel W. Bruce and L. Kay Webster, contributing editor George Garrett (1997)

1997 edited by Matthew J. Bruccoli and George Garrett, with the assistance of L. Kay Webster (1998)

1998 edited by Matthew J. Bruccoli, contributing editor George Garrett, with the assistance of D. W. Thomas (1999)

1999 edited by Matthew J. Bruccoli, contributing editor George Garrett, with the assistance of D. W. Thomas (2000)

2000 edited by Matthew J. Bruccoli, contributing editor George Garrett, with the assistance of George Parker Anderson (2001)

Concise Series

Concise Dictionary of American Literary Biography, 7 volumes (1988-1999): *The New Consciousness, 1941-1968; Colonization to the American Renaissance, 1640-1865; Realism, Naturalism, and Local Color, 1865-1917; The Twenties, 1917-1929; The Age of Maturity, 1929-1941; Broadening Views, 1968-1988; Supplement: Modern Writers, 1900-1998.*

Concise Dictionary of British Literary Biography, 8 volumes (1991-1992): *Writers of the Middle Ages and Renaissance Before 1660; Writers of the Restoration and Eighteenth Century, 1660-1789; Writers of the Romantic Period, 1789-1832; Victorian Writers, 1832-1890; Late-Victorian and Edwardian Writers, 1890-1914; Modern Writers, 1914-1945; Writers After World War II, 1945-1960; Contemporary Writers, 1960 to Present.*

Concise Dictionary of World Literary Biography, 10 volumes projected (1999-): *Ancient Greek and Roman Writers; German Writers; African, Caribbean, and Latin American Writers; South Slavic and Eastern European Writers.*

Dictionary of Literary Biography® • Volume Two Hundred Forty-one

American Sportswriters and Writers on Sport

Dictionary of Literary Biography® • Volume Two Hundred Forty-one

American Sportswriters and Writers on Sport

Edited by
Richard Orodenker
Penn State Abington

A Bruccoli Clark Layman Book
The Gale Group
Detroit • San Francisco • London • Boston • Woodbridge, Conn.

Matthew J. Bruccoli and Richard Layman, Editorial Directors
C. E. Frazer Clark Jr., Managing Editor
Karen L. Rood, Senior Editor

Printed in the United States of America

The paper used in this publication meets the minimum requirements of American National Standard for Information Sciences–Permanence Paper for Printed Library Materials, ANSI Z39.48-1984. ∞™

Library of Congress Cataloging-in-Publication Data

American sportswriters and writers on sport / edited by Richard Orodenker.
p. cm.–(Dictionary of literary biography: v. 241)
"A Bruccoli Clark Layman book."
Includes bibliographical references and index.
ISBN 0-7876-4658-X (alk. paper)
1. Sportswriters–United States–Biography–Dictionaries. I. Orodenker, Richard. II. Series.

GV742.4.A64 2001
797.4'49796'0922–dc21 2001023165
[B]

10 9 8 7 6 5 4 3 2 1

For my world—Robyn, Emily, and Todd

Contents

Plan of the Series

... Almost the most prodigious asset of a country, and perhaps its most precious possession, is its native literary product–when that product is fine and noble and enduring.

Mark Twain*

The advisory board, the editors, and the publisher of the *Dictionary of Literary Biography* are joined in endorsing Mark Twain's declaration. The literature of a nation provides an inexhaustible resource of permanent worth. Our purpose is to make literature and its creators better understood and more accessible to students and the reading public, while satisfying the needs of teachers and researchers.

To meet these requirements, *literary biography* has been construed in terms of the author's achievement. The most important thing about a writer is his writing. Accordingly, the entries in *DLB* are career biographies, tracing the development of the author's canon and the evolution of his reputation.

The purpose of *DLB* is not only to provide reliable information in a usable format but also to place the figures in the larger perspective of literary history and to offer appraisals of their accomplishments by qualified scholars.

The publication plan for *DLB* resulted from two years of preparation. The project was proposed to Bruccoli Clark by Frederick G. Ruffner, president of the Gale Research Company, in November 1975. After specimen entries were prepared and typeset, an advisory board was formed to refine the entry format and develop the series rationale. In meetings held during 1976, the publisher, series editors, and advisory board approved the scheme for a comprehensive biographical dictionary of persons who contributed to literature. Editorial work on the first volume began in January 1977, and it was published in 1978. In order to make *DLB* more than a dictionary and to compile volumes that individually have claim to status as literary history, it was decided to organize volumes by topic, period, or genre. Each of these freestanding volumes provides a biographical-bibliographical guide and overview for a particular area of literature. We are convinced that this organization–as opposed to a single alphabet method–constitutes a valuable innovation in the presentation of reference material. The volume plan necessarily requires many decisions for the placement and treatment of authors. Certain figures will be included in separate volumes, but with different entries emphasizing the aspect of his career appropriate to each volume. Ernest Hemingway, for example, is represented in *American Writers in Paris, 1920–1939* by an entry focusing on his expatriate apprenticeship; he is also in *American Novelists, 1910–1945* with an entry surveying his entire career, as well as in *American Short-Story Writers, 1910–1945, Second Series* with an entry concentrating on his short fiction. Each volume includes a cumulative index of the subject authors and articles.

Since 1981 the series has been further augmented by the *DLB Yearbooks,* which update published entries, add new entries to keep the *DLB* current with contemporary activity, and provide articles on literary history. There have also been nineteen *DLB Documentary Series* volumes which provide illustrations, facsimiles, and biographical and critical source materials for figures works, or groups judged to have particular interest for students. In 1999 the *Documentary Series* was incorporated into the *DLB* volume numbering system beginning with *DLB 210, Ernest Hemingway.*

We define literature as the *intellectual commerce of a nation:* not merely as belles lettres but as that ample and complex process by which ideas are generated, shaped, and transmitted. *DLB* entries are not limited to "creative writers" but extend to other figures who in their time and in their way influenced the mind of a people. Thus the series encompasses historians, journalists, publishers, book collectors, and screenwriters. By this means readers of *DLB* may be aided to perceive literature not as cult scripture in the keeping of intellectual high priests but firmly positioned at the center of a nation's life.

DLB includes the major writers appropriate to each volume and those standing in the ranks behind them. Scholarly and critical counsel has been sought in

**From an unpublished section of Mark Twain's autobiography, copyright by the Mark Twain Company*

deciding which minor figures to include and how full their entries should be. Wherever possible, useful references are made to figures who do not warrant separate entries.

Each *DLB* volume has an expert volume editor responsible for planning the volume, selecting the figures for inclusion, and assigning the entries. Volume editors are also responsible for preparing, where appropriate, appendices surveying the major periodicals and literary and intellectual movements for their volumes, as well as lists of further readings. Work on the series as a whole is coordinated at the Bruccoli Clark Layman editorial center in Columbia, South Carolina, where the editorial staff is responsible for accuracy and utility of the published volumes.

One feature that distinguishes *DLB* is the illustration policy–its concern with the iconography of literature. Just as an author is influenced by his surroundings, so is the reader's understanding of the author enhanced by a knowledge of his environment. Therefore *DLB* volumes include not only drawings, paintings, and photographs of authors, often depicting them at various stages in their careers, but also illustrations of their families and places where they lived. Title pages are regularly reproduced in facsimile along with dust jackets for modern authors. The dust jackets are a special feature of *DLB* because they often document better than anything else the way in which an author's work was perceived in its own time. Specimens of the writers' manuscripts and letters are included when feasible.

Samuel Johnson rightly decreed that "The chief glory of every people arises from its authors." The purpose of the *Dictionary of Literary Biography* is to compile literary history in the surest way available to us–by accurate and comprehensive treatment of the lives and work of those who contributed to it.

The *DLB* Advisory Board

Introduction

DLB 241: American Sportswriters and Writers on Sport continues the plan developed in *DLB 171: Twentieth-Century American Sportswriters,* but the present volume also includes the work of nineteenth-century sportswriters and certain writers born after 1930. As Herbert Warren Wind noted in *The Realm of Sport* (1966): "the hundred years between 1815 and 1915 may well have been the heyday of the literary reporter. In those days, when travel was hard and few people really got around, when concerts and plays and lectures were about the only diversions even in capital cities and when, to be sure, there were no such mass media as the movies, radio, and television, the writer was the great entertainer. How well the best ones knew their craft, from Nimrod to Churchill."

The essence of sports, distinguished from the business of sports, reflects Josef Pieper's description, from *Leisure: The Basis of Culture* (1952), of leisure as "an attitude of mind, a condition of the soul." Early sportswriters, Henry Chadwick most prominent among them, regarded sports in this way and connected them to the life of the nation and the nature of man. Sports became part of the record of American culture and its phenomena, although many early influences were English, including the aforementioned Nimrod (Charles James Apperley), Pierce Egan, and Robert Smith Surtees, whose subjects were the manly sports of hunting, horses, and boxing. Chadwick was born in England, but he became an American citizen and the first important baseball scribe. He extolled American core values and beliefs, such as self-reliance, sportsmanship, and healthy competition, values that were essential to juvenile sports literature at the turn of the century. Ray Robinson, in his *Matty: An American Hero* (1993), compares early-twentieth-century pitching great Christy Mathewson to the fictional hero Frank Merriwell, noting of the latter:

> From 1896 to 1914 Merriwell was the beau ideal of millions who read about his singular exploits and feats of derring-do in *TipTop Weekly,* the most popular five-cent novel of its era. Merriwell played every sport under the sun. He was a dominant pitcher in baseball, a superb halfback in football, a powerful stroke on the crew . . . , and he was also a whiz in boxing, lacrosse, golf, track, and billiards. More important, Merriwell possessed a spotless character: he didn't drink or smoke, stood for truth, justice, family, loyalty, duty, patriotism, friendship, right over wrong. He was anti-snob, anti-bully, and pro-tolerance. In short, he represented the heroic residue of late nineteenth century passions.

Sportswriters after 1914 began to branch out into different schools of writing. John R. Tunis, in his *$port$: Heroics and Hysterics* (1928), was critical of sportswriters who encouraged what he called the "Great Sports Myth":

> These gentry–the newsgatherer, and the new professional sports uplifter–tell us that competitive sport, as well as informal, unorganized, sport, is health-giving, character-building, brain-making. They imply, more or less directly, that its exponents are heroes, possessed of none but the highest moral qualities; tempered and steeled in the great, white heat of competition; purified and made holy by their devotion to intercollegiate and international sport. Thanks to them–and to others not entirely disinterested–there has grown up in the public mind an exaggerated and sentimental notion of the moral value of great, competitive, sports spectacles.

The writers that Tunis objected to made up the "Gee Whiz" school of hyperbolic, grandiose sportswriting, including figures such as Paul Gallico and Richards Vidmer, who were often capable of tempering their excesses with excellent writing. Others worked out of the comic tradition of Mark Twain, whose "Celebrated Jumping Frog of Calaveras County" (1865) is often considered to be one of the first great works of American sports literature; these writers, Ring Lardner and Dan Parker among them, formed the "Aw Nuts" school. The writing was funny, often acerbic, and sometimes derisive. Many sportswriters still wrote in the tradition of the nineteenth century and gradually settled into Stanley Woodward's "On the Button" school of sports journalism, characterized by straight reportage and fidelity to the source, whether it was the game they were covering or the player they were interviewing. This group included writers Frank Graham and Jesse Abramson.

Sportswriting in the twentieth century was also characterized by regionalism and occasionally a bit of local color. *The Oxford Companion to American Literature* defines regionalism as laying "stress upon quaint oddities of dialect, mannerism, and custom and . . . basic philosophical or sociological differences." Malcolm Bingay in Detroit, Halsey Hall in Minnesota, and Fred Russell in Nashville, as well as sportswriters from Brooklyn to Boston, regularly employed elements of regional writing in their stories. Such writing usually focused on oddball fans and other local characters, familiar settings (such as taverns), and rivalries between nearby cities. J. Roy Stockton of the *St. Louis Post-Dispatch,* for example, caught the Midwest sensibility in his profile of Iowa-born pitching great Bob Feller and Feller's father, Bill, for his *The Gashouse Gang and a Couple of Other Guys* (1945):

> Neighbors thought that William Andrew Feller, of Van Meter, Iowa, must have fallen on his head when he was a boy. Bill Feller did the strangest things. He was forever playing catch with his boy, throwing and catching a baseball, while other farmers were putting in, tending, or harvesting their crops.
>
> It is fine to have a strong son when you are tilling a 360-acre farm. The boy can feed and water the stock, plow the corn, and he's no end of help generally. But Bill Feller didn't even a plant corn and oats, which, generally are considered the best crops in that part of Iowa. He planted wheat. Wheat didn't require so much attention. That left more time for playing catch.

Between the two world wars African American newspapers turned to sports, focusing mainly on the issue of integration after World War II. At first, integration was an issue mainly in the black press, but from there it entered the mainstream of the national media. Black sportswriters became key players in the sports integration saga. Because black newspapers often operated on low budgets, writers frequently found themselves wearing several hats. Black sportswriters such as Joe Bostic and Dan Burley doubled as editors, columnists, and entertainment reporters. African American sportswriters could also be "Gee Whiz," "Aw Nuts," or "On the Button" types; as Jim Reisler further notes in his *Black Writers/Black Baseball* (1994), black writers, upon the abandonment of "bland, longish game summaries, with the occasional analysis sounding more like summaries of military strategy and few, if any, player or manager profiles or quotes," took up the practice of writing regular sports columns about the same time white columnists did, in the mid 1920s. Their writing was heightened by the appearance of several distinctive black sports figures of the era, especially Joe Louis and Satchel Paige. In addition to Bostic and Burley, Frank A. Young of the *Chicago Defender* and A. S. "Doc" Young are other African American sportswriters to appear in this volume.

The sports-feature writer, represented in this volume by Jim Murray, Al Stump, Ed Linn, George Plimpton, and David Halberstam, was an outgrowth of the development of sportswriting during the last century. In the late 1880s a major newspaper was likely to print fewer than one hundred columns of sports news during the year. Yet, that number was a significant increase from the previous decades, and it appeared to be growing. By the late 1930s nearly one hundred columns–a twelve-page sports section–were likely to appear in the typical Sunday edition alone. Sportswriting, fairly or unfairly, long had been considered, as Stanley Woodward noted in *Sports Page* (1949), "a low form of art." By the 1940s, however, it had risen in stature, so much so that the novelist Dawn Powell could remark about a newspaper reporter in her 1954 book *The Wicked Pavilion* that he "had hoped for assignments in the field of sports but the editor felt that literary training and education were required for that." As sports magazines flourished in the 1950s and 1960s and the number of newspapers diminished, the sports column became a regular and lasting feature of the genre.

Also of importance were sports editors, such as J. G. Taylor Spink of *The Sporting News,* F. C. Lane of *Baseball* magazine, and Nat Fleischer of *Ring,* all of whom demonstrated a high degree of professionalism and influence. Fleischer helped set the tone for much of the journeyman boxing prose written during the twentieth century, while Spink, according to Fred Lieb in *Baseball as I Have Known It* (1977), was a "fearless" and "daring" editor, "famous for . . . his unflagging energy for work" and "for his knowledge of baseball and all sports people."

Sports books have earned a secure niche in the marketplace, but they have undergone a publishing boom in the last several years, encompassing not just the traditional categories, but also works on professional wrestling and NASCAR. In an issue devoted entirely to the subject (20 March 2000), *Publishers Weekly* observed: "Sports publishing continues to strive as it diversifies. It takes nothing for granted anymore and has become one of our fastest moving, alternative areas of the publishing industry." Some small publishers and university presses have devoted themselves to reprinting older, "classic" titles in the field, particularly baseball. These books in many cases often provide the only examples of extant sportswriting from past eras. Without these primary works, one must turn to historical and biographical books to find some early examples of sportswriting, where they appear as secondary sources and usually in snippets.

The authors of these books and other sports literature still exhibit the influence of sportswriters of the past centuries. Some sportswriters portray modern champions with a certain amount of awe, if not quite in the manner of Merriwell or Mathewson. After he became the youngest player ever to win a Grand Slam in golf and become, at age twenty-four, arguably the greatest golfer in history, Tiger Woods was seen by *Time* magazine, in a 14 August 2000 cover story, as a different kind of Frank Merriwell for the new millennium: "It's that personality almost as much as his athletic prowess that has allowed him to become all things to all people. He is youthful but not callow, self-assured but never cocky, intelligent without seeming intellectual. And he remains, in his megastardom, a wary and private man." The lineage of those observations was set down long ago, from the early days of baseball to the Golden Age of sports in the 1920s and 1930s.

Other sportswriters prefer to dispel myths–even those myths worth preserving–left behind by sportswriters of old. Did Walter Camp himself (as Grantland Rice asserted) come up with the idea of the All-American college football team? No doubt he developed it, promoted it, and created its modern equivalent, but, as Jack Newcombe writes in *The Fireside Book of Football* (1964), "he must at least share authorship of the very earliest All Americans with one Casper Whitney, who began picking them for *The Week's Sports* in 1889." Did Bill Veeck indeed plan to buy the 1943 Philadelphia Phillies and stock the team with Negro League ballplayers, as he attests in his autobiography, *Veeck–As in Wreck*? Not according to David Jordan, Larry Gerlach, and John Rossi in *The National Pastime* (1998): "The major difficulty with this oft-told story is that it is not true. Veeck did not have a deal to buy the Phillies. He did not work with Abe Saperstein and others to stock any team with Negro League stars. No such deal was quashed by Landis or Frick. In fact, there was hardly any Veeck-Phillies connection at all."

As the entries in this volume try to show, on the one hand, sportswriters have written with much originality and variety, even when they are not gifted stylists and sometimes when they stray far from the field. They cannot be defined by a single adjective, even when they seem to fall into one of the three schools of sportswriting and whether or not they are classified as reporters, columnists, or feature writers. Richard P. Goldman, an anthologist of sportswriting, assembled for his 1958 collection *Sportswriters' Choice* "several examples of excellent straight reporting, a historical essay, a poem, biography, several analytical articles, a piece that could be termed fact-fiction, some expose stories, humor, anger, nostalgia, whimsy, sorrow, bitterness. They are all part of the broad field of sportswriting."

On the other hand, sportswriters have often been some of the best critics of their own field. Robert Lipsyte once quipped: "Well-meaning people often ask sportswriters, even middle-age sportswriters, what they are going to do when they grow up." Each paragraph of Bob Addie's famous piece "The Sportswriter," which appeared originally in *The Washington Post and Times Herald* on 13 August 1957 and was reprinted in *Best Sports Stories 1958: A Panorama of the 1957 Sports Year,* points to what Addie thought was "a composite picture of a sportswriter . . . with all his foibles and his eternally juvenile heart." Among his many qualities is that "He is quick to defend and slow to offend. He can count on the fingers of one hand the number of athletes who have ever thanked him for a story but if he had a dime for every guy who threatened him when he wrote a critical story, he'd be too rich to write sports." Roger O'Gara, a sportswriter for the *Berkshire* (Mass.) *Evening Eagle,* wrote what it was like to be a "Small-Town Sports Writer" in a 7 November 1952 column: "You climb into the rickety press box, argue with some hanger-on that he has your seat, and prepare to cover the game. You're a study in concentration, because you realize that you must be. If you should miss a play, it's gone, brother, irretrievably gone. Turn to the student spotter, if there is such a bird, and he'll tell you that he was looking the other way, or lighting a cigarette. No, he didn't catch who made the tackle." The lot of the small-town sportswriter has likely remained essentially the same.

Finally, contemporary sportswriting has shed itself of certain antediluvian fashions, although it has lost some of its zing because of political correctness and tendentiousness. More women, for example, now cover major sports–a long way from Blackie Sherrod's lament in the *Fort Worth Press* (29 October 1954) after a female reporter was assigned to cover a Southern Methodist University–Kansas game: "Shove a skillet in their hands, and they'll play ping pong with it. They fly airplanes, charge into bullrings and race downhill on bobsleds. But press boxes, please no. Someone help, we are sinking into the gulf. Spare the last straw. Keep the last standard, tattered though it is, nailed to the mast." In the early part of the century, women sportswriters were seen as something of novelties. As Harold Seymour reports in *Baseball: The People's Game* (1990), "Ina Eloise Young, sports editor of a Trinidad, Colorado, daily, received national publicity when she covered the 1908 World Series. Two years later a Pittsburgh paper sent one of its women reporters to cover the Pirates during spring training, but the editor published her stories on the society page instead of the sports page." Nonetheless, women writers have made some lasting contributions to the genre. Julia Harpman, who occasionally covered women's sports in the 1920s, wrote a piece in 1926 on Gertrude Ederle, the first woman to swim the English Channel. Recent times have seen women writing on sports, from novelist Joyce Carol Oates to historian Doris Kearns Goodwin. To a greater degree women's sports are commanding more attention and respect, as are the writers who cover them regularly. Associated Press sportswriter Beth Harris's reports from a sold-out Rose Bowl on the U.S. victory over China for the 1999 FIFA Women's World Cup soccer title were particularly notable. Other beat reporters, such as Claire Smith of the *Philadelphia Inquirer,* also write about mainstream sports.

The best sportswriting demonstrates what Alistair Cooke, in *Fun and Games: On Sport and Other Amusements* (1995), called "the 'isle of joy' offered by sport in an ocean of anxieties." For others, the formula is simpler. Jim Murray wrote in the introduction to *The Best of Jim Murray* (1965): "The only thing I know for sure about sports is that they need dramatizing." In his *The Joy of Sports* (1967), the religious philosopher Michael Novak calls to mind the daunting task the sportswriter faces in attempting to dramatize the familiar:

> There is no substitute for the squeak of sneakers on the court and the sound of the ball slipping through the cords. No words are as adequate as the cool sheen of a baseball fresh from its paper wrapper, tossed to the pitcher at the height of the last game of the World Series. No analysis does justice to the instantaneous decision of a quarterback, trapped on his goal line in the waning seconds of a game, to snap the pigskin toward a blurred target at his distant 30-yard line. To talk about sports without recreating their drama, feel, and excitement would render one worthy of death by continuous committee meetings, from which fate God spare us all.

Acknowledgments

This book was produced by Bruccoli Clark Layman, Inc. Karen L. Rood is senior editor. Charles Brower was the in-house editor. He was assisted by Philip B. Dematteis, Nicole Lyles, and George Anderson.

Production manager is Philip B. Dematteis.

Administrative support was provided by Ann M. Cheschi, Amber L. Coker, and Angi Pleasant.

Accounting supervisor is Ann-Marie Holland.

Copyediting supervisor is Phyllis A. Avant. The copyediting staff includes Brenda Carol Blanton, Brenda Cabra, Allen E. Friend Jr., Melissa D. Hinton, William Tobias Mathes, Rebecca Mayo, Nancy E. Smith, and Elizabeth Jo Ann Sumner.

Editorial associates are Andrew Choate and Michael S. Martin.

Database manager is José A. Juarez.

Layout and graphics supervisor is Janet E. Hill. The graphics staff includes Karla Corley Brown and Zoe R. Cook.

Office manager is Kathy Lawler Merlette.

Photography supervisor is Paul Talbot. Photography editors are Charles Mims and Scott Nemzek.

Permissions editor is Jeff Miller.

Digital photographic copy work was performed by Joseph M. Bruccoli.

The SGML staff includes Frank Graham, Linda Dalton Mullinax, Jason Paddock, and Alex Snead.

Systems manager is Marie L. Parker.

Typesetting supervisor is Kathleen M. Flanagan. The typesetting staff includes Patricia Marie Flanagan, Mark J. McEwan, Pamela D. Norton, and Alison Smith. Freelance typesetters are Wanda Adams and Vicki Grivetti.

Walter W. Ross did library research. He was assisted by Steven Gross and the following librarians at the Thomas Cooper Library of the University of South Carolina: circulation department head Tucker Taylor; reference department head Virginia W. Weathers; Brette Barclay, Marilee Birchfield, Paul Cammarata, Gary Geer, Michael Macan, Tom Marcil, Rose Marshall, and Sharon Verba; interlibrary loan department head John Brunswick; and interlibrary loan staff Robert Arndt, Hayden Battle, Barry Bull, Jo Cottingham, Marna Hostetler, Marieum McClary, Erika Peake, and Nelson Rivera.

Dictionary of Literary Biography® • Volume Two Hundred Forty-one

American Sportswriters and Writers on Sport

Dictionary of Literary Biography

Jesse Abramson

(10 March 1904 - 10 June 1979)

Adam R. Hornbuckle

MAJOR POSITIONS HELD: Sportswriter, *New York Herald* (1922–1924); sportswriter, *New York Herald Tribune* (1924–1967).

SELECTED PERIODICAL PUBLICATION–UNCOLLECTED: "New Records for Old," *Princeton Athletic News,* 15 June 1935, p. 7.

OTHER: "Hagg vs. Rice," in *A.A.U., National Track and Field Championships* [program], 19–20 June 1943;

"Olympian Heights," in *Sports Extra: Classics of Sports Reporting,* edited by Stanley Frank (New York: Barnes, 1944), pp. 213–218;

"Agony in Atlanta," "Patience + Persistence + Power = 4:07.3," in *Best Sports Stories of 1944: A Panorama of the 1944 Sports Year,* edited by Irving T. Marsh and Edward Ehre (New York: Dutton, 1945), pp. 89–92, 159–162;

"'Pore Little Boys' Get Rich," in *Best Sports Stories of 1945: A Panorama of the 1945 Sports Year,* edited by Marsh and Ehre (New York: Dutton, 1946), pp. 91–94;

"End of a Dynasty," in *Best Sports Stories of 1946: A Panorama of the 1946 Sports Year,* edited by Marsh and Ehre (New York: Dutton, 1947), pp. 197–199;

"Home Come the Sailors," in *Best Sports Stories of 1947: A Panorama of the 1947 Sports Year,* edited by Marsh and Ehre (New York: Dutton, 1948), pp. 227–231;

"Track and Field," in *Sport's Golden Age: A Close-Up of the Fabulous Twenties,* edited by Allison Danzig and Peter Brandwein (New York: Harper, 1948), pp. 228–242;

Jesse Peter Abramson

"Middie Miracle," in *Best Sports Stories of 1948: A Panorama of the 1948 Sports Year,* edited by Marsh and Ehre (New York: Dutton, 1949), pp. 17–23;

"Wreck of the Ram," in *Best Sports Stories of 1949: A Panorama of the 1949 Sports Year,* edited by Marsh and Ehre (New York: Dutton, 1950), pp. 91–95;

"No Upset?" in *Best Sports Stories of 1950: A Panorama of the 1950 Sports Year,* edited by Marsh and Ehre (New York: Dutton, 1951), pp. 105–109;

"Architect of Triumph," in *Best Sports Stories of 1951: A Panorama of the 1951 Sports Year,* edited by Marsh and Ehre (New York: Dutton, 1952), pp. 145–148;

"Melted Sugar," in *Best Sports Stories of 1952: A Panorama of the 1952 Sports Year,* edited by Marsh and Ehre (New York: Dutton, 1953), pp. 19–23;

"Legalized Mayhem," in *Best Sports Stories of 1953: A Panorama of the 1953 Sports Year,* edited by Marsh and Ehre (New York: Dutton, 1954), pp. 195–197;

"Bobo and the Kid," in *Best Sports Stories of 1954: A Panorama of the 1954 Sports Year,* edited by Marsh and Ehre (New York: Dutton, 1955), pp. 158–161;

"Bannister Says Olympics Tougher than 3:59.4 Mile," in *Wake Up the Echoes, from the Sports Pages of the New York Herald Tribune,* edited by Bob Cooke (Garden City, N.Y.: Hanover House, 1956), pp. 58–60;

"The Tables Turn," in *Best Sports Stories of 1957: A Panorama of the 1957 Sports Year,* edited by Marsh and Ehre (New York: Dutton, 1958), pp. 21–25;

"The Perils of Archie," in *Best Sports Stories of 1958: A Panorama of the 1958 Sports Year,* edited by Marsh and Ehre (New York: Dutton, 1959), pp. 25–27;

"The Right Was the Might," in *Best Sports Stories of 1959: A Panorama of the 1959 Sports Year,* edited by Marsh and Ehre (New York: Dutton, 1960), pp. 139–142;

"Winter–Book on Olympics," in *Annual Indoor Games: New York Athletic Club, 1868–1960* [program], 13 February 1960;

"How to Select an Olympic Team," in *84th Annual Outdoor Track and Field Championships of the Intercollegiate Association of Amateur Athletes of America* [program], 27–28 May 1960, p. 5;

"NYAC Brings Back the Nationals," in *Annual Indoor Games: New York Athletic Club, 1868–1961* [program], 17 February 1961;

"ICAAAA Loses Two Old Friends," in *40th Annual Indoor Track and Field Championships of the Intercollegiate Association of Amateur Athletes of America* [program], 11 March 1961, pp. 14, 45;

"The Best Bet That Lost," in *Best Sports Stories of 1960: A Panorama of the 1960 Sports Year,* edited by Marsh and Ehre (New York: Dutton, 1961), pp. 163–167;

"Miler Jim Beatty–Giant Killer," in *Annual Indoor Games: New York Athletic Club, 1868–1962* [program], 16 February 1962, p. 11;

"The I.C.A.A.A.A. Welcomes Uncle Eddie," in *41st Annual Indoor Track and Field Championships of the Intercollegiate Association of Amateur Athletes of America* [program], 10 March 1962, pp. 4, 54;

"Dateline Moscow: Yanks Beat Reds," in *Best Sports Stories of 1961: A Panorama of the 1961 Sports Year,* edited by Marsh and Ehre (New York: Dutton, 1962), pp. 255–259;

"2 Minutes 6 Seconds After 2 Years," in *Best Sports Stories of 1962: A Panorama of the 1962 Sports Year,* edited by Marsh and Ehre (New York: Dutton, 1963), pp. 126–129;

"Meet the Olympic Coach," in *57th Annual Invitational Indoor Games of the Millrose Athletic Association* [program], 30 January 1964, pp. 11, 82;

"30th Reunion–Baxter Mile," in *Annual Indoor Games: New York Athletic Club, 1868–1964* [program], 13 February 1964, pp. 11, 44;

"45 Years–K. of C. Meets," in *45th Anniversary Indoor Athletic Meet of the New York Chapter, Knights of Columbus* [program], 27 February 1964, pp. 6–7;

"First, Let's Beat the Russians," in *76th Annual National Amateur Athletic Union Track and Field Championships* [program], 27–28 June 1964, p. 39;

"The Newest Fastest Human," in *Best Sports Stories of 1963: A Panorama of the 1963 Sports Year,* edited by Marsh and Ehre (New York: Dutton, 1964), pp. 255–257;

"Rollie's Revenge," in *Best Sports Stories of 1964: A Panorama of the 1964 Sports Year,* edited by Marsh and Ehre (New York: Dutton, 1965), pp. 113–115;

"Robinson's Pipedream," in *Best Sports Stories of 1965: A Panorama of the 1965 Sports Year,* edited by Marsh and Ehre (New York: Dutton, 1966), pp. 23–25;

"Stalemate," in *Best Sports Stories of 1966: A Panorama of the 1966 Sports Year,* edited by Marsh and Ehre (New York: Dutton, 1967), pp. 95–97;

"Meet Director Turns Author," in *The Wanamaker Millrose Story: History of the Millrose Athletic Association: 1908–1967,* by Fred Schmertz (Yonkers, N.Y.: Millrose Athletic Association, 1967), p. 11;

"A Centennial for Indoor Track," in *Annual Indoor Games: New York Athletic Club, Centennial Anniversary, 1868–1968* [program], 16 February 1968, pp. 25, 29, 50;

"They Stamped Their Names on the Games," in *48th Annual Indoor Track and Field Championships of the Intercollegiate Association of Amateur Athletes of America* [program], 28 March 1969, pp. 4, 43;

"The Bushnell Years," in *94th Annual Outdoor Track and Field Championships of the Intercollegiate Association of Amateur Athletes of America* [program], 29–30 May 1970, pp. 4–5;

"The Millrose Pantheon . . . Three-Time Winners Only," in *65th Annual Invitational Indoor Games of the Millrose Athletic Association* [program], 28 January 1972, pp. 16–17;

"State of the Union–Dept. of Track," in *66th Annual Invitational Indoor Games of the Millrose Athletic Association* [program], 26 January 1973, pp. 14–16;

"In 1973 U.S. Trackmen Recover," in *67th Annual Invitational Indoor Games of the Millrose Athletic Association* [program], 25 January 1974, pp. 12, 14;

"Finally, a Wanamaker Mile that begins with a '3'," in *68th Annual Invitational Indoor Games of the Millrose Athletic Association* [program], 31 January 1975, pp. 59–61;

"Millrose Memories . . . and Afterthoughts," in *71st Annual Invitational Indoor Games of the Millrose Athletic Association* [program], 30 January 1976, pp. 14, 15, 87;

"Millrose Memories with Footnotes," in *72nd Annual Invitational Indoor Games of the Millrose Athletic Association* [program], 27 January 1978, pp. 17, 43;

"Confessions of a Meet Head," in *United States Olympic Committee (USOC) Invitational Indoor Track and Field Meet* [program], 4 February 1978, pp. 10, 38.

Jesse Peter Abramson, longtime sportswriter for *The New York Herald Tribune,* was known as "The Book" among his contemporaries for his profound knowledge of sports and his extraordinary recollection for detail. An encounter between him and a former Intercollegiate Association of Amateur Athletes of America (IC4A) track-and-field champion, recalled by Red Smith in his 11 June 1979 obituary for Abramson in *The New York Times,* illustrates the appropriateness of that nickname. As Abramson and other journalists were checking into the Poland Spring Hotel near Lewiston, Maine, to cover the 1965 rematch between Cassius Clay and Sonny Liston for the world heavyweight boxing championship, he recognized James L. Reid, then a prominent Maine judge, in the hotel lobby. As a Harvard undergraduate Reid had won the IC4A two-mile championship in 1928 and 1929. Asked by one reporter his best time in that race, the judge proudly replied "about 9:20." Instantly, Abramson's authoritative voice declared: "Oh, no, Jim, you were never that fast. You did 9:22." To settle the issue Reid sent a courier to his chambers in Augusta for his scrapbook. With the evidence in hand the judge turned to a faded clipping, which proved that "The Book" was indeed correct: Reid's winning time was 9 minutes, 22 seconds.

Although his expertise was most apparent with respect to track and field, Abramson wrote authoritatively about boxing, college football, baseball, swimming, fencing, rowing, and automobile racing. Smith described him as "a fanatically accurate reporter: tireless, inquisitive and informed, with a healthy skepticism and gift for weaving color, background and incident into the fabric of a news story." These traits brought Abramson exceptional recognition from the E. P. Dutton Publishing Company: his stories appeared in each volume of its *Best Sports Stories* series from 1944 to 1967. Five times, in 1948, 1952, 1957, 1958, and 1965, his stories were included among Dutton's prizewinning stories of the year. Dutton judge Quentin Reynolds described Abramson's first prizewinning essay, "Middie Miracle," which described the 1948 Army-Navy football game that ended in a 21–21 tie for the undefeated cadets and winless midshipmen, as "the kind of story Abramson writes day in and day out for the *New York Herald Tribune.*" The following passage from that article demonstrates his ability to thread color, background, and incident into a story.

> President Harry S Truman sitting throughout on the Navy side, remaining to the last play, standing with the rest and craning his neck over a midshipman guard of honor in front of him, lent plausibility to another implausible score to which Navy, reasonably enough, reacted as though it were one of the greatest triumphs in its gridiron history. It was a Trumanesque kind of incredible battle that the midshipmen fought to achieve their fully-earned tie with less than five minutes to go.

Abramson began writing about sports for *The New York Herald* in the early 1920s, a decade known as the Golden Age of American sports. During the 1920s the popular appeal of sports rose dramatically, as the public became fascinated with the exploits of sports heroes such as baseball player Babe Ruth and boxer Jack Dempsey. Perhaps most responsible for this phenomenon was a new generation of journalists, the "gee whiz" school of writers, who created images of athletes that often overwhelmed the individual's actual achievement. Although influenced in the beginning by their exaggerated hyperbolic style, Abramson nevertheless developed his own deliberate and authoritative approach, in which he reported the evolution of a football game, a track-and-field meet, or a prizefight in such a way that the reader had the sense of witnessing the event himself.

Born on 10 March 1904 in Mountaindale, a small village in the Catskill Mountains, near Spring Valley, New York, Jesse was the son of Louis, a tailor, and Minnie Virship Abramson. His birth, however, was recorded officially as 11 May, because the courier whom his family had sent to register his birth procrastinated for an entire day. Moreover, he was registered only as Peter Abramson. Soon after his birth the family moved to the Brooklyn borough of New York City. In 1922 Abramson served as editor of the Stuyvesant High School yearbook and graduated valedictorian from the Manhattan-based public high school.

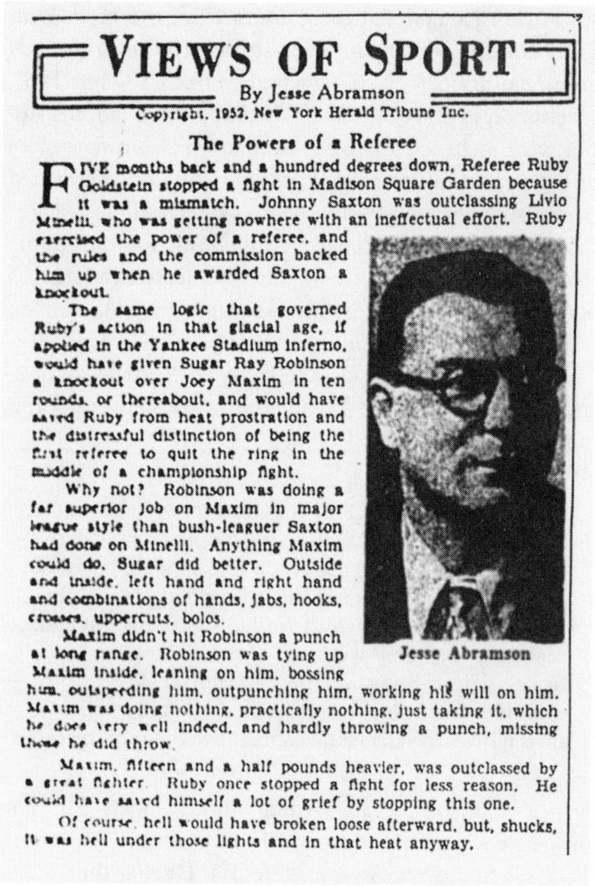

VIEWS OF SPORT

By Jesse Abramson

Copyright, 1952, New York Herald Tribune Inc.

The Powers of a Referee

FIVE months back and a hundred degrees down, Referee Ruby Goldstein stopped a fight in Madison Square Garden because it was a mismatch. Johnny Saxton was outclassing Livio Minelli, who was getting nowhere with an ineffectual effort. Ruby exercised the power of a referee, and the rules and the commission backed him up when he awarded Saxton a knockout.

The same logic that governed Ruby's action in that glacial age, if applied in the Yankee Stadium inferno, would have given Sugar Ray Robinson a knockout over Joey Maxim in ten rounds, or thereabout, and would have saved Ruby from heat prostration and the distressful distinction of being the first referee to quit the ring in the middle of a championship fight.

Why not? Robinson was doing a far superior job on Maxim in major league style than bush-leaguer Saxton had done on Minelli. Anything Maxim could do, Sugar did better. Outside and inside, left hand and right hand and combinations of hands, jabs, hooks, crosses, uppercuts, bolos.

Maxim didn't hit Robinson a punch at long range. Robinson was tying up Maxim inside, leaning on him, bossing him, outspeeding him, outpunching him, working his will on him. Maxim was doing nothing, practically nothing, just taking it, which he does very well indeed, and hardly throwing a punch, missing those he did throw.

Maxim, fifteen and a half pounds heavier, was outclassed by a great fighter. Ruby once stopped a fight for less reason. He could have saved himself a lot of grief by stopping this one.

Of course, hell would have broken loose afterward, but, shucks, it was hell under those lights and in that heat anyway.

Jesse Abramson

Head for Abramson's column for 27 June 1952

Although accepted by Columbia University for enrollment in the fall of 1922, Abramson instead took a position as a stringer in the sports department of *The New York Herald* about a week before the beginning of the semester. "I was only being paid per story," Abramson told Chuck Stogel in a 24 June 1978 *Sportscope* interview, "but I was lucky to have a friendly editor who would put one column of mine in the first edition and then a fresh copy in the second edition. I was able to make about $125 a week as a stringer, which was as much as anybody working full-time back then." As a young journalist Abramson "was doing all right," as he modestly recalled, working for one of the oldest and most prestigious newspapers in the nation with some of the nation's best sportswriters.

As a stringer Abramson covered local high-school sports for *The New York Herald.* His report of the 1922 Public School Athletic League (PSAL) cross-country championship demonstrated his penchant for accuracy and attention to vivid detail. Abramson's description of the winning performance by Samuel Greenefege of Flushing High School, from the 9 October 1922 *New York Herald,* exemplifies his early craft: "The Flushing lad left his mark very slowly when the starter sent the field away, and he was far back of the pacemakers during the running of the first mile. Unlike the average schoolboy, he did not attempt to make up the lost ground at the start. He decided to wait on the pacemakers comparatively fresh to move up rapidly toward the end. Passing one runner after another as if they were standing still Greenefege went to the front in the last half mile and won by 100 yards."

Abramson continued to hone the authoritative journalistic style that came to characterize his writing with reports on high-school football games and track-and-field meets and profiles of outstanding prep performers. He also wrote a weekly column, "With the Scholastic Athletes," which summarized the highlights of high-school and college freshman sports in the New York metropolitan area.

One of Abramson's most memorable moments covering high-school track and field came in 1923 when he witnessed the establishment of an apparent world record in the hundred-yard dash. "It was at Wingate Field in Brooklyn," as he told Stogel, "and Frank Hussey ran a would-be world record 9.6 seconds in the 100 yard dash at the PSAL championships." Public School Athletic League officials, however, did not believe it and did not allow the record to stand. The officials concluded that "no man can run that fast," Abramson observed. "Something like that had also happened in the 1890s." Hussey's 1923 performance, official or not, was a portent of things to come, as he won the hundred-yard dash in the 1925 Amateur Athletic Union Championships in 9.8 seconds.

In 1924 *The New York Herald* became *The New York Herald Tribune* and hired Grantland Rice to cover the 1924 Summer Olympic Games from Paris. Transmitted by cable, his reports arrived to the sports desk in a condensed text that needed to be rewritten for publication. Abramson was given the assignment of rewriting Rice's stories. "You see, at that time," Abramson explained to Stogel, "all overseas copy was sent in cable-ese. It was an abbreviated transmission of mostly verbs and nouns to save money. We'd rewrite the stories by filling in the rest of the needed words." Although it is difficult to determine which stories Abramson rewrote himself, he more than likely wrote the following description, from the 8 July 1924 edition of the *Herald Tribune,* of the raising of the British flag following the unexpected victory of Harold Abrahams in the 100 meters, over the highly acclaimed Americans Charley Paddock, Jackson Scholz, Chester Bowman, and Loren Murchinson: "Throughout most of the hazy sunlit afternoon the Stars and Stripes had been flying from the masthead of victory, but just after sunset the American flag gave way to the

Union Jack in one of the most sensational triumphs in the history of the Olympic 100-meter dash, when a tall, long-legged Cambridge sprinter outraced an all-star field." Rewriting Rice's reports marked Abramson's break as a sportswriter; afterward he not only garnered his own byline–"J. P. Abramson"–but was assigned the Olympic Games, track and field, and amateur sports in general as his permanent principal beat for the *Herald Tribune*.

Abramson provided firsthand coverage of the Olympic Games in Amsterdam in 1928, Los Angeles in 1932, Berlin in 1936, London in 1948, Melbourne in 1956, Rome in 1960, and Tokyo in 1964 for *The New York Herald Tribune*. In 1968 he worked for the Mexican Olympic Committee as the foreign press chief at the games in Mexico City and covered the event for *The Washington Post*. Abramson reported on the 1972 games in Munich for both *The International Herald Tribune* and *The Washington Post*. In 1976 he served as the press liaison for the U.S. Olympic Committee at the games in Montreal. Because of his knowledge of the Olympics, especially track and field, Abramson's presence at the games was, for many reporters, essential. Red Smith, who worked with Abramson at the *Herald Tribune* before the newspaper folded in 1967, told Frank Dolson of *The Philadelphia Inquirer* (28 April 1978) that "there are a lot of us who would be reluctant to cover the Olympics without Jesse to lean on." Often their reliance on Abramson became a source of frustration: Smith recalled that Shirley Povich, at the Tokyo games in 1964, once blurted out "Aw shut up, Jesse! Who needs you?" when Abramson suggested story ideas to him and Smith on the final day of the games.

As a journalist Abramson witnessed and wrote about more than fifty years of the modern Olympic Games movement. During that time American Olympic athletes virtually dominated the games, winning more gold, silver, and bronze medals than any other nation, until 1952, when the Soviet Union entered a team (its first since 1912) that came within five medals of the seventy-six garnered by the United States. In 1956 the Soviet Union surpassed the United States in total medals, ninety-eight to seventy-four, leading many Americans to question how America selected its Olympic team. A staunch defender of the Olympic trials system, Abramson wrote in the official program to the annual IC4A track-and-field championships in 1960 that "it's the best, soundest, most democratic, most non-political way of determining Uncle Sam's delegates." Although he sympathized with the athletes, some of them national champions or world-record holders, that failed to make the Olympic team, he refuted the idea of the selection of the team becoming a "popularity contest." In defense of the system he pointed to little-known athletes such as Lindy Remigino, who prior to qualifying for the U.S. Olympic Team and winning the gold medal in the 100 meters in 1952 had never won a national championship. Although Abramson wrote glowingly about America's Olympic performers, he had recognized by the early 1960s that the rest of the world, especially the Soviet Union and the Eastern Europeans, had caught up with and, in some events, surpassed the United States.

In more than a half-century of covering the Olympic Games Abramson witnessed the rise, decline, and resurgence of women's participation. Women first participated in the Paris games in 1900, despite the fact that Pierre de Coubertin, the founder of the modern Olympic movement, discouraged their participation. In 1928 the women's Olympic track and field included, for the first time, the 800-meter run, an event won by Germany's Karoline Radke with a time of 2 minutes, 16.6 seconds, a world record that lasted for sixteen years. After the race most of the participants, including the winner, collapsed from exhaustion and had to be given medical assistance. For many antifeminists in the International Olympic Committee (IOC) and International Amateur Athletic Federation (IAAF), the aftermath of the women's 800 meters demonstrated that women could not run distances longer than 200 meters. Abramson, who observed the race firsthand, told Stogel that the women "were crawling up the stretch. It was the kind of race where they said we better cut out this women's racing. They may be great at sprints, but they'll never make it at distances." In 1960 the IOC restored the 800 meters to the women's track-and-field program, demonstrating, according to Abramson, that one should "never say 'never.'"

Many authorities on the Olympic Games consider track and field the showcase sport of the quadrennial event. Similarly, many track-and-field correspondents, such as Bob Hersh of *Track and Field News* (August 1979), regarded Abramson as "the dean of American track and field writers and scholars." Abramson distinguished himself from other track-and-field correspondents by his unmatched memory for statistical details, as demonstrated in his encounter with Judge Reid in 1965, and by his appreciation for the philosophical foundations of the sport. Before publications such as *Track and Field News* began compiling yearly lists of performances in each event, Abramson amassed these statistics himself in spiral notebooks, which he carried from meet to meet. According to Hersh in an unpublished interview from January 1998, Abramson's notebooks were "legendary," and many correspondents, especially novices, benefited from them in reporting various meets. One such novice who profited from Abramson's unmatched knowledge of track and field and personal cache of statistics was Red Smith, who during his tenure with *The Philadelphia Record* often covered the Penn Relays. As he revealed to Dolson in 1978, "I was never that conversant with track and field, and I discovered if I had to thumb through the program after each event to check the records I'd get there four events behind. I soon learned just to wangle a seat next to Jesse."

As with the Olympic Games, Abramson chronicled more than a half-century of track-and-field competition in the United States. Many of the same themes developed in his Olympic coverage also emerged in his track-and-field writing. In track and field, as in the larger Olympic movement, he saw the United States dominate the sport internationally, only later to be challenged by the Soviet Union and other emerging nations. From the late 1950s to the 1970s the two nations regularly held track-and-field competitions either in the United States or the Soviet Union. In the program for the 1 February 1963 Invitational Indoor Games of the Millrose Athletic Association, Abramson pointed out that in the four meets held between the two countries, U.S. trackmen had "accounted for 13 of 14 firsts (of 22 events) and their winning total was pretty much always the same, 124 to 128 points." The American women, however, were routinely defeated by the Soviets. Nonetheless, Abramson supported competition against the Soviet Union and welcomed Soviet track-and-field athletes to the United States. On the eve of the 1963 Millrose Games he reviewed the records of Soviet high jumper Valery Brummel and long jumper Igor Ter-Ovanesyan against Americans in those same events. Whereas Brummel had not lost to an American, Ter-Ovanesyan had never defeated one, leading Abramson to conclude that the "Millrose meet should be jumping tonight."

The Millrose Games, first held in 1908, is one of the oldest and most prestigious indoor invitational track-and-field meets in the United States. Abramson's association with the event began in 1928, after he had gained a few years of experience on the track-and-field beat for *The New York Herald Tribune.* One of his first articles on the Millrose Games criticized Fred Schmertz, director of the meet, for not inviting Pinky Sober, a City College of New York runner and local hero, to compete in the 600-yard dash. In "Meet Director Turns Author" (1967) Abramson recounts how this article introduced him to the "emollient manner of Mr. Schmertz," who said that "it was unfortunate that Sober had achieved his track stardom so recently," since the selection committee had already filled the 600-yard field. Instead, he asked Abramson if he "would consider the cause of track and justice served if Sober were invited to run a special 880 against Eddie Swinburne and others? Sober won the race and set a meet record and was third best, among the hundreds of competitors, in the outstanding-athlete vote." This encounter between Abramson and Schmertz marked the beginning of a long and intimate association, and Abramson soon became the media director of the Millrose Games.

Unlike some sports journalists, whose careers began in the "gee-whiz" era of the 1920s, Abramson did not write sentimentally about outstanding performances of the past when reporting current events but instead provided the reader with skeptical but healthy perspective based on facts and figures. In "New Records for Old" (*Princeton Athletic News,* 15 June 1935), an essay on the rapid turnover of track-and-field world records during the 1930s, he remarked:

> Considering that (Paavo) Nurmi's 4:10.4 lasted eight years, one would think Jack Lovelock's 4:07.6 would endure for ten or twenty years. But no! Before it can be assimilated by the International Amateur Athletic Federation and officially inscribed among the world records, it has been surpassed. For, consider, if you will, that Lovelock's record was never spread upon the books of the I.A.A.F., because when they met to approve it there was a faster record by (Glen) Cunningham awaiting approval. In the rush of things one hasn't much time to admire the flawless performance that is a new record. The popular reaction seems to be that a 4:06.7 mile is all right while its lasts, but it won't last long.

Abramson's observation that Cunningham's world record would not last was correct, as Sydney Wooderson of Great Britain lowered the standard by three-tenths of a second in 1937. Nor would the four-minute barrier in the mile last forever, as Roger Bannister of Great Britain crashed through it with a 3:59.4 performance in 1954. In accessing the Oxford medical student's feat for *The New York Herald Tribune* (7 May 1954), Abramson once again viewed it from the perspective of facts and figures rather than superhuman awe: "Ever since Paavo Nurmi, on his 1925 tour made the track world aware that the 4:00 mile was in reach in our time, cinderpath pundits have been trying on the 4:00 mile for size. How will it run? Now the formula comes out of the laboratory. It's tested and proved. It's 57.5, 60.7, 62.3, 58.9 for successive quarters. Just as the experts had said–a fast early quarter, a half in less than 1:59, a three-quarters around 3:00 and a final quarter under 60."

Dutton included Abramson's track-and-field articles in its *Best Sports Stories* series four times during his career. His first article so recognized, which appeared in *Best Sports Stories of 1944: A Panorama of the 1944 Sports Year* (1945), is "Patience + Persistence + Power = 4:07.3," about the Knights of Columbus meet in New

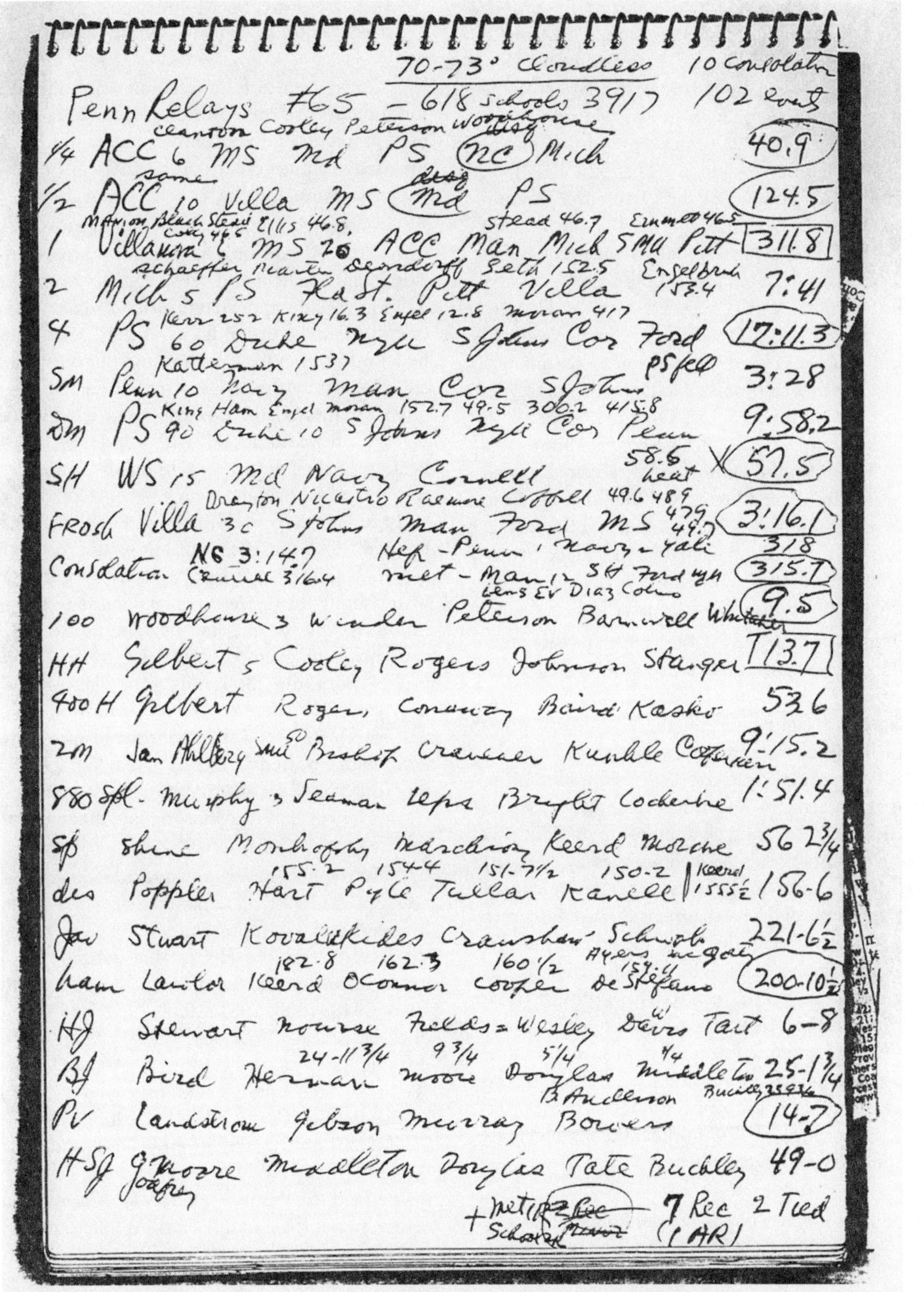

Page from Abramson's notebook recording results of the 1959 Penn Relays at the University of Pennsylvania (Collection of Bob Hersh)

York, at which Gilbert Dodd established an indoor world record in the mile. "Somehow Dodds husbanded his power for the stretch wallop," he wrote of the Boston mile ace, who "ran his fastest last quarter of the year, 63.9 seconds, and though he was slowing down agonizingly in the last forty he got there in the nick of time." In 1961 Dutton included "The Best Bet That Lost," Abramson's account of the Olympic high-jump competition in 1960, in which another Bostonian, John Thomas, "the world's highest, most consistent, most unruffled, most unbeatable leaper, the best bet everyone on the face of the earth conceded was most likely to win a gold medal here, placed third." Jerry Nason of *The Boston Globe* echoed Abramson's sentiments, describing Thomas's bronze-medal performance as "one of the major upsets in all Olympic history." In "Dateline Moscow: Yanks Beat Reds," Abramson's 1962 contribution to the Dutton series, about the third meet between the United States and the Soviet Union, also featured a hapless Thomas, who suffered yet another loss to 1960 Olympic champion Valery Brummel. A profile of Bob Hayes, "The New Fastest Human," appeared in *Best Sports Stories of 1963.*

Although Abramson wrote most passionately about track and field, he also excelled as a boxing correspondent for *The New York Herald Tribune.* His boxing articles appeared eight times in the *Best Sports Stories* annuals, with four of them receiving recognition for "Best News Coverage" in 1952, 1957, 1958, and 1965. Joey Maxim's defeat of Sugar Ray Robinson for the world middleweight boxing championship in 1952 was the subject of Abramson's prizewinning essay "Melted Sugar," which captured the fervor of the relentless match "fought in brutal heat that registered 104 degrees under the Yankee Stadium lights on the hottest June 25 in New York history." The fight, scheduled for fifteen rounds, ended after the thirteenth, which proved to be the most draining for Robinson, who fell to the mat not from a blow by Maxim but rather from the momentum of a punch that missed. Abramson's description of the final moments of the thirteenth round provides the reader with a sense of Robinson's vulnerability to fatigue rather than Maxim's punch:

> That fall, not from a punch, drained Robinson's last ounce of strength. When he got up they exchanged hard rights, and Maxim followed with a one-two that sent Robinson reeling crazily along the ropes on the northern side of the ring–not so much from the blows, but from his own unutterable weariness. The bell rang. His seconds, Harry Wiley and Peewee Beal, rushed from the corner and had to lift and carry Robinson to his stool. Dr. Alexander Schiff, commission physician, went to the corner. It was clear that Robinson, completely exhausted from his brilliant fight, had gone as far as a human could in that torture chamber.

According to John Chamberlain, one of the Dutton judges, "the way (Abramson) made the brutal heat of that night of the Robinson-Maxim fight a living, breathing, omnipresent part of the story easily stamps (it) as the winner in the 'coverage' category."

Although not an award-winning story, "Legalized Mayhem," Abramson's account of Jimmy Carter's lopsided lightweight title defense against an inexperienced Tommy Collins appeared in *Best Sports Stories of 1953.* In one of the most brutal fights of the 1950s, Carter won by a knockout in the fourth round but only after knocking Collins to the canvas ten times. Abramson eloquently captured the powerlessness felt by the Boston Garden crowd of 12,477 who witnessed the merciless beating of their hometown hopeful "until (the referee) was forced to halt the match when Collins's manager and trainer finally took matters in their own hands and jumped into the ring–an automatic disqualification under Massachusetts boxing laws." For the critics of prizefighting the Carter-Collins fight demonstrated how unmanageable boxing had become in the 1950s, especially with the promoters standing to gain considerable profits from the thousands of dollars generated by nearly nightly televised fights. Abramson pointed out that gamblers stood to profit handsomely from the fight, which posted "a record gate of $197,172. The betting fraternity, aware that Collins could be another Chuck Davey, a boy against a man, made Carter an 11-to-5 favorite."

In the fall Abramson covered college football. An accomplished football correspondent, he was one of the founders and a past president of the New York Football Writers Association. His football writing was selected for inclusion in the *Best Sports Stories* annuals for 1944, 1945, 1948, 1950, 1951, 1952, 1964, and 1967. In each of these articles Abramson hooks the reader with the opening line, as in "Agony in Atlanta" from 1944: "Georgia Tech's undefeated, unscored-on, untried firebrands defeated Navy, 17 to 15, before 35,000 on Grant Field this summery day in the wildest and most fantastic game of football in many a long year." He then maintained the reader's interest with a vivid narration of the game; for example, in "Architect of Triumph," included in *Best Sports Stories of 1951,* he portrays quarterback Dick Kazmaier, winner of the 1951 Heisman Memorial Trophy, leading Princeton to a 53–15 victory over Cornell:

> Always throwing on the run, hitting his receivers between the eyes, as they say, throwing them hard, lobbing them soft, the flawless artist completed fifteen of

> his seventeen passes for 236 yards. Ripping through and around the Big Red Line, cleverly sidestepping, weaving, feinting, driving, Kazmaier picked up 124 yards on the ground, averaging seven yards with his rushes, for a total offense of 360 yards against a strong foe.

The New York Herald Tribune ceased circulation in May 1967, while Abramson was covering the Marine Corps Relays in Quantico, Virginia. Although his forty-five-year association with the paper had ended, he continued to serve as the media director for the Millrose Games and IC4A Indoor Championships. While serving as the Olympic Games press liaison in 1968, Ed Mosler of the New York State Olympic Committee asked Abramson if he would be interested in participating in the organization of a new indoor track-and-field meet to benefit the United States Olympic Fund. Naturally, Abramson thought Mosler wanted him to handle public relations for the proposed meet, but Mosler wanted him to be the meet director. Abramson's experience in administrating sporting events was limited; in 1942, as the president of the New York Track Writers Association, he had participated in the organization and sponsorship of the Navy Relief Fund Meet. In his program notes for the ninth United States Olympic Committee (USOC) Invitational Indoor Track and Field Meet, held on 4 February 1978, Abramson wrote that "the only way to learn the meet-directing business was by doing it, and there was not much time to prepare for the 1969 inaugural." At any rate, the first USOC Invitational was successful, with a world record in the rarely contested 1500-meter walk, the first of several world-record performances that have graced the meet over the years.

In March 1978 physicians discovered that Abramson had developed abdominal cancer. Paul Zimmerman, then a sports correspondent for *The New York Post,* interviewed Abramson at his home in Mount Vernon, New York, on the eve of the tenth USOC Invitational. Although Ray Lumpp of the New York Athletic Club was the acting director of the meet while in Abramson's absence, Abramson, as the title of Zimmerman's 11 January 1979 article suggested, was "still in command." In his vociferate style Abramson admonished Sam Sloan, a meet volunteer and former executive director of the New York State Olympic Committee, for a typographical error in a press release.

On the evening of 10 June 1979, Abramson passed away at his Mount Vernon home. In the program notes for the 1979 IC4A Indoor Track and Field Championships, a meet for which Abramson had served as the media director since 1928, Frank Litsky, track-and-field correspondent for *The New York Times,* was quoted as remarking that "we shouldn't mourn Jesse, we should celebrate having known him." Several awards distinguished Abramson's career, including the Grantland Rice Award of the Sportsmanship Brotherhood, the James J. Walker Award for service to boxing, and the award for meritorious service from the New York Track and Field Writers Association. At the conclusion of the American indoor track-and-field season the New York Track and Field Writers Association awards the outstanding male athlete a trophy in Abramson's honor. After his death the USOC Invitational also created the Jesse Abramson Memorial Award to recognize meritorious service to track and field. As the program notes for the nineteenth Vitalis/USOC Invitational reported, Maury Allen of *The New York Post,* a 1988 recipient of the award, held "the honor with particular pride because the late Jesse Abramson was one of his 'journalistic heroes.'" For his career achievements, especially in reporting track and field, Abramson was elected to the Track and Field Hall of Fame in Indianapolis, Indiana, in 1981.

References:

Frank Dolson, "A Matchless Track Record," *Philadelphia Inquirer,* 28 April 1978, B, pp. 1, 4;

Bob Hersh, "Jesse Abramson," *Track and Field News* (August 1979): 57;

Jay Horwitz, "Jesse 'The Book' Abramson," in *1979 IC4A Indoor Championships* [program], pp. 6, 26;

Stan Saplin, "Abramson of the 'Trib,'" in *55th Annual Invitational Indoor Games of the Millrose Athletic Association* [program], 2 February 1962, p. 11;

Red Smith, "Jesse P. Abramson, Sportswriter for Herald Tribune, Dead at 75," *New York Times,* 11 June 1979;

Chuck Stogel, "Abramson: A Gold Medal Career," *Sportscope* (24 June 1978): 10, 38;

Paul Zimmerman, "Abramson Still in Command," *New York Post,* 11 January 1979, p. 78.

Papers:

Most of Jesse Peter Abramson's notebooks are owned by Bob Hersh, the senior editor of *Track and Field News,* in New York, New York.

David Anderson

(6 May 1929 –)

Jack Ziegler
Cochise College

MAJOR POSITIONS HELD: Sportswriter, *Brooklyn Eagle* (1951–1955); sportswriter, *New York Journal-American* (1955–1966); sportswriter, columnist, *New York Times* (1966–).

David Anderson

BOOKS: *Great Quarterbacks of the NFL* (New York: Random House, 1965);
Great Pass Receivers of the NFL (New York: Random House, 1966);
Great Defensive Players of the NFL (New York: Random House, 1967);
Upset: The Unexpected in the World of Sports, by Anderson and Milton Lancelot (New York: Doubleday, 1967);
Countdown to Super Bowl (New York: Random House, 1969);
Sugar Ray, by Anderson and Sugar Ray Robinson (New York: Viking, 1970);
Always on the Run, by Anderson, Larry Csonka, and Jim Kiick (New York: Random House, 1973);
The Return of a Champion: Pancho Gonzalez' Golden Year 1964 (Englewood Cliffs, N.J.: Prentice-Hall, 1973);
Frank: The First Year, by Anderson and Frank Robinson (New York: Holt, Rinehart & Winston, 1976);
The Yankees: The Four Fabulous Eras of Baseball's Most Famous Team, by Anderson, Murray Chass, Robert Creamer, and Harold Rosenthal (New York: Random House, 1979);
Sports of Our Times (New York: Random House, 1979);
Hey, Wait a Minute: I Wrote a Book, by Anderson and John Madden (New York: Villard, 1984);
Shooting for the Gold: A Portrait of America's Olympic Athletes, photographs by Walter Iooss Jr. (Ottawa, Ill.: Jameson, 1984);
The Cubs (New York: Random House, 1985);
The Story of Football (New York: Morrow, 1985);
One Knee Equals Two Feet (And Everything Else You Need to Know about Football), by Anderson and Madden (New York: Villard, 1986);
The Story of Basketball (New York: Morrow, 1988);
One Size Doesn't Fit All, by Anderson and Madden (New York: Villard, 1988);
In the Corner: Great Boxing Trainers Talk about Their Art (New York: Morrow, 1991);
Pennant Races: Baseball at Its Best (New York: Doubleday, 1994);
The Story of the Olympics (New York: Morrow, 1996);
All Madden: Hey, I'm Talking Pro Football! by Anderson and Madden (New York: HarperCollins, 1996);
The Story of Golf (New York: Morrow, 1998).

OTHER: "Fury on Ice," in *Best Sports Stories 1959: A Panorama of the 1958 Sports Year,* edited by Irving T. Marsh and Edward Ehre (New York: Dutton, 1959), pp. 197–209;

"Million-Dollar Baby," in *Best Sports Stories 1963: A Panorama of the 1962 Sports Year,* edited by Marsh and Ehre (New York: Dutton, 1963), pp. 222–225;

"Mess on the Ice," in *Best Sports Stories 1964: A Panorama of the 1963 Sports Year,* edited by Marsh and Ehre (New York: Dutton, 1964), pp. 250–254;

"The Longest Day of Sugar Ray," in *Best Sports Stories of 1965: A Panorama of the 1964 Sports Year,* edited by Marsh and Ehre (New York: Dutton, 1965), pp. 35–48;

"He Turns Footballs into Golden Eggs," in *Best Sports Stories 1966: A Panorama of the 1965 Sports Year,* edited by Marsh and Ehre (New York: Dutton, 1966), pp. 89–99;

"Injuries: They Upset Football's Odds," in *Best Sports Stories 1967: A Panorama of the 1966 Sports Year,* edited by Marsh and Ehre (New York: Dutton, 1967), pp. 136–147;

"I'll Forgive, But I'll Never Forget," in *Best Sports Stories 1972: A Panorama of the 1971 Sports Year,* edited by Marsh and Ehre (New York: Dutton, 1972), pp. 23–28;

"The Lady Was an Umpire," in *Best Sports Stories 1973: A Panorama of the 1972 Sports Year,* edited by Marsh and Ehre (New York: Dutton, 1973), pp. 78–80;

"The Greatest Is Now the Tiredest," in *Best Sports Stories 1974: A Panorama of the 1973 Sports Year,* edited by Marsh and Ehre (New York: Dutton, 1974), pp. 177–179;

"A Hockey Lesson for Dr. Kissinger," in *Best Sports Stories 1977: A Panorama of the 1976 Sports Year,* edited by Marsh and Ehre (New York: Dutton, 1977), pp. 196–198;

"The Best of Al McGuire," in *Best Sports Stories 1978: A Panorama of the 1977 Sports Year,* edited by Marsh and Ehre (New York: Dutton, 1978), pp. 181–183;

The Red Smith Reader, edited by Anderson (New York: Random House, 1982);

"Long Live the Revolution," in *The Armchair Quarterback,* edited by John Thorn, with David Reuther (New York: Scribners, 1982), pp. 1–11;

"1977: Reggie," in *The Fireside Book of Baseball,* fourth edition, edited by Charles Einstein (New York: Simon & Schuster, 1987), pp. 13–14;

"Sandwiches at an Execution," in *The Armchair Book of Baseball II,* edited by Thorn (New York: Scribners, 1987), pp. 14–16;

Martin Davis, *The Greatest of Them All: The Legend of Bobby Jones: Classic Photography of the Incomparable Bobby Jones,* includes essay by Anderson (Greenwich, Conn.: American Golfer, 1996);

Jules Alexander, *The Hogan Mystique: Classic Photographs of the Great Ben Hogan,* includes essay by Anderson (Greenwich, Conn.: American Golfer, 1996).

SELECTED PERIODICAL PUBLICATIONS–UNCOLLECTED: "Final Whistle," *Saturday Evening Post,* 230 (16 March 1963): 34–35;

"Gentlemen Prefer Golf," *New York Times Magazine* (9 March 1986): 70–71;

"Howie Young: Hockey's Abominable Iceman," *Saturday Evening Post,* 237 (22 February 1964): 30–31.

Dave Anderson covers a multitude of sports and covers them well. Aside from an interest in an athlete's skill, Anderson shows more concern for the content of his character. Perhaps because of his intellectual Catholic training in high school and college, Anderson seems preoccupied with whether an athlete evinces an Aristotelian balance in his or her life. Anderson focuses on the golden mean–the athletes he profiles may have too little confidence, such as Jerry Quarry, who felt deep in his heart he could never beat Muhammad Ali; or too much, such as Ron Stander, who believed selected sycophants that he could beat Joe Frazier. The dedicated, serious athlete will first of all have genuine self-knowledge. Thus, Anderson's heroes, including Ali, Joe Namath, and, above all, Joe DiMaggio, have just the right amount of confidence. Such frank confidence is sometimes construed as arrogance by the less Aristotelian minded, however–Ali, Namath, and DiMaggio have all been construed as egotists.

Anderson is also interested in character in the more dramatic sense as a commentary on human behavior. As was fellow sportswriter Grantland Rice, Anderson is interested in how athletes "play the game," rather than if they win or lose. Anderson likes to examine people under athletic stress and comment on how they behave. For him, sports are a kind of moral laboratory. Thus, an article on Henri "the Pocket Rocket" Richard dwells not only on this smaller, reserved player's success in the rugged National Hockey League but also on his difference from his bigger, brawling brother, Maurice "the Rocket" Richard. Typical of Anderson, he is interested not just in athletic achievement but the story behind the story.

David Poole Anderson was born on 6 May 1929 in Troy, New York. His father, Robert P. Anderson, was an advertising executive, while his mother, Josephine David Anderson, was an insurance broker. Later, the Andersons moved to a middle-class section of Brooklyn, Bay Ridge. Located at the present-day eastern terminus of Verrazano Bridge, Bay Ridge was characterized by two-story, two-family homes and smaller, well-maintained apartment houses. Anderson grew up in Bay Ridge playing street sports such as baseball, touch football, basketball, and roller hockey. Though not a particularly skilled athlete, he enjoyed all sports. As a teenager he expanded his athletic horizons by taking the Staten Island ferry to the public Silver Lake Golf Course there. Robert Anderson nurtured his son's interest in reading and sports by bringing home a

Anderson with boxer Joe Frazier (Jack Ballith/UPI)

half dozen newspapers daily, which Dave would spread out and read on the living room floor. He was thus introduced to the writings of Arthur Daley of *The New York Times,* Frank Graham of *The New York Journal-American,* W. C. Heinz and Grantland Rice of *The New York Sun,* Dan Parker of *The New York Daily Mirror,* Joe Williams of *The New York World-Telegram,* and Tommy Holmes of *The Brooklyn Eagle.* The sportswriters Anderson most admired, however, were Red Smith of *The New York Herald Tribune* and Jimmy Cannon of *The New York Post.* He became close friends with both men in later years.

As a teenager Anderson wanted to be a baseball writer like his idols Smith and Cannon. To that end he worked every Saturday as a copyboy for *The New York Sun.* By that time he had developed catholic tastes, favoring the high-octane 1940s St. Louis Cardinals over the local Dodgers. When not attending Xavier High School in Manhattan, Anderson took the subway to the Polo Grounds or Yankee Stadium to broaden his baseball education.

Anderson attended Holy Cross College, taking a Bachelor of Arts in English in 1951, and served as sports editor of the college newspaper, the *Tomahawk.* Anderson had hoped to get a job at *The New York Sun,* but the paper folded. Instead, in August 1951 Anderson went to work for *The Brooklyn Eagle* editing racing charts. Anderson's arrival at *The Eagle* coincided with the Dodgers' late-season collapse. Anderson often cites Bobby Thomson's "shot heard 'round the world," his ninth-inning home run that won the National League pennant for the New York Giants on 3 October 1951, as his most vivid recollection in sports. He heard Russ Hodges's play-by-play as he was looking at the already-made-up Eagle headline, "Dodgers Win Pennant."

Anderson's professional break came in 1953 when the Dodgers beat reporter for *The Eagle,* Harold Burr, broke his hip in Cincinnati. Anderson became a permanent fill-in, covering the "boys of summer" until 1955, when The Eagle folded. From 1955 to 1966 Anderson worked as a sportswriter for *The New York Journal-American,* moving in 1966 to *The New York Times.* There, in 1971, together with his former idol, Red Smith, Anderson became the designated "Sports of the Times" columnist. In 1981 Anderson won a Pulitzer Prize for commentary, following the leads of Smith and Daley.

Aside from his newspaper work, Anderson has written hundreds of articles for quality publications such as *Sport, Sports Illustrated, Reader's Digest,* and *True.* He is the author of several important books on sports and sports history, including *Countdown to Super Bowl* (1969), *Sports of Our Times* (1979), *In the Corner: Great Boxing Trainers Talk about Their Art* (1991), and *Pennant Races: Baseball at Its Best* (1994). Anderson is married to the former Maureen Ann

Young. They have four children: Stephen, Mark, Mary Jo, and Jean Marie.

In 1959, at age twenty-nine, eight years after breaking in with *The Brooklyn Eagle,* Anderson was writing a lengthy article for a major weekly magazine, *The Saturday Evening Post.* "Fury on Ice," the saga of the Richard brothers–which appeared in the 1 March 1958 issue and was selected for inclusion in *Best Sports Stories 1959: A Panorama of the 1958 Sports Year*–may be considered a major apprentice piece, along with two other articles for *The Saturday Evening Post,* "Final Whistle" (16 March 1963) and "Howie Young: Hockey's Abominable Iceman" (22 February 1964). In "Fury on Ice" Anderson sketches the nuances of sibling relationships in the younger Henri's growing up in Montreal, where Maurice is a revered athletic hero. Almost in the manner of a psychological novelist, he explores the contradictory emotions of both men. On the roster of the Montreal Canadiens, Henri, a rookie, has a million things to prove, while Maurice, his teammate, must decide to either play the protective big brother or let his brother struggle on his own. Maurice ultimately decides to let his brother make his own way; Henri establishes himself as a star in his own right, and Maurice even begins to emulate his little brother's more finessed style of play. Together, they play a seamless kind of hockey, relying on technique instead of Maurice's formerly more brawling style.

Anderson's interest in good sportsmanship, the interior game, is reflected in "Final Whistle," which centers on Bob Cousy's retirement. As a college journalist, Anderson covered Cousy while the two attended Holy Cross. As "Final Whistle" indicates, Anderson is a proponent of the "great man" theory of sports history, feeling that some athletes tower over their era. Thus, when someone like DiMaggio, Namath, Ali, or Cousy retires, society is diminished: "All sports will be the poorer, and all of us will feel a little older." Anderson perceptively notes that it was by no means a free ride for Cousy. From the tough German Yorkville section of Manhattan, the French-surnamed Cousy, who had a slight speech impediment, was nicknamed "Flenchy." Drawing on interior strength, Cousy surmounted incessant teasing, just as at 6'1" he found his way around larger opponents in the National Basketball Association (NBA) with skill and grace. Cousy embodies the quiet nobility and stoicism Anderson so values in all humans, refusing the hoopla the NBA and Boston Celtics would gladly have provided. Instead, he insists on a plain vanilla farewell: "None of the supermarket stuff, with a dozen cases of this and a lifetime supply of that. Just make sure it's simple."

Anderson focuses on the darker aspect of sport in his 1964 article on Howie Young. Young is like Maurice Richard run amok, a tortured athlete whose behavior borders on the psychotic. At age twenty-six, Young is intelligent but impulsive and immature, the exact opposite of the controlled, mature Cousy. Young revels in self-destructive behavior: "I'm a hood. . . . It's an outlet for me." For Richard violence seemed an outgrowth of the game; for Young it seems rooted in a flawed character. The perceptive Anderson envisions such behavior rooted in Young's ambition. As a youngster Young played hockey with older, bigger boys and always felt compelled to be the toughest guy on the ice. This overcompensation that made him so gifted athletically exacted a heavy moral and psychological toll.

Anderson depicts a married Young who lives with three bachelors and roams Chicago's streets at night by himself and whose play on the ice is suicidally aggressive. Anderson's interviewing skills illuminate Young's driven, restless, self-destructive personality: "I can't sit around like some guys . . . some nights I just go. It's an outlet for me."

In 1964, at age thirty-five, Anderson showed maturation in talent with his "The Longest Day of Sugar Ray," which won the award for best magazine story in the Dutton Press *Best Sports Stories of 1965: A Panorama of the 1964 Sports Year.* The essay details the decline of boxer Sugar Ray Robinson. At age forty-four, Robinson is reduced to filling halls in places such as Pittsfield, Massachusetts, against unknowns for small purses.

Anderson's article notes that the great fight stories–Budd Schulberg's *The Harder They Fall* (1947), Ring Lardner's "Champion" (1916), Ernest Hemingway's "The Killers" and "Fifty Grand" (both 1927)–are essentially morality plays in which characters confront the fact that their skills will not last forever. Once Robinson fought Jake LaMotta and Carmen Basilio, packed in the spectators at the Palais de Sport in Paris and Chicago Stadium, and owned several businesses in Harlem. Now he fights Clarence Roiley in Wahcunah Park for $700. As Robinson, without irony, observes of himself: "I'm not desperate . . . but I don't have the money like I used to." Robinson has become a kind of sideshow, yesterday's champion. Yet, Anderson notes that in Robinson's warm-ups one can sometimes glimpse his quickness and skill, now largely hidden in slower reflexes and weaker punches.

Anderson continued to expand both skill and subject matter with his 1965 award-winning piece on New York Jets co-owner Sonny Werblin, "He Turns Footballs into Golden Eggs," reprinted in *Best Sports Stories 1966: A Panorama of the 1965 Sports Year.* Always an admirer of intelligence and tact, he sees Werblin as the man who has resuscitated an expiring American Football League (AFL). Perhaps wrongly in the eyes of football purists, Werblin, a former talent agent, perceived the new league as sports entertainment and brokered peace between the AFL and the National Football League (NFL) on the basis of economic self-interest. Anderson also admires Werblin's knack of treating athletes like human beings, a touch absent in most NFL negotiations. He notes how a small gesture to Matt Snell's parents–bringing them hot chocolate at a chilly Jets game–translated into Snell's signing with the Jets and not the New York Giants. In Anderson's eyes Werblin had vision in realizing that the Jets had to be new and different. Thus, he moved them out of the decaying Polo Grounds to Shea Stadium, gave them distinctive green-and-white uniforms, and, perhaps most importantly, changed their name from Titans to Jets. Perhaps owing to his background as a talent scout, Werblin saw in Joe Namath an athlete the city would clasp to its bosom as it did with Jack Dempsey, Babe Ruth, and Frank Gifford: "He reminds me of Joe DiMaggio. And Sinatra, and the way Sinatra would come on in a nightclub and light up a room all by himself."

Anderson received further recognition in 1967, winning a best sports story award for "Injuries: They Upset Football's Odds," initially published in *True* magazine. In "Injuries" he indicts the on-the-hoof mentality of pro football, later the subject of Pete Gent's novel *North Dallas Forty* (1973). Anderson pictures pro football as a kind of blood sport in which athletes must play hurt or lose their jobs. He feels pro football is the most demanding of any sport, citing players hurtling toward each other at twenty miles per hour as a case in point. He notes that while players seem to be in magnificent shape, it is not the case: Johnny Unitas wears a special vest to protect his damaged ribs, Namath's weak right knee is braced and wrapped, and Gary Cuozzo is shot full of novocaine. Players, he observes, are routinely expected to play with detached retinas, concussions, and debilitating knee injuries. The article also takes on the heroes of the game. Anderson recalls Green Bay Packers coach Vince Lombardi as especially demanding, having once seen him order a vomiting Jim Taylor back in the game. His conclusion to this take on training-table heroes is typically laconic: "The team with the smallest medical bill is likely to be the one that ends up with the title."

Anderson's first major book, *Countdown to Super Bowl,* was published in 1969. Profusely illustrated by Leroy Neiman with sparse line drawings, the book covers the eleven days up to and including Super Bowl III, on 12 January 1969, between the Jets and the Baltimore Colts. Anderson, at this time a beat reporter for the Jets, understandably focuses on the seventeen-point underdog New Yorkers. Starting with Weeb Ewbank, the Jets head coach, who was fired by Colts owner Carroll Rosenbloom after the 1962 season, many among the Jets felt like they had been pushed around by the NFL long enough. Jets tackle Winston Hill, for example, is described as having nightmares about going up against his old nemesis, Colt defensive end Ordell Braase.

At the center of the drama is Namath. As with his portrait of Frazier, Anderson gives the reader something different than the conventional viewpoint. He introduces "Broadway Joe" as he is buying a gold brooch for his mother. Namath emerges as a considerate, sensitive, physically courageous man who works hard at his job. Anderson presents Namath's so-called guarantee of a Jets win as more a plain statement of fact. After carefully reviewing game footage of the Colts, Namath decided that the Baltimore defense was overrated and Earl Morrall had a tendency to throw lobbing passes. Far from portraying Namath as egocentric, Anderson records his gracious acceptance of the game's most valuable player award: "This should be a most valuable player award for the entire team."

While Anderson's account of the Jets' 16–7 win is clear, crisp, and concise, it is almost anticlimactic. The focus in *Countdown to Super Bowl* is on the building suspense and the grace under pressure that individual Jets show as the clock ticks down to game day. As Namath deduced, Morrall did indeed throw "balloon balls," while Ewbank's squad showed masterful poise and execution.

Anderson's "I'll Forgive, but I'll Never Forget," which was included in *Best Sport Stories 1972: A Panorama of the 1971 Sports Year,* chronicles Joe Frazier's return to his childhood home in South Carolina. Anderson, as is his wont, offers a different take on the "Black Marciano" created by many white sportswriters as an adversary to the flamboyant Ali. Anderson's Frazier is a much angrier, embittered man than other writers have indicated. Anderson shrewdly notes that behind Frazier's reserve exists a childhood during which he once picked vegetables for fifteen cents a crate. While his mother, Dolly, has a relaxed attitude toward race relations, Frazier is suspicious, almost paranoid. Explaining his admiration for Joe Louis, Frazier notes that "down in the South, the black goes for the black." Furthermore, his ambition, like the fighters' ambitions in Hollywood B movies, seems fueled by resentment: "I live on a challenge basis; life is a challenge."

Sports of Our Times is a seminal work in the Anderson canon. Composed of columns culled from Anderson's years at *The New York Times,* the book is also notable for Anderson's introduction and headnotes, in which he offers insights into his writing. He reflects on the enthusiasm and joy in craft that often comes across in his prose: "I have a job that many people would love to have." He also notes the challenge of turning out four thousand-word columns per week, especially when he and alternating columnist Red Smith had to avoid repetition. In *Sports of Our Times* Anderson examines the interaction of athletic achievement and character. Like Dick Young, Anderson has a tendency to look backward, although he never becomes the revenant Young was. However, along with Young, Anderson sees baseball as a "roots game," the game "most Americans grow up with," at its best before the Dodgers and the Giants moved west in 1958. For

Anderson, "sports were simpler" and "horizons were closer" in the period immediately following World War II.

Anderson still finds plenty to admire in selected modern athletes such as Hank Aaron, however. He pictures Aaron as excelling both physically and morally. Anderson's compliments on Aaron could equally be addressed to literary characters like Odysseus or Horatio, steady, high achievers whose exploits speak for themselves. As Anderson remarks on Aaron, "Throughout his career he has performed the same way–stoically, without flair, without emotion. He seldom creates headlines with anything except as his home runs." Anderson sees strength of character as internal, a frank yet modest self-confidence that needs no approval from the wider world. Thus, Anderson prefers Aaron's "durability and consistency" to Babe Ruth's "charisma." Anderson further admires Aaron's almost Odyssean control of emotion. As Aaron neared Ruth's career record of 714 home runs, he did not physically wilt, as the more high-strung Roger Maris did when approaching Ruth's single-season record in 1961. For Anderson steadiness and reliability are cardinal virtues.

In the "Football" chapter of *Sports of Our Times* Anderson notes that along with many other city kids he preferred the quality of the professional game to the rah-rah atmosphere of college football. Though respectful of old pros such as Unitas, he devotes an entire chapter to columns on Namath, expanding on many of the themes covered in *Countdown to Super Bowl.* He finds Namath a kind of Janus–the public face, cocky, cynical, hedonistic; the private face, honest, forgiving, thoughtful. Anderson particularly praises Namath for his physical courage in routinely undergoing painful knee-draining procedures at Lenox Hill Hospital. Like Aaron, Namath meets his inevitable physical deterioration with calmness, stoicism, and grim humor. Coming from treatment for his wobbly knees, Namath sees a broken-down old derelict outside Lenox Hill. Turning to Anderson, he remarks, "Must be an old quarterback."

One of Anderson's major points is that character is where you find it, not just in marquee names. So in "The Little Names" chapter of *Sports of Our Times,* he examines the different faces of boxer Ron Stander and wheelchair-bound marathoner Bobby Hall. As portrayed by Anderson, Stander lacks the ability to see the world realistically and pays the price with his health and the dissolution of his marriage. Mismatched in 1972 with slugger Joe Frazier, Stander started believing the prefight hype and suffered a horrible beating. Stander's wife, Earlene, is a realist who at first pities her husband's delusions ("He was an excellent husband until he turned pro. You can't raise two kids on fantasy"), then reluctantly drops him when he chooses dreams over responsibility.

A more positive story is the account of Bobby Hall, a paraplegic athlete who competed in the Boston Marathon despite heavy pressure from the organizers of the race. Hall, well conditioned by anyone's standards, got a fifteen-minute head start and stayed ahead for eighteen miles. Anderson admires not only Hall's physical skills but also his moral victory over his handicap. Hall, "smiling even when he was laboring to wheel his wheelchair up the hills," was a man devoid of self-pity who wants recognition as an athlete, not a special athlete. And he was recognized–by the applause of onlookers and literal pats on the back from his fellow contestants. One New York Marathon official privately told Anderson he was upset with his column on Hall–it would cost the organization a lot of money to fund "special" accommodations. Anderson's response: "More than ever, I was glad I had written it."

Anderson devotes the last and longest chapter in *Sports of Our Times* to Muhammad Ali. While Dick Young had a long love-hate relationship with Ali, Anderson always viewed him with a more balanced eye. What irritated the more conservative Young–Ali's flamboyance and devotion to the Nation of Islam–troubles the more tolerant Anderson not at all. Anderson perceives Ali's brashness more as honest self-confidence, much like Namath's, and his devotion to the Black Muslims as sincere religious feeling. The aspect of Ali's character that Anderson finds distasteful is his treatment of women–his routine infidelity and casual cruelty. Anderson notes that he usually does not write about subjects' private lives unless they choose to make them public.

Anderson feels that Ali is the greatest heavyweight of all time. He found it personally difficult to watch Ali's long decline in the 1970s. As Ali's "fighter's hands" began to ache and time slowed his lightning jab and quick legs, Anderson sensed an aging boxer's yearning for a quiet life where he could be an "ordinary citizen, go to the hardware store, cut the grass."

If there is one athlete that epitomizes skill and character for Anderson, it is Joe DiMaggio. Anderson's section in *The Yankees: The Four Fabulous Eras of Baseball's Most Famous Team* (1979), "The Joe DiMaggio Years," centers on the New York Yankees from 1936 to 1951. For Anderson, DiMaggio defines class: "his presence demanded decorum." He is especially interested in DiMaggio's aloofness, his tailored suits, and the glacial reserve that made him seem at times an "Italian nobleman." Yet the truth, as Anderson piquantly observes, was a bit different. DiMaggio was a fisherman's son from San Francisco who developed his reticence in response to his family's teasing about his poor grammar. Despite his regal bearing, he was indifferently educated, a high-school dropout who preferred baseball to books.

Anderson's discussion of DiMaggio centers on his fifty-six-game hitting streak in 1941. As Anderson remarks:

Anderson sitting next to New York Yankees manager Joe Torre, 1998

"Occasionally a baseball player has a year that is his alone, a year with which he is identified forever." Again, the hitting streak is not only a superior athletic feat, it also sheds light on DiMaggio's character. Demanding excellence from himself–he refused to extend the streak by bunting–he encouraged others to rise to new heights. American League pitchers declined to intentionally walk him, instead going straight at him. When the streak finally ended, DiMaggio accepted it with a laconic "Well, that's over."

Anderson particularly extols DiMaggio's strong work ethic. He disdained his onetime roommate, the hard-living Joe Page. Rather than put up with Page's late-night disruptions, he roomed alone, to better prepare himself for the next day's game. DiMaggio always shone in adversity, especially toward the end of his career. By 1949 bone spurs made each game an agony for him. Yankee management wanted to keep him in the lineup and offered him all sorts of inducement–switching his defensive position from outfielder to first baseman, removing him from the game in the late innings, shifting him to primary duty as a pinch hitter. Moved to fifth in the batting order, he saw the writing on the wall and hung up his cleats after the 1951 World Series. For DiMaggio retirement was knowing when to look for the exit. As he remarked at the time, "It's not the money, it's me. . . . I don't want to play baseball like this."

In *In the Corner: Great Boxing Trainers Talk about Their Art* (1991), Anderson shows his knack for looking at the unusual angle by focusing on the cornermen behind a fighter's success. He writes a general introduction and a headnote to each chapter, which consist primarily of edited transcripts, with the trainers speaking for themselves. The trainers Anderson profiles range from father figures such as Eddie Futch and Emmanuel Steward to more irascible types such as Lou Duva and Richie Giacetti. Despite the ostensibly brutal subject matter, however, the book is also about tenderness and love. Most of the trainers see their charges as surrogate sons, and all have a fierce love for the sport. Thus, Steward carefully prepares a meal for Michael Moorer of vegetables from his own garden, while Goody Petronelli recounts how he first coached boxing for free after long days as a construction worker. As Petronelli asks, "Where would the fighter be without the trainer?"

For virtually all the cornermen the keys to victory are discipline and the mentor-protégé relationship. Most trainers are suspicious of a fighter's friends, especially in training camp, where they can create a "party atmosphere." Petronelli feels a training camp should be a time of almost monastic preparation; Steward recalls how Tommy Hearns's Detroit "friends" distracted him from the task at hand. George Benton, who managed Leon

Spinks in his upset of Ali, points to the chaos in Spinks's corner during their rematch, after Spinks had let him go for flashier company. Gil Clancy identifies Emile Griffith as the ideal fighter, a willing pupil who let a cornerman direct his considerable skills in the right direction. As Clancy notes, a between-rounds conference with Griffith was like a business meeting.

Many trainers have incisive points of view about their charges. For example, Angelo Dundee provides some insight about Ali different than the public perception. He notes that while Ali missed three years late in his professional life because of the draft imbroglio, he came back a more mature and intelligent fighter. Dundee further relates how Ali always made himself available to the public and how, during his involuntary hiatus, he humbly worked as a sparring partner in Dundee's Miami gym for pocket money. A key point Dundee makes is that the trainer must provide calm leadership in unsettling situations. As an example, he cites Ali's first fight with Sonny Liston, when the panicky fighter wanted to quit after the first round because of a burning sensation in his eyes (probably caused by something on Liston's gloves). Dundee spoke slowly and quietly to Ali and wiped his eyes. He settled down and went on to beat Liston. Dundee also reflects how much of the trainer's job revolves around research. In preparing Sugar Ray Leonard for Marvin Hagler, he spent hours watching tapes of Hagler in the ring, finally figuring out that he had a weak left hand–such "little keys," in Dundee's words, often open the way to victory. Benton seems to echo that sentiment: "That's how you win fights. Styles."

Some of Anderson's interviews–for example, that with Ray Arcel, born in 1899 and manager of eighteen champions–evoke the most illustrious figures in the sport. As Eddie Futch said of Arcel, who worked with Jack Dempsey, Benny Leonard, and Ezzard Charles, "He brought class, dignity, and a high degree of professionalism to boxing." Arcel, Petronelli, and Dundee all seem cut from the same cloth–they perceive boxing as a kind of religious vocation demanding total dedication. As Arcel notes, "Boxing is brains over brawn . . . if you can't think, you're just another bum in the park." He feels that good trainers teach their charges "mental energy. Self-control. Determination." Arcel remarks sadly that too much contemporary boxing compares poorly with times past: "Boxing is not really boxing today. It's theater."

In the Corner includes chapters on less-successful trainers, as well. Jackie McCoy, for example, works on the Los Angeles docks, along with two former charges who did not take their craft seriously, Mando Ramos and Don Jordan. McCoy portrays the bleaker side to the fight game–picturing many fighters living in a dream world, believing the stamina, the punching power, and the good times will last forever–and asserts that many fighters have dark, self-destructive personalities. Even after all the disappointment McCoy has endured, however, he cannot stay away from the sport: he devotes his spare time to helping young fighters at the Westminster Gym.

In many ways *Pennant Races* is Anderson's most ambitious book. As usual, Anderson advances a cogent argument for his book in the introduction: pennant races are "longer and tighter" than the World Series, a "season long ordeal" that takes the true measure of the worth of a team. In *Pennant Races* Anderson selects fifteen seasons from 1908 to 1993 based upon their "theatrical dimensions." For source material Anderson utilized the newspaper files of the New York Public Library, his personal files, published materials, rare photographs, and more than one hundred interviews.

Anderson often succeeds in furnishing a fresh perspective on old events. For example, most baseball historians concentrate only on the three-way National League race between Chicago, Pittsburgh, and New York in 1908. Anderson points out that the American League was equally competitive, with Chicago, Detroit, and Cleveland all in the hunt. Typical of Anderson, he writes that the outcomes in both leagues were decided by resolution of character, as shown by Cubs pitcher Ed Reulbach, who pitched two shutouts in one day in a doubleheader against Brooklyn on 26 September. Yet the game was changing, with Bucknell University graduate and Giants pitcher Christy Mathewson bringing class to what some viewed as a game for hooligans. Anderson catalogues the strain that the 1908 pennant races levied on their participants. Addie Joss, the great Cleveland pitcher, who threw a perfect game against the White Sox on 8 October, died of meningitis in 1910 at age thirty-one; Cleveland second baseman Nap Lajoie said he never recovered from the pressure of the 1908 campaign; National League president Harry Pullian fell into a depression over the tough decisions demanded in September 1908 and shot himself fatally the following year. Perhaps the most tragic figure was Fred Merkle, the normally intelligent player for the Giants who neglected to touch second base in a crucial game between the Giants and the Cubs. Though vigorously defended by Giants manager John McGraw and accumulating a first-rate professional record, Merkle died a recluse in Daytona Beach, Florida, in 1956. Shortly before his death Merkle remarked: "I suppose when I die . . . they'll put on my tombstone, 'Here Lies Bonehead Merkle.'"

Anderson identifies several bizarre instances in the 1920 American League race, perhaps the most shocking being the 16 August fatal beaning of Cleveland shortstop Roy Chapman by Yankee fastball pitcher Carl Mays. Anderson notes that Chapman was playing in his final season. His wife was pregnant and he was going into business in the fall of 1920. In an historical note often missed, he

Anderson (center of photo) watching David Duval in August 1999 at the PGA Championship, Medinah Country Club, Chicago (AP Photo/Michael Conrad)

remarks how Chapman actually stood up and walked around after the fatal pitch before collapsing near home plate. No one was more shocked at Chapman's subsequent death than Mays, whose statement to the local district attorney is brimful with pain and regret. Anderson also recalls two other important events of that year. Babe Ruth hit fifty-five home runs with the new "lively ball," thus ushering in the era of the power hitter. The second was the unraveling of the Chicago White Sox in September, after the revelation of the Black Sox betting scandal from the World Series the previous fall. Enraged White Sox owner Charlie Comiskey suspended the eight players involved, and the pennant chances collapsed for the White Sox.

Anderson also provides a fresh look at another well-researched race, for the 1951 National League pennant. While almost all baseball historians focus on Bobby Thomson's game-winning home run, Anderson emphasizes a key double play third baseman Thomson effected earlier in the game. He also provides a new take on Giants manager Leo Durocher, who many writers portray as a foul-mouthed neurotic. Anderson draws a more subtle portrait of an intelligent man who excelled at motivating players–especially, in this instance, Thomson and Willie Mays–and whose temper tantrums were calculated motivational tools. Anderson even manages to bring new insights to the "shot heard 'round the world," which left Thomson and Brooklyn gopher-ball pitcher Ralph Branca, in the author's words, "handcuffed in history." With an eye toward notable coincidences Anderson observes that Thomson once played for a Brooklyn farm team on Staten Island and that Branca grew up a Giants fan. Anderson's depiction of the two players' reactions to the Giants victory exemplifies his attention to detail: Thomson celebrated with a quiet dinner with friends, while Branca, still living with his parents in the Bronx, found consolation from a priest who told him: "God chose you . . . because he knew you'd be strong enough to bear the cross."

In a playoff series filled with heroes and greats, Anderson feels the two managers played pivotal roles. Durocher imparted a sense of well-being and confidence to the Giants–even when trailing in the bottom of the ninth inning, they still felt they would win. Charlie Dressen, the Brooklyn manager, was nursing a psychologically wounded club who had squandered a sizable mid-August lead. Anderson types Dressen as irrational and petulant and wonders why he would choose Branca, the loser in the first game of the series, as a relief pitcher.

A theme common to virtually all of Anderson's writing is the necessity of tempering physical skill with moral choice. If anything, Anderson places more weight on the choices an athlete makes under stress–handling great good fortune or personal reversal, withstanding egoism, coming to terms with aging and inevitable decline. Along with Aristotle, Anderson sees such decisions as challenges in degree and timing. An ethical act should be performed at the right time, in the right amount, for the right reason. Thus, Hank Aaron realized that when he started using reading glasses his days in baseball were numbered. He accepted the end of his playing days and moved on to a productive career in management. On the other hand, Sugar Ray Robinson had lived all his life in the present and had developed no other skills than boxing. When his body gave out, he had nothing else to do and was reduced to fighting for nickels and dimes in backwoods venues. For Anderson sports resonates with chances missed and taken and the inevitable consequences contingent upon choice.

Golf, the least violent sport, is also the one in which Anderson perceives the toughest test of character. For him it is the ideal sport. Mentally demanding, ethically constricting, physically exhausting, golf taxes all aspects of a participant's character. It provides the ultimate contest in sports–against the course and against oneself. In "Gentlemen Prefer Golf," a short but incisive article Anderson wrote for *The New York Times Magazine* in 1986, these character-related issues are addressed. Anderson repeats the story of Bobby Jones assessing himself a penalty stroke in the 1925 U.S. Open, even though no one else saw the violation. As he almost sternly notes, "A golfer is his own umpire." In the same article Arnold Palmer recalls a lesson in character-building on the links from his father, the pro at the Latrobe Country Club. After a temper tantrum by the teenage Palmer, his father advised him: "If you ever throw a club again, that will be the last time you play competitive golf."

Perhaps the best summation on golf, and sport in general, as a moral laboratory comes from Jack Nicklaus in "Gentlemen Prefer Golf." Nicklaus hopefully observes that young men coming to the professional tour learn not just skills from the older men but also manners and sportsmanship. Nicklaus notes that there is no room for immaturity on the golf course, a testing ground where young men and women serve moral, as well as athletic, apprenticeships. For Anderson golf, with its emphasis on self-scoring, sportsmanship, and integrity, is a litmus test for effective living. Golf, like life for Anderson, is a "strict game that demands self-control."

Red Smith summed up Anderson's abilities perhaps better than anyone else when he commented on "I'll Forgive, but I'll Never Forget" for the Dutton Best Sports News-Feature Prize in 1972. Although Smith was unaware that Anderson was the author of the piece at the time, he wrote: "A superlative blend of honest reporting and lean writing by a man of perception and sensitive awareness. Obviously, this sports writer's horizons are wider than the boundaries of the playing field."

Malcolm Bingay

(16 December 1884 – 21 August 1953)

Martin J. Manning
United States Information Agency

MAJOR POSITIONS HELD: Reporter, *Detroit Today* (1900); editor, *Detroit News* (1900–1930); editor and sports columnist, *Detroit Free Press* (1930–1953).

Malcolm Bingay

BOOKS: *Iffy's Book of Tiger Tales,* as "Iffy the Dopester" (Detroit: Stair-Jordan-Cerre, 1935);
Detroit Is My Own Home Town (Indianapolis & New York: Bobbs-Merrill, 1946);
Of Me I Sing (Indianapolis: Bobbs-Merrill, 1949).

OTHER: *He Who Went About Doing Good* (Detroit: Privately printed, Press of the Round Circle, 1939);
"We Want Tigers–Not Tame Kittens," in *The Detroit Tigers,* by Frederick G. Lieb (New York: Putnam, 1946);
Good Morning: A Collection of Some of the Best Liked Columns of Malcolm W. Bingay, Late Editorial Director of the Detroit Free Press (Detroit: Detroit Free Press, 1954).

SELECTED PERIODICAL PUBLICATIONS–UNCOLLECTED: "Detroit Tradition," *Current History,* 39 (October 1933): 45–50;
"The Good Doctor," *Hygeia,* 15 (December 1937): 1071;
"Baseball's Bouncing Betsey," *Saturday Evening Post,* as Iffy the Dopester, 211 (21 January 1939): 12–13, 30, 33, 35;
"Baseball's Troubadour: The Saga of Germany Schaefer," *Saturday Evening Post,* as Iffy the Dopester, 212 (27 January 1940): 16–17, 65–68;
"Get a Horse!: When Detroit Roared Like a Mining Camp, and the World Was Remade," *Saturday Evening Post,* 212 (29 June 1940): 12–13, 71–75;
"The Motor Boys in Action: When Detroit Roared Like a Mining Camp, and the World Was Remade," *Saturday Evening Post,* 213 (6 July 1940): 30, 32, 46, 48–49;
"Eddie Guest, Himself!" *Rotarian,* 57 (September 1940): 22–24;
"The Fan Who Bought the Ball Park," *Saturday Evening Post,* 215 (6 March 1943): 18, 83–84;
"What I Saw in Europe," *Vital Speeches of the Day,* 11 (1 August 1945): 623–627;
"It Could Happen Here," *Reader's Digest,* 47 (August 1945): 45–46;
"Life on Loo-Choo," *Forum,* 104 (September 1945): 44–45;
"When Kids Were Giant-Killers," *Forum,* 104 (November 1945): 258–259;
"Tie Wages to Profits? No!–Says Malcolm Bingay," *Rotarian,* 68 (March 1946): 20–21, 50–52;
"By Default," *Forum,* 105 (June 1946): 907–908.

Malcolm Bingay tried as early as 1904, when he was only nineteen years old, to become a sportswriter when he lobbied unsuccessfully to become the Ann Arbor correspondent for the *Detroit News.* His goal was to cover the celebrated "point-a-minute" football teams at the University of Michigan and get a college degree. When the same newspaper hired him as a sports editor the same year, however, football was the one sport he did not get a chance to cover in the job.

Bingay devoted his professional career as a newspaper editor and reporter to other pursuits, as well. In his early days he covered the Detroit waterfront, its hotels, and its labor unions. As managing editor of the *Detroit News* Bingay cultivated friendships with Henry Ford and other titans of the automobile industry and became involved in state politics; but, above all, he promoted Detroit.

Bingay witnessed the profession of sportswriting, especially in the daily newspaper, take off in the late nineteenth century and early twentieth century as Americans had more time for leisure and sports as well as more disposable income than ever before. With the creation of sports journalism in newspapers and in publications such as *The Sporting Times* in 1890–which was devoted entirely to the coverage of the first professional American sport, baseball–there was an increasing demand for writers to describe the color and the action, the thrills and the excitement, of sports for the reader not privileged to participate personally at the event.

Malcolm Wallace Bingay was born in Sandwich, Ontario, 16 December 1884, the son of John George Bingay and his wife, Isabelle McIntyre. He had two sisters and a brother. As an infant he came to the United States and was educated in Detroit, where his family settled. He never considered himself much of a scholar and was expelled from Central High School as "rebellious, ignorant and arrogant," as he recalled in his autobiography, *Of Me I Sing* (1949), after an argument with a teacher over Bingay's contention that a pig in the mud under a fence started the War of 1812. He worked briefly for a baker and a messenger before starting his newspaper career as a printer's apprentice with the *Michigan Farmer*. Bingay continued his education with YMCA evening classes and in special courses at the University of Michigan, although he never received a college degree.

At the *Michigan Farmer* Bingay learned the art of printing; in return, he cleaned type, swept floors, ran errands, and did other jobs. In 1901, at age seventeen, he started as an office boy with the *Detroit News* before becoming a reporter, city editor, and managing editor for the paper. One of his initial duties was to go out to Bennett Park to pick up copy on the first five innings of the baseball games in order to save the newspaper telegram tolls. On 6 September 1901 Bingay was in the ballpark when the flash came over the wires that an anarchist, Leon Czolgosz, had shot President William McKinley at the Pan-American Exposition in Buffalo, New York. He rushed back to his office, thinking he had a scoop, to find the first edition of the news already in print.

Bingay worked other positions at the *Detroit News,* including sports editor from 1904 to 1908, city editor from 1908 to 1912, and managing editor from 1912 to 1928. As sports editor his major responsibilities were to write about the Detroit Tigers baseball team and their superstar, Ty Cobb; to travel with the team; and to produce at least four columns a day. Bingay never really had the chance to cover football, as he hoped. He did write about prizefighting, however, which was briefly barred in Michigan at the time, and he established himself as something of an authority on the sport. He earned this reputation, he admitted in *Of Me I Sing,* by rewriting what columnists at other newspapers such as the *Chicago Tribune* and the *New York World* had already said. Bingay also covered horse racing, but he did not like it. As he recounts in *Of Me I Sing,* he was turned off by "the smells and the dust and the dirt; the complete artificiality of it all; the beetle-eyed betters howling hysterically in the hope of getting something for nothing; the inane chatter of foolish women who have aberrations that some system can be devised to beat the races; the touts, the petty chiselers, the gangsters who never look at a horse but only at the results and the odds." He gave up covering the races in the course of his career.

The *Detroit News* fired Bingay as managing editor in 1928 because "I was saying the right things in the wrong way and doing a lot of drinking." Detroit Tigers player Billy Rogell remarked in Richard Bak's *Cobb Would Have Caught It: The Golden Age of Baseball in Detroit* (1991) that Bingay could be vindictive when he drank: Rogell recalled an incident when he was staying in a "nice hotel on the northeast side of Chicago," where the Tigers were playing the Cubs in the 1935 World Series. Bingay came into the lobby looking like "he'd vomited all over himself and slept out on the street." Rogell's wife made a remark about the hotel letting "these drunks in here." Bingay heard her and promptly became a strong critic of her husband. Rogell had thought he and Bingay had a good relationship before the incident.

The newspaper made Bingay its London bureau chief in 1928–1929, but Bingay was not entirely comfortable as a foreign correspondent and was unhappy with the lack of appreciation from the newspaper for his work in Europe. He left this position because of the illness of his first wife, Sarah Ross, whom he married on

A cartoon rendition by Floyd S. Nixon of "Iffy the Dopester," the fictional character created by Bingay for his baseball column in the Detroit Free Press *(from Bingay,* Detroit Is My Own Home Town, *1946)*

28 October 1908; she died 14 October 1930. They had one daughter, Sibyl Ross. A year after his wife's death Bingay married Cecelia Fuhrman, on 4 December 1931.

Upon his return to the United States, Bingay left the *Detroit News* and served as a consultant to a national advertising agency for about a year. In 1930 he edited the centennial edition of the *Detroit Free Press,* to which he soon transferred his experience as editorial director. Bingay was associated with the *Free Press* until his death, although his relationship with the staff was often quite stormy. *Newsweek* (16 August 1948) noted that in Detroit half of the people who read the *Detroit Free Press* read his "Good Morning" column (which he began in 1930) on the editorial page to find "the truth and the light" while the other half read him "to see what the Old Coot is crabbing about today."

Bingay's columns ranged from sports coverage to opinions on local politics as well as on the world situation, but many of them ignited controversy and generated much criticism. In his "Good Morning" column, which he often claimed reflected his own personality–"arrogant, conceited, impatient, rough, crude, bitter"–and which highlighted his flamboyant and highly personal style, Bingay became one of the best-known newspapermen in Michigan. Nonetheless, he alienated much of the staff of the newspaper, while his hard-line conservative politics angered many readers. He attacked President Franklin Delano Roosevelt and the United Auto Workers Union, and his sharply critical obituary of James Couzens, one-time partner of Henry Ford, Detroit mayor, Michigan governor, and U.S. senator, almost got him fired in 1936. Bingay reprinted many of these columns on personalities and sports, especially baseball, which he considered Detroit's safety valve, in *Detroit Is My Own Home Town* (1946).

Perhaps Bingay's most popular creation was "Iffy the Dopester," which started as an unsigned sports column during the 1934 baseball season. The name had its origins in Bingay's early days as a sportswriter for the *Detroit News,* when every sports section ran a schedule of the day's games, accompanied by standings that showed a team's record "if they win" and "if they lose." According to Iffy, he was born "with two strikes on me" that "even the doctor agreed to . . . and my old man was pretty much disgusted but Abner Doubleday who invented baseball said not to worry." Bingay wrote the column in a breezy, anecdotal, and folksy style that mocked the sportswriters who were keeping Detroit citizens excited about the pennant chances of the Tigers.

"Iffy" remained anonymous, identified only by a drawing of a gaffer created by *Detroit Free Press* artist Floyd S. Nixon, until *The Saturday Evening Post* (21 January 1939) published a piece on Bingay that disclosed his pseudonym as a "white-whiskered old coot whose ball memory ran back to Abner Doubleday" and whose "articles were compounded of mythological and literary illusions, a sound knowledge of the game and a close acquaintance with the diamond heroes of the past." The column soon expanded to a few daily paragraphs that tried to start feuds with almost any public character, sports or otherwise, including Soviet dictator Joseph Stalin and union leader John L. Lewis. To promote the column the *Detroit Free Press* distributed over a half million Iffy buttons, encouraged the establishment of Iffy clubs throughout Michigan, and sponsored such public-relations gimmicks as Iffy cushions and cocktail glasses, Iffy songs, and Iffy tigers modeled after the drawings with which Nixon decorated the columns. Many of Bingay's one-liners from his columns, collected in *Of Me I Sing,* demonstrate his characteristically American wit: "'I'm just crazy to be in the newspaper business,' he said, and I explained, 'You have to be'"; "Matthew, Mark and Luke were great reporters while John was just an editorial writer"; "Any woman without a heart can make a fool of any man without a head"; "You discipline yourself in the social amenities so that you can tolerate being bored."

One of Iffy's favorite individuals, both personally and professionally, was Walter O. Briggs, the owner of the Detroit Tigers, "the fan who bought the ball park," as Bingay highlighted in his columns, his book *Detroit Is My Own Home Town* (1935), and in a 6 March 1943 article for *The Saturday Evening Post.* Another was Detroit Tigers player Herman Schaefer, whom Bingay considered "the finest natural comedian baseball has ever known." Bingay, writing as "Iffy," profiled Schaefer in "Baseball's Troubadour: The Saga of Germany Schaefer" (*Saturday Evening Post,* 27 January 1940) as a player of whom "the world will know his like no more, because baseball now is serious big business and holds no place for the troubadour of the diamond. For Schaef . . . was not a master clown like Altrock nor a vaudevillian like Al Schacht. His humor came out of the spontaneity of the game itself, bubbling from him in the head of play. Doing such mad things as stealing first after reaching second and forcing the lawmakers to pass a law forbidding it." Bingay's admiration of Ty Cobb, whom he considered the best ever as he wrote in *Detroit Is My Own Home Town*–"after he had hung up his spiked shoes for good, the game was never quite the same for me"–reflects his style when he was totally supportive and enthusiastic about his subject despite knowledge that the athlete, although a star on the field, was not the most likable human being off it.

In *The Detroit Tigers* (1946), author Frederick G. Lieb reprinted one of Bingay's columns, "We Want Tigers–Not Tame Kittens," written at the end of September 1933, after the Tigers had another losing season and manager Bucky Harris resigned. Always loyal, Bingay expressed his dissatisfaction as Iffy the Dopester with a two-column editorial that the *Detroit Free Press* ran, as Lieb put it, in "12-point Roman type, big enough to smack [owner] Frank Navin and anyone else interested, right in the face." After noting that the Detroit Tigers had won their last pennant twenty-four years earlier, Iffy mourned that "Detroit, long one of the best baseball towns in America, has been steadily losing interest in the sport because of lifeless teams under a lifeless management. If baseball is a sport, then Frank Navin should bestir himself to present to the paying public some form of competition." After admonishing Navin to "show some sporting blood, take a gambler's chance, spend some money, get an aggressive leadership," Bingay declared professional baseball is a business that "must also be a sport in order to survive," one that requires enthusiasm behind the ownership.

Another Bingay invention for his "Good Morning" column was a series of one-sentence "Intercepted Letters," signed by "Pipeline Pete." One column in 1948, for example, printed an intercepted letter to Secretary of State George C. Marshall: "Dear George: Does President Truman give you hourly reports on his changes of mind, or do you just have to guess a foreign policy?"

Bingay increasingly used undisguised sarcasm against his opponents, especially in his columns during the 1930s. His 7 April 1936 "Good Morning" piece, for example, "The Unwritten Letter of an Exasperated Small Town Editor," was addressed to Eleanor Roosevelt in response to her popular syndicated column, "My Day."

Despite the wit and sarcasm frequently expressed in his columns, however, Bingay was a serious journalist. As editorial director he was responsible for all news, sports, and features, as well as the editorial pages. In this role he coordinated a story on an American Legion parade during its 1931 convention in Detroit that won a Pulitzer Prize the next year for five *Detroit Free Press* reporters. Bingay had the reporters research statistics and background material on places where American Legion posts fought during World War I and connect this information to the parade. He claimed in *Of Me I Sing* that the resulting story was "more than a parade story" but "in marching formation, a history of the American Army's participation in the war." In 1933 he received an honorable mention citation for correspondence from the Pulitzer Prize committee for "the brilliantly written obituary of Sir Donald Ross," the Nobel laureate who discovered the mosquito cycle in malaria.

One of Bingay's most frequently reprinted columns is "He Who Went about Doing Good," which first appeared in the *Detroit Free Press* on Christmas Day in 1930 and reveals a spiritual side to Bingay that he rarely exhibited in print. The column declares that "this day is celebrated by people of many faiths, and by many of no faith, the birth of Him Whom the world calls Jesus of Nazareth. What is His significance today?" Bingay ends with an observation that "those of you who have gone forth this Christmas in the joy of unselfish service, who have soothed the suffering, strengthened the weak and aided the needy now find your reward in your own hearts, for you have but followed in the footsteps of Him 'Who went about doing good.'"

As a concerned journalist Bingay started a national campaign in 1933 against the "yellow press" to counter the assistance and favorable coverage many newspapers gave to criminals, which he called "reportorial burglary." The International Association of Police Chiefs adopted a resolution at their annual convention that supported Bingay's actions; in 1949, however, Bingay earned the animosity of police organizations when as editorial director he spoke out against the Detroit

Bingay (right), mid 1930s, during a radio broadcast with (from left) Free Press *colleague Edgar A. Guest, Tigers owner Frank J. Navin, and Tigers player-manager Mickey Cochrane (from Bingay,* Of Me I Sing, *1949)*

Police Department, which required a loyalty oath from *Free Press* reporters seeking access to the police and fire departments. Bingay felt that "the only guarantee of freedom given by the constitution is the freedom of a printing press from being licensed." Bingay's position as editor also afforded him influence in Michigan state politics. When William Randolph Hearst bought the *Detroit Times* and began printing horse-racing odds, a move that drew away *Free Press* readers, Bingay pushed through a state law banning the publication of such odds.

After the end of World War II, Bingay traveled to Europe in April 1945 with a group of American publishers and editors at the request of General Dwight David Eisenhower "to testify to the world" of the atrocities of the Nazi slave-labor prison camps. As Bingay recounts in *Of Me I Sing,* Eisenhower wanted the most authoritative voices in journalism to report what they saw so that Americans would accept that the accounts of "the most horrible hells ever devised by the warped minds of madmen" were not exaggerated. He was a last-minute replacement for John S. Knight, the publisher of the *Free Press,* whose oldest son was killed in action shortly before the trip.

During Bingay's travels his dispatches from Dachau and from Buchenwald were widely syndicated, and he signed a group statement urging the United States to adopt a strong policy toward war criminals. From this experience he produced some of his most heartfelt writing. "It Could Happen Here," an article that first appeared in the 10 May 1945 *Detroit Free Press* and was reprinted in the August issue of *Reader's Digest,* expressed his feelings after his return from Europe. On 16 May 1945 Bingay expanded these remarks in "What I Saw in Europe and What We Must Do About It," an address before a special meeting of the Economic Club of Detroit that was published in *Vital Speeches of the Day* (1 August 1945). Bingay unsparingly described his anger and his outrage at the Nazi atrocities that he witnessed. Comparing Nazism to the Ku Klux Klan, gangster Al Capone, and "the political, rabble rousing genius" Huey P. Long, Bingay saw his "own beloved America through that hideous nightmare that was once Germany."

Bingay (center) with Walter O. Briggs, owner of the Detroit Tigers from 1936 to 1952 (left), and commissioner of baseball Kenesaw Mountain Landis (from Bingay, Detroit Is My Own Home Town, *1946)*

Bingay published his *Detroit Is My Own Home Town* in 1946; the book is an enthusiastic account of the automobile capital of the world by a newspaperman who had grown up with the city since the days when it was almost literally a one-horse town. Featured are stories of the auto industry and of some of the "fabulous fellows" of the city, such as Henry Ford and Father Charles E. Coughlin, the "radio priest." The volume also offers a generous selection of Iffy's baseball stories, varying in tone from masterful praise, such as his sometimes adulatory prose about Ty Cobb or his genuine respect for Briggs, to a breezy, irreverent style when he is writing about someone like Schaefer, "the old Detroit second-sacker," and his antics on the field. Most of all, the reader is constantly made aware that Bingay loved Detroit baseball with a passion he did not feel for other sports. This bias is especially apparent in his disdainful descriptions of prizefighting and horse racing as he experienced them in his earliest days as a sports editor on the *Detroit News.* Bingay could be sarcastic, even harsh, when writing about individuals he did not like or approve of, and his egotistical style celebrates his irascibility.

Reception of the book was mostly positive. The reviewer for *Kirkus Reviews* (1 February 1946) found it "a labor of love which catches the spirit of the city," while the reviewer for *The New York Times* (26 May 1946) thought it raced along in "a style as breezy as Detroit itself" and was "an outstanding contribution to folklore, fact and fantasy." For the reviewer in *Book Week* (21 April 1946), however, Bingay's memoir seemed to be "written entirely in the Detroit Athletic Club, where the auto moguls gather to play high finance like poker." The reviewer in the *Springfield Republican* (21 April 1946) praised the readable yarns and the "much intriguing out-of-school talk about the days when the 'auto game' was considered the proper territory of the sports department" but claimed that the book lacked the sense of the personality of the city, describing instead a Detroit equipped with "a carburetor instead of a soul."

After his trip to Europe, Bingay tried to promote Eisenhower as a presidential candidate, but he blundered seriously when he wrote an editorial on 3 November 1948, the day after the presidential election, that falsely declared Thomas E. Dewey as the winner, an incident similar to the infamous "Dewey Defeats Truman" headline that appeared that same day in the *Chicago Daily Tribune.* The newspaper staff asked Bingay to drop the editorial after election returns declared Harry Truman the winner, but, true to character, he stubbornly refused, possibly because he was attempting to establish his credentials with the Republican Party.

Bingay had varied interests, which were reflected in his memberships in the American Society of Newspaper Editors, the Newcomen Society of Baseball Writers' Association of America, the Board of Commerce, and the Sigma Delta Chi fraternity. He was elected an honorary member of the Wayne County Medical Society and received honorary doctor of law degrees from Wayne University in 1932 and Olivet College in 1946.

Bingay's autobiography, *Of Me I Sing,* is an incomplete but still entertaining account. Bingay was selective in his inclusion of important events in his life. He devotes a chapter to his early experience as a sportswriter for the *Detroit News* from 1904 to 1910, a journalistic experience he considered one of the best of his life since it exposed him not only to sports greats but also to the major figures in the automobile industry. Otherwise, the book includes little on his sportswriting. *Of Me I Sing* is impartial in his depiction of personalities, however, especially those he had already attacked in his newspaper columns, such as Father Coughlin. When Coughlin used his radio show to attack Wall Street and stock speculation, Bingay published an exposé of the priest's stock-market deals. His fascinating and revealing profile of Couzens showed "a man of contradictions" who was "one of the richest men in America, but one of the loneliest," who wanted friends but "spurned with bitterness every proffered companionship."

The reviewer for the *Saturday Review of Literature* (9 April 1949) found *Of Me I Sing* "a lively and authentic addendum to the saga of American journalism"; the reviewer for the *San Francisco Chronicle* (24 July 1949), on the other hand, thought the book was "as egotistical as it sounds." A more balanced opinion came from the writer for the *New York Herald Tribune/Weekly Book Review* (20 February 1949), who described it as "a backward-looking book" but one of "a happy warrior, a man who has spent half a century collecting scars and contusions more abundantly than cash, but having a rousing good time anyhow." To young men, the review concluded, the book was a warning as well as an invitation. Journalists may end up battered and bankrupt, but "you will not be bored."

Malcolm Wallace Bingay died 21 August 1953, one day after suffering a cerebral hemorrhage while writing his "Good Morning" column. After his death the *Free Press* published *Good Morning: A Collection of Some of the Best Liked Columns of Malcolm W. Bingay, Late Editorial Director of the Detroit Free Press* (1954).

A 22 August 1953 obituary in *The New York Times* called Bingay "one of the most colorful newspaper personalities in the Midwest," who "sparked the enthusiasm and incurred the wrath of both his readers and fellow-journalists." The article attributed this reputation both to Bingay's celebrated irascibility and to his proven skills. A former colleague found Bingay "a dread figure to municipal malefactors and a source of holy terror to cub reporters and office boys." In a sense Bingay represented an embodiment of Detroit, the city he praised and criticized all his professional life. He was not the most likable man, especially with the abusive attacks he hurled at opponents and his political prejudices, but his sports column countered these negative qualities with its mostly positive boosterism for the sports teams and athletes of Detroit.

References:

"Bing's Song," *Time,* 53 (7 March 1949): 64;

"Good Morning Bingay," *Newsweek,* 32 (16 August 1948): 54–55;

"Malcolm Bingay, Detroit Newsman," *New York Times,* 22 August 1953, p. L15;

James S. Pooler, "The Legend of Malcolm Bingay, As Remembered by His Friend Jimmy Pooler," *Detroit Free Press,* 25 December 1966, pp. 1, 8–9.

Papers:

The libraries of the *Detroit Free Press* and the *Philadelphia Inquirer* have clipping files on Malcolm Bingay. His papers are in the Bentley Historical Library, Ann Arbor, Michigan, which also has material on Bingay in its Frank Dwight Fitzgerald, Emerson R. Boyles, and Frank Murphy collections.

Joe Bostic

(21 March 1908 - 29 May 1988)

Kelly E. Rusinack

MAJOR POSITIONS HELD: Broadcaster, WCBM radio, Baltimore (1932–1935); correspondent, *Baltimore Afro-American* (1935–1937); broadcaster, WMCA radio, New York (1937–1939); broadcaster, MCMW radio, New York (1939–1942); sports editor, radio and entertainment columnist, *New York People's Voice* (1942–1945); sports editor, *New York Amsterdam News* (1945–circa 1950); announcer, Madison Square Garden (1972–1988).

A flair for the dramatic characterized Joe Bostic's approach to his professional endeavors. As a sports announcer, radio broadcaster, journalist, socialite, and educator, Bostic was never demure. The hallmark of Bostic's attitude was his refusal to be intimidated–by his peers, by social standards, and especially not by organized crime or even by the so-called Mahatma of baseball, Brooklyn Dodgers general manager Branch Rickey. Bostic was confident of his abilities and aspired to positions few men of color had held before him, and he did so without worrying about his reputation from either the black or white communities. It is perhaps his audacity as a sportswriter that overshadows all his other accomplishments, though his sportswriting career was the shortest-lived of all.

Joseph William Bostic was born in Mt. Holly, New Jersey, on 21 March 1908 to Lawrence and Lillian Eldridge Bostic. His parents helped their son attain something that most sportswriters–or members of his race in general–did not have in the 1930s: a college education. Bostic worked his way through Morgan State College (later University) in Baltimore, financing his education in part by boxing under an assumed name (so that his father would not find him out). He was already an accomplished pugilist, having won two boxing championships at Atlantic City High School; he also earned four letters in sports between the two high schools he attended, Mt. Holly High and Atlantic City High. His father did not approve of an athletic career for Bostic, who also played collegiate varsity baseball while at Morgan State. Bostic was close to his father, and out of respect for his father's support of his future the younger Bostic compromised with his family–he majored in journalism and kept his love of sports on the sidelines as a journalist and announcer. The fearlessness and self-esteem Bostic learned from his family and drew upon as an athlete seem to have served him well all his life, as evidenced later in his writings.

Joe Bostic (from Jim Reisler, Black Writers/Black Baseball, *1994)*

After graduating in 1932, Bostic took his first job, as a gospel-music radio broadcaster for WCBM in Baltimore, perhaps the career closer to his heart than sports. Bostic was the first African American broadcaster at the station, and perhaps in the history of Baltimore radio. He also worked for a few years as a correspondent for the *Baltimore Afro-American* newspaper, one of the premier black publications of the twentieth century. He married a Baltimore native, Morgan State alumna and teacher Dorothy Mitchell, in 1930. As their three children, Joe Jr., Lee, and Debra, came along, the Bostics moved from racist Baltimore to the more liberal New York City, where opportunities existed for a young, educated black couple.

Bostic continued his radio broadcasting career in New York and began graduate studies at Columbia University, though he never received a degree. He also began announcing Negro League baseball games. New York City boasted the best baseball in the country, black and white, and Bostic added his radio-trained voice to the excitement surrounding Negro League baseball in its heyday.

Bostic began his sports announcing career in an unusual way. He was working the third shift as a stevedore at the New Jersey docks at the time and would indulge his love of baseball by attending day games at the Dyckman Oval, host to many local and Negro League baseball games. At one such game the stadium announcer took ill and suddenly left the ballpark without warning, leaving the announcer's booth empty. Bostic soon noticed that no one was announcing the game, so he left his seat, entered the booth, and began to call the game himself. When questioned by the stadium authorities as to what he thought he was doing, Bostic simply stated the obvious: their announcer left and he was calling the game. Impressed by Bostic's initiative and abilities, the team owner offered Bostic the position full-time by the end of the game.

This scene was repeated, with variations, many times as Bostic took the initiative to earn positions in sports announcing that men of color had never before held. When a new boxing arena opened in Harlem, the Rockland Palace, Bostic introduced himself to the owners and told them that they needed a man of his talent and experience, someone "from the community"–that is, the black community–as their new announcer. In a later interview Bostic said that he had to pass through the scrutiny of Tammany Hall and the mob in order to obtain his license to announce boxing in New York. Given the racial climate of the time, however, greasing the right palms was a small task in comparison to the difficulty in just getting the white owners to take him seriously.

At the same time, the Negro National League, impressed with Bostic's announcing at the Oval, appointed him to announce their games at Yankee Stadium and the Polo Grounds, where Negro League games often outdrew the all-white major-league teams who made their homes at those ballparks. For four consecutive years Bostic was selected to announce the annual East-West All-Star Classic in Chicago, the major Negro League event of the season. The East-West games easily drew more than fifty thousand fans each year. To be selected to announce the games was a great tribute to Bostic's abilities as an announcer. On the difficulty of starting his career as a sports announcer in the 1940s, Bostic commented in a 1977 interview with *Black Sports* magazine, "You had no sympathies, you had no radio or television or Black movement, or the desire of whites to placate us. . . . It was like trying to dig a career out of concrete."

From 1942 to 1945 Bostic held his most famous–or infamous–job, as sports editor and entertainment columnist for the New York *People's Voice* newspaper. Owned and operated by Adam Clayton Powell Jr., a black New York City politician and former preacher with decidedly Communist leanings, the *People's Voice* gave Bostic the opportunity to pull no punches as a journalist. He insisted in his columns, for example, that the Indianapolis Clowns Negro League team did a disservice to all African Americans by perpetuating the stereotype of blacks as clowns, though he conceded that such showmanship drew crowds to see the team play. He acknowledged the dichotomy between the need to gain respect in a white-dominated society and the need to keep baseball alive through gate receipts and was graceful enough to admit his personal trepidation over these conflicting interests.

Bostic drew the ire of the major-league baseball establishment with his articles, characterized later by Howie Evans in his obituary of Bostic for the *Amsterdam News* (4 June 1988) as "blistering." From his editorial column, "Scoreboard," always written in the third person as if it was an alter ego, Bostic shot darts at the racists of baseball, poking holes in their arguments of the racial inferiority of blacks. Making his "Weekly Slam" lists in early 1944 were the "Operators" of major-league baseball, Judge Landis (separately), and Adolph Hitler. Much like the Communist *Daily Worker,* Bostic criticized those who would conspire to oppress blacks in general and African American baseball players in particular.

Unlike some of the more famous black sportswriters of the early 1940s, such as Sam Lacy and Wendell Smith, Bostic did not fear the retribution of, and did not wish to placate, the racist sports establishment. He sometimes wrote scathing articles in which he criticized his fellow journalists for what he believed to be their lack of courage. He was not afraid of being labeled as a troublemaker–in fact, he seemed to thrive on the challenge. He dealt head-on with the subject of race and sports, not by begging whites for a chance but by demanding equality for people he knew to be equal or superior to their oppressors. Bostic himself was better educated than most of the whites who conspired to keep blacks disfranchised for most of the 20th century, and his race awareness formed the substance of his articles. In keeping with the tradition of the black press, Bostic did not cover major-league baseball or other all-white sports. His coverage included anything in which African Americans were involved, however, from Negro League baseball to local handball, golf, boxing, the Amateur Athletic Union (AAU) leagues, and basketball.

His "Weekly Salute" column, for example, highlights black achievements in sports nationwide. Bostic conducted interviews with people he found to be proponents of racial equality, such as white Catholic priest Father Campion, who spoke out against racism in baseball. He also recognized racial pioneers such as Dr. Charles Drew, who had been a standout athlete at Amherst College. Bostic applauded Dr. Drew, noting, "now you're scoring point[s] for a bigger 'team'–the entire human race!" In highlighting such achievements he educated his readers to the pride of their race, often obscured by the silence of a white media.

One of his more famous articles came in a column in "Scoreboard" from March 1942. Simply titled "Dreamin'," it was his fantasy of being the first "broker" for Negro League stars, who Bostic kept in cages in the fantasy, for sale to a clamoring major-league baseball establishment. The government wants to shut down the operation as a monopoly, however; baseball commissioner Kenesaw Mountain Landis refuses to allow desegregation; and the presidents of the Negro National and American Leagues object to the sale of their investments. In this last respect Bostic was ahead of other desegregationists in dealing with the issue of decimating the Negro Leagues without remuneration. When baseball eventually desegregated, the ever financially tenuous Negro Leagues quickly declined.

On a more serious note, about four months later Bostic addressed the issue in an 11 July 1942 "Scoreboard" column, "In Re Negroes in Big Leagues." Saying that all black sportswriters had an opinion on the issue, he offered his, admitting, "our notions about the whole idea don't exactly see eye-to-eye with the popular point-of-view." Outlining his position, he explained, "Our approach to the question is strictly mercenary. We're deadly practical about the entire situation. We're not convinced that the baseball played in the organized leagues necessarily represents the best caliber of ball played per se, and therefore, the Negro players would not be moving into faster company than that in which they were already playing." He went on to assert that desegregation would mean the death of not only the Negro Leagues but also the industries that supply goods and services to black baseball, which were mostly

SPORTS EXTRA

By JOE BOSTIC

CLEVELAND—Here in the Forrest City it's good cutting up old touches with the boys on the sports beat . . . Sam McAllister, lone race member on the municipal boxing commission setup, may do a Jim Farley and parlay the post into a bigger spot on the national scene. What with the increasingly strategic influence that Ohioans are exerting in the national political arena. It's a cinch that if Mr. Lausche goes any great distance that he's a sure shot to carry Samuel along. So as a future book reminder, we say keep an eye on him. One thing this writer knows; he's a mighty handy fellow to know around these parts.

in the national political arena. It's a cinch that if Mr. Lausche goes any great distance that he's a sure shot to carry Samuel along. So as a future book reminder, we say keep an eye on him. One thing this writer knows; he's a mighty handy fellow to know around these parts.

Joe Bostic

Square Garden Friday (tonight). . . You are naturally inclined to pick Jake because he has turned the trick twice already. However, there is also the performance chart which shows that Tommy improved as the series progressed. He COULD have the complete answer this time. Certainly if he can attain the physical and mental peak that he reached for the Robinson fight, he'd have enough to win. After all, Robbie has beaten Jake five times (true, he didn't get the official nod that night in Detroit although he won six heats) and Tommy came mighty close to shading Mr. Slick on the title contest. He hits sharp and he'll have more weight. But that's where we think the edge lies. The Bronxite is no super scrapper but, he's a good man and a good big man figures to take a good little man, even if his name is Tommy Bell and he weighs around 150.

Bostic's 15 March 1947 column in the New York Amsterdam News. *He served as sports editor for about five years, beginning in 1945.*

black-owned institutions. He also listed African Americans who would be out of jobs–such as secretaries, umpires, scorekeepers, and announcers.

Bostic argued further that subjecting players to "the humiliation and indignities associated with the problems of eating, sleeping and traveling in a layout dominated by prejudice-ridden southern whites" had no merit. He suggested the introduction of an all-black team into major-league baseball, an idea that had more supporters at the time than Bostic supposed. He summarized: "From the idealist and democratic point of view, we say 'yes' to Negroes in the two other leagues. From the standpoint of practicality: 'No.'" While his arguments were reasonable for his time, Bostic eventually acceded to the idealistic approach, to the detriment of the all-black establishments represented and supported by Negro League baseball.

Bostic also took the Black Yankees, for whom he announced games, to task for their lack of talent for the 1944 season. Comparing them to the perennial powerhouse Homestead Grays, and even to the New York Cubans and the Newark Eagles, he expressed his dismay that his hometown team did not appear ready for competition. He had an obligation, he asserted, to criticize the team's chances: "as a newspaperman with even an ounce of integrity, I owe it to my readers to call 'em as I see them or suffer the humiliating alternative of having the age-old indictment of the Negro press hurled at me, to wit: Negro sportswriters don't know what the hell they're talking about."

In April 1944 Bostic surmised that the desegregation of baseball was dealt a blow straight from the White House, as Presidential Secretary Stephen Early accepted a lifetime pass from the owner of the Washington Senators, Clark Griffith, an outspoken opponent of integration. Bostic astutely analyzed this act as confirmation that the government saw nothing wrong with major-league baseball. After the death of Judge Landis, the racist baseball commissioner, Bostic even publicly requested an audience with Ford Frick and William Harridge, presidents, respectively, of the National and American Leagues, to extract statements from them officially denouncing Jim Crow baseball.

Bostic, though, did not limit his barbs to whites. He also served notice on other members of his race that they, too, were being scrutinized. He took on the foolishness of the problems plaguing Negro League baseball, which had a long history of administrative and labor strife. In September 1942, for example, he complained of how poorly the Negro Leagues treated their fans; in an August 1944 article he chastised Satchel Paige's latest demands, noting that Negro League promoters had "given Leroy the exaggerated notion of his importance." He went on to give statistics of Paige's true drawing power, in comparison to the popular myths, targeting some criticisms at Abe Saperstein, promoter of Negro baseball, and his portrayals of Paige to the media. In doing so Bostic attacked a black baseball legend–almost unheard of in the black media. The challenge exemplified his belief that African Americans must hold themselves to the same standards to which white Americans held themselves.

In January 1944 Bostic endorsed Wendell Smith of the *Pittsburgh Courier* for the position of Negro National League statistician, an idea that Smith himself developed and even offered to do for free. Instead, the Negro National League owners–with the exception of the astute and irascible Effa Manley of the Newark Eagles–chose to hire the all-white Elias Sports Bureau. When this announcement was made in March of that year, Bostic lashed out at the owners in two separate columns. He considered the hiring of the Elias Sports Bureau to be a betrayal of the entire race–that even the black baseball owners bought into the inferiority of blacks. Bostic saw these attitudes within his race to be even more stifling of progress than the oppression faced from whites.

Bostic's most glorious moment as a sports journalist, though, was a story of his own making. In April 1945, on the heels of the passage of the Ives-Quinn antidiscrimination bill in New York, he teamed up with Nat Low of *The Daily Worker* to take Dave "Showboat" Thomas and Terris McDuffie, two Negro League ballplayers, to the Dodgers training camp at Bear Mountain for tryouts. Branch Rickey was furious at having been blindsided, but Bostic was unflappable. He detailed their two-day stay at the facility on his sports page, counting it as a victory, though he knew it had not tangibly changed anything. Bostic's critics said that he had gone about it all wrong, that his approach only angered Rickey, hurting the cause even more. He responded that no approach would have been flawless given the racial climate in baseball at the time, but that he believed the time was right to take some sort of action and that his approach was better than taking no action at all.

Though tough and direct, Bostic also displayed a keen sense of humor. He wrote an entertaining column, "Home Boy Says," in which he "translated" letters written in jive, then popular with the Harlem jazz crowd. He also wrote "Man About Harlem," a gossip column, for a while. In this respect he followed the lead of Dan Burley, also a popular black newspaperman at that time, who wrote similar columns as editor of the *Amsterdam News,* another New York black paper. Bostic also had a radio column, in which he never missed an opportunity to promote his own shows. He believed that "the greatest single media for the dissemination of propaganda is the radio," and he continued with careers in both radio and newspapers simultaneously for many years.

Bostic left the *People's Voice* for the *Amsterdam News* a few weeks before Jackie Robinson signed a minor-league contract with the Brooklyn Dodgers in late 1945. Bostic followed Robinson's progress for the *Amsterdam News.* He almost missed the most important baseball story of his time, however. Having accidentally eaten inedible mushrooms at a Harlem restaurant the night before the Dodgers' opening day in 1947, Bostic was home in bed ill on the day that Robinson was promoted to the Brooklyn club from the Montreal Royals minor-league club. He explained the emotions of that long-anticipated moment in his "Scoreboard" column the next day:

> A flinthearted sawbones had ordered us to bed. We were obedient up to a point. Listening to Red Barber's descriptions of the goings on, we stood it as long as we could . . . jumped up, grabbed our duds and made a bee line to Ebbets Field. . . . There wasn't anything you could say. What words could be adequate? You just felt a warm glow inside.

In September 1947, at the end of Robinson's first major-league season, Bostic gave Rickey his due, while reasserting his personal disapproval of the Mahatma's tactics. In "It Seems Rickey, Alone, Was on the Level," Bostic admitted that "there is no love lost between Rickey and Bostic, so this piece is hardly a matter of back slapping for a personal friend. . . . We resented his implication that we were dishonest and will continue to do so until such time as we receive an appropriate apology." He explained that his lengthy diatribe was meant to prove just how deeply his personal resentment of Rickey went, in order to highlight some glowing recommendations.

Bostic then had enough integrity to admit to an admiration for Rickey: "But, it took plenty of guts to face the ridicule on one hand and snide insinuations on the other, that he had violated a sacred 'agreement' that was in the form of an understanding. . . . Therefore, *Scoreboard* makes this specific recommendation: That the sports fans and a comprehensive citizens' committee give him the most impressive inter-racial testimonial dinner that this town ever saw . . . to pay a deserved tribute to a man, who, in our estimation, has struck the most important and significant blow for sports democracy in the past 20 years."

Bostic proved time and again in his sportswriting that he was a man of integrity, not afraid to take a stand, to admit publicly when he was wrong, and to admit publicly when he was right. His forthrightness and tenacity stood in marked contrast to most other newspapermen of his time, black and white, who did not take strong stands unless it was in support of the popular argument and who were afraid to hold opinions that might offend the social elite.

In addition to his sportswriting and radio broadcasting, Bostic produced and promoted theatrical talent shows and gospel concerts, including the first all-black gospel program to play at Carnegie Hall, the Negro Gospel and Religious Musical Festival, featuring the premier gospel singer of that time, Mahalia Jackson. He was known as the "Dean of Gospel Disk Jockeys" for his production of the Sunday morning "Gospel Train" on WLIB radio in New York. When television began to replace radio, Bostic transferred some of his loyalties to the new medium, as there seemed always to be room for one more professional endeavor in his busy life.

Bostic had a long and storied career as a boxing and wrestling announcer. Building upon his success announcing at Rockland Palace and for the Negro Leagues, as well as using his connections, he was able to secure positions at all-white venues such as Queensboro Arena in 1947. A friend who owed Bostic a favor and who was influential in the New York boxing circles spoke with the owners of Queensboro about an excellent announcer they should hire–at Bostic's insistence, his race was not mentioned, for it was a sure hindrance to being offered the job. He was given the job based on his experience and on the word of his friend. Bostic and his friend arranged that he would show up five minutes before the first bout he was to announce, not enough time for the owners to find a replacement once they found he was African American. Bostic figured that at least he would have one night of work at Queensboro. He was confident that his talent and ability as an announcer would earn him the position from there.

Bostic's first night at Queensboro happened to be the day Babe Ruth died, and before the fight began he broadcasted an enthralling tribute to the Babe for the audience. As he finished, the crowd stood on their feet and cheered. The owners of the arena later told him that they had never heard a boxing announcer receive a standing ovation–and Bostic had the job.

Bostic was next offered the announcing duties at Ridgewood Grove. There was one catch–he was required to announce professional wrestling matches, then considered to be a lowly assignment. He accepted the position and took the wrestling announcing in stride, a decision that turned out to be a blessing in disguise. As professional wrestling became more popular and took to television, Bostic's inside knowledge was invaluable and opened yet another new career for him.

Bostic stayed in sports as an announcer for many years. He went on to announce boxing at Sunnyside Gardens, White Plains Arena, the Old Broadway, and St. Nick's Arena. When longtime Madison Square Garden announcer Johnny Addie died in 1972, the same friend who secured Bostic's position at Queensboro petitioned for him to succeed Addie as the main ringside boxing announcer for the Garden. The competition for the prestigious position was fierce. For a job with such a high profile, which would catapult an announcer into the national spotlight, the top announcers from around the country–white announcers, as the Garden had never had a nonwhite announcer–offered to do the job for free, to relocate at their own expense. Bostic did not waiver in his application for the position, though he did not have the credentials of most of his competition.

As with the Queensboro job, Bostic triumphed. He became the first African American announcer in Madison Square Garden history. He also became the first black admitted to the Boxing Writers and Track Writers Associations. He helped to open the press boxes at the Garden to the black press through his boxing connections there. He also organized the National Negro Sportswriters Association and wrote sports articles through the association over the years.

Bostic's career encompassed more than his sports and journalistic endeavors; he and his wife cofounded the Junior Academy in Brooklyn in 1965, a private educational academy for African Americans. Dorothy Bostic received much attention in the black community for her work at the academy and appeared in the African American version of "Who's Who" many more times than did her husband, the racial pioneer, for her work as an educator. Of his opinion on the importance of the molding of black imagery in society, Bostic said in a 1977 *Black Sports* interview, "It is all important that we put our best image forward if we're going to make an impact in this total society in which we find ourselves. Because everyone else is doing it for his side." The Bostics lived their lives as cornerstones to that ideal of heightened awareness of the role of African Americans in modern American society.

Bostic died in a Long Island hospital on 29 May 1988, from long-standing heart ailments, at the age of eighty. His wife, who was also ill at the time of her husband's death, passed away less than two months later. He was relatively forgotten at the time of his death, even in the black community. Nevertheless, the *Amsterdam News* eulogized him, citing the opportunities he helped create for African Americans in sports, in journalism, in television, in education, and in society: "Joe Bostic was one of the most respected and at the same time, one of the most feared Black journalists of the '40s. Feared by those who practiced racism."

References:

"Joe Bostic," *Black Sports,* 2 (March 1977): 40–46;

Benedict Cosgrove, *Covering the Bases: The Most Unforgettable Moments in Baseball in the Words of the Writers and Broadcasters Who Were There* (San Francisco: Chronicle, 1997);

D. L. Cummings, "The Key Players: Black Reporters Pressed the Issue," *New York Daily News,* 13 April 1997, p. 12;

Howie Evans, "Negro League celebration needs lessons in history," *New York Amsterdam News,* 19 November 1994, p. 56;

Evans, "75th Anniversary of Negro Baseball League celebration slated," *New York Amsterdam News,* 2 December 1995, p. 48;

John Freeman, "History show offers great histrionics," *San Diego Union-Tribune,* 6 December 1991, p. D-6;

Jim Reisler, *Black Writers/Black Baseball: An Anthology of Articles from Black Sportswriters Who Covered the Negro Leagues* (Jefferson, N.C.: McFarland, 1994), pp. 75–76;

Dick Zander, "Joe Bostic, Sports Journalist Who Broke Racial Barriers," *New York Newsday,* 1 June 1988, p. 41.

Warren Brown

(3 January 1894 - 19 November 1978)

Joel Sternberg
Saint Xavier University

MAJOR POSITIONS HELD: Sportswriter, *San Francisco Bulletin* (1916–1917); sports editor, *San Francisco Call-Post, San Francisco Call-Bulletin* (circa 1918–1921, 1922); sports editor, *New York Evening Mail* (1922); reporter, *New York Journal* (1923); sports editor, columnist, *Chicago Herald and Examiner* (1923–1939), *Chicago Herald-American* (1939–1941); sports editor, columnist, reporter, *Chicago Sun* (1941–1946); columnist, reporter, *Chicago Herald-American* (1947–1953), *Chicago American* (1953–1969); occasional columnist, *Chicago Today* (1969–1974).

BOOKS: *Rockne* (Chicago: Reilly & Lee, 1931);
The Chicago Cubs (New York: Putnam, 1946);
Win, Lose, or Draw (New York: Putnam, 1947);
The Chicago White Sox (New York: Putnam, 1952).

OTHER: "A World Pennant Comes to Washington," in *Sport Writing of Today and Selections from The Best Sport Stories,* edited by Lawrence W. Murphy (Champaign, Ill.: The Service Press, 1925);
"Bedlam in Bengaltown," in *Best Sports Stories of 1945,* edited by Irving T. Marsh and Edward Ehre (New York: Dutton, 1946).

Warren Brown (from Harold Johnson, Who's Who in Major League Baseball, *1933)*

SELECTED PERIODICAL PUBLICATIONS–UNCOLLECTED: "Warren Brown Gets Line on Firpo by Day in Camp," *Chicago Herald and Examiner,* 7 September 1923, p. 17;
"Grange Could Make Up Camp's Entire Backfield," *Chicago Herald and Examiner,* 20 October 1924, p. 11;
"Gabby Likes 'Em Hot," *Saturday Evening Post,* 211 (11 February 1939): 14–15, 84–86, 88–89;
"Hall of Fame Door May Close on Schalk if He Misses This Year," *Chicago Herald-American,* 6 January 1953, part 2, p. 18;
"It Could Only Happen to the White Sox," *Chicago,* 1 (July 1954): 46–51;
"Don't Believe Everything You Read," *Sport,* 17 (August 1954): 36–37, 68–71;
"What's Happening at Halas U?" *Sport,* 17 (November 1954): 10–11, 87–90;
"Has the American League Gone Minor?" *Sport,* 18 (February 1955): 10–11, 86–89;
"It's Now or Never for the White Sox!" *Sport,* 18 (June 1955): 14, 59–61;
"Jim Rivera Talking," *Sport,* 20 (October 1955): 20–21, 84–87;
"The Lane of Many Turnings," *Sport,* 21 (March 1956): 30–33, 90–92;

"Three Kinds of Players: Casey Stengel," *Baseball Digest,* 19 (August 1960): 81–82;

"Fence Busters Make the Game: Ted Williams," *Baseball Digest,* 20 (September 1960): 32;

"Down Memory Lane: Landis Protected Rights of the Players," *Baseball Digest,* 29 (September 1970): 52–55;

"Down Memory Lane: Nothing Compares to Glitter of World Series," *Baseball Digest,* 29 (October 1970): 64–68;

"Down Memory Lane: San Francisco, Fertile Ground for Major Leaguers," *Baseball Digest,* 30 (March 1971): 70–74;

"Down Memory Lane: Name Changes Common in Baseball," *Baseball Digest,* 30 (May 1971): 60–63;

"Down Memory Lane: Obscure Records Have an Allure of Their Own," *Baseball Digest,* 30 (July 1971): 84–87;

"Down Memory Lane: Odd Things Happened to Cubs in World Series," *Baseball Digest,* 31 (May 1972): 70–72.

Warren Brown was considered one of the premier sports editors and sports columnists in the United States in a career that began in 1916 and continued successfully for more than half a century. Recognized as a versatile and prolific writer, Brown was as comfortable and adept at covering the so-called hard news stories as he was in covering sports. Educated as a classical and Latin scholar, he was renowned for his exceptional mastery of the English language, his encyclopedic memory, and his razor-sharp wit. He excelled at coining memorable phrases, whether behind a typewriter or behind a podium, and in either venue his humor could be sarcastic or benign–as easily capable of deflating as well as inflating. In his selection to The National Baseball Hall of Fame in 1973, Brown was cited as a "Californian who worked in New York and made his reputation in Chicago" and was heralded for consistently giving "composition and expertise" to sports pages around the country.

Born in the coal-mining town of Somersville, California, on 3 January 1894, Warren William Brown was the son of Patrick and Hanore Boyle Brown. By his recollection, his father operated a sort of second-rate "Stork Club," the fate of which seemed to hinge on the well-being of the mines in the area. When the mines flooded and the miners moved away, so too did the Browns. Eventually they settled in San Francisco, where Warren began to encounter the people and events that fashioned his career. He became an avid reader with a strong interest in sports performers, past and present. He was especially interested in baseball and prizefighting, and to his delight he found many of his heroes living in close proximity to his new hometown.

Entering the grammar-school section of St. Ignatius College, later the University of San Francisco, Brown made significant progress, and in September 1905, at the age of eleven, he was promoted into the high school at St. Ignatius, where he proceeded to struggle. The following April, in the aftermath of the devastating San Francisco earthquake, Brown's schoolwork was disrupted and his family scattered to nearby Oakland and Sacramento. Moving back to San Francisco in 1907, a more mature Warren reentered the St. Ignatius secondary school. This time, he found academic life easier, which gave him more opportunity to read the sports pages and to develop his athletic skills.

Brown's love for baseball and his athleticism were a natural combination. Playing with the Telegraph Hill Boy's Club as a teammate of Swede Risberg–later to become infamous as one of the 1919 Chicago "Black Sox"–Brown had demonstrated potential. In 1909 he made the St. Ignatius College varsity team as a first baseman and center fielder while still a junior in high school. As he recalled in his autobiographical *Win, Lose, or Draw* (1947), "in my days elastic wasn't quite the word for eligibility codes." Nevertheless, Brown's abilities were noteworthy, and he was cited in *The San Francisco Call* when he and future major-leaguer Harry Heilmann hit the only two home runs as opponents in the 1911 city high-school championship. Overall, while playing concurrently for the St. Ignatius high school and college, Brown was awarded seven athletic monograms.

In 1913 Brown played semiprofessional baseball in Sebastopol, California, and within a year he began receiving offers from various professional baseball organizations, including Connie Mack's Philadelphia Athletics. He signed with nearby Sacramento in the Pacific Coast League, which provided him the opportunity to return to St. Ignatius College at the end of the season. In his first appearance for Sacramento as a pinch hitter, Brown hit safely off former Chicago White Sox pitching star Doc White. The art of fielding did not come quite so easily, however. "My floundering around," he later recalled in *Win, Lose, or Draw,* "prompted a Los Angeles baseball writer to say that I had all the grace of an underfed elephant on a waxed ballroom floor." Despite more auspicious moments of glory, including hitting two bases-loaded triples in one inning to drive in six runs, at the conclusion of the 1914 season Brown resumed his studies and, with no regrets, gave up thoughts of baseball as a career.

Upon his graduation from college in 1915 Brown contacted Hy Baggerly, the sports editor of *The San Francisco Bulletin,* who informed him that while no full-time position was available, he did need someone to write notes on semiprofessional baseball twice a week. Brown took the assignment and, as he indicated in his autobiography, contributed "a batch of bright and breezy banter, boots and bingles about the bushers," for which he was paid five dollars a week. When Francis J. Mannix, the baseball writer for the *Bulletin,* suddenly resigned, Brown, in the right place at the right time, wrote a story about a visiting Salt Lake City team. The story was published with Brown's byline, and his career was officially under way.

During World War I Brown interrupted his newspaper activities by enlisting in the Coast Artillery Corps. Stationed at Ft. Winfield Scott, he was transferred to Corps Intelligence for the duration of the war, and, as he writes in *Win, Lose, or Draw,* he "fought like hell through several western states and Alaska to keep the dread Hun and his loathsome agents at bay." After the war he returned to the *Bulletin* but soon followed several of his colleagues to William Randolph Hearst's *San Francisco Call-Post,* where he worked as a reporter and, while still in his early twenties, was named sports editor. When the *Bulletin* experienced financial difficulties, a merger with the *Call-Post* occurred, and Brown's newspaper was transformed into the *Call-Bulletin.* Brown survived these changes, and, with his position secure, on 23 August 1919 he married Mary Olive Burns, whom he had met while playing for Sebastopol.

As a reporter in San Francisco, Brown covered sports, qualified as a drama critic specializing in vaudeville and musical comedy, and assisted in covering local assignments, including political conventions and murder trials. Working under the guidance of Edward T. "Scoop" Gleeson, a knowledgeable and enthusiastic journalist, Brown was encouraged continually to experiment. The only house rule at the *Call-Bulletin* was a dislike for phoniness. In one memorable instance Gleeson and Brown set their sights on possible wrongdoings in the Pacific Coast League. When their investigation was completed, the league president was deposed and several team owners were replaced. Brown's antipathy toward phonies continued throughout his life, and, as he noted, it brought him peace of mind. "Eventually," said Brown as reported by David Condon in *The Chicago Tribune* (7 November 1964), "you'll find that peace of mind is more important than most of the other rewards."

Through the years the "Hearst style" to which Brown was exposed was often identified by trick idiom, beautiful phrasing, and vivid imagery. Brown, however, held steadfastly to the concept of simplicity–a concept he learned early in his career from T. A. Dorgan, better known as Tad, a cartoonist, accomplished sportswriter, and former Baggerly employee. In conversation with Dorgan, the young reporter mentioned that he liked to read Arthur Brisbane on general subjects and Damon Runyon in sports. They were easy to read and easy to understand even if he did not always agree with them. Dorgan held up for contrast and criticism an ornate story that Brown had written. From that moment Brown discarded his flowery expressions, which he acknowledged as better suited for his English classes at St. Ignatius. To his knowledge, Brown asserted, he had knowingly confused readers only once since that time, over the coverage of a Northwestern–Notre Dame football game. A fan from each team wrote him to complain that he was biased for their opponents.

When the temperamental boxing expert for the *Bulletin,* Marion Salazar, resigned unexpectedly, Brown was again in the right place at the right time. Cited as the first writer to predict that Jack Dempsey would succeed Jess Willard as heavyweight champion, Brown had speculated that Dempsey would knock out Willard in the first round of their 4 July 1919 match. Brown was threatened with dismissal for daring to make this rash prediction but was vindicated as Willard was knocked down seven times in the first round. Only the timekeeper's inaccurate counting kept Brown's prediction from coming true.

Brown's knowledge of boxing and admiration of Dempsey provided another career opportunity in 1921 when he was asked by Dempsey's flamboyant manager, Jack "Doc" Kearns, to supervise the champion's press relations for his upcoming bout with Georges Carpentier. Despite his lack of experience for this task, Brown took a leave of absence from his newspaper and traveled east to Atlantic City, where, as he later recalled in *Win, Lose, or Draw,* "there were as many newspapermen . . . as there were candidates for the Miss America contest, before they began eliminating the outsized numbers and culled the lilies from the tomatoes."

Having rubbed shoulders with an array of American and foreign journalists, in 1922 Brown returned to the *Call-Bulletin* but with an eye toward a more prestigious journalistic position in New York. He requested and was refused a salary increase and promptly served notice that he would consider offers from other newspapers. The opportunity came quickly. When sports editor Hugh Fullerton left the *New York Evening Mail* for a post in Chicago in 1922, Brown applied for the position and was accepted. To his mind, he had made the big leagues, although the *Evening Mail* was in the second rank of New York newspapers.

As reporter and columnist Al Laney recalled in his autobiography, *Covering the Court: A 50-Year Love Affair with the Game of Tennis* (1968), the *Evening Mail* had a small sports staff "housed in a back corner of the city

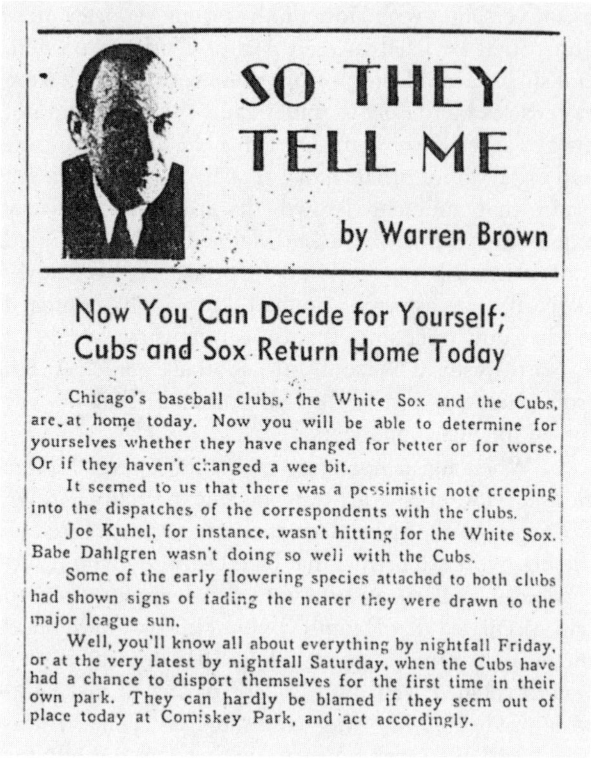
SO THEY TELL ME

by Warren Brown

Now You Can Decide for Yourself; Cubs and Sox Return Home Today

Chicago's baseball clubs, the White Sox and the Cubs, are at home today. Now you will be able to determine for yourselves whether they have changed for better or for worse. Or if they haven't changed a wee bit.

It seemed to us that there was a pessimistic note creeping into the dispatches of the correspondents with the clubs.

Joe Kuhel, for instance, wasn't hitting for the White Sox. Babe Dahlgren wasn't doing so well with the Cubs.

Some of the early flowering species attached to both clubs had shown signs of fading the nearer they were drawn to the major league sun.

Well, you'll know all about everything by nightfall Friday, or at the very latest by nightfall Saturday, when the Cubs have had a chance to disport themselves for the first time in their own park. They can hardly be blamed if they seem out of place today at Comiskey Park, and act accordingly.

Brown's column in the 10 April 1942 Chicago Sun. *He was the first sports editor for the newspaper, which began publishing in December 1941.*

room." At that time a wealth of legendary sportswriters were working in the city, including Heywood Broun, Damon Runyon, Grantland Rice, Gene Fowler, Ring Lardner, and Westbrook Pegler; but, said Laney, Brown–"one of the adornments of our craft"–was the one willing to lend a young writer a helping hand. As sports editor for the *Evening Mail,* Brown observed that no specialists on tennis were working on any New York newspaper at that time, and he encouraged Laney to cover that sport. Brown's assistance started the writer on a successful career as one of the premier tennis and golf writers in the United States.

Brown and the *Evening Mail* came to a fairly swift parting of the ways, and he was succeeded as sports editor by Ed Sullivan–another aspiring young journalist who Brown had helped in the early stages of his career. Brown was unemployed in New York until boxing promoter Tex Rickard found a position for him at Madison Square Garden in late 1922 or early 1923, which he held until the Hearst organization's *New York Journal* hired him as a boxing expert and sent him to Shelby, Montana, to cover Dempsey in his successful decision against Tommy Gibbons on 4 July 1923.

In fall 1923, *Journal* executives informed Brown that he was being transferred to Chicago to work at Hearst's *Chicago Herald and Examiner.* On assignment covering the upcoming Dempsey-Luis Firpo match, Brown wrote a bylined series of reports and in-depth interviews from the fighters' training camps that were featured in the Chicago newspaper beginning on 7 September 1923. But his actual first assignment upon his move to the Midwest was to report on the upcoming national amateur golf championship in a suburb of Chicago. Not well versed in golf, Brown relates in his autobiography that he knew there was a game and "that it was not played on horseback." To prepare himself, he followed the publisher of the *Herald and Examiner,* George Buckley, and friend Rice around a golf course to pick up pointers. His first column published after his move, "Evans and Jones Tie When Chick Misses Putt," appeared on 18 September 1923. Two months later, on 9 November 1923, he initiated his column "So They Tell Me." Focusing on a variety of sports performers, athletic competitions, sport oddities, and general human-interest items, the column was soon appearing six days a week alongside Brown's daily coverage of various sporting events.

Much to Brown's liking about his Chicago assignment was collegiate football. Located in the heart of Western Conference territory and close in proximity to South Bend and the University of Notre Dame, the new Chicagoan quickly became a fan and friend of Knute Rockne and the legendary "Four Horsemen" of Notre Dame, and a lifelong fan and avid follower of Red Grange at the University of Illinois. Credited with coining the "Galloping Ghost" nickname for Grange, Brown also recommended that Walter Camp install the halfback as the entire backfield for Camp's 1924 all-American team after Grange scored four touchdowns in the first twelve minutes of his legendary game against the University of Michigan on 18 October. In 1925, Grange's final year as a collegian, Brown offered him a job on the *Herald and Examiner* as a football expert. Recalling Grange's refusal in *Win, Lose, or Draw,* Brown wrote, "I have taken consolation in the fact that mine was not the only attempted tackle that had missed Red Grange."

Brown's friendship with Rockne did lead to a writing assignment for the Notre Dame coach. In combination with Glenn "Pop" Warner of Stanford University and Tad Jones at Yale, Rockne was a charter member of the All-America Board, formed to select all-American teams. The *Herald and Examiner* was the Midwest outlet for the stories, which the coaches contributed on a weekly basis. Brown reorganized Rockne's initial offering for impact but says that after the first story he never again had to show him what was news and what was filler.

Drawing on his friendship and admiration for the Notre Dame coach, Brown published his first book, *Rockne,* in 1931–a highly complimentary biography that was released after Rockne's death in a plane crash earlier in the year, on 31 March. In the foreword to Brown's book, Notre Dame president Reverend Charles L. O'Donnell praised Brown, noting that his sketches provide a truthful portrait of Rockne–a sentiment echoed by Casswell Adams in his 21 June 1931 *New York Herald Tribune* review: "He writes of Rockne the man, and from him we learn of the humor, the genius, the generosity, the sincerity of the stocky, bald-headed coach. He, in a terse, not unpleasant style, hurriedly sketches the coach by telling us wisecracks, his satirical shafts."

After Rockne's death Brown's relationship with Notre Dame proved to be somewhat difficult for other Chicago reporters, especially Arch Ward, the sports editor for the *Chicago Tribune.* A former publicity director at Notre Dame, Ward's close association with the university had been seen as a valuable asset for attracting readers from the large Catholic community in Chicago. The mantle of Notre Dame football, however, had passed to Heartley "Hunk" Anderson, a former player under Rockne who did not readily accept Ward. Brown, on the other hand, was viewed as a hardworking journalist and a friend of the "Fighting Irish." Problems boiled to a head in 1932 when pool reporters, including Ward, were denied admission to the Notre Dame locker room in Los Angeles after Notre Dame's defeat by the University of Southern California. The explanation offered reporters was that a statement had already been given to Brown. Mounting a vigorous protest to Notre Dame president O'Donnell, Ward ultimately gained a more equitable standing with the university.

From his earliest days Brown applauded and encouraged those writers who supplied their readers accurate information, sufficient opinion to provoke discussion, and an entertaining style. Typically, his own writing was precise, insightful, and, at any given moment, witty, funny, angry, or scathing. Two early samples of his work are illustrative. Commenting on a rash of injuries to National League baseball players, *The Sporting News* (19 June 1930) quoted Brown as saying that the National League pennant should "be constructed of adhesive tape with surgical bandage trimmings. 'Instead of being presented with wrist watches for home runs,' Brown said, 'the boys should be given clinical thermometers.'" Listing the various injuries, he went on to say: "The Giants have had mumps, the regulation run of spavins and bowed tendons. The Phillies, the Reds and the Braves haven't needed any misfortunes. They are the Phillies, the Reds and the Braves, which is misfortune enough."

On 2 November 1935 Chicago's weekly black newspaper, the *Chicago Defender,* reprinted Brown's coverage of the Illinois-Iowa football contest from the preceding week–a report highly complimentary to African American halfback Oze Simmons. In this commentary Brown took to task those writers and coaches who encouraged fans to pay close attention to the blockers, whom they felt seldom received any credit for making successful runs happen. "Well," wrote Brown, "Oze Simmons made a run of 71 yards against Illinois last Saturday":

> His backfield companion, Dick Crayne, blocked out one man to let Oze get through the line, as was duly reported, but after that, for at least 69 of the 71 yards, who-in-hell else was there to watch but Oze Simmons? . . . The only persons running interference for him were four members of Bob Zuppke's eleven, and they haven't caught Simmons yet, though they had him surrounded at least twice as he ran down the field. . . . I'm rather happy I didn't try to watch the blockers, 'cause I wouldn't have cared to miss Simmons. . . . Illinois missed him enough for all of us on that run. . . .

In the 1930s Brown also began to gain recognition as a toastmaster and master of ceremonies. He claimed to have gotten his start when Coach Rockne practically shoved him in front of a microphone before Notre Dame left for its 1925 Rose Bowl appearance with Stanford. In his *Chicago Daily News* entertainment column on 2 November 1933, however, John Lawson observed that the reputation began in 1933 when Brown's wife, Olive, talked him into an evening of cabareting. Identified by orchestra leader Vincent Lopez in the Urban Room of the Congress Hotel in Chicago, Brown was asked to speak. He responded with a few sports witticisms and then teased Lopez and various other celebrities in attendance. Reported Lawson: "Warren sat down with a storm of applause ringing in his ears." Building on his success, he emceed orchestra leader Ted Weem's "Chicago Night" in the Walnut Room at the Bismarck Hotel, and, again, captivated the audience. Lawson predicted that some day Brown, who was always straight-faced and serious about his humor, "will close up his reportorial typewriter and hie himself off in show business. A guy with a line of lingo like Warren is too good wasting his time writing sports."

Throughout the 1930s Brown continued to report and edit sports for Hearst's *Herald and Examiner* and the *Herald-American,* which succeeded the *Examiner* in 1939. In the 1940s he transferred his allegiances to the *Chicago Sun,* begun on 4 December 1941 by publisher Marshall Field. The newspaper, taking an editorial stance opposite that of the conservative, isolationist *Chicago Tribune,* found it difficult to operate at the outset due to the impending war. Printing facilities, supplies, and experienced newspaper personnel were not easily available. Working out an arrangement to share presses with the *Chicago Daily News,* the newspaper began recruiting employees. The uncertainty of the venture intimidated many, but Brown took the gamble and signed on as the newspaper's first sports editor and reporter, also bringing with him his "So They Tell Me" column.

During his time at the *Sun,* Brown uttered perhaps one of the most quoted lines in baseball history. In 1945 the Associated Press contacted members of the Baseball Writers' Association for opinions on who would win the World Series between the Detroit Tigers and the Chicago Cubs. Most contacted selected one of the teams and predicted the number of games it would take to win the series. In his inimitable style Brown responded: "I don't think either one of them can win it." The aptness of Brown's quip was borne out by the series, often cited as the worst World Series ever played. Brown summed up the seven-game series in his book *The Chicago Cubs* (1946):

> It went the full seven games before the Tigers took the odd contest and became world's champions. Long before that point was reached even the players themselves had given up trying to figure out what might happen next. Fly balls were dropping beside fielders who made no effort to catch them. Players were tumbling going around the bases. The baseball was as far removed from previous major league standards as was possible without its perpetrators having themselves arrested for obtaining money under false pretenses.

As Brown told an after-dinner audience some years later, if the Tigers' catcher, Paul Richards, had not gotten a hit in the last game, "the silly thing might be going on yet."

On 28 December 1946 Brown wrote his final column for the *Chicago Sun* and left to rejoin the Hearst organization. On 18 January 1947 the *Herald-American* advertised his return: "You will find day by day his suave drollery, his disarming irony, his trenchant satire, and his smart whimsicalities just the flavoring to set your day right." Maintaining his critical edge and sharpening his one-liners, Brown continued to sting with great accuracy. When Minnie Minoso joined the Chicago White Sox in 1951, Brown observed that the team was "off and running, but now, for the first time since 1920, they had a general idea of why and where." On 27 July 1951, when the struggling Chicago Cubs promoted first baseman Phil Cavarretta to manager status, Brown noted that he would seem to be taking over with two strikes against him. "I'd worry more about that were it not for the fact that I have to go very far back in Cub history to come up with a manager who didn't have two strikes on him when he took the job." Watching the team struggle to stay out of last place in the National League, Brown eventually commiserated with Cavarretta, suggesting that Cub management give the manager a bonus for having to watch the team play every day.

Continually in demand as an after-dinner speaker, Brown extended his reach with featured guest appearances on Bing Crosby's national network radio programs–reputedly the only sports columnist to appear on an annual basis. He often wrote his own material for these appearances, and in one particular episode of *Philco Radio Time,* broadcast on the American Broadcasting Company network on 14 May 1947, a low-key Brown can be heard trading quips easily with Crosby, baseball slugger Hank Greenberg, and comedian Groucho Marx. But he had his greatest success in the more familiar surroundings of a baseball dinner. When asked to introduce Dr. Allan Dafoe, the physician who brought the Dionne quintuplets into the world, Brown brought the house down when he identified him as "a man with the greatest delivery in the history of the national pastime."

From the mid 1950s into the 1960s, in addition to his newspaper work, Brown contributed feature articles to national and regional magazines. With an eye toward separating fact from fancy, in an August 1954 *Sport* magazine feature, "Don't Believe Everything You Read," he examined the famed Chicago Cubs double-play combination, Joe Tinker to Johnny Evers to Frank Chance. In researching their statistics, however, Brown found no evidence of their having accomplished anything extraordinary. In fact, said Brown, from 1906 to 1909 the Hall of Fame trio turned in a mere fifty-four double plays–twenty-nine sequenced from Tinker to Evers to Chance and, giving them the benefit of the doubt, another twenty-five from Evers to Tinker to Chance.

Brown's interest in Tinker to Evers to Chance may have developed through his work with the National Baseball Hall of Fame. In 1953 Brown had been elected to Cooperstown's first Veterans' Committee, and, as committee chairman in 1955, he was present when Chicago White Sox catcher Ray Schalk was voted into the prestigious museum. In his *Whatever Happened to the Hall of Fame?: Baseball, Cooperstown, and the Politics of Glory* (1995), baseball historian Bill James implies that Brown's presence and the vote for Schalk's entry were not coincidental–an innuendo to which Brown would agree. Of all living major leaguers he had known high-school teammate Dutch Reuther and Schalk the longest, having met the catcher in

1913 when St. Ignatius College played the barnstorming White Sox. After a close loss to the Chicago team, Brown struck up an acquaintance with Schalk, and the two men began a lifelong friendship that culminated in Brown providing the boost necessary for Schalk to enter Cooperstown. Writing in his book *The Chicago White Sox* (1952), Brown noted that despite Schalk's somewhat ordinary statistics, he felt that his friend's catching record "was studded with extraordinary feats of 'iron-man' activity," including catching more than one hundred games in each of a dozen seasons. On 6 January 1953 in the *Herald-American,* Brown went on to cite Schalk as one of the four or five greatest catchers of all time and detailed his integrity, sportsmanship, and character as established "in the dire days of the ill-fated 1919 World Series." The Veterans' Committee vote for Schalk was unanimous.

In late fall 1964, in tribute to his fiftieth year as a sportswriter and journalist, Brown's newspaper, now the *Chicago American,* sponsored a lavish celebration. By virtue of a decree issued by Mayor Richard J. Daley, on 8 November 1964 Brown was honored as the city's number-one citizen. Celebrities in the world of sport and other dignitaries assembled at Chicago's Pick-Congress Hotel for a dinner with former White Sox owner Bill Veeck performing as toastmaster and featuring a televised appearance by former associate Ed Sullivan in New York.

The praise leading up to and surrounding Brown's day was extensive. Commenting on his prolific output, his keen insight, and his knowledge of sports and athletes, former *Herald and Examiner* employee and longtime *Chicago Daily News* competitor John P. Carmichael wrote on 7 October 1964 that for more than fifty years Brown had seen everything and, as a lifelong teetotaler, perhaps more clearly than most "although those who don't know him well suspected he had to be a drinking man from the company he kept." But, noted Carmichael, while Brown was the confidant of many he was "the reserved friend of fewer"–most notably, the legends of sport.

Echoing Carmichael's sentiments, Condon of the *Tribune* (7 November 1964) noted that Brown was never one to be swayed by public opinion. "During World War II," said Condon, "the veteran had the courage to clamor that we start paying more attention to fighting than to baseball. For the moment, that did not endear Warren Brown to the baseball owners, but they eventually came to secret agreement that he had been right."

Never resting on his laurels, Brown continued to write well into his senior years. In the early 1970s, at the age of seventy-eight, he penned a series of articles under the column title "Down Memory Lane" for *Baseball Digest* magazine. When the *Chicago American* became *Chicago Today* in 1969, he was still contributing columns and continued to do so until it ceased publication on 13 September 1974.

Cover for the 1946 Armed Services Edition of Brown's book, in which he describes the 1945 World Series between the Detroit Tigers and the Cubs as the worst ever played (Bruccoli Collection, Thomas Cooper Library, University of South Carolina)

Just after Brown's eightieth birthday, on 5 January 1974, the Chicago Headline Award, presented annually by the Chicago chapter of the Baseball Writers Association of America, was renamed the Warren Brown Award in his honor. Observed Brown's longtime associate Bill Gleason in his 7 January 1974 *Chicago Sun-Times* column, "That Warren Brown was a giant of our business is one of the truths that the Chicago baseball writers have agreed upon. I'm sure that Warren finds wry amusement in the fact that he is the first writer for whom an award was named and takes sublime pleasure from the fact that the first 'Brownie' will go to a fellow named Henry Aaron."

On 12 August 1974 Brown was enshrined into the National Baseball Hall of Fame. Awarded the J. G. Taylor Spink Award for sportswriters by the Baseball Writers' Association of America the previous December, he and fellow inductees, *The New York Times* journalists John Drebinger and John Kieran, brought to sixteen the number of writers so honored in Cooperstown.

Brown passed away in his sleep at his Forest Park, Illinois home on 19 November 1978. He was survived by two of his three sons, a daughter, and eleven grandchildren. As a reporter, editor, and columnist, Brown covered forty-five World Series, forty Kentucky Derbies, and many of the great sporting events of his time. As he was fond of saying, he had written "about every damn thing under the sun."

Described by friends and colleagues as aristocratic and imposing, kind and helpful to those below him, albeit sometimes frosty and abrasive to his superiors, Brown was considered by many to be a giant–to some, perhaps the biggest name in Chicago journalism for more than half a century. In fitting tribute, Condon captured the essence of Brown's life and career in his 22 November 1978 "In the Wake of the News" column for the *Chicago Tribune:* "Yes, Warren Brown ran with our craft's giants. Most often, he outdistanced them."

References:

Bob Broeg, "Brown, Kieran, Drebby Typewriter Titans," *Sporting News,* 176 (22 December 1973): 36;

Broeg, "Two Hall of Famers: Of Warren Brown . . . Dick Young," *Sporting News,* 187 (3 February 1979): 36;

John P. Carmichael, "The Barber Shop," *Chicago Daily News,* 7 October 1964, VIII: 73;

Robert J. Casey, *Such Interesting People* (Indianapolis: Bobbs-Merrill, 1943), p. 98;

David Condon, "In the Wake of the News," *Chicago Tribune,* 7 November 1964, II: 1;

Condon, "In the Wake of the News: Hail and Farewell to Warren Brown," *Chicago Tribune,* 22 November 1978, V: 1;

James Enright, "Warren Brown Joins Hall of Fame Today," *Chicago Today,* 12 August 1974, p. 44;

Bill Gleason, "A Chicago Giant of Journalism," *Chicago Sun-Times,* 22 November 1978, p. 98;

Gleason, "It's 'Fame' Day for Brown, Too," *Chicago Sun-Times,* 12 August 1974, p. 102;

Gleason, "Writing Great Warren Brown in Hall of Fame," *Chicago Sun-Times,* 7 January 1974, p. 84;

Bill James, *Whatever Happened to the Hall of Fame?: Baseball, Cooperstown, and the Politics of Glory* (New York: Simon & Schuster, 1995), pp. 51, 111, 159, 259;

Al Laney, *Covering the Court: A 50-Year Love Affair with the Game of Tennis* (New York: Simon & Schuster, 1968), pp. 46–48;

Jim Langford, comp., *Runs, Hits & Errors: A Treasury of Cub History and Humor* (South Bend, Ind.: Diamond Communications, 1987), p. 120;

John Lardner, "Shelby, 1923," in *The Fireside Book of Boxing,* edited by W. C. Heinz (New York: Simon & Schuster, 1961), pp. 229–237;

John Lawson, "Householder Yields to 'Emcee' Lure," *Chicago Daily News,* 2 November 1933, p. 26;

Richard Lindberg, *Stealing First in a Two-Team Town* (Champaign, Ill.: Sagamore, 1994), pp. 204–205;

Thomas B. Littlewood, *Arch: A Promoter, Not a Poet: The Story of Arch Ward* (Ames: Iowa State University Press, 1990), pp. 49, 61, 63–64;

James Mote, *Everything Baseball* (New York: Prentice Hall, 1989), p. 108;

Daniel Okrent and Steve Wulf, *Baseball Anecdotes* (New York: Oxford University Press, 1989), pp. 73, 139, 174–175, 236;

"Scribbled by Scribes," *Sporting News,* 89 (19 June 1930): 4;

Ed Stone, "Chicago Salutes Warren Brown at Testimonial Tonight," *Chicago American,* 8 November 1964, VI: 1–2;

Stone, "Old Friends Pay Tribute to Warren Brown," *Chicago American,* 9 November 1964, III: 19;

"Three Writers to Share Spink Award," *Sporting News,* 176 (15 December 1973): 38;

Oswald Garrison Villard, *The Disappearing Daily: Chapters in American Newspaper Evolution* (New York: Knopf, 1944), pp. 150–157;

"Warren Brown Day Tomorrow," *Chicago American,* 7 November 1964, II: 11;

"Warren Brown Joins H-A Sports Lineup," *Chicago Herald-American,* 18 January 1947, I: 6.

Dan Burley

(7 November 1907 - 30 October 1962)

Kelly E. Rusinack

MAJOR POSITIONS HELD: Sports editor, columnist, and reporter, *Chicago Defender* (1928–1931, 1935–1937); city editor, columnist, sports and theatrical editor, *Chicago Sunday Bee* (1932–1935); city editor, reporter, columnist, theatrical and sports editor, *New York Amsterdam News* (1937–1948); staff writer, *Ebony* (1951–1957); associate editor and staff writer, *Jet* (1951–1957).

BOOKS: *Dan Burley's Original Handbook of Harlem Jive* (New York: Jive Potentials, 1945);
Diggeth Thou? (Privately printed, 1959?).

OTHER: *South Side* [Chicago] *Civic Telegram* (newspaper), edited by Burley, 1932;
"Major League 'Dozens' Playing," in *The Phillies Reader,* edited by Richard Orodenker (Philadelphia: Temple University Press, 1996).

SELECTED PERIODICAL PUBLICATIONS–UNCOLLECTED: "I'll throw this one out and then duck," *New York Amsterdam News,* 25 June 1947;
"The Love Life of Joe Louis," *Ebony,* July 1951, pp. 22–34;
"The Bathtub Murder Case," *Ebony,* November 1951, pp. 108–117;
"Why Walcott Won't Fight," *Ebony,* December 1951, pp. 64ff;
"Why Fight Managers Hate Women," *Ebony,* October 1952.

Dan Burley

Dan Burley spent his career studying the contemporary African American life in New York and Chicago, a culture and society particular to blacks in the first half of the twentieth century. Burley socialized amid the celebrities of Harlem, yet never lost his admiration for the average people whose stories would not otherwise be noticed. Burley's intelligence and inquisitive nature led to a wide range of interests, from playing jazz piano to investigative writing, all of which he patently mastered. He spread his considerable understanding of contemporary black culture to the denizens of Chicago and Harlem as a musician, newspaper editor, socialite, and author. He possessed a natural ability to analyze his cultural observations and to set them forth in an entertaining yet informative fashion. Best known as a jazz musician and cultural icon, Burley also left an indelible mark on African American journalism. With a career that spanned more than three decades for the most widely read black publications of his time, he earned a highly respected reputation among his peers. His smooth prose veiled a biting wit, and his polished writing style proved apropos for his social commentary.

Daniel Gardner Burley was born in Lexington, Kentucky, on 7 November 1907, the son of James and

Anna Seymour Burley. His father, a former slave, was a Baptist evangelist, and his mother taught at the Tuskegee Institute under Booker T. Washington. His family lived in Fort Worth, Texas, then moved to Chicago when Dan was eleven years old. There he was introduced to big-city life, which became and remained the subject of his fascination.

Burley's interest in journalism began early in life; he started his career as a writer when he graduated from Wendell Phillips High School in Chicago in 1928 and went straight to work as sports editor, columnist, and reporter for the *Chicago Defender,* one of the more outspoken of the nationally popular black newspapers. In 1932 he continued his journalistic career with the *Chicago Sunday Bee,* another black newspaper, as city editor, columnist, and sports and theatrical editor, already exhibiting his versatility and leadership abilities as a journalist. He was concurrently a staff correspondent for the Associated Negro Press before moving to New York City in 1937.

Burley's interest in and talent for jazz music also became evident early in his life. By the age of seventeen he was playing the tinkling piano sounds that characterized house-rent parties of the era of the Great Depression, called "skiffle," which Burley is popularly credited with having invented. He helped popularize not only the skiffle–known as "riffling" in Harlem–but also barrel-house blues. Throughout his life Burley created approximately twenty original musical compositions and gave them colorful titles, including "Pig Foot Sonata" and "The Chicken Shack Shuffle." Burley took his individual style of piano playing with him to Harlem, the mecca of black culture for his generation.

In New York, Burley made his most notable mark on black journalism and culture. Already an accomplished jazz musician and newspaperman, Burley used his social skills and connections to quickly gain entrée into Harlem society. Harlem was in decline as a cultural center by the late 1930s, its heyday having peaked just prior to the Depression. Few writers had taken the opportunity to record for posterity the influences on entertainment and society that had their roots in Harlem, however.

In 1937 Burley took what was perhaps his most notable journalistic job as reporter, city editor, columnist, and theatrical and sports editor of the *New York Amsterdam News,* a black weekly. The *Amsterdam News* was considered to be one of the premier multiethnic papers in New York, even touted by *The New York Times* as always having "a great deal of persuasive power in Harlem and other Black Communities." Burley worked concurrently as a jazz musician and also as an editor and columnist for the *New York Age.* By 1941 the *Amsterdam News* touted Burley as its most widely read writer, advertising that "His columns, 'Back Door Stuff' and 'Confidentially Yours,' stand out like gems in contemporary Negro newspaper literature and have countless readers both colored and white."

"Back Door Stuff" was mostly a social scene gossip column. Sometimes written in jive, a language created by and for musicians and street people, the column "read like pure gibberish, though not to any hep cat who was in the habit of reading," as Jervis Anderson characterized it in his *This Was Harlem: A Cultural Portrait, 1900–1950* (1982). For the "unhep"–the uninitiated–Burley would "translate" the jive into mainstream English. For example, one installment of "Back Door Stuff" included this exchange:

> You're slicing your chops about these fine young hens tripping down the crunching straight in the cool of the evening. But, ole man, you're really nowhere with that larceny you're laying, because if you were up on the stickers, like I am: you'd dig that they, themselves, are just out there mugging, hoping that some Cat, without his boots, might broom by, and knock 'em to some fine dried barkers, or at least a scarf that won't choke 'em, or a glass with a little head on.
>
> The translation:
>
> Slicing your chops is a dignified way of beating your gums or doing a lot of talking. And the fine young hens tripping down the crunching straight, are just pretty gals out for a walk. And the larceny you're laying is the play you're making. "You'd know all the fine points, if you were up on the stickers." And the hens out there are just muggin' (standing around) hoping that a Square like you will make a down payment on a fur jacket (dried barkers) or a dinner (scarf that won't choke 'em–presumably a heavier meal than cold cuts and crackers); or a glass with a little head on (a drink, my friend).

Burley was distinguished by his ability to connect with all people, no matter their race or social standing, without losing himself in their world. His Harlem was equally famous and infamous, rich and poor, hope and hell, as Mel Tapley recalled in a tribute to Burley for the *Amsterdam News* (12 February 1994): "His uptown tales were in the era when some of the most beautiful girls around were Lena Horne, Winnie Johnson, the Brown twins, Tondelaya, Ruby Dallas, Chinkie Grimes and the other shapely competitors for the title of "Miss Fine Brown Frame" or "Naturally." . . . But there were belt-tightening, financially-strapped times, too. Editor Burley used to mention the dudes who showed up at those invitation-only black-tie affairs at the Savoy or Golden Gate, but slept in their Cadillacs and Lincolns. . . . these Caddypad guys dined on cornflakes and gravy

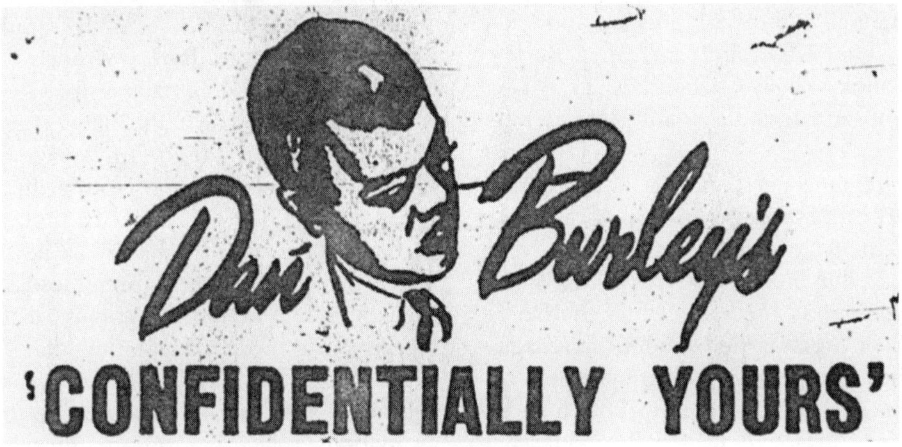

Heads for Burley's Amsterdam News *column*

and hot dogs." In addition to theatrical and musical entertainers, anyone who was someone in the African American community became part of Burley's Harlem experience, including notable athletes such as Joe Louis, Paul Robeson, Roy Campanella, and Jackie Robinson.

In 1945 Burley put some of his street knowledge on paper, personally publishing what became the bible of jive, *Dan Burley's Original Handbook of Harlem Jive*. Burley's book was not just a dictionary of terminology but an explication of the evolution of inner-city life and language. Burley traced the emergence of jive to Chicago, circa 1921. In his handbook Burley presents a well-researched history of black culture and subculture. Without either deriding or excessively glorifying the use of slang, Burley colorfully yet intellectually ties this history in with the purpose of language in culture:

> The language of Jive presents an unusual opportunity for experimentation in rhymes. . . . As to meter, it is desirable that the syllables form a correct measure, but this is not essential. . . . That's why, dear reader, you must constantly review what has gone before, and why you must insist on perfection before attempting ambitious steps in this hitherto uncharted division of Americana. . . . Soon you will be talking in such a manner that your friends will think you have gone completely looney and belong in a strait-jacket. But don't let that worry you. They tried to put Shakespeare in the dog-house, and even attempted it with Edgar Allan Poe.

Almost twenty years after its publication, Burley's book was described in the *Amsterdam News* as "an imaginative compilation of 'hep' talk that created and spread abroad an in-group language of humor, gut, wit, hardness and softness that still is the coin of common exchange among musicians and 'the cats.'"

In the foreword to the handbook, Earl Conrad, author of *Harriet Tubman: Negro Soldier and Abolitionist* (1942) and a fellow New York journalist, praised Burley's effort as a "masterly handling of Negro idiom and dialect and colloquial expression." Conrad, who said he had occasion to critique Burley's writings on jive in the scholarly *Journal of Negro Education,* hailed Burley as a link between the African American and white worlds: "he could show us how and why one world influences the other, why the two are constantly merging in myriad ways." Conrad introduced Burley as a scholar of merit, rather than just a chronicler of idioms, and cast intellectual legitimacy on Burley's study of jive. By explaining that semantics is a science of living language, Conrad described Burley's handbook as an essential "study of Negro life and the inter-impact of Negro and white on each other." In Conrad's estimation the handbook elevated Burley to the status of semanticist: historian, linguist, and lexicographer, all in one. Fifty-four years after Burley published the book, Tony Scherman in "The Theresa" (1998) observed that it "is still used by ethnolinguists."

The social commentary offered in the handbook came at a crucial time in the history of relations between African Americans and the white majority, a point also emphasized in Burley's sportswriting. Without meaning to expose all the "secrets" of the black subculture in which jive was the standard language, the terms identified and defined by Burley spoke for themselves. Terms such as "ballroom without a parachute" (defined as "reefer den without reefers"); "chamber of commerce," which refers to a toilet; "john" ("a square jaded white male seeking thrills in colored communities"); and "main drag of many tears" ("126th Street where disappointment tinges the loud laughter") all speak to a culture outside the realm of white American experience. The handbook served as much to celebrate Harlem as to educate white America to the richness and complexity of black urban culture.

More than just a dictionary of slang, *Dan Burley's Original Handbook of Harlem Jive* explains in detail how to use jive. In chapters such as "Jive Rhyming and Meter" and "Simple Construction of Statements in Jive," Burley carefully builds upon the standard rules of English to initiate his readers to an understanding of jive as a form of speech. The handbook even features translations of well-known writings into jive, such as Clement Moore's "The Night Before Christmas," Hamlet's soliloquy, and even Edgar Allan Poe's "The Raven." In doing so, Burley displayed his depth of understanding not just of the jive dialect but also of literary construction in translation, a further testament to his intelligence and writing skills.

Burley's journalistic endeavors were equally meritorious. Unlike his explorations of jive, Burley's sports coverage was written in plain English, direct and to the point. He apparently preferred to keep the worlds of entertainment and serious journalism apart, and his sportswriting belonged in the latter category. Burley used his space on the sports page, particularly his "Confidentially Yours" column, to highlight the triumphs of black athletes, touting them for their significance in the black community and to American athletics. He reported on the advancements of African Americans in sports, locally and nationally.

Burley was an outspoken proponent of integration and wrote often and passionately for the desegregation of all facets of American society. He was convinced that his ideas had popular support, noting the nods of approval and slaps on the back he received when he was seen out in public. In October 1941, for example, Burley wrote a piece when Sam Pierce, a black football player for Cornell University, took the field against the navy team at Annapolis. Burley's article made the front page of the *Amsterdam News* (25 October 1941). Noting that "So significant was the fact that a Negro had played against the Naval Academy and at Baltimore in the heart of what is said to be the most prejudiced area outside of Washington," he put the gravity of the game in perspective by further suggesting that "perhaps, President Roosevelt, may be behind the complete change of heart attitude, and prospectus that marked the Annapolis relaxation of one of the nation's most long-drawn out and concentrated vigils to keep all black faces off the gridiron when Uncle Sam's middies were at play." Burley's articles during the war highlighted Jim Crow in the military through the trials of Joe Louis, heavyweight champion. Burley outspokenly opposed Louis's fighting for the navy while it remained virulently racist.

Burley also noted ethnic strife within the black community, especially with respect to sports. He often reported on Effa Manley's problems with her investments–better known as the Newark Eagles–and with the other Negro National League team owners. In September 1944 an umpire for the Negro National League asked Burley to address the issue of "chicken-feed pay for Negro umpires." He did not hesitate: "But when an umpire has to take the burdens of the baseball world on his back and then doesn't get enough pay for an honest day's work to pay his rent, buy food and other necessities of life, then something should be done about it, not alone by baseball officials, but by the fans who follow the game and want to see Negro baseball advance." Again Burley was able to demonstrate that Manley bucked the system, noting that she "seems to be about the only owner in the N.N.L. who can see the disparity of pay and the treatment of umpires. . . . It was she who broke up the sorry spectacle of umpires running from club owner to club owner after each game trying to collect their pay, or standing on the sidewalk until late in the night to get their measly salary."

Burley did not only point a finger at racial problems. In early 1942 he wrote about Joe DiMaggio's father, an Italian immigrant, who was detained during the war as an alien. Burley noted the ethnic problems white America faced through immigration, though he never lost sight of the fact that European immigrants came to the United States unshackled, unlike members of his race. He also noted that the baseball owners' winter meetings had done nothing to advance desegregation, though the public outcry, started by men like Burley, was gaining national attention.

Burley did not mince words when it came to talking about the desegregation of baseball, and he did not shy away from the controversy. In an August 1942 article from his 'Confidentially Yours' column in the *Amsterdam News* Burley lauded and vilified Satchel Paige in the same breath, for his statement that major-league baseball would have to come up with at least $37,000 a year in salary if they wanted him, because that was what he had made the previous year in the Negro Leagues and that was what was necessary to draw him into the situation of traveling through the South on a racially mixed team and dealing with overt racism.

While Burley agreed that Paige was worth every penny and more, he felt that the pitcher's stance was a setback to the other Negro League players getting "their long-denied and long-deserved opportunity," by giving the white baseball establishment "ammunition" with which to continue denying this opportunity. Burley complained that Paige's statements threatened

> to tear down all that has taken newspapers and other public-spirited groups and individuals years to build. In other words, it has been a long road leading up to the present when public pressure can and has forced major league club owners to make public statements. . . . The long road traveled by those fighting for a renaissance in baseball has had little aid and support from the fellows for whom the fight is being waged. . . . However, Paige will find that his latest squawk won't deter those who are committed to the fight to open the door of opportunity to all players, no matter what their color. The line is down, and even if it doesn't come this year, the big moment for Negro ballplayers is bound to roll around soon.

Burley was even instrumental in finding a black photographer to take the picture of Jackie Robinson signing with the Brooklyn Dodgers organization, pulling Austin Hansen, a photographer for the *Amsterdam News,* from his lunch to get to manager Branch Rickey's office in time to get the famous shot.

At about the same time, Joe Bostic, the sports editor of the *People's Voice,* himself an outspoken journalist, intimated in his "Speaking of Sports" column of 12 September 1942 that Burley and Wendell Smith of the *Pittsburgh Courier* were engaging in a journalistic feud. Bostic did not elaborate, however, and any such feud was not publicly apparent from Burley's articles.

After baseball began to desegregate, Burley took on an even touchier topic–racism within integrated baseball. Burley began his controversial 25 June 1947 column about Jackie Robinson's treatment in major-league baseball, "I'll throw this one out and then duck." Burley decided to address the issue of racial epithets hurled at Robinson, mostly by Ben Chapman of the Philadelphia Phillies. Burley cut to the chase, noting that, to a certain extent, Chapman's explanation that ethnic epithets had always been a part of professional baseball was a valid argument; he then dug more deeply into the necessity of turning the other cheek. Burley suggested that African Americans should "learn not to flinch at the word we all hate so thoroughly that others use to describe and embarass us. . . . If we stopped letting it make us feel so badly or inferior, we would overcome a major barrier toward our advancement." He goes on to explain that all great black athletes, such as Jack Johnson, Sam Langford, Paul Robeson, and Rube Foster, had racial epithets hurled at them but did not allow that "air thus used" to destroy their sense of self-worth or to inhibit their desire to win. Burley demonstrated time and again his own desire to tackle the tough subjects facing athletics and members of his race, and he did so with the belief of the importance of his message.

Burley continued to make musical appearances, which were also advertised in the *Amsterdam News.* The self-taught pianist played with the likes of the Emmy Award–winning composer Dick Hyman, who could credit his first job in a jazz band to Burley, and with blues guitarist Walter "Brownie" McGhee. Burley became more renowned for taking part in the Harlem social scene than for writing sports; his presence in the Harlem nightlife helped to sell papers, as Burley used the information he uncovered for his gossip column, "Back Door Stuff." Burley was considered to be one of the "bards" of Harlem, a fixture at the bar of the pop-

1830-125TH ST. ANNOUNCES 111TH ANNIVERSARY JAMBOREE-1941
OCTOBER 24TH TO NOVEMBER 1ST

Navy Team Ends Jim Crow Policy

A Bigger Paper A Better Paper 32 Pages

NEW YORK Amsterdam STAR NEWS Star-News

VOL. XXXII, No. 46 SATURDAY, OCTOBER 25, 1941 IN TWO SECTIONS SECTION ONE 10c

Indicts 10 in Fight on Lynchings

Headline for Burley's front-page report on the first college football game in which an African American player–Cornell University running back Sam Pierce–played against the U.S. Naval Academy team

ular Hotel Theresa at Seventh Avenue and 125th Street, soaking up the atmosphere and taking note of the myriad tales of uptown life.

Burley moonlighted as a musician and a radio disc jockey. Among the stations for which he spun records were WLIB and WWRL in New York. He was also instrumental in establishing the famous *Amsterdam News* midnight shows at the Apollo Theater on 125th Street in Harlem, which drew entertainers from all facets of the entertainment industry.

Burley left the *Amsterdam News* after eleven years, his longest-running full-time journalistic position. Returning to Chicago, he plied his trade with *Ebony* and *Jet,* magazines published by the Johnson Publishing Company–the first, an established magazine, widely respected for its concentration on and celebration of black life in the United States; the latter, a spinoff black entertainment magazine that quickly became as popular as its predecessor. Burley did not concentrate on sports for these magazines. When he did, he often used his substantial knowledge of boxing–he was the first black member of the New York Boxing Writers Association–and his connections in sports and in Harlem to create sports articles unrivaled in their depth of research.

Ebony rarely credited the writers of its articles in the 1950s, but Burley was credited with at least four articles while on staff at the magazine. His first bylined article for *Ebony* was a sports piece, "The Love Life of Joe Louis," in which he linked Louis to at least twenty-nine women, mostly "showgirls, dancers, models, actresses, glamour girls, one or two secretaries and one society girl." Some of these women were married, which Burley was not ashamed to point out. Burley appeared to have intimate knowledge of Louis's dating habits, including how much each woman meant–or did not mean–to the fighter emotionally.

In addition to his sports-related articles, Burley penned some articles of a different nature, such as a true-crime story, "The Bathtub Murder Case." He appears to have done the investigative work himself for the article, which is exemplary of Burley's superlative abilities as an investigative reporter.

He also predicted an early retirement for "Jersey Joe" Walcott after having spoken with Walcott's wife for a December 1951 article. Burley reported that Walcott was more interested in "fighting juvenile delinquency" than in further pursuing his boxing career. Burley also disclosed that Walcott had always lied about his age and that he was forty-one at the time of the article, not thirty-seven, as was widely believed.

Burley tackled a timeless subject in "Why Fight Managers Hate Women," (*Ebony,* October 1952) explaining the tribulations that wives, girlfriends, and other female hangers-on imposed on fighters. He tactfully explained, through the use of real-life examples, that women often distracted fighters from their main focus, which alone would displease a fighter's manager. Burley also detailed how many women who became involved with fighters were far more interested in the man's money than in the man himself, and how often fighters were in great financial trouble because they allowed this deception to happen. Thus, Burley explained, fight managers hated the women who would destroy a fighter and, presumably, jeopardize the manager's income.

Burley concurrently wrote for *Jet* magazine as an associate editor. *Jet* cited its authors even less frequently than *Ebony,* however, and no articles were ever credited to Burley. In addition to the more prominent papers and magazines for which he wrote, Burley authored his own newspapers; *The Owl* was his last journalistic endeavor and his occupation at the time of his death.

Burley's death of a heart attack in his Chicago home on 30 October 1962, just shy of his fifty-fifth birthday, stifled a voice of Harlem and black culture unrivaled in its sapience. *Jet* waxed eloquently in its obituary of the writer:

> Dan Burley, the poet laureate of straw-bosses and Southern sheriffs, of cornfield preachers and fifth floor walk-up flats, of barbecued pork and fried chicken, of pimps and prostitutes and lonesome tramps, was born in Lexington, Kentucky. But he was a big city man. He loved the sounds and the smells and the cries of the Harlems and the South Sides of America . . . he immersed himself in the tragedies and triumphs of the little nobody people, in the way they talked, in the way they laughed, in the way they went to the wall and died. . . . The texture of Negro life in the ghetto was also the theme of his two books . . . and his more than twenty musical compositions.

The *Amsterdam News* ran a front-page obituary for its longtime editor, explaining his success: "Combining a wide-ranging eye with a 'nose for news' and an immense number of personal contacts in both the upper and lower strata of Negro life, Dan Burley quickened his reporting and commentary with his own special brand of wit and often sharp insight into Negroes as people and their society as a tragi-comic brand of American folkways." Burley, who had been predeceased by his first wife, singer Gustava McCurdy, was survived by his second wife, Gladys; his daughter, Dianne; and two stepchildren, Sharon Chiles and Peter Burley.

Burley's name remains among those respected names of black journalism of the 1940s, along with Wendell Smith, Sam Lacy, Joe Bostic, and Frank "Fay" Young, all of whom voiced their displeasure at the white sports establishment for its treatment of blacks. Burley also left a legacy of scholarship with respect to jive, a twentieth-century phenomenon that might otherwise have gone unrecorded. Burley's versatility–as a writer, musician, and associate of both the poor and the rich–reveals the depth of character of the "heppest cat" of them all.

References:

Jervis Anderson, *This Was Harlem: A Cultural Portrait, 1900–1950* (New York: Farrar, Straus & Giroux, 1982), p. 316;

Earl Conrad, "The Philology of Negro Dialect," *Journal of Negro Education* (Spring 1944);

Conrad, foreword to *Dan Burley's Original Handbook of Harlem Jive* (New York: Jive Potentials, 1945);

Tony Scherman, "The Theresa," *American Legacy* (Winter 1998);

Mel Tapley, "Hansen's Harlem says G'bye," *New York Amsterdam News,* 10 February 1996, p. 21;

Tapley, "Stirring up sweet memories of Sugar Hill," *New York Amsterdam News,* 12 February 1994, p. 21;

"Dan Burley," in *Black Writers/Black Baseball: An Anthology of Articles from Black Sportswriters Who Covered Negro Leagues,* edited by Jim Reisler (Jefferson, N.C.: McFarland, 1994), pp. 127–144.

Walter Camp

(7 April 1859 – 14 March 1925)

Jack Morris

BOOKS: *Foot-ball: How to Coach a Team* (Boston: Wright & Ditson, 1886);

American Football (New York: Harper, 1891; enlarged, 1894; enlarged again, 1896);

Walter Camp's Book of College Sports (New York: Century, 1893; revised, 1900);

Football, by Camp and Lorin F. Deland (Boston: Houghton, Mifflin, 1896);

Drives and Puts: A Book of Golf Stories, by Camp and Lilian Brooks (Boston: L. C. Page, 1899);

Yale, Her Campus, Class-Rooms, and Athletics, by Camp and Lewis Sheldon Welch (Boston: L. C. Page, 1899);

The Substitute: A Football Story (New York: Appleton, 1908);

Condensed Bridge for the Busy Man (New York: Collier, 1909);

Jack Hall at Yale: A Football Story (New York & London: Appleton, 1909);

The Book of Foot-ball (New York: Century, 1910);

Old Ryerson (New York & London: Appleton, 1911);

Football for the Spectator (Boston: Badger, 1911);

Frank Armstrong at Queen's, as Matthew M. Colton (New York: Hurst, 1911);

Condensed Auction for the Busy Man (New York: Platt & Peck, 1912);

Auction Up-to-date, Including Nullos (New York: Platt & Peck, 1913);

Danny Fists (New York: Grosset & Dunlap, 1913);

Captain Danny (New York & London: Appleton, 1914);

Danny the Freshman (New York & London: Appleton, 1915);

Keeping Fit All the Way: How to Obtain and Maintain Health, Strength and Efficiency (New York & London: Harper, 1919);

Athletes All–Training, Organization and Play (New York: Scribners, 1919);

Football Without a Coach (New York & London: Appleton, 1920);

Handbook on Health, and How to Keep It (New York: Appleton, 1920);

Walter Camp (from Harford Powel Jr., Walter Camp, the Father of American Football, *1926)*

The Daily Dozen for Men and Women (New York: Reynolds, 1921);

Training for Sports (New York: Scribners, 1921);

A Pocket Bridge Book (Garden City, N.Y.: Doubleday, Page, 1923).

OTHER: *Football Facts and Figures: A Symposium of Expert Opinion on the Game's Place in American Athletics,* compiled by Camp (New York: Harper, 1894);

Sports and Games, edited by Camp (New York: Collier, 1903);

Spaulding's How to Play Football: A Primer on the Modern College Game with Tactics Brought Down to Date, edited by Camp (New York: American Sports Publishing, 1904);

The Book of Sports and Games, edited by Camp (New York: Crowell, 1923);

The Daily Dozen (New York: Reynolds, 1925).

SELECTED PERIODICAL PUBLICATIONS–UNCOLLECTED: "Letter to the 'Editor's Open Window,'" *Outing,* 9 (January 1888): 379–381;

"The Games and Laws of American Football," *Outing,* 11 (October 1888): 68–76;

"The American Game of Foot-ball," *Harper's Weekly,* 32 (10 November 1888): 858;

"A Day's Foot-ball Practice at Yale," *Harper's Weekly,* 32 (24 November 1888): 890;

"Base-ball–For the Spectator," *Century Magazine,* 17 (October 1889): 831–837;

"Intercollegiate Football in America," *St. Nicholas,* 17 (November 1889): 37–40;

"Track Athletics in America," *Century Magazine,* 18 (June 1890): 203–212;

"First Paper: The Ground and the Outfit," *St. Nicholas,* 17 (July 1890): 555–562;

"Second Paper: Fielding, Throwing, and General Practice," *St. Nicholas,* 17 (July 1890): 667–673;

"Third Paper: The Basemen and the Shortstop," *St. Nicholas,* 17 (August 1890): 752–758;

"Fourth Paper: The Battery," *St. Nicholas,* 17 (August 1890): 825–832;

"Fifth Paper: Batting and Base-Running," *St. Nicholas,* 17 (September 1890): 945–949;

"Sixth Paper: Reminiscences," *St. Nicholas,* 17 (October 1890): 1017–1021;

"College Football," *Outing,* 17 (February 1891): 384–390;

"Team Play in Foot-ball," *Harper's Weekly,* 35 (31 October 1891): 845–846;

"Football of 1891," *Outing,* 19 (November 1891): 153–157;

"Review of the Football Season," *Outing,* 21 (October 1892): 52–59;

"'Interference' in Football," *Harper's Weekly,* 36 (19 November 1892): 1115;

"Battles of the Football Season of 1891," *Outing,* 21 (November 1892): 102–106;

"A Plea for the Wedge in Football," *Harper's Weekly,* 37 (21 January 1893): 67;

"Undergraduate Limitations in College Sports," *Harper's Weekly,* 37 (11 February 1893): 143;

"Junior Promenade at Yale," *Harper's Weekly,* 37 (18 February 1893): 159;

"College Athletic Outlook," *Harper's Weekly,* 37 (1 April 1893): 315;

"The Yale Side of the Athletic Question," *Harper's Weekly,* 37 (8 April 1893): 339;

"College Athletics," *Century Magazine,* 24 (June 1893): 204–210;

"Football of 1893: Its Lessons and Its Results," *Harper's Weekly,* 38 (3 February 1894): 117–118;

"Current Criticism of Football," *Century Magazine,* 25 (February 1894): 633–635;

"The New Rules and the Forwards," *Harper's Weekly,* 38 (3 November 1894): 1053;

"Athletic Extravagance," *Outing,* 26 (April 1895): 81–84;

"A Yale View of the Football Situation," *Harper's Weekly,* 39 (6 April 1895): 334;

"Inter-collegiate Baseball–The Yale Nine," *Harper's Weekly,* 39 (27 April 1895): 403, 405;

"Football of '95. A Forecast of the Season," *Outing,* 27 (November 1895): 169–176;

"Winning a Football Goal," *Outlook,* 28 (May 1896): 980;

"Football. Review of the Season of 1895," *Outing,* 29 (October 1896): 62–71;

"Football. Review of the Season of 1896," *Outing,* 31 (October 1897): 26–33;

"Opening of the Football Season," *Harper's Weekly,* 41 (9 October 1897): 1017–1018;

"Football Notes," *Harper's Weekly,* 41 (16 October 1897): 1042;

"Football Notes," *Harper's Weekly,* 41 (23 October 1897): 1066;

"The Football Season," *Harper's Weekly,* 41 (30 October 1897): 1090;

"Football of '97. A Forecast of the Season," *Outing,* 31 (November 1897): 133–136;

"College Football," *Harper's Weekly,* 41 (6 November 1897): 1114;

"College Football," *Harper's Weekly,* 41 (13 November 1897): 1138;

"Football at the Colleges," *Harper's Weekly,* 41 (20 November 1897): 1161–1162;

"College Football," *Harper's Weekly,* 41 (27 November 1897): 1185–1186;

"Football Notes," *Harper's Weekly,* 41 (4 December 1897): 1210;

"A Review of College Football," *Harper's Weekly,* 41 (11 December 1897): 1233–1234;

"Football in Nebraska and Kansas," *Harper's Weekly,* 41 (25 December 1897): 1298;

"Call for a High Standard in College Athletics," *Harper's Weekly,* 42 (8 January 1898): 46;

"The College Man in War–Part I," *Collier's,* 27 (June 1898): 14–16;

"The College Man in War–II," *Collier's,* 28 (July 1898): 20–22;

"Intercollegiate Boat-Racing of 1898 and Its Results," *Collier's,* 28 (July 1898): 18–19;

"Sports of the Amateur on Field and Water," *Collier's,* 28 (August 1898): 22;

"Sports of the Amateur on Field and Water," *Collier's,* 28 (10 September 1898): 119;

"Sports of the Amateur on Field and Water," *Collier's,* 28 (17 September 1898): 19;

"Football. Review of the Season of 1897," *Outing,* 33 (October 1898): 40–48;

"Football in America," *Frank Leslie's Popular Monthly,* 47 (November 1898): 56–65;

"Football Prospects at New Haven," *Collier's,* 30 (September 1899): 20;

"College Athletics," *Frank Leslie's Popular Monthly,* 48 (October 1899): 584–594;

"Some Abuses in Athletics," *Independent,* 52 (22 March 1900): 714–717;

"A Historical Game of Football," *Youth's Companion,* 74 (November 1900): 625–626;

"Methods and Development in Tactics and Play," *Outing,* 37 (November 1900): 171–176;

"College Training-Tables. Their Use and Abuse," *Century Magazine,* 40 (June 1901): 307–317;

"The Present Condition of Football," *Independent,* 53 (10 October 1901): 2394–2397;

"A Summer's 'Roughing It': The Story of a Single Long Vacation," *World's Work,* 6 (June 1903): 3588–3596;

"The Eleven Greatest Football Players of America," *Independent,* 57 (27 October 1904): 949–956;

"The Solid Old Man of Business," *St. Nicholas,* 32 (July 1905): 828–829;

"Satisfactory Referees and Umpires Needed," *Harper's Weekly,* 49 (28 October 1905): 1556, 1576;

"Straight Road to an Open Game in Football," *Outing,* 51 (December 1905): 370;

"New Phases of the Season's Football Play," *Collier's,* 40 (October 1907): 20–21;

"American Sports," *Century Magazine,* 48 (November 1909): 60–73;

"Great Teams of the Past," *Outing,* 55 (December 1909): 284;

"Personality in Football," *Century Magazine,* 49 (January 1910): 443–445;

"All-Time All-American Football Team," *Century Magazine,* 49 (February 1910): 601–603;

"New Ideas in Athletics," *Outing,* 56 (March 1910): 651–661;

"The American National Game," *Century Magazine,* 49 (April 1910): 936–948;

"Track Athletics," *Century Magazine,* 49 (June 1910): 269–279;

"The Mystery of Rowing," *Century Magazine,* 49 (July 1910): 323–334;

"Lawn Tennis, the Queen of Games," *Century Magazine,* 49 (August 1910): 545–557;

"Golf, the Game of Courtesy," *Century Magazine,* 49 (October 1910): 820–833;

"Influence of the Tackle Play," *Collier's,* 46 (October 1910): 23–26;

"The New Football," *Outing,* 57 (October 1910): 17–25;

"Rugby Football in America," *Outing,* 58 (March 1911): 707–713;

"The Canoe Race," *The Congregationalist and Christian World,* 96 (August 1911): 284–285;

"All-America Football Team of 1911," *Collier's,* 48 (December 1911): 18–19;

"Progress in American Sport," *Country Life,* 11 (April 1912): 29–30;

"Olympic Games of 1912," *Collier's,* 50 (July 1912): 22–23;

"The New Football," *Outlook,* 102 (28 September 1912): 171–177;

"Making a Football Team," *Outing,* 61 (November 1912): 143;

"All-America Football Team of 1912," *Collier's,* 50 (December 1912): 10–11;

"All-America Eleven," *Collier's,* 52 (December 1913): 3–4;

"What Are Athletics Good For?" *Outing,* 63 (December 1913): 259–272;

"Camp's All-America Eleven, 1914," *Collier's,* 54 (December 1914): 20;

"Baseball and Life," *Collier's,* 55 (20 March 1915): 25;

"Camp's All-America Eleven, 1915," *Collier's,* 56 (December 1915): 13;

"Patriotic Services by Men over 45," *Rotarian,* 8 (June 1917): 577–579;

"Our Government Plant," *Outlook,* 117 (5 September 1917): 12–13;

"Uncle Sam's Athletic System," *Outlook,* 118 (27 March 1918): 482–484;

"Keeping the Nation Fit," *Independent,* 71 (December 1918): 400–401;

"Review of the Football Service and All-America Team," *Collier's,* 63 (January 1919): 13;

"Reconstruction of the Man," *Outlook,* 121 (5 February 1919): 224–225;

"Walter Camp's Daily Dozen Set Up," *American Magazine,* 87 (March 1919): 33–36;

"Industrial Athletics," *Outlook,* 122 (11 June 1919): 252–253;

"What Is New about the Young Man of Today," *American Magazine,* 88 (November 1919): 14–15;
"True Training," *Outing,* 76 (February 1920): 204–206;
"Keeping Young at 40," *Collier's,* 65 (June 1920): 11–13;
"Live Faster: Don't Die Faster," *Collier's,* 66 (July 1920): 9–11;
"Football in Business," *Collier's,* 66 (October 1920): 9;
"Walter Camp's All-America Team," *Collier's,* 66 (December 1920): 8–9;
"Come Out of the Cave," *Collier's,* 67 (January 1921): 7;
"Keeping Fit," *Woman's Home Companion,* 48 (January 1921): 4–5;
"The Broad Folk Highway of American Sport," *American-Scandinavian Review,* 9 (April 1921): 257–267;
"Beautifying Exercises," *Women's Home Companion,* 48 (May 1921): 16;
"Don't Be a One Sport Man," *Collier's,* 67 (May 1921): 5–6;
"You Pass Your Physical Zenith between 31 and 35," *American Magazine,* 91 (May 1921): 31;
"How I Pick the All-America Team," *Collier's,* 68 (December 1921): 17;
"Walter Camp's All-America Team," *Collier's,* 68 (December 1921): 5, 20;
"Fit for a Fight or a Frolic," *Collier's,* 70 (November 1922): 9–10;
"What Sports Can Do for Girls," *Women's Home Companion,* 49 (November 1922): 10;
"Not Only Fit, but Ready," *Collier's,* 70 (December 1922): 9–10;
"Walter Camp's All-America Team," *Collier's,* 70 (December 1922): 24;
"Spend Thrift Golf," *Collier's,* 71 (January 1923): 3–4;
"Don't Burn Up the Fast Boys," *Collier's,* 71 (May 1923): 17;
"Are City Golfers Free and Equal?" *Collier's,* 72 (July 1923): 9–10;
"What Makes a Champion," *Collier's,* 72 (September 1923): 9–10;
"What I Am Trying to Do," *World's Work,* 47 (October 1923): 600–604;
"The Frankenstein of College Athletics," *World's Work,* 47 (November 1923): 101–105;
"Round the Course in 1923," *Collier's,* 72 (November 1923): 20;
"After All, the Scotch Invented Golf," *Collier's* (December 1923): 15–16;
"Walter Camp's All-America Team," *Collier's,* 72 (December 1923): 6–7;
"Craze for Costliness in Golf," *World's Work,* 48 (July 1924): 313–317;
"Under Forty Too Young for Golf," *World's Work,* 48 (October 1924): 602–604;
"How Clean Is Sport?" *World's Work,* 49 (January 1925): 319–321;
"Walter Camp's All-America Team," *Collier's,* 75 (January 1925): 12–13, 43;
"What Does It Cost to Be Fit," *Collier's,* 75 (February 1925): 17;
"It's Easy to Keep Fit," *Collier's,* 75 (March 1925): 17–19;
"All-Time All-American," *Collier's,* 75 (May 1925): 10;
"Getting the Most Out of Life," *Collier's,* 76 (September 1925): 18–19.

By the age of thirty-three, a scant twelve years after graduating from Yale University, Walter Camp was already known as the "Father of American Football." Sports columnist Caspar Whitney first used the nickname in a column in the popular magazine *Harper's Weekly* (5 March 1892). The title was appropriate, because by 1892 Camp had almost single-handedly fashioned the game of American football. The rising popularity of the game was almost solely his doing. He had taken the game of rugby and changed it, in his way of thinking, into an American game.

For almost fifty years Camp served on the football rules committees. His opinions, especially in his early years, dominated the sessions. Camp knew that developing the game was not enough, however. For it to catch on, the word had to be spread. So despite having a full-time job at the New Haven Clock Company and serving as an unpaid adviser to the Yale football team, Camp wrote articles and books on football and sports in general. By his death he had written nearly 30 books and more than 250 magazine articles. His articles appeared in national periodicals such as *Harper's Weekly, Collier's, Outing, Outlook,* and *The Independent* and in juvenile magazines such as *St. Nicholas, Youth's Companion,* and *Boys' Magazine.* His stories also showed up in major New York City and Philadelphia daily newspapers. According to his biographer, Richard P. Borkowski, "Camp was instrumental through writing and lecturing in attaching an almost mythical atmosphere of manliness and heroism to the game not previously known in American team sport."

Camp became one of the highest paid nonfiction writers in America, and he wrote to instruct Americans on his beloved game of football. In the 1870s and early 1880s, the game was played mainly in the eastern colleges, and the fans were students and professors of the schools. In 1880 the first Thanksgiving game played in New York City drew only five thousand spectators. By 1884 that figure rose to ten thousand. By the late 1880s the Thanksgiving games were much anticipated. A crowd of twenty-five thousand was estimated at the 1889 Thanksgiving Day game between Yale and

Camp (back row, fourth from left) with teammates from the first Yale University varsity football team, 1876

Princeton in New York. In the early 1890s crowds of thirty to forty thousand people were not unusual for championship games, usually involving Yale, Princeton, Harvard, or Pennsylvania.

While initially his writings were mostly on football, Camp also wrote on other sports as well. His belief that amateur sports developed qualities in youth such as self-control, leadership, citizenship, and rugged individualism caused him to be a champion of most sports. Historian John Rickards Betts, in *America's Sporting Heritage: 1850–1950* (1974), identifies the years from 1860 to 1890 in American history as "the athletic impulse" and the period from 1890 to 1920 as "the triumph of athletics." Camp straddles those two eras as a huge presence. Ronald A. Smith, in his book *Sports and Freedom: The Rise of Big-Time College Athletics* (1988), wrote: "Camp, more than any one individual, created the American version of football that became the dominant college sport, and thus in a way, shaped the course of all intercollegiate sports in America. . . . Camp is a prime example of how powerful men helped give direction to American college sport during the period it was growing most rapidly."

By his later years his role within Yale University had diminished. During this time he became a proponent of physical fitness for all ages and wrote much on the subject. He developed a physical fitness routine he called "the Daily Dozen," which became so popular that the U.S. government requested his help in training military personnel. By the time of Camp's death in 1925, his name was not just synonymous with football but with physical fitness as well. During his writing career his articles touched on everything from commentaries on recent collegiate football games to advice for fighting the common cold; from information on what a young girl should expect at the Yale Junior Promenade to advice to people on how to keep physically fit.

Walter Chauncey Camp was born on 7 April 1859 in New Britain, Connecticut. He was an only child. His father, Leverett Lee Camp, was a schoolteacher. His mother, Ellen Cornwall Camp, was also briefly a schoolteacher. The two were married in 1855 and moved to New Haven in 1864 when Leverett Camp took a job at the highly respected Dwight School. He later became the principal at the school. He was a strong supporter of physical exercise and formed a military-type student group, the Dwight School Cadets. Leverett Camp also sold real estate on the side. His father's love of physical exercise and industriousness evidently influenced Camp.

Camp spent almost the entirety of his life in New Haven. Growing up, he was a tall, thin boy who probably was a little more serious-minded than other children his age, although that quality, as Borkowski notes, was probably exaggerated by some of his contemporaries: "He was in general an average boy growing up in a middle class neighborhood and only slightly more serious-minded than his friends in regard to work and play. This characteristic of total seriousness, so obvious in his adult years, seems to have been attached to his youth by a few later writers. Young Walt more than likely played for the same reason most young people play–to have fun." Camp attended Hopkins Grammar School, where he wrote for the school paper. Other than a baseball team, there were no organized sports at Hopkins. He graduated sixth out of a class of thirty-five boys, and in 1876 he began his collegiate years at Yale University.

Camp entered Yale as a seventeen-year-old freshman, standing six feet tall and weighing 157 pounds. He joined the football team and played six seasons and part of a seventh (at this time, graduates were allowed to play intercollegiate football). A knee injury in his seventh season ended his playing career. Camp's athletic endeavors did not stop with football, however. He made every varsity team in existence at the time. He played baseball, captaining the freshman team, then playing with the varsity his junior, senior, and graduate-school years. During the 1880 season Camp had the highest batting average in the Intercollegiate Association. Camp played shortstop, left field, and pitcher. He also participated to a lesser extent in swimming, tennis, track, and rowing. According to football historian Parke H. Davis, Camp invented the hurdle step while running hurdles in track; up to that point, runners had stopped and jumped over the hurdles. Davis also claims that Camp won every swimming race he ever entered, regardless of length–anywhere from short distances to five miles. He also played in the first intercollegiate tennis tournament in 1883. That he did so a year after withdrawing from graduate school shows the looseness of eligibility standards in intercollegiate activities during this time.

His activities on the football field won him the most attention, however. He was a great dropkicker and punter as well as an excellent runner, but Camp was best at looking at a tactical situation within the game and finding a way to capitalize on it. His analytical mind revolutionized the game, first from a playing standpoint and later on from a rules standpoint. In 1876 he was elected the captain of the freshman football team and became a member of the varsity as well. Camp played every game that year, including the first Yale-Harvard game, on 17 November 1876. In fact, in his first six years he played every minute of every game, never leaving the field for injury or substitution. Yale's record during that time was 25–1–6. Camp was also team captain his junior and senior years. Camp entered Yale medical school in 1880; he continued to play football for two more years but turned down the captaincy, a role he believed belonged to undergraduates.

In his capacity as team captain, Camp attended his first rules meeting during his junior year, on 9 October 1878. From that time until his death he was a member of every football rules committee. This work with the rules committees earned Camp his reputation as the "Father of American Football." When Camp enrolled at Yale, the "football" being played was actually English rugby, with a few differences. The main emphasis of the game was kicking. Blocking was not allowed, although players were surreptitiously getting in the way of opposing players by this time. Tackling was permitted only above the waist. Forward passes were not allowed. The ball had to be thrown laterally to move it from player to player. The game was played with fifteen players to a side.

Camp's first two suggestions at his first rules committee meeting were to reduce the players per side to eleven and to have safeties count in the scoring, although both suggestions were rejected. Soon, though, Camp's persuasive manner of debating began to win people to his way of thinking. He eventually perfected a strategy to get the rules committee to listen to his views. He would sit back and let his colleagues debate the issues until they were exhausted and asked him for his opinion. By 1880 his eloquent speech and gallant manner, as well as his on-field exploits, had gained him considerable respect. His suggestions slowly started to become adopted. He was responsible for introducing the ideas of the line of scrimmage, downs (starting with three and later adding a fourth), and five yards for a first down (which he later had changed to ten yards). He changed the point values for touchdowns, field goals, and safeties. He was also responsible for the neutral zone and for plays beginning with six men on the line of scrimmage. His initial ideas were formed to transform the game from a kicking game to a running game. Over the years, more rule changes were brought about to make the game more palatable to the average fan and make it less brutal. With all these changes happening so rapidly, Camp found it to the game's advantage to write about football and explain the various rule changes in the national media.

Camp spent two years in medical school, then withdrew because, according to Tim Cohane, he could "not bear the sight of blood." In 1882 he joined the sales staff of the Manhattan Watch Company. One

Camp, 1918, demonstrating the "grate," one of the Daily Dozen exercises he developed for President Woodrow Wilson's cabinet (Yale University Library)

year later he took a New York sales office job with the New Haven Clock Company, where he worked for forty-two years, until his death. He became the president of the company in 1903 and chairman of the board in 1923. Five years after taking the job with the New Haven Clock Company, he married Alice Graham Sumner on 20 June 1888. She was the sister of Camp's favorite professor at Yale, William Graham Sumner. The Camps had two children. Walter Camp Jr. was born in 1891 and Janet Camp in 1897. The family lived in New Haven, close to both Yale and the New Haven Clock Company.

After graduation, Camp continued his ties to the Yale football team though it was limited by his responsibilities with the New Haven Clock Company. Between 1883 and 1919, with a few exceptions, he was either a coach or adviser to the football team. In either capacity his contributions were extensive. When he could not make practices, his wife would attend and take thorough notes. He would review the notes and then talk with the coaches and captains at his home that evening. He was years before his time with the use of still photos to study the individual play of his athletes. He also insisted that his players diagram plays using lines, arrows, and X's, a system that has remained in use.

In the midst of his obligations to his employers, his work with the Yale football team, and his responsibilities with the football rules committees, Camp started to find the time to write. He was as much a natural-born writer as an athlete. In his senior year at Yale he won both the Ivy Ode and Class Poem competitions. In the 1880s, however, he found it difficult to get anything about football published. In his article "Current Criticism of Football," published in *The Century Magazine* (February 1894), Camp wrote of the lack of availability of newspaper space for the game back in the 1880s and how "zealous" he had to be to sell the game. In 1886 he was able to get a thirty-five-page pamphlet, *Foot-ball: How to Coach a Team,* published by a Boston company, Wright and Ditson, but he published little else during this time. Eventually, his reputation, and the increasing popularity of the game, opened doors for him. One such opportunity in late 1889 led to a small article that listed the best football players of the previous season, which he called the "All-America Football Team."

There is a debate as to who actually had the idea for an All-America team. The first All-America team appeared in a short-lived publication, *The Week's Sport.* The article included no byline. Several historians credit Caspar Whitney, the editor of *The Week's Sport,* with the idea. While most people believe there was collaboration between the two, there are those who believe that Whitney used Camp's name to legitimize the picks and little else was of Camp's doing. Camp himself confused the issue. In an article in *Collier's* dated 14 January 1899, he lists all the teams from 1889 to 1898. Two weeks later, in the same magazine Camp wrote: "In giving the list of All-America teams for a number of years in a recent issue, it was my intention to state that the selections were those of Mr. Caspar Whitney in *Harper's Weekly.*" Writing in *The Independent* on 27 October 1904, however, Camp wrote about the popularity of the All-America team. "The selection of 'All-America' teams seems to have become a mania, and the only excuse that I can put forth for further contribution is that of habit, for in 1889, I first introduced the idea and selected the first eleven." Whitney, two years after Camp's death, said in a 1927 article for *Collier's:* "I don't know whose idea it was. My memory is very treacherous and I simply cannot remember. Maybe the idea was mine, maybe it was Camp's. At any rate we worked closely together and we had a lot of fun doing it. Certainly it never occurred to either one of us, in those early days, that it would ever make anyone famous some day. If you're going to write something, give Camp the credit–I don't want any credit." A receipt of payment, signed by Whitney for Camp's work on the first All-America team, was found within Camp's papers at the Yale University Library and suggests a collaboration of some type.

The All-America team was published for the last time in *The Week's Sport* in 1890. Again, there was no byline on the story. From 1891 to 1899 the teams were presented in *Harper's Weekly*. Whitney had joined *Harper's* as sporting editor and had begun writing a weekly column, "Amateur Sport." The All-America teams began appearing in this column. Camp likely collaborated with Whitney on all the teams except in 1897, when Whitney went on an extended trip and Camp's name was bylined on the story. That year also marked the first time that second- and third-team All-Americans were selected. In 1899 Camp selected an All-America team for *Collier's*. It was exactly the same team as Whitney's in *Harper's Weekly,* lending credence that Camp continued to collaborate with Whitney for one last time. From 1900 to 1924, with the exception of 1917, Camp's All-America teams appeared solely in *Collier's*. He was now picking the teams himself. In 1917, because many collegiate athletes were serving in the military during World War I, Camp picked an All-Service team. Upon Camp's death in 1925, famed sportswriter Grantland Rice took over the duties. So popular was the All-America team that one year a thief broke into the printer of *Collier's,* stole the list, and tried to sell it to another publication. After that incident Camp began sending the teams in three different parcels to *Collier's*. The teams were reunited only at press time. Sport pages across the nation ran the list soon after it appeared in *Collier's*. Other publications attempted to put together similar teams, but Camp's was the one everybody wanted to see. As Kathleen D. Valenzi and Michael W. Hopps quote in their *Champion of Sport: The Life of Walter Camp, 1859–1925* (1990), Harold "Red" Grange, the University of Illinois football great, once remarked: "Camp was the No. 1 name in football; if you weren't on the Camp team, it didn't mean a thing."

The relationship between Whitney and Camp was a rocky one, with many ups and downs. The two were the preeminent authorities and spokesmen for football in the 1890s. They were sometimes friends, though often they found themselves on opposite sides of the issues. They worked together on *The Week's Sport* and then moved together to *Harper's Weekly*. Camp was paid twenty-five dollars a month to provide material for Whitney's column. During their first two years at *Harper's,* Whitney's "Amateur Sport" column used unaccredited Camp writings on several occasions. On the other hand, Whitney helped Camp by editing his first book, *American Football,* published by Harper and Brothers in 1891. The two worked together into the 1910s at *Harper's, Collier's,* and *Outing,* with Whitney as editor and Camp as writer. Michael Oriard, author of *Reading Football: How the Popular Press Created an American Spectacle* (1993), points out that although Camp and Whitney appeared to be linked, "the pages of these magazines suggest something very different from complete agreement between the two men." When Whitney was with *Harper's,* Camp was an occasional contributor except in 1897, when Whitney took his extended trip. At the same time, Camp was the principal football writer for *Outing*. When Whitney moved to *Outing* in 1900, Camp began to appear less frequently there. Camp moved on to *Collier's,* where he was sporting editor. He later joined *Harper's* in the same capacity. When Whitney changed jobs again in 1908 to *Collier's,* Camp's stories ran less frequently.

In private, the two also had their difficulties. In 1894 they argued, through letters, over pay for Camp's contributions to *Harper's*. In the end Camp wrote a letter to Whitney, stating, "You know better than I can tell you that up to a short time ago there was no man who stood higher in my opinion for squareness than you. . . . Perhaps of late you have been misrepresented to me, or we have been at cross purposes for it has seemed impossible to make my belief in you gibe with what seemed to be facts." Whitney returned Camp's letter to him with a note written on the bottom and the back: "What in the Hades are you talking about. . . ? No one ever had cause or assumption to write to me in such a way." Camp's byline appeared only three more times in *Harper's Weekly* in the next three years.

In 1900, however, the two put aside their differences to invest in *Outing*. Whitney got Camp and Camp's friend R. S. Bertron to put $5,000 into the deal. This business arrangement soon led to a second blowup between the two. In 1901 Whitney wrote a harsh story in *Outing* condemning the failure at Yale to enforce eligibility requirements among the school's athletes. Camp immediately asked for his money back and expressed his intention to withdraw from the advisory board of the magazine. Whitney was angry that Camp would assume that the magazine would be a partisan publication rather than an unbiased journal. Eventually, Camp held onto his stock but did not contribute an article to the publication for four years. Oriard opined that the two men's conflicting fundamental values led them to clash: "Camp and Whitney both stood for high-minded football untainted by abuses, yet their ultimate commitments led them in different directions. Whitney, the Anglophile, wanted football to mirror a social structure rooted in tradition and class distinctions. Camp, the Yankee businessman, promoted football for a competitive, democratic, pragmatic, corporate America."

There is no doubt, though, that it was Whitney who helped Camp start to promote football. Prior to

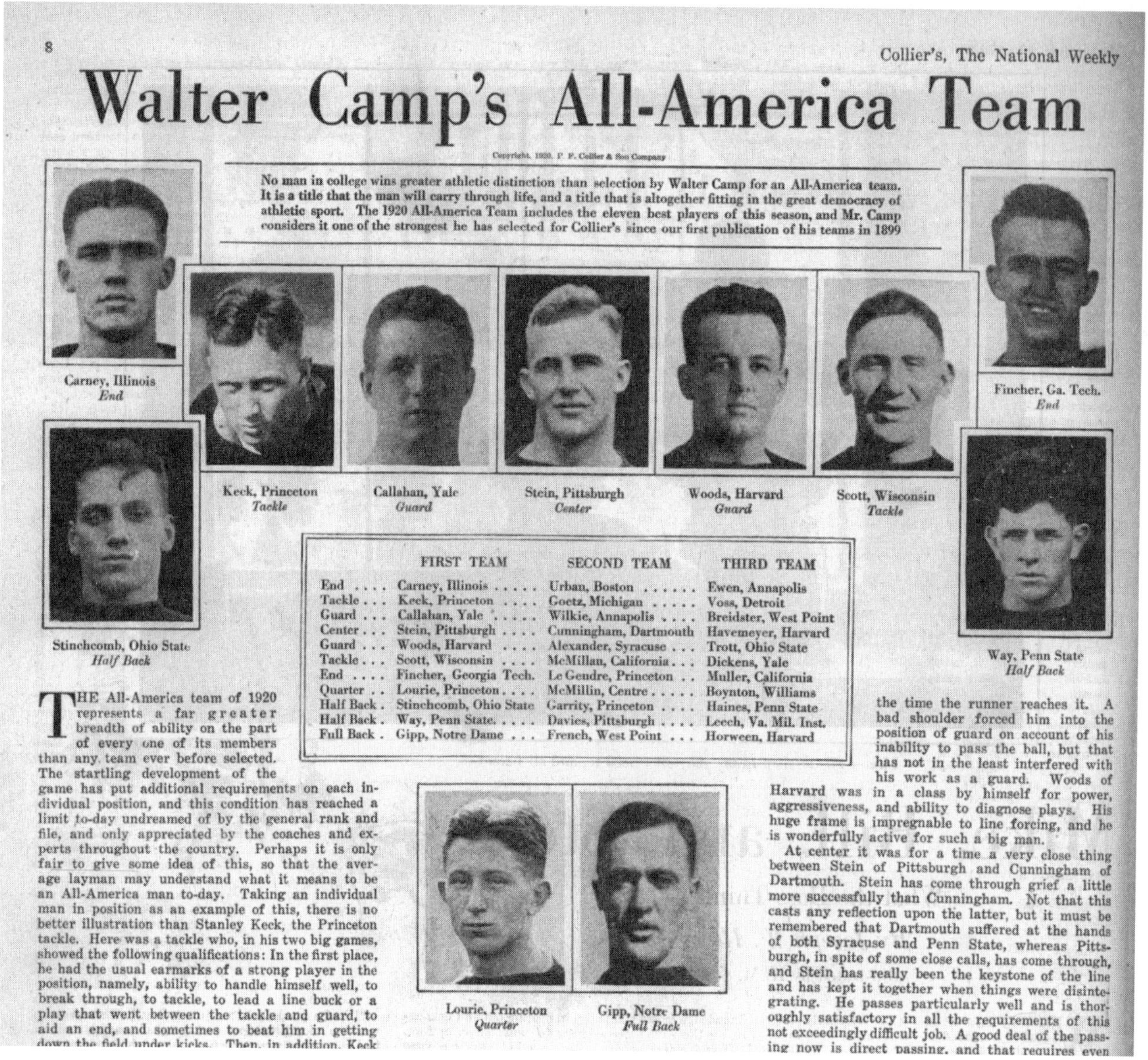

8 Collier's, The National Weekly

Walter Camp's All-America Team

Copyright, 1920, P. F. Collier & Son Company

No man in college wins greater athletic distinction than selection by Walter Camp for an All-America team. It is a title that the man will carry through life, and a title that is altogether fitting in the great democracy of athletic sport. The 1920 All-America Team includes the eleven best players of this season, and Mr. Camp considers it one of the strongest he has selected for Collier's since our first publication of his teams in 1899

Carney, Illinois
End

Keck, Princeton
Tackle

Callahan, Yale
Guard

Stein, Pittsburgh
Center

Woods, Harvard
Guard

Scott, Wisconsin
Tackle

Fincher, Ga. Tech.
End

Stinchcomb, Ohio State
Half Back

Way, Penn State
Half Back

	FIRST TEAM	SECOND TEAM	THIRD TEAM
End	Carney, Illinois	Urban, Boston	Ewen, Annapolis
Tackle ...	Keck, Princeton	Goetz, Michigan	Voss, Detroit
Guard ...	Callahan, Yale	Wilkie, Annapolis	Breidster, West Point
Center ...	Stein, Pittsburgh	Cunningham, Dartmouth	Havemeyer, Harvard
Guard ...	Woods, Harvard	Alexander, Syracuse ...	Trott, Ohio State
Tackle ...	Scott, Wisconsin	McMillan, California ...	Dickens, Yale
End	Fincher, Georgia Tech.	Le Gendre, Princeton ..	Muller, California
Quarter ..	Lourie, Princeton	McMillin, Centre	Boynton, Williams
Half Back .	Stinchcomb, Ohio State	Garrity, Princeton	Haines, Penn State
Half Back .	Way, Penn State.	Davies, Pittsburgh	Leech, Va. Mil. Inst.
Full Back .	Gipp, Notre Dame ...	French, West Point ...	Horween, Harvard

THE All-America team of 1920 represents a far greater breadth of ability on the part of every one of its members than any team ever before selected. The startling development of the game has put additional requirements on each individual position, and this condition has reached a limit to-day undreamed of by the general rank and file, and only appreciated by the coaches and experts throughout the country. Perhaps it is only fair to give some idea of this, so that the average layman may understand what it means to be an All-America man to-day. Taking an individual man in position as an example of this, there is no better illustration than Stanley Keck, the Princeton tackle. Here was a tackle who, in his two big games, showed the following qualifications: In the first place, he had the usual earmarks of a strong player in the position, namely, ability to handle himself well, to break through, to tackle, to lead a line buck or a play that went between the tackle and guard, to aid an end, and sometimes to beat him in getting down the field under kicks. Then, in addition, Keck

Lourie, Princeton
Quarter

Gipp, Notre Dame
Full Back

the time the runner reaches it. A bad shoulder forced him into the position of guard on account of his inability to pass the ball, but that has not in the least interfered with his work as a guard. Woods of Harvard was in a class by himself for power, aggressiveness, and ability to diagnose plays. His huge frame is impregnable to line forcing, and he is wonderfully active for such a big man.

At center it was for a time a very close thing between Stein of Pittsburgh and Cunningham of Dartmouth. Stein has come through grief a little more successfully than Cunningham. Not that this casts any reflection upon the latter, but it must be remembered that Dartmouth suffered at the hands of both Syracuse and Penn State, whereas Pittsburgh, in spite of some close calls, has come through, and Stein has really been the keystone of the line and has kept it together when things were disintegrating. He passes particularly well and is thoroughly satisfactory in all the requirements of this not exceedingly difficult job. A good deal of the passing now is direct passing, and that requires even

Camp's selection of the year's best college football players, which appeared in the 18 December 1920 issue of Collier's *magazine*

Camp's writings, infrequent and short articles appeared in national periodicals. In 1878 *Harper's Weekly* began to print occasional football stories, often without attribution and with short titles such as "Foot-ball." In 1887 Frederick Evans began writing fairly regular articles on football for *Harper's,* and Camp's first articles for the magazine brought him to national attention soon thereafter. His articles of the late 1880s and early 1890s informed the public on the game of football and explained the many rules changes that occurred during this time. The opening paragraph of his "The American Game of Foot-ball" (10 November 1888) illustrates his approach to educating the public:

The football game of to-day is a scientific contest, for which during three months, upward of fifty men have carefully trained, practised [*sic*], and perfected themselves in all the strategies of a studied campaign. Out of this fifty have been selected twenty-two men, eleven from each university, and these the very picture of muscular agility, and endurance. And the audience! Never until the advent of this sport has anything like it been assembled. Ten thousand people, the bulk of them flying college colors would make a grand site anywhere. . . .

To Camp, sport was a wonderful character builder that perfected the mind and body. Sports, especially his beloved football, taught students self-control and the ability to be gracious in defeat. He saw football in particular as a sport that would prepare a young man for his life to come. In the 31 October 1891 issue of *Harper's* he wrote: "If ever a sport offered inducements to the man of executive ability, to the man who can plan, foresee, and manage, it is certainly the modern American foot-ball." This article was accompanied by one of the most famous football drawings of the nineteenth century, W. A. Rogers's "Out of the Game," which pictures a football player lying motionless on the playing field while a teammate kneels beside him, and in obvious distress, waves for help from the sidelines. The picture epitomized the feelings of critics of the game who believed that it was too brutal. Camp recognized the savageness of the game and tried to enact rules that would help ease the problems, but his two-page article next to the picture was an emotionless piece that sought to be a primer on the game. Explained within the article were the finer points such as "The Wedge or V," "How to Meet a Wedge," "End Run," and "Using the Wind." According to Oriard, "Neither Camp nor Rogers misrepresented the game; each simply represented it from a particular perspective." Camp's perspective, however, was the one that won favor with most Americans.

Camp continued to write articles for a variety of national periodicals. He also began to write for juvenile periodicals. In November 1889 his article "Intercollegiate Football in America" appeared in *St. Nicholas.* He wrote about sports other than football as well, however. In June 1890 he wrote on the sport of track for *The Century Magazine,* in which he makes a statement that became a prevailing theme for him later in life–the necessity of physical fitness for all people: "Americans are already realizing that the unfailing laws of nature demand more attention to the physical welfare of the body." The article highlights the different events involved in track athletics at that time, including bicycling and tug-of-war. According to Camp, the popularity of track "means that more men are enjoying the benefits of open-air exercise, and by the help of the pleasant stimulus of contest are being drawn towards a better physical development."

In 1891 Camp published his first book, *American Football.* The book, 175 pages long, explains the game and the different positions to the average fan. In his preface Camp explains why he wrote the book and gives an underlying motive for his early periodical writings: "The progress of the sport of football in this country, and a corresponding growth of inquiry as to the methods adopted by experienced teams, have prompted the publication of this book. Should any of the suggestions herein contained conduce to the further popularity of the game, the object of the writer will be attained."

The book was written for fans of all interest levels who wanted greater insight into the game. The last chapter, "A Chapter for Spectators," lays out the rules simply. Laurence Hutton, literary critic for *Harper's New Monthly Magazine,* reviewed the book in his February 1892 "Literary Notes" column: "To the uninitiated, therefore, it is naturally obscure; but it is not written for the uninitiated, and those that carry a glossary and diagrams in their mind's eyes, and know what Mr. Camp is talking about, will unquestionably appreciate his scientific treatment of his subject, and profit by his remarks."

Hutton's review was obviously biased, written in a Harper and Brothers periodical about a Harper and Brothers book. The attention the book received, however, indicates that football, with Walter Camp's prodding, was becoming a growing phenomenon. His articles appeared with more frequency every year, not only in *Harper's Weekly,* but also in *Outing,* a monthly devoted exclusively to recreation and sports.

Camp himself was also growing in stature. His Yale teams were the standard of American football, and his name was becoming closely associated with the sport. On 26 February 1892 a dinner was held in his honor in the concert room of Madison Square Garden in New York. Nearly four hundred people attended the festivities. Whitney even took the occasion to write a story for *Harper's Weekly,* noting that Camp's "efforts have been ever directed towards placing sport on a healthier and better planet." Camp's articles continued that trend, but he faced a bigger challenge as the 1890s wore on.

Camp eventually addressed those critics who attacked football because they believed the game was too violent. President Grover Cleveland abolished the annual Army-Navy game following the 1893 season, when word reached him that twenty-four Annapolis players had been admitted to the hospital during the season and that the college had granted players eighty-two sick days and issued an additional sixty excuses from drills because of injury. Harvard, led by college president Charles Eliot, considered banning the sport.

At the same time that Camp continued writing his informative articles, he was privately sending out a series of questionnaires to several hundred former players. The survey asked them to list, among other things, the most serious injury they had received playing football, as well as their present physical condition. The final question asked what overall effects the player felt football had on him. Camp compiled the responses into a book, published as *Football Facts and Figures: A Symposium of Expert Opinions on the Game's Place in American Athlet-*

Cover for Camp's 1921 manual for the calisthenics routine he developed

ics (1894), which has been the source of debate because of its bias. According to Oriard, Camp falsified the evidence only to prove his point and omitted evidence that would have gone against his point. Camp appears to have cut out at least one particularly damaging statement from the draft report of his findings in preparing *Football Facts and Figures.* He found that 20 percent of former players reported some permanent injury–a fact that never made it to publication. Although Borkowski concedes that Camp did leave negative responses out of the book, he also points out that there were positive responses left out as well. Positive responses, in fact, counted for 95 percent of the replies.

Camp himself at least partially believed that the rules needed to be changed to make the game less brutal. In his early writings he defended the "momentum" play, in which the offensive team amassed from five to seven players before the snap of the ball to run at one player on the defensive side. The play frequently resulted in injuries and occasionally in death. By 1894 attempts were made to limit momentum plays, but a split between Harvard and Yale caused complications. Eventually the two schools were united under one organization, which adopted rules to stop the deadly play. With the publication of *Football: Facts and Figures* and the abolishment of momentum plays, the critics were somewhat quieted, albeit temporarily.

Despite its critics and infighting, football continued to grow in popularity. As Camp wrote in "Football of 1893: Its Lessons and Its Results" (*Harper's Weekly,* 3 February 1894), "Whatever be said of the football season of 1893. . . , it stands pre-eminent as the year in which more public attention was attracted to the sport than ever before." Midway through the 1890s Camp's articles changed from an instructional tone to more stories on actual games and the many rule changes. He continued to write on other sports as well, publishing *Walter Camp's Book of College Sports* in 1893. Three years later he published *Football,* co-authored with Harvard coach Lorin F. Deland. Camp's final instructional book on the game, *The Book of Foot-ball,* appeared in 1910.

By 1897 Camp's popularity was such that he was asked to help fill in for Whitney while the *Harper's* sporting editor took "a sporting tour around the world." Writing in Whitney's "Amateur Sports" column in *Harper's* for ten straight weeks, Camp commented on the 1897 season. It culminated in his All-America team on December 11. *Harper's* also carried a story by Camp two weeks later clarifying a situation between the University of Nebraska and the University of Kansas. While the article was only three paragraphs long, it showed that Camp had become a major factor in the sport. He stated the problem and explained what the solution should have been, then closed by lecturing: "Prominent institutions should remember the responsibilities they bear of setting the example to others, and uphold the highest standards."

Camp found himself in great demand as a sports journalist. *Collier's* chose him to be their sporting editor, and in 1898 he was the first person to have a sports story appear in that magazine. The demand for his writings, along with his work at New Haven Clock Company, made him well off financially. With all his duties, including writing, he was an extremely regimented person. He would sit in his parlor with a large book propped across his knee and fashion his stories in longhand on a yellow legal pad. He then would place the copy in an envelope and walk a block to drop it in a mailbox. In this manner he was able to keep up with his commitments.

Camp's articles dealt with the issues gripping sports at the time. The 1905 season brought another attack from football critics alarmed at the number of football-related deaths. Newspapers posted casualty lists alongside football stories. The uproar reached such a level that President Theodore Roosevelt invited Camp and other recognized leaders of the sport–Arthur T. Hildebrand; John B. Fine, founder of the Princeton Preparatory School; Edward M. Nichols; and Harvard Coach William T. Reid Jr. of the Unitarian Club of Boston–to the White House on 5 October 1905 for a four-hour meeting on the problem. Prior to the meeting Roosevelt had made his wishes known to Camp in a letter: "I want you to make the game not soft but honest" (7 October 1905). In an article in *Harper's Weekly,* "Satisfactory Referees and Umpires Needed," which appeared three weeks after the meeting, Camp saw the problem as a matter of applying the rules as they were written. He felt there was a need for better officiating. Others saw the problem as being the rules committee itself, however. A new committee was formed that challenged the authority of Camp's committee. Early in 1906 the two committees met and formed a new board. In doing so Camp's position as leader of the ruling football committee was usurped. He was given the duty of editing the rule book, a job he had held since its inception. The new combined committee made some major changes, the biggest being the addition of the forward pass, which, in the past, Camp had not supported. This rule changed the emphasis of the game to speed rather than brute force and made it less deadly, and the majority of public criticism died down after the 1906 season.

Starting in 1909 and continuing through the 1910s, Camp started to write juvenile fiction. His first series, known as the Yale sports series, comprises the novels *The Substitute* (1908), *Jack Hall at Yale* (1909), and *Old Ryerson* (1911). A second trio of novels featured the character Danny Fists: *Danny Fists* (1913), *Captain Danny* (1914), and *Danny the Freshman* (1915). He also lent his name to a series written by Matthew M. Colten about an athletic boy named Frank Armstrong. Camp invented the character and began writing the series, but by the second book he was only consulting Colten. He asked that his name not be associated with the books after the third book was published, although they sold well, the first three having sold more than twenty-three thousand copies.

Late in the first decade of the twentieth century, Camp was receiving between $50 and $125 per article. He had received $2,000 from a publisher just for the right to put his name on the Frank Armstrong series. He was receiving more than $600 a month from *Collier's* for his work. While his career in writing was still going strong, however, his role with the Yale football team was diminishing, and he resigned from his connection with Yale football in 1910. There are various reasons given for his resignation from the program he loved. His critics felt he was responsible for the poor showing, by Yale standards, during the 1910 season: the team had suffered two defeats and a tie. His age played a part, as well. At more than fifty years old, he was considered to be out of touch. He did continue his presence, as always, on the various rules committees.

He was not gone from Yale football for long, though. For the next few years he alternated between helping and distancing himself from the program. There was no doubt, however, that football was not his sole interest. Physical fitness, which he had emphasized from time to time during his writing career, now became particularly important to him.

Harford Powel Jr., in his book *Walter Camp, the Father of American Football: An Authorized Biography* (1926), asserts that the advent of World War I rejuvenated Camp after years of declining prestige at Yale, although Camp was still involved with the Yale team in 1916. More likely, as he aged Camp began to realize that staying in shape was a difficult matter and turned much of his attention to helping Americans stay physically fit. He organized a local group that he called the Senior Service Corp, the objective of which was "to provide that citizens, whose age is beyond that of active military duty, but who desire to be of service to their government, may be made as physically fit as possible." Many of his articles at this time were geared toward this end. As Camp published articles with titles such as "Uncle Sam's Athletic System" (*Outlook,* 27 March 1918), "Keeping the Nation Fit" (*The Independent,* December 1918), and "Reconstruction of the Man" (*Outlook,* 5 February 1919), his name became associated not just with football but also with physical fitness.

In recognition of this fact, during the war the U.S. government gave Camp the position of director of the athletic division of the Navy Commission on Training Camp Activities. During World War I he held such titles as athletic director and chairman of athletics for the Navy Commission. Later Camp also became involved in the same manner with the Army Aviation Corps. For his work in the Navy he achieved the rank of captain. Camp also traveled to Washington, D.C., during the war years to start a physical-fitness program for the members of President Woodrow Wilson's cabinet. The group met mornings at 7:30 behind the Treasury Building. One member of the group, known as the "Walter Scamps," was Assistant Secretary of the Navy Franklin D. Roosevelt. Using his experiences with the "Walter Scamps," Camp put together a pamphlet about the "Athletic Cocktail" he had invented, which he called "The Daily Dozen."

Camp used his Daily Dozen in his position as athletic director to help military men. It was his idea to "duplicate the home environment" as much as possible to improve morale in the camps. The twelve exercises were easy to remember and were broken into four alliterative groups: "Hands, Hips, and Head"; "Grind, Grate, and Grasp"; "Crawl, Curl, and Crouch"; and "Wave, Weave, and Wing." Camp promoted the Daily Dozen enthusiasti-

The Walter Camp Memorial Gateway at Yale University

cally, estimating at one point that more than sixty-five thousand men in the Navy were using it. When the war ended, Camp continued to push the Daily Dozen by modifying it for different groups such as women, office workers, or children.

In March 1919 he publicized the workout routine in an article for *American Magazine,* "Walter Camp's Daily Dozen Set Up." The next month it was reprinted in a steel-company magazine, *Forge,* and in chart form in *American Boy.* The regimen gained public recognition when Camp's article about it appeared in *Collier's* in August 1920. The issue sold out immediately, and *Collier's* received a huge amount of requests for reprints of the article. Camp next published the routine as a pamphlet, *The Daily Dozen for Men and Women* (1921), and in April 1923 he printed another twenty-five thousand copies. It was sold out by October. In his position as physical-fitness expert Camp was brought to the House of Representatives in 1921 to speak. He not only addressed the assembly but also persuaded three congressmen to help him demonstrate the exercises.

Camp laid out his objectives for this period of his life in "What I Am Trying to Do," an article for *The World's Work* (October 1923):

> To induce people to take proper and systematic exercise and thus gain and keep good health.
>
> To persuade colleges to modify the extravagances of their present Frankenstein method of athletics.
>
> To demobilize the expensive side of golf and other athletic sports.

Golf had become an interest of Camp's as early as 1899, and that year he co-authored a work of fiction, *Drives and Puts: A Book of Golf Stories,* with Lilian Brooks. Through the years he published articles on golf, but he did not begin to write regularly on the subject until the 1920s. In his later years much of his focus shifted from team sports to individual sports that the average American could enjoy. In an article in 1923 Camp wrote: "Every American should be entitled to the right of life, liberty and the pursuit of golf balls!"

In 1919 Camp stepped away from the Yale football team for the final time, but he still served on the football rules committees of the new National Collegiate Athletic Association (NCAA). At his death on 14 March 1925, in fact, he was attending the annual meeting of the Intercollegiate Football Rules Committee at the Hotel Belmont in New York City. He was found by several of his friends in his hotel room, having died in his sleep a month prior to his sixty-sixth birthday. At the same time he had been working on a series of physical-fitness articles for *Collier's*. Two of these articles were published posthumously, the final article, "Getting the Most Out of Life," appearing in the September 1925 issue.

On 15 June 1925 a memorial service was held at Battell Chapel at Yale during commencement week. Professor William Lyon Phelps remembered how Camp had "wisely used his experience, his knowledge, and his capacity for leadership in teaching young America the highest ideals of sportsmanship during just the period when such teaching was most needed." Grantland Rice, who had replaced Camp at *Collier's,* wrote:

> How often must have come to Walter Camp the memory of old football battles in rain and snow, in sun and shadow–the flying tackle and the savage line thrust–the forward wall braced for the shock–the graceful spiral careening against a sky of blue and gray–the long run down the field–the goal line stand–the forward pass–the singing and the cheering of great crowds–young and old. America gathered together on a golden afternoon, with bands playing and banners flying.
>
> It may have been in the midst of such a dream that the call to quarters came, and Taps were sounded as the great knight came down the field.

Three years after Walter Camp's death, Yale erected a gateway in his memory. Contributions from more than 1,000 Yale graduates, 224 universities, and 279 prep schools paid for the seventy-foot-wide, fifty-foot-high white portal. It was the entrance not only to the Yale Bowl, the university football field, but also to all athletic fields. Tablets on the ends of the gateway read: "Given by American colleges and schools Uniting with Graduates of Yale to Honor Walter Camp and the traditions of American College Sport which he exemplified." Twenty-six years after his death, in 1951, he was elected into the National Football Foundation Hall of Fame.

In the end, Camp had written for more than twenty different magazines and many newspapers, including the *Philadelphia Press, Boston Globe, Boston Herald, San Francisco Call, New York Evening Post,* and the *New Haven Evening Register*. In addition to the more than twenty books he wrote and edited, he also edited the official intercollegiate *Football Rules & Guide* and the "How to Play Football" series. Camp's football accomplishments have certainly overshadowed his writing accomplishments, but in the end his writing made him a nationally known figure and allowed him to gain his objectives in promoting and popularizing the game he loved.

Biographies:

Harford Powel Jr., *Walter Camp, the Father of American Football: An Authorized Biography* (Boston: Little, Brown, 1926);

Richard P. Borkowski, "The Life and Contributions of Walter Camp to American Football," dissertation, Temple University, 1979;

Kathleen D. Valenzi and Michael W. Hopps, *Champion of Sport: The Life of Walter Camp, 1859–1925* (Charlottesville, Va.: Howell, 1990).

References:

John Richards Betts, *American Sporting Heritage: 1850–1950* (Menlo Park, Cal.: Addison Wesley, 1974);

Tim Cohane, *The Yale Football Story* (New York: Putnam, 1951), pp. 27–69, 110, 188–189, 238;

Albert Beecher Crawford, ed., *Football Y Men 1872–1919,* 3 volumes (New Haven: Yale University Press, 1962–1963) I: 38;

Parke H. Davis, *The American Intercollegiate Game* (New York: Scribners, 1911);

Richard Goldstein, *Ivy League Autumns: An Illustrated History of College Football's Grand Old Rivalries* (New York: St. Martin's Press, 1996), pp. 10–19;

David Otto Hennins, "The Role or the 'Newspaper in the Development of Football 1869–1929,'" dissertation, University of Wisconsin-Milwaukee, 1997, pp. 26–38;

Robert Leckie, *The Story of Football* (New York: Random House, 1969), pp. 7–10, 12–14, 16–17;

Michael Oriard, *Reading Football: How the Popular Press Created an American Spectacle* (Chapel Hill: University of North Carolina Press, 1993), 35–56, 145–165, 208–216;

Ronald A. Smith, *Sports and Freedom: The Rise of Big-Time College Athletics* (New York: Oxford University Press, 1988), pp. 83–98.

Papers:

The Walter Camp papers are housed in the Manuscript Department of the Yale University Library.

O. P. Caylor

(17 December 1849 – 19 October 1897)

David Ball

MAJOR POSITIONS HELD: Reporter, *Cincinnati Enquirer* (1874–1881); official scorer, club secretary, Cincinnati Reds (1876–1886); editor, *Cincinnati Commercial* (1882–1886).

BOOK: *A Fated Promise* (New York: Dillingham, 1890); republished as *The Rockwell Case* (New York: Dillingham, 1896).

O. P. Caylor

Relatively little-remembered by sports historians, O. P. Caylor was one of the most-influential baseball writers of the last quarter of the nineteenth century and for several years was an important official of the Cincinnati Reds and the American Association, the major league to which the Reds then belonged. Baseball club officials have from time to time dabbled in journalism, and many newsmen in Caylor's day followed his example in serving as club secretaries; a few were even important figures in league management. Rarely if ever has one man simultaneously achieved such prominence in both roles as Caylor did at the height of his career, however.

Born near Dayton, Ohio, on 17 December 1849, Oliver Perry Caylor graduated first in his high-school class in Dayton. After studying law he was admitted to the bar in 1872 and moved to Cincinnati. His legal practice led him to newspaper correspondence, then employment by *The Cincinnati Enquirer* in late 1874. Soon he was made responsible for baseball coverage for the newspaper.

The *Enquirer* in the middle and late 1870s was an ideal platform for a bright young writer eager to make his name as a baseball writer. Interest in baseball was then on the upswing in the Queen City of the West. After the famous Cincinnati Red Stockings had disbanded following the 1870 season, the city had been without professional ball for several years. In August 1875, however, local businessmen organized a team that played some games during the last months of the season and then became a charter member of the National League in 1876. At the same time the young publisher of the *Enquirer,* John McLean, was leading the way for a new kind of newspaper–more respectable than the penny press but discreetly sensationalistic. By the standards of the day, McLean's *Enquirer* put relatively little emphasis on partisan politics, concentrating instead on feature stories, society and crime news, and other items of interest to more apolitical readers. A talented amateur catcher in his earlier years, McLean understood that baseball news had the potential to pull in the kind of readers he was after, and he was willing to give the game–and Caylor–plenty of space.

By the 1876 inaugural season of the National League, Caylor already served as the Reds' official scorer, perhaps as much a tribute to the position of the *Enquirer* in Cincinnati as to Caylor's individual standing at that time. By 1880, however, he had established close relations with Reds president Justus Thorner and was prominent enough that some baseball reference works in later years listed Caylor as the Reds' manager.

As a result, other newspapers attacked Caylor as a power behind the throne; Charles Scanlon of the *Cincinnati Commercial* complained bitterly of favoritism toward the *Enquirer* correspondent. The scorer's position was something of a plum. One story relates that Deacon Jim White, the manager of the 1879 Reds, had brought in his own brother-in-law to do the scoring, thereby angering Caylor, who supposedly retaliated by criticizing White's signing of infielder Ross Barnes. In fact, a review of Caylor's *Enquirer* coverage reveals that he was always on particularly friendly terms with both Barnes and White, and in 1879 was far more critical of the Reds front office. He wrote that either White or Cal McVey, who replaced White as manager early in the season, could do an adequate job if club president Wayne Neff would stop meddling with the team. The tale that Caylor opposed Jim White out of spite over the loss of the scorer's job is clearly untrue, but it serves as an example of the kind of stories put out by Caylor's enemies as he grew more prominent.

At the end of the 1880 season the Reds were expelled from the National League because of reluctance to accept all of the National League rules. In the *Enquirer* an angry Caylor denounced the expulsion and reportedly became a key figure in two attempts to organize a second league during the winter of 1880. Nothing came of these, but in June 1881 Caylor and three other local men came together to organize a new professional team to replace the departed Reds. Each man put in $100, with which the new organization rented the Reds' old ballpark and used it to raise more money by staging games between independent professional and semiprofessional teams, meanwhile planning to field its own team during the next season. That fall Caylor played an important organizational role as representatives from independent teams met in Cincinnati and founded a second major league, called the American Association, with the Reds as a charter member. An article from the *Cincinnati Enquirer* (3 November 1881) announcing the birth of the new league also demonstrates his distinctive prose style:

> An Independent League has been formed. To-day it is a certainty, and its enemies can laugh as scornfully as they wish and ridicule it as much as they desire, still it has started out most bravely and most determinedly. The old League had not its backing when it began life, and to-day its members are not as wealthy as those who compose the new Association. The organizers of the latter have worked most zealously to perfect it, and success never crowned their efforts until yesterday. With the wreck of the International [League] staring them in the face, the energetic founders of this last organization commenced their labors during the past months, and, although certain failure beset them at nearly every corner, they continued their exertions until they triumphed. Their struggles have been crowned with brilliant success, and stand forth to this country requesting patronage in the shape of the American Association of Base-ball Clubs. The latter has chosen as its motto, "Liberty to all." It believes fully that the League has done much to foster and improve the national pastime, even advancing it to a point far beyond what it had ever reached. It fully recognizes the experience its elder rival has had with crooked professionals and black sheep, and proposes to support it in those particulars. It is doubly peaceful. It is liberal. It extends its hand to the old League and asks its co-operation in the advancement of this truly national sport.

Soon after the new team formed, Caylor left the *Enquirer*. He later testified in a legal deposition that he left the paper on 18 August 1881, but its baseball coverage since about the middle of July had been notably perfunctory. According to the testimony in his lawsuit, he intended to concentrate on his law practice but within a few months was engaged by the *Cincinnati Commercial,* for which he at first provided only occasional pieces. By the time the 1882 baseball season began, he was serving as editor for his new paper, whose coverage of the sport was soon comparable to that of the *Enquirer*. For the next five years he remained with the *Commercial,* which soon became the *Commercial Gazette* as the result of a merger.

During the early and middle 1880s Caylor reached the height of his influence in the baseball world. Cincinnati was then only beginning to lose its status as the urban center of the Midwest to Chicago, and its newspapers circulated widely throughout the region, so that writing for the two leading newspapers in the city had made Caylor known on a wider, regional stage. By mid decade his columns were carried by other newspapers, and his national visibility was further increased by a column in *The Sporting Life,* the leading sports weekly of the day.

Although Caylor soon sold out his interest in the Reds, he continued to serve as the club secretary, a position roughly equivalent to that of a modern general manager, even while holding his newspaper job. He also served in important positions on the rules and schedule committees of the American Association. In the spring of 1883 he was a member of the association's conference committee, which negotiated peace with the National League after a commercial war, and he served for a while as secretary of the joint committee, which oversaw relations between the rival leagues. For a time he also edited the official guide for the association.

Because newspapers of the day rarely gave bylines, it is difficult to determine what kind of writing Caylor did besides his employment as baseball reporter–or "baseball critic," as he once described himself–for the *Enquirer* and *Commercial Gazette*. He testified in court that he had been originally hired by the *Commercial* to do "occasional literary and other work," without specifying what that might mean. However, while he was traveling with the Reds on an 1879 road trip his "O.P.C." byline did appear in the *Enquirer* on an interview with a boxer and a travel piece describing cities in Upstate New York through which the team had passed. In 1887, after he had moved to New York, the same byline appeared in the *Cincinnati Times-Star* on an article about the New York theatrical season. He may well have written similar pieces without credit for the *Enquirer* and the *Commercial Gazette*. It is not unlikely, however, that he functioned as an ordinary reporter, at least when he was with the *Commercial Gazette*. The long hours demanded by the profession would have left little time for his many other interests.

When Caylor began writing, a rather ornate and heavy style was in common use on sports pages. About the mid 1880s younger reporters in Cincinnati such as James Faulkner and Ren Mulford began to experiment with a racier, colloquial style of reporting game stories; but Caylor, although he was on friendly terms with both these men, never emulated their stylistic experiments. He could write well at times but was rarely first-rate as a stylist. His occasional forays into narrative and descriptive writing were uninspired at best, and he was often guilty of sloppiness–for example, a tendency to repeat the same word excessively. This stylistic carelessness was perhaps due to the fact that he had so many irons in the fire at one time. Besides his duty as the Reds' secretary and his various services in American Association affairs, he held the concession on the team's scorecards for a few years, and he may have continued to practice law in a low-key way. Although enemies scoffed at him as an attorney without clients, he did maintain an office for his legal practice until he left Cincinnati in 1886 and featured his legal practice on the letterhead of his stationery.

More than style, at any rate, Caylor's real distinction lay in his sharp intelligence and an analytical ability honed, on the one hand, by broader practical experience in baseball politics than most of his colleagues could boast, and, on the other, by his training and practice in law. His comments on the business aspects and on the playing rules–both rapidly evolving in the early days of professional sports–are particularly interesting.

At the same time, Caylor's background as an attorney was perhaps responsible for a tendency to rely too heavily on legalistic argument. At times this trait could make him seem merely pedantic and even endearingly quixotic, as in his constant insistence that by finishing first in the American Association's 1882 pennant race, the Reds had become the defending champions of the association for 1883, not 1882, as the rest of the world insisted on saying. Caylor's bent for legalistic thinking was not always so trivial, however. Even the friendly Mulford complained that Caylor had "used the tactics of a lawyer" by imposing on Mulford's trust to print in the *Cincinnati Times-Star* half-truths concerning an embarrassing incident during Caylor's tenure as manager of the Metropolitans of New York.

While Caylor's official standing with the Reds gave his reporting of club affairs a distinct authority, it was not without its drawbacks. Aside from the fundamental conflict of interest involved in covering a ball club he himself was running, Caylor also used his columns to promote his scorecards and baseball guides (including *Reach's Official Base Ball Guide,* which he edited) without revealing his connection with them. Even by the comparatively relaxed ethical standards of contemporary journalism, Caylor recognized his position as problematic, and he was careful to maintain a low profile in his dual role, referring to himself when necessary in the *Commercial Gazette* simply by the title of "the secretary of the Cincinnati Club." Hostile reporters for other papers, especially the *Enquirer,* alluded to Caylor's double role occasionally, but few were in a position to throw stones. At one time or another all the important Cincinnati baseball writers of Caylor's day were in the employment of some local baseball team.

In the 1870s Caylor's skills were particularly suited to covering the National League Reds. While a better team might have given more scope to a writer of real stylistic distinction, Caylor's analytical abilities made him perfect for covering the original ugly duckling of the National League, a franchise bedeviled by a series of inept and financially unstable managements and unskilled or underachieving teams. Although Caylor generally tried to be supportive of the interests of the club, in 1876 he laid out for his readers the futility of an attempt to compete at the highest level with a team of amateurs and unknown young professionals, and in 1877 he criticized the team's accumulation of hard hitters without regard to their defensive positions. During the disappointing season in 1879 his targets included Neff's meddling in team discipline, the imbalance produced when the signing of four high-priced players left little money for the rest of the team, and the foolishness of starting on a road trip with only one pitcher. In the 1880s Caylor rarely provided such sharp

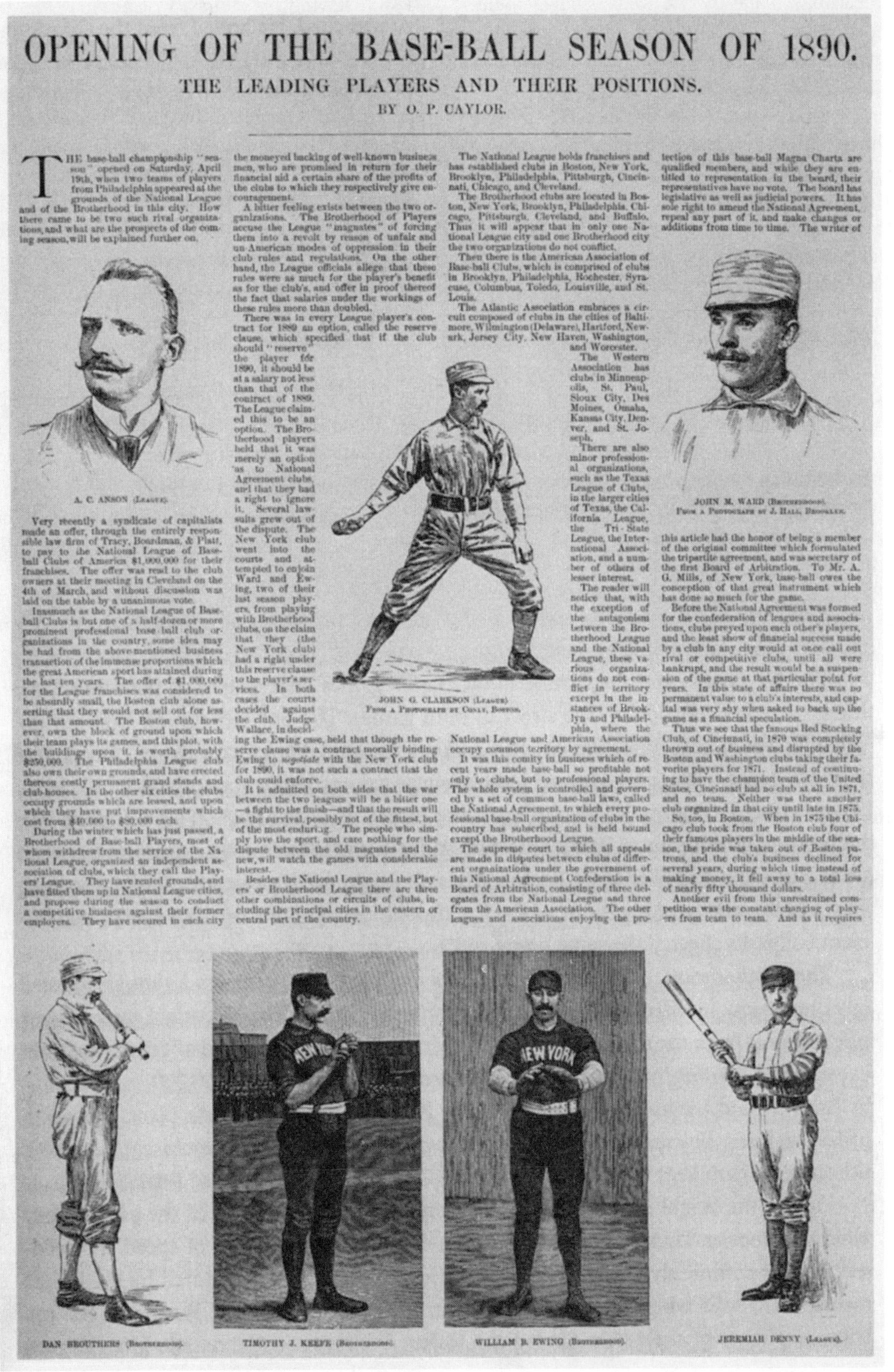

OPENING OF THE BASE-BALL SEASON OF 1890.

THE LEADING PLAYERS AND THEIR POSITIONS.

BY O. P. CAYLOR.

THE base-ball championship "season" opened on Saturday, April 19th, when two teams of players from Philadelphia appeared at the grounds of the National League and of the Brotherhood in this city. How there came to be two such rival organizations, and what are the prospects of the coming season, will be explained further on.

A. C. ANSON (League).

Very recently a syndicate of capitalists made an offer, through the entirely responsible law firm of Tracy, Boardman, & Platt, to pay to the National League of Base-ball Clubs of America $1,000,000 for their franchises. The offer was read to the club owners at their meeting in Cleveland on the 4th of March, and without discussion was laid on the table by a unanimous vote.

Inasmuch as the National League of Base-ball Clubs is but one of a half-dozen or more prominent professional base-ball club organizations in the country, some idea may be had from the above-mentioned business transaction of the immense proportions which the great American sport has attained during the last ten years. The offer of $1,000,000 for the League franchises was considered to be absurdly small, the Boston club alone asserting that they would not sell out for less than that amount. The Boston club, however, own the block of ground upon which their team plays its games, and this plot, with the buildings upon it, is worth probably $250,000. The Philadelphia League club also own their own grounds, and have erected thereon costly permanent grand stands and club-houses. In the other six cities the clubs occupy grounds which are leased, and upon which they have put improvements which cost from $40,000 to $80,000 each.

During the winter which has just passed, a Brotherhood of Base-ball Players, most of whom withdrew from the service of the National League, organized an independent association of clubs, which they call the Players' League. They have rented grounds, and have fitted them up in National League cities, and propose during the season to conduct a competitive business against their former employers. They have secured in each city the moneyed backing of well-known business men, who are promised in return for their financial aid a certain share of the profits of the clubs to which they respectively give encouragement.

A bitter feeling exists between the two organizations. The Brotherhood of Players accuse the League "magnates" of forcing them into a revolt by reason of unfair and un-American modes of oppression in their club rules and regulations. On the other hand, the League officials allege that these rules were as much for the player's benefit as for the club's, and offer in proof thereof the fact that salaries under the workings of these rules more than doubled.

There was in every League player's contract for 1889 an option, called the reserve clause, which specified that if the club should "reserve" the player for 1890, it should be at a salary not less than that of the contract of 1889. The League claimed this to be an option. The Brotherhood players held that it was merely an option as to National Agreement clubs, and that they had a right to ignore it. Several law-suits grew out of the dispute. The New York club went into the courts and attempted to enjoin Ward and Ewing, two of their last season players, from playing with Brotherhood clubs, on the claim that they (the New York club) had a right under this reserve clause to the player's services. In both cases the courts decided against the club. Judge Wallace, in deciding the Ewing case, held that though the reserve clause was a contract morally binding Ewing to *negotiate* with the New York club for 1890, it was not such a contract that the club could enforce.

JOHN G. CLARKSON (League).
From a Photograph by Conly, Boston.

It is admitted on both sides that the war between the two leagues will be a bitter one—a fight to the finish—and that the result will be the survival, possibly not of the fittest, but of the most enduring. The people who simply love the sport, and care nothing for the dispute between the old magnates and the new, will watch the games with considerable interest.

Besides the National League and the Players' or Brotherhood League there are three other combinations or circuits of clubs, including the principal cities in the eastern or central part of the country.

The National League holds franchises and has established clubs in Boston, New York, Brooklyn, Philadelphia, Pittsburgh, Cincinnati, Chicago, and Cleveland.

The Brotherhood clubs are located in Boston, New York, Brooklyn, Philadelphia, Chicago, Pittsburgh, Cleveland, and Buffalo. Thus it will appear that in only one National League city and one Brotherhood city the two organizations do not conflict.

Then there is the American Association of Base-ball Clubs, which is comprised of clubs in Brooklyn, Philadelphia, Rochester, Syracuse, Columbus, Toledo, Louisville, and St. Louis.

The Atlantic Association embraces a circuit composed of clubs in the cities of Baltimore, Wilmington (Delaware), Hartford, Newark, Jersey City, New Haven, Washington, and Worcester.

The Western Association has clubs in Minneapolis, St. Paul, Sioux City, Des Moines, Omaha, Kansas City, Denver, and St. Joseph.

There are also minor professional organizations, such as the Texas League of Clubs, in the larger cities of Texas, the California League, the Tri-State League, the International Association, and a number of others of lesser interest.

The reader will notice that, with the exception of the antagonism between the Brotherhood League and the National League, these various organizations do not conflict in territory except in the instances of Brooklyn and Philadelphia, where the National League and American Association occupy common territory by agreement.

It was this comity in business which of recent years made base-ball so profitable not only to clubs, but to professional players. The whole system is controlled and governed by a set of common base-ball laws, called the National Agreement, to which every professional base-ball organization of clubs in the country has subscribed, and is held bound except the Brotherhood League.

The supreme court to which all appeals are made in disputes between clubs of different organizations under the government of this National Agreement Confederation is a Board of Arbitration, consisting of three delegates from the National League and three from the American Association. The other leagues and associations enjoying the protection of this base-ball Magna Charta are qualified members, and while they are entitled to representation in the board, their representatives have no vote. The board has legislative as well as judicial powers. It has sole right to amend the National Agreement, repeal any part of it, and make changes or additions from time to time. The writer of this article had the honor of being a member of the original committee which formulated the tripartite agreement, and was secretary of the first Board of Arbitration. To Mr. A. G. Mills, of New York, base-ball owes the conception of that great instrument which has done so much for the game.

JOHN M. WARD (Brotherhood).
From a Photograph by J. Hall, Brooklyn.

Before the National Agreement was formed for the confederation of leagues and associations, clubs preyed upon each other's players, and the least show of financial success made by a club in any city would at once call out rival or competitive clubs, until all were bankrupt, and the result would be a suspension of the game at that particular point for years. In this state of affairs there was no permanent value to a club's interests, and capital was very shy when asked to back up the game as a financial speculation.

Thus we see that the famous Red Stocking Club, of Cincinnati, in 1870 was completely thrown out of business and disrupted by the Boston and Washington clubs taking their favorite players for 1871. Instead of continuing to have the champion team of the United States, Cincinnati had no club at all in 1871, and no team. Neither was there another club organized in that city until late in 1875.

So, too, in Boston. When in 1875 the Chicago club took from the Boston club four of their famous players in the middle of the season, the pride was taken out of Boston patrons, and the club's business declined for several years, during which time instead of making money, it fell away to a total loss of nearly fifty thousand dollars.

Another evil from this unrestrained competition was the constant changing of players from team to team. And as it requires

DAN BROUTHERS (Brotherhood). TIMOTHY J. KEEFE (Brotherhood). WILLIAM B. EWING (Brotherhood). JEREMIAH DENNY (League).

Caylor's preview of the upcoming baseball season in the 3 May 1890 issue of Harper's Weekly analysis of decisions made by the Reds' management. The team was certainly far better run at the time, and even so, Caylor was not expected to attack the conduct of a club in which he himself was a leading figure.

When the Reds were under fire in 1880 for selling liquor in the stands and renting their park out to amateur teams on Sundays, Caylor replied to criticism by a newspaper in Worcester, Massachusetts (then a National League city), by writing: "Puritanical Worcester is not liberal Cincinnati by a jugful, and what is sauce for Worcester is wind for the Queen city. Beer and Sunday amusements have become a popular necessity in Cincinnati." This quotation is probably Caylor's best-remembered, but while it is true to the character of nineteenth-century Cincinnati, it does not reflect well the kind of man its author was. Far from the raffish free spirit implied by the quotation, Caylor was a Methodist, a man of traditional values who as club executive and journalist always preferred the respectable middle classes rather than "that noisy element which has so often rendered base ball fields the scene of disgraceful riots" and whose contract permitted him to be absent from games played on Sunday.

Caylor was a small man, often in poor health. One of the better stories of his career has him describing a ball player from a visiting team under the headline "A Keg of Beer Will Catch for Louisville Today." The angry player is supposed to have stormed into the newspaper office, ready to give the author of the article a good beating, only to retreat quietly after meeting the diminutive Caylor. Asked why, the player later said, "Oh, I couldn't hit him. He's just a pimple on a stick." Highly educated by the standards of the day, Caylor perhaps at times mixed uneasily with the spirited men who played and followed professional baseball in the nineteenth century.

Caylor is generally remembered for his flair for sarcastic writing, along with a sharp temper and conceit. He is depicted as "a vituperative bantam" possessing "a sharp tongue and a great vanity . . . never one to spare a player's feeling." Even in his own day the affable Frank Richter of *The Sporting Life* said that Caylor made more enemies than friends due to "a pugnacious disposition . . . an eagerness to enter in to controversy . . . a positive nature which could brook neither opposition, advice, or suggestion." Contemporary baseball historian David Quentin Voigt, in his *American Baseball: From the Gentleman's Sport to the Commissioner's System* (1983), described Caylor's prose style as "sneering" and "scornful." Harold Seymour, in *Baseball: The Early Years* (1960), called him "that expert of sarcasm." Player strikes and unions were often a target for Caylor's venom, as were outside challenges to organized baseball such as the Union Association of 1883, started by Henry V. Lucas. When brewer Ellis Wainwright helped establish a St. Louis Union club, Caylor labeled the team, filled with some baseball outcasts, "The Lucas-Wainwright Lunatic Asylum." He particularly targeted baseball writers, as quoted in Voigt's *American Baseball,* "who actually imagine that the success of the game is raised or lowered by the leverage of their pen, with their ego as a fulcrum."

Caylor could write harshly at times and did not shirk controversy. He was an emotional man, given to explosions of temper. Frank Wright of the *Cincinnati News Journal,* another well-disposed journalist and a personal friend, wrote that "As a secretary, business manager, or representative at meetings, he has no superior; but his quickness of temper is his fault." Normally a judicious reporter, Caylor, at stressful moments, could sometimes write intemperately. This problem seemed to have worsened in the 1880s, and certainly his temper became a more serious liability when he carried the dual responsibility of representing his club officially and reporting the news to the public.

For example, in 1882 his newspaper baiting of umpire Joe Simmons after the arbiter's last-inning decision had cost the Reds an important game ("outrageously partial in his decisions . . . remarkable ignorance and lack of judgment . . . certainly the worst that has been seen here yet") encouraged a crowd at the next day's game to mob Simmons. The following year he angrily denounced several Reds for failing to sacrifice in another crucial ninth-inning situation in St. Louis and then ordered the benching of veteran shortstop Charlie Fulmer. Although he never said so openly, the *News Journal* later revealed that Caylor had suspected St. Louis Browns' owner Chris Von der Ahe of bribing Fulmer to play poorly, as the *News Journal* later revealed. Other local journalists, although they probably knew of Caylor's suspicions concerning Fulmer, were unconvinced. An avalanche of criticism from press and public met the shortstop's benching, Caylor's position as club secretary may have been threatened, and the club directors gave control of the team on the field to team captain Charlie Snyder, who promptly reinstated Fulmer. A chastened Caylor spent the next few weeks writing about Fulmer and Snyder in an ostentatiously friendly way.

Caylor's penchant for sarcasm, however, has been exaggerated. Caylor wrote in a day of "personal journalism," when unbridled vituperation was common currency among newspaper writers. The publishers of Caylor's two Cincinnati papers, McLean of the *Enquirer* and Murat Halstead of the *Commercial Gazette,* engaged in a running battle, which climaxed when Halstead nearly challenged McLean to a duel. Many of Caylor's targets were themselves journalists with the will and ability to repay in kind to his attacks. For example, during the controversy over the office of scorer in 1879, Scanlon of the *Commercial* described Caylor as "an annual plant or fungus of unhealthy growth that blooms somewhere along in April, emitting a rank odor all through the summer months extremely offensive to every one save himself . . . this unsavory jack o'lantern . . . the base ball wrecker of the *Enquirer*." While Caylor could write sharply when engaged in quarrel, he almost never indulged in clownish personal abuse of this sort.

Many of the controversies he was involved in resulted from his actions as league and team official. The *Indianapolis Times* spoke of him with considerable respect as a baseball authority until a day in the summer of 1883 when Caylor stole into town and signed an Indianapolis player for the 1884 Reds. After that he was "O. P. Caylor, the agent of perfidy" to the *Times,* as well as "cucumber-headed Caylor" and "the gilt-edged crank of the *Commercial Gazette*." The St. Louis–based *Sporting News* similarly mocked him and ridiculed him as "Offensive Partisan Caylor" and "O. Pensive Caylor," in part at least because of his role in signing Tony Mullane, a star pitcher who was pirated away by the Reds after promising to sign a contract with the St. Louis Browns. Although Cincinnati club president Aaron Stern actually seems to have taken the leading part in signing Mullane, Caylor had been active in the *Commercial Gazette* in defending the Reds and Mullane from attack.

In writing about players Caylor generally showed forebearance. The 1876 Reds, for instance, won only fifty-six league games. Yet, for the most part Caylor was gentle with them, recognizing that the players were doing their best and that the real blame lay with management, who were trying to compete in the new National League with amateurs and unknowns. Similarly, he recognized the great difficulty of the umpires' job and treated them in a similarly restrained fashion (except on the relatively rare occasions when his temper got away from him, as it did with Simmons).

All in all, whoever reads Caylor's writing not in the form of isolated quotations but as a body of work in the context of the journalism of his day will find him remarkable less for a habit of occasional sarcasm shared with many contemporaries than for a certain charm and sensitivity, qualities much rarer in the sportswriting of his or any day. Perhaps nothing illustrates this quality better than his treatment of Mike Burke, a young Cincinnatian who had signed with the Reds for the 1879 season after running up an enviable record as a minor-league player.

Installed as the starting shortstop, Burke got off to a bad start. Evidently a sensitive person and somewhat insecure, he began pressing and his play deteriorated still further. Caylor took a liking to the young man and encouraged him in his *Enquirer* notes (and no doubt in person); but Burke was benched and then made critical errors when injuries to other players gave him another chance to get into the lineup. One day, club secretary J. C. Howe met Burke as he entered the ball park and handed him his unconditional release. At this, the player snapped, threatening to assault Howe and a security guard who interfered and attacking manager Cal McVey. Finally he was led to the dressing room, where he broke down crying. Caylor described the incident in the *Enquirer* and explained:

> It is not a cause for reproval, but rather of compassion. No more conscientious or earnest ball player ever stepped upon the field than Burke. . . . He has a young wife and baby whom he worships depending on him for a living, and their welfare made him anxious for the future–too anxious. When his release was offered to him the thought of it drove him completely beside himself, and under the half-crazed excitement he did what he afterward expressed abject sorrow for. He was manly enough to apologize to those he had threatened or assaulted, and nobody speaks of him in other terms than kindness. Had he played through indifference of improper care of himself he would not now have the sympathy of every one. But Burke has at least until lately been perfectly temperate and honest in his profession. It is the general belief of ball players who know him that he will to some other city and play as brilliantly the rest of the season as he did with the Tecumsehs last year. . . .

During the mid 1880s Caylor's associations with the *Commercial Gazette* and the Reds increasingly involved him in interrelated feuds in his home city. When Caylor changed his original plans to devote his time to his law practice and went to the *Commercial Gazette,* he joined a newspaper that was locked with the *Enquirer* in what has been called "one of the longest, most savage, and at the same time most spectacular newspaper wars in American history." McLean may have resented Caylor's desertion to the camp of the bitter enemy. Between 1883 and 1886 McLean and Justus Thorner engaged in fierce battles either to take over management of the Reds or establish a successful rival club in Cincinnati, and Caylor, highly exposed as both club secretary and the Reds' spokesman through his columns in the *Commercial Gazette,* became the chief target of attacks in the *Enquirer.*

What might have been a minor skirmish in the war for the favor of Cincinnati baseball fans suddenly took another turn when Harry Weldon of the *Enquirer* published a violent attack on Caylor for alleged penurious and inept management of the Cincinnati club, theft of his share in the Reds from McLean, and even what

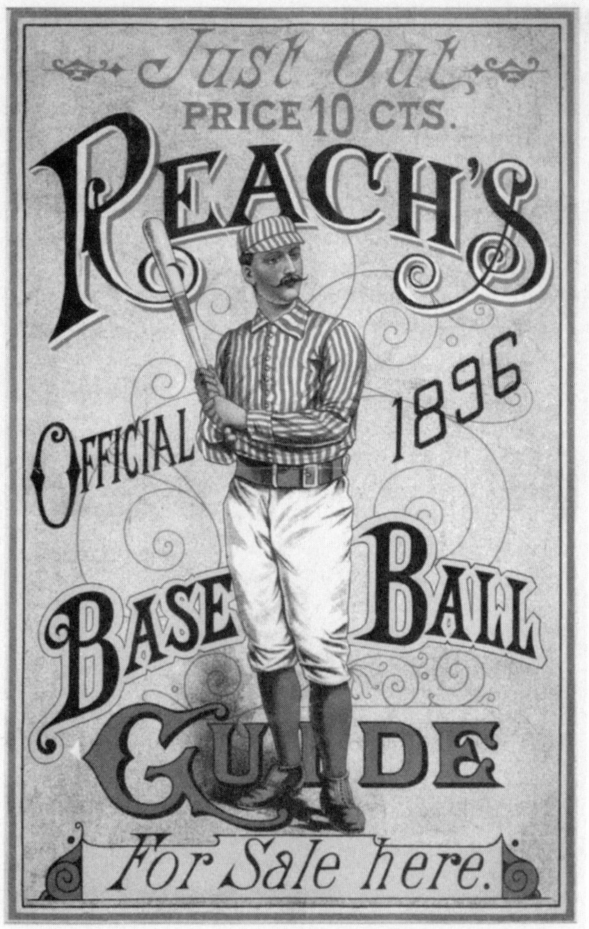

Advertising poster for the baseball guide that Caylor edited for the Reach sporting-goods firm, which manufactured baseballs

Weldon claimed was Caylor's role in having the Reds expelled from the National League in 1880. Without using Caylor's name, he identified him unmistakably by alluding to the diminutive stature, calling him "the skeleton who presides over the destinies of the Cincinnati club . . . the great disorganizer [whose] despotism, combined with his egotism and penuriousness, has brought the officials of the Cincinnati organization into such disrepute . . . the lizard-like individual who prostitutes the columns of a morning contemporary to advance his own interests."

Caylor was not slow to react. In characteristically lawyerly fashion he replied to Weldon's article on his conduct point by point, but only after he first attacked Weldon personally. These articles show Caylor's writing at its best, as he cleverly parries the *Enquirer* reporter's bludgeon blows with rapier strokes:

> Thought so! That fiery-brained, fiery-headed Professor of Belles Lettres, who works the base ball exchanges for the *Enquirer,* has made a second excursion into the fields of polite and elegant diction so characteristic of his pure mind. Again has the object of this mighty mental effort been the human base ball editor of the *Commercial Gazette,* who seems to be the *bete noire* of the terra-cotta-headed youth. Only one short week ago this bright youth was daily accustomed to call each afternoon upon the writer hereof and in those sweet dulcet tones which are shadowed in his literary gems, was wont to inquire, "Anything new to-day?" Then, while the *Commercial Gazette* base ball "lizard" proceeds to load up the *Enquirer* mechanic with choice bits of base ball information and "points," the said *Enquirer* mechanic would tip himself back in his chair and make notes or draw diagrams of the news according to the orthography necessary, and his sweet violet eyes would bulge out with gratitude while the milk of human kindness, resembling tobacco juice, would trickle down over his soft, tender chin from the two corners of his mouth, and soak away in the soft sponge-like folds of his plush waistcoat.

In 1886 Weldon left Cincinnati to become secretary of the St. Louis Browns, and Caylor had kind words for a former enemy who had joined the American Association, which Weldon had continued to taunt since 1884: "Mr. Weldon and the writer have several times engaged in little base ball tilts with the pen—very foolishly, as both are now ready to confess. But that belongs to base ball history. Mr. Weldon comes squarely over to the right side at last."

When ownership of the Reds fell into the hands of John Hauck, a brewer and banker, Caylor became the team manager, the first holder of that actual title since the club had been organized in 1881. Caylor promptly announced his new appointment to newspapers across the country, although he had always functioned as manager de facto. The highly public announcement was the sort of thing that fueled public belief in his vanity. As the *St. Louis Post-Dispatch* later jeered, Caylor telegraphed the news "all over the country, in double-leaded style, and signed the messages himself."

Under Caylor the Reds played well early, but floundered enough at times that several local newspapers began to complain, and the *Enquirer* again began its abuse of both players and Caylor with a bit of uninspired doggerel:

> There is a ball club in our town
> Each member of which is a clown,
> Their manager, Caylor, has made it a failure,
> And the sport-loving public is on.
> Moral: go down to the Millcreek bottoms to see the amateurs play.

On 9 June 1886, with the end of a long and painful road trip approaching, Caylor did not hesitate to complain to his readers about the abuse he was suffering from the new managing editor of the *Enquirer,* Allen O. Myers, a writer and sometimes politician who was threatened with expulsion for repeated disorderly conduct on the floor of the Ohio House of Representatives: "The new managing editor, who radiates from Vine street, is heating his alcoholic brain with an expressed fear that there will be no suitable mark of reception for the Cincinnati Club on its return home to-day. His recollection of the last enthusiasm he witnessed on the Cincinnati grounds is that of 2,000 spectators standing up in the grand stand and pavilion and cheering, while two policemen carried his kicking, struggling and foul-mouthed form out of the crowd and pitched it over the fence." Myers was a tougher customer than the sportswriters Caylor was used to jousting with, however, and the Reds' continued disappointing play put him on the defensive. By September it was apparent that his time with the Reds was at an end. Soon after he decided to leave Cincinnati.

Caylor kept his plans close to the vest at first, telling the *Cincinnati Star-Times* he was heading to Philadelphia, where according to one rumor he would open an employment office for baseball players. There was even talk of electing him president of the American Association, although he categorically denied interest in the office. By the time he left Cincinnati in January 1887 he had revealed that he was going to New York to edit a new national daily baseball newspaper, to be published by John B. Day and Erastus Wiman, owners of the two major-league clubs in New York. The American Association recognized his valuable service by making him a lifetime member. Caylor's *Base ball Tribune* duly appeared at the beginning of the baseball season, but the readership and the superstructure to support a daily national sports publication did not exist in 1887. Within a few weeks the *Tribune* had disappeared.

Caylor remained in New York, where he may have supported himself for a while as a freelance writer; but in June 1887 Wiman named Caylor manager of his Metropolitan club. While Caylor worked hard to improve the perennial last-place ball club, nothing seemed to work and he was harassed by a succession of unpleasant and embarrassing incidents. On 5 September 1887 he was excluded from a special meeting of the American Association along with other newspaper reporters. Caylor immediately resigned his honorary association membership and stormed out of the room, his "face whiter than the Saratoga chips at the end of the lunch counter." From this time forward Caylor became an enemy of the association and a partisan of the National League, which had never had easy relations with the younger circuit, in spite of the peace between them that Caylor himself had helped broker.

At the end of the season Wiman folded his Mets, although Caylor had already announced that he would not be back to lead the team in 1888. Indeed, his years as a mover and shaker in the baseball world were coming to an end, and for a while he was not to have much of a platform even to comment about baseball affairs. He now changed directions drastically, moving to Carthage, Missouri, where he bought and edited a newspaper. In May 1889 a Cincinnati paper noted that Caylor had come up to Kansas City but gone away disappointed after watching his old team the Reds lose to the Kansas City Cowboys. By the end of the year he had sold out his interest in the Carthage paper, reportedly at a handsome profit.

After his western sojourn Caylor again returned to New York, where he became editor of *The Sporting Times and Theatrical News.* An old rival of *The Sporting News* and *The Sporting Life,* which was in serious decline, the weekly had come into the hands of Albert Spalding, the sporting-goods magnate and Chicago White Stockings president, who was a power in National League circles. Caylor stepped into the *The Sporting Times* editorial chair just as league players, joined in a union known as the Brotherhood, were preparing to organize a new league to free them from the reserve clause, which controlled their freedom of movement from team to team and was a cornerstone of the system of player sales and trades. Caylor had on occasion supported the interests of players against owners, but he was a firm proponent of the reserve clause and as editor of the *The Sporting Times* gladly pitched in to support the league against the Brotherhood-sponsored Players League. While players of his day were not nearly as well paid as their modern counterparts, it was nevertheless easy for Caylor to lampoon the "wage slaves" parading at meetings of the new league in their diamond rings and expensive coats. After one year of conflict the Players League died, and Caylor, having been unable to revive the *The Sporting Times,* saw Spalding fold the paper.

Upon his return to New York, Caylor had also become a baseball writer for *Harper's Weekly,* writing preview articles for the coming baseball season and longer essays, such as a 3 May 1890 piece on "Baseball's Contribution to the Economy," in which he noted "the tremendous strides professional base-ball has taken during the last fifteen years, until it has become an established business all over the United States." Along with the National League and American Association clubs Caylor even considered "the eight Brotherhood clubs, embracing about one hundred and twenty players, whose salaries will aggregate

$250,000, swelling the grand total to 1620 players and $1,750,000 in salaries."

In 1890 Caylor tried his hand at something different, writing a novel called *A Fated Promise,* published by G. W. Dillingham. A lurid romantic mystery set in the aftermath of the Civil War, it was republished in 1896 under the title *The Rockwell Case.*

After five years of wandering, Caylor at last regained stability in 1892 when he became the baseball editor of the *New York Herald.* Although he was no longer a member of the inner circle of baseball's power brokers, the *Herald* position was an enviable one for a sports journalist. His most famous line for the paper was "The Giants without [Amos] Rusie would be like *Hamlet* without the Melancholy Dane." Caylor served as official scorer for the New York Giants as well, and he continued to write for the sporting weeklies.

Among Caylor's many admirers was Henry Chadwick, and contemporary writers have also recognized his importance. Noted Voigt: "Caylor wrote articles that made lively reading for those who were not the object of his attention. Always an independent thinker, he tried in his own way to elevate the image of major-league baseball in general, and baseball writing in particular." Not much of a forward thinker, he remained skeptical, even condescending, about some innovations–for example, he wrote, "every base ball player and manager knows that no artificial light, however powerful, can ever be used for professional base ball playing."

In 1897 his always fragile constitution began to give way to tuberculosis, and he left his wife and daughter in New York to seek treatment in a clinic at Winoa, Minnesota. He died in Winoa on 19 October. *Reach's Official Base Ball Guide,* remembering its old editor on the occasion of his death, remarked how Caylor had visited the ball grounds one last time before his fated trip out west: "though scarcely able to reach his old seat . . . his courage never faltered."

References:

Lee Allen, *The Cincinnati Reds* (New York: Putnam, 1948);

Donald Walter Curl, "The Cincinnati *Commercial,*" *Bulletin of the Cincinnati Historical Society,* 24 (July 1966): 221–235;

Curl, *Murat Halstead and the Cincinnati Commercial* (Boca Raton: University Presses of Florida, 1980);

Frederick G. Lieb, *Connie Mack: Grand Old Man of Baseball* (New York: Putnam, 1945);

Preston D. Orem, *Baseball (1845–1881) from the Newspaper Accounts* (Altadena, Cal.: Privately published, 1961);

Frank V. Phelps, "Oliver Perry Caylor," in *Baseball's First Stars: The Second Volume of Biographies of the Greatest Nineteenth Century Players, Managers, Umpires, Executives, and Writers,* edited by Frederick Ivor-Campbell (Cleveland: Society for American Baseball Research, 1996);

Harold Seymour, *Baseball: The Early Years* (New York: Oxford University Press, 1960);

Dean A. Sullivan, ed., *Early Innings: A Documentary History of Baseball, 1825–1908* (Lincoln: University of Nebraska Press, 1995);

David Quentin Voigt, *American Baseball: From the Gentleman's Sport to the Commissioner's System,* 3 volumes (University Park: Pennsylvania State University Press, 1983).

Henry Chadwick

(5 October 1824 - 20 April 1908)

Jerry J. Wright
Penn State University

MAJOR POSITIONS HELD: Senior cricket and baseball writer and editor, *Brooklyn Eagle* (1856–1894); *New York Clipper* (1857–1888); editor, *Beadle's Dime Base-ball Player* (1860–1881); editor, *The Base Ball Player's Book of References* (1866–1881); editor, *Base Ball Players' Chronicles* (1867–1869); editor, *DeWitt's Base Ball Guide* (1869–1880); editor, *Spalding's Base Ball Guide* (1881–1908); editor, *The Metropolitan: A Journal of the Polo Grounds* (1882–1884).

Henry Chadwick (National Baseball Library and Archive)

BOOKS: *Base Ball Rules* (New York: Beadle, 1858);

Beadle's Dime Book of Cricket: A Desirable Cricketer's Companion, Containing Complete Instructions (New York: Beadle, 1860);

Beadle's Dime Book of Cricket and Base-Ball (New York: Beadle, 1867);

The Game of Base Ball. How to Learn It, How to Play It, and How to Teach It (New York: Munro, 1868);

Chadwick's American Cricket Manual (New York: DeWitt, 1873);

Our Boy's Baseball Rules, 2 volumes (New York: Munro, 1877–1878);

The Art of Batting and Base Running (New York: A. G. Spalding, 1878; revised, 1886);

Chadwick's Baseball Manual (London: Routledge, 1883);

Sports and Pastimes of American Boys (London: Routledge, 1884);

The Art of Baseball Batting (New York: A. G. Spalding, 1885);

The Art of Fielding, with a Chapter on Base Running (New York: A. G. Spalding, 1885);

Technical Terms of Baseball (New York: A. G. Spalding, 1887);

The American Game of Baseball (Philadelphia: Holland, 1889);

How to Play Base Ball (New York: A. G. Spalding, 1889).

OTHER: *Beadle's Dime Base-Ball Player,* edited by Chadwick (New York: Beadle, 1860–1881);

DeWitt's Base Ball Guide, edited by Chadwick (New York: J. C. Haney, 1866–1881);

Base Ball Players' Chronicles [weekly], edited by Chadwick (1867–1869);

DeWitt's Base Ball Umpire's Guide, edited by Chadwick (New York: R. M. DeWitt, 1875);

Spalding's Base Ball Guide, edited by Chadwick (New York: A. G. Spalding, 1881–1908);

The Base Ball Player's Book of References (New York: J. C. Haney, 1866–1881);

The Metropolitan: A Journal of the Polo Grounds, edited by Chadwick (1882–1884);

Spalding's Minor League Guide, edited by Chadwick (New York: A. G. Spalding, 1889).

SELECTED PERIODICAL PUBLICATIONS–UNCOLLECTED: "New Rules of Baseball, 1887," *Lippincott's Monthly Magazine,* 39 (1887): 830–833;

"Baseball," *Outing,* 12 (August 1888): 117–120;

"Reporting Baseball," *Writer,* 11 (Winter 1898): 82–84;

"Commentary," *Sporting Goods Dealer,* 1 (October 1899): 8;

"Old Time Baseball," by Chadwick and Clarence Deming, *Outing,* 38 (July 1901): 420–422;

"The Art of Playing Baseball," *Baseball Magazine,* 1 (July 1908): 25–29;

"The Albert G. Spalding I Knew," *Baseball Magazine,* 2 (March 1909): 13–15.

Henry Chadwick once wrote, "Thanks to Base Ball–the entering wedge of the great reformation which has since taken place–we have been transformed into quite another people, and, as we never do things by halves, but generally rush into furors and extremes, the chances are that from being too neglectful of out-of-door sports we shall become too fond of them." Chadwick had a lifelong love affair with the sports of his time, from cricket, to sailing, to billiards, to chess, and though his fondness abounded in them, he took none for granted. While he wrote about such recreational diversions, he developed a particular interest and enthusiasm for baseball. A prolific writer and editor, he was the first to chronicle the game and its various appurtenances in more than one hundred newspapers, magazines, pamphlets, guides, and books during a journalism career that spanned more than a half century. His descriptive, insightful game accounts and careful statistical compilations created a public awareness of the fledgling sport and later served as the historical record of an emerging national pastime. He was universally accepted as the greatest authority on baseball in the country, and from behind the scenes he posed a powerful, influential force for shaping the game. To facilitate his writing and statistical accounts of contests he developed the first truly informative box score. He was the architect for many of the rules of the game and became their arbiter as a member and chair of the rules committee for the National Association of Base Ball Players and later the National League. While his passion and devotion for the game accorded him the moniker "Father of Baseball" early in his career, his writing, vision, innovation, and continuous reformation of the game is largely responsible for its growth and popularity and for the way Americans have come to know, understand, and appreciate baseball. In his own time he was the philosopher of the game, as well as its historian and one of its early entrepreneurs, helping to create a baseball industry and a specialist role for sports journalism.

Henry Chadwick was born in St. Thomas Exeter, Devon, England, on 5 October 1824, to James and Henrietta Chadwick. He attended the Devonshire Academy, where he studied a traditional grammar-school curriculum and explored an aptitude for music. At school he played respectable games of rounders and cricket, but generally his early recreational activity ran toward less-strenuous pursuits such as fishing, billiards, chess, and music. His musical interest was encouraged by both parents, in particular his mother, from whom he learned to play the piano at an early age. For a time his parents felt young Chad would pursue a career as a musician, but in the end he learned and successfully applied his father's craft of journalism.

As editor of the Exeter *Western Times,* James Chadwick was well known in England as a voice of radical reform for many causes. Social causes and reformation ran in the family, as Henry's half brother, Edwin Chadwick, was one of the most respected public-health reformers in England. James Chadwick was a strong-willed individual with high standards for discipline, ethical character, and moral values, which were reflected in his work and the rearing of his sons. As a journalist he wielded considerable influence and did not hesitate to voice strong opinions on issues ranging from national politics to social reform. The popularity and acceptance of his sometimes radical views gradually became less prevalent, however, leading to career frustration and the family's immigration to America.

The Chadwicks arrived in the United States on 21 September 1837, two weeks before Henry's thirteenth birthday. They settled in Brooklyn, New York, where James Chadwick worked initially as a freelance journalist and Henry continued his education in the public-school system, along with further cultivating his musical interests. Chadwick developed his interest in journalism at about age seventeen, when he began work as a newspaper stringer turning in local cricket match scores to *The New York Times.* In 1844, at age twenty, he became a regular contributor to the *Long Island Star* in Brooklyn, reporting on cricket, sailing, horse racing, and other popular sports of the period. One of his first contributions was a feature story about a race among members of the newly formed New York Yacht Club in July 1844. His direct and authoritarian style, with careful attention to the most minute detail of events, quickly brought Chadwick and the sports he covered to the attention of a larger audience. The *Star* increased its circulation, and other

Chadwick (middle row, far right) with the teammates in his cricket and baseball club, New York City, 1863 (The Spalding Collection, Miriam and Ira D. Wallach Division of Art, Prints and Photography, New York Public Library)

newspapers sought his contributions. During the next ten years Chadwick's essays and accounts of sporting practices, as well as the theater, appeared in nearly every New York–area newspaper.

Despite early demands of New York papers for Chadwick's sporting accounts, the games and recreational pursuits of the city did not consume all of his waking hours. His mother's early artistic influence stirred a lifelong interest in music and the theater. He wrote music, including a baseball song, played and taught piano, and was a respected theater critic. Chadwick's musical interest led to his introduction to Jane Botts, a music student from Virginia, whom he married on 19 August 1847. Throughout his dedicated journalism career Chadwick was also devoted to his family and delighted in his wife, two daughters, grandchildren, and great-grandchildren.

From his earliest days with the *Long Island Star* Chadwick pursued a simple career ambition: to make a living promoting sports, especially baseball, as a wholesome form of recreation for the urban masses. The changes to the urban environment brought about by the industrial advances of the early nineteenth century had, in his view, created greater potential for both recreation and leisure pursuits but also moral decay. He wrote with great concern about the newly formed cricket and yacht clubs. Writing about the typical cricket club in *The New York Times* (7 November 1853), he charged that "the exclusiveness of its members, drawn wholly from a distinctive class, and foreign at that, and the slightest inducement they held for the propagation of the game among native-born citizens particularly, has alienated all respect and esteem from them on the part of the general public to which cricket is a novelty." He later reputed the clubs' competitions.

With this article and other critical exposés, Chadwick was carrying on in the reform-minded tradition of his father and half brother. Sport in general, and baseball in particular, was the theater through which Chadwick promulgated his father's teachings of moral values, advocacy, and social reform. Though his vision for sport in America developed early in his career as a journalist, he only discovered his life's work in 1856, when returning from a cricket match on Fox Hill. In his instructional book *The Game of Base Ball. How to Learn It, How to Play It, and How to Teach It* (1868), Chadwick wrote:

> I chanced to go through the Elysian Fields during the progress of a contest between the noted Eagle and Gotham Clubs. The game was being sharply played on both sides, and I watched it with deeper interest than any previous ball match between clubs I had seen. It was not long before I was struck with the idea that base ball was just the game for a national sport for Americans, and, reflecting on the subject, it occurred to me, on my return home, that from this game of ball a powerful lever might be made by which our people could be lifted into a position of more devotion to physical exercise and healthful out-door recreation than they had hitherto, as a people, been noted for.

Chadwick thus decided that baseball could do for America what cricket had done for England. Baseball, like cricket, had the necessary elements: structure of rules, disciplined styles of play with strategy and training, club organization, and morality through fair play, health, and manliness. With an authoritative pen Chadwick embarked on a mission to promote the game and, through it, reform the ills of society.

In 1856 William Cauldwell of the *New York Sunday Mercury* was the only reporter covering baseball regularly in the city. Upon his return to New York, however, the enthusiastic Chadwick asked for and received permission from the managing editor of *The New York Times* to cover the game of baseball. Though he continued to cover other sports for many papers, from this point baseball consumed his journalistic life. He began his proselytizing for the game immediately. When there were no games to cover he wrote nonpaying baseball pieces for the *Times* and other area papers. He became the chief protagonist and expert of the game, selling baseball to what was becoming, in part by his own contrivance, a sports-crazed public. In a 13 December 1856 column for the *New York Clipper,* Chadwick proclaimed that "the game of base ball is generally considered the National Game amongst Americans."

In 1857, after attending the first baseball convention called by the Knickerbockers, the formation of the National Association of Base Ball Players, and the Massachusetts Association of Base Ball Players, Chadwick sold his first feature article to *The New York Times.* It was an exposé comparing these organizations, specifically rule variations and styles of play. It marked the beginning of his passion for scientific structure of the game.

Chadwick joined the staff of the *New York Clipper* in 1858, becoming the first baseball editor of a newspaper. In this capacity he covered the first baseball game to attract wide attention in the New York area when all-star players from New York and Brooklyn crossed bats at the Fashion Race Course on Long Island. Chadwick wrote four variations of his account of the game, which appeared between 21 July and 24 July 1858 in the *Times,* the *Long Island Star,* and the *Brooklyn Eagle,* while retaining the most detailed account for the *Clipper.* The multiple accounts of this game truly introduced baseball and Henry Chadwick to the newspaper-reading public.

Chadwick's fascination with the rules of the game led him to publish *Base Ball Rules,* the first book of its kind, in 1858. Because of this book he was immediately recognized as the authority on the subject and was selected chairman of the rules committee for the National Association of Base Ball Players. From this position he interpreted rules and settled disputes, while exercising tremendous power and influence to direct the structure of the game to fit his moralistic crusade.

By the late 1850s and early 1860s the concern for physical health and manly sport that Chadwick had exhorted for nearly a decade was suddenly in vogue. The sporting press, especially, published many articles extolling the benefits of fresh air, exercise, and all kinds of outdoor sports. To Chadwick's delight many of the articles defended, praised, and advertised baseball as a healthful recreation. Feeling vindicated, he methodically wrote articles–especially in the annual *Beadle's Dime Base-Ball Player,* for which he served as editor beginning in 1860–arguing "that base ball is an invigorating exercise and manly pastime."

During the strife-torn years of the American Civil War, the national pastime passed through a dormant period in its development. Chadwick continued his promotional influence on the game, however. On 21 October 1861, exactly three months following the Battle of Bull Run, he arranged the "Silver Ball Match" between teams picked from nine in Brooklyn and New York, with sponsorship from his employer, the *New York Clipper.* Later, as a war correspondent, he took the opportunity to write not only of the conflict but also of baseball in uniform and how entire ball teams frequently joined military service together. In an article for *The New York Times* (10 June 1863) he quoted Nicholas E. Young, then secretary and later president of the National League: "In my regiment we had a full cricket team and a Base Ball team, all of whom had played together at home."

As Chadwick was often opinionated in his writings on baseball and morality, he was objective in issues related to the war. As a northerner and a journalist with a wife who was southern by birth, he found it to be not in his best interest to take sides. His wife did accompany him on his occasional trips to Washington, where she could meet with family members and both she and her husband could attend the theater. On one such occasion, 19 November 1864, the couple saw a performance of *Hamlet* at the new Grover Theatre that was also attended by President Abraham Lincoln along with several Union generals and their wives. Chadwick wrote of the experience, and although outside his element as a sports journalist he was able to convey insight as to the character of the president and the situation at hand:

> . . . Mr. Lincoln was evidently an interested and attentive spectator of the performance throughout, as he sat leaning his arms on the edge of the box with his chin on his hand in true western style. I must confess I was not taken by the appearance of his profile while viewing him in this position. Though he gave an attentive ear to the play, it was not till the gravedigger's scene in the fourth act was presented that his particular fancy seemed to have been struck by the occurrence of the drama. . . . From the manner in which Mr. Lincoln enjoyed the whole scene, it was manifest to me he had seen this witty publication; certainly there were others in the house who had. It is well that the occupant of the White House possesses this mental safety valve of humor, or otherwise the immense weight of cares incident to his position must long since caused him to succumb to the great pressure. . . .

After the war ended Chadwick returned to full-time sportswriting and a position as baseball writer for the *New York Herald*. This same period gave rise to what is perhaps Chadwick's most significant contribution to baseball, and particularly to baseball journalism. In 1867, to keep pace with his writing demands for game coverage and detailed scoring, he expanded his 1861 development of the scorecard to include a standardized box score. His scoring system enabled documentation of every type of play with a coding of letters: *A* was for an out at first base, for example, and *B* for an out at second base. He used *F* for fly-ball out, *S* for sacrifice, and *L* for foul out, because *F* was already used and *L* was the other prominent phonetic element in the term. Similarly, he chose *K* for a strikeout because "It was the prominent letter of the word strike, as far as remembering the word is concerned." Before Chadwick's standardized invention box scores listed only the participants, their outs made, and runs scored. Like the scorecard, at first his new system was difficult to use; but he refined his method, effectively utilizing codes for plays from his scorecard, and eventually produced the first genuinely informative box score, along with many of the most basic player statistics, such as the earned-run average and the batting average.

Chadwick had always felt that for the game to be an effective reformer, it should be played with technical prowess and expertise. His early tinkering with rules and innovations as directed toward perfecting the game and developing its strategic, scientific features. In *How to Play Base Ball* (1889), perhaps his most influential work promulgating the scientific approach, Chadwick drew upon a reference in the *New York Clipper* (16 March 1876) by his publisher, A. G. Spalding, to baseball as a "bloodless battle." The book abounds with military metaphors stressing the importance of a well-placed attack, with tactics coordinated by the captain, or "commander on the field," who is responsible for the overall strategy. The pitcher and catcher are the battery of the regiment (team). The pitcher, the artillerist of the squad, lays siege to the "home base" of the batting team and "is the main reliance of the attacking force of the field corps," also known as infielders, who "are the immediate supporting force of the 'battery'" and "the defenders of the citadel of the field."

An example of the more skillful, scientific approach was his long-standing argument for the "fly game" over the "bound game." Prior to and during the Civil War a batted ball caught by a fielder in the air (on the fly) or after one bounce disqualified the batter as out. Some advocates of the game argued that only a ball caught on the fly should count as out, and there was much editorializing in the newspapers on both sides of the issue. Chadwick equated the two techniques with manliness: the fly game was for the adult player, and the bound game "a feat a boy ten years of age would scarcely be proud of." In the 1860 *Beadle's Dime Base-Ball Player* he urged fielders to "try their utmost to take it on the fly, and not wait until it is almost touching the ground, and then, Boy-like, try to take it on the bound. Nothing disappoints the spectator, or dissatisfies the batsman so much, as to see a fine hit to the long field caught on the bound in this simple, childish manner." Through Chadwick's lobbying efforts the rules committee of the National Association of Base Ball Players adopted the fly-ball game on 14 December 1864. This victory was the first in a series of major rules battles that Chadwick won.

As the popularity of baseball increased, Chadwick's advocacy and cultivation of the game as the moral savior of mankind confronted a new problem: professionalism in the guise of amateurism. For some years he had recognized the emergence of professional players on amateur teams coupled with increasing instances during the 1860s of professional teams masquerading as amateurs. He felt that such deception was unethical, and in support for perfection of the scientific features of the game he editorialized vigorously for open professionalism as a cure for the hypocrisy that discolored the supposedly amateur game. Harry Wright took the lead in 1869, when he announced publicly that his Cincinnati Red Stockings club were highly

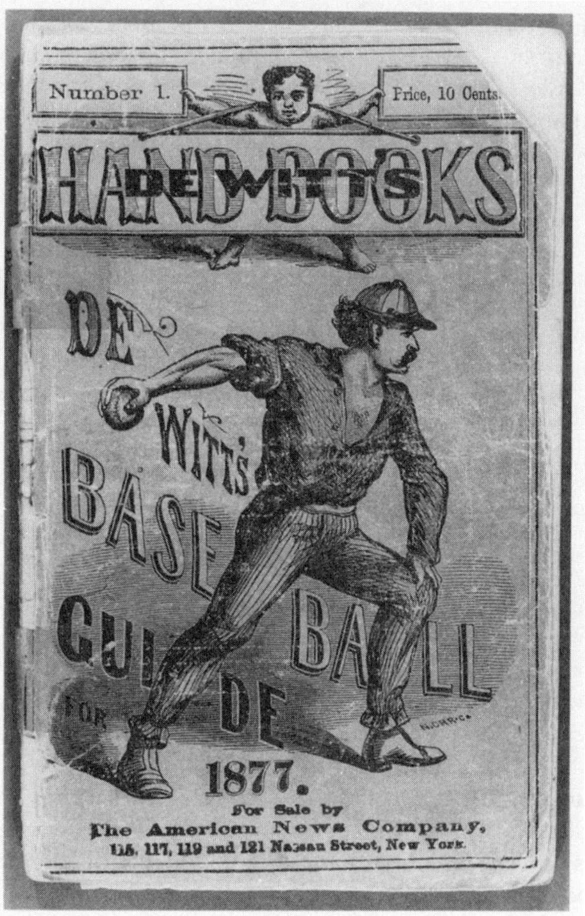

Front covers for annual baseball guides edited by Chadwick. He edited the Beadle's *survey from 1860 to 1881 and* DeWitt's *from 1869–1880 (National Baseball Library and Archive).*

paid professionals. As Chadwick reported in the *New York Clipper* (25 March 1871), his efforts bore full fruit on St. Patrick's Day when representatives of ten clubs met in "a smoky gaslit hallroom adjoining the café" at Callier's Rooms on the corner of Broadway and Thirteenth Street in New York City and formed the National Association of Professional Base Ball Players.

Despite some early victories, not all of Chadwick's lobbying efforts and rule proposals became law. In 1874, at the fourth meeting of the National Association of Professional Base Ball Players in Boston, the group adopted his new rule proposals for the establishment of the batter's box and the prohibition against players betting on their own team. Chadwick's proposition to increase the number of players to ten per side and the length of games to ten innings was soundly defeated. Yet, even in defeat Chadwick was never discouraged. He continually pressed for rule changes to improve the scientific balance between offense and defense, alterations in the scoring system, and policies to eliminate the influence of gambling. Ultimately, Chadwick won far more of these battles than he lost, and baseball, the media, and his readership continued to award him great respect for his insight on rule formulation, codes for fair play, and arbitration.

By the late 1860s the fly game and other changes influenced by Chadwick brought about a more technical, scientific approach that elevated the level of play and thus ushered in a new era of professionalism. While Chadwick initially voiced his approval, the game was soon plagued with the immoral elements for which Chadwick's game was intended to rid society: unsportsmanlike play, greed, gambling, intoxication, and lazy spectatorship. To Chadwick these five sins were the greatest threat to baseball. He was optimistic, however, that even at a professional level the game could remain virtuous.

In an effort to ensure the virtuousness of baseball, Chadwick increased his prolific assault on each of these vice-laden elements. From 1866 to 1881 he served as editor of the annual *The Base Ball Player's Book of References,* published by J. C. Haney, and from 1867 to 1869 he edited the first baseball weekly, *Base Ball Players' Chronicles.* Additionally, he began editing *DeWitt's Base Ball Guide,* all while maintaining his tireless campaign of newspaper columns and feature articles. On the field cheating by players became more widespread, but Chadwick vehemently deplored greed, gambling, and intoxication as the most serious threats to the sport.

For Chadwick both the players and the owners were guilty of greed. The loss of revenue by the league had prompted a steady increase in admission price to fifty cents, of which players demanded their share. The price increase served to drive attendance down further, however, resulting in fewer profits for owners and the league. In his *New York Clipper* column for 16 January 1876, Chadwick solemnly urged an earnings reduction for both parties: "Say what you will, gentlemen of the League, you must come down . . . to the twenty-five cent admission fee, and you must proportionately lower your salaries. . . . catchers and pitchers deserve more than players at other positions but $1000 is good pay even for them, and a hundred dollars a month (for six months) is sufficient for the other positions."

While Chadwick's abetment for scientific method and structure successfully elevated baseball to a professional level in terms of technical skill, he was greatly disturbed by escalating problems regarding unsportsmanlike behavior and player discipline and morality. He turned his writing to players' behavior on and off the field, and he encouraged the drafting of club constitutions to provide standards for player conduct. He wrote vehemently on the five sins and his perception of a deteriorating game and extolled players' hard work and clean living. In the 10 August 1887 edition of his "Chadwick's Chat" column which appeared occasionally in *Sporting Life,* he wrote: "If this season teaches anything, not to mention that of past seasons, it is the utter folly of expecting good play and thorough team work out of a party of players, the majority of whom take no care of themselves in keeping their bodies in a healthy condition for the exacting work of the diamond field. To suppose that a man can play ball properly who guzzles beer daily, or indulges in spiritous liquors, or who sets up nightly gambling or does worse by still more enervating habits at brothels is nonsense." Chadwick was himself a specimen of personal discipline. A man of average physique and structure, he began his daily regimen at 5:00 A.M. with a cold plunge, followed by a light breakfast and work. In the evening he took a brisk walk before bed, even in winter, and only rarely a drink of spirits. He credited his longevity to the frequent taking of Turkish baths.

Philosophically, Chadwick no doubt fully expected ballplayers and even fans to follow his own strict regime for life. Even if they lacked such discipline, however, he did expect them to exercise control of their actions during contests. He wrote in the 1871 *Beadle's Dime Base-Ball Player* that "gambling on baseball, either by players or fans, takes considerable moral self-control for a man in a spirited state, who has bet heavily on a game to keep from interfearing [*sic*] in one way or another with the proceedings." He continued to exhort the evils of gambling, particularly the growing dangers of fraudulent play by "hippodroming," the deliberate throwing of games in the interest of professional gamblers. In 1876 his crusade resulted in the abolition of selling betting pools on stadium grounds. He reluctantly gave up the fight to prevent Sunday games, however, fully realizing the potential for advancing the sport through play on work holidays.

By the mid 1870s, in his own mind, Chadwick's advocacy for baseball as the moralistic reformer of culture was continually being challenged on all fronts. At the professional level the actions of players, owners, umpires, and fans increasingly mirrored the disreputable elements found in urban society. Chadwick's mechanism for reform was itself in need of reforming. The first such attempt, the formation of the National League in 1876, left Chadwick critical of the founders for acting in secrecy and for failing to consult him in their plans. In his *New York Clipper* column for 12 February 1876 he praised their efforts but criticized the new code of rules and governing structure. His strong belief in the game soon calmed his anger, however, and he became a strong supporter of the new league.

The same could not be said of the formation of the Players' League in 1890. Chadwick had always been critical of player-revolving (which allowed players a kind of free agency while still under contract), viewing it as a lack of trust and loyalty to the club and parent organization. When John Ward formed the Brotherhood of Professional Base Ball Players in 1881 and the Players' League, rival to the National League, in 1890, Chadwick labeled him "a greedy, self-seeking, and power-mad revolutionist, a liar, conniver, a contract breaker, and all-round corrupter of youth" in *Sporting Life* (4 October 1890). In *The New York Times* (17 July

Cover for the 1883 British edition of Chadwick's rules of American baseball (Mark Rucker Collection)

1890) he assessed the situation with the clear and parental vision that had made him the dean of baseball journalists: "The baseball war . . . is not a war of labor or capital as the Brotherhood leaders and their partisan organs would have the baseball world believe. Neither is it a war for the emancipation of so-called 'baseball slaves.' On the contrary it is simply a big strike on the part of high salaried star players for the purpose of ultimately becoming baseball capitalists instead of employees at $5,000 a season salaries, aided by a syndicate of Wall Street operators who thought they saw a big bonanza in the hands of the National League magnates." Chadwick's journalism had a powerful influence. With the loss of public patronage and continued drain of expenses, the brotherhood was unable to survive financially. Consequently, with the end of the 1890 season, the Players' League collapsed and disbanded, and its players scrambled to rejoin the still-solvent National League and American Association, where Chadwick felt they belonged.

The initial reformation of baseball represented by the National League included elements of freedom and physicality that frustrated Chadwick's vision. For example, he regretted the rise of the slugging game that became prominent during the 1890s and greatly overshadowed the finer skills of fielding, hitting, and base running. He wrote in *Harper's Weekly* (8 June 1907) that "the true estimate of good pitching is based on the chances offered the fielders for outs" and that "it is to excellence in infielding and strategically placed hits that we are to look for the beauty of base ball." He viewed the new approach as trouble in the ever-increasing neglect of the finer points of batting. In *The New York Times* (14 September 1905) he asserted that "too much attention is given to the method of batting known as 'slugging for homers,' a habit that marks what is called 'record batting,' which takes the place of what is called 'teamwork at the bat.'" At this late period in his career Chadwick never had time to correct this flaw in the scientific regimen of baseball.

As much as Chadwick delighted in perfecting the game, he championed the cause that British standards of sportsmanship and fair play should dominate organized baseball. The realities of competition, however, often threatened this vision, and the sport was constantly sullied in his eyes by inebriation, rowdiness, and umpire abuse by players, managers, fans, and even media. In a letter to the editor of *Sporting Life* (27 April 1887), Chadwick wrote: "hissing by fans makes no sense. What good does it do? Not a particle in any respect. On the contrary, it acts against good umpiring, and is encouraging to that nuisance of our ball field–kicking." Chadwick would not tolerate kicking and rowdiness as tactics for winning. Although his authority with respect to the structure of the game was generally accepted, Americans were much less receptive of his conception of sportsmanship and fair play. His colleagues, similarly, were largely undaunted by his furious criticism of "cowardly" writers guilty of abusing umpires and players in print.

In an interview for the 8 June 1907 issue of *Harpers' Weekly* Chadwick identified kicking and rowdiness as the most recent abuses that threatened the integrity of professional baseball. He proclaimed that such "rowdy blackguardism" had grown due to the "laxity in discipline on the part of club-team managers and the aid and countenance given the managers and their players by the majority of the magnates." Although he concluded the interview with mixed feelings about the future of sportsmanship and fair play in the professional game, Chadwick's entire journalism career was an ardent crusade toward this end.

A man of modest means, Chadwick drew personal satisfaction from the social contribution he felt he had made. While his work afforded him extensive opportunities for travel, he resided his entire American life in Brooklyn. In 1887, after fifty years in the city, he

The plaque to Chadwick at the National Baseball Hall of Fame, Cooperstown, New York, where he was one of the initial inductees in 1939

delighted in his membership in the Society of Old Brooklynites. In 1894 the National League awarded him an honorary membership and, two years later, a lifetime annual pension of $600 for his contributions to baseball and service to the league. He was honored at a White House reception by President Theodore Roosevelt in 1903, and in 1904 received the only medal awarded to a journalist by the Louisiana Purchase Exposition "World's Fair" in St. Louis.

In 1905, at age eighty-one, Chadwick was still a vibrant journalist ready to take on what was probably his last reform battle–a battle that ultimately, depending on one's view, he would win–establishing baseball as an American institution. The rise of sports journalism was linked to the rapid growth of the sporting goods industry, particularly during the latter part of the nineteenth century. Chadwick wrote in the first issue of the *Sporting Goods Dealer* (October 1899) that "our Yankee manufacturers now control the supply of sport goods the world over." His many columns promoting sport and baseball had effectively conveyed the need for expertise and regimen that could only be attained with proper sports equipment. Thus, because of Chadwick, sports journalism and the sporting-goods industry cast a huge influence on sporting culture. This particular aspect of the growth of sports helps to explain the working relationship between Chadwick, the journalist, and Albert G. Spalding, the baseball player turned sporting-goods manufacturer.

During his playing career Spalding was the industrious, sober professional that Chadwick worked so diligently to promote. He also violated many of Chadwick's cardinal principles, however, twice revolving to other teams and manipulating rules and policies, particularly as the player-manager and eventual owner of the Chicago White Stockings. Regardless, from 1881 to 1908 Chadwick was the editor and principal writer of *Spalding's Base Ball Guide.* The guide was an annual publication that included the National League rules, records, history, and playing instructions as well as advertisements for Spalding products and, most importantly for Chadwick, his editorializing on all facets of baseball and other sports. While ostensibly devoted to the good of the game, the guide was a valuable promotional tool for Spalding and for Chadwick was another venue to promote baseball in his own image.

The Chadwick-Spalding connection worked well despite some philosophical differences and disagreement about the origin of baseball. Spalding maintained that baseball was created wholly and more or less spontaneously in the United States, while Chadwick contended that the game had developed in evolutionary fashion. In November 1905, Spalding, knowing well that Chadwick had virtually formulated the history of the game, approached him about writing an account of the origins of baseball. Chadwick was not responsive to the task, expounding his theory of the development of the game in a 28 November 1905 letter to Spalding: "you cannot go back on the fact that Base Ball derived its origin from the old English game of Rounders because the basic principle of both games is the field, use of a bat, and a ball and bases."

Chadwick had indirectly thrown down another gauntlet, and Spalding was quick to pick it up. To support his argument for the American origin of the game, he assembled a prestigious commission headed by former league president Abraham G. Mills to investigate and uncover the truth. Chadwick, on the other hand, had referred to baseball as the "national game" many times in his writings and in fact probably coined the phrase. Despite his conviction that baseball evolved from British rounders, Chadwick also felt equally strongly that the United States needed a game to consecrate its national sporting identity.

On 30 December 1907 Spalding announced the finding of the Mills Commission that baseball was invented by Abner Doubleday in 1839 in Cooperstown, New York, thus establishing the enduring myth of the origin of the game. In response Chadwick sent a revealing note to Mills: "your decision in the case of Chadwick vs. Spalding . . . is a masterly piece of special pleading which lets my dear old friend Albert escape a bad defeat. . . . The whole matter was a joke between Albert and myself." Chadwick then had the dubious task of editing the report for the 1908 edition of Spalding's guide. After Chadwick's death his widow gave Spalding all the documentary material her husband had collected and produced on the origins of the game. Spalding's history of baseball, *America's National Game* (1911), maintained the account of its exclusively native origins.

When Chadwick died of pneumonia and heart failure on 20 April 1908, flags flew at half-staff in all ballparks throughout the country in his honor. In 1939, the centennial year of baseball according to the Mills Commission, the National Baseball Hall of Fame opened in Cooperstown, the mythic site of the birth of the sport, and the Centennial Committee elected Chadwick as one of the initial inductees.

For the many sportswriters who followed him, Henry Chadwick set a precedent. He was part of the action, on and off the field, that he described to the public. He not only wrote the news, he made it. Equally important, his columns and books conveyed to readers that real sport was not a fantasy but a reality to be taken seriously, with rules and codes and structure to transcend their lives. Further, he felt that the public should consume performed sporting contests that were developed, packaged, and delivered by a diverse industry of sport providers. As a sports journalist Chadwick was a major innovator and developer in the evolution of that industry.

References:

Melvin L. Adelman, *A Sporting Time: New York City and the Rise of Modern Athletics, 1820–70* (Urbana: University of Illinois Press, 1986), pp. 103, 106, 107, 111, 117, 118, 122, 131, 136–137, 137–138, 148, 151, 161–162, 163, 154–165, 166–167, 170–171, 173, 174–175, 258–259, 277–278, 282;

L. J. DeBekker, "The Father of the Game," *Harper's Weekly,* 51 (8 June 1907): 838–840;

Donald Dewey and Nicholas Acocella, *The Biographical History of Baseball* (New York: Carroll & Graf, 1995), pp. 70–71;

Warren Goldstein, *Playing for Keeps: A History of Early Baseball* (Ithaca, N.Y.: Cornell University Press, 1989), pp. 9, 11, 31, 34–37, 43–44, 49–50, 52, 54–56, 67–68, 71, 83, 87–89, 92, 105, 108–111, 144–145;

Frederick Ivor-Campbell, Robert L. Tiemann, and Mark Rucker, eds., *Baseball's First Stars* (Cleveland: Society for American Baseball Research, 1996), pp. 26–27;

John Allen Krout, *Annals of American Sport* (New York: United States Publishers Association, 1956), pp. 125, 130, 137;

Irving A. Leitnew, *Baseball: Diamond in the Rough* (New York: Criterion, 1972), pp. 27, 42, 55, 58–59, 77, 105, 176, 196, 214;

Peter Levine, *A. G. Spalding and the Rise of Baseball: The Promise of American Sport* (New York: Oxford University Press, 1985), pp. 8, 13, 16, 19, 23–24, 28, 53, 62, 99–100, 112–116, 133;

Jacob C. Morse, "In Memory of Henry Chadwick," *Baseball Magazine,* 1 (June 1908): 9–11;

Thomas S. Rice, "Henry Chadwick," *Sporting News* (21 May 1936), p. 11;

Robert Smith, *Baseball* (New York: Simon & Schuster, 1970), pp. 23–24, 26, 28, 29, 155, 225, 293, 392, 395–396, 399;

Joel Zoss and John Bowman, *Diamonds in the Rough: The Untold Story of Baseball* (Chicago: Contemporary Books, 1996), pp. 42–44, 49, 52, 63, 73, 77–78, 83, 121, 390.

Papers:

Henry Chadwick's papers, including scorebooks, scrapbooks, diaries, and letters, are included in the Henry Chadwick file at the National Baseball Hall of Fame Library, Cooperstown, New York; the Albert G. Spalding Collection at the New York Public Library; and the Abraham G. Mills Papers at the National Baseball Hall of Fame.

Bob Considine

(4 November 1906 – 25 September 1975)

Joe Marren

Business First of Buffalo

MAJOR POSITIONS HELD: Sportswriter, reporter, feature writer, *Washington Post* (1929–1933); sports editor, *Washington Herald* (1933–1937); syndicated sports columnist, reporter, feature writer, *New York American* (1937); sports columnist, *New York Daily Mirror* (1937–1942); sports and news reporter, International News Service (1942–1950); columnist and news reporter, King Features and Hearst Headline Service (1950–1975).

Bob Considine

BOOKS: *MacArthur the Magnificent* (New York: McKay, 1942);

The Babe Ruth Story, by Considine and Babe Ruth (New York: Dutton, 1948);

Innocents at Home (Garden City, N.Y.: Doubleday, 1950);

The Maryknoll Story (Garden City, N.Y.: Doubleday, 1950);

The Panama Canal (New York: Random House, 1951);

Man against Fire: Fire Insurance–Protection from Disaster (Garden City, N.Y.: Doubleday, 1955);

Dempsey: By the Man Himself, by Considine and Bill Slocum (New York: Simon & Schuster, 1960);

Ask Me Anything: Our Adventures with Khrushchev, by Considine, William Randolph Hearst Jr., and Frank Conniff (New York: McGraw-Hill, 1960); republished as *Khrushchev and the Russian Challenge* (New York: Avon, 1961);

The Men Who Robbed Brink's: The Inside Story of One of the Most Famous Holdups in the History of Crime, by Considine and Specs O'Keefe (New York: Random House, 1961);

It's the Irish (Garden City, N.Y.: Doubleday, 1961);

Ripley: The Modern Marco Polo, as Robert Considine (Garden City, N.Y.: Doubleday, 1961);

The Unreconstructed Amateur: A Pictorial Biography of Amos Alonzo Stagg (San Francisco: Amos Alonzo Stagg Foundation, 1962);

General Douglas MacArthur (New York: Fawcett, 1964);

It's All News to Me: A Reporter's Deposition (New York: Meredith Press, 1967);

The First Hundred Years: A Portrait of the NYAC, by Considine and Fred G. Jarvis (New York: Macmillan, 1969);

Toots (New York: Meredith Press, 1969);

The Remarkable Life of Dr. Armand Hammer (New York: Harper & Row, 1975);

They Rose Above It: True Stories about Men, Women, and Children Who Fought Back in the Face of Pain, Doubt, and Dismay (Garden City, N.Y.: Doubleday, 1977).

OTHER: Ted W. Lawson, *Thirty Seconds over Tokyo,* edited by Considine (New York: Random House, 1943);

Sammy Schulman, *Where's Sammy?* edited by Considine (New York: Random House, 1943);

Jonathan Wainwright, *General Wainwright's Story: The Account of Four Years of Humiliating Defeat, Surrender, and Captivity,* edited by Considine (Garden City, N.Y.: Doubleday, 1946);

Robert E. Stripling, *The Red Plot against America,* edited by Considine (Drexel Hill, Pa.: Bell, 1949);

True War Stories: A Crest Anthology, compiled by Considine (New York: Fawcett, 1961).

PRODUCED SCRIPTS: *Ladies' Day,* original play by Considine, Edward C. Lilley, and Bertrand Robinson, RKO, 1943;

The Beginning or the End, motion picture, original story by Considine, M-G-M, 1947;

Hoodlum Empire, motion picture, screenplay by Considine and Bruce Manning, Republic, 1952.

Bob Considine began his sportswriting career during the so-called Golden Age of sports, which lasted from shortly after World War I until about the time of the Great Depression. During the 1920s journalism was generally dedicated to the process of celebrity making, and sports pages around the country contributed such luminaries as Jack Dempsey ("The Manassa Mauler"), Red Grange ("The Galloping Ghost"), Babe Ruth ("The Sultan of Swat"), and "Big" Bill Tilden. The typical prose of sportswriters of the time bordered on mawkishness and sometimes endowed athletes with mythical abilities–what some scholars have termed as "fakelore." There were those sportswriters, such as Grantland Rice, Damon Runyon, and Ring Lardner, who usually rose above such sentimentality; yet, even they still built their essential sporting heroes in the magazines and New York City papers.

Considine became a sportswriter while working as a State Department clerk in Washington, D.C., in 1927. He was also making a name for himself on the local tennis scene. Although he won nearly fifty state and regional titles, the *Washington Herald* regularly misspelled his name. As he described in his autobiography, *It's All News to Me: A Reporter's Deposition* (1967), he eventually decided to take up the matter personally with the editors of the *Herald:* "I had begun to reach the third and sometimes even the fourth round of local tennis tournaments and was consequently injured one morning, while still suffused in the blush of a previous day's victory, to read in the *Herald* that the match had been won by Robert Constantine. I repaired to the desk of the paper's sports editor, William Henry Coyle, who silently accepted the correct spelling of a name he had seen only in the agate type beneath 'other results.'" As Considine recalled, Coyle told him: "If you want to see any tennis news in the paper, you'll have to write it yourself."

Considine spins similar yarns in his account of his forty-five-year professional life, during which he was chiefly known for ghostwriting and for churning out yards of newspaper copy. He was also famous for his zest for work: in addition to the demands of a reporter's profession, he wrote or cowrote more than twenty books, worked on three movies, wrote fiction and feature stories, took part in various radio and television news programs, and also wrote a syndicated column. He helped everyone from bank robbers to media stars, soldiers, and sports heroes tell their stories.

Robert Bernard Considine was born on 4 November 1906 in the Swampoodle section of Washington, D.C., near Union Station, a neighborhood then heavily populated by Irish immigrants and their families in St. Aloysius Parish. His father, James William Considine, was a tinsmith, and his mother, Sophie (Small) Considine, was a homemaker with five children. His father died when Considine was nine years old, and his oldest brother went to work to help support the family. Considine himself dropped out of Gonzaga High School at age seventeen, in 1923, to work as a messenger boy for the Census Bureau and later for the Bureau of Public Health. Then he became a typist in the Treasury Department and, in 1927, a clerk in the State Department.

While working at the State Department and taking night-school courses in creative writing and journalism at George Washington University, Considine won several Middle Atlantic singles titles in tennis. At about the same time, in 1929, he parlayed his semiregular freelance writing into a weekly column, "Speaking of Tennis," for the *Washington Post* at $5.00 per week. At the time the *Post* was fourth in circulation among five papers in the city, and life in the newsroom under publisher Edward B. McLean was austere. Shirley Povich was sports editor at the *Post* at the time; in a 1989 *Post* article reflecting on his tenure he wrote that he liked Considine's writing style, and in late summer 1930, Povich was able to stretch the entry-level salary for cub reporters from $20.00 per week to $35.00 in Considine's case.

Considine was initially reluctant but took the job on the advice of his future wife, Mildred (Millie) Anderson. She and Considine were married on 21 July 1931. They had four children–Michael, Barry, Dennis, and Deborah. Millie Considine was also a writer, the author of *Just a Minute, Mrs. Gulliver: Being an Account of the Travels and Travails of One Mrs. Bob Considine in the Wicked Cities of the World, Wherein the Wacky Doings of High and Low Are Hilariously Set Forth* (1967), about her own encounters with celebrities, and co-author with Ruth Pool of *Wills: A Dead Giveaway* (1974), a look at the wills of famous people.

In January 1933 Povich assigned Considine to cover the Washington Senators baseball team. The pieces Considine wrote from spring training that year caught the attention of Mike Flynn, managing editor of the *Washington Herald,* who hired him away from the *Post* at $110 a week. Flynn named Considine the sports editor later that year. His first act as editor was to assign himself the task of writing a daily column, as he recalled in his autobiography.

Considine's first "On the Line" column was about Ring Lardner, who died the day the column debuted, on 25 September 1933. "On the Line" followed Considine from one paper to another and grew to cover more than sports as he met and wrote about world leaders during and after World War II. By the time of his death in 1975, it had been distributed to 105 newspapers. The column was much more successful than Considine's tenure as an editor at the *Herald.* After a few months he was replaced and told to stick to writing. He continued to cover his baseball beat and wrote some editorials as well as a series on government clerks, "Uncle Sam's Children."

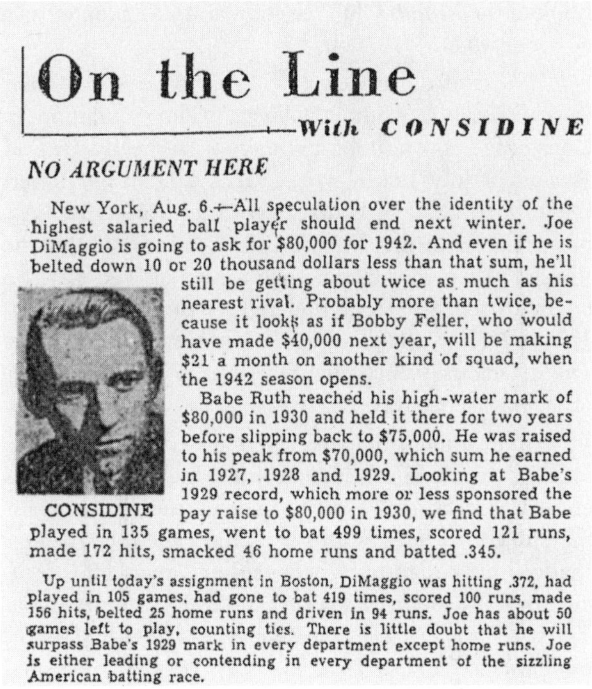

On the Line

—With CONSIDINE

NO ARGUMENT HERE

New York, Aug. 6.—All speculation over the identity of the highest salaried ball player should end next winter. Joe DiMaggio is going to ask for $80,000 for 1942. And even if he is belted down 10 or 20 thousand dollars less than that sum, he'll still be getting about twice as much as his nearest rival. Probably more than twice, because it looks as if Bobby Feller, who would have made $40,000 next year, will be making $21 a month on another kind of squad, when the 1942 season opens.

Babe Ruth reached his high-water mark of $80,000 in 1930 and held it there for two years before slipping back to $75,000. He was raised to his peak from $70,000, which sum he earned in 1927, 1928 and 1929. Looking at Babe's 1929 record, which more or less sponsored the pay raise to $80,000 in 1930, we find that Babe played in 135 games, went to bat 499 times, scored 121 runs, made 172 hits, smacked 46 home runs and batted .345.

CONSIDINE

Up until today's assignment in Boston, DiMaggio was hitting .372, had played in 105 games, had gone to bat 419 times, scored 100 runs, made 156 hits, belted 25 home runs and driven in 94 runs. Joe has about 50 games left to play, counting ties. There is little doubt that he will surpass Babe's 1929 mark in every department except home runs. Joe is either leading or contending in every department of the sizzling American batting race.

A 1946 Considine column in the New York Daily Mirror

The *Herald* was a part of the Hearst newspaper chain, and Considine moved to New York in January 1937 to take over Damon Runyon's sports column on another Hearst paper, the *New York American.* He was transferred to yet another Hearst newspaper, the *New York Daily Mirror,* in June 1937, after the *American* went bankrupt. (It later briefly emerged as the *Journal-American.*) At that time, the International News Service (INS), the Hearst wire service that later merged with United Press Association to form United Press International, assumed half of Considine's contract, since it was already syndicating his "On the Line" column. This change meant Considine was soon assigned other stories besides what took place on various ball fields.

Yet, Considine's best-known sportswriting pieces were also written during this time. Generally, sportswriting was in a transitional phase from the end of the Golden Age of the 1920s to a more-cautious realism as the world dealt with financial chaos and drifted closer to World War II in the 1930s. (Considine distinguished the two approaches in his autobiography as the "Gee Whiz" style of the 1920s and the "Aw Nuts" approach of the 1930s.) His most celebrated short piece, "Louis Knocks Out Schmeling," is a description for the *Daily Mirror* of Joe Louis's victory against German champion Max Schmeling on the night of 22 June 1938. The article demonstrates Considine's ability to combine the flourishes of the "Gee Whiz" school, the relatively restrained style of the 1930s, and his own social observations, and has been included in several sportswriting anthologies. Perhaps what makes the article most distinctive is its heroic characterization of Louis, an unusual portrayal of an African American at the time: "He was a big, lean copper spring, tightened and retightened through weeks of training until he was one pregnant package of coiled venom." The article also shows that Considine was conscious of the political implications of the fight, in which Schmeling had been touted as a representative of the superiority of Nazi Germany:

> But once he crawled down in the belly of the big stadium, Schmeling realized the implications of his defeat. He, who won the title on a partly phony foul, and beat Louis two years ago with the aid of a crushing punch after the bell had sounded ending a critical round, now said Louis had fouled him. That would read better in Germany, whence earlier in the day had come a cable from Hitler, calling on him to win.

By 1942 Considine was writing exclusively for the INS and traveling extensively as a war correspondent. He collaborated with a U.S. Army Air Force captain, Ted Lawson, who had lost a leg in thc 18 April 1942 bombing raid on Tokyo led by Lieutenant Colonel Jimmy Doolittle. Lawson's account, edited by Considine, appeared in serialized form in *Collier's* magazine in 1942 before it was published as a book, *Thirty Seconds over Tokyo,* by Random House in 1943. It became a

Book-of-the-Month Club selection and was adapted as a movie in 1944.

Most of the reviews for *Thirty Seconds over Tokyo* were favorable. Rodney Gilbert, calling attention to Considine's contribution to the book in the *Weekly Book Review* (11 July 1943), wrote: "It is 'edited' by Robert Considine. That, of course, may mean anything. . . . but whatever he did, Mr. Considine did so well that the story is just such a tale as such a man as Ted Lawson ought to tell." Vincent McHugh, writing in *The New Yorker* (17 July 1943), disagreed, however: "It isn't by any means as well written as some of the other personal-experience records."

Considine usually received an "edited by" or "as told to" credit for the books for which he served as ghostwriter. His role was to provide the structure for the subject to tell his story, taking care not to overshadow his collaborator. Considine's next ghostwriting effort, *General Wainwright's Story: The Account of Four Years of Humiliating Defeat, Surrender, and Captivity* (1946), was also related to World War II. Congressional Medal of Honor winner General Jonathan Wainwright was a Japanese prisoner of war from December 1942 to September 1945.

As Considine recalls in his autobiography, his experiences during World War II served to broaden his horizons considerably: "It was rewarding being a part of the world of sports. . . . But the War pulled back a vast curtain and gave me my first view of the world, its wonders and its peoples." He reflected that he sometimes missed sportswriting because "there is always something special about a good sportswriter that the best in the other departments seldom attain. He attracts more and tenacious readers and holds them longer than the other featured stars."

Considine might have missed the sports world, but he continued to write occasionally on the subject for the INS and for freelance magazine assignments. His 12 October 1946 INS article about Boston Red Sox slugger Ted Williams demonstrates a more-cynical perspective and a more-measured style than his early, "Gee Whiz" writing:

> He is a mixed-up adolescent who recoils from the vivid daffiness of his idolaters. As a ball player who served his country and hit .340 in his first post-war year, he instinctively resents abuse from fans whose lives were unaffected by the war. His sense of hearing is so acute he hears every blunt remark. And his eyes are so sharp he can read between the lines of every Boston baseball writer's story.

Considine did not completely abandon the more-colorful style, however. A July 1950 article for *Flair* demonstrates that he was still capable of "Gee Whiz" writing when appropriate for the subject:

> The American athletic scene does not need new blood as much as it needs simply blood. It cries out to be weaned from the Pablum-like morass into which it has been lowered by the twin devils of listlessness and subjection. It needs red meat; a renaissance of the maverick vulgarity that produced the Golden Age of Sport. This seemlier generation of athletes of all three sexes, and the unbridled rise of dictatorial power among officials have bred most of the guts out of the sports scene. The public hungers for a chew-tobacco oaf with 20-20 vision and supernatural muscular control who, like his forebears, accepts the fact that he was placed on earth to raise hell with law, order and the record books.

Considine may well have been thinking of Babe Ruth when he wrote the *Flair* article. He had taken on the job of helping to write Ruth's autobiography two years before. The writing of *The Babe Ruth Story* (1948) proved more difficult than Considine anticipated, however, because of the fact that Ruth was dying of cancer at the time. Despite those troubles, the book was well received by reviewers. Rex Lardner, in *The New York Times Book Review* (2 May 1948), wrote: "Bob Considine, who wrote the book in the first person, has done much more than describe Ruth's vagaries and exploits. He has captured the team personality of the Yankees of the Twenties and Thirties."

Considine also did uncredited screenplay work on the movie adaptation, which was released by Allied Artists Pictures in 1948 and widely criticized for its artificial, sentimentalized portrayal of its subject. Bosley Crowther wrote in *The New York Times* (27 July 1948): "Ruth was a great one with the kid fans, but it smacks of sheer artifice to show his bulbous counterfeit in this movie maundering over pathos-coated tots." Baseball scholars have also rejected the contrivances of the movie; Ruth biographer Robert Creamer, author of *Babe: The Legend Comes to Life* (1974), told *The Sporting News* (6 February 1995) that the movie was largely responsible for perpetuating the myth that Ruth "called his shot" in a 1932 World Series game at Wrigley Field, pointing to the center-field stands before hitting a home run in that direction: "There's no question he did not point to the center-field stands. . . . It was because of that stupid William Bendix movie that people thought otherwise."

Considine's next collaborative sports book was *Dempsey: By the Man Himself* (1960), written with prizefighter Jack Dempsey and another ghostwriter, Bill Slocum. As Considine recalled in *It's All News to Me: A Reporter's Deposition,* "Jack spared nothing: the grinding poverty of his early days, his saloon fights to stay alive, the brutish beatings he took as a boy (one so savage that he was carted away from the fight unconscious in a wheelbarrow), his slacker trial after World War I, his wives. . . . He told me his story in the only way it could be told, in basic English that was always closer to the Anglo-Saxon than to Mayfair. And so we faithfully recorded it." Dempsey's attorney, however, objected to the candidness of the manuscript and demanded significant cuts. Although *Look* magazine asked Dempsey to publish the story as originally written, the fighter refused.

Despite the legal blandishments, the book was generally well received. Sportswriter W. C. Heinz, in *The New York Times Book Review* (15 May 1960), called it the best of the books about Dempsey: "This is a franker, more intimate effort, put together by two veteran newspaper men skilled in the mining and refining of the concise, revealing anecdote. . . . Most of it sounds like Dempsey, but it was inevitable that somewhere in the clicking of two typewriters some of the sounds of the Man Himself would be lost."

Considine wrote in *It's All News to Me* that he disliked writing for sports figures. Major league baseball players were the hardest to work with because of their desire to avoid controversy: "Years ago a Philadelphia baseball writer assigned to spook a daily article signed: 'By Jimmy Foxx,' during the World Series conscientiously called on the slugger and asked him if he had thoughts about the tone of the upcoming articles. 'Yeah,' Jimmy said, 'don't hurt nobody's feelings.'"

Considine derived more satisfaction from interviewing generals, politicians, and world leaders. During his career, he covered presidents Dwight Eisenhower, John Kennedy, Lyndon Johnson, and Richard Nixon on tours around the world, including Nixon's historic trips to Beijing and Moscow. In 1975 Gerald Ford granted Considine an exclusive interview in the White House about a month before the writer died. Considine considered one of his greatest successes as a newsman his reportage on the meeting between Eisenhower and General Douglas MacArthur shortly after Eisenhower was elected president in 1952–he beat his competition by twelve hours when he filed an exclusive story that the pair had met to discuss the Korean War.

Considine also wrote about political leaders and potentates as a member of the so-called Hearst Task Force. Considine, William Randolph Hearst Jr., and Frank Conniff were granted an exclusive interview with Soviet premier Nikita Khrushchev in Moscow in 1957, at the height of the Cold War. The syndicated news stories that resulted from the four-hour interview won the three men the Overseas Press Club Award for best reporting from abroad, and the material was also shaped into a book, *Ask Me Anything: Our Adventures with Khrushchev* (1960). Reviewing the book for *The New York Times Book Review* (31 July 1960), Harrison Salisbury wrote: "The result is a series of fascinating close-ups of Nikita Khrushchev and his political lieutenants. . . . Here, too, is healthy advice to Americans that it is time to substitute knowledge for superstition in evaluating the Soviet problem."

Considine and Babe Ruth celebrating the 1948 publication of Ruth's autobiography, on which the two collaborated

Considine also received an Overseas Press Club Award in 1959 for his reporting on the death of Pope Pius XII. A devout Catholic, he felt a deep personal interest in the story. He was recognized throughout his career with awards from religious organizations. For his work in "restoring spiritual values," Considine was awarded a Christopher Medallion on 14 January 1953 in New York City. Considine also received the Catholic Writers Guild Award in 1949 and the Catholic Institute of the Press Award, also in 1949. During his life he received an American Jewish Congress Award and a Christian Athletic Foundation Award.

He also received honors from more-secular organizations, including the George R. Holmes Memorial Award in 1947 for stories on the hydrogen bomb tests; Sigma Delta Chi Award for distinguished service in journalism, based on his series on underworld figures in 1949; and the Albert and Mary Lasker Foundation award in 1952 for a series on the fight against cancer. In 1975 he was named to the New York City chapter of Sigma Delta Chi's professional hall of fame for journalists, along with Walter Cronkite and Lowell Thomas, both of CBS, and Homer Bigart and James Reston of *The New York Times*. He was a member of the Overseas Press Club (serving as president in 1947), Sigma Alpha Epsilon, and Sigma Delta Chi. St. Bonaventure University in southwestern New York State established the Bob Considine Award in 1978 to recognize the outstanding accomplishments of journalists. The Overseas Press Club also awards an annual Bob Considine Award for the best newspaper or wire-service analysis of international affairs.

In addition to the awards and the professional memberships, Considine was widely respected by his colleagues and contemporaries. African American sportswriter Sam Lacy credited him with helping to integrate the press box of Griffith Stadium in Washington, D.C., by inviting Lacy to sit next to him during a prizefight. Red Smith's column in *The New York Times* for 27 September 1975, two days after Considine's death, noted that he "poured out books and magazine pieces and radio and movie scripts and always had time to be kind to young guys in our business." Povich's column on 26 September 1975 in the *Washington Post* noted Considine's "friendliness and concern for others. For 10 days in Washington baseball camp at Biloxi, Miss., he covered up for a fellow reporter who . . . was preoccupied with a drinking problem. After 10 days of filing stories to his own paper as well as to his competition, Bob Considine was finally heard to complain, 'I've just realized I've been writing better stuff for his paper than I have for my own.'"

Considine died of a stroke on 25 September 1975 in New York City at the age of sixty-eight. He remained committed to his profession until the end of his life. Just months before he died, he was a participant in a hot-air balloon race in Nevada. His balloon crashed and he was hospitalized with a back injury, but he continued to write, and four of his columns were about his injury and his treatment. In one of his last columns, written shortly before his death, he told readers:

> I'll croak in the newspaper business. Is there any better way to go? In what other trade can a man hope to build a bridge between himself and others every day of every week of every year. On what other field of endeavor is a competitor called upon to come up each day with words and thoughts he did not use the day before. Every time a reporter picks up a phone to call in a story, swings aboard a plane to go on an assignment, or spins a fresh sheet of copy paper into his typewriter, he shoots his roll–like a craps player going for broke.

References:

David Davis, "Roger Kahn–Sports and Sensibility," *Book* (September/October 1999);

Mark Newman and Steve Gietschier, "TSN's Greatest 100 Baseball Players!" *Sporting News,* 6 February 1995;

Shirley Povich, "A Sporting Life," *Washington Post,* 29 October 1989, p. W22.

Nat Fleischer

(1887 - 25 June 1972)

Scott A. G. M. Crawford

MAJOR POSITIONS HELD: Assistant sports editor, *New York Press* (1912–1916); sports editor, *New York Sun* (1916–1918), *New York Telegram* (1918–1927); publisher, editor, and writer, *The Ring* magazine (1922–1972).

Nat Fleischer

BOOKS: *Training for Boxers* (New York: Ring, 1927);

Young Griffo, the Will O' the Wisp of the Roped Square (New York: C. J. O'Brien, 1928);

Jack Dempsey, the Idol of Fistiana: An Intimate Narrative, with Numerous Illustrations (New York: Ring, 1929);

How to Second a Boxer (New York: C. J. O'Brien, 1929);

Gene Tunney, the Enigma of the Ring, with Numerous Illustrations (New York: F. Hubner, 1931);

How to Box (New York: Ring, 1932);

How to Referee and How to Judge a Fight (Tenafly, N.J.: Tenafly Printing Co., 1933; revised edition, New York: C. J. O'Brien, 1962);

Nat Fleischer's Universal Boxing Course (Tenafly, N.J.: Tenafly Printing Co., 1933);

"How to Second" and "How to Manage a Boxer" (Tenafly, N.J.: Tenafly Printing Co., 1934);

Modern Wrestling: Its Holds and Methods, by Fleischer and Jack Curley (New York: Ring Book Shop, 1935);

From Milo to Londos: The Story of Wrestling through the Ages, with Numerous Illustrations (New York: C. J. O'Brien, 1936);

Black Dynamite: The Story of the Negro in the Prize Ring from 1782 to 1938, 5 volumes (New York: C. J. O'Brien, 1938–1947)–comprises volume 1, *Black Dynamite: The Story of the Negro in Boxing* (1938); volume 2, *Jolting Joe: The Story of Joe Louis and Homicide Hank: The Drama of Henry Armstrong* (1938); volume 3, *The Three Colored Aces, Story of George Dixon, Joe Gans and Joe Walcott and Several Contemporaries* (1938); volume 4, *Fighting Furies: The Story of the Golden Era of Jack Johnson, Sam Langford and Their Negro Contemporaries* (1939); volume 5, *Sockers in Sepia: A Continuation of the Drama of the Negro in Pugilistic Competition* (1947);

Max Baer, the Glamour Boy of the Ring (New York: C. J. O'Brien, 1941);

Reckless Lady: The Life Story of Adah Isaacs Menken (New York: C. J. O'Brien, 1941);

The Boston Strong Boy: The Story of John L. Sullivan, the Champion of Champions (New York: C. J. O'Brien, 1941);

The Flaming Ben Hogan: Pugilist, Pirate, Gambler, Civil War Spy, Oil Magnate, Evangelist (New York: C. J. O'Brien, 1941);

Commando Stuff (New York: C. J. O'Brien, 1942);

"Gentleman Jim": The Story of James J. Corbett (New York: C. J. O'Brien, 1942);

"Terrible Terry," the Brooklyn Terror: The Fistic Career of Terry McGovern (New York: C. J. O'Brien, 1943);

Jack McAuliffe, the Napoleon of the Prize Ring (New York, 1944);

"The Michigan Assassin": The Saga of Stanley Ketchel, World's Most Sensational Middleweight Champion (New York: C. J. O'Brien, 1946);

Leonard the Magnificent: Life-story of the Man Who Made Himself "King of Lightweights" (New York, 1947);

The Heavyweight Championship: An Informal History of Heavyweight Boxing from 1719 to the Present Day (New York: Putnam, 1949; London: Sportsman's Book Club, 1954; revised edition, New York: Putnam, 1961);

The Louis Legend: The Amazing Story of the Brown Bomber's Rise to the Heavyweight Championship of the World (New York: Ring, 1956);

Simple Exercises for Height Increase (London: Thorsons, 1957);

50 Years at Ringside (New York: Fleet, 1958);

A Pictorial History of Boxing, by Fleischer and Sam Andre (New York: Citadel, 1959; London: Spring Books, 1964).

Editions: *Jack Dempsey* (New York: Arlington House, 1972);

An Illustrated History of Boxing, by Fleischer and Sam Andre (Secaucus, N.J.: Carol, 1997).

OTHER: *Scientific Blocking and Hitting and Other Methods of Defense,* edited by Fleischer (New York: Ring, 1935);

Nat Fleischer's All-Time Ring Record Book, 4 volumes, edited by Fleischer (New York: Ring, 1941–1944);

Nat Fleischer's The Ring Record Book, 8 volumes, edited by Fleischer (New York: Ring Book Shop, 1945–1952);

Nat Fleischer's The Ring Boxing Encyclopedia and Record Book, 11 volumes, edited by Fleischer (New York: Ring Book Shop, 1953–1973).

Nathaniel Stanley "Nat" Fleischer was born in New York City in 1887, one of nine surviving children of Haskell and Anna Fleischer. He never knew his exact birth date; when he was about twenty-one he selected 3 November so as to be able to vote in an upcoming election. He grew up on the Lower East Side of Manhattan, an area that was a proving ground for fledgling prizefighters. He was introduced to boxing at age eight when his father gave him pictures of fighters that were included in Sweet Caporal and Murad cigarette packs. When he was twelve he saw "Terrible" Terry McGovern fight Thomas "Pedlar" Palmer and was, according to his obituary in *The New York Times* (26 June 1972), "bitten by the bug and never recovered." Two weeks after watching the McGovern-Palmer bout he took up boxing; eventually he became captain of the boxing team, as well as president, of the Oregon Athletic Club in New York City; he also played first base and catcher on the club baseball team and in a 1962 *Sports Illustrated* interview recalled becoming adept at "trick bicycle riding." When the five-foot, two-inch, 122-pound Fleischer was knocked out by a professional fighter posing as an amateur, he decided that boxing was not for him.

After graduating from Townsend Harris High School, Fleischer entered City College of New York. Although he continued to enjoy watching and reading about boxing, he was more interested in track and field–he ran the 100 yards in 10.2 seconds, the 220 yards in 25 seconds, and long-jumped 19 feet, 6 inches–and in managing the basketball team. He began his journalistic career in college by working as campus correspondent for two daily newspapers and as a stringer on the sports desk of the *New York Press.*

In 1908 Fleischer was a member of a reception committee for the American Olympic team returning from London. The group was invited to President Theodore Roosevelt's Oyster Bay Estate, where Roosevelt officially welcomed the athletes. In his autobiography, *50 Years at Ringside* (1958), Fleischer noted that Roosevelt's reaction to being called a sissy as a boy had been to take up boxing; he proudly quotes the president as saying, "If boxing were taught in every public and secondary school and in college, this nation would soon find itself rid of bullies and would develop in our youth a spirit of manhood, a spirit that teaches fairness to our fellow men."

Fleischer graduated with a bachelor of science degree in 1908 and began teaching at Public School 7 in the daytime and working on the sports desk of the *New York Press* at night. He disliked teaching, however, and began studying chemistry at New York University. The result, according to a 1947 *Collier's* profile of Fleischer by Kyle Crichton, was that "A slight mishap in an ammonia experiment resulted in Nat's blowing up the laboratory and departing without a refund on his $400 tuition fee." He then spent a year in postgraduate study at the Yale School of Forestry. Although he abandoned that career, he maintained a lifelong interest in horticulture; on his later travels around the world he brought home orange seeds from Bangkok, fig roots from Sorrento, and corn kernels from Nova Scotia.

In *50 Years at Ringside* Fleischer recounts meeting the writer Jack London at Jack Cooper's New York Gymnasium in the early 1900s: "London was exercising with the mitts and he surprised me with his skill."

London believed that he needed to know how to fight if he were to survive the dangers of hobo life. Fleischer encountered London again in Reno, Nevada, on 4 July 1910 at the fight in which Jack Johnson successfully defended his heavyweight championship against James J. Jeffries; Fleischer describes London as Jeffries's "most ardent rooter."

By 1912 Fleischer was assistant sports editor at the *New York Press.* The paper was purchased that year by Frank A. Munsey, a pioneering press mogul who bought, sold, and merged newspapers to such an extent that he was known as the "Great Consolidator." Munsey promoted Fleischer to sports editor in 1916, the same year he merged the *Press* into the *New York Sun.* Fleischer married Gertrude Augusta Phillips of Pittsburgh, a former actress and the daughter of sportswriter A. D. Phillips, in New York City on 22 October 1917. In 1918 he moved to the *New York Telegram* when Munsey bought that paper. The Fleischers' only child, Joan Phillips Fleischer, was born on 24 May 1920.

In 1922 a bill was proposed in the New York legislature to repeal the 1920 Walker Law, which had legalized boxing in the state. To give themselves a forum to oppose the measure Fleischer and three partners launched a magazine, *The Ring,* with offices in the old Madison Square Garden on Eighth Avenue. Fleischer invested $4,000 in the enterprise, which he pursued on a part-time basis while continuing to work at the *Telegram.* The first issue of *The Ring* appeared on 15 February. Two of the partners sold their shares to Fleischer after the bill was defeated.

One of the many dramatic fights at which Fleischer was ringside during his career was the Jack Dempsey–Luis Angel Firpo clash on 2 September 1923. In round one Firpo knocked Dempsey through the ropes after having been knocked down himself seven times. Fleischer's description of Firpo's loss to Dempsey in the second round is a masterful example of psychological insight into what defines a champion:

> Had Firpo possessed brain power in proportion to his enormous strength, he would have been crowned that day as heavyweight champion of the world. The Wild Bull, with all his powerful strength to give and take punishment, showed that he lacked the one essential quality to pugilistic greatness. He saw Dempsey with his back against the ropes, his jaw an open target, his hands hanging loosely at his sides, stunned from the impact that had sent him into the laps of the newspapermen at the ringside. But Firpo's brain was not quick. When he finally did come to the full realization that a beaten man stood before him and a championship was at his feet, his opportunity was gone. Luis gave Jack time to recover. In a moment the Manassa Mauler shifted into action, and then there was no stopping him.

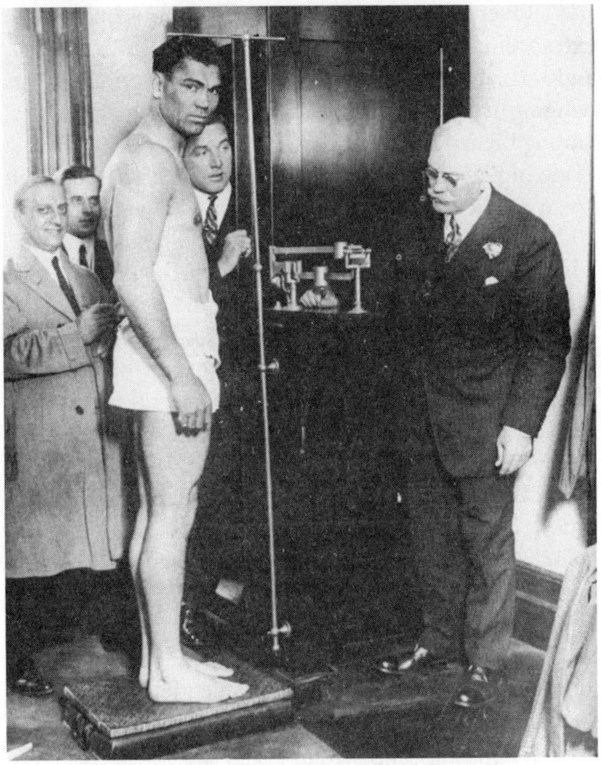

Fleischer (left) observing Jack Dempsey being weighed in by New York State Athletic Commissioner William Muldoon for Dempsey's 2 September 1923 fight with Luis Angel Firpo

In *Beyond the Ring: The Role of Boxing in American Society* (1988) sports historian Jeffrey T. Sammons calls Fleischer "the prime mover" in the early 1920s on the issue of removing the racial barrier from the heavyweight championship. Fleischer consistently used *The Ring* to advance the claims of Harry Wills, "the Black Panther," to be given the opportunity to fight Dempsey for the championship. Despite the public support generated by *The Ring,* however, a Wills-Dempsey bout never materialized.

Munsey died in 1925; in 1927 Roy A. Howard bought the *Telegram,* and Fleischer returned from a trip to Europe to find himself out of a job. He decided to make publishing *The Ring* his full-time undertaking and bought out his last remaining partner. Although *The New York Times,* the *Washington Post,* the *Chicago Tribune,* and the *Los Angeles Times* ran serious boxing commentaries by such first-rate writers as James R. Harrison, James P. Dawson, Joseph C. Nichols, and John Kicran, *The Ring* captured a growing readership because Fleischer treated boxing not just as a sport but as a way of life. By the end of the 1930s *The Ring* was the authoritative voice of boxing in the United States and around the world.

Over the years the *Ring* offices accumulated an extraordinary collection of boxing memorabilia, arcana, and artifacts, including hundreds of boxing gloves hanging from the ceiling and many boxer's watches, among them a one-pound favorite of John L. Sullivan's. Pride of place in Fleischer's collection was the gold belt given to the English fighter Charley Mitchell after his 10 March 1888 bout with Sullivan in Chantilly, France. The belt had been made for Mitchell by a group of a hundred London gentlemen for the equivalent of $10,000; when Mitchell's son was killed in World War I he put the belt up for auction on behalf of the War Relief Fund. It was bought and sold several times from 1916 to 1922, raising a total of $2 million. The belt was finally purchased for $1,200 by the British boxing manager Ted Broadribb, who gave it to Fleischer. Some indication of its value can be gauged by the fact that Fleischer had to pay $624 in duty to bring the belt into the United States. Other items specially treasured by Fleischer were a nearly complete collection of Joe Louis's boxing gloves and the timekeeper's bell used in the 4 July 1910 fight in Reno in which Jeffries knocked out Johnson to retain the world heavyweight title.

By the time he wrote *The Boston Strong Boy: The Story of John L. Sullivan, the Champion of Champions* (1941), Fleischer could say in the foreword that for more than half a century he had "been at the ringside for every important championship fight in the heavyweight division. Willard, Dempsey, Tunney, Schmeling, Jack Sharkey, Primo Carnera, Max Baer, Braddock, Louis, Ezzard Charles–I have watched and studied them all." Fleischer was a passionate supporter of boxing who had the ability to generate a prodigious outpouring of words; he is reputed to have written his thirty-chapter *"Gentleman Jim": The Story of James J. Corbett* (1942) in thirty-six hours. Often he was both writer and editor of his own work, resulting in material that is verbose and lacks focus. But his treatment of boxing luminaries from Bob Fitzsimmons to Louis deftly integrates sports history into journalistic reporting, and his essays on lesser-known boxers, such as Baer, Tommy Burns, and Jim Braddock, have endured more than a half century since they appeared in print. Fleischer's account of Baer's introduction to boxing in *Max Baer, the Glamour Boy of the Ring* (1941) retains its freshness today:

> It was at a dance in Livermore that Baer was first bitten by the pugilistic bug. He and four companions had purloined a demijohn of wine that belonged to a locomotive engineer, and when the owner discovered his loss, he was in no mood for explanations of boyish pranks. He rushed at the miscreants, swinging right and left. Max's pals scampered for safety, but Max himself was too slow getting underway. A haymaker caught him on the chin. Max went crashing back against a wall. As the infuriated engineer rushed again, Max let go a wild right. It landed flush on the attacker's jaw, and down he went, out. The thrill of that one-punch victory gave Baer ideas. He bought a punching bag and a pair of gloves and set up a small gymnasium on the ranch. A few informal set-tos with the cowhands convinced Max that his destiny was in the ring.

During World War II Fleischer was permitted to print only fifty-four thousand copies of *The Ring* a month because of paper rationing. He presented the U.S. Army with thirteen thousand free copies a month, which paid off in a circulation gain of thirty thousand less than a year after the war. In 1944 he narrated the Hollywood documentary *Kings of the Ring;* among the boxers featured were Johnson, Louis, Dempsey, Baer, Billy Conn, Burns, Bill Squires, Lou Nova, George Carpentier, Carnera, and Gene Tunney. By the end of the war Fleischer had established himself as boxing's most widely recognized raconteur.

In 1947 circulation of *The Ring* reached 117,000, including 9,000 copies sold in London, 4,000 in Australia, and 5,200 in South Africa. As Crichton noted in a *Collier's* magazine profile that year, Fleischer saw himself as "Mr. Boxing"–a "self-appointed historian" who "rules over boxing like a brood hen." Crichton portrays Fleischer as an enlightened athletic despot who remade boxing according to his image of what it ought to be. For example, he thought that champion boxers should receive recognition similar to that accorded other athletes. Obviously, they would not fight without the incentive of cash, but trophies–and especially championship belts–seemed to Fleischer a more-fitting reward for stellar fighters. He started handing out *Ring* belts in 1922; when Rocky Graziano beat Tony Zale at the Chicago Stadium for the world middleweight championship on 27 September 1946, he became the 126th boxer to receive a belt from Fleischer. The belts helped to promote *The Ring,* kept Fleischer's name on the sporting pages of the world's press, and allowed Fleischer to wear the mantle of boxing's premier authority. The presentation of such awards also allowed Fleischer an extraordinary podium from which to pontificate. As Crichton observes somewhat hyperbolically:

> When Mr. Fleischer enters a ring to present a belt there are observers who swear that a halo appears around his head. In a gravelly voice tinged with New York East Side nuances he launches into a sweet and reverent eulogy of the art of mayhem. As the hours pass his voice grows in fervor and there are tears in the eyes of those members of the audience still awake. The tension became so great one night in Detroit that some kindly individual doused the lights. When they were turned on again five minutes later Nat was still speaking but the crowd had left.

It was Fleischer's idea for *The Ring* to publish annual rankings of boxers. Initially he drew on the expertise of promoter Tex Rickard, one of his original partners in the magazine, and Dempsey made the selections one year. Early on, however, Fleischer took over the drawing up of the rankings. For Crichton, Fleischer rated the top ten heavyweights of all time, in order, as Johnson, Jeffries, Fitzsimmons, Dempsey, Corbett, Sam Langford, Louis, Tom Sharkey, Tunney, and Burns. The most-eccentric fighter he had ever seen, Fleischer told Crichton, was Battling Siki, the Senegalese. The greatest boxing thriller was the 1923 Dempsey-Firpo bout. Johnson had the "best left hand in boxing" and was also the best feinter, jabber, and counterpuncher. Dempsey and Jackie "Kid" Berg were the most-aggressive fighters. Tunney was the coolest fighter. Fitzsimmons was the hardest hitter. Jeffries was the "most durable" heavyweight. Sullivan and Dempsey were the greatest boxing heroes. Boxing's greatest upsets were Max Schmeling's knockout of Louis in 1936 and Louis's knockout of Schmeling in 1938. The most-thrilling era in boxing was the "White Hope" period that followed Johnson's defeat of Burns in December 1908: when the African American Johnson became heavyweight champion of the world, boxing promoters embarked on an international hunt to locate a "Great White Hope" who could beat him. For Fleischer, the selection of the greatest boxer of all time posed no difficulty; he told Crichton:

> Dempsey was a tiger, Jeffries was a stone wall, Fitzsimmons was a killer, Corbett was a magician, Joe Louis is dynamite with both hands, but Johnson was daddy of them all. He was a wonderful boxer, a splendid jabber, and the best feinter who ever lived and he could catch a blow with his left and counter with his right, all with such speed that it became almost a simultaneous movement. And no matter what anybody says, he could take it and dish it out. He's my boy.

While Fleischer fine-tuned his list of top boxers during the last twenty-five years of his life, he never wavered in his high regard for Johnson.

In his 1966 anthology *The Realm of Sports* Herbert Warren Wind brought together what he called a corps of the sporting world's "most distinguished writers." Among his selections was "The Brown Bomber," from Fleischer's *The Heavyweight Championship: An Informal History of Heavyweight Boxing from 1719 to the Present Day* (1949). Fleischer compresses the first of Louis's twenty-five title defenses, that against Tommy Farr of England on 4 August 1937, into four sentences that capture the elemental aspect of pugilistic engagement:

Fleischer presenting featherweight and welterweight championship belts to Henry Armstrong and a medal to Joe Louis as the outstanding fighter of 1938

> Louis went into the ring to end the fight as quickly as possible. Instead he caught a tartar, and it was lucky for him that Farr lacked a knockout punch. By staying the limit, Tommy routed the critics who had predicted his speedy fall. Tossing caution to the winds, he stood up for fifteen rounds of savage fighting, and at times he battled with a viciousness that made the thirty six thousand spectators wonder whether he was really a representative of the country that in recent years had specialized in horizontal heavyweight kings.

On 22 June 1938 Louis faced the German Schmeling at Yankee Stadium. The fight engendered a national frenzy as the United States hoped for Louis to avenge his surprising and humiliating defeat by Schmeling in 1936. Fleischer's opening paragraph on the fight is succinct, and the effect is savage: "At the bell, Louis tore into Schmeling with rights and lefts and bore the German to the ropes. Those drives were no long swings. The punches went barely eight inches, and they took all the fight out of Max. They paralyzed him." Although he admired Louis, Fleischer was unsentimental when he commented on Louis's waning powers. On 5 December 1947 Jersey Joe Walcott fought Louis for the heavyweight championship. Louis, according to

Cover for a 1939 issue of Fleischer's magazine

Fleischer, was fortunate to scrape out a narrow decision in fifteen rounds: "He was awkward. He looked foolish as he tried to catch up with the sprinting Jerseyite. His timing was terrible and his coordination was lacking. He was listless. He often looked bewildered as he tried to get close enough for action. It was a depressing exhibition from a champion." Fleischer sums up Louis's appeal to the American public, describing him as:

> the boy from Alabama who became heavyweight King, the Negro who has not only proved himself the master boxer of his age but who has demonstrated by his fine behavior in and out of the ring that the color of a man's skin is an irrelevant factor in determining his worth. Not the least of Joe's achievements was a reign of nearly twelve years without a single demand that he be dethroned by a *white* man. The explanation lies partly in the fact that the American people have become more mature since the days of Jack Johnson, partly in the fact that Louis was a great champion and a fine citizen.

Fleischer's wife died on 20 November 1949 while the couple was vacationing in Havana, Cuba. Fleischer never remarried.

Fleischer rated the Jimmy Carruthers–Chamrern Songkitrat world bantamweight championship bout in Bangkok on 2 May 1954 as the "most dramatic" fight he ever attended. Fleischer's account of the fight for *The Ring,* "Title Battle in Typhoon," describes the 59,760-person crowd as a "mass of humanity of many nations": "It was a picture to behold, to see fight fans, men, women and children, many carrying bags of food, coming to the fight in their gayest festival garments, paying respects to Buddha and their national idol, Chamrern Songkitrat." His one-paragraph pen sketch of the challenger shows the *Ring* publisher at his vintage best:

> Songkitrat, known as the "Fiery Lizard," is a handsome Thai boy of twenty-four, who took his name from a boxing school he attended. He toughened himself for Siamese-style fighting by plowing behind a water buffalo in the rice paddies as a youth, and so clever was he in the Thai rough-and-tumble style of fighting that he was urged to turn his talents to the European and American style [boxing], in which he has met with success.

After twelve bruising rounds, Carruthers won "by a hairline margin," with Fleischer, one of the ringside judges, scoring the fight 31 to 29 in favor of the Australian. Fleischer quotes Songkitrat as saying at the end of the contest, "I am personally satisfied that the decision was fair and beyond doubt. If I am not sorry, my friends and my country men, why are you?" Never hesitant to moralize, generalize, and pontificate, Fleischer concludes: "Thus in Songkitrat, Thailand has a boxer who lives up to the tradition of fair play and sportsmanship for which his country is noted."

In 1954 the arrival of the weekly *Sports Illustrated* put a dent in the preeminent position of the monthly *Ring* as the journal of boxing. Nevertheless, *The Ring* continued to be the dominant voice of the sport. By 1962 the U.S. circulation of the magazine was 157,000, with 93,000 more copies sold around the world; a British and British Commonwealth edition was printed in London. A price increase that year from 35¢ to 50¢ was followed by a 7 percent gain in circulation. Although one-eighth of the pages of the magazine were devoted to professional wrestling, Fleischer told Gilbert Rogin in a 1962 interview that he thought that "true wrestling" was a thing of the past and that the 1960s variety was simply "burlesque." But if he dropped wrestling from the magazine, he said, he would lose twenty thousand readers.

Fleischer railed against those who criticized boxing; while he knew that corruption and brutality existed in prizefighting, Fleischer–referred to by other sportswriters as "Mr. Boxing," "the Boswell of Jacobs' Beach," and "the Great Father of *La Boxe*"–saw his sport in a more-romantic vein. For Fleischer, boxing

Fleischer in 1947, with part of his collection of boxing gloves from championship fights (photograph by Hans Knopff)

was a stage for memorable and mighty events: "Boxing can never be killed," he was quoted as saying in his obituary in *Newsweek* (10 July 1972). "It's a sport bred into the race of man." Fleischer had a standing order for his correspondents: "If you can't praise a guy, keep quiet. He'll take enough licks from the other guy anyhow."

For many years *The Ring* carried a high-minded paragraph on the contents page:

> *The Ring* is a magazine which a man may take home with him. He may leave it on his library table safe in the knowledge that it does not contain one line of matter either in the text or the advertisements which would be offensive. The publisher of *The Ring* guards this reputation jealously. It is entertaining and it is clean.

Fleischer could not, however, resist telling Rogin the story of the time he refereed the Harry Jeffra-Spider Armstrong featherweight title bout in Baltimore on 29 July 1940, when the ringside temperature stood at 102 degrees:

> After the 11th round I took my tie off. After the 12th I unbuttoned my shirt. After the 13th I pulled off my shirt. After the 14th I took off my undershirt. After the 15th I held up the hand of Jeffra and slumped against the ropes, hardly able to budge. A lady came up to me and said, "So you're the Nat Fleischer who preaches morals in *The Ring!* You should be ashamed of yourself, taking off your underwear in public!"

Fleischer told Rogin that he had a standard response to letters from parents of aspiring fighters:

> I tell the mothers that if the boy likes boxing as an exercise, by all means don't discourage him, otherwise he may become a street fighter. I tell the lads that they should take up a job instead, that that will be their future, that the chances of becoming wealthy through boxing are practically nil and not to turn professional unless they have real ability.

In 1958 Fleischer published his autobiography, *50 Years at Ringside*. Like much of his writing, the book combines good reporting and taut boxing commentary with long-winded accounts of famous occasions at which he was in attendance and important people who enjoyed his company. The short chapter "Birth of *The Ring*" takes the reader into "a cubbyhole in the Old Madison Square Garden," where, in February 1922, he made a "wavering debut" to "combat attacks against boxing." One delightfully told vignette reports on a trip Fleischer made to Germany in mid August 1926. It was his third visit to the country, and he was tracking down a promising heavyweight named Max Schmeling. In the small town of Bernau, thirty miles from Berlin, he watched an amateur boxing match:

> The spectators, more than a thousand, kept themselves in good humor guzzling beer from German mugs and eating sausages and sauerkraut. Men, women and children crowded the place. Some women dangled nursing babies, others played with dachshunds. It was the strangest gathering I had ever seen at a fight.

Fleischer likens the enthusiastic Bernau boxing audience to the crowd scenes in William Hogarth's narrative painting *Southwark Fair* (1733), then goes on to describe his first meeting with Schmeling–"six feet of gangling brawn."

Fleischer's account of his dealings with Schmeling and Schmeling's unofficial manager, Arthur Buelow, and the intrigues that surrounded Schmeling's first visit to the United States in 1928 are worthy of a Phillip Marlowe mystery. Backers, dealers, attorneys, crooks, the wily promoter Rickard, and the pugnacious manager Joe Jacobs slip in and out of various subplots that go into the masterminding of a new world heavyweight champion. Fleischer shows himself to be a man of principle in a crowd of rogues, rascals, simpletons, and tough-minded fight entrepreneurs:

> I had a [10 percent] contract [with Schmeling] I never made use of. Had I exercised my rights, I would have collected close to $220,000 as my share of Max's U.S. earnings. I never participated in the management of a fighter, though I did collect for services rendered at times as a scout for Rickard and his successor, Mike Jacobs, after I had left the New York *Telegram*. . . . Schmeling's contract rests in my Garden Museum.

Fleischer concludes the autobiography: "Were I to live my life over again, there is nothing I would cherish more than to be a part of the boxing scene and play the role that has been mine during the past half century."

Fleischer's *A Pictorial History of Boxing* (1959), co-authored with Sam Andre, is the most popular boxing book of all time. Hundreds of black-and-white photographs are juxtaposed with a minimalist commentary. Fleischer's genius as writer, editor, and commentator is his ability to highlight boxing's primitive drama in clipped prose. For example, the account of the Sugar Ray Robinson–Randy Turpin rematch on 12 September 1951 at the Polo Grounds in New York City includes a photograph of Robinson, with bloodied face, moving to a neutral corner as Turpin lies stretched out on the canvas. The caption reads:

> Sugar Ray was in trouble in the 10th round of his return match with Turpin. His left eye was sliced open and bleeding profusely. If he could go one more round, the bout might possibly be stopped. In desperation, he went all out with a barrage of blows, until Turpin lay flat on his back.

Boxing took Fleischer all over the world. By 1962 he had visited Europe on thirty-seven occasions and had circumnavigated the globe six times. The vast majority of the trips had to do with boxing. Boxing brought Fleischer the La Medaille d'Hononeur d'Or de l'Education Physique et des Sports from France, the Constantiniano Ordine Militaire di San Giorgio di Antiochia and the Commandatore della Stella al Merito Sportive from Italy, and the Order of the White Elephant, Third Class, from King Bhumibol Adulyadej of Thailand. Around the world Fleischer was recognized not just for *The Ring* but for his official roles in the ring and at ringside: he refereed and judged more than one thousand fights, including world championships that, while of little interest to American fight fans, were events of monumental cultural importance in their home constituencies–for example, the May 1961 Pone Kingpetch–Kyo Noguchi world flyweight championship in Tokyo and the September 1962 Eder Jofre–Joe Medel world bantamweight championship in São Paulo, Brazil. Such events offered the garrulous Fleischer the opportunity to regale audiences with boxing tales in which he was every bit as colorful as the fighters.

On 25 February 1964 at Miami Beach, Florida, Cassius Marcellus Clay outboxed and exhausted Sonny Liston, the world heavyweight champion, to the point that Liston could not start the seventh round. Following his victory over Liston, Clay embraced the Nation of Islam and changed his name briefly to Cassius X and then, in March, to Muhammad Ali. Ali applied to the Selective Service System for conscientious objector status on religious grounds; the request was denied, and on 28 April 1967 he refused induction into the army and was stripped of his title by the World Boxing Association, the New York State Athletic Commission, and other state boxing authorities.

Fleischer was never impressed by Ali, whom he did not regard as a great fighter on the level of a Johnson, Jeffries, or Fitzsimmons. Throughout the 1960s he continued to refer to Ali as Cassius Clay, refusing to use the fighter's Muslim name, and he thought that Ali's claim to be a conscientious objector was insincere. Nevertheless, Fleischer did not agree with the stripping of Ali's world heavyweight title, and *The Ring* continued to designate Ali the champion. Fleischer claimed that 90 percent of *Ring* readers supported his stand. A 1967 *Sports Illustrated* "Scorecard" sidebar called Fleischer's position "absurdly idealistic" but concluded: "we applaud Fleischer, if for no other reason than in an age in which what is just is increasingly overwhelmed by what is merely expedient, he has stuck to his guns."

In 1970 Fleischer played himself in the movie *The Super Fight,* which featured a computer-generated match between Ali and Rocky Marciano. Fleischer agreed with the computer, which projected that Marciano would have knocked Ali out in the twelfth round.

Fleischer was a founding member of the Boxing Writers Association. On two occasions he received the association's James J. Walker Award for his services to boxing, and the organization created the Nathaniel S. Fleischer Award in his honor. His most significant contribution to boxing literature was *Nat Fleischer's The Ring Boxing Encyclopedia and Record Book,* which he edited from 1953 to 1973 but which appeared annually under various titles from 1941 until 1987.

Fleischer's prediction as to the fiscal future of boxing is uncanny in its accuracy:

> As for the future, I don't agree with those who predict nothing but gloom for boxing while they lament the lost glories of Rickard and Dempsey, Jacobs and Louis. Studio television will dominate professional efforts during the coming years and eliminate the fear of financial failure. There is no end to the fabulous returns the future holds for world championship matches with television wired for theater and home pay viewing exclusively. The receipts of the golden era of boxing will seem insignificant measured against what can be grossed with this new medium.

Fleischer's final residence was at 151 Bayside Drive, Atlantic Beach, Long Island. He died of a heart ailment at University Hospital in New York City on 25 June 1972. His lifetime total of words in print surpasses forty million; at his death he had a dozen unpublished manuscripts, including a 268,800-word bibliography of boxing as treated by authors such as Victor Hugo, Charles Dickens, and Sir Arthur Conan Doyle. He was survived by his daughter, who had married the managing editor of *The Ring,* Nat Loubet, and three grandchildren. *Time* (10 July 1972) mourned the passing of one of boxing's "most pugnacious defenders." *Newsweek* (10 July 1972) described him as a "boxing historian" who "saved his own Sunday punch for the typewriter." Fleischer also had an obituary notice in the French magazine *L'Express* (7–9 July 1972).

The October 1972 issue of *The Ring* celebrated its founder in "The Life and Times of Nat Fleischer," noting that Fleischer had lived to enjoy the fiftieth anniversary of the magazine. Fleischer, the piece said, was "honest. He was fearless. He was for God, for Country and for Boxing. . . . a seeker after the truth, and a fighter for the right." *The Ring* thanked the more than one thousand men and women from all over the world who had sent their condolences. The issue included Fleischer's final rankings of fighters: as "most colorful" he placed Robinson third and Baer second; the leader was Ali. Fleischer, however, still referred to Ali as Cassius Clay.

In spite of the adulation accorded Fleischer, by the end of his life his impact on boxing had diminished. Critics regard *Muhammad Ali: The People's Champ* (1995), a collection of essays edited by Elliot J. Gorn, as a seminal study not just of the Ali era but of the evolution of modern boxing; Fleischer's name does not appear in the index, and of the nine contributors only Randy Roberts lists any Fleischer sources (*Ring* essays of April and September 1964). While recent sports historians have made limited use of Fleischer's vast body of work, Arthur Ashe drew on the third volume (1938) of Fleischer's five-volume *Black Dynamite: The Story of the Negro in the Prize Ring from 1782 to 1938* (1938–1947) for his *A Hard Road to Glory: A History of the African-American Athlete, 1619–1918* (1988). David Wiggins also used Fleischer as a source in his *Glory Bound: Black Athletes in a White America* (1997).

Fleischer in the boxing museum and hall of fame at the Ring *offices in Madison Square Garden in 1962 (photograph by Will Blanche)*

In *The Boxing Register* (1997) James B. Roberts and Alexander G. Skutt point out that Fleischer's moralizing in *The Ring* elevated boxing and sought practical remedies to improve the sport. Fleischer garnered public support for more-extensive physical examinations for fighters, padded rings, and a halt to fights when one of the boxers had been seriously cut. Ralph Hickok's *Encyclopedia of North American Sport History* (1992) notes that the monthly and yearly ratings in *The Ring* were "accepted as authoritative and helped to prevent mis-matches."

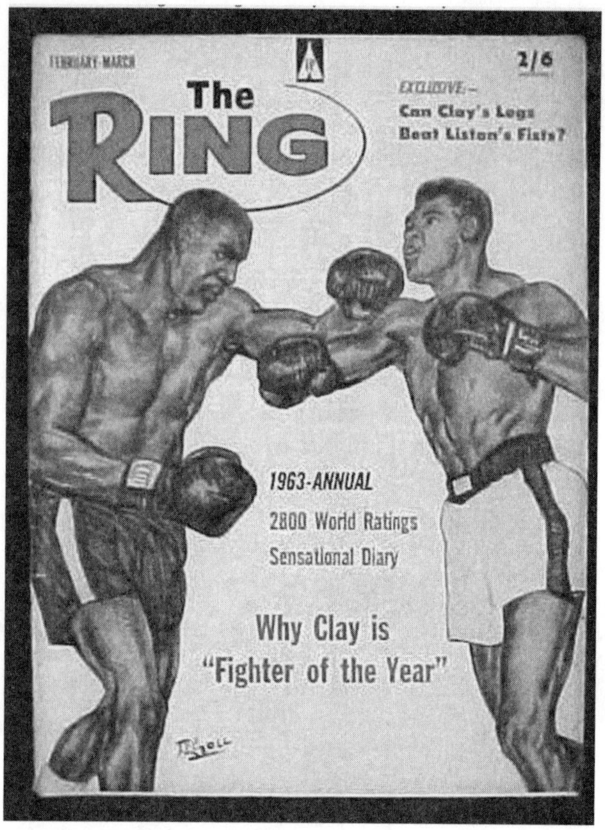

Cover for a 1964 issue of Fleischer's magazine promoting the upcoming heavyweight championship fight between Sonny Liston and Cassius Clay, who later changed his name to Muhammad Ali

A rival publication to *The Ring* for some years has been another New York City publication, *International Boxing.* In the November–December 1997 issue Don Majeski lists his choices for the fifty most influential boxing figures of all-time. The list is headed by boxing's first superstar, Sullivan; in the seventh place, just behind Dempsey, is Nathaniel S. Fleischer. Majeski comments:

> Nat Fleischer did not do any one thing better than anyone else. . . . He was not a great writer or even an efficient historical scholar. Fleischer was, however, boxing's linchpin, the glue that held the sport together. He provided a sense of continuity, the keeper of the flame in a largely disorganized, rather catch-as-catch-can business. . . . For almost three generations Fleischer was there, an oracular figure–the final arbiter and authority who brought a perceived integrity, knowledge, objectivity, and sense of absolutism to boxing.

The Ring editor Nigel Collins said in an unpublished 28 July 1998 interview that Fleischer was a good but not outstanding sportswriter; he was, however, boxing's "greatest publicist." His greatest legacy may be, according to Collins, that he was a man of Victorian ideas in a modern age. His help to African American boxers "has never been fully appreciated," and the sport of boxing will never again see his like as a man whose sense of fairness was impeccable. Herbert G. Goldman, the editor of *International Boxing Digest,* said in an unpublished 29 July 1998 interview:

> He was a desperately needed mortar for the sport. In every sense he was the official and unofficial anchor of boxing. Boxing has always been a sport where chaos is the rule. Fleischer provided a foundation and a sense of continuity. There is a deep need for such a figure today and none exists.

Interview:

Gilbert Rogin, "Mr. Boxing Himself," *Sports Illustrated,* 17 (6 August 1962): 54–60.

References:

Kyle Crichton, "Mr. Boxing," *Collier's,* 120 (6 December 1947): 58–63;

"The Life and Times of Nat Fleischer," *Ring,* October 1972, pp. 9–10, 68;

Don Majeski, "The 50 Most Influential Boxing Figures of All-Time," *International Boxing,* 39 (November–December 1997): 20;

Dan Parker, "Mr. Boxing," *Saturday Evening Post,* 218 (16 March 1946): 17, 125–128;

James B. Roberts and Alexander G. Skutt, *The Boxing Register* (New York: McBooks Press, 1997), p. 423;

Randy Roberts, "The Wide World of Muhammad Ali," in *Muhammad Ali: The People's Champ,* edited by Elliot J. Gorn (Urbana: University of Illinois Press, 1995), p. 52;

Jeffrey T. Sammons, *Beyond the Ring: The Role of Boxing in American Society* (Urbana: University of Illinois Press, 1988);

"Scorecard," *Sports Illustrated,* 27 (23 October 1967): 12;

David Wiggins, *Glory Bound: Black Athletes in a White America* (New York: Syracuse Press, 1997), p. 45.

Frank Graham

(12 November 1893 - 9 March 1965)

Edward J. Tassinari

Frank Graham

MAJOR POSITIONS HELD: City reporter (1914–1915), sports reporter (1915–1934), sports columnist, *New York Sun* (1934–1943); sports editor, *Look* (1943–1944); sports columnist, *New York Journal American* (1945–1964).

BOOKS: *Andy Blue* (Racine, Wis.: Whitman, 1932);

Davy Lane (Racine, Wis.: Whitman, 1932);

Lou Gehrig: A Quiet Hero (New York: Putnam, 1942);

The New York Yankees: An Informal History of a Great Baseball Team (New York: Putnam, 1943; revised edition, 1948; revised again, 1958);

McGraw of the Giants: An Informal Biography (New York: Putnam, 1944);

The Brooklyn Dodgers: An Informal History (New York: Putnam, 1945);

Al Smith, American: An Informal Biography (New York: Putnam, 1945);

The New York Giants: An Informal History of a Great Baseball Team (New York: Putnam, 1952);

Baseball Extra (New York: Barnes, 1954);

Third Man in the Ring, by Graham and Ruby Goldstein (New York: Funk & Wagnalls, 1959);

Baseball Wit and Wisdom: Folklore of a National Pastime, by Graham and Dick Hyman (New York: McKay, 1962).

OTHER: "The Dark Horseman," in *Sports Extra: Classics of Sports Reporting,* edited by Stanley Frank (New York: Barnes, 1944), pp. 230–233;

"Ex-Champion," in *Best Sports Stories 1946: A Panorama of the 1945 Sports Year,* edited by Irving T. Marsh and Edward Ehre (New York: Dutton, 1946), pp. 178–181;

"Bob Feller's Finest Victory," in *Best Sports Stories 1952: A Panorama of the 1951 Sports World,* edited by Marsh and Ehre (New York: Dutton, 1952), pp. 123–127;

"My Friend Grantland Rice," in *Best Sports Stories 1955: A Panorama of the 1954 Sports World,* edited by Marsh and Ehre (New York: Dutton, 1955), pp. 284–291;

"Fellow Named Archie Moore," in *Sportswriters' Choice: Their Best Stories,* edited by Richard P. Goldman (New York: Barnes, 1958), pp. 131–134;

"All the Way to the Grave," in *The Fireside Book of Boxing,* edited by W. C. Heinz (New York: Simon & Schuster, 1961), pp. 165–166;

"The Ups and Downs of Conn McCreary," in *The World of Sport: The Best from Sport Magazine,* edited by Al Silverman (New York: Holt, Rinehart & Winston, 1962), pp. 192–198;

"Boy at Wrigley Field," in *Roads to Greatness,* edited by Louise Galloway (New York: Crowell-Collier, 1962), pp. 123–150;

"Five O'Clock Lightning," in *The Realm of Sport: A Classic Collection of the World's Great Sporting Events and Personalities as Recorded by the Most Distinguished Writers,* edited by Herbert Warren Wind (New York: Simon & Schuster, 1966), pp. 51–55;

"'Nice Guys Are in Last Place,' Says Leo," in *From Cobb to "Catfish": 128 Illustrated Stories from Baseball Digest,* edited by John Kuenster (Chicago: Rand McNally, 1975), pp. 122–123;

"Tell Me about Babe Ruth . . . " and "Whitey Ford: Hard-Boiled Yankee," in *Sport Magazine's All-Time All Stars,* edited by Tom Murray (New York: Atheneum, 1977), pp. 170–191, 225–232;

"Kenesaw Mountain Landis," in *The Baseball Anthology: 125 Years of Stories, Poems, Articles, Photographs, Drawings, Interviews, Cartoons, and Other Memorabilia,* edited by Joseph Wallace (New York: Abrams, 1994), pp. 143–145, 147.

SELECTED PERIODICAL PUBLICATIONS–UNCOLLECTED:

FICTION

"Hail and Farewell," *Collier's,* 108 (13 December 1941): 72, 84–85.

NONFICTION

"Friendliness–The Babe Knows Its Worth," *American Magazine,* 112 (August 1931): 71, 135;

"Katie's Hero," *Collier's,* 106 (20 July 1940): 12, 44;

"Big League Hotfoot," *American Magazine,* 130 (October 1940): 53, 116;

"Right Field, New York," *Collier's,* 108 (13 September 1941): 34, 36–38;

"The Care and Feeding of Jockeys," *Collier's,* 109 (7 February 1942): 26, 42, 44;

"The Bullpen," *Saturday Evening Post,* 214 (13 June 1942): 26, 70, 72–73;

"The Kid from Sunnyside," *Collier's,* 110 (5 December 1942): 13, 58;

"Weep No More My Lady: The Derby Comes Once More to Kentucky," *Look,* 8 (2 May 1944): 56–59;

"Indestructible Shortstop," *Collier's,* 124 (9 July 1949): 32, 40;

"Here Come the Dodgers Again," *Look,* 17 (8 September 1953): 58–59.

A mild-mannered, soft-spoken, diminutive man, once described by a friend, Bob Reilly, as being "psychopathically polite," Frank Graham was recognized in his day as one of the finest sportswriters: a consummate reporter, a master of precise prose, and the man who revolutionized his profession through his unsurpassed talent with the conversational sports column. Few have ever approached his ability to reproduce the talk of the dugouts, clubhouses, and locker rooms of sport; none have created more artful material from casual, behind-the-scenes banter. Graham never intruded upon the scenes he described, instead stepping out of the picture while letting the story unfold. He crafted consistently fine columns without ever taking notes, relying on a faultless memory, a talent he characteristically downplayed. Graham was widely liked and respected both within and outside the sporting world and sportswriting fraternity.

Frank Graham was born on 12 November 1893 in the East Harlem borough of New York City, the youngest of four children of David Graham and Frances Sullivan Graham, who died giving birth to Frank. His son, Frank Graham Jr., recounts much of his father's early life in his autobiographical memoir, *A Farewell to Heroes* (1981). He was raised by a grandmother and a sister and saw little of his father, a Tammany Hall functionary. As a boy Graham suffered from a form of spinal meningitis, which cost him the sight in his right eye. An indifferent student, he dropped out of high school in the ninth grade and through the efforts of a brother, Harold, obtained work as a telephone company messenger, a job he held for six years.

Although only five feet, five inches tall and weighing little more than one hundred pounds, and despite his impaired vision, Graham was a capable sandlot ballplayer and went undefeated in six amateur boxing matches. His passion for boxing and his desire to write about the sport began as a young teenager as he watched other fighters train. While still working for the telephone company, he began to write, selling freelance boxing pieces to New York daily newspapers and to Ned Brown, a sportswriter who published *Boxing* magazine. Recommended by Brown, Graham was hired by *New York Sun* sports editor Joc Vila in late 1914. Initially he worked as a crime reporter but later returned to the sports department. When one of the staff baseball reporters fell ill, Graham was assigned to cover the New York Giants during spring training in 1916. His concise, authoritative prose so impressed Damon Runyon, then writing for the *New York American,* that Runyon praised his work to Vila.

Although a product of the verbose, grandiloquent age of sportswriting, Graham, from his earliest work for the *Sun,* revealed a facility for the language and a respect for accuracy and precision. A careful observer, he eschewed hyperbole and conveyed atmosphere effectively. In a time when mass tastes hungered for sporting entertainments and savored every scrap of information about athletic heroes, Graham neither debunked nor sanctified the athletes about whom he wrote. As his close friend Red Smith pointed out in his *To Absent Friends* (1982), Graham

Graham, at a dinner in 1943 commemorating his retirement from the New York Sun, *receiving a parody cover of* Look *magazine from restaurateur Toots Shor*

"had been a newspaperman in the purest sense, a digger for truth, a reporter of facts." Graham wrote about a variety of sports, his favorites being boxing, baseball, and horse racing.

In autumn 1921 Graham took a one-month leave of absence from the *Sun* to write about European sports while touring battlefields with a brother, Wade, who had fought in World War I. While in Europe, Graham was based at the *Paris Herald;* he met and wrote about many interesting American expatriates and immersed himself in the vibrant life and culture of postwar Paris. His European travels and experiences widened his perspective through comparisons with American sports, athletes, and sporting environments, and his writing skills were honed by his vivid pen portraits of colorful characters and locales; but his chief interests remained in American playing fields, racetracks, and boxing arenas. On 17 October 1923 Graham married a distant cousin, Gertrude Lillian Whipp. They had four children, the eldest of whom, Frank Jr., also became a sportswriter, though he later switched to environmental writing.

Graham was a self-taught writer, whose lack of extensive formal education and disdain for higher education and educators generally belied an appreciation for reading and literature. His personal library, explored by his son Frank after his father's death, included travel literature, books of the sea, novels set in Paris and London, the early works of Ernest Hemingway, and Rudyard Kipling's *Ballads and Barrack-Room Ballads* (1892). He especially admired the lean, spare prose and stoic virtues of Hemingway's heroes in such short stories as "Fifty Grand," "The Killers," and "The Undefeated." The *Sun* featured a solid, highly regarded sports section, including the syndicated column of Grantland Rice, the most influential sportswriter of his time. Graham ghostwrote Rice's column at times when Rice was overwhelmed by other responsibilities. He formed lasting friendships with Rice and Smith, arguably the two most influential sportswriters of the twentieth century. Stylistically, however, he traveled his own distinctive path.

Graham covered the Giants through 1926 and became emotionally attached to the team and manager John McGraw, developing deep admiration and friendships with McGraw and many of his players. In later years he revisited the Giants of that era in several books and many articles and columns. From 1927 through the 1933 season he covered the New York Yankees. With Vila's death in the spring of 1934 Graham stood to become the sports editor of the *Sun* but preferred instead to assume Vila's sports column. It proved to be a perfect decision. As Frank Graham Jr. commented: "The column was, and remained, all that he ever really wanted out of his professional life. He had almost total freedom to make up his mind about what he wanted to do every day and how he wanted to treat what he saw."

Between 1 May 1934 and 31 August 1943, for six days per week, Graham used his column, "Setting the Pace," to transform the sportswriting craft with his ability to capture scene and atmosphere while re-creating the kind of nonchalant talk that sports fans almost never hear. His first column, an interview with heavyweight challenger Max Baer and his manager, Ancil Hoffman, shortly before Baer's defeat of champion Primo Carnera, was typical of much of his best work with its crisp, concise description, precise word choice, and totally realistic talk:

> There was the sudden crash of knuckles against the door and it swung open to admit the challenger for the heavyweight championship. He wore a gray and plaid suit, a gray shirt, a brown and white plaid tie and gray suede shoes. He was hatless, but a belted top coat hung in the crook of his left arm.
>
> "I was just saying," said Hoffman, "that you are sure that you are going to knock out Carnera."
>
> "I will lay him out flatter than a tablecloth," said Max.
>
> "You see?" said Hoffman. "He knows all the answers."
>
> "Sure," said Max. "I can't miss. Everybody who ever fought that big bum has hit him on the chin, but none of them can hit like I can. When I hit him on the chin he will go down and stay there."
>
> He flung the top coat across the chair.
>
> "How do I look?" he demanded. "Pretty good, eh? I look better than that. I look wonderful."

Graham accepted Baer's braggadocio because it was a natural component of the fighter's personality. As a perceptive, analytical critic, however, he was unsparing in detecting the many gaps and flaws in Baer's unlettered boxing technique.

On another occasion, a casual conversation with Yankees pitcher Charley Ruffing while waiting for the Yankees to depart from Grand Central Station for Cincinnati during the 1939 World Series provided candid comments for Graham's 6 October 1939 column:

> Charley Ruffing stood near the gate to the train. Nobody in the crowd of commuters hurrying by recognized him. He stood there talking to a couple of newspaper men.
>
> "How's your arm?" the other newspaper man asked.
>
> "Sore," Ruffing said. "It feels just like I had lead in my elbow."
>
> "How did it feel yesterday?"
>
> "It felt pretty good," he said. "It don't hurt me so much when I pitch, but it hurts the next day. I'm going to have it looked at as soon as the series is over."
>
> "How about your head?" The newspaper man asked.
>
> "My head's all right," Ruffing said. "If my arm was as good as my head I would be all right."

In the 1930s Graham was already being recognized as one of the finest sports columnists of his time. In his book *City Editor* (1934), Stanley Walker, city editor of the *New York Herald Tribune,* praised Graham's column, calling it "one of the best ever seen. Graham's stuff is pleasant, lucid and informative." During the Depression, Graham began to supplement his newspaperman's income with freelance writing, contributing regularly to *Baseball Magazine* and, in 1932, writing two children's books for a small midwestern publishing house. His salary at the *Sun,* a notoriously parsimonious organization, was never commensurate with his talents. After having achieved considerable success with a juvenile biography, *Lou Gehrig: A Quiet Hero* (1942), he wrote his final *Sun* column on 31 August 1943 and left to become sports editor of *Look* magazine.

His time spent at *Look*–little more than a year–was not enjoyable. Although toiling diligently to inject professionalism and style in the sports section, he was handicapped by editorial decision-making by committee, coupled with the necessity to write and edit copy, produce a sports quiz, and achieve a reasonable balance between topical sports news and lightweight fare. While sharpening the focus of the magazine and eliminating some of its pictorial fluff pieces, Graham was unable to significantly upgrade its overall sporting content. He found himself writing about a variety of sports that little interested him–college basketball, women's tennis, high-school track and field–and professed a desire to return to newspaper work. Only in an atmospheric, nostalgic look at the Kentucky Derby, "Weep No More My Lady: The Derby Comes Once More to Kentucky" (2 May 1944), did his love for the subject combine with his literary skill to dramatize the emotional attraction of the event:

> The field for the Kentucky Derby is coming to the track. The crowd stands silent, and from the massed bands come, softly, the strains of "My Old Kentucky Home."
>
> In this moment the spectators reach the highest emotional pitch achieved at any sports event, surpassing even that breathless space when a heavyweight champion and his challenger shuffle their feet in their corners, waiting for the opening bell. This moment at Churchill Downs tightens your throat, and once having known the thrill of it, you'll never again hear "The sun shines bright in the old Kentucky home . . ." without being whisked back in fancy, to the Downs on Derby day, without seeing the motionless crowd, its multiple voices stilled, and the jockeys in their bright silks on the backs of the sleek three year olds, coming to the paddock.

Graham left *Look* in December 1944 and worked as a freelance writer until, through Runyon's efforts, he received and accepted an offer to write a daily sports column for the *New York Journal American.* He wrote "Graham's Corner" from 10 September 1945 until 21 December 1964, returning to the life he loved best: covering his favorite sports, often accompanied by close friends and colleagues Rice, Smith, and W. C. Heinz. During this time Smith and Graham, upon entering the Hialeah racetrack clubhouse, were described by *Journal American* racing writer Pat Lynch as "1 and 1-A," comparing them to a perfectly complementary pair of thoroughbreds from the same racing stable entered in the same championship race.

Graham was in many ways a traditionalist, seeking comfort in time-honored rituals, long-standing institutional verities, and familiar environments such as the Twentieth Century Fight Club in the "Jacobs Beach" section of Manhattan, major-league dugouts, and racetrack clubhouses. As sport and society changed in the years after World War II, he was less comfortable confronting those changes. The role of the sportswriter and sports columnist, who once represented the only practical source of information for the avid sports fan in the years between the world wars, altered as increased radio and television broadcasts opened new vistas for viewers and listeners, who began to demand more facts, quotes, and colorful asides from the sports pages. Aggressive, ambitious younger sportswriters such as Dick Young, Jimmy Breslin, and Roger Kahn emerged, eager to obtain exclusives through arduous digging for inside information. What they and others presaged was a more personal style of sports journalism that probed behind the scenes and explored controversial issues. Brash, iconoclastic writers generated blunt, provocative questions in confrontational fashion, seeking sharp quotes and finding ironic bits of humor in tangential or totally irrelevant matters.

Graham never passed judgment on his fellow sportswriters in print and retained a light touch even when writing critically. In a 12 August 1963 column in the *Journal American* on former middleweight champion Gene Fullmer, Graham advised the fighter to retire after suffering a bad beating at the hands of champion Dick Tiger. Graham noted that Fullmer's manager, Marv Jensen, had been unable to teach his fighters to box properly, yet conveyed that thought in such a manner that it did not seem offensive. Remaining faithful to his basic writing style, he kept his distance from the concerns of the new sports journalism and reverted more often to past heroes or memories stirred through chance encounters with old friends on the sports beat. Frank Graham Jr. related how his father once told him that he was no longer a part of the "dugout fixtures," that he was now perceived as an elder by the players, which minimized the kind of spontaneity he had preserved in his best prewar columns. Many of Graham's columns and articles of the 1950s and 1960s recycle older material and subject matter. Yet some of his finest magazine work was produced during that period.

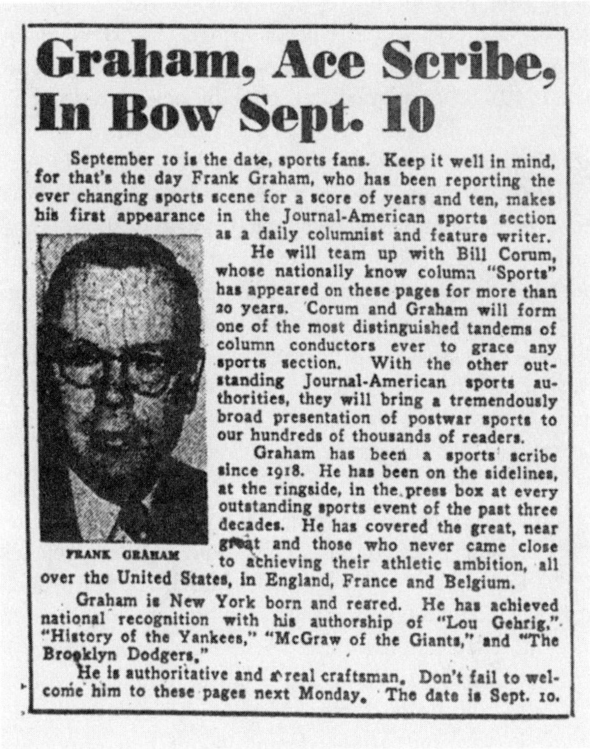

Graham, Ace Scribe, In Bow Sept. 10

September 10 is the date, sports fans. Keep it well in mind, for that's the day Frank Graham, who has been reporting the ever changing sports scene for a score of years and ten, makes his first appearance in the Journal-American sports section as a daily columnist and feature writer.

He will team up with Bill Corum, whose nationally know column "Sports" has appeared on these pages for more than 20 years. Corum and Graham will form one of the most distinguished tandems of column conductors ever to grace any sports section. With the other outstanding Journal-American sports authorities, they will bring a tremendously broad presentation of postwar sports to our hundreds of thousands of readers.

Graham has been a sports scribe since 1918. He has been on the sidelines, at the ringside, in the press box at every outstanding sports event of the past three decades. He has covered the great, near great and those who never came close to achieving their athletic ambition, all over the United States, in England, France and Belgium.

Graham is New York born and reared. He has achieved national recognition with his authorship of "Lou Gehrig," "History of the Yankees," "McGraw of the Giants," and "The Brooklyn Dodgers."

He is authoritative and a real craftsman. Don't fail to welcome him to these pages next Monday. The date is Sept. 10.

FRANK GRAHAM

Announcement in the New York Journal American, *4 September 1945*

Graham contributed articles for *Collier's, The Saturday Evening Post,* and *American Magazine* and wrote for *Baseball Digest* for nearly twenty-five years until his death. His best-known magazine work appeared in *Sport,* a magazine that premiered in September 1946 and featured in-depth articles from the leading sportswriters of the day. Graham wrote for *Sport* almost from its inception, mixing his fund of sporting lore and history with profound respect for the greats, near-greats, and colorful fringe characters in an ongoing series, "One for the Book," that began in February 1949 and continued well into the next decade. The series reflects both his strengths and weaknesses as a magazine writer–at worst, an overreliance on hackneyed material, loosely connected anecdotes, and abrupt, formless endings. In other pieces, notably in his writing about horse racing, boxing, and reminiscences of special friends and heroes, he creates elegiac word pictures and transports the reader to a time and ambiance that he knew well and re-created with fidelity. As in his newspaper work, Graham was never obtrusive. He remained outside his recollections, never referring to himself in the first person; yet his presence is clear, his descriptions vivid.

Two of his finest pieces in *Sport* profile great fighting champions, Henry Armstrong ("They Called Him Hammerin' Henry," November 1952) and Stanley Ketchel ("The Legend of Stanley Ketchel," March 1953)–rugged, aggressive crowd favorites separated by time, weight, and race but reflecting the style and verve that Graham valued highly. Describing Armstrong's style, Graham writes: "Even the old timers around New York admitted they'd never seen a fighter just like Henry before. If an opponent elected to stand and slug, Henry blanketed him with punches. If he tried to run, Henry herded him along the ropes, or pinned him in a corner and hit him until he fell down–or a merciful referee intervened. Hammerin' Henry, his newspaper nickname, served him well." Ketchel was shot and killed by a jealous ranch hand in 1910. Graham recounted the reaction of two of his friends at the time:

> In New York, Hype Igoe, sportswriter, and Wilson Mizner, wit and cynic, both pals of Ketchel's, heard that he had been shot, that he had been moved to a hospital and that his condition was critical.
>
> "Steve's going to die," Hype whispered, as they huddled over a drink.
>
> Mizner shook his head. "No," he said. "All they have to do is count over him and he'll get up."
>
> But Mizner was wrong. Ketchel never even heard the count.

A subsequent piece, "Galento–The Grotesque Gladiator" (April 1957), reveals another facet of Graham's talent: writing a lead paragraph that combines a definitive anecdote, perceptively related, to delineate the essence of his subject:

> On the June night in 1935 that Jim Braddock won the heavyweight championship from Max Baer, there was a preliminary bout between a fighter called Young Hippo, six feet four inches tall and wrought in the classic mold, and a short, pot-bellied bruiser out of Orange, New Jersey. In his corner, before the bell, Hippo appeared to be bored. Crossing his legs, he leaned back against the ring post and yawned as he looked over the crowd jamming the Madison Square Garden Bowl in Long Island City. Within a very short time after the bell rang, he completely lost interest in the proceedings; the squat one hit him on the chin with a left hook and knocked him unconscious.
>
> Thus did Tony Galento, with one punch, broaden his horizons.

Although Graham was universally considered a gentle man with a gentle writing style, he could be blunt when he saw fit. In a June 1956 piece for *Sport,* "Say, Isn't That Willie Pep in There?"–on the ring wanderings of the broke, embattled former featherweight champion, reduced to fighting nonentities for meager purses before sparse crowds–Graham flatly asserts that Pep had thrown his controversial 1954 fight against Lulu Perez. Throughout his career Graham admonished once-great veterans to quit the ring when their skills had clearly eroded. In other *Sport* pieces he was sharply critical of baseball greats Bob Feller, who he chided for a materialistic, self-centered approach to the game that included rejecting several All-Star Game appearances, and Joe DiMaggio, regarding his surly, self-imposed isolation as his skills diminished during a final, injury-plagued season in 1951.

Many of Graham's pieces reflect the New York ambiance of the 1920s and the influences of Runyon and Hemingway in terms of characterization, atmosphere, and dialogue. Graham loved the offbeat, shadowy figures and rogues that dwelt on the fringes of his favorite sports–the gamblers, bookies, struggling horse trainers and injury-riddled jockeys, and fight managers and promoters hustling for a buck or demonstrating the resiliency to continue in search of that elusive big payday. His zeal for savage brawlers and rowdies sometimes exceeded normal literary parameters, lapsing into florid grandiloquence. In a piece for *Sport,* "The Fabulous Harry Greb" (May 1952), for example, Graham writes: "When it came to brawling in the ring, he and Harry were kindred souls. To each, the crash of skull against the other's was sweet music, the scratch of the laces across the face a feeling sublime. They were two of a kind." Yet, Graham often sought to check himself when his enthusiasm for the untamed primitives rumbled to the surface. He often gently qualified his statements or prefaced them with a kind of bemused retrospection, reflecting on an earlier era and viewpoints he held that were no longer secure. Writing in *Sport* (December 1949), Graham chronicles the promotional career of Jack Hurley during professional wrestling's greatest era in the

Graham being congratulated by heavyweight champion Floyd Patterson after receiving the James J. Walker Memorial Award from the Boxing Writers Association (from Frank Graham Jr., A Farewell to Heroes, *1981)*

1920s and 1930s and rhapsodized about many classic matches. He noted, however, in regard to the present dubious legitimacy of the sport, that he was unsure when "the change was made and the script rewritten." He ruefully concluded, "Am I naive in believing that this, and many other matches that followed it, were on the level? It must seem so, in light of what has happened in the years between." He also came to realize the need to temper his romanticism and stylistic digressions, especially when speculating on a subject's course of action, or the basis for specific behavior. In "Tell 'Em What I Done to Philadelphia Jack O'Brien" (December 1954), Graham ruminates as to why his subject chose a boxing career, only to curtail his musings with an abrupt "Let's stop being romantic." Yet he could also state the following: "The names of most of the men he met that year [1901] have been forgotten. Some of them will be remembered always. . . . Remembered by whom? It is a question well advanced and well-taken. The answer is by those who saw or heard of them in their youth, and who pore over the boxing records." Such a comment illustrates an idiosyncrasy Graham exhibited throughout his career–his habit of resurrecting the memories of past heroes to better preserve their exploits in a world he believed was rapidly losing its ability and desire to remember.

Graham was a member of the editorial board of judges for the first volume of the E. P. Dutton series *Best Sports Stories,* which appeared in 1945. He was represented several times in that series; in 1955 his sensitive piece "My Friend Grantland Rice," initially published in *Sport* (November 1954), was awarded second place among the magazine articles of that year. During his career Graham wrote many articles and columns that served as literary memorials for deceased friends, fellow writers, and sporting notables. These pieces reflect his reporter's knowledge and understanding of his subjects, together with the ability to make them real without conferring layers of sanctification.

Graham had known Rice for forty years, and the two men were close friends for half that period. In the years after World War II, together with Red Smith, they shared a predilection for an obscure Florida racetrack, Sunshine Park, that gained a measure of fame through their writings. Years before, Rice had defended Graham and other baseball writers when their credibility was questioned in a verbal scrap with McGraw, who had disavowed some incendiary remarks he had made about National League officials after being fined for an altercation with an umpire in Cincinnati. In his tribute Graham confronts some of the exaggerated notions written about Rice after his death and proceeds to reveal essential aspects of Rice's personality and character through judicious anecdotes and personal insights. In a strikingly similar vein Graham's retrospective piece "Tell Me about Babe Ruth . . . " (*Sport,* October 1954) provides a penetrating, well-rounded account, combining anecdotal and controversial passages and Graham's familiarity with Ruth and many of the events described. Writing from memory, Graham commits several factual errors, but his restrained style conveys the remarkable essence of the man without any recourse to sensationalism nor any need to expound on his excesses. Describing Ruth, Graham writes, "He was warmhearted, fabulously generous, genuinely fond of children, greatly moved by the ills and trials of others, devoted to his family and his friends–and would not have known how to deal with an enemy for the simple reason that he never had one."

Graham's first book with a sports-oriented theme, *Lou Gehrig: A Quiet Hero,* is a popular biography aimed at younger readers; the book was a best-seller, garnered good reviews, passed through multiple printings, and, as noted by Frank Graham Jr., played a significant role in getting countless adolescent boys interested in reading while creating a cottage industry for baseball biographies that has not yet expired. Graham relates the broad outlines of Gehrig's life with relatively brief attention paid to his statistical achievements and individual seasonal highlights. He builds chapters upon informative anecdotes and realistic, if hypothetical, conversational passages that blend well and make for enjoyable, effortless reading. The Gehrig biography is entertaining and well-crafted but not probing, avoiding controversy. Writing of Gehrig's fatal illness and early death is nearly impossible without manifesting excessive sentiment; inevitably Graham fell victim, devoting an inordinate amount of space to that period and at times resorting to maudlin hypothetical musings on Gehrig's state of mind and thought processes in his final weeks. He writes nothing of substance concerning Gehrig's antipathy toward McGraw, linked to his loss of amateur status for one year after playing minor-league baseball briefly at Hartford under an assumed name, nor about the basis for his falling out with Ruth, nor about the delicate relationship between Gehrig's wife and his extremely protective and domineering mother. Graham undoubtedly knew more than what he wrote but never sought sensationalism for its own sake, and so simply avoids sensitive subject areas.

Graham's next baseball biography is *McGraw of the Giants: An Informal Biography* (1944). Having covered the team for a decade, Graham knew McGraw and many of his players well. Loved by his friends and reviled by his enemies, McGraw was a complex personality, and Graham provides a fuller portrait than in writing about the relatively colorless Gehrig. Reviewing the book in *The New York Times* (21 May 1944), James Hutchins said that Graham "does not altogether explain" McGraw. "He chooses instead to tell his story, quite objectively and in valid, easy prose–never making a superman of him and never whitewashing him." Typically, Graham's biography confines itself almost exclusively to McGraw's baseball career. No mention is made of his brief first marriage, nor of the loss of his mother and four siblings in a diphtheria epidemic when he was twelve years old. Nor does the reader encounter a rationale for the murkier aspects of McGraw's character–his drinking, brawling, gambling, and business connections with the underworld gambler and moneyman Arnold Rothstein, and the many bribe allegations linked to team functionaries and supporters. Graham's experiences in a world populated by assorted gangsters, fixers, rogues, scoundrels, and sinners developed within him a remarkable tolerance of human frailties and flaws.

For the purist and baseball historian the omissions and factual errors are annoying. Graham excelled in his ability to encapsulate his subjects, describing them at various stages of their lives, which was the hallmark of the perceptive powers of a careful observer and professional wordsmith. On the opening page of the book he portrays McGraw, warts and all, and clearly defines the parameters circumscribing the biography:

> He was, distinctly, a robust temperament. He was generous and loyal to his friends, implacable toward his foes. He was vain about some things, extremely modest about others. He irritated persons in the mass and charmed them as individuals. His charities were numerous, and he genuinely resented any attempt to publicize them. He forgave many injuries done to him–but forgot none of them. He enjoyed many fine friendships and had many quarrels.
>
> It has been said of him that he would have been as successful in any other field as he was in baseball because he possessed the qualities that would have made him a leader wherever his choice had rested. Perhaps. Yet there is nothing in the record to bear this out. The record is that whenever he ventured beyond baseball he failed dismally, and that he lost tremendous sums playing the races, dabbling in oil and speculating in Florida real estate.
>
> But in fairness to him, since he devoted his life to baseball, he should be judged only in that field–and in that field he was touched with genius.

Graham (right) and fellow sportswriter Red Smith at the Saratoga Racetrack, Saratoga Springs, New York

Despite the passage of more than half a century, Graham's McGraw biography can be read today and retains a wonderfully entertaining quality.

Graham's two other biographies were less successful. His editor at G. P. Putnam's Sons, Wallace Hanger, suggested that he expand his literary horizons. Fresh from the success of his earlier works, Graham left *Look* in December 1944 to work as a freelance writer. He agreed to write a biography of Al Smith, the recently deceased former governor of New York and unsuccessful Democratic Party candidate for the presidency in 1928. The result, *Al Smith, American: An Informal Biography* (1945), was, partly due to Smith family interference, an unpleasant experience for Graham to write and a disappointing book. In *A Farewell to Heroes* Frank Graham Jr. relates that his father never glanced at the final galleys of the book before it went to print.

What successfully enlivened McGraw's career fails to energize the life and times of the quintessential New York machine politician who transcended his humble ethnic origins to gain national prominence. Graham was certainly comfortable portraying the Lower East Side of New York City at the turn of the century and the political ambiance of Tammany Hall with its colorful cast of characters. Smith's political progression is related in workmanlike fashion, but the essence of the man and his family remains elusive, as does any true understanding of the major issues he confronted and the basis for his policy decisions and core beliefs. The anecdotes that animate sports-related subjects seem in *Al Smith, American* more like a collection of sketches that portray Smith in a pleasant light without any real substance or depth. Too often the book is suffused with banalities that add little. Graham treats Smith's later life superficially and makes no attempt to evaluate his political significance. Reviewers considered the book a popular and sympathetic work, providing a vivid picture of time and place but too readily passing over Smith's errors and omissions and inadequate from the analytical viewpoint. Graham never intended his biographies to be comprehensive, but he never again ventured beyond the world of sports in his literary endeavors.

Boxing referee Ruby Goldstein told his life story to Graham in *Third Man in the Ring* (1959). A promising lightweight contender whose career fell short of expectations after several knockout defeats in key bouts and a strangely ambivalent attitude toward his profession, Goldstein stumbled uncertainly through life for years after his boxing career ended until he found his true calling as a referee while serving as an army physical-training instructor during World War II. He became a nationally recognized celebrity with the arrival of television in the 1950s, officiating many televised bouts during the brief period of public infatuation with boxing.

In recounting Goldstein's story (told in the first person), Graham traverses familiar New York city terrain. Goldstein was the youngest of four children of a poor immigrant Jewish family, attracted early on to the neighborhood boxing milieu with its fight clubs, local rivalries, and an unpredictable blend of selfless, decent individuals hoping to mold and create champions, and assorted gamblers, mobsters, and scoundrels waiting to exploit young talent. Graham conveys this environment skillfully. At its core, however, this book also seems hollow. Too little is known about the origin of Goldstein's self-doubt, nor why his mother's presence and his religious beliefs so strongly influenced his career, nor why he failed in critical bouts. The reader learns much behind-the-scenes information of the referee's craft and can take heart in Goldstein's successful efforts to reconstruct his life, but the excessively sentimental tone (criticized by an unnamed reviewer in the 28 November 1959 issue of *The New Yorker*) mars the overall effect.

Graham's finest books are his trilogy of baseball team histories: *The New York Yankees: An Informal History* (1943), *The Brooklyn Dodgers: An Informal History* (1945), and *The New York Giants: An Informal History of a Great Baseball Team* (1952), part of a series of books published by Putnam in the 1940s and 1950s. Writing in the *Cooperstown Review* (1993), baseball historian Peter C. Bjarkman, in a comprehensive review article on literature related to the Dodgers franchise, refers to Graham's "unsurpassed tome in the landmark Putnam series of the 1940s" as the standard source on the era before Roger Kahn's *The Boys of Summer* (1972). The next year, in "The Home Team: Team Histories as Baseball Literature," also published in the *Cooperstown Review,* Bjarkman reiterated his praise for both the Putnam series and Graham. He contended that, in the genre of baseball team histories, the best of them emphasize plot structure akin to well-crafted novels, a wealth of memorable characters, and a clearly defined team personality. Graham's trilogy consistently adheres to those standards. They combine his flawless narrative skills, firsthand knowledge of the principals, fringe characters, and long-forgotten lore, and a striking sense for the dramatic moments. The books have remained fresh, wonderfully informative, and lively, and their factual errors are relatively few and generally minor.

The New York Yankees went through many reprintings, three editions, and was excerpted in each of Charles Einstein's three-volume anthology *The Fireside Book of Baseball.* In an appreciation note at the beginning, Graham extends his gratitude to former Yankees pitcher Waite Hoyt, a team member from 1921 to 1930, for much background information and insights. Hoyt provided similar material for many Yankee team histories and individual player biographies. Graham's Yankees team history merges plot, characters, and team personality in typically fluid, facile, unhurried fashion. His portrayals of greats and near greats are deft, key games and incidents are concisely described, and conversational passages carry a ring of authenticity. He relates, for example, an exchange that took place after the Yankees had won the first two games of the 1927 World Series from the Pittsburgh Pirates in Pittsburgh:

> Now the series shifted to New York. As the Yankees were riding down to the station that night, a newspaperman in a cab with Lazzeri and three other players said:
>
> "If you fellows don't wind this series up in the next two games, I'll shoot you."
>
> And Lazzeri said: "If we don't beat these bums four in a row, you can shoot me first."

Graham's history handles smoothly the few and straightforward changes within team ownership and management. The narrative adheres to clearly delineated periods in the development of the team, each coherently leading into the next. Writing in the *SABR Review of Books* (1986), in a survey of New York Yankees baseball literature, baseball historian Mark Gallagher began his assessment with Graham's team history, which he terms "a solid and candid book . . . Graham didn't stir controversy, and neither did he duck it." No other history of the Yankees provides a better sense of the team's origins and its advance toward a position of dominance from the days of Ruth and Gehrig in the 1920s and 1930s to the DiMaggio era in the 1940s.

When Graham wrote his Brooklyn Dodger team history, that franchise had moved beyond its "Daffiness Boys" image of bumbling, congenial mediocrity and was on the brink of its most successful decade. Bjarkman writes that Graham's *The Brooklyn Dodgers* suffers "only from the unavoidable fact that the greatest moments of Brooklyn baseball history had not yet happened. For the early foundational years of the franchise birth and struggle, the entrepreneurship of Charlie Ebbets, and the incomparable Daffiness sagas of the Wilbert Robinson years, Graham simply can not be matched as an authoritative source." Contemporary reviewers praised the book as "easily readable," "authoritative, appreciative," "temperate and tolerant, painstaking and accurate." Richard Maney, writing in *The New York Times Book Review* (3 June 1945), viewed the Dodgers in rather condescending fashion, stating that Graham "goes slumming" in contrast to his previous books and contending that the team deserved as interlocutor "a literary Hogarth, not a man trapped in the vise of fact." Nevertheless, Graham carefully threads his way from the origins of the team in 1883 into the twentieth century through seasons mired in the second division until the arrival of Larry MacPhail and Leo Durocher heralded a dramatic change in the fortunes of the team.

Graham's New York Giants team history is less of an original work; two-thirds are a condensation of his biography of McGraw, and the two decades under managers Bill Terry, Mel Ott, and Leo Durocher are distilled from many of his articles. More than with the Yankees and Dodgers, the history of the Giants is in large part the story of their managers, a fact Graham fully understood. The formula utilized in his earlier team histories again serves well, mixing narrative and anecdotes with a leavening of key games, incidents, and colorful characters while minimizing controversy.

In 1954 twenty of Graham's baseball pieces for *Sport* were anthologized in *Baseball Extra.* His final book, co-authored with Dick Hyman, is *Baseball Wit and Wisdom: Folklore of a National Pastime* (1962), an eclectic collection of drawings, cartoons, anecdotes, and oddities built around baseball themes.

In 1960 Graham underwent a serious stomach operation. He cut back to three columns weekly and focused more on nostalgic sporting memories and the passing of older athletic heroes. In one column he jested that he wished to be buried under a tree in the infield at Saratoga Racetrack. His last column appeared on 21 December 1964, a piece on Larry Doyle, a former Giant. Afflicted with terminal cancer, Graham suffered a skull fracture in a fall at his home in late February and died on 9 March 1965.

Graham was a member of several sportswriting associations and received countless awards and honors during his life and posthumously. He was awarded the J. G. Taylor Spink Award by the Baseball Writers Association of America in 1971, and with it, inclusion into the Writers Wing of the Baseball Hall of Fame. The Boxing Writers Association of America honored Graham's memory in 1997 with its A. J. Liebling Award for Outstanding Boxing Writing.

Respected for his honesty and journalistic integrity, Frank Graham was a man without pretense or artifice who shunned the spotlight but actively reached out to and assisted talented young writers and maintained consideration for the sensitivities of others. Such writers as Red Smith and Jimmy Cannon wrote of his profound impact in their field. Of the many words of tribute that were published after his death, Cannon's, in the 10 March 1965 *Journal American,* may sum him up best:

> A gentle man who seemed to walk on the tips of his toes as if he intended to pass through the world without disturbing anyone. He was, this shy and noble man, exactly as he wrote. The copy was pure and so was he. He typed it quickly on the toy machine with the dainty tapping of polite fingers. He frisked the characters of even the rogues for their good traits and cherished them for that. He was an original, this embarrassed poet, who changed sports writing, and brought to it the dignity of folk literature.

Like Smith and Cannon, Graham was one of the few sports columnists who was read not for what he said but for how he said it. He commented rarely about the nature of his craft, but in one instance, cited by Smith, he revealed his writing philosophy in basic terms: "My job is to take the reader behind the scenes where his ticket doesn't admit him–in the dugout and clubhouse, the football locker rooms, the jockeys' quarters, the fighter's locker room–and let him see what goes on there and hear what is said."

References:

Ira Berkow, *Red: A Biography of Red Smith* (New York: Times Books, 1986), pp. 82, 103–104, 128–129, 164–165;

Peter Bjarkman, "Bums Lit: The Literary Boys of Summer," *Cooperstown Review,* 1 (1993): 54–70;

Bjarkman, "The Home Team: Team Histories as Baseball Literature," *Cooperstown Review,* 2 (1994): 161–183;

Charles Fountain, *Sportswriter: The Life and Times of Grantland Rice* (New York: Oxford University Press, 1993), pp. 268–270, 273–274;

Frank Graham Jr., *A Farewell to Heroes* (New York: Viking, 1981);

Mark Gallagher, "A Tour of Yankee Literature," *SABR Review of Books,* (1986): 21–35;

Harold Rosenthal, "Two Crackerjack Books in the Graham Manner," *Editor and Publisher,* 91 (5 July 1958): 48;

Fred Russell, *Bury Me in an Old Press Box: Good Times and Life of a Sportswriter* (New York: Barnes, 1957), pp. 168, 195–196, 221;

Red Smith, "My Press Box Memories," *Esquire,* 84 (October 1975): 202–203, 250;

Smith, *To Absent Friends* (New York: Atheneum, 1982), 58–59;

Stanley Walker, *City Editor* (New York: Stokes, 1934), p. 130;

Stanley Woodward with Frank Graham Jr., *Sportswriter* (Garden City, N.Y.: Doubleday, 1967), pp. 47–51, 157–158.

David Halberstam

(10 April 1934 -   )

Adam R. Hornbuckle

MAJOR POSITIONS HELD: Reporter, *West Point (Mississippi) Daily Times Leader,* 1955–1956; reporter, *Nashville Tennessean,* 1956–1960; staff writer, *The New York Times,* 1960–1967; contributing editor, *Harper's,* 1967–1971.

David Halberstam (photograph by Bruce Plotkin; from the dust jacket for October 1964, *1994)*

BOOKS: *The Noblest Roman* (Boston: Houghton Mifflin, 1961);

The Making of a Quagmire: America and Vietnam During the Kennedy Era (New York: Random House, 1965);

One Very Hot Day (Boston: Houghton Mifflin, 1968; London: Bodley Head, 1968);

The Unfinished Journey of Robert Kennedy (New York: Random House, 1969; London: Barrie & Jenkins, 1970);

Ho (New York: Random House, 1971; London: Barrie & Jenkins, 1971);

The Best and the Brightest (New York: Random House, 1972; London: Barrie & Jenkins, 1972);

The Powers That Be (New York: Knopf, 1979; London: Chatto & Windus, 1979);

The Breaks of the Game (New York: Knopf, 1981);

The Amateurs (New York: Morrow, 1985; London: Hodder & Stoughton, 1986);

The Reckoning (New York: Morrow, 1986; London: Bloomsbury, 1987);

Summer of '49 (New York: Morrow, 1989);

The Next Century (New York: Morrow, 1991);

The Fifties (New York: Villard, 1993);

October 1964 (New York: Villard, 1994);

The Children (New York: Random House, 1998);

Playing for Keeps: Michael Jordan and the World He Made (New York: Random House, 1999; London: Yellow Jersey, 2000).

OTHER: *Stephen Crane, Great Stories of Heroism and Adventure,* edited, with an introduction, by Halberstam (New York: Platt & Munk, 1967);

Best American Sports Writing, 1991, edited, with an introduction, by Halberstam (New York: Houghton Mifflin, 1991);

"The Art of Robert Riger," in *The Sports Photography of Robert Riger* (New York: Random House, 1995), pp. 59–62;

Mark Vancil, ed., *The NBA at Fifty,* foreword by Halberstam (New York: Park Lane, 1996);

"The Passion, the Intensity, the History," in *The Kansas Century: 100 Years of Championship Jayhawk Basketball,* edited by Rich Clarkson (Kansas City: Andrews McMeel, 1997), pp. 22–25;

"History's Man," in *Jackie Robinson: Between the Baselines,* by Glenn Stout and Dick Johnson (San Francisco: Woodford, 1997), pp. 63–69;

Kenneth S. Robson, ed., *A Great and Glorious Game: Baseball Writings of A. Bartlett Giamatti,* foreword by Halberstam (Chapel Hill, N.C.: Algonquin Books, 1998);

"A Dynasty in the Making," in *ESPN SportsCentury,* edited by Michael MacCambridge (New York: Hyperion Press, 1999), pp. 21–31;

The Best American Sports Writing of the Century, edited, with an introduction, by Halberstam (New York: Houghton Mifflin, 1999);

"He Got a Shot in the NBA, and It Went In," in *The Best American Sports Writing 2000,* edited by Dick Schaap (New York: Houghton Mifflin, 1999), pp. 70–76;

"Jordan's Moment," in *The Best American Sports Writing 1999,* edited by Richard Ford (New York: Houghton Mifflin, 1999), pp. 57–68.

SELECTED PERIODICAL PUBLICATIONS–UNCOLLECTED: "An Instinct for the Game," *Atlantic Monthly,* 248 (October 1981): 76–84;

"Jackie Robinson," *Sport,* 77 (December 1986): 10–14;

"The Stuff Dreams Are Made Of," *Sports Illustrated,* 66 (29 June 1987): 38–40;

"The Great Joe D.," *New Yorker,* 22 (8 May 1989): 42–52;

"A Hero for the Wired World," *Sports Illustrated,* 75 (23 December 1991): 75–78;

"Anatomy of a Champion," in *The Best American Sports Writing 1996,* edited by John Feinstein (New York: Houghton Mifflin, 1996), pp. 138–147;

"How He Got Up There," *Time,* 151 (22 June 1998): 62–63.

Perhaps better known to most readers for titles such as *The Best and the Brightest* (1972), *The Powers That Be* (1979), *The Reckoning* (1986), *The Fifties* (1993), and *The Children* (1998), David Halberstam is also recognized as one of the leading American sportswriters. Although he never covered sports routinely for newspapers or sports magazines, Halberstam has written or edited seven books and several articles and other pieces on major-league baseball, professional and collegiate basketball, amateur rowing, and fencing. Each of his sports books occupied several weeks on *The New York Times* best-sellers' list. Yet, despite Halberstam's achievements in sportswriting, the genre is not his principal vocation but rather provides him with a break from more serious projects. He completed *The Amateurs* (1985), a character study of four young men contesting to represent the United States in the 1984 Olympic Games in the single-sculls rowing event, while researching and writing *The Reckoning,* an examination of American postindustrial decline. "When David is occupied with a big, bone-crushing masterwork, he gets in up to his armpits and needs to take a break," Harrison Salisbury observed in *People* magazine (4 November 1985), "he writes something for pure enjoyment. And that means sports, since he's the ultimate sports fan."

Salisbury's observation of Halberstam as the "ultimate sports fan" is obviously an exaggeration, but he has been an avid fan for most of his life. Although he describes himself as a nonathletic youth in the introduction to *Best American Sports Writing, 1991,* he competed in track and field at Roosevelt High School in Yonkers, New York. Rather than becoming an athlete himself, Halberstam became a sportswriting aficionado, and as a boy he admired sportswriters Red Smith, Jimmy Cannon, Leonard Gross, and Bill Heinz. He has observed that sports, unlike politics, provides writers the freedom to experiment with language and form and develop their own literary voice. Halberstam especially enjoyed reading *Sport,* one of the few nationally distributed sports magazines of the 1930s and 1940s. In *Best American Sports Writing, 1991* he refers to *Sport* as "one of the few places where the writing seemed serious, and one could sense the beginning of a literary touch, and an attempt to break out of the routine format of magazine writing of the day."

Like most young boys growing up in America during the first half of the twentieth century, David Halberstam followed baseball with great interest. Born in the Bronx borough of New York City on 10 April 1934 to Charles and Blanche Halberstam, he spent his early childhood within seven blocks of Yankee Stadium. In *Summer of '49* (1989), an examination of the American League pennant race between the New York Yankees and the Boston Red Sox that year, he reminisces about the first game he and his father attended together at Yankee Stadium in 1939. His father pointed out Joe DiMaggio to him, explaining why the Yankee outfielder was such a remarkable player, especially as a base runner. "Watch him go from first to third on a single," Halberstam recalls his father saying to him and vividly remembers that he "tried to see what I could not really comprehend: the grace of the great Yankee outfielder." Halberstam's father, a former military physician, returned to active duty during World War II, and as a result the family moved around the country, finally settling in Winstead, Connecticut. There Halberstam renewed his interest in the New York Yankees through reading his favorite sportswriters and listening to Mel Allen's radio broadcasts of the games. Boston Red Sox loyalties, however, extended into Connecticut, and Halberstam grew to appreciate the Red Sox and admire their superstar slugger, Ted Williams. His appreciation of the Red Sox came in part from his Uncle Harry, who visited the family often in Winstead from his home in

Dust jacket for Halberstam's account of the 1984 U.S. Olympic trials in single-sculls rowing

Boston. Halberstam impressed his uncle with his knowledge of baseball statistics and trivia, derived from reading *Sport* and the local sports pages. Uncle Harry, who owned season tickets to the Red Sox home games, in turn impressed his nephew, because he had seen the "players' faces up close" from his seat behind first base. Moreover, Uncle Harry knew intimate details about the players unrevealed by the sportswriters and broadcasters, such as the fact that Johnny Pesky's last name was actually Paveskovich. Halberstam, who attended Red Sox games with his uncle after the war, remembers "the seats being as good as he promised."

After World War II the Halberstams moved near Tuckahoe, in Westchester County, New York. In *Summer of '49* Halberstam remembers not feeling "accepted there, and, in turn, never accepted" his new home. "I was not particularly good at things boys are supposed to be good at," he confessed; "instead I was good at things (schoolwork) grown-ups want them to be good at but which, of course, win them no approval from their peers." In 1948 his father suffered a debilitating heart attack, thus compounding Halberstam's feelings of isolation and abandonment, and died after a second heart attack the following year. Halberstam found solace in baseball, becoming completely absorbed in the pennant race that year between the Yankees and the Red Sox, the two teams that had divided his loyalties over the previous decade. He went to several games at Yankee Stadium, sometimes sneaking off from school with his friends. Halberstam remembers how he "felt that season with remarkable clarity: my concern when DiMaggio was unable to play at the beginning of the season, and my elation when Tommy Henrich, who was my favorite player, carried the team in his absence."

After graduating from Roosevelt High School in 1951, Halberstam entered Harvard University. In *Best American Sports Writing, 1991* he recalls as a freshman "taking one of Red Smith's early collections, *Out of the Red,* from Harvard's Lamont Library and keeping it so long that I had to pay $13 in library fees, no small sum in 1951 dollars." Halberstam joined the editorial staff of the school newspaper, the *Harvard Crimson,* eventually becoming its managing editor. Although the position provided the prerequisite experience for a career in journalism, he did not feel truly prepared to be a reporter. Managing the *Crimson,* as he told Brian Lamb in an interview on C-SPAN (11 July 1993), only prepared him to "put out a paper six times a week for a very sophisticated audience," but not how to "interview ordinary people." Although he probably could have gained a position on a major metropolitan newspaper after graduation from Harvard in 1955, Halberstam decided to apprentice himself with a small newspaper and learn how to interview people. His apprenticeship took place at the *West Point Daily Times Leader,* the "smallest daily in the state of Mississippi," as he told Lamb. Halberstam described his time in West Point as "the greatest experience" of his life, as he "learned how to deal with ordinary people, to listen to them, to see the value in people who didn't agree with the same things I agreed."

In Mississippi Halberstam's journalistic efforts were focused mostly on stories about racial desegregation in the South. After joining the *Nashville Tennessean* in 1956 he got his first assignment from the sports desk, to cover the opening day of the Nashville Volunteers of the minor-league Southern Association. "The Nashville Volunteers played at a wondrous old ballpark called Sulphur Dell," which Halberstam describes in detail in the introduction to *Best American Sports Writing, 1991:*

> There where right field should have been were the old L&N railroad tracks, in effect decapitating right field and making it, as I recall, about 250 feet at the foul pole. In order to give the right fielder a chance, the

> architects of the park had landscaped right field so that it rose ever higher, and the fielder, not unlike a Swiss mountain climber, had to play on an incline. It was a disaster for some young left-handed Nashville hitters who, because of the temptation posed by the wall, developed what became known as the Sulphur Dell chop, a quick, controlled upswing at an unusually sharp angle, which, if the hitter connected, almost guaranteed a home run, but which finished the hitter forever with line drives.

Halberstam joined the staff of *The New York Times* in the fall of 1960. Initially assigned to the Washington bureau, he covered the presidential inauguration of John F. Kennedy in January 1961 and the early days of the Kennedy administration. Early in his career at the *Times,* Halberstam had the opportunity to meet and spend an evening with Jimmy Cannon, one of the sportswriting heroes of his boyhood. He admired Cannon especially, as he recalls in *Best American Sports Writing, 1991,* because his writing "gave the reader a sense of what . . . an important sports event had felt like to those deeply involved" in it. Their meeting, however, disappointed Halberstam because he could sense the "unbearable quality" of Cannon's loneliness. "If there is such a thing as the beginning of the end of innocence for a young man, then it comes at moments like that, of seeing someone who had been a hero, indeed perhaps a role model, and knowing instantly, that there is something dreadfully wrong with the way he has lived, that the price was too great."

In the fall of 1960 the *Times* sent Halberstam to the Congo to cover the political turmoil in the central African republic. That assignment, which proved to be both thrilling and life-threatening, marked the beginning of an award-winning career as a foreign correspondent. Halberstam won the Page One Award from the Newspaper Guild of New York for his reporting from the Congo in 1962. That year the *Times* assigned him to cover the war in South Vietnam and the increasing American involvement in it. Upon his arrival he encountered an official policy of reporting the war optimistically, but the misrepresentation of disasters such as the 1963 Battle of Ap Bac as victories convinced Halberstam to write frankly about what he observed in Southeast Asia. In 1963 Halberstam won the George Polk Memorial Award, and in 1964 he shared the Pulitzer Prize with Malcolm W. Browne of the Associated Press. Halberstam, Browne, and Neil Sheehan of United Press International shared the first Louis M. Lyons Award from the Nieman Fellows of Harvard University in 1964 for Conscience and Integrity in Journalism, for reporting "the truth as they saw it . . . without yielding to unrelenting pressures."

Beginning in 1964, Halberstam served a succession of assignments at the New York, Warsaw, and Paris bureaus of *The New York Times.* While working in New York he completed *The Making of a Quagmire: America and Vietnam During the Kennedy Era* (1965), a personalized account of his experience in Vietnam and an assessment of American policy. In January 1965 Halberstam worked in Warsaw, where he encountered opposition to his forthright reporting style. The Polish government accused him of maliciously representing Poland as racist and anti-Semitic and eventually expelled him from the country. While in Warsaw Halberstam married Elzbieta Cryzewska, then the most popular actress in Poland (whom he later divorced in 1977). After a brief period in Paris in 1966 Halberstam returned to New York, where he worked another year before resigning from the *Times* in April 1967.

When Halberstam worked at *The New York Times,* sportswriters ranked at the bottom of the hierarchy of journalists. Halberstam remembered the paper not placing much emphasis on sportswriting then, and writers such as Red Smith at the rival *New York Herald Tribune,* he writes in *Best American Sports Writing, 1991,* "were a source of embarrassment, if not to the editors of the paper, then to the reporters." Nevertheless, he remembers a certain "magnetic attraction that pulled some of our best-known journalists . . . to the sports department to talk to the sportswriters." Halberstam sensed in them and himself "a certain envy" when they talked to the sportswriters. Whereas the foreign correspondents may have been the stars of the newspaper, they realized "that the sportswriters had more fun, and also that they were allowed to earn a living and remain–as most people in the city room, for all of their fame, could not–little boys."

After resigning from *The New York Times* Halberstam became a contributing editor of *Harper's Magazine.* He spent four years with *Harper's,* writing about American politics and politicians, the 1968 presidential election campaign, and the Vietnam War. He completed three books during this time: *One Very Hot Day* (1968), a novel about Vietnamese troops and their American advisers; *The Unfinished Journey of Robert Kennedy* (1969), a chronicle of the political career of the assassinated presidential candidate; and *Ho* (1971), a biography of Ho Chi Minh, the political leader of North Vietnam. In 1971 Halberstam resigned from *Harper's* and became a freelance author, writing for a variety of magazines, including the *Atlantic Monthly, Esquire, Harper's Bazaar,* and *McCall's.* In 1972 he published *The Best and the Brightest,* a critically acclaimed study of the domestic origins of the Vietnam War, the men who made the decisions to go to war, and the men who conducted it.

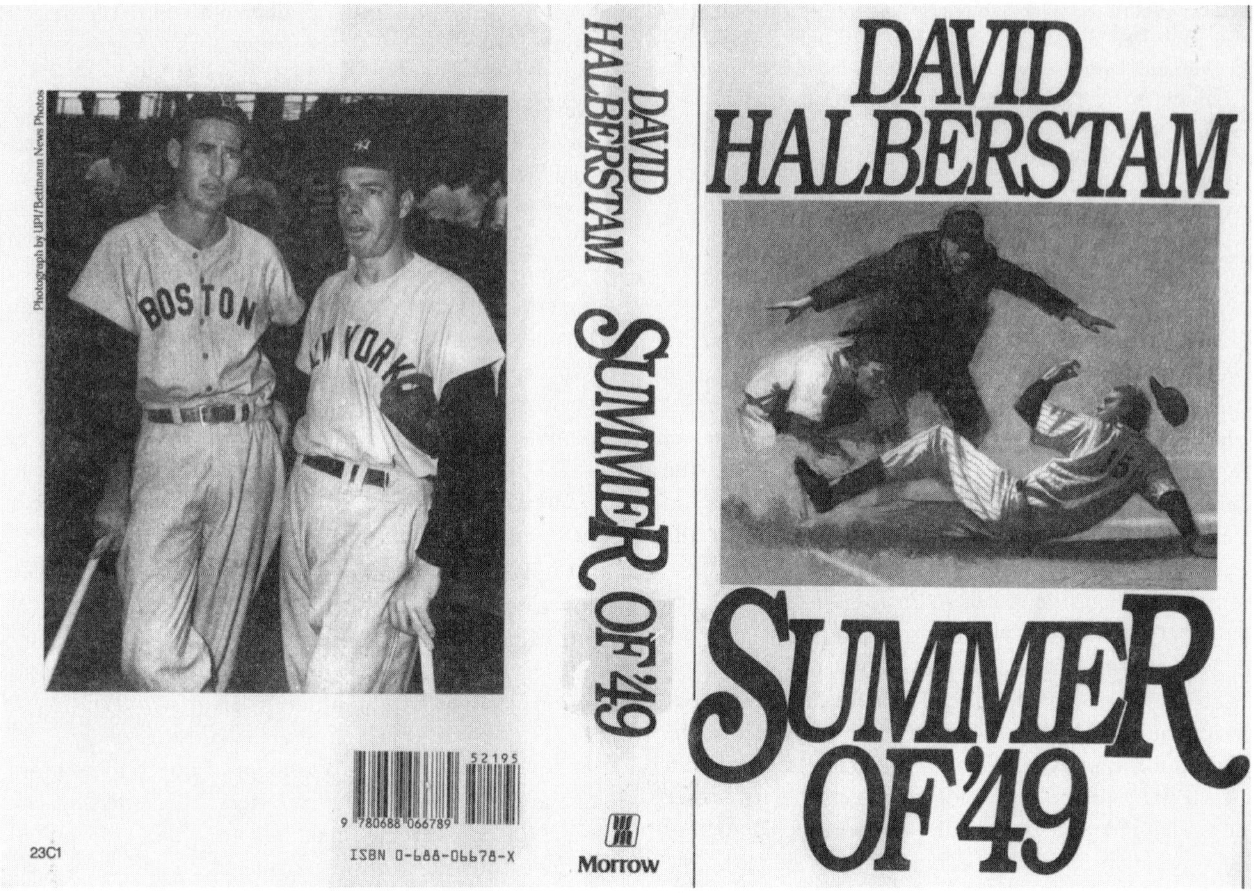

Dust jacket for Halberstam's 1989 memoir recounting his obsession, in the wake of his father's death, with the 1949 American League pennant race

Halberstam's writing, by the 1970s, reflected the style and form of the "new journalism," which Leonard Downie Jr. described in *The New Muckrakers* (1976) as "detailed reporting presented with the techniques of fiction: colorful style, extensive description, experimental use of language and punctuation, changing points of view, personal commentary from the writer, juxtaposed facts creating a desired dramatic effect, and even views from inside the minds of the characters in the narrative." As a practitioner of the new journalism Halberstam approached his subject as a novelist, exhibiting a flair for the dramatic, a highly personal appreciation for his material, and exhaustive character development and analysis. He asserts in *Best American Sports Writing, 1991* that the new journalism had its roots in sportswriting. In writing about sports, "authors could experiment, find their voice, and be rewarded for breaking out of form (after all, a beat writer who covered 154 baseball games using the same form every day was not only boring his readers, he was boring himself)."

Following the publication of *The Powers That Be* in 1979, Halberstam began to work on his first sports project, an examination of professional basketball focusing on the Portland Trail Blazers of the National Basketball Association (NBA). The Trail Blazers, in only their sixth season in the league, won the 1977 NBA championship, defeating the Philadelphia 76ers. Halberstam's research consisted of spending the 1979–1980 season with the team, traveling across the country and interviewing its management, owners, coaches, players, and opponents. The book that emerged from this project, *The Breaks of the Game,* was published in 1981, but he first wrote "An Instinct for the Game," an article published in the *Atlantic Monthly* in October 1981. "An Instinct for the Game" profiles two Portland personnel, Morris Buckwalter, a Trail Blazer scout and former NBA player of the late 1950s and early 1960s, and Billy Ray Bates, a rookie recruited and signed by Buckwalter. Through these individuals Halberstam shows how professional basketball had evolved from a game of fundamental passes, layups, and two-hand set shots played predominantly by whites in the 1950s to one of blind, behind-the-back passes, long-range jump shots, and slam dunks played predominantly by African

Americans in the 1970s. Buckwalter, who represented the old style of play, recognized at the end of his career that "the coming of the black athletes had changed the game and made players like himself obsolete." Bates, a promising young black player from Mississippi, epitomized Buckwalter's observation, as he "had something extra, something that could be neither studied nor taught, and that was an instinct for the game."

Halberstam examined professional basketball when the NBA was undergoing a period of great expansion, which had begun in the mid 1960s, fueled by an ever-increasing amount of money from television contracts. In 1979, when he traveled with the Trail Blazers, the NBA had just agreed to a four-year, $74–million television contract with the CBS network. The first television contract for NBA games came in 1964, when the ABC network bought the rights to televise regular-season Sunday afternoon games for $650,000. Over the course of its lucrative fifteen-year marriage with television, the NBA expanded from nine to twenty-one teams, the franchises grew richer, and the players earned and demanded bigger salaries. Portland reflected not only the burgeoning fortunes of the NBA, quickly assembling the talent to secure the championship after only six years in the league, but also the tribulations accompanying success, such as holding on to highly paid players in an increasingly competitive market. For instance, Maurice Lucas, then the second-most-valuable Trail Blazer behind Bill Walton, earned $300,000 in 1979 but wanted more money to remain in Portland another year. "Money," as Halberstam put it in *The Breaks of the Game,* "now clouded not only the relationships between management and player, but between player and player."

Published by Knopf two years after *The Powers That Be,* Halberstam's examination of the corrupting influences of power and money in the media, *The Breaks of the Game* was promoted as a similar exposé of professional basketball. Critics, however, disagreed, arguing that *The Breaks of the Game* was not about power and money solely; they were mere backdrops to a larger story of a sport, the individuals involved in it, and the society in which it was played. Taylor Branch argued in *The New Republic* (10 February 1982) that the book revealed "the madness basketball creates around the curse of winning and the joy of the pure game." Halberstam's penchant for biographical anecdote shines in *The Breaks of the Game,* as in the following vignette about Jack Ramsay, which illustrates Branch's observation:

> Ramsay sweated heavily now, anxiety sweat, not just through his shirt, but through his jacket and even his shoes. Earlier in his career he had been self conscious about it, and about the tell-tale stains. Once in college, in a desperate attempt to hide the signs of so delicate a nervous system, he had taped sweat socks to his armpits. That had worked for a time, but as the evening wore on the tape had given out, the sweat socks had slipped and has started coming out of his sleeves, flapping in the air as he moved his arms. That ended the sweat socks and he had decided to go to Pampers instead, which had worked admirably for a time, protecting him as they had protected the finer sensibilities of millions of mothers and fathers. But the Pampers were clumsy, or at least a whole Pamper was, and so he had gotten crafty, and he had cut a Pamper in half, placing a half in each armpit. That had worked well for a time, until during a game in Buffalo, the Pampers had started to unravel. Buffalo fans in those days were accustomed to seeing almost anything, but that night they were treated to the sight of the Buffalo Braves coach shedding damp pellets all over the floor. That was his last night in Pampers. . . .

For his second sports project, begun in July 1984, Halberstam turned his attention to the 1984 Olympic trials in the men's single-sculls rowing event. Appalled by the commercial hype preceding the games, he recognized "that amateur athletics suddenly meant money, commercialism, drugs," as he told *People.* In rowing, Halberstam found "a sport where there was absolutely no chance for endorsement or money or fame." The resulting book, *The Amateurs,* which came out sixteen months later, focuses on four of the top American oarsmen, John Biglow, Joe Bouscaren, Brad Lewis, and Christopher "Tiff" Wood. Although Biglow won the Olympic trials, the central character in the book is Tiff Wood, a 1975 Harvard graduate, a world-championship bronze medalist, and at the time the reigning national champion in the single sculls. Norman Hildes-Heim, who reviewed the book for *The New York Times* (11 August 1985), speculated that Halberstam made Wood the centerpiece of the book so as to soothe the disappointment of Harry Parker, longtime Harvard and 1984 Olympic rowing coach, over Wood's loss. "Despite the effort," observed Hildes-Heim, "Mr. Halberstam expends explaining the other oarsmen, his story reads as though ghostwritten, with Mr. Wood the ghost behind the writer."

For Halberstam the world of amateur rowing provided a stark contrast to that of professional basketball. Rowing, as he observes, "had in no way benefited from the extraordinary growth of sports, both amateur and professional, which had been caused by the coming of television." In fact, rowing seemed to exist in what Halberstam described in *People* as "a hermetically sealed world peopled with articulate, obsessed young men." Throughout the book he tries to convey what it meant to be an amateur sportsman in the late twentieth century, nearly a century after the concept had been articu-

Dust jacket for Halberstam's 1994 examination of the racial issues underlying the 1964 World Series

lated and codified in Great Britain. Halberstam seems to capture the meaning of amateurism best in this description of the pride instilled in oarsmen by Harvard coach Harry Parker:

> In a commercial world, he was able to create an environment where exceptional young men sacrificed themselves neither for love nor for money but for certain goals and a certain pride. The true victory for one of his oarsmen was not over the person next to you or the person in another boat but over his standards. Above all, he sensed why it was that they were amateurs, why they gave so much in a society that gave back so little reward. For his men, rowing was as much theology as sport; it was built entirely upon faith. The oarsman's self-esteem and membership in this elite circle depended completely on what he did; if he worked hard enough, he would be rewarded.

Halberstam returned to professional basketball in 1987 to write an article for *Sports Illustrated* on the NBA championship finals between the Boston Celtics and the Los Angeles Lakers. In "The Stuff Dreams Are Made Of" (29 June 1987) he profiled Boston and Los Angeles in terms of their respective superstars, Larry Bird and Earvin "Magic" Johnson. Bird and Johnson, who joined the NBA in 1979 after confronting each other in the National Collegiate Athletic Association finals earlier that year, had made the 1980s their decade in professional basketball. Halberstam noted that in addition to each improving his own game every year since joining the NBA, Bird and Johnson possessed "the rare gift of the truly great basketball player–the ability to make other players better." In doing so, Bird and Johnson led their respective teams to the NBA championship tournament every year since the two had joined the league. Led by Johnson, a three-time playoff most valuable player (MVP), the Lakers captured four NBA titles in the 1980s. Conversely, Bird, a two-time playoff MVP, led the Celtics to three titles that decade.

The Lakers won the 1987 NBA title, defeating the defending champion Celtics in six games. That championship, according to Halberstam, showed that the Lakers had finally coalesced under Johnson, completing the transformation from a team dominated by the imposing center Kareem Abdul Jabbar to one showcasing "a 6'9" point guard who grabs the rebound himself and pushes it relentlessly upcourt, on occasion sacrificing control for tempo." Until the arrival of Pat Riley as head coach at the start of the 1986–1987 season, the tension between Jabbar and Johnson tugged at the team, resulting in Paul Westhead, who emphasized Jabbar's game, losing his job as coach. Riley succeeded, according to Halberstam, by "paying homage to the Kareem team, while expediting the emergence of the Magic team." The Lakers finally emerged as Magic's team in 1986–1987 through the efforts of players such as Michael Cooper and the acquisition of new players such as James Worthy, who not only complemented Johnson but could keep up with his unfettered style of play.

Inescapably, the central theme of "The Stuff Dreams Are Made Of" is race, given the fact that Johnson is black and Bird is white. This difference, as Halberstam observes, distinguished the teams, as the top seven players on the Lakers were black. For nearly a decade Boston stood out as "one of the whitest teams in the league" and, at that time, started three whites and often played four at a time. Despite the apparent lack of racial diversity on the Celtics, Halberstam rightly noted that Boston led the way in the desegregation of professional basketball, as it "was the first integrated team and the first team to start five blacks." Bird's race, nevertheless, became an issue before the start of the championship finals. Dennis Rodman and Isiah Thomas of the Detroit Pistons remarked that Bird was overrated and had achieved superstardom because of his race, a fact that "white fans and media seized on and magnified." In this context Halberstam acknowledged the frustration felt by black players over the perception of Bird "as the lunch-box player who only by dint of hard work and high intelligence has created himself as a great basketball player, whereas what is seen of Johnson is simply his natural skills, not the endless hours spent honing those skills and the intelligence to employ them constantly in making split second decisions."

For his third book-length sports project, *Summer of '49,* Halberstam turned his attention to major-league baseball. In one of the most exciting pennant races in major-league history, the Red Sox returned from an eleven-game deficit out of first place in July to surpass the Yankees in the team standings, only to lose the league championship to their archrivals in the last game of the season. In describing the disappointment and hopelessness felt by the Red Sox, Halberstam wrote that they "had no desire . . . to replay the game. No one wanted to talk about the next season. No one wanted to take solace in the cliches about how close they had come, and how they had made up the eleven games on the Yankees."

Critics praised *Summer of '49* for its portrayal of major-league baseball and the society in which it was played during the first half of the twentieth century. Martha Duffy, who reviewed the book for *Time* (22 May 1989), wrote that Halberstam captured "both the glamour and the quaintness of the late '40s, when the corner bar, the movie palace and the ball park were the major entertainment centers." Sports as national entertainment, a theme ventured tentatively in *The Breaks of the Game,* is examined in greater detail in *Summer of '49:* "With the exception of the rare heavyweight fight or college football game that attracted national attention, baseball dominated American sports entertainment" in the years immediately following World War II. Professional football, then "a minor league ticket," did not surpass baseball as the chief source of sports entertainment around the nation until the next decade through television. Similarly, golf and tennis were of interest only to the "few who played those sports" in the 1940s.

After World War II, sports heroes, in Halberstam's words, "mesmerized" America. Major-league stars such as Joe DiMaggio, Ted Williams, Bob Feller, and Stan Musial, each of whom had served in the military during the war, had returned to the game, signaling to Americans "a return to life . . . as it had been before Pearl Harbor." Although Halberstam admired Red Sox slugger Ted Williams, he held a special place in his heart for DiMaggio. His portrayal of the Yankee center fielder in *Summer of '49,* later excerpted in *The New Yorker* as "The Great Joe D.," suggests Ernest Hemingway's archetypical protagonist, "who exhibited grace under pressure, who withheld any emotion lest it soil the purer statement of his deeds. DiMaggio was that kind of hero; his grace and skill were always on display, his emotions always concealed." Halberstam notes that he paid a heavy price for his stoicism, however, suffering from insomnia, ulcers, and tobacco and caffeine addiction.

In 1991 *Sports Illustrated* named Michael Jordan, who led the Chicago Bulls to the NBA championship that year, as its sportsman of the year. Halberstam authored the lead article, "A Hero for the Wired World," for the special 23 December 1991 issue devoted to Jordan. In Jordan, who had established himself as arguably the greatest professional basketball player of all time since joining the Chicago Bulls in 1984, Halberstam finds the "kind of fame that exceeds sports; he is both athlete and entertainer. He plays in the age of the satellite to an audience vastly larger than was possible in the past and is thus the first great

Dust jacket for Halberstam's 1999 examination of the worldwide celebrity of the man named by ESPN as the greatest North American athlete of the twentieth century

athlete of the wired world." Jordan's celebrity had transcended national borders, even into countries where basketball had not gained a foothold. Halberstam identifies Muhammad Ali as possessing the same transnational appeal until his conversion to Islam and refusal to serve in the military during the Vietnam War politicized his image unfavorably with the general public. Moreover, boxing does not enjoy the same public appeal as basketball, especially among young people, "with whom the idolatry enjoyed by Jordan must begin."

In writing about Jordan, Halberstam returned to the subject of professional basketball and, subsequently, to the theme of race. Jordan–unlike many of the black athletes before him, except probably Magic Johnson–seemed to have transcended the racial perceptions and prejudices of white America. Halberstam describes him and Johnson as "cross-over heroes," in that they had "received more commercial endorsement deals from the predominantly white, middle-class purveyors of public taste than . . . white athletes." Jordan's commercial appeal redefined "American male beauty," Halberstam argues; "his good looks . . . are a surprise to older white Americans, who by cultural instinct grew up thinking that Gary Cooper and Gregory Peck and Robert Redford and Paul Newman" epitomize American male beauty.

In 1991 Halberstam was asked by Glenn Stout, editor of the *Best American Sports Writing* series, to serve as the guest editor of the series' first volume. On one hand, Halberstam's selection as guest editor signaled the acceptance of the former foreign correspondent into the sportswriting fraternity, while on the other, it signaled his breakout from the sportswriting pack. In selecting and assembling the stories for the anthology, Halberstam was struck by the impact of television on sportswriting, recognizing that "the job of the skilled sportswriter is to go where the cameras can't go, to find out exactly what hungry readers who already know the outcome need to know, and to beat television at a story it thinks it has already covered."

The 1964 World Series between the New York Yankees and the St. Louis Cardinals provides the subject for *October 1964* (1994), Halberstam's second book-length treatment of major-league baseball. He examines the season that led up to the series, in which the Cardinals defeated the Yankees, thus bringing to an end the latter team's fifteen-year domination of the sport. One reason for the Yankees' defeat was the team's long-standing policy against signing black players, which was predicated upon the fear of George Weiss, who managed the Yankees from 1947 to 1960, that white, middle-class fans would be unwilling to share the bleachers with black fans. In 1964 the Yankees started one African American player, Ellison Howard, a veteran catcher from the Negro Leagues who, according to Halberstam, bore accusations of "tokenism" with stoic dignity.

Race, a theme that Halberstam had developed at length in his previous studies of professional basketball, plays a prominent role in *October 1964.* Whereas the Yankees failed because of their conservative racial views, the Cardinals succeeded because of their liberal attitudes toward race. For financial reasons as well as moral ones the Cardinals had rejected the old racist practices of major-league baseball and by 1964 had assembled a formidable core of black players, including Bob Gibson, Lou Brock, Curt Flood, and Bill White. More important, these players received support from older white players such as Dick Groat, Curt Simmons, and Ken Boyer, as well as Tim McCarver and Ray Sadecki, two younger white players. For Halberstam, Gibson's win over the Yankees in the final game of the series represented a team of power and prejudice defeated by a club led by a determined young black man. In Halberstam's baseball tale, as James Breslin observed in *The New York Times Book Review* (14 August 1994), "we find less social history than moral parable: we live, Mr. Halberstam assures us, in a just and even politically progressive cosmos."

In *October 1964* Halberstam also examines how the relationship between baseball and the media had changed in the postwar years. By 1964 baseball had evolved from a radio to a television game. As a result teams no longer represented cities so much as television markets that competed for an ever-increasing share of the audience. Television ultimately undermined a team's loyalty to a city, as in the case of the Milwaukee Braves, which moved to Atlanta in 1964, "where they would have a market all to themselves, instead of sharing the greater Chicago market with two Chicago teams." In New York, baseball competed with football for the market share, which for the Yankees meant competing against the upstart New York Jets of the fledgling American Football League, which had signed a lucrative television contract with ABC in 1964. That infusion of cash enabled the Jets to sign Joe Namath, the dashing quarterback from the University of Alabama, to a three-year contract worth more than $400,000, an unheard-of sum for a rookie. Namath's success translated to a further loss of the market share for the Yankees, because he possessed the "star quality" lacking in most of their players.

In 1995 Halberstam wrote "The Art of Robert Riger," an essay for *The Sports Photography of Robert Riger,* a collection of photographs by the celebrated sports photojournalist and illustrator. Riger's photographs and illustrations graced *Sports Illustrated* and other magazines in the years following World War II. According to Halberstam, Riger, through his art, "had the unique capacity to slow the action down, to show you what you had just seen and give it a sense of permanency, lest one surpassing moment be pushed aside by the next brilliant moment." By the 1970s, however, the speed of football, for instance, had increased such that "it struck him that he was falling behind in his ability to capture the action." Many of Riger's photographs capture calmer moments in sport, such as one between football players "Kyle Rote and Frank Gifford in their T-shirts in the locker room before a game, warriors made curiously mortal by how ordinary they seem just before they don their gladiators' armor." Riger's athletes "were warriors," Halberstam observes, "largely unheralded by the society around them, men living in their own world and bonded by the rules of their own culture, their egos not yet inflated by skyrocketing salaries and constantly escalating fame."

Halberstam's reputation as an authority on the cultural significance of professional basketball in America solidified in 1996 with his foreword to *The NBA at Fifty,* a book celebrating the fiftieth anniversary of the league. Just as he had written in 1991 that Michael Jordan was the athlete for the "wired world," Halberstam identifies professional basketball, as played by the NBA in 1996, as the sport for the wired world. He observes that "in a nation where the pace of life, driven by jet planes, by television, by computers and faxes and e-mail gets faster all the time," basketball had surpassed baseball and football in satisfying the national appetite for sport. When the NBA (then known as the Basketball Association of America) played its first game in 1946, the slow pace of baseball, characterized by long, predictable moments punctuated by quick bursts of action, corresponded to the mood of a nation weary after nearly two decades of depression and war. Although football provided a quicker pace than baseball, the even more accelerated pace of basketball, switching from "offense to defense and back to offense again in micro seconds," best satisfied the needs of the burgeoning television culture.

Although the NBA celebrated its fiftieth anniversary in 1996, the sport of basketball itself was more than one hundred years old by then, and many colleges and universities around the nation had been playing the game since its invention in 1891. In 1998 the University of Kansas reached the centennial of its men's basketball program, and for *The Kansas Century: 100 Years of Championship Jayhawk Basketball,* a book commemorating that event, Halberstam wrote "The Passion, the Intensity, the History." He points out that the University of Kansas had made significant contributions to the development of college basketball, as several of the most successful programs in the nation had links to Kansas. Halberstam identifies Adolph Rupp of Kentucky, Dean Smith of North Carolina, and Ralph Miller of Oregon State as part of the "long line of other prominent coaches" that could be traced back to Phog Allen, who coached at Kansas from 1908 to 1954. Allen, who compiled a record of 590 wins and 219 losses, learned the game from Dr. James Naismith, who established the Kansas basketball program after inventing the sport in Springfield, Massachusetts.

In 1997 the nation commemorated the fiftieth anniversary of the desegregation of major-league baseball with various tributes to Jackie Robinson, who broke the long-maintained "color line." In *Jackie Robinson: Between the Baselines,* one of the many books that appeared that year in honor of Robinson, Halberstam argues passionately that "he was history's man. Nothing less." In paving the way for the scores of African Americans that followed him into both professional and amateur sports, Robinson disproved all the myths that white America believed about black athletes: that they were lazy, that they would fold under pressure, that they simply were not good enough to play against white sportsmen. In a broader sense Robinson's integration of baseball "helped put an end to other arguments" against preventing blacks from participating in other arenas of American life. As Halberstam writes, the segregation of American sport was simply contradictory to the doctrine of fair play: "We had as a nation always thought of sports as a place where American democracy proved its own validity and where generation after generation of new immigrants showed their worthiness as Americans by prospering first here before they went on to excel in other fields."

In 1998 Halberstam wrote the foreword to *A Great and Glorious Game: Baseball Writings of A. Bartlett Giamatti.* The former president of Yale University, who became the commissioner of major-league baseball in 1988 and died the following year, was more than an acquaintance to Halberstam; the two men were close friends who had shared a great interest in baseball, which had provided both men with more comfort and order than the volatile world around them in their youth. Halberstam writes of his indebtedness to Giamatti, who helped him "understand why baseball had proven such an important link to the world of his father": "baseball was something that children could understand; it provided the first entrée into the world of adults, and its stars were the first great men whose deeds a child could comprehend and calibrate." Despite Giamatti's passion for baseball, however, Halberstam doubted that he could have held "the line against the power of modern greed and materialism" that led to the strike in 1994.

For his fifth sports book Halberstam again wrote about Michael Jordan. Published by Random House in 1999, less than a year after Jordan led the Chicago Bulls to its sixth NBA championship of the decade, *Playing for Keeps: Michael Jordan and the World He Made* was not Halberstam's idea but that of Doug Stumpf, his former editor at *Vanity Fair.* In an interview with Geoff Edgers of the online magazine *Salon* (18 February 1999) Halberstam said that he resisted the idea because he had already written a book on professional basketball, other books had already been written on Jordan, and the "monstrosity of big-time celebrity" would limit his access to his subject. Although Halberstam was unable to interview Jordan for *Playing for Keeps,* he nevertheless delivered–according to sportswriter Ira Berkow, who reviewed the book for *The New York Times* (31 January 1999)–"insight, balance, analysis, an assemblage of pertinent anecdotes and the kind of digging for information you would get from" archeological researchers.

In *Playing for Keeps* Halberstam elaborates upon his 1991 observation of Jordan being the "hero for the wired world." Jordan, by 1999, had become more than a household name; his image was also a commodity marketed globally by companies such as Nike, Gatorade, Coca-Cola, McDonald's, General Mills, and Hanes, who used it to peddle their goods to the world. In this sense he is not the maverick crusader for civil rights and social justice that Jackie Robinson, Muhammad Ali, and Paul Robeson were before him, but rather the promoter of an image carefully crafted by media and advertising interests. Halberstam illustrates the extent to which Jordan protects his image, quoting his rationale for his reluctance to support Harvey Gantt, the black former mayor of Charlotte, North Carolina, in his 1996 campaign against archconservative incumbent Jesse Helms for the U.S. Senate: "Republicans buy sneakers, too."

Besides *Playing for Keeps,* Halberstam published two other pieces of sportswriting in 1999, both broader in scope, which reveal his take on the history of sports and sportswriting in America during the twentieth century. In "A Dynasty in the Making," the introduction to *ESPN SportsCentury,* Halberstam writes that at the beginning of the twentieth century "sports, both amateur and professional, had limited importance; ordinary people lacked the time to play them, and more important, the money to watch them." For Halberstam, early-twentieth-century America was a dour, frugal, joyless Calvinist society in which sports and entertainment had little value. Except for the 1920s, when Americans devoured the exploits of Babe Ruth and other sports heroes, the first decades of the twentieth century were dominated by economic depression and war. As the century progressed, however, growing prosperity and the rise of mass-communications media provided people more time and money to consume sports entertainment. In the 1950s and 1960s television brought sports into American homes to an unprecedented degree. By the end of the century U.S. entertainment culture was pervasive, with leisure, sports, and recreation ends in themselves for most Americans.

Sportswriting and the role of sportswriters changed dramatically during the twentieth century. In the introduction to *ESPN SportsCentury* and *The Best American Sports Writing of the Century,* which Halberstam edited with Glenn Stout, he discusses the impact of the broadcast revolution on sportswriting, sports reporters, and the print media in general. With the advent of radio in the 1920s "the print media no longer ranked as the fastest or the most important means of communication." In competition with the broadcast media for much of the century, sportswriters "had to assume that in most cases their readers knew the score and the essentials of what had taken place; increasingly their job was to explain what happened and why it had happened, and what these athletes whom they had seen play were really like." For Halberstam the quality of sportswriting, as well as journalism in general, did not diminish in the age of mass communication but flourished, giving rise to a generation of more thoughtful and probing reporters.

Interviews:

Brian Lamb, "Booknotes," 11 July 1993 <www.booknotes.org/transcripts/10198.htm>;

Geoff Edgers, "Writing on Air," *Salon* [online magazine], 18 February 1999 <www.salon.com/books/int/1999/02/18int.html>.

References:

Christopher P. Anderson, "After 'The Best and the Brightest,' David Halberstam Reels in Another Whopper, 'The Powers That Be,'" *People,* 17 (7 May 1979): 100, 103, 105;

Anderson, "Fed Up with Big-Bucks Athletics: David Halberstam Explores the Passion of Unknown Olympians," *People,* 24 (4 November 1985): 73–76.

Halsey Hall

(23 May 1898 – 30 December 1977)

Stew Thornley

MAJOR POSITIONS HELD: Reporter-columnist, *Minneapolis Tribune* (1919–1922); *St. Paul Pioneer Press* (1922–1926); *Minneapolis Journal* (1926–1939); *Minneapolis Star-Journal* (1939–1941); *Minneapolis Star* (1941–1961).

WORKS: "Not in the Book," in *Best Sport Stories 1947: A Panorama of the 1946 Sports Year,* edited by Irving T. Marsh and Edward Ehre (New York: Dutton, 1947), pp. 85–87;

"The Catch," in *Best Sport Stories 1948: A Panorama of the 1947 Sports Year,* edited by Marsh and Ehre (New York: Dutton, 1948), pp. 100–103;

"Right as Roe," in *Best Sport Stories 1950: A Panorama of the 1949 Sports Year,* edited by Marsh and Ehre (New York: Dutton, 1950), pp. 44–46;

"The Kids' Lost Fight," in *Best Sport Stories 1951: A Panorama of the 1950 Sports Year,* edited by Marsh and Ehre (New York: Dutton, 1951), pp. 62–65;

"Advice to the Football-Lorn," in *Best Sport Stories 1958: A Panorama of the 1957 Sports Year,* edited by Marsh and Ehre (New York: Dutton, 1958), pp. 130–132.

Halsey Hall

Baseball fans who grew up in Minnesota in the 1960s knew Halsey Hall as the color analyst on radio and television broadcasts for the Minnesota Twins. Hall was a masterful raconteur who wove tales of baseball from an earlier era into his patter. His career as an announcer and sportswriter went back well before the Twins came to Minnesota. He was a newspaperman first but later combined the career with other sidelines, including announcing, public speaking, and sports officiating.

Halsey Lewis Hall was born on 23 May 1898 in Greenwich Village to Smith B. and Mary Hall. Smith Hall had become a journalist at the instigation of his father and his great-uncle, who founded several daily newspapers in Minnesota, including the *St. Paul Globe* and the *St. Paul Dispatch.* He initially managed another of his uncle's papers, the *Fergus Falls Telegram,* before becoming assistant to the city editor of the *Globe* in its Minneapolis branch office. After his uncle sold the *Globe,* he became the city editor for the *Minneapolis Times.*

After ten years in Minneapolis, Smith Hall left to become the associate editor of the *Kansas City Globe.* In his capacity as drama critic for the paper he met a young actress, Mary deLuce White, whom he married in September 1895. Hall's parents relocated briefly to New York, where his father had accepted a position with an Eastern news service; soon after Hall's birth, however, they returned to Kansas City, and shortly thereafter separated. Hall's mother, intent on her acting career, divorced Smith Hall in 1904 and left the rearing of her son to the Hall family. By 1900 much of the clan was in Minnesota, congregated within a few blocks of one another in the Ramsey Hill neighborhood of St. Paul, with many of them living under the same roof. Hall's father, however, also took an itinerant path, traveling extensively as a press agent for circuses, church conventions, and political candidates.

Thus, Hall (called "Bundles" by his family) grew up constantly surrounded by family members and in relative comfort, but he received little affection. He was briefly under the care of a nanny who induced drowsiness by giving him whiffs of gas from the stove, a practice that led Hall to develop rickets and lifelong spindly legs, a condition he bore with good humor. According to Hall's daughter, Sue Kennedy, her father did not speak until he was four years old. The woman most responsible for raising Hall, however, was his step-grandmother, Corinne Hall.

Hall was, on the surface at least, a happy child. He played baseball in a vacant lot and basketball at the YMCA. In a May 1908 letter Smith Hall wrote to his son: "I hope you have learned to play baseball better than the Minneapolis team does. Maybe I'll be home about July 1st to see how well you can catch and bat." Despite the transient nature of his job, Hall's father tried to spend as much time as he could with him. They attended Minneapolis Millers baseball games at Nicollet Park as well as vaudeville shows at the Unique Theater and the Pantages Theater. Smith Hall served as the publicity agent for these theaters and would often let young Halsey write the reviews, which appeared in the *Minneapolis Tribune* the following morning.

Hall graduated from Central High School in June 1916, where he served as the manager for the hockey team and earned a letter in track and field by running the half-mile. A line under his name for his senior class picture reads, "His heart is as far from study as Heaven is from earth." Even so, he apparently was a diligent student. He took summer courses in typing and bookkeeping at the Minneapolis Business College while still in high school and upon graduation from Central enrolled at the University of Minnesota. Hall also worked as a stenographer for the Provident Life & Trust Company, which occupied suites in the McKnight Building in downtown Minneapolis. He enlisted in the U.S. Navy on 30 July 1918 and was stationed at a recruiting office in Duluth, Minnesota. Hall's father had died of pneumonia in 1917, and at the time he left for the service few of his family members remained in the Twin Cities.

Hall rarely saw his mother, who achieved her goal of becoming a renowned stage actress and married six more times. In 1915 he visited her in New York, and together they witnessed an unforgettable performance by Enrico Caruso at the Metropolitan Opera House. A few years later, while visiting dressed in his Navy uniform, Hall was introduced by Mary Hall as her nephew because she did not want people to know she had a son old enough to be in the armed service. She eventually moved to Buenos Aires, from where she sent Hall a postcard in 1945 that concluded: "Look me up some time." It was the last contact the mother and son ever had.

On 18 September 1919 Hall returned to civilian life and immediately secured his first newspaper position, a reporting job with the sports department of the *Minneapolis Tribune*. So rapid was this transition that he spent his first night at the *Tribune* in his sailor uniform. Soon enough, however, he had adopted what became his familiar outfit of bow tie and striped shirt, and on 27 November his first byline appeared in the newspaper. The event was the championship game of the state high-school football tournament, which was staged under the auspices of the University of Minnesota. The two semifinal games had ended in ties, and school officials decided to let coin flips determine the entries in the championship game.

On 27 November 1919 Virginia and Montevideo High Schools, the winners of the coin tosses, squared off at the University of Minnesota's Northrup Stadium for the state title. Hall was in the press box and reported the outcome in the *Tribune* the next day: "It required no toss of a coin to decide the winner of yesterday's state high school championship battle between Virginia and Montevideo, for Virginia broke the tie that binds in a most emphatic manner and ground the light but plucky Montevideo team into the sod at Northrup field by a score of 18 to 7."

For the next forty-one years Hall's descriptive and highly colorful writing style was enjoyed by sports fans in both Minneapolis and St. Paul (and even across the country, as he also served as a correspondent for *The Sporting News,* a national sports weekly). He worked for a variety of newspapers and covered an even greater variety of assignments. "He was never a fan of the obvious," said Dick Gordon, who worked with Hall at the *Minneapolis Star*. "Because he composed the story in his head *en route* from the game site to the newspaper office, he could bang out his account in practically no time," said Glen Gaff, another colleague at the paper. "He was an unusually rapid typist." Tom Briere, who also worked there, noted that it was Hall's custom to write the headline for his story before getting to the details. "One time he was about to send a page to be printed when he remembered that he had written nothing in the story concerning the headline. He had to rush in a last second paragraph."

Hall's assignments on the sports beat were varied. He attended wrestling matches ("before the days of stomping and kicking and stuff like that," he once said), reported bowling and golf scores, and for many years wrote a billiards column in the winter called "Cue Tips." Billiards was one of his favorite hobbies, and he won handicap tournaments in the balk-line and three-cushion variations of the game at Snyder's Recreation Hall in Minneapolis and at the Minneapolis Athletic Club. Moreover, his newspaper work could include more than just sports. In a 1976 interview with Irv Letofsky of the *Minneapolis Tribune,* Hall remembered that on one occasion he covered a statewide cornhusking bee and, on another, a sewing bee at a downtown Minneapolis department store.

Sports were Hall's main beat, though, and while he got to know many athletes, Hall made a point of not socializing with them. "He always said that a writer should never get too close to the players because it could make it difficult in case he had to write something bad about them," said his daughter in an unpublished interview. Rather, he hung out with his sportswriting cronies, especially Dick Cullum, Ed Shave, and George Edmond.

Hall did not stay long at his first sportswriting job. In 1922 he switched not only newspapers but also cities, as he went from the *Tribune* to the *St. Paul Pioneer Press.* On 22 December 1922 Hall married Marguerite Sula Bornman in London, Wisconsin, where her brother was a Moravian minister. They had one daughter, Sue.

Part of the lure in switching newspapers may have been the chance to cover the hockey team of the St. Paul Athletic Club ("A. C.") that competed in the United States Amateur Hockey League and played its home games at the Hippodrome (now the Coliseum) on the State Fairgrounds. "Down the ice in uncheckable rushes came the men of the A. C.," Hall wrote in a 20 December 1922 account of this powerful aggregation, which was regarded as one of the top amateur squads in the country. "Nothing in sports could ever beat the sight of Moose Goheen taking the puck, circling behind his own net, and then taking off down that rink, leaping over sticks along the way," Hall recalled.

In 1926 Hall switched newspapers again, returning to Minneapolis to join the *Journal.* By this time the balance of power in hockey also had shifted across the Mississippi River. The Minneapolis Millers hockey team had lured Taffy Abel from St. Paul and brought in the legendary Ivan (Ching) Johnson from the Mesabi Iron Range in northern Minnesota, additions that put the team on the verge of a dynasty. The reign of the Millers over the hockey world was brief, however, and came to an end when the National Hockey League (NHL) expanded and formed a U.S. division for the 1926–1927 season. The new NHL franchises raided the rosters of many midwestern teams, including the Millers, who never completely recovered from this blow. Hall, however, remained an avid hockey fan for many years; in 1944 he was elected president of the American Association of Hockey Writers.

Hall's first year at the *Journal* was spent primarily covering college sports, but in 1927 he received the prime assignment as the beat writer for the Minneapolis Millers baseball team of the American Association, a Class AAA minor-league team only one step away from the majors. He quickly became known among the press-box denizens of Nicollet Park for his peculiar superstitions, particularly the belief that he could incite Miller rallies by standing in certain places. On one occasion he elbowed his way through a crowded press box, exclaiming, "I've got to get to the other side. We need a double!" He often roamed the roof of the press box, which offered a more panoramic view, and he could easily become so engrossed in the action that he forgot his fear of heights. To get a better look he would sometimes lean so far over the edge that his colleagues feared for his safety.

One of Hall's more memorable early accounts resulted from the Millers' Independence Day game with the St. Paul Saints in 1929. The rivalry between Minneapolis and St. Paul extended to the diamond at that time, and meetings between the Millers and Saints were always intense affairs. When a spiking incident triggered a brouhaha, Hall provided a detailed blow-by-blow account:

> McMullen grounded out, Roettger to Betts who covered first. McMullen stepped on Betts' foot. Betts took the little white pellet and fired it hard at McMullen's neck. Bohne landed a right to Betts' jaw, grounding him. Roettger rushed Bohne. Bohne landed a left and right on Roettger's face and the playing reserves arrived. . . . The cops charged in, pulling right and left. . . . Bruno Haas came running in to remonstrate with the cops who were taking Campbell away. Wingfield broke in and battled with Campbell. Three cops took Campbell away while listening to Haas' impassioned oratory. Roettger walked to the bench, his eye a messy sight. Betts, Bohne and Roettger excused for the day. Much hubbub in the stands. Batboys peaceful.

The headline over Hall's story the next day read "Sammy Bohne Doesn't Play, But Gets More Hits Than Those Who Do."

Three months later Hall covered his first World Series, a match between the Philadelphia Athletics and Chicago Cubs that produced a pair of memorable events. One highlight, which occurred in game 4–an incredible rally in which the A's scored ten runs in the last of the seventh inning to wipe out an 8–0 Chicago lead–Hall remembered as one of his "biggest sports thrills ever"; but the series opener provided him with his first national recognition.

The first game of the 1929 World Series is remembered most for Philadelphia manager Connie Mack's choice of a starting pitcher. Most expected Mack to open with George Earnshaw, who won twenty-four games that season, or Lefty Grove, who won twenty games while leading the American League in earned run average. Instead, Mack opted for aging right-hander Howard Ehmke, who had pitched only fifty-four innings all season. In a 1974 interview with Patrick Reusse of the *St. Paul Pioneer Press,* Hall recalled the reaction of his journalist colleagues at the sight of Ehmke loosening up in the Philadelphia bullpen before the game: "Everyone thought Grove was warming up under the stands and Ehmke was just a decoy. . . . When the game started and Ehmke took the mound, someone in the press box said, 'The gamblers have gotten to Connie. The only honest sports left are wrestling and horse racing!'"

Ehmke crossed up the Cubs with his slow curveball and other off-speed pitches. He hurled a six-hitter and not only won the game, 3–1, but also struck out thirteen Chicago batters to set a new World Series record. His outstanding performance provided Hall with a rich source of material for his first World Series story:

> Chicago, Oct. 9–It is reported that Abraham Lincoln, once the manager of the United States, was told that General Grant had been drinking and Abraham Lincoln said, "Find out what he drinks and give it to the rest of my generals."
>
> Wherefore, we find today the unusual situation in which Howard Ehmke, a pitcher who has been disciplined by Connie Mack for being a trouble maker and disturber and anything but a right sort of liver, is the hero of an opening World Series game. It is natural to suppose, therefore, that Mr. Mack now will insist all his pitchers become trouble makers and castoffs and then how will you stop the Athletics?

Hall's account of this game was included in a journal published annually at that time by the *New York Herald Tribune* to recognize the top sports reporting of the year. He received similar recognition in other national publications in the late 1940s and 1950s.

Most of his articles so honored are about World Series games, although one, "Not in the Book," included in *Best Sport Stories 1947: A Panorama of the 1946 Sports Year,* published by Dutton Press, concerns the first major-league playoff series, between the Brooklyn Dodgers and St. Louis Cardinals for the National League pennant in 1946: "And so the National League toga is edged in cardinal instead of the blue and white of the Bums, and that blue and white was black and blue this sunny Thursday." Another, "Advice to the Football-Lorn," collected in *Best Sports Stories 1958,* is a tongue-in-cheek piece on how to watch a game: "When there is a rest period and a fellow in white runs out with a bottle to a group of players, don't plead: 'Please send for that man to come up to our section. I'm thirsty.' 'That man' is the trainer or one of his assistants and not a stadium vendor."

In 1932 Hall had the opportunity to cover two World Series that were played simultaneously. Most of the nation watched the series between the Chicago Cubs and New York Yankees; of equal interest to Minnesota residents, however, was the Junior World Series, a postseason contest between the champions of the American Association and International League that had been held off and on since 1903. The combatants in the 1932 Junior World Series were the Minneapolis Millers, who had won their first American Association pennant since 1915, and the Newark Bears, who had won 109 games to capture the International League flag by 15½ games. Both World Series opened in the East, and Hall stayed abreast of each by shuttling back and forth between Bears Stadium in Newark and Yankee Stadium in the Bronx.

The Millers held a 2–1 edge in their series as they boarded a train for home. Hall rode with them as far as Chicago and was present at Wrigley Field on 1 October 1932 to witness one of the legendary events in the history of the World Series. The Yankees led the series 2–0 and were tied with the Cubs in the fifth inning of game 3 when Babe Ruth stepped to the plate and, according to baseball lore that has persisted ever since, pointed toward center field before hitting a mammoth shot into the bleachers to untie the game. Lou Gehrig followed with another home run, and the Yankees went on to win the game; the next afternoon they completed the sweep of the series. Whether or not Ruth actually "called his shot" has been debated ever since. Hall later said that Ruth "definitely indicated he was going to hit a home run on that pitch."

While his account of the game that appeared in the *Minneapolis Journal* the next day made no mention of

Hall (center) with his colleagues, Ray Scott (left) and Herb Carneal, with whom he announced Minnesota Twins baseball games beginning in 1960

any such indication, Hall nonetheless was clearly impressed with the enormity of Ruth's blast:

> It was an explosion that carried far, far out past the center-field side of the scoreboard in right center and, as the Babe circled around the precious sacks, the roars and boos mingled with cheers. So once again George Herman Ruth shoved it right down the Cub throats for he had been a target from the time the game opened. The Chicago bench rode him, the fans showered vocal razzberries upon him but the big Bam laughed and slugged, slugged and laughed. He had passed the sceptre to his understudy in brutality, Mr. Gehrig of Columbia, but he took it back again today.

Meanwhile, the Junior World Series between the Millers and the Bears provided its own share of drama. The series was tied at two games apiece, and the fifth game, at Nicollet Park, was also tied, 8–8, entering the ninth inning. A play occurred in which Harry Rice, the Millers' center fielder, dived for the ball and appeared to have snatched it before it hit the ground. Both the second- and third-base umpires signaled out, but an argument ensued, and the four umpires reversed their decision five times. The Millers came out on the short end of the "Play of Six Decisions," as the lead of Hall's article on the game indicates: "Minneapolis fandom has a hangover today from sitting in on a debauch of baseball inefficiency." Of the rhubarb he added: "The sum and substance of it is that nobody saw the ball on the ground. Therefore, justice rises up to ask, why is the decision reversed purely on circumstantial evidence when it would have raised no more havoc to have stuck to the guns that were fired in the first place."

The next day Newark rallied for three runs in the top of the ninth to win the game by a score of 8–7 and the Junior World Series, 4–2. While many in the Minneapolis media were quick to blame the umpires for the Millers' loss, Hall passed on the opportunity and instead praised the victors: "A rousing toast to the Newark Bears. A tribute to this flaming youth outfit of glorified speedsters with their college spirit, their heads-up baseball and their splendid balance."

Hall became recognized as one of the most knowledgeable baseball writers in the region. In 1934 he was elected president of the American Association of Baseball Writers. Major-league baseball commissioner Happy Chandler tapped him to be a charter member of the Baseball Scoring Rules Committee, which wrote and reviewed the rules under which the game is played. Hall was reappointed each year by Chandler and his successors.

Besides his reporting on particular teams or specific events, Hall also wrote a regular column that appeared in whichever newspaper he was working for at the time. His two longest-running columns, "Here's How" and "It's a Fact," included regular characters such as Simple Suzie and Neuritis J. Bile and the features "The Barbershop Chord for Today" and "Do You Remember?" Neuritis J. Bile was a curmudgeonly alter ego who regularly expounded opinions usually unrelated to the world of sports, as in Hall's October 1929 column for the *Journal:* "NEURITIS J. BILE coughed explosively into his cup. Then he blurted–'I would like to go out sometime in a congenial company where everyone wants to go to the same show. I have been invited to a dinner and the movies and a dance and vaudeville and the stock company and a hockey game in one and the same night and I should like to ask how a guy with only normal equipment can fill all these engagements at once.'" Hall used Simple Suzie as a lead-in for a play on words each day: "Simple Suzie supposes football players sleep under a nice light quilt made out of touchdown"; "Simple Suzie is doing her canning now and says she's made some delicious traffic jam."

"The Barbershop Chord for Today," a regular part of Hall's "Here's How" column, ranged from paraphrased aphorisms to sports-related one-liners: "You can lead a pitcher to the shower water, but you cannot make him think"; "The rooters hollered 'Stonewall' and the line fell down like a ton of brick"; "Do you manage the Cardinals or have you got a job?" For many years his column concluded with the nostalgic "Do You Remember?" feature, in which he printed recollections from his readers (always crediting the contributor) of events and places from an earlier era:

> Do You Remember the time–
>
> . . . when (going back is Burt E. Hallquist) kids went swimming in the raw at the creek where the Glenwood Chalet now stands?
>
> . . . when (old time a-hunting goes Ed Murphy of the Soo Line) you opened a bottle of pop by giving the cap a resounding smack to release it?
>
> . . . when (help arrives from Howard Ries, the Shakopee bottling gentleman) there was a horse trough at Broadway and James Avenue N.?
>
> . . . when (thanks to E. W. Evenson) women wore black sateen underthings?

The observations he made in his column were sometimes sarcastic and biting, often humorous, and, on occasion, poetic. In April 1929 Hall was referee of a high-school basketball game between De La Salle of Minneapolis and St. Mel of Chicago. The Chicago squad came from behind with a furious fourth-quarter rally to defeat De La Salle, and Hall's next column included a wry reference to the game: "St. Mel did more shooting in the last quarter than the leading citizens of its community." When Joe Louis scored a first-round knockout of Germany's Max Schmeling–who had become an unwilling symbol of Aryan supremacy–on 22 June 1938, Hall opened his "It's a Fact" column in the *Journal* the next day with "Heil, little ADOLF! And how are you?. . . That shower of small particles in Berlin this morning was merely ADOLF's moustache popping out, hair by hair."

At times Hall also doubled as a sports photographer, although he altered his name slightly when assuming this role. A picture of Danny Taylor of the Millers sliding into home during a spring-training game in Daytona Beach appeared on the front page of the Sunday, 20 March 1938, sports section of the *Journal.* Under the caption was the credit line "Photo by Journal staff photographer, H. Lewis Hall."

On 1 August 1939 the other evening daily in the city, the *Minneapolis Star,* purchased the *Journal.* Hall retained his job and soon became an institution at the new *Minneapolis Star-Journal.* One of Hall's coworkers, Eddie Brietz, commented in his 10 August 1939 column on how smoothly Hall handled the transition: "Halsey Hall didn't miss a comma when the Minneapolis *Star* annexed him and the *Journal.* He started a column in the *Journal* building and finished it in the *Star*'s."

Hall retained his "It's a Fact" column and continued most of his regular duties, including his coverage of the Minneapolis Millers, at the new paper. With the merger Hall was reunited with his original boss in the newspaper business, Charlie Johnson, who had been sports editor for the *Star* since 1922 and who continued in that role with the *Star-Journal.* In 1941 another realignment of the newspapers in the city took place with the purchase of the *Star-Journal* by the *Minneapolis Morning Tribune.* Both newspapers (the *Tribune* and the *Star,* which finally dropped the *Journal* name from its masthead) continued to function as separate entities. Eventually, Johnson was made executive sports editor of both the *Star* and the *Tribune*. Hall remained an employee of the *Minneapolis Star,* although his stories appeared in both newspapers with his byline, an uncommon practice at the time. Hall's colleague, Jimmy Byrne, recalled that Johnson published Hall in the *Tribune* in an attempt to bolster readership of the morning paper. "Halsey had such a great reputation as a baseball writer that often Charlie would have him cover the games for the *Tribune* instead of the *Star*." Hall became known for his keen insight of players' strengths and weaknesses; for his unlimited knowledge of teams in all leagues; for his shrewd appreciation of the strategy of the game; for his many friends among players, managers, and owners; and for his vivid style and humor in his daily stories. In 1947 the *Star* and *Tribune* purchased a full page in *Editor & Publisher* magazine to promote Hall as the "Little Giant Argument Settler for all sports fans of the Upper Midwest."

Hall is credited by many as being the reporter who alerted fans in the Twin Cities about the arrival of a great new center fielder to the Millers spring-training camp in March 1951. Willie Mays reported to the Millers on 16 March, and within a few days Hall devoted his entire "It's a Fact" column to the new sensation: "You watch him run and throw and hit and you are on his side in a minute," he wrote. "Willie is lithe, beautifully muscled, just under six feet, weighs 170 pounds and doesn't vary in his weight off and in season. Right-handed all the way, he has great power to right center and here the dear old memory of Nicollet's fences in that direction comes back." Less than a month into the regular season, however, Mays was called up by the New York Giants, who by that point owned the Millers; recalls of other Miller players followed, and, as usual, Hall had the last word on the subject. "Let Rosy Ryan and Tommy Heath have the gold removed from their teeth and send it to the New York front office. They'll get it sooner or later anyway."

The Millers carried on for several more years, and fans continued to enjoy Hall's colorful narration of the games. On an eighth-inning rally featuring Ray Broome, Marv Blaylock, Ray Katt, and Ray Dandridge: "The eighth was altogether jolly, what ho! Broome walked and Katt's double brought him over. Blaylock's single to center counted the big Pussy and Ray Dandridge's singleton let Marvin romp home." Regarding a fine mound performance turned in by slugger-turned-pitcher Jack Harshman: "Harshman, with pitches carrying the relentless timing of a parking meter, was the winner."

In August 1952 Hall reported on a game at Nicollet Park that took only eighty-six minutes to play and featured five home runs by the Millers, with a final shot by Ray Broome in the sixth inning capping the team's scoring: "In a game as rapid as a Manville divorce, Minneapolis whippeted to its ninth-consecutive victory Tuesday, hammering Charleston to defeat, 7–2. . . . The slug-for-the-circuit symphony being as pronounced as it was, Roy Broome tuned in during the sixth cadenza." Hall could be withering, however, when reporting on less-than-sterling performances by the Millers: "The Minneapolis Millers stood around on base longer than Martin Luther at the Lyceum Friday night and wound up losing to St. Paul, 6–2"; "Technically, it was Minneapolis *Star* and *Tribune* night at Nicollet Park Monday night but, as the Toledo Sox defeated the Millers, 12–6, it had all the appearance of Lakewood Cemetery night."

Since he was regarded as one of the experts on the game, Hall was often asked to pick his all-star baseball team. On these occasions he rattled off the names without hesitation: "First base, George Sisler; second base, Rogers Hornsby; shortstop, Honus Wagner; third base, Brooks Robinson; outfield, Babe Ruth, Tris Speaker, and Ty Cobb; catcher, Gabby Hartnett; right-handed pitcher, Walter Johnson; left-handed pitcher, Lefty Grove." Hall was remembered even more for his "Celestial All-Star Team," an aggregation he made reference to when writing of the passing of a former great. On 16 August 1948 he reported on the newest addition to the team–Babe Ruth, who died that day:

> There's a one-two, cleanup punch on the Celestial All Stars now.
>
> Once again George Herman (Babe) Ruth is hitting ahead of Lou Gehrig. With the passing of the Babe, this peerless tandem of batting torture is reunited in pastures where all infields are green and from where they may look down upon current mortals weakly trying to emulate their feats. . . .

Hall was never one to turn his back on innovation, according to Angelo Giuliani, a St. Paul native who caught for the Millers and Saints as well as several major-league teams. Giuliani recalled that once, when the Western Union operators were on strike, "Halsey was worried how his story would get back in time for the next day's edition." Giuliani, who had raised homing pigeons since 1927, put one of his birds in a crate for Halsey, and he hauled it down to Kansas City. "When he finished his story, he put it into the capsule attached to the bird's leg and let it go. As I recall, the pigeon delivered Halsey's story on time and he made his deadline."

At the same time Hall was writing for newspapers, he was pursuing a full-time career in sports announcing. He started in 1923 with the Jack Dempsey–Tommy

Gibbons heavyweight title fight in Shelby, Montana. Hall called the fight, not from Shelby but from a second-floor window of the *Pioneer Press* building in St. Paul. Because Gibbons was from St. Paul–he later served as Ramsey County sheriff for twenty-three years–there was great local interest in the bout. Hall re-created the action from a Western Union wire and delivered a blow-by-blow account through a megaphone to the fight fans gathered on the street below. He soon took to announcing in a more conventional manner, and his voice became a familiar one to people throughout the Upper Midwest. His friendly delivery and contagious laugh were once described in a *Sports Illustrated* article as "redolent of happy days at Grandpa's house."

Hall was also one of the most highly regarded referees of football and basketball games in the area. He officiated primarily at the high school and college levels, although he also worked a handful of games in the National Football League on the two occasions that Minneapolis had a team in the NFL in the 1920s.

On some occasions he did double duty, combining his roles as referee and reporter. After officiating a game he grabbed his typewriter and banged out a story of the contest that appeared in the newspaper the next day. He also became the number-one toastmaster in the area, regaling hundreds of audiences as a speaker and as a master of ceremonies. Hubert Humphrey, himself a prolific orator, once called Hall "one of the few men who has given more speeches in Minnesota than I have."

In 1960 a new opportunity emerged for Hall. The newly founded Minnesota Twins franchise brought major-league baseball to the area, and he was selected as a member of the broadcast crew. For many years Hall had juggled the dual jobs of newspaper reporter and radio announcer, but this time he devoted himself primarily to the broadcasting position with the Twins.

Hall never did leave newspaper writing completely, however. Up until his death he had articles and regular columns in a variety of publications, including *The Skyway News,* a newsletter for Midwest Federal Savings and Loan, and *Minnesota Motorist,* a magazine published by the American Automobile Association of Minneapolis. He also had a column in the *Minneapolis Daily Herald,* a short-lived newspaper started when publication of the *Star* and *Tribune* was interrupted in the spring and summer of 1962 by a sixteen-week employee strike. The *Minneapolis Daily Herald* ceased publication shortly after the strike, but the editor of the *Herald,* Francis McGovern, then started a newspaper of his own, the *Minneapolis Daily American,* which also featured a column by Hall for many years.

Hall's last newspaper stint was with the *Twin Cities Free Press* in 1977–shortly before his death on 30 December of that year–and still he ended his column with the "Do You Remember?" feature, although by this time his reminiscences concerned events from the days when he first began writing a column. Shortly after Hall's death Dick Cullum campaigned to have the new domed stadium in downtown Minneapolis named after him. Instead, the stadium was named for another noted Minnesotan, Hall's longtime admirer Hubert Humphrey.

Hall's influence on sports journalists in the region extended beyond his circle of personal acquaintances. Joe Soucheray, who started his reporting career with the *Minneapolis Tribune* in 1973 and later moved to the *St. Paul Pioneer Press,* never worked directly with Hall but said that he was influenced by his writing nonetheless. "I went through back issues of the papers, started reading Hall's accounts of the game, and discovered many differences between his style and that of a modern sportswriter. . . . Halsey was a wonderful writer. He would describe beautifully what a certain player looked like when he caught a ball and how he threw it, or how the sun shadowed half the field–things that quite accurately left the reader with a sense of having been there. I then began to realize that this was the way I wanted to write sports."

Interviews:

Patrick Reusse, "At 76, Halsey in 'Pretty Good Shape,'" *St. Paul Pioneer Press,* 15 December 1974, p. 9;

Irv Letofsky, "Halsey Hall as Popular as the First Day of Spring," *Minneapolis Tribune,* 8 July 1976.

Arnold Hano

(2 March 1922 -)

George Tuttle
Library of Hattiesburg, Petal, and Forrest County

BOOKS: *The Big Out* (New York: Barnes, 1951);
Valley of Angry Men, as Matthew Gant (New York: Fawcett Gold Medal, 1953);
A Day in the Bleachers (New York: Crowell, 1955);
The Flesh Painter, as Ad Gordon (New York: Lion Books, 1956);
Flint, as Gil Dodge (New York: New American Library, 1957);
The Manhunter, as Gant (New York: New American Library, 1957);
Slade, as Gordon (New York: Lion Books, 1957);
So I'm a Heel, as Mike Heller (New York: Lion Books, 1957);
The Last Notch, as Gant (New York: Dodd, 1958);
The Raven and the Sword, as Gant (New York: Coward, 1960);
Willie Mays: The Say-Hey Kid (New York: Bartholomew House, 1961); revised as *Willie Mays* (New York: Grosset & Dunlap, 1966);
Queen Street, as Gant (New York: Regency, 1963);
The Executive (New York: New American Library, 1964);
Sandy Koufax: Strikeout King (New York: Putnam, 1964; revised, 1967);
Marriage, Italian Style (New York: Popular Library, 1965);
Bandolero (New York: Popular Library, 1968);
Greatest Giants of Them All (New York: Putnam, 1968);
Roberto Clemente: Batting King (New York: Putnam, 1968; revised, 1973);
Why Me? by Hano and William Gargan (Garden City, N.Y.: Doubleday, 1969);
Running Wild (New York: Popular Library, 1973);
Kareem!: Basketball Great (New York: Putnam, 1975);
Muhammad Ali: The Champion (New York: Putnam, 1977).

OTHER: *Western Roundup,* edited by Hano (New York: Bantam, 1948);
Western Triggers, edited by Hano (New York: Bantam, 1948);
"How the Home Run Is Shaking Up the Game," in *The World of Sport: The Best from Sport Magazine,* edited by Al Silverman (New York: Holt, Rinehart & Winston, 1962), pp. 3–12;
"Tension and Torment," in *Best Sports Stories 1963: A Panorama of the 1962 Sports Year,* edited by Irving T. Marsh and Edward Ehre (New York: Dutton, 1963), pp. 73–82;
"CBS Calls the Signals," in *Best Sports Stories 1965: A Panorama of the 1964 Sports Year,* edited by Marsh and Ehre (New York: Dutton, 1965), pp. 298–301;
"Jim Ryun and the Philosophy of Pain," in *Best Sports Stories 1968: A Panorama of the 1967 Sports Year,* edited by Marsh and Ehre (New York: Dutton, 1968), pp. 210–221;
"Orlando Cepeda," in *The Third Fireside Book of Baseball,* edited by Charles Einstein (New York: Simon & Schuster, 1968), pp. 189–194;
"Stan Musial's Last Game," "How I Wrecked My Life–How I Hope to Save It" [by Hank Thompson as told to Hano], "John F. Kennedy: His Legacy to Sports," "Jim Ryun: What's He Trying to Prove?" in *The Best of Sport: 1946–1971,* edited by Silverman (New York: Viking, 1971), pp. 299–311, 321–336, 359–366, 594–604;
"Willie Stargell: Some Man!" in *Baseball Stars of 1972,* edited by Ray Robinson (New York: Pyramid, 1972), pp. 100–106;
"The Willie Mays Decade," in *Sport Magazine's All-Time All Stars,* edited by Tom Murray (New York: Atheneum, 1977), pp. 376–394;
"A Week with the Phillies," in *The Phillies Reader,* edited by Richard Orodenker (Philadelphia: Temple University Press, 1996), pp. 145–161.

SELECTED PERIODICAL PUBLICATIONS–UNCOLLECTED: "A Family Affair," *Sports Illustrated,* 7 (7 October 1957): 62–66;
"The Duke of Los Angeles," *Sport,* 29 (April 1960): 56–64;

"The Wacky World of Bo Belinsky," *Sport,* 34 (September 1962): 42–45, 82–84;

"The Pitcher, Whitey Ford–The Batter, Stan Musial," *Sport,* 36 (November 1963): 14, 15, 72–75;

Felipe Alou [as told to Hano], "Latin-American Ballplayers Need a Bill of Rights," *Sport,* 36 (November 1963): 20, 21, 76–79;

"Roberto Clemente: Man of Paradox," *Sport,* 39 (May 1965): 68–74;

"Mickey Mantle: The Twilight of a Hero," *Sport,* 40 (August 1965): 66–73;

"Black Rebel Who Whitelists the Olympics," *The New York Times Magazine* (12 May 1968): 32, 33, 39, 41, 42, 44, 46, 48, 50;

"The Form of the New Decade," *Sport,* 48 (December 1969): 16, 17, 73–75;

"The Lonely War of Alex Johnson," *Sport,* 50 (October 1970): 39, 40, 84, 85;

"Interviewing: It's More than a Q. & A.," *Writer,* 94 (September 1981): 9–12;

"Spring Training on the Sandlot," *The Diamond,* 2 (March/April 1994): 26–28.

Arnold Hano is noted for two things. He was the founding and primary editor of Lion Books, a paperback publisher, during the 1950s, of several important works of noir fiction, including novels by Jim Thompson. He was also a sportswriter and the author of *A Day in the Bleachers* (1955). The two careers are unrelated, even though one, in a roundabout way, led to the other. *A Day in the Bleachers* is the cornerstone of Hano's work as a sportswriter, a book that received great reviews (in such publications as *The New York Times, The New Yorker, Saturday Review,* and *Time*) but was a commercial failure. It sold only 3,500 copies initially. Still, word of mouth has kept it alive, and over the years recognition has grown. This recognition helped Hano land a job as a regular contributor to *Sport* magazine from the late 1950s to the early 1970s. In 1957, when *Sports Illustrated* wanted someone to report on the closing of the Polo Grounds, the setting for *A Day in the Bleachers,* it contacted Hano. By 1982 interest in the book was such that Da Capo Press purchased the publication rights to it, and it has been in print ever since. The work is noteworthy because it captures the experience of attending a baseball game as well as any piece of literature can. *A Day in the Bleachers* is Hano's best-known work, but his work at *Sport* as a magazine writer is equally important. A talented interviewer, Hano did many fine articles on sport personalities, both in and out of baseball. He was also in tune with the changes occurring during the 1960s and wrote opinion pieces and other articles that capture the spirit of the times. Along with Roger Kahn, Ed Linn, Myron Cope, Dick Schaap, and John Lardner, Hano was part of the gifted stable of writers that distinguished *Sport.*

Arnold Hano was born in the Bronx on 2 March 1922, a few blocks from the Polo Grounds, home of the New York Giants. He is the son of Alfred, a lawyer turned salesman, and Clara, sister of screenwriter Bertram Millhauser. Hano's first assignments as a writer came at the age of eight. His brother, Alfie, who was eleven at the time, produced a neighborhood newspaper, which the brothers sold door-to-door for a nickel. Initially Arnold rewrote newspaper stories, but he quickly tired of this practice and started writing his own material.

Hano's interest in journalism was reignited during his sophomore year at Long Island University, when he wandered into the offices of the school newspaper and was instantly captivated. At that point he decided to change his major to English and journalism and, soon after, joined the newspaper staff. In his junior year he was sports editor, and in his senior year he was co-editor. After graduating in June 1941 he accepted a job with the *New York Daily News* as a copyboy and junior reporter, and he stayed with that position until he enlisted in the army in 1942. He rose to the rank of second lieutenant and was awarded combat ribbons for his service in the Pacific theater, including the Bronze Arrowhead for an initial landing on a hostile shore. His brother, Alfie, died when fighter and anti-aircraft fire hit his B-17, although he had helped save several enlisted men before going down with his plane.

After the war Hano enrolled in graduate school at Columbia University but found it dull. He quit school and took a job as news bulletin editor for the New York State Department of Labor. Later, he added an extra income by teaching a night class at the Robert Louis Stevenson School and also found time to write short stories. One of his manuscripts made its way to literary agent Scott Meredith, who did not find the story marketable but did offer Hano a job as a manuscript reader. In 1948 Bantam Books hired him to edit their Western novels. He quickly worked up to the rank of managing editor before accepting the position that led to the creation of Lion Books.

In 1950 the Magazine Management Company, publisher of various magazines and of Marvel Comics (which later became famous for the superhero Spider-man), decided to make a serious foray into paperback publishing. The company hired Hano as editor in chief. Magazine Management had previously released a handful of titles under the Red Circle Books imprint, but Hano upgraded the line by securing the reprint rights to better novels and changing the name to Lion Books. Lion also published paperback originals, and

Cover for the November 1963 issue of the magazine for which Arnold Hano was a regular contributor from the 1950s to the 1970s. Hano wrote the article on Ford and Musial and ghostwrote the piece by San Francisco Giants outfielder Alou.

these books helped secure a place for the mass-market publisher in literary history. Lion was not the best-paying market for the crime fiction that flourished in paperbacks of the 1950s, but thanks to Hano's skill and his willingness to publish novels too dark for other publishers, it became one of the most important. The company published Jim Thompson's *The Killer Inside Me* (1952) and eleven other titles by him as well as some of the better works by David Karp, Day Keene, and David Goodis.

Hano was the top man at Lion until 1954. As he explains in an interview published in *The Big Book of Noir* (1998), "I left Lion Books when Martin Goodman [Magazine Management's publisher] offered all of the editors a ten percent cut because of one of the recessions. I had an ex-wife and two kids and a new wife and ten percent removed my margin. Since I had been dabbling in freelance writing, I decided I would just try the freelance life. If I was going to starve, I would rather starve at my own rate." Hano and Marjorie Mosheim had married on 4 October 1942. They had two children, Stephen and Susan. They divorced in 1951. He married Bonnie Abraham on 30 June 1951. They had a daughter, Laurel.

As one who had dabbled in freelance writing, Arnold had published both in pulp and slick magazines. His first short story appeared in 1948, and his baseball novel, *The Big Out,* was published by A. S. Barnes in 1951. This novel was followed by a Western, *Valley of Angry Men,* written under the pseudonym "Matthew Gant" for Gold Medal Books in 1953.

The year 1954 marked a turning point for Hano. He became a full-time writer, and his beloved New York Giants won the pennant and faced in the World Series the Cleveland Indians, who that season had one of the best records in baseball history. *A Day in the Bleachers* is about a single baseball game, the first of the 1954 series. The book begins on the previous day, with Hano at home with his wife and his decision to attend the game, and follows his thoughts and observations leading up to and including the event.

One of the profound insights in the book is how a common experience, in this case a baseball game, can create a bond between strangers, which usually disappears once the experience has concluded. While Arnold is waiting in line outside the Polo Grounds, he meets a man from North Carolina who is a cousin of former Giants pitcher Max Lanier. They strike up a conversation about Lanier and other baseball-related topics. Five times in the narrative Hano refers to the man as "my friend" and once as "my North Carolina friend." As the line splits, however, the two men are separated; Hano writes at the end of chapter 2: "It was the last I saw of him." The same phenomenon is replayed between Hano and the chief antagonists of the story at the conclusion of the game.

Once inside the Polo Grounds, Hano hunts for a seat, explaining the best area for viewing a game. While many fans have a favorite place from which to view a game, Hano states specifically why. In a similar fashion he provides an analysis of why Giants fans are superior to other fans. In the process of supporting his conclusion he invites readers into the mind of the bleacherites.

In a way the game is a subplot of the book. The focus of the story is in the bleachers. Hano portrays himself as the protagonist; the chief antagonists are the "man directly behind him," a faceless Indians fan, and a "woman in a red beret," who is the old nemesis of a Giants fan, a Dodgers fan. Although outnumbered two to one, Hano relies on his superior knowledge and his faith in the Giants. Throughout the game the three exchange barbs, their comments serving to punctuate the play on the field. Hano's faith is rewarded when Dusty Rhodes's pinch-hit home run in the tenth inning wins the game for the Giants. He looks for his adversaries, but the woman in the red beret has disappeared and the Cleveland fan is lost in the crowd. Hano is alone but content that his team has won.

The reviews for *A Day in the Bleachers* were positive. Novelist James T. Farrell commented in *The New York Times Book Review* (7 August 1955) that Hano "describes the practice before the game, gives vignettes of other bleacher denizens, and writes us a dramatic account of the game itself–and, though we know its outcome, our interest is held here as it might be in a novel." Elaine Simpson wrote in the *Saturday Review* (12 November 1955): "Woven into and through the play-by-play report of the game are short sketches of players and fans, tales of baseball history and its lore, and facts inconsequential but amusing–all told with warmth, humor, and journalistic skill. Any reader over twelve who is a baseball fan will not want to miss this book."

Scholars have continued to praise *A Day in the Bleachers.* Mike Shannon included the book in his *Diamond Classics: Essays on 100 of the Best Baseball Books Ever Published* (1989), calling it a "little classic." Despite its brevity–the first edition is 153 pages in length–and relatively modest focus, *A Day in the Bleachers* deals with more than the outcome of a particular game, as Shannon asserts: "the abiding attraction of *A Day* remains its understated presentation of the meaning of fanship." Richard Orodenker, in *The Writers' Game: Baseball Writing in America* (1996), echoes Shannon's assessment: "from the outset Hano identifies with every other bleacherite who 'felt the urge' to attend the game that day. These shared feelings and expectations are vital in shaping the 'constantly shifting and exciting vista(s)' and understanding how baseball figures into the daily lives of citizens."

Although it depicts an atmosphere born of cheap seating that is no longer common in major-league sports, *A Day in the Bleachers* offers a view of how to watch a game that has remained relevant. A bleacherite is a fan who enjoys the game with the same enthusiasm with which it is played. As Hano writes, "Though we are patently the watchers, we are really the participant, as the racing hearts attests, the tight chest, the rushing blood hot in the temples." *A Day in the Bleachers* is a tribute to live sports, to the camaraderie and rivalry of a stadium as opposed to watching a broadcast of the event.

In addition to its successful evocation of the experience of a live game, the book is also noted for capturing one of the great moments in sport history: "the catch" by Willie Mays of Vic Wertz's fly ball to deep center field. Hano devotes chapter 10 to the play, putting Mays's achievement in context with other players and other plays. His description has a restrained quality, and he is careful not to overembellish. Yet, he reaches the conclusion that Mays is "not merely a great ball player, but the great ball player of our time." Shannon writes that "Hano is at his descriptive, narrative, and analytical best" in the passage. Orodenker states: "Hano crystallizes the moment by focusing on the interplay between the imposing figure of the batter, Vic Wertz . . . and the new pitcher, Don Liddle, . . . as well as on the image of the indomitable player who will come between them, Mays himself."

In 1957 *Sports Illustrated* gave Hano the chance to write an epilogue to *A Day in the Bleachers.* "A Family Affair" (7 October 1957) is a fitting obituary to a legendary ballpark, the Polo Grounds. In writing the piece Hano attended both of the last two games the Giants played there, going to the penultimate game in case the last game was rained out. The first game had an attendance of about three thousand people; the last game, twelve thousand. Hano focuses on the last game, but he also counterpoints the two games to create a tribute to those fans for whom the Giants were more than their favorite team, but also part of their family.

Hano's early freelance work was mostly fiction, but as the 1950s continued, he found increasing work in nonfiction. Ray Robinson, a former editor at Magazine Management, was the editor at *Pageant* magazine in 1957. He sent Hano to interview actor Mickey

Rooney for a celebrity profile, and Hano exhibited a talent for doing personality pieces. For this article he earned a nomination for a Franklin award, given for the best nonfiction magazine writing. He thus quickly established a reputation as a writer of stories about movie and sport celebrities.

A Day in the Bleachers created an additional opportunity for Hano when *Sport* published an excerpt from the book. After he moved to Laguna Beach, California, in the mid 1950s, Hano accepted assignments from the magazine. Most of his articles on sports personalities appeared in *Sport.*

As Hano states in an article for the September 1981 issue of *Writer,* "Observation is a key element in interviewing. An interview is not just question and answer." "At its best," he adds, "an interview is a slice of life." Hano's personality pieces are often not just about the celebrity but about the process involved in getting the story. A fine example is "The Lonely War of Alex Johnson," which appeared in the October 1970 issue of *Sport.* Johnson, an outfielder for the California Angels, had a reputation for having a nasty disposition. Hano quotes the Angels public-relations man: "Alex is moody. Don't bother him before 11 a.m. He'll want the interview at the ballpark, not his apartment. I doubt that he knows the difference between preparing a magazine piece and a newspaper story, so I don't know how much time he'll give you." Upon encountering Johnson, however, Hano finds him to be different from the man reported in the press and warned about by his front office. Johnson does not snarl, is willing to be interviewed at home and at the ballpark, and wants to be interviewed early, before eleven o'clock. Hano does not simply contradict the predominant opinion about his subject, however; he paints a balanced picture, illustrating Johnson's defensiveness by describing a scene where he reacts to a comment Hano makes about his cleats:

> "You're wrong about their being old. That's the first thing."
>
> "I give up." I said. "You win. I made a mistake."
>
> "Yes," he said. "You did." Mollified, he said, "I tore them the first day of spring training. They were one size too small and I put them on the stretcher. They tore. I wear them only during batting practice."
>
> Defensive. Edgy. But he was right. I had assumed something about Alex Johnson that was not factually correct. This has been the story of Alex Johnson and his relations with the press.

Dust jacket for the revised edition (1966) of Hano's 1961 biography of the Giants outfielder

The article provides a well-developed portrait of Johnson, offering not just a series of quotations but also Hano's careful observations of how he behaves. Hano creates the effect of having invited the reader along to witness the interview.

Besides his magazine work, Hano wrote frequent pieces for Ray Robinson's Baseball Stars series, published by Pyramid Books. For the 1972 edition Robinson assigned Pittsburgh Pirates slugger Willie Stargell to Hano and suggested that he report on Stargell's abilities as a clutch player. When Hano asked Stargell about playing in pressure situations he replied: "I don't consider that pressure. I consider it a beautiful challenge. I enjoy the game at its climax. I enjoy a close game. I enjoy it when I come up, with the whole game riding. Pressure? That's excitement. Pressure is being black and trying to live from one day to the next." Stargell had given Hano a new angle, and he went with it, opening the article with a story about Stargell's trip to the South for his first professional training camp in 1959 and a racial incident in a Mississippi restaurant.

The Stargell piece is an example of how Hano did not shy from such topics as civil rights. He took advantage of the opportunities sportswriting provided to comment on broader social issues, such as the November 1963 *Sport* article he wrote for Felipe Alou on the treatment of Hispanic players in the United States or the piece for *The New York Times Magazine* (12 May 1968) on Harry Edwards, the former star athlete and college instructor who was behind the black boycott of the 1968 Olympic Games. Unintimidated by Edwards's rhetoric, Hano neither supports or opposes the boycott but instead analyzes a complex man who seems to have a mixed message, militant and moderate, for white America. He concludes, "He talks about the Olympics . . . but he really is talking about the nation's cities, and the world. For openers–at least as a gesture of good faith–we should start listening."

At times as an interviewer Hano has had to dig for a story and to use creative methods of obtaining the facts. As he explains in his article for *Writer,* he had to be inventive when interviewing Hank Thompson for the autobiographical "as told to" piece "How I Wrecked My Life–How I Hope to Save it." Thompson, a former Giants star, was in prison for robbing a liquor store of $270. When Hano asked him what was the final straw that had made him take such a drastic action, Thompson could not answer the question. Hano explains, "When the why question doesn't work, shift to how. I said, 'Show how you held up that bar, Hank.'" As Thompson acted out the scene, he used his left hand to reach for an imaginary gun. Hano asked him why he used his left hand, and Thompson responded, "Didn't I tell you? The night before I was riding in a car and we were in an accident. The glass from the window broke and gashed my arm. I had to go to the emergency room of the hospital for twelve stitches. That was the last straw."

Hano received recognition for his sportswriting from several sources in 1963. He won an award from the National Sportscasters and Sportswriters Association; and "Tension and Torment," his article on the Giants' loss to the Yankees in the 1962 World Series, was reprinted in *Best Sports Stories 1963: A Panorama of the 1962 Sports Year.* During the same year he won the Sidney Hillman Award for his article for *Saga* magazine about California farm labor, "The Burned Out Americans." In a statement for *Contemporary Authors,* Hano describes himself as "a generalist–it's hard to imagine a subject that does not interest me. I particularly enjoy writing about people in the public eye–learning who they really are and what makes them tick." He has thus written articles on a host of Hollywood stars, including Rooney, John Wayne, Henry Fonda, and Marlon Brando, with the same skill as his articles on Johnson, Roberto Clemente, and Mickey Mantle.

Most of the articles for *Sport* can be divided into three categories: personality pieces, opinion pieces, and tributes. Hano has contributed memorable examples of all three types to the magazine. His opinion pieces range from purely sports-related topics, as in "How the Home Run Is Shaking Up the Game," in which he writes on the home-run mania ignited by the 1961 season, to speculation as to how the social changes of the 1960s would effect athletics in "The Form of the New Decade" (December 1969). Hano's most memorable tribute for *Sport* was not on a sports figure but on President John F. Kennedy. Written after his death, "John F. Kennedy: His Legacy to Sports" is a moving piece of prose, although it might be considered too sentimental by contemporary readers.

Monthly magazines such as *Sport* rarely did straight reporting, since they lacked the immediacy to do so effectively. Hano was an able reporter, though, as his articles "A Family Affair" and "Tension and Torment" indicate. Another notable example of his reporting is "A Week with the Phillies," in which Hano documents the Phillies' performance in the first week in September during the 1964 pennant race. The team was "steady," as manager Gene Mauch observed, winning five games and losing three. Hano does not limit himself to the Phillies and their play on the field, however. He also tells of the August 28 race riots in Philadelphia, the aftermath of the riots, dropping attendance at Phillies' games, and fans who seem to be more interested in booing than cheering. Hano does not draw any conclusions but reports what he sees: "This is how the Phillies went into the stretch. You know how they came out of it." (The team collapsed.) As when writing about Mays's famous catch in *A Day in the Bleachers,* Hano is understated and thorough. Although he did not write many stories about sports outside of California, he observed the Phillies while on a separate assignment for *TV Guide.* The *TV Guide* article, "CBS Calls the Signals," which sent Hano to the East Coast to cover the $28.2 million broadcast contract between the CBS network and the National Football League, later appeared in *Best Sports Stories 1965: A Panorama of the 1964 Sports Year.*

Besides *A Day in the Bleachers* Hano has written other books, including five sports biographies for young adults. In 1967 he won the Boys' Clubs of America junior book award for the revised edition of his Willie Mays biography. In 1968 he received the opportunity to select his all-time Giants team in a collection of biographical sketches, *Greatest Giants of Them*

All, once again targeted for the young adult audience. Hano has remained a Giants fan, even after the team moved to California.

In 1966 Arnold returned to teaching, working as an instructor in writing at the University of California, Irvine. In 1977, at the age of fifty-five, he attended graduate school at California State University, Fullerton, and graduated with a M.A. in journalism in 1979. After graduation he moved from the University of California, Irvine, to a position as senior lecturer at the University of Southern California, where he stayed until 1985. Throughout the 1970s he gradually did less freelance writing. He also wrote less for *Sport* after Al Silverman quit as editor. He was, for the most part, no longer involved with sportswriting, when he accepted a position in 1980 as editorial director at Pacific Mutual Insurance, where he worked until he retired in 1989. In June 1991 Hano and his wife joined the Peace Corps and traveled to Costa Rica. After their service in the Peace Corps ended in September 1993, they built a home abroad and maintain residences in both California and Costa Rica.

Hano is a man who took advantage of opportunities. He was not the only writer to sit in the bleachers of a baseball game, but he was the first to realize that there was a story there and to remind readers that there is more to a sporting event than the sport itself and that the fan is a participant and part of the experience. Hano has also reached into his own experiences for story ideas. "Spring Training on the Sandlot" (*The Diamond,* March/April 1994), for example, is a touching personal story about Hano, his brother Alfie, and baseball. The article shows Hano at his best, demonstrating that he is still quite capable if the opportunity presents itself.

Interview:

George Tuttle, "An Interview with Arnold Hano," in *The Big Book of Noir,* edited by Lee Server, Ed Gorman, and Martin H. Greenberg (New York: Carroll & Graf, 1998), pp. 227–230.

References:

Richard Orodenker, *The Writers' Game: Baseball Writing in America* (New York: Twayne, 1996);

Mike Shannon, *Diamond Classics: Essays on 100 of the Best Baseball Books Ever Published* (Jefferson, N.C.: McFarland, 1989);

David L. Ulin, "Notes from a Fan," *SABR Review of Books,* 4 (1989): 121–128.

Dan Jenkins

(2 December 1929 -)

Scott A. G. M. Crawford

MAJOR POSITIONS HELD: Reporter and sports editor, *Fort Worth Press* (1948–1960); reporter and editor, *Dallas Times Herald* (1960–1962); contributing editor, *Sports Illustrated* (1962–1984); senior writer, *Golf Digest* (1990-).

BOOKS: *Sports Illustrated's The Best Eighteen Golf Holes in America* (New York: Delacorte, 1966);

The Dogged Victims of Inexorable Fate (Boston: Little, Brown, 1970);

Saturday's America (Boston: Little, Brown, 1970);

Semi-Tough (New York: Atheneum, 1972);

Dead Solid Perfect (New York: Atheneum, 1974);

Limo, by Jenkins and Edwin Shrake (New York: Atheneum, 1976);

Baja Oklahoma (New York: Atheneum, 1981);

Life Its Ownself: The Semi-Tougher Adventures of Billy Clyde Puckett and Them (New York: Simon & Schuster, 1984);

Football, photographs by Walter Iooss Jr. (New York: Abrams, 1986);

Fast Copy (New York: Simon & Schuster, 1988);

You Call It Sports, but I Say It's a Jungle Out There (New York: Simon & Schuster, 1989);

You Gotta Play Hurt (New York: Simon & Schuster, 1991);

Bubba Talks of Life, Love, Sex, Whiskey, Politics, Foreigners, Teenagers, Movies, Food, Football, and Other Matters That Occasionally Concern Human Beings (New York: Doubleday, 1993);

Fairways and Greens: The Best Golf Writing of Dan Jenkins (New York: Doubleday, 1994);

Rude Behavior (New York: Doubleday, 1998);

I'll Tell You One Thing: The Truth about Texas, America, and College Football (Emeryville, Cal.: Woodford, 1999).

OTHER: *The Best American Sports Writing, 1995,* edited, with an introduction, by Jenkins (New York: Houghton Mifflin, 1995);

Dan Jenkins (photograph © by Dan Jenkins Jr.; from the dust jacket for Rude Behavior, *1998)*

Greatest Moments in TCU Football, edited by Jenkins and Francis J. Fitzgerald (Louisville, Ky.: AdCraft, 1996);

The Hogan Mystique: Classic Photographs of the Great Ben Hogan, by Jules Alexander, includes essay by Jenkins (Greenwich, Conn.: American Golfer, 1996).

PRODUCED SCRIPT: *Dead Solid Perfect,* television movie, screenplay by Jenkins, Home Box Office, 1988.

Dan Jenkins has combined a lifelong enthusiasm for the sports of football and golf with an inimitable brashness and irreverence. From his days as a young Fort Worth, Texas, journalist to his post as senior columnist for *Golf Digest,* Jenkins has been a creative, sometimes crusty, and frequently contentious commentator. In more than four decades of celebrated sportswriting he has entertained, stimulated, and provoked his readers by transforming clichéd and caricatured sporting figures–the dumb jock, the crazy fan, the demoniacal coach–with his witty, eccentric prose.

Daniel Thomas B. Jenkins was born 2 December 1929 in Fort Worth, Texas. He was the son of a salesman and an antiques dealer. In a November 1984 interview with Stephanie Mansfield for the *Washington Post* Jenkins mourned the fact that his father, "a sports nut," packed up and left the household when he was a boy. His mother was often ill, and Jenkins, an only child, was raised by a grandmother and an aunt.

Jenkins's earliest memories are of being a rabid sports fan. He read everything available on the subject. His favorite source of information and inspiration was the daily issue of the *Fort Worth Star.* He told Stephanie Mansfield in the *Washington Post* (10 November 1984) that he wanted to be a newspaper reporter at the age of ten, when he saw Clark Gable in an old movie playing an irresponsible reporter, "a guy with his press card in his hat." Jenkins has consistently acknowledged his debt to his grandmother in the early development of his ambition: "My grandmother bought a typewriter. It sat on the kitchen table. I would take the paper every day, put a piece of paper in and start copying the newspaper story word for word. One day, I started trying to improve on it. I thought, 'This guy's an idiot. I can do better than this.' It hasn't stopped since."

After graduating from R. L. Paschal High School, Jenkins enrolled at Texas Christian University and then worked for the *Fort Worth Press* from 1948 to 1960 as sports editor and columnist. He then spent two years with the *Dallas Times Herald* before joining *Sports Illustrated* in 1962.

At the start of his journalistic career Jenkins revealed a special affection for two very different forms of athletic activity. He enthused over the individual, noncontact sport of golf and the violent world of college and professional football. Some of his early *Fort Worth Press* writing is extremely well crafted. The paragraphs are short; the sentences are taut; and the action is nicely interwoven with social commentary. In 1958 Jenkins wrote about Tommy Bolt winning the U.S. Open on a "vicious course" that "broke Sam Snead in two days" and "wrenched Ben Hogan's wrist." He also demonstrates a knack for the apt metaphor, describing South African Gary Player as a "young diamond." Jenkins sets his descriptions of golf action against a social backdrop, revealing a sharp eye for the sort of detail that elevates sportswriting to the level of authentic and memorable essay writing. In the middle of the piece he writes of the 70,000 soft drinks and the 48,000 hot dogs that were consumed by 20,000 spectators who saw firsthand "the course's brutal rough."

Jenkins's concluding paragraph is a model of crisp sportswriting. His prose is solid and workmanlike, just like Bolt's golf game:

> Bolt was equal to a glamorous finish before the TV cameras by hitting straight down the 18th fairway and slamming a wood directly on the green for two putts, a par, and the title. This was a toughie that he had made six on Friday and five on this morning–but now he was hamming it up for the swarm of reporters who accompanied him up the steep hill to the green. He curtsied, removed his hat, threw up his arms, and enjoyed the good feeling.

Despite such well-rounded narratives on the competitiveness of serious golf, early on Jenkins attracted more attention–not all of it praise–for his comedic essays and satirical pieces. In "Letter of Thanks," for example, which appeared in the *Fort Worth Press* in 1959, Jenkins writes a fictional, semiliterate letter from Clarance "No. 41" Watkins to a college coach about his recent recruitment visit:

> I don't guess I never got a recepsion like you gave us up there when we were there. I never been to a high class place like that where the coaches all wear school t-shirts and school socks. I sure appreciate you telling me I could live in the air condition dorm and get me an extra big bed and that Mr. McCarmeck would see to it I wouldn't have to walk ever where I went. I guess that means I might get me a car and believe me I would sure keep it quite like you instricted me to if I came to school there.

Clarance's letter was Jenkins's way of poking fun at the recruiting philosophy of Texas colleges and the lengths to which they would go to produce winning football teams. "Letter of Thanks" and similar pieces from the time indicate that Jenkins was one of the earliest critics of the excesses, abuses, and faults of modern football, which in the 1960s began to take over the mantle of the "National Pastime" from baseball. Jenkins's irreverent jibes at the sport served to deglamorize a violent activity in which too often toughness and hardness were seen to be synonymous with good character and honest effort. His voice was clearly distinct from other football writers of the time, who tended to treat the sport with reverence.

Jenkins (left) and Edwin "Bud" Shrake, with whom he later co-authored the novel Limo *(1976), at the* Fort Worth Press *in the mid 1950s (courtesy of Gary Cartwrighttesy)*

While "Letter of Thanks" was illustrative of Jenkins's jaundiced perspective on football, he also sought to focus on the moral, social, and intellectual complexities of a college game that demanded so much of its participants. In "A Look at a Footballer" (1960) Jenkins writes in a serious, even somber vein as he considers the demands placed upon a successful college player. He argues that players "may receive some concessions from certain instructors, but they probably are deserved because no sport is more time-consuming than football. And the lessons to be learned in the stadium are as vital to the nation as those in the classrooms." The final paragraph of the essay offers one of Jenkins's characteristically keen observations about the complex relationship between player and sport: "The strange part is, it wouldn't mean nearly so much to him if the cheers weren't accompanied by the boos. It wouldn't mean as much to all of us, either. When it's over he understands that and finally identifies himself."

In 1962 Jenkins moved to New York City and began a career as a writer for *Sports Illustrated.* Roy Blount, Jenkins's colleague at *Sports Illustrated* for seven years in the 1960s and early 1970s, noted in the *Washington Post* (10 November 1984) that Jenkins "was the quintessential *Sports Illustrated* writer . . . He knew everything and everybody. And his way of covering golf tournaments was legendary. He would sit there in the bar drinking and wait for the golf players to come in and tell him what they did."

Jenkins published his first book, *Sports Illustrated's The Best Eighteen Golf Holes in America,* in 1966. The collection of his *Sports Illustrated* essays has him hopping from the Merion Golf Club in Ardmore, Pennsylvania, to Pebble Beach in Monterey, California, with many stops between, including the Augusta National Golf Club, home of the Masters, where he describes the twelfth hole as "gorgeous and alluring as it sits at the foot of a hill covered with azalea and pine and even some golden bell . . . , but it is actually a blithe spirit, full of deviltry."

In 1970 Little, Brown published two collections of Jenkins's essays for *Sports Illustrated. Saturday's America* consists of stories or parts of stories on football that appeared in the magazine from 1962 to 1969. Jenkins discusses personalities, teams, and rivalries and does not hesitate to pour his scorn and ridicule on such hallowed American cultural icons as the sports movie and the Heisman Trophy. Reviewing the book in the January 1971 issue of *Harper's,* Larry L. King observed: "There is social commentary in Jenkins' work, delightful airings of the latest cultural absurdities, and some of the funniest one-liners since Mel Brooks or Woody Allen sat down to tickle the typewriter."

In *Saturday's America* Jenkins can be teasing, as in his description of Purdue alumni and fans: "Does a Boilermaker sound like the kind of a guy you would want your sister to date? Does he sound like *fun?* He's got to drive a '57 Buick, come from a family of fourteen in Gary, and spend his vacations breathing rivet dust." Another vignette, "The Disciples of Saint Darrell" (a reference to University of Texas coach Darrell Royal), is a rollicking tale of two Texas couples who drive huge distances to squeeze four games–three college and one National Football League–into a tortured, lost weekend. In the words of the central character, Joe Coffman, football is "as essential as air conditioning." Coffman recalls "Nasty" Jack Kilpatrick and his determination to see the University of Texas Longhorns play. "Toughest man I ever knew. Hitchhiked all the way from Miami to Austin with nothing but an old toothbrush and a Johnnie Ray record of 'Cry.' Think he wasn't tough?"

In the last section of the book, "The Immortals," Jenkins offers a decade-by-decade listing of the greatest players of the sport. He writes of "the miracle man of the 1920's," Red Grange, and his famous single-game performance, scoring five touchdowns and rushing 402 yards for the University of Illinois in its 18 October 1924 game against Michigan. Considering O. J. Simpson's career at the University of Southern California, Jenkins asserts that he was "all of the greatness that had come before him in one dynamic package."

Throughout *Saturday's America* Jenkins's skill at recording the colorful trappings of football fandom and his ear for dialect are in evidence. In the epilogue, for example, he recalls an old, tobacco-chewing coach, Abe Martin, who called his best players "pine knots" and spoke of a game as "a choir practice, a formal dance, an ear roastin' or a story tellin'." As Jenkins notes, Martin provided him with the title of the collection. "'Danny,' he said. 'You know what that is up there in those stands and down here on this foo-ball field? What we got around us here is the greatest thing in the whole world. What we got here is Saturday's America.'"

Jenkins's other book published in 1970, *The Dogged Victims of Inexorable Fate,* is also a collection of *Sports Illustrated* pieces. The collection is similar to *Saturday's America* in its wicked humor and its gallery of unusual characters. Jenkins eschews the approach of Herbert Warren Wind, Alistair Cooke, P. A. Ward-Thomas, and Henry Longhurst, who wrote paeans to the glories and traditions of the game. Jenkins dissects golf good-naturedly, from the early days of the professional tour, circa 1930–when the purses were small but the players enjoyed themselves–to the 1960s, by which time pro golfers had become globe-trotting businessmen who were being eyed enviously by the younger players attempting to establish themselves on the tour.

The Dogged Victims of Inexorable Fate reveals Jenkins to be happily trapped in a love-hate relationship with golf. The opening sentence of the work establishes the breezy tone that dominates the collection: "It first occurred to me that golf was not particularly the grimmest game in the world one afternoon when I was reading *The Brothers Karamazov* on an electric cart. There is nothing in *The Brothers Karamazov* about golf, of course, and very little in the novel about electric carts."

Jenkins shifts effortlessly from the perspective of traveler to that of golfer or social historian. He describes the legendary "birthplace of golf," St. Andrews, Scotland, as "an old university town. Spires rise up over narrow streets littered with shops and cozy pubs. Students wearing red cloaks are bicycling around. Statues confront the stroller. An inn is here and there, and the North Sea just beyond." Jenkins recounts a round of golf that he played on the "Old Course" at St. Andrews, noting the unusual names for various holes: "In rapid order, I was lost in Elysian Fields, lost in the Beardies, trapped in Hell Bunker, gouged in the Principal's Nose, over the fence, smothered in heather, and even out of bounds on an overhang of The Old Course Hotel at the Road Hole. Finally, I limped up the 18th fairway en route to the Valley of Sin. Par for 86." Another notable piece in the collection is his account of young, bustling, cigarette-smoking Arnold Palmer's first Masters victory at Augusta, in 1958: "He won it with his pants too long, his shirt-tail out and no one sure at that time whether Latrobe was in Pennsylvania or Poland."

By 1970 Jenkins had garnered a loyal readership with his writing for *Sports Illustrated.* He became famous, however, not as a journalist, but as a novelist with the publication of *Semi-Tough* in July 1972. By October of that year the novel was in its third printing. Narrated by football player Billy Clyde Puckett, the book immediately establishes his cheerfully profane, blunt voice:

> I guess by now there can't be too many people anywhere who haven't heard about Billy Clyde Puckett, the humminest sumbitch that ever carried a football. Maybe you could find some Communist chinks someplace who don't know about me, but surely everybody in America does if they happen to keep up with pro football, which is what I think everybody in America does. That, and jack around with somebody else's wife or husband.

Puckett begins with his thoughts on the "racial question," in an epithet-filled discourse clearly intended to capture the reader's attention. He insists, however, that he is not prejudiced: "nobody can help being what he is, whether it turns out to be black as a cup of coffee at a truck stop, or a white Southern dumb-ass like most of our parents."

Puckett, along with his crony, Shake Tiller, and their teammates on the New York Giants are in Los Angeles for a Super Bowl meeting with the New York Jets. The novel comprises Puckett's notes for his memoirs, tape-recorded during the week prior to the championship game. Jenkins uses the format to satirize not only football but celebrity, sportswriting, politics, the publishing industry, and many incidental targets. At the same time, *Semi-Tough* addresses more-serious underlying themes, such as the physical toll the sport takes on its participants.

Stylistically the novel is reminiscent of Jenkins's sports reporting, with its short sentences, laconic dialogue, thoroughgoing irreverence, and absence of any literary arrogance. Puckett's narration is a mix of prankishness, double entendres if not outright lewdness, grossness, occasional charm, and repeated forays into moralizing and philosophizing.

Critical response to the novel was fairly evenly divided. Jonathan Yardley, writing in the *Washington Post* (17 September 1972), accepted the vulgarity of *Semi-Tough* in the interest of verisimilitude; he was less forgiving of the "slip-shod plotting, cliched characterizations and slick sentimentality." Yardley described Jenkins as "an able and clever sports writer" but lamented that the novel "has no momentum." Pete Axthelm, on the other hand, writing in *Newsweek* (19 September 1972), labeled *Semi-Tough* "an outrageously funny novel and a devastating satire on jocks and jock journalism" and asserted that the "Texas-football-vulgar jargon" was perfectly pitched.

Jack Spencer, writing in *The Saturday Review*, described the players that populate the novel as "Neanderthals with killer instincts, sexually overwhelming . . . but supposedly lovable withal." Noting that Jenkins sought to translate the objectionable into humor by the sheer weight of outrageousness, Spencer concluded that "*Semi-Tough* takes a subject ripe for satire and treats it with all the humor of a towel slap in a locker room–without the sting."

One of the more-perceptive analyses of the combination in the novel of full-blooded comedy and serious themes was written by King for *Publishers Weekly* (23 October 1972). King interviewed Jenkins as well as Billy Clyde Puckett. The conversation allowed Jenkins to address serious issues about the interpenetration of sport and society. Asked why the dialogue in the novel was so offensively racist, Jenkins responded that it was "a device to show, within the context of a larger fictional structure, those traditional racist reflexes even now prevalent among certain of our accepted social

Dust jacket for Jenkins's satirical 1972 novel about professional football players

institutions. Including professional football teams." He also opined that "Most football players seem to like regimentation. They need to be led and motivated: after all, they're grown men playing the games of boys. The coaches . . . are good at exploiting that need, and advertised as having exceptional organizational abilities."

Semi-Tough was an immediate popular success, however, becoming a Book-of-the-Month Club alternate selection and earning Jenkins $250,000 for the paperback rights. While he admitted to being overwhelmed by the fame and the money that accompanied the success of the novel, he bought two houses, one in Hawaii and one in Florida, and a Park Avenue apartment in New York.

In 1977 United Artists released a movie version of *Semi-Tough,* directed by Michael Ritchie. Jenkins did not contribute to the screenplay, and the screenwriter, Walter Bernstein, eschewed the raunchiness of the novel. Jenkins did labor in Hollywood for two months on a pilot for a television series based on the novel, although the project was a failure.

Jenkins next published *Dead Solid Perfect* (1974), a golf novel that features the author's typically outrageous plotting, profane language, and satirical take on big-money sports. The protagonist is thirty-four-year-old Texan Kenny Puckett, who has been married three times and had an up-and-down career as a professional golfer for a decade. He finds success as a final-round contender at the United States Open. With Jack Nicklaus already watching from the clubhouse, Puckett realizes that scoring a par on the eighteenth hole will make him the surprise and sensational victor. As he approaches the last green his comment to his caddie is distinctively Jenkinsian: "God damn, Rose . . . We may not even have to putt that son of a bitch." After the tournament is over, Puckett chuckles, "I think that even an Egyptian mummy might have enjoyed that walk I took to the last green. I sincerely recommend the cheering for anybody's ego."

Axthelm, writing in the November 1974 issue of *The Saturday Review,* thought that *Dead Solid Perfect* featured Jenkins's first believable female character in Beverly Tidwell, Puckett's second wife, and that the most consistent quality of the novel was its succession of one-liners. In 1988 Jenkins was executive producer and screenwriter for an adaptation of the novel for the Home Box Office cable network, with Randy Quaid in the role of Puckett.

Jenkins returned to the characters of *Semi-Tough* in *Life Its Ownself: The Semi-Tougher Adventures of Billy Clyde Puckett and Them* (1984), which was advertised in *The New York Times Book Review* with half a page of endorsements from sportswriting and novelist colleagues such as Roy Blount Jr., Elmore Leonard, and Bob Greene of *The Chicago Tribune.* Greene has held Jenkins in high esteem throughout his career. Writing in his *Tribune* column for 28 October 1981, he observed that Jenkins was his favorite author. Much of the regard was born out of one journalist recognizing the other's work ethic: "Jenkins is a man who knocks a story out and picks up a paycheck and then knocks another story out so he can pick up another paycheck." Ever the iconoclast and debunker, Jenkins told Greene that commerce, not literary integrity, is the cornerstone of successful writing: "Hell, I'd give a quote to Hitler if he was a friend of mine."

In *Life Its Ownself* Puckett's career as a running back has ended because of a medial collateral injury to his knee; he is four years into marriage with Barbara Jane Bookman, his and Tiller's childhood friend from the original novel. Other characters from *Semi-Tough* have made their own transitions from their football careers: Tiller becomes a popular but critically savaged novelist, and the profane and bigoted T. J. Lambert has become a coach at Texas Christian University. Puckett's injury strains his marriage, as he comes to terms with his new life as a former football star. As both he and Barbara Jane pursue careers in television, she as a sitcom actress and he as a color commentator for CBS, they begin to drift apart. Although the novel has much the same humorously raunchy tone as its predecessor, it ends on a sentimental note, with Puckett and his wife reuniting on the field during halftime at a TCU football game: "I pulled Barbara Jane to me. We kissed as if we were all alone on the field. And then we kept walking. And in the stadium where I'd heard so many cheers, where the scent of winning was in the air again, it occurred to me that I'd scored the greatest victory of my life. Barbara Jane had come back."

Jenkins takes aim at different satirical targets in this novel, including college football as a big-money game, sports coverage on television, and the relationship between pro players and team and league management. Jim Tom Pinch, "sports editor and columnist for *The Fort Worth Light & Shopper*" and Puckett's collaborator for *Semi-Tough,* expresses outrageous opinions on the sports he hates, "which included almost every sport but college football," Puckett relates. He quotes one of the sportswriter's "Pinch's Palaver" columns, in which he writes he deplores television's corruption of the National Football League:

> Wake me up when the Super Bowl's over, but don't bother to tell me who won. I already know.
> CBS.

Jenkins also includes extended passages from Tiller's "A Not So Fond Farewell to the NFL," which he writes for *Playboy* magazine: "The owners ought to walk with a goose step. The general managers should wear black cloaks. The coaches need to be locked up in rubber rooms. And the zebras–the game officials–belong in correctional institutions."

In *The New York Times Book Review* (21 October 1984) D. G. Myers credited *Semi-Tough* as being the best novel to date about professional football but considered *Life Its Ownself* to be "filled with gall" and little else. Jenkins's "raw satiric talent," Myers asserted, was offset by his "smug knowingness." The novel did receive some accolades, however. Carolyn Banks found it "side-splittingly" funny and noted in the *Washington Post Book World* (7 October 1984) that "even a feminist can love Billy Clyde" and that Jenkins possessed the special ability to "ensnare a person in a single phrase." Like *Semi-Tough, Life Its Ownself* was a Book-of-the-Month Club alternate, but it did not sell as well as its predecessor.

Two years after the publication of *Life Its Ownself* Jenkins wrote the text for *Football* (1986), a photography book produced by the publisher Harry N. Abrams. *Football* shows off Walter Iooss Jr.'s brilliant photographs, the majority of which were first published in *Sports Illustrated.* Jenkins's writing style in *Football* is far removed from the narrative voice he gives Billy Clyde Puckett. His text is both knowledgeable and intimate, as in his description of Bobby Layne, the high-living Detroit Lions quarterback: "Layne was a true competitor and as much of a leader off the field as he was on, which was why so many people other than his faithful teammates sought the pleasure of his company. He liked to close establishments, he could tell good stories, and he always picked up the biggest checks. It was part of his temperament, part of his style. He craved action, he enjoyed good company, and evidently he didn't care much for sleep."

In 1988 Jenkins published his third novel, *Fast Copy,* with football again as the principal subject. The novel is set in Texas in the 1930s, when oil was the backbone of the state economy and quarterback "Slingin'" Sammy Baugh led the TCU Horned Frogs to several bowl victories. Like Jenkins's other novels, *Fast Copy* is filled with cheerful profanity and raucous characterizations. He also writes nostalgically about the daily routine of a small newspaper and Texans' passion for football.

Gary Dretzka, reviewing the book for the *Chicago Tribune* (3 November 1988), relished Jenkins's penchant for well-placed one-liners but summed up the novel with a less-than-complimentary football analogy. "It just seems that instead of going for a touchdown here, Jenkins settled for a field goal, and 3 points weren't enough to cover the spread." Author Fanny Flagg approved of Betsy Throckmorton, the maverick heroine of *Fast Copy*–"who smokes, drinks and cusses up a blue streak and knows her football better than you or me"–but argued that the crude language intended to capture the ambience of macho football talk got in the way of the story. Christopher Lehmann-Haupt, writing in *The New York Times* (27 October 1988), praised Jenkins's novelistic eye for period detail and likened him to a trick bicyclist, relying on sheer momentum to carry the novel along because of his "awareness that if he stops he is bound to fall."

While Jenkins is clearly identified with sportswriting, he has delved into other topics. In 1976 he collaborated with fellow Texan Edwin Shrake to write *Limo,* a show-business satire written in Jenkins's usual fast-paced comic style. John Mariani, writing in *The Saturday Review* (2 October 1976) saw *Limo* as sharing common ground with *Semi-Tough* in that both were exposes of "inept and insufferable yes-men." In 1981 Jenkins published *Baja Oklahoma,* set in the world of country-and-western music. The novel features some of Jenkins's typical sports characters in minor roles. Tommy Earl Bruner, for example, "had been a football immortal at Paschal High and TCU. Although he was now 35 and those days were well behind him, he still thought of himself as a local celebrity. This gave him the right to be drunk in public."

Jenkins in New York circa 1972 (courtesy of Stephanie Salter)

Jenkins himself was known on the sports circuit for his penchant for hard living. Axthelm observed in *Newsweek* (19 September 1972) that he "will drink his way through a big game week, then pop a dexedrine, prop his typewriter amid the prone bodies of less durable celebrants–and produce a witty and informative *Sports Illustrated* piece." Stephanie Mansfield's 10 November 1984 *Washington Post* profile opens: "Dan Jenkins takes a swig of J and B. It is served in a glass the size of a vase. He's been known to down 30 or 40 of those suckers between sunsets."

In 1984, after twenty-two years and more than five hundred articles for *Sports Illustrated,* Jenkins feuded with the senior editorial staff about the quality of his golf writing. Despite his significant contributions to writing on the sport overall, he could be rambling, self-absorbed, and even silly. A 1982 *Sports Illustrated* piece, "Getting the Shaft," illustrates the point. Ostensibly a review of 1981 golf highlights, the article recounts Jenkins's visit to his dentist and vacation on another continent and reports that the author missed the United States Amateur Championship because "I was home transferring all of my Bing Crosby 78s onto cassettes."

Following his departure from *Sports Illustrated* Jenkins began a stint as a regular contributor for *Playboy* magazine and later was a contributor to *Golf Digest.* David L. Vanderwerken, writing in *Modern Fiction Studies* (Spring 1987), sees Jenkins as a significant American satirist, "a Mark Twain of the NFL": "In his journalism, especially his regular monthly column for *Playboy,* Jenkins has become our Mencken, outrageously and unabashedly prejudiced, jaundiced, eccentric, ornery, taking well-aimed slapshots at all sorts of tomfoolery across the spectrum of contemporary sport." A sampling of the titles of his *Playboy* articles demonstrates his reliance on parody, burlesque, and invective: "The Dunces of College Sports," "Football for Foreigners," "God Save Wimbledon, the Queen," and "The Stupor Bowl." Vanderwerken argues that Jenkins's writing serves as a counterbalance to the celebrity worship that dominates the world of sports.

In 1989 Jenkins published *You Call It Sports, but I Say It's a Jungle Out There,* another collection of essays, with sections devoted to the author's usual topics, football and golf, as well as on "Other Games," "The Real World," and "Sports Movies." The book collects Jenkins's pieces from *Playboy* and *Golf Digest* in the 1980s, in addition to some *Sports Illustrated* writing from the 1970s. As the dedication indicates, Jenkins had not mellowed with age: "For all the poets who've had their funniest leads rewritten by imbeciles, their best quotes killed by quote Nazis, their favorite kickerlines chopped off by mysterious phantoms, and their expense accounts chewed on by eunuchs who've never been to Beverly Hills." Another retrospective collection, *Fairways and Greens: The Best Golf Writing of Dan Jenkins,* was published by Doubleday in 1994.

In 1995 Jenkins served as a guest editor of *The Best American Sports Writing.* In his introduction he takes jabs at literary pretension, suggesting, for example, that one New York literary fixture should be renamed the "*New York Review of Each Other.*" His favorite sports book for the year, he jokes, is about a flabby, forty-five-year-old fighter, Big Bob Lord, who knocks out "an exceptionally large piece of Samsonite luggage" in the eighth round and, after retirement, "becomes even more famous for his oils of airport conveyor belts."

Jenkins's third wife, June Burrage of Fort Worth, Texas, is a restaurant owner. They have three children. One son, Marty, is also a restauranteur, while a daughter, Sally, has written for the *San Fransisco Examiner,* the *Washington Post,* and *Sports Illustrated;* another son, Danny, is a sports and commercial photographer based in New York City. Many of Jenkins's books are dedicated to his family.

In 1993 Jenkins was voted into the Texas Golf Hall of Fame, and in 1994 he received the Metropolitan Golf Writers Lifetime Contribution to the Game Award. As Harvey Penick said about Dan Jenkins: "No one has ever written about the game with more wit and insight." Jenkins's writings on golf and football, considered in the context of a long and varied career, ensure his place as a sportswriter of the first rank.

References:

Pete Axthelm, "Scotch on the Jocks," *Newsweek,* 80 (19 September 1972): 106–107;

Bob Greene, "Dan Jenkins, Writer: Not Even Semi-phony," *Chicago Tribune,* 28 October 1981, II:1;

Stephanie Mansfield, "Dan Jenkins, All Tough," *Washington Post,* 10 November 1984, p. D11;

David L. Vanderwerken, "Dan Jenkins' Needle," *Modern Fiction Studies,* 33 (Spring 1987): 125–134.

F. C. Lane

(25 October 1885 - 20 April 1984)

Leverett T. Smith Jr.
North Carolina Wesleyan College

MAJOR POSITIONS HELD: Editor, *Baseball Magazine* (1912–1937); editor, *The Little Red Book of Major League Baseball* (1937–1948).

BOOKS: *Batting: One Thousand Expert Opinions on Every Conceivable Angle of Batting Science* (New York: Baseball Magazine, 1925);
The Mysterious Sea (Garden City, N.Y.: Doubleday, 1947);
The World's Great Lakes (Garden City, N.Y.: Doubleday, 1948);
Earth's Grandest Rivers (Garden City, N.Y.: Doubleday, 1949);
The Story of Mountains (Garden City, N.Y.: Doubleday, 1951);
The Story of Trees (Garden City, N.Y.: Doubleday, 1952);
All About the Sea (New York: Random House, 1953);
All About the Insect World (New York: Random House, 1954).

F. C. Lane

SELECTED PERIODICAL PUBLICATIONS–UNCOLLECTED: "Is There Room for a Third Big League?" *Baseball,* 13 (June 1914): 43–52;
"The Firebrand of the Federal League," *Baseball,* 13 (July 1914): 25–32, 98, 100, 102, 104, 106, 108, 112, 114;
"Baseball Mismanagement That Costs a Fortune," *Baseball,* 14 (February 1915): 19–24;
"Collins the Great," *Baseball,* 14 (March 1915): 47–63;
"Why Not Recognize the Federal League?" *Baseball,* 14 (March 1915): 25–30, 104, 106, 108, 110, 112;
"Eventually There Will Be a Third Big League Why Not Now?" *Baseball,* 14 (April 1915): 25–32, 108, 110, 112, 114;
"The International League, the Belgium of the Baseball War," *Baseball,* 15 (May 1915): 29–32, 106, 108, 110, 112, 114, 116, 118, 120, 122, 124;
"Reulbach, the Man Who Was Run Out of Baseball," *Baseball,* 15 (May 1915): 63–74;
"Famous Magnates of the Federal League," *Baseball,* 15 (July 1915): 24–32, 102, 104, 106, 108, 110, 112, 114, 116; 15 (August 1915): 28–32, 106, 108, 110, 112, 114, 116; 15 (September 1915): 52–61;
"The High Road to Peace," *Baseball,* 16 (January 1916): 25–32;
"Peace and Prosperity," *Baseball,* 16 (February 1916): 23–30, 106;
"Why the System of Batting Averages Should Be Changed," *Baseball,* 16 (March 1916): 41–47;
"Why the System of Batting Averages Should Be Reformed," *Baseball,* 18 (January 1917): 52–60;

"A Brand New System of Batting Averages," *Baseball,* 18 (February 1917): 7–12;

"The Base on Balls," *Baseball,* 18 (March 1917): 93–95;

"Revising the Fielding Records," *Baseball,* 19 (June 1917): 305–306;

"The True Value of a Baseball Star," *Baseball,* 20 (February 1918): 337–340;

"The Need for Drastic Reform in Baseball Records," *Baseball,* 21 (May 1918): 157–158, 160;

"The Season's Sensation," *Baseball,* 21 (October 1918): 471–472;

"Has the 'Lively' Ball Revolutionized the Game?" *Baseball,* 27 (September 1921): 435–439, 477–478;

"Why Babe Ruth Has Become a National Idol," *Baseball,* 27 (October 1921): 483–484;

"The Hidden Risks in Base Stealing," *Baseball,* 29 (June 1922): 295–297;

"The Decline in Run Scoring Efficiency," *Baseball,* 29 (July 1922): 339–340, 373–374;

"Natural Slugging vs. Scientific Batting," *Baseball,* 29 (August 1922): 337–339, 428;

"The Wizard of the Dope," *Baseball,* 30 (April 1923): 509–510, 521–522;

"The Changing Trend in Present-Day Baseball," *Baseball,* 32 (May 1924): 535–536, 572–573; 33 (June 1924): 297–298; 33 (July 1924): 345–346, 373; 33 (October 1924): 493–494;

"A Review of the Recent Scandal," *Baseball,* 34 (December 1924): 299–300, 329;

"Has Judge Landis Made Good?" *Baseball,* 34 (February 1925): 393–395, 428–430;

"Should the Lively Baseball Be Abolished?" *Baseball,* 35 (August 1925): 407–408;

"Cutting Straight to the Heart of the Baseball Dope," *Baseball,* 38 (February 1927): 387–388, 420; 38 (March 1927): 449–450, 468–469;

"A Better Method of Rating Baseball Pitchers," *Baseball,* 38 (April 1927): 483–485, 516;

"Many Homers–Many Runs–Is the Baseball Trend," *Baseball,* 39 (June 1927): 309–310;

"On the Ten Year Track of the Extra Base Clout!" *Baseball,* 39 (July 1927): 364, 372–373;

"Back to a Better Balanced Ball Game!" *Baseball,* 39 (August 1927): 408;

"Changing Base Hits into Runs," *Baseball,* 39 (September 1927): 464, 469;

"The Faulty Foundation of Batting Averages," *Baseball,* 42 (January 1929): 347–348, 372–373;

"The Much Discussed Menace of the Lively Ball," *Baseball,* 43 (October 1929): 503–505, 521–522;

"A New Era in Baseball," *Baseball,* 48 (May 1932): 533–534, 569;

"The Changing Trend in Modern Baseball," *Baseball,* 49 (June 1932): 293–294, 326;

"Serious Problems Which Confront Baseball," *Baseball,* 50 (January 1933): 339–340, 376;

"New Fields for Major League Enterprise," *Baseball,* 50 (March 1933): 435–436, 473–474;

"What's Wrong with Baseball, Anyway?" *Baseball,* 50 (April 1933): 483–484, 521;

"When Is a Home Run Not a Home Run?" *Baseball,* 51 (July 1933): 349–351, 374;

"Cashing in on Safe Hits," *Baseball,* 51 (August 1933): 405–406, 426;

"Hard Times Are Baseball's Golden Opportunity," *Baseball,* 51 (September 1933): 435–436, 472;

"Baseball Problems of the Winter Meetings," *Baseball,* 52 (December 1933): 291–292, 333–334;

"Baseball Takes the Air," *Baseball,* 57 (June 1936): 293, 331–332.

F. C. Lane's career as a sportswriter comprised only a part of a long and various life. Joining the staff of *Baseball Magazine* sometime in 1910 or early 1911 at the age of twenty-five, he is first listed as co-editor with the founder of the magazine, J. C. Morse, in the December 1911 issue. Beginning with the January 1912 issue, he is listed as sole editor, a position he held for twenty-six years, ending in December 1937. During his editorship, and in the many signed articles he contributed to the magazine, he broadened and deepened its original purposes: to be a celebrator and an independent but friendly critic of all dimensions of the National Game of baseball. Published monthly and year-round, *Baseball* could take a longer view of events than the daily papers or the weekly *Sporting News* and *Sporting Life.* The staples of *Baseball* were interviews with players and others attached to the game in various ways, monthly and seasonal reports on doings in the organized, independent, collegiate, and industrialized (but not the Negro) leagues, biographical essays, discussions of the business and politics of baseball, and various attempts to measure the effectiveness of offensive and defensive styles of play. Lane himself became an excellent interviewer and profiler, and he was a constant critic of the statistics that purported to measure the game. His goal was to establish an objective, scientific basis for evaluating player performance. He was, perhaps, handicapped in this quest by an affection for the scientific game as it was played before 1920.

Ferdinand Cole Lane was born near Morehead, Minnesota, on 25 October 1885, the fourth child of Alpheus Ferdinand Lane and the third of his second wife, Mary Cole. Family economic troubles caused them to move east, to Akron and Canton in Ohio, and then to Lowell, Truro, and finally Marion, Massachusetts, where the family settled. Lane says in *Twentieth-Century Authors* (1955) he attended school for six years "under the shadow of Hog's Back Church" near Truro and then graduated from Tabor Academy in Marion. He received a B.A. from Boston University in 1907. He then attended law school for three years at Boston University, as well as pursuing graduate studies at the Massachusetts Institute of Technology. Simultaneously he served part time as assistant biologist at the Massachusetts Department of Fisheries and Game. During these years he also developed a habit of extensive travel. Both the extent of his education and its scientific emphasis would have a significant impact on the nature of his sportswriting. He always presented himself as an "objective observer," and he enjoyed presenting material about baseball in the context of Western history and literature, as in the following defense of the stolen base from his 1922 article "The Hidden Risks of Base Stealing": "'Opportunity,' said Napoleon. 'I make opportunity.' The baserunner can say no less." Lane and his wife, Emma, were married in her Brooklyn home on 30 June 1914. She outlived him by some ten months. There is no evidence that they had any children.

Lane's routine as editor of *Baseball Magazine* included writing yearly appraisals of the potential opponents in each World Series and then evaluating the outcome of the series. In addition, each year he named an all-star team for both the National and American Leagues and an All-American team comprised of the best players from both. Beginning in 1927, he also developed a system that would reveal the most valuable offensive player in the league each year. And throughout his tenure he published interviews with many players and officials of the game. Lane's interests encompassed both the game on the field and the politics and business side of the game. In all, he produced more than eight hundred signed articles for the magazine, and in addition undoubtedly wrote many of the unsigned editorials. He also did "much ghost writing," he told *Twentieth-Century Authors,* though there has been no positive identification of anything he wrote under anyone else's name.

Lane best describes his sense both of himself as a sportswriter and of the vast changes occurring in the way baseball was played in a September 1921 article, "Has the 'Lively' Ball Revolutionized the Game?" There he refers to himself as an "investigator . . . who, free from all prejudice, is trying to get at the facts." He reveals his own prejudice about how the game should be played in describing the batting revolution of the time. "Baseball which would by rights consist of the four-square edifice of pitching, batting, fielding, and base running, has shifted during the chaotic conditions of the present into a towering batting structure which quite overshadows other departments of the game." Here Lane's uneasiness about the ascendancy of the slugging style exemplified by Babe Ruth is underlined.

Lane consistently stressed the importance of statistics in making baseball a distinctive sport. He articulates this principle in a 1923 article profiling Al Munro Elias, whom he called "The Wizard of the Dope." In the article he states that the "most important improvement in baseball is the development in the vital statistics of the game" and that "the great preponderance of baseball over all other athletic sports rests upon the facility with which it may be expressed in permanent form in statistics."

Lane often compared those with an interest in baseball statistics to scientists. "Researches into the dope," he writes in "Should the Lively Baseball Be Abolished?" (August 1925), "are always of interest to the vast army of fans to whom records and averages are a fascinating study. Besides there is an element of scientific value in such investigations. For just as the botanist can tell by rings in the stump of a giant Sequoia that the year, it may be that Columbus discovered America, was marked by a prolonged drouth in the Yosemite Valley, so may the baseball dopester trace the influence of sudden changes in the game itself by corresponding changes in the written records." Later in the same essay he compares the "dopester" to a geologist.

That Lane concerned himself with the business side of the game as well as the game on the field is particularly evident in times of turbulence: the war over the Federal League, the "Black Sox" scandal and Judge Kenesaw Mountain Landis's commissionership, and the effects of the Depression in the early 1930s, for example. In 1914 and 1915 Lane became especially interested in the issues presented by the Federal League. In the June 1914 *Baseball* he asked "Is There Room for a Third Big League?" His answer was affirmative, and he cited population statistics, the wealth of the Federal League owners, and the eventual presence of enough major-league-caliber players in support. Even before the advent of commercial air travel opened up the whole country to major-league baseball, Lane was able to imagine expansion. Several of his other articles in *Baseball* underscored these points and served to support the cause of the Federal League.

One source of players for the Federal League was, of course, the existing major leagues, and frequently Lane's biographical articles of the time focus on the dubious legality and general unfairness of player contracts, particularly the reserve clause, which he nevertheless regarded as essential to the health of the game. "Is There Room for a Third Big League" was followed the next month by an article on George Stovall, "The Firebrand of the Federal League," that focuses on his treatment in Cleveland and St. Louis. A March 1915 celebration of the career of Eddie Collins, "Collins the Great," focuses in part on his contractual relations with Philadelphia and his trade to Chicago. In the May 1915 *Baseball* Lane focuses more directly on contractual injustices in "Reulbach, the Man Who Was Run Out of Baseball," the blurb for which reads: "it is the aim of the following article to trace that career, to reveal the high-handed injustice which made success to a man like Reulbach an impossibility, and to expose the dark intrigues whereby a player of the highest capacity and integrity can be summarily read out of baseball." Lane's sense of contractual unfairness eventually disappeared as the reserve clause appeared more and more essential to order in the game.

Lane was not at all happy with the behavior of the major-league owners. Beginning in the February 1915 issue, in which his "Baseball Management That Costs a Fortune" disparaged the building of new baseball parks, he chided them for their business practices, and urged the official recognition of the Federal League. In "Why Not Recognize the Federal League?" (March 1915) he identified team owners as the principal obstacle to this goal: "the progress of American baseball is a story of perpetual strife against the obstinate, pigheaded stubbornness of the leaders in possession against any innovation, however vital to the welfare of the game." In "Eventually There Will Be a Third Big League Why Not Now?" (April 1915) he rehearses his arguments for expansion, and in "The International League, the Belgium of the Baseball War" (May 1915) he worries about the effects of the dispute on the minor leagues, announcing "the 'Baseball Magazine' has been laboring for some weeks to bring the contending factions together on mutually agreeable terms of peace."

Lane did not consider all owners pigheaded, however. In the summer 1915 issues of *Baseball* Lane published "Famous Magnates of the Federal League," profiling the Federal League owners. In the profile of Robert D. Ward, which appeared in the July issue, Lane writes: "it is our purpose to show the baseball public the type of men who have made the Federal League, and are now waging the fight which they believe to be in the interest of the national game. . . . clean-cut, masterful men who have made a fortune in other lines of business and would render a conspicuous service to baseball, having seen what manner of men they are and the prospect they offer for a new era in the game, if the public prefer the beer-guzzling, whiskey-befuddled magnate of the old school, why, that is their own lookout." This depiction of Ward is followed in the August and September issues by equally positive profiles of Harry Sinclair and Chicago owners Charles Weeghman and William Walker.

Lane concluded his meditations on the Federal League war in the January and February 1916 issues of *Baseball.* In his January article, "The High Road to Peace," responding to "rumors of peace in baseball," he moderates his call for recognition of the Federals as a third major league, suggesting instead a "middle road," on which both sides would make concessions. In "Peace and Prosperity" he declared the war over and prosperity at hand, even as he expressed his preference for expansion and a third major league.

Lane did not respond much to the developing Black Sox scandal, at least not in his signed articles. He attacked sportswriter Hugh Fullerton's claim that the 1919 World Series had been fixed, not on the grounds of the purity of baseball but rather because the statistical evidence suggested that the two leagues were pretty evenly balanced. Fullerton's claim, he felt, was a result of the myth of American League superiority. The Black Sox scandal, as well as subsequent ones, is a definite presence in *Batting: One Thousand Expert Opinions on Every Conceivable Angle of Batting Science* (1925), Lane's only baseball book. "Shoeless Joe" Jackson, often cited and discussed in the book, is described as "the unfortunate Joe Jackson." Ed Cicotte is referred to as "that great pitcher with a blackened reputation," and Joe Gedeon, a St. Louis Browns player who became caught up in the scandal, is described as "one of the best hit and run men in baseball before he was banished from the game as a melancholy aftermath of the Black Sox scandal." "Shufflin' Phil" Douglas, a New York Giants pitcher who was banished from the game by Landis in 1922 for suggesting that he could be bribed to desert the team in the heat of a pennant race, is referred to as "the unfortunate Phil Douglas."

Lane also kept an eye on the political side of the game. When Judge Landis was appointed commissioner, Lane was supportive, but he bristled at some of Landis's decisions and found him a distasteful individual. Lane's coverage of Landis's handling of the O'Connell–Dolan scandal is a case in point. Just before the World Series of 1924, in which the New York Giants and Washington Senators were to compete, Landis barred Giants outfielder Jimmy O'Connell and coach Cozy Dolan for life for allegedly offering a bribe to Phillies shortstop Heinie Sand to throw a game. Landis exonerated three Giants regulars who were also implicated. Lane interviewed everyone involved for an article he published in the December 1924 issue of *Baseball,* "A Review of the Recent Scandal." He had trouble interviewing Landis and reported in the article that "Judge Landis treated our well meant efforts with personal abuse."

Lane followed up in the February 1925 issue with an assessment of Landis, "Has Judge Landis Made Good?," presenting him as "a man with conspicuous faults no less than conspicuous virtues." He worried that Landis as commissioner "is responsible to no one in baseball for his conduct," and he worried about his character. Alluding to the incident mentioned above, Lane wrote: "we have done not a little for Judge Landis. He has never done anything for us. On the contrary, his violent temper has led him to personal insult as surprising as it was unprovoked." Lane concluded his article with a list of five "defects of temperament" he finds in Landis: "a theatrical love for effect," "a domineering manner," "a cold, self-centered, merciless strength of purpose," "utterly lacking in tact," and "a truly colossal egotism and a personal vanity quite as astonishing." "On the whole we are inclined to believe that the Judge has made good," Lane concludes. "But his exploits represent far from one hundred percent efficiency. And personally, we would have a higher respect for the man if he did not remind us so much of a famous quotation from Shakespeare's tragedy, 'Macbeth,' of 'The poor player who struts and frets his hour upon the stage and then is heard no more.'" This assessment could not have pleased the judge.

In a series of articles in 1933 Lane considered the ills (mainly brought on by the Depression) of professional baseball, concluding that as a sport and as a business the game was fundamentally healthy. His December 1933 article, "Baseball Problems of the Winter Meetings," summarizes these issues and proposes some tentative solutions:

> First: A possible readjustment in the sale of tickets and in the distribution of receipts of World Series games. Second: A sweeping downward revision in expenses involving a reduction in many player salaries. Third: a serious attempt, by trades and otherwise, to attain a better balance of club strength in both major circuits. Fourth: a thoughtful consideration of double-headers and other possible means of stimulating public interest. Fifth, an equally thoughtful consideration of far-reaching innovations such as: First: The All-Star game inaugurated during the past season between picked teams of the two great circuits. Second: The more ambitious project which calls for a general series of inter-league games between the two great circuits during the closing weeks of the season.

These proposed solutions were themselves problematic, however. One reason was the nature of the ownership of a major-league team. Lane identifies the problems of baseball as "problems of any large business in hard times, problems which call for initiative, courage and a fair insight into future conditions." The owners tended not to exhibit these qualities, though; "with few exceptions," he writes, owners "have been cautious, ultra-conservative and, in a sense, shortsighted." The owner "is usually so engrossed with his individual cares and worries that he slights, if he does not ignore, the needs of baseball as a national institution."

Lane also felt that too much income was going to the players and argued that more of the income for the World Series should go back to the teams and the game itself. He also felt that players' salaries should be reduced–a reform about which owners could be enthusiastic–emphasizing that the problem lay with owners' attitudes and not necessarily with players' greed. "The owners have engaged in a mad scramble to spend their money in the effort to create a winner. The result is, mounting expenses, diminishing receipts." Lane seemed occasionally sympathetic with the players' position, saying in an article in the April 1933 issue, "What's Wrong with Baseball, Anyway?," that "ballplayers . . . are driven by a kind of necessity to get all they can while 'the getting is good.' They realize that their own hold upon a job is insecure and may slip at any moment. They are too familiar with the accidents and hazards of their highly competitive profession to bank very strongly on the future. Their philosophy is simple. It is 'make hay while the sun shines.'" Nevertheless, in the January 1933 article that inaugurated these meditations, "Serious Problems Which Confront Baseball," he referred to salary expenditures as "stark insanity."

Lane considered the owners the source of another problem, the "regrettable situation," as he calls it in "New Fields for Major League Enterprise" (March 1933), in which major-league crowd size "in most of these parks . . . has begun to lag in July, to dwindle in August and to die away to an apathetic handful of spectators in September." A related problem was that "in striving for a pennant, the interests of each individual owner clash with the interest of the league as a whole." The pennant had become more important than the game itself. In "What's Wrong with Baseball, Anyway?" Lane deplores both owners' and fans' obsession with winning: "By assigning wholly fictitious values to success, the individual ball game has declined in importance. The game, as a contest, has become obscured in the lengthening shadow of the pennant." To restore interest in the contest Lane recommended something like parity among all major league teams.

He also wanted to see interleague play. He listed the All-Star Game as something that should continue and proposed interleague play in the last third of the season as a remedy for lagging attendance. As he emphasizes in "New Fields for Major League Enterprise," the idea was not a new one. "Who originated this proposition, I cannot say. I do know that I discussed it at length with Barney Dreyfuss, then President of the Pittsburgh Ball Club, nearly twenty years ago. He favored the plan. It has been broached many times since. Not a few sport writers have written about

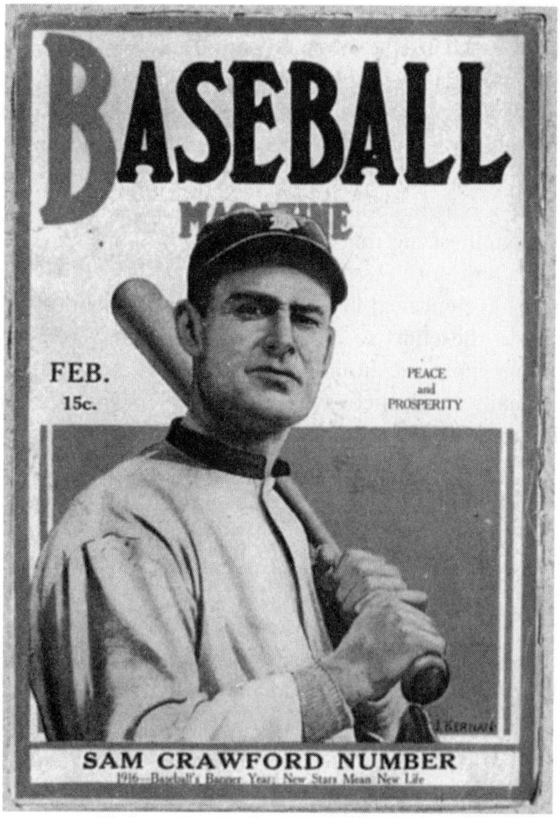

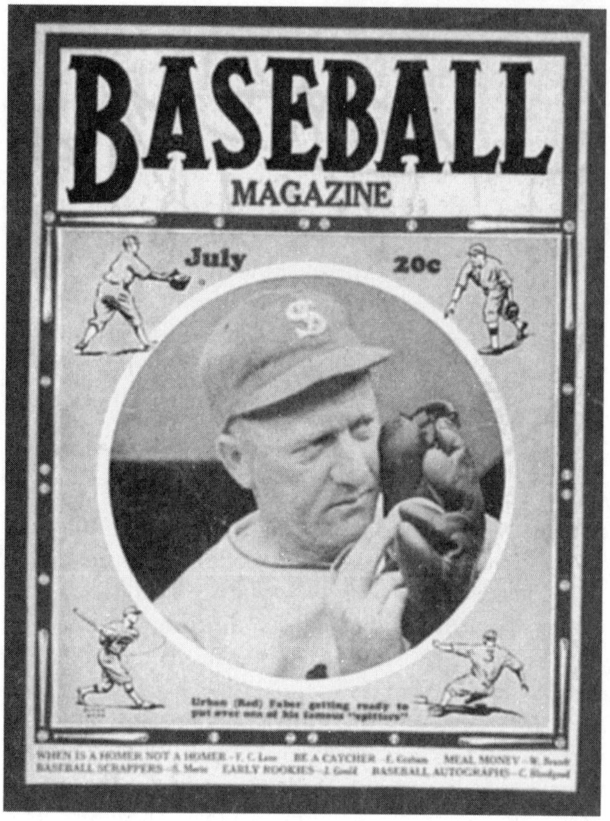

Covers for 1916 and 1933 issues of the magazine Lane edited from January 1912 until December 1937

it in their columns." In spite of Lane's recommendations, it was the mid 1990s before interleague play was introduced. Lane was hopeful, however, that the present crisis would overcome the owners' innate conservatism, as he suggests in "Hard Times Are Baseball's Golden Opportunity" (September 1933): "the progress of baseball has come almost entirely from periods of stress like the present." In "What's Wrong with Baseball, Anyway?" he concludes that "baseball is as sound at the core, as a sturdy oak, as strong and as unassailable."

Lane saw the business history of baseball as essentially progressive. In a June 1936 article on the role of radio in baseball, "Baseball Takes the Air," he complained that "too many may feel inclined to believe that baseball has arrived, that little further change is possible or even desirable. That point of view," he continued, "is in error. Baseball is still progressing, developing along new lines, evolving into something broader, better and more universally appealing." Innovations that increased the popularity of the game, such as radio, were always welcome, though Lane noted that a minority of the owners saw radio as "an invisible enemy, a rival" and feared that fans would be "prone to stay at home and listen to the game rather than to journey to the ballpark and see it in person."

On the field Lane also hoped for constant improvement, but here he had more difficulty arranging the facts to suit his theories. The slugging revolution of the 1920s violated his sense of the constant improvement in offensive play, so he settled for a more dialectical sense of the development of the game, saying in the third of his four 1924 articles on "The Changing Trend in Present Day Baseball," "the history of baseball may be briefly stated as an effort to maintain a normal equilibrium between the offensive and defensive forces of a baseball club." *Normal* is the key word here. Lane always regarded the home run as an abnormal event.

Lane was a statistician at heart, and he looked to the records in formulating his understanding of the game. In fact, he maintained that records were what distinguished baseball from all other sports. In "Cutting Straight to the Heart of the Baseball Dope" (February 1927), he announced that "Baseball owes an immeasurable debt to the records. The history of the game is a story of the growing accuracy and complexity of the records. Plodding statisticians, toiling in obscurity and for a meagre recompense, have been the creators of baseball greatness no less than star players and far sighted owners. The records have sustained baseball's enduring popularity and assured it a well deserved eminence over all other athletic sports." At the center of his sportswriting lies a continuing examination of these records.

He wondered how to evaluate players accurately and began to analyze the records as early as 1916. In the March 1916 issue of *Baseball* Lane focused on the question of batting averages and found the statistic an unreliable one in judging the value of a hitter. His article "Why the System of Batting Averages Should Be Reformed" (January 1917) begins by raising the following questions: "Suppose you asked a close personal friend how much change he had in his pocket and he replied 'Twelve coins,' would you think you had learned much about the precise state of his exchequer? Would a system that placed nickels, dimes, quarters, and fifty-cent pieces on the same basis be much of a system whereby to compute a man's financial resources?" Lane then points out that "it is precisely such a loose, inaccurate system which obtains in baseball and lies at the root of the most popular branch of baseball statistics." Later in the article he characterizes the system of batting averages as "absurd."

Lane then asks "what constitutes the value of a hit" and answers his own question: "a hit is valuable in so far as it results in a score." He proceeds to give values to each kind of hit and to conclude, on the basis of their performances in the 1915 season, that Cactus Cravath was a far better hitter than Jake Daubert, even though the latter's batting average was twenty points higher. Lane continued to analyze batting, pitching, and fielding records throughout his editorial stay at *Baseball,* and even though none of them caught on with major-league baseball, they stand as precursors to the sophisticated computer analysis of baseball records made these days by Bill James and others.

In fact, Lane returned to the subject early the next year, this time armed with figures gleaned from a representative selection of games from the previous year. In a series of three articles in the January, February, and March 1917 issues, Lane improved on his speculative figures of the year before and added the base on balls to his calculations. In the first article, "Why the System of Batting Averages Should be Reformed," Lane offered some "essential facts" and described his method: "This summer we kept strict account of a large number of major league games. In order that these games might be as representative as possible they extended from the opening contest in April to the closing curtain scene in October and included a world's series game for good measure. They comprised games played by every club in both major leagues." From this data Lane was able to calculate a value for each kind of hit, based on "the effect that hit may have in producing a run," as he reminded his readers in "A Brand New System of Batting Averages" (February 1917). The current system "manifestly exaggerates the importance of the chop hitter who makes few extra base hits, while it is grossly unfair to the slugger who makes many triples or home runs." Lane's system, he promises, will "offer a much fairer and more comprehensive view of the batting ability of the professional baseball player."

Lane applied his system to the leading batters of the 1916 season, finding enhanced value in such players as Zack Wheat, Cy Williams, and Wally Pipp. Eddie Collins, on the other hand, "was a man of many singles" and his value as an offensive player thereby diminished. In the March 1917 issue Lane addressed himself to the question of the offensive value of "The Base on Balls." In this article Collins makes a sort of comeback, as he had received eighty-six bases on balls the year before. "Collins has a double toe hold on the base on balls column. He is known to be a good batter and he is also a past master in the art of waiting them out." Lane went on to calculate the value of a base on balls, using the same data he had for calculating the value of hits. In addition, he surmises that "the effect of a base on balls, in short, is more damaging to the pitcher's nerve than is an ordinary hit."

That June Lane began to think about fielding records, calling them a "dreary chaos" and "a dark chapter in baseball history." The trouble, he felt, was that although there was a single standard in batting, "in fielding there should be as many standards as there are positions." He tried comparing individual fielding averages against the major-league average at that position but reported that he was not happy with the results: "the figures mean something perhaps, but just what isn't very clear." He satisfied himself with the conclusion that "if we are going to use the records at all, let's use them intelligently. They tell us nothing when they say that Hans Wagner fielded for .942 at shortstop, unless they also give us a fair standard by which to judge that mark. Such a standard might readily be found by approximating the fielding average of all shortstops in the major leagues."

But it was offense that fascinated Lane most, and he was witness to the radical change in offensive play instituted by Babe Ruth. Lane had already been writing about Ruth for several years, beginning with an article in the October 1918 issue, "The Season's Sensation." In "Why Babe Ruth Has Become a National Idol" (October 1921) he resorts to quoting William Shakespeare in order to describe the sources of Ruth's popularity.

"Greatness in any line breeds its critics. We cannot help recalling Cassius' comments on Julius Caesar, in Shakespeare's famous drama, they apply so aptly to Babe Ruth in his own particular domain of baseball. 'Upon what meat does this our Caesar feed that he has grown so great?' is a fair echo to the chorus of the knockers; and that other line of grudging appreciation, 'Why, man, he doth bestride the narrow world like a Colossus,' is a literal and timely description of how the battering Babe towers above the diamond." Ruth's figure continued to fascinate Lane, perhaps because he violated all the norms of scientific baseball, to which Lane was committed.

Three articles that appeared in the summer of 1922 reveal Lane's apprehensions about the emerging slugging style of offensive play. In "The Hidden Risks in Base Stealing" (June 1922) Lane deplores the decline of "one of baseball's most sparkling features, that act of skill, daring and initiative which spells a stolen base." He proceeds to argue, using figures from the preceding year, that the risk of getting thrown out at second on a steal attempt was no greater than the risk of getting put out as a result of staying at first. He concludes: "baseball needs stolen bases."

In "The Decline in Run Scoring Efficiency" (July 1922) Lane begins by asserting that "it isn't the hit that counts so much, for hits in themselves do not win ball games. Runs are the essential and hits are valuable only insofar as they produce runs." Lane complains of a situation in which there is "a mad scramble for safe hits which has been the major league obsession for the past two or three years" and consequently "the proper use of these hits has not received the attention it deserves." He mentions "three methods of making hits productive: Slugging, the timely wallop, and base running." He graphs the decline in run production and notes that its recent rise is due to slugging rather than baserunning, which has declined. He reminds the reader that "we have deplored this sensational decline because the stolen base is one of the flashy, brainy plays in baseball and one of the chief elements of a well directed offense."

Lane reports that slugging "has raised the general average of run scoring efficiency in spite of a continued decline in base stealing." He notes, however, "that all the home run records . . . have not sufficed to raise the run scoring average to what it was ten years ago." "Extra base hitting," he concludes, "is at best a poor substitute for scientific base running." In "Natural Slugging vs. Scientific Batting" (August 1922) Lane's bias can be seen clearly in the way he describes the two kinds of hitters. The place hitter overcomes "brute force by science." The advent of the slugger he describes as follows: "Then came Babe Ruth and his fifty-six ounce bat and his two hundred and twenty pounds of gorilla like strength and he assaulted not only the home run record but the long established system of major league batting." Science is being overcome by brute force.

In a series of four articles published between May and October 1924 with the umbrella title "The Changing Trend in Present-Day Baseball" Lane systematically examines the changes he saw. He states his thesis at the beginning of the first article of the series, speaking of "an essential change in the very nature of baseball which is at present in full operation. A few years back Baseball was a pitching duel. Then the lid blew off and it became a slugging orgy. Now, . . . the game is slowly returning to sanity, where it will presumably become a better balanced, more evenly rounded contest of skill." In the third article of the sequence, "Is Pitching Growing Stronger?" (July 1924), Lane imagines a happy ending to the slugging "epidemic." Under the conditions of slugging, he writes, games "become too uncertain, too much the sport of blind chance, too much the product of brute slugging. Many of the finer points of baseball were ignored or used but seldom. The sacrifice and the stolen base are quite as much a part of baseball as the two-bagger. They have been greatly neglected, however, in recent years. Baseball was a little one-sided in 1917, too much of a pitching affair. But baseball was much more one-sided in 1921 when the sluggers were indulging in an orgy of extra base hits." Lane felt, however, that he could refer to these trends in the past tense. As he said later in the article, "Major League batting found the turning point in the season of 1921. It is now on the decline. The trend is plainly downward."

Offensive play forms the subject of Lane's only book on baseball. It was called *Batting: One Thousand Expert Opinions on Every Conceivable Angle of Batting Science.* Published by *Baseball* in 1925, it sold for a dollar. Lane describes *Batting* as "the essence of thousands of interviews." He wanted readers to know that in this case the author is simply an objective scientific observer, assembling data from as many sources as possible. "The Editor of this book," as he calls himself, "has expressed no opinion. He has merely painstakingly collected and contrasted a vast array of opinions from all the acknowledged experts of batting that baseball has produced in fifteen years." Fifteen years was exactly the amount of time Lane had spent editing *Baseball,* interviewing ballplayers both on the job and in their homes.

Despite Lane's aspiration to be an objective, scientific observer, his own opinions about batting periodically show through the many quotations from players that comprise the bulk of the book. He longed to see continual improvement in offensive skills. "Keen observers of batting, however, will admit that certain features have improved. The bunt, for example, was an offshoot of legitimate batting, that has now fixed its place in the club offensive. The hit and run play has also developed greatly, and place hitting, the crowning achievement of the batter's skill, has been more evident in later seasons than it was before the dawn of the present century." Lane later defines place hitting as "the ability to direct the course of the batted ball at will to some point on the playing field where it will fall out of reach of the waiting fielder" and characterizes it as "this most difficult of batting arts." He cites Willie Keeler's "pointed epigram . . . 'Hit 'em where they ain't.'" Lane also includes the art of bunting as one of the essential dimensions of batting–"there would be more great hitters in baseball if the bunt were better developed"–and underlines his progressive sense of the development of batting by adding: "the bunt marks a distinct advantage in batting science over the old days of pure slugging."

Lane was writing, however, in the new days of pure slugging; not only had Babe Ruth been setting new home-run records, but many lesser hitters were emulating his batting style. Lane quotes Ruth just ten times in the book, while he cites Ty Cobb–the master of place hitting–some fifty times. On the other hand, the other players cited by Lane speak of Ruth and Cobb equally often. Otherwise, Lane is silent on the resurgence of slugging, mentioning only that "slugging has not received the credit it deserves in the playing records." The chapter on slugging, "The Secret of Heavy Hitting," is the longest in the book, indicating that the players themselves have a great deal to say about it.

For Lane, though, slugging was not scientific; and he regarded baseball as "an exact science." Comments on scientific hitting, on the team as a machine, and on players as specialists in technical areas can be found throughout the book. Lane at one point imagines himself an experimental scientist, measuring the speed of the bat as it meets the ball. *Batting* is by no means a scientific tract, however; instead, it is a kind of medley of players' voices, orchestrated by Lane himself. The reader is treated to the opinions not just of batters but of pitchers, umpires, managers, owners, and miscellaneous others, all culled from fifteen years of Lane's interviewing.

Lane spent much of 1927 meditating about the meanings of the statistical record baseball left behind. He was plainly still uneasy about the ability of the records to reveal the value of players. In "Cutting Straight to the Heart of the Baseball Dope," which appeared in the February and March issues of *Baseball,* he used various offensive figures to determine who the best players in the National and American Leagues were the preceding year. Lane felt that these records had "never been properly codified." His solution was to "combine all the necessary facts about a player in one comprehensive total." Lane identified a dozen categories of offensive play, listed the leading five players in each category, and assigned five points to the first-place player down to one for the fifth. In the National League, Lane was impressed that Hack Wilson got the most points even though he was not among the top five in batting average. In the American League, he was impressed by how many more points Babe Ruth got than anyone else. He was careful to observe that his "aim is to suggest a substantial improvement upon the existing method," not to arrive at a perfect one. This evaluation became an annual event in *Baseball.*

Lane did not think the player with the highest batting average was the best hitter, nor did he think the pitcher with the lowest earned run average was the best pitcher; thus, in the April 1927 issue he applies the same method to the 1926 pitching records. He discusses the limitations of both win-loss record and earned run average as indicators of pitching excellence and concludes that "no single column of figures, taken as it stands, can rate Major League pitchers and do justice in the rating." Lane combines eight categories and finds that George Uhle of Cleveland was by far the best pitcher in the majors and Pete Donohue of Cincinnati was the best National League pitcher. Though Uhle was first in winning percentage and second in earned run average in the American League, the fact that Donohue appeared on neither list in the National League consoled Lane.

Over the next four months Lane produced articles each month examining the slugging style and its effectiveness in producing runs. In "Changing Base Hits into Runs" (September 1927) he reminds himself and his readers that "ability to change hits into runs is the test of a well organized offensive. . . . In general, the club with the best balanced and most intelligently directed attack will score the maximum number of runs on the hits it has made." Lane charted the number of runs made per hit for the past fifteen years and found that the number had sunk back nearly to its 1912 low. For him this fact confirmed the ineffectiveness of the slugging offense, for he felt that longer hits ought to have produced more runs. "The present system of blind slugging," he concludes, "is not only unscientific, but extremely wasteful. The team no longer gets the utmost from its safe bingles."

Lane, though, had given himself reason to be optimistic in the three previous articles in the series, the first two on extra-base hits and a third, "Back to a Better Balanced Ball Game!" (August 1927). He began his study of extra-base hits by noting that their dramatic increase "marked a fundamental change in the very texture of the game." A result of this was "a looser, more hazardous affair." Wondering if it were not possible to overestimate the influence of these extra-base hits, Lane concludes his article on the home run by announcing that "the day of the home run is already past the meridian. . . . The pitchers are gradually getting back some lost ground. Baseball is becoming less of a slugging match, more of a well-rounded contest. Exit the surplus homer and its accompanying brood of too common and unimpressive scored runs." "Back to a Better Balanced Ball Game!," in which Lane's charts showed a drop in both batting averages and total bases between the 1925 and 1926 seasons, concludes on a similar note: "the tide has evidently turned. Batting no longer dominates the game. Pitching and fielding have at length succeeded in halting the devastating slugging which threatened to throw all established checks and balances into absolute chaos."

In "The Faulty Foundation of Batting Averages" (January 1929) Lane returns to his examination of the batting average as a meaningful offensive statistic and develops a comprehensive rejection of it. He begins by saying that "this is no idle slam at batting averages" and admitting that batting averages were "at once the most popular and the most accurate" of baseball statistics. But, Lane argues, "the true test of a batter should be not what he does for himself, but what he does for his team." What was wrong with batting averages was that "they glorify individual effort," not team play.

Lane asks what the purpose of a baseball team is and answers "to score runs and to prevent the opposing team from scoring runs." "Runs are the thing," he continues, "hits are merely incidental." Batting has no other value than "to assist in scoring runs." Lane then asks "what is a safe hit, anyway?" The answer is "a hit is a fraction of a run. So far as actual results go, it has no other value." Runs are created through three factors: "getting on base, advancing, and scoring."

Having focused his readers on scoring runs as the meaningful dimension of batting, Lane turned his attention to the relation of batting average to "batting ability." "A hit is a fraction of a run, but there other fractions just as important, just as expressive of true batting ability." Lane proceeded to list the others–the walk, the sacrifice, the hit by pitch, the infield out or fly ball–that advance baserunners and wondered "are they . . . expressed in the batting averages which are supposed to disclose a batter's ability?" The answer was no–for Lane one fundamental weakness of the batting average as a baseball statistic.

Lane adds a second fundamental weakness. "Wherein lies the fundamental weakness in batting averages? It is this. They exaggerate the importance of one particular feature of batting skill. They minimize or ignore or penalize other factors which also have their place. They are one-sided and therefore inaccurate. They are inaccurate and therefore unjust." Lane went on, "Batting averages consider only safe hits. To that extent they are unfair even to those who make them, for safe hits, as every schoolboy knows, vary greatly in importance."

Although Lane did not propose a specific solution to this problem, he understood the principles on which he thought batting ability should be based. "The unit of a batting average is a safe hit. The unit of a batting average ought to be a single base, and it makes no difference in the final result whether that single base is gained by the batter himself or is vicariously transferred to the base runner." Scoring runs was the thing, and "there are four bases in every run. The man who has contributed one or more of those bases by whatever batting method, is entitled to due consideration for his contribution to the coveted run scored." Lane concludes that "the batter should receive credit for all the bases he gains for himself, for all the bases he advances a fellow teammate by virtue of his ability to hit, to sacrifice, to work the pitcher for a pass or to advance the runner by an infield out. His final average, rated according to the number of bases which he has contributed to his club's total, is a far more accurate and comprehensive expression of his batting ability than the present long accepted method which considers only safe hits."

In the October 1929 issue of *Baseball* Lane returned to the issue of the batting surge of the decade and its meaning in "The Much Discussed Menace of the Lively Ball." He was more sanguine about the changes to the game in this article, saying that "the slump in science is a loss; the bulge in uncertainty is a gain. And there you are." Lane spent some time on the limitations of the scientific game, concluding that "the . . . pendulum . . . had swung too far in favor of defense." The number of home runs still seemed excessive, however, and Lane wondered about the causes. He concluded that "the lively ball is not quite so much of a villain as it has been painted" and that there were three other important factors: "the geography of the playing field" (with Baker Field in Philadelphia an especial villain), "changing styles in batting" brought on by Babe Ruth's success, and "the everlasting 'new' ball," a product both of umpires' discarding discolored and roughened baseballs and fans' not returning those hit into the stands. Lane concludes that with time hitting would return to its "normal" levels.

Then, looking back at the records of the 1931 season, Lane again detected a change in the offensive styles of play, a change he discusses in two articles, "A New Era in Baseball" (May 1932) and "The Changing Trend in Modern Baseball" (June 1932). "A New Era in Baseball" begins with the fact that batting averages declined precipitously between 1930 and 1931. Lane hoped that this was a sign that a balance between pitching and batting would be achieved. Looking back at the league batting averages of the past twenty years, he concluded that in the 1910s "the pitcher had the game by the throat," while in the 1920s "the era of the famous rabbit ball was in full swing." Lane looked for reasons for the current balancing and found three. Umpires had been instructed to keep baseballs in play longer, giving pitchers the advantage of worn baseballs. In addition, a change in the manufacture of the ball resulted in raised seams and a thickened cover, deadening the ball and making it easier for pitchers to throw curve balls. The sacrifice fly was also abolished, lowering batting averages slightly. Lane hoped these changes signaled a trend back to the scientific ball of earlier days and revealed his distaste for the slugging game when he referred to it as "the mad hysteria of batting which ruled the game for at least ten years" while welcoming a "soberer, saner viewpoint."

In "The Changing Trend in Modern Baseball" Lane looked at the home-run and stolen-base figures for the past twenty years and found more evidence for hope. Even though the figures do "disclose very graphically the enormous ascendancy of the home run and the corresponding fall of the stolen base," Lane found that "last year two significant things occurred in the records. Stolen bases increased slightly and home runs took a decided drop. The variation in stolen bases was slight indeed, but homers fell off more than thirty per cent." Lane attributes the drop in home runs to the same changes in the use and manufacture of baseballs he mentioned the previous month. Lane saw the home run and the stolen base as "roughly complementary," but he could only hope that the use of the stolen base as an offensive weapon would increase.

During 1933 Lane found time to return to some of his favorite topics of the game on the field: the significance of the home run and of batting averages. Lane had always been ambivalent about the home run, regarding it on the one hand as the most efficient way of scoring runs and on the other as the harbinger of a style of play he despised. His July 1933 article "When Is a Home Run Not a Home Run?" introduced the notion of park dimensions as a factor in players' home run totals. In the August issue Lane interrogated the value of batting averages again in the article "Cashing in on Safe Hits." He calculated the average length of hits in terms of bases, team by team, and then calculated the number of hits it took to produce a run for each team. Once again Lane identified runs as the key element of the game. "Every incident upon the field of action centers about the run. Every act of managerial strategy, every deed of player initiative, base stealing, batting, fielding, and pitching are all designed to produce or to prevent the production of runs." Lane continued, "This basic thought requires emphasis in these days when the hit has been granted an exaggerated importance." Lane still regarded the hit as an individual act and runs as the result of team play, but he could not avoid the knowledge that "the longer a hit, the more likely it is to score runs."

Lane left *Baseball* at the beginning of 1938; he is last listed as its editor in the December 1937 issue, and no more articles appear with his byline. For the next eleven years, through the 1948 issue, he edited *The Little Red Book of Major League Baseball,* published by his friend Al Munro Elias. After that he left the study of baseball behind him, spending his remaining professional years teaching at Piedmont College in Georgia, where he was awarded an honorary doctorate, and writing books about nature for both adults and children. He made Cape Cod his home until his death on 20 April 1984 at the age of ninety-eight.

References:

Frederick Ivor-Campbell, "Lane, Ferdinand Cole 'F. C.,'" in *Biographical Dictionary of American Sports. 1992–1995 Supplement for Baseball, Football, Basketball, and Other Sports,* edited by David Porter (Westport, Conn.: Greenwood Press, 1995), pp. 116–117;

Jack Kavanaugh, "F. C. Lane," *National Pastime,* 16 (1996): 58–59.

Papers:

Several letters by F. C. Lane are housed in the F. C. Lane File of the Baseball Museum in Cooperstown, New York.

Bill Leiser

(26 April 1898 - 16 January 1965)

Raymond Schmidt
College Football Historical Society

MAJOR POSITIONS HELD: Sports reporter, *San Francisco Examiner* (1925–1933); sports editor, *San Francisco Chronicle* (1934–1965); sports columnist, *Illustrated Football Annual* (1942–1953).

WORKS: "O'Dea of Wisconsin," in *Best Sports Stories 1935,* edited by Irving T. Marsh and Edward Ehre (New York: Dutton, 1935), pp. 188–196;
"Goat to Glory," in *Best Sports Stories 1946: A Panorama of the 1945 Sports Year,* edited by Marsh and Ehre (New York: Dutton, 1946), pp. 95–99;
"The Ceiling Was Zero," in *Best Sports Stories 1947: A Panorama of the 1946 Sports Year,* by Marsh and Ehre (New York: Dutton, 1947), pp. 128–131;
"End of an Era," in *Best Sports Stories 1948: A Panorama of the 1947 Sports Year,* edited by Marsh and Ehre (New York: Dutton, 1948), pp. 139–142;
"Bear Escape," in *Best Sports Stories 1949: A Panorama of the 1948 Sports Year,* edited by Marsh and Ehre (New York: Dutton, 1949), pp. 125–130;
"Brunk of the Bears," in *Best Sports Stories 1950: A Panorama of the 1949 Sports Year,* edited by Marsh and Ehre (New York: Dutton, 1950), pp. 101–107;
"From the Ivory Tower," in *Best Sports Stories 1961: A Panorama of the 1960 Sports Year,* edited by Marsh and Ehre (New York: Dutton, 1961), pp. 278–279.

SELECTED PERIODICAL PUBLICATIONS–UNCOLLECTED: "The Coast," *Illustrated Football Annual,* 13 (1942): 74–83;
"The Coast," *Illustrated Football Annual,* 14 (1943): 37–45;
"The 10-Year Roundup," *Illustrated Football Annual,* 14 (1943): 78–81;
"The Coast," *Illustrated Football Annual,* 15 (1944): 23–31;
"The Coast," *Illustrated Football Annual,* 16 (1945): 18–24;
"The Coast," *Illustrated Football Annual,* 17 (1946): 46–54;
"The Coast," *Illustrated Football Annual,* 18 (1947): 45–53;
"The Coast," *Illustrated Football Annual,* 19 (1948): 54–62;
"The Coast," *Illustrated Football Annual,* 20 (1949): 54–63;
"The Coast," *Illustrated Football Annual,* 21 (1950): 54–63;

Bill Leiser

"The Coast," *Illustrated Football Annual,* 22 (1951): 28–37;
"The Coast," *Illustrated Football Annual,* 23 (1952): 29–38;
"The Coast," *Illustrated Football Annual,* 24 (1953): 57–64.

Bill Leiser was a San Francisco–based sportswriter whose newspaper career spanned across a period of nearly five decades. During this time he became known as one of the preeminent football writers in the country, but he was also a consummate newspaperman in his role as sports editor of the *San Francisco Chronicle* for thirty-one years. Under his direction the image, content, and style of sports reporting in the *Chronicle* was uplifted; as a columnist he explored the entire range of the sporting world in a fashion that appealed to even the most casual fan. While never relenting in his support of amateur athletics, Leiser was always ready to champion civic improvements for his adopted Bay Area.

Many sportswriters labor through their careers without a nationally syndicated column, a stack of published books, or a regular byline in one of the popular magazines, and so their work is usually destined to be known almost exclusively by the regional newspaper audience for whom they wrote. Leiser was able to overcome these obstacles, however; he established a solid reputation among his peers around the country with a journalistic style that combined color, drama, and skepticism, as well as a real knowledge of the games and personalities he covered.

William Frederick Leiser was born on 26 April 1898 on a farm near Madison, Kansas, his mother's home state, to Mederick Leiser and his wife, Mabel Tocht Leiser. After brief stops in Minnesota and Wisconsin, the family soon moved to Twin Falls, Idaho, where Bill was eventually joined by two brothers, Edwin and John, and one sister, Ruth. After completing high school in Twin Falls, Leiser began college at Stanford University in Palo Alto, California, but the U.S. entry into World War I soon caused the young student to alter his plans. Leiser joined the army and was assigned to a student battalion for his time in the military, which was all spent on the West Coast.

Returning to his classes at Stanford, Leiser worked at odd jobs in order to pay his way through school. For one year he had to live in a loft, something that he had in common with a well-known college football figure of whom he later wrote, Amos Alonzo Stagg. Majoring in political science, he was a member of the Stanford debate team through all four of his undergraduate years, serving as the manager of the debate squad during his senior year. Leiser intended to continue on in law school and was also a member of the professional law fraternity, Phi Delta Phi. His budding skills in politics and debate were put to good use as a major campaign manager in several of the student body elections at Stanford, earning for himself the nickname "Colonel House," after Woodrow Wilson's political crony.

Leiser, although not an athlete himself, had always been attracted to the world of sports, and he was active in two significant areas of Stanford athletics. After returning the college to intercollegiate football in 1918, Stanford officials soon became envious of the prestige and money being generated by the great gridiron teams of its archrival, the University of California. The coming of Glenn "Pop" Warner as head football coach at Stanford was still a few years away, but in 1920 the university decided to proceed in the building of a sixty-thousand-seat football stadium. Beginning in March 1921, Leiser served as one of the leaders in the selling of stadium subscriptions, and in just six weeks virtually all the necessary $200,000 in funding had been pledged.

More significant to his eventual career was Leiser's work as a sportswriter during his collegiate days. While he served as associate editor of the Stanford yearbook for 1921, it was the newspaper business that was beginning its siren call to the prelaw student. While an undergraduate he worked as a sportswriter for the student newspaper, the *Daily Palo Alto,* and in his senior year he served as editor of the paper.

During this same period Leiser was also picking up occasional stringer assignments covering sports for the *San Francisco Examiner* and the *Los Angeles Times,* frequently using the byline of "William Frederick." After graduating from Stanford in 1921 with a degree in political science he continued with his studies for two more years in Stanford Law School while continuing to work as a stringer for the two West Coast newspapers. He received his Juris Doctor degree from Stanford in June 1923, but when it came time for him to prepare for the bar examinations in early 1924, Leiser could no longer ignore his interest in newspaper journalism and college athletics.

Turning his back on six years of study, Leiser decided to try his hand as a professional sportswriter, and so he never took the state bar exams. In later years he facetiously told people that the main reason he had decided against the legal profession in favor of sportswriting was to insure that every November he would have football tickets to the big game between Stanford and the University of California. After working as a part-timer for a year, Leiser was hired in 1925 as a full-time sportswriter by the *San Francisco Examiner* and assigned to cover yachting in the Bay Area, along with college football.

The *Examiner* was part of William Randolph Hearst's chain of newspapers and billed itself as the "Monarch of the Dailies." The lively material on its pages helped to achieve a dominant sales position over the other three major dailies in San Francisco at this time. Much of the success of the *Examiner* was also generated by its sports section, which had a modern and spacious appearance that was the equal of any newspaper in the country. Its coverage of West Coast college football was without peer in Northern California.

Leiser joined an *Examiner* sports staff that included such capable football writers as Curly Grieve, Brent Metzler, Abe Kemp, and Martin Burke. With five schools in the Bay Area playing major college football, Leiser, known throughout his career as a prolific writer, went right to work pounding out reams

Rousseau's Perfect Race Turns Back Challenger Tommy Lee

Every Tuesday morning special amateur sports page, covering bowling, billiards, bush baseball and other minor sport. Managers, send in your scores early.

San Francisco Examiner Sports

Monarch of the Dailies

MONDAY SAN FRANCISCO, AUGUST 28, 1933 MONDAY

Baseball, football, basketball, boxing, swimming, track and field, tennis and all the leading sports covered by best observers and writers in the West.

SEAVER TRIMS DR. BAKER 3 AND 1, FOR STATE GOLF TITLE

YACHT MAYBE BEATS CAPRICE IN CUP CLASSIC

Perpetual Trophy Remains in S. F. as Result of 'Old Fox's' Ninth Victory for Corinthians

By William Leiser

Nine times he has been on the spot and still he claims a perfect score!

He won again yesterday, "The Old Fox," resorting to few of the tricks, stunts, and aces in the hole for which he is famous, but sailing a race without a mistake and turning back the challenge of young Tommy Lee and the Caprice of Los Angeles by 2 minutes and 14 seconds.

It was a big, comfortable margin at the end. It was anything but that at the start when the challenger slipped out to a nice lead, and it was anything but that four-fifths of the way through the 14 mile course as ships and masters matched wits less than sixty seconds apart, but in the end Skipper Arthur Rousseau, sailing a perfect race, romped home with the traditional reputation more than ever intact—"unbeatable on San Francisco Bay."

Beating Back From Southampton--Old Fox Moves Up--Wins 9th Cup

HERE THEY GO. The "Old Fox," Art Rousseau, and the Maybe, leading the challenging Caprice and Don Lee of Los Angeles in race for the perpetual challenge cup yesterday on San Francisco Bay.

THE PICTURE was snapped back of Angel Island, where the breeze was still and the "race began." The two great six meters were this close together almost all the way through the fourteen-mile course.

ROUSSEAU AND THE Maybe eventually won by two minutes and fourteen seconds, most of the margin being accumulated in the last leg. It was the ninth successful annual cup defense for the "Old Fox."

SEAVER WINS GOLF HONORS FROM BAKER

California Youth Has Little Trouble Scoring Victory in State Tournament

Cards

By Harry M. Hayward

DEL MONTE, Aug. 27.—"Charlie, three or four years ago they told me you were a great golfer but could never win a tournament because you were too good natured. But it seems that ever since the telling I have been presenting championship trophies to you. Twice in succession it has been the northern California amateur cup and now it is the California championship which you have so gloriously won today."

Lead article written by Leiser during his final year as sports editor of the Examiner

of football material from August through December. Frequently he filed multiple articles on the same day, and on those occasions he used his regular byline on one article while other features carried the byline "By W.F.L." or no credit line at all. The style of many of these unsigned pieces clearly marks them as Leiser's work, however.

The 1920s was an ideal time for following college football on the West Coast, as teams struggled fiercely throughout the decade for regional dominance. In the early years of the decade the University of California had reigned with its "Wonder Teams," but soon Stanford and the University of Southern California were considered to be among the top programs in the country. Meanwhile, one of the big stories of West Coast football during the 1920s was the emergence of a small Catholic college called St. Mary's. Under the direction of coach Edward "Slip" Madigan, St. Mary's openly aspired to be the "Notre Dame of the West" in college football. Madigan's aspirations began with the idea of challenging Stanford, the University of California, and the University of Southern California for dominance on the Pacific Coast, and for nearly two decades the colorful gridiron coach provided Leiser with story material.

Leiser quickly established himself as the top football writer at the *Examiner,* and the newspaper assigned him to most of the top games on the coast, such as the early-season showdown between Stanford and St. Mary's in 1927. The lead to his game story on 2 October 1927 demonstrates the early development of his style, one that could also be found in many eastern press boxes at this same time: "Playing through four quarters of intense fighting, the determined, consistently brilliant defensive football that only a great team can produce, little St. Mary's College tied the Stanford champions in knots at Palo Alto yesterday and beat them, 16 to 0." Another example of his early style is an article he wrote two weeks later, after being on hand as USC and Stanford battled to a 13–13 tie in one of the great games of West Coast football history. On the front page of the *Examiner* of 16 October 1927 Leiser wrote: "A milling mob of 60,000, limp and exhausted, but football mad, poured out through the Stanford stadium gates at sundown yesterday, murmuring the name of the man with the punch, who averted defeat, and almost won, for Coach Glenn Warner's Cards."

By 1927 Leiser had already expanded his regular football writings to include an occasional weekday feature column, although he did not receive his own regular column until he joined the *Chronicle*. Leiser's writings for the *Examiner* frequently display an intimate understanding and love for the excitement of football, as in his 16 October 1927 piece: "It was not a perfect game by far, but perfection is likely to be monotonous, while a game with breaks, spirit, fight, and last minute drive that characterized Saturday's argument will send the crowds home raving."

By 1930 Leiser was commonly regarded as one of the best football writers on the West Coast, even if he was not yet recognized nationally. His personal life had been substantially altered by this time, with his marriage to Alice Lyle (Billie) Parks on 31 August 1930. Billie, originally from Minnesota, was working on the staff of the *Examiner* as the foods editor (writing under the byline of "Prudence Penny") when the couple met. The Leisers had no children during their marriage of thirty-five years.

In the realm of college football USC had by this point ascended to the top of the gridiron wars on the West Coast, with Stanford, California, and St. Mary's regularly challenging the Trojans with powerhouse teams of their own. During the seasons of 1930 and 1931 Leiser covered games that carried both regional and national significance, including a November 1930 visit to the Bay Area by Dartmouth for a major intersectional game against Stanford. These assignments provided opportunities for him to become more widely known among writers from the East.

Typical of his story leads at this time was his opening to an account of a surprising win by California over St. Mary's, as he wrote on 12 October 1930: "Bullet footballs from the trigger-like arm of Opportunist Henry Shaldach, everlasting fired into the heart of the St. Mary's defense, sprung the Bears into the open yesterday at Memorial Stadium." Throughout his career Leiser always had a great appreciation for outstanding football players; yet, only a few made enough of an impression on him to warrant a detailed description for his readers. On 25 October 1930 Leiser was on hand to watch USC, with standout running back Orv Mohler, dismantle an overhyped Stanford outfit by a score of 41–12. Describing the brilliant Mohler, Leiser wrote that "there aren't superlatives in the English language that can properly describe the wheeling, twisting, driving, slippery 160-pounder as he was moving through the open field spotted with Stanford men, shifting the ball from one arm to the other."

Along with covering his beloved Stanford, Leiser wrote most often about the Galloping Gaels of St. Mary's during his time at the *Examiner*. In 1931, just one week after a stunning upset of USC, ranked first in the nation, the St Mary's football team produced another shocker, this one a 14–0 win over California. Leiser, already known for the amount of copy he could generate, pumped out an exciting account of California's attempt to hold off St. Mary's wide-open offense that ran to forty-four column inches.

Throughout Leiser's years at the *Examiner* he also served as the yachting writer, a busy assignment during the spring and summer months along San Francisco Bay. Leiser revisited various forms of boat racing frequently throughout his career, but the early 1930s at the *Examiner* represents his most extensive coverage of the sport, as he penned boating and university crew racing articles throughout the summer and well into the fall. Every August since 1895 the Bay Area had hosted the Perpetual Challenge Cup, a fourteen-mile race for yachting-class craft, and Leiser's prerace and race-day coverage incorporates all the techniques of style that typified his football material. The Perpetual Challenge Cup was a big-time race that drew yachts from around the country, along with occasional foreign entries, but the trophy generally found a home each summer in Northern California at the Corinthian or San Francisco Yacht Clubs.

Leiser's articles previewing the race typically combine historical reminiscence of the event, along with plenty of technical material dealing with race strategy. His stories of the actual races include detailed descriptions of the yachts struggling through the choppy bay waters around Alcatraz Island. Leiser produced readable accounts of the yachting races, reflecting a real understanding of the sport while also entertaining even the most casual devotee of the sports section. For good measure he also used a sprinkling of his typical "scene-setting," such as his lead on 28 August 1933 about longtime Bay Area yacht skipper Arthur Rousseau: "He won again yesterday, the Old Fox, resorting to few of the tricks, stunts, and aces in the hole for which he is famous, but sailing a race without mistake in turning back the challenge of young Tommy Lee." While at the *Examiner,* Leiser played a major role in organizing the annual W. R. Hearst Regatta, which quickly became one of the largest yachting events on the West Coast.

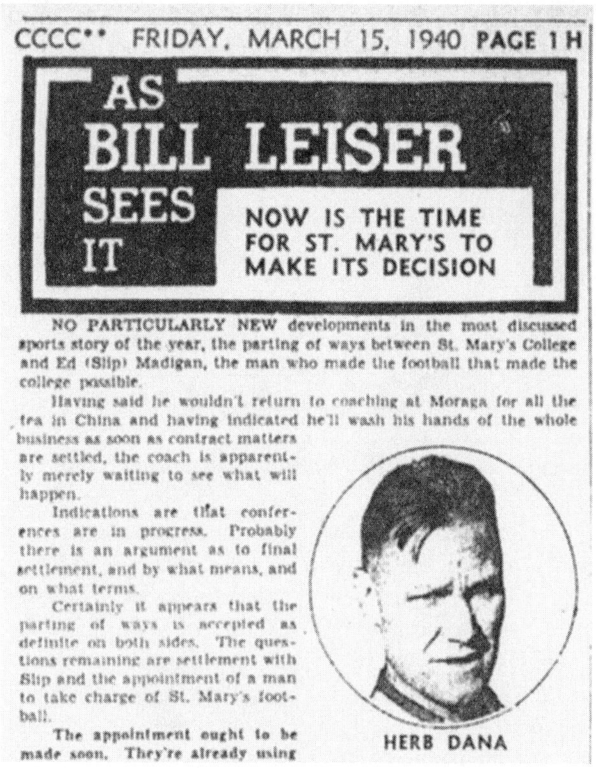

CCCC** FRIDAY, MARCH 15, 1940 PAGE 1 H

AS BILL LEISER SEES IT

NOW IS THE TIME FOR ST. MARY'S TO MAKE ITS DECISION

NO PARTICULARLY NEW developments in the most discussed sports story of the year, the parting of ways between St. Mary's College and Ed (Slip) Madigan, the man who made the football that made the college possible.

Having said he wouldn't return to coaching at Moraga for all the tea in China and having indicated he'll wash his hands of the whole business as soon as contract matters are settled, the coach is apparently merely waiting to see what will happen.

Indications are that conferences are in progress. Probably there is an argument as to final settlement, and by what means, and on what terms.

Certainly it appears that the parting of ways is accepted as definite on both sides. The questions remaining are settlement with Slip and the appointment of a man to take charge of St. Mary's football.

The appointment ought to be made soon. They're already using

HERB DANA

Head and opening paragraphs of one of Leiser's columns for the San Francisco Chronicle

Leiser's first love was still college football, however, no matter how good a boat racing analyst he might be, and by 1933 his writings reflected a desire to expand the boundaries of his material beyond that of the basic game previews and analysis. On 19 August 1933, before the preseason football training camps had even opened, Leiser broke an exclusive story in the *Examiner* about the decision to sign "Navy" Bill Ingram, head football coach at the University of California, to a new two-year contract, putting to rest the rumors that he might be leaving Berkeley despite having good seasons in 1931 and 1932. Throughout that autumn Leiser produced a series of articles that included such diverse gridiron topics as talk of a possible series between USC and St. Mary's, a discussion of a proposed new Pacific Coast Conference, a defense of Coach Warner against his Stanford alumni critics, a debate on the merits of various rules changes and offensive philosophies, and a consideration of the relative merits of football as played in the Big Ten and Pacific Coast Conferences.

By 1933 Leiser was also chafing at the restrictions of the West Coast boundaries that were imposed upon his subject material. That season the sports editor of the *Examiner,* Curley Grieve, sent Leiser along with the St. Mary's team on its trip to New York City for the annual game against Fordham, a series that Madigan had initiated in 1930. Leiser filed dispatches along the way on the trip east, as the luxurious special train carrying the team and a large party of fans made stops in Chicago at the Century of Progress Fair and at Niagara Falls. In New York City Leiser wrote extensively about the frenzy of anticipation over the approaching showdown between the two powerhouses. Fordham came into the game with an undefeated record, along with ideas about a possible trip to the Rose Bowl and a national championship.

This fourth renewal of their intersectional rivalry was also a major part of the struggle between the two Catholic college football powers, as each sought to become the next Notre Dame of the gridiron world now that the Fighting Irish seemed to be tailing off after the death of the legendary coach Knute Rockne. Leiser reveled in this newfound media spotlight, and while he was filing his usual pregame stories back to the West Coast he was also finding time for writings on the national football scene. A typical example was a column from New York that appeared on 3 November 1933, devoted completely to a discussion of the rumors of an impending coaching change at Notre Dame, and his views on the most likely successor.

Leiser's time in New York in November 1933 also brought him into regular contact with all the major writers and members of the sporting media who had converged on the city for the intersectional showdown. His pregame stories frequently mention conversations with prominent media personalities such as Ted Husing, Sid Mercer, and Bill Corum. When the *Examiner* ran its extensive game coverage on 5 November 1933, it presented an account of the action written by Leiser and another by Damon Runyon, who was writing for the Universal News Service. Runyon had long ago established himself as one of the best of the college football writers, but in 1933 his technique seemed antiquated and out of fashion when compared to the more contemporary football writing of the West Coast newsman. By this time Leiser's game accounts combined an exciting, colorful, and dramatic style of leads and scene setting with an ability to present readable and factual descriptions of what had happened on the field. When the traveling party eventually made it back to San Francisco, Leiser continued to combine occasional articles on the national football scene with his regular coverage of the Bay Area schools. With his career evolving beyond that of a regional football writer, Leiser was hired in early 1934 as the sports editor for the rival paper to the *Examiner,* the *San Francisco Chronicle.*

In the years prior to 1934 the *Chronicle* sports pages had never been a serious challenger to the Hearst-owned *Examiner.* The *Chronicle* itself was a privately owned newspaper, founded in 1865 by M. H. de

Young, and for many years it carried a subcaption below its logo banner on the front page that read: "Leading Newspaper of the Pacific Coast." Since late 1921 the sports editor of the *Chronicle* had been Harry B. Smith, a newsman who soon became widely known on the West Coast as a major boxing writer. The sports section of the *Chronicle,* printed on green paper since the mid 1920s and subtitled the "Sporting Green," had always been considered somewhat old-fashioned in overall appearance, an exception being the day of the annual California–Stanford football game coverage. The four mainstay sportswriters at the *Chronicle* by the early 1930s included Smith, Ed Hughes, Art Rosenbaum, and Will Stevens, with Hughes being highly regarded for his coverage of the football program at California along with his work on the Pacific Coast League baseball beat.

Leiser was brought into the *Chronicle* as sports editor by Paul C. Smith, then the executive editor, and according to Rosenbaum, who eventually compiled a fifty-eight-year career at the *Chronicle,* Harry Smith was not pleased about the change. In an unpublished interview Rosenbaum explained that Smith, despite his reputation as a boxing expert, was not considered to be a good writer by the other staff members. Also, under his direction as editor, the *Chronicle* sports section was felt to be lagging behind the competition.

Leiser had a considerable amount of respect for Smith as an individual, according to Rosenbaum, so he obtained the approval of the *Chronicle* management to continue listing Smith's name on the banner of the sports page as the sports editor, with Leiser's name eventually being added at a later date. Until the early 1940s the *Chronicle* sports page logo included the wording "Edited by Harry B. Smith and Bill Leiser"; according to Rosenbaum, however, Leiser was in complete command of the sports department from his first day at the *Chronicle.* Another of the agreements Leiser obtained on coming to the *Chronicle* was that any stories dealing with criminal or scandalous activities involving sports personalities would not appear in the sports section but would be consigned to the pages of the city news department. This policy continued at the *Chronicle* until a management change at the newspaper in the late 1940s.

While Leiser was already regarded as an important writer on the Pacific Coast, his name was really brought into the national spotlight in September 1934 with the publication of his exclusive story locating Pat O'Dea, the college football great. O'Dea, an Australian, had played for the University of Wisconsin from 1896 to 1899, during which time he had accomplished phenomenal kicking feats that established him as the greatest punter and dropkicker ever to play the game of college football. By 1917 O'Dea could no longer take all the attention and adulation that constantly intruded into his personal life, and so he had disappeared and was thought to have been killed during World War I.

Nearly two decades later Leiser heard rumors about O'Dea living on the West Coast. Following up these leads, in early September 1934 he located O'Dea, who had been living in Westwood, California, for the previous fifteen years under the assumed name of "Charles J. Mitchell." By this time O'Dea, who worked as a statistician at the Red River Lumber Company, was ready to resume using his real name. The exclusive story was carried in the *Chronicle* on 19 September 1934, and Leiser opened with a classic lead: "They said he had moved on to the next world–this man who crashed through with football records never surpassed or equaled in the gridiron history of America and then vanished as completely and mysteriously as Aladdin's Genii." Leiser's article about O'Dea was later selected for inclusion in the annual collection published by E. P. Dutton of the year's best sports stories, the first of seven times that his writings would be so honored.

Under Leiser's guidance the layout and writing style of the *Chronicle* sports section were soon upgraded. By 1935 Leiser was also leading the way in a gradual shift of the method of football coverage at the paper, away from the usually lengthy pieces that included considerable detail and liberal amounts of insider commentary. In its place the *Chronicle* began presenting more of a "review" style of writing, which launched the sports section into the more-modern method of coverage. There was still room for some creativity, however, especially in the story leads, as in Leiser's postgame analysis of a 1935 showdown between the Universities of California at Los Angeles and California, when he wrote of the scene in Los Angeles: "They were steamed to white heat. Intensely they craved the scalp of the Golden Bear, and there were 80,000 of them storming the huge concrete bowl today to celebrate the drive of the South to the top, but they found the old big brother Bear too smart."

The sports page was not the only place at the *Chronicle* where Leiser made his presence known. While writing for the *Examiner,* in 1933 Leiser had been among the original members of the newspaper union that was called the San Francisco–Oakland Newspaper Guild. Within a year of joining the *Chronicle* Leiser was considered to be one of the prime movers in the highly successful efforts on the part of the union to enlist the editorial and sports staff personnel of the *Chronicle* into its membership. Leiser served as chairman of the Pension Fund Committee of the guild until his death in 1965.

In 1935 Leiser's reputation as a newspaperman was continuing to grow, as evidenced by his debut that fall as the host of a weekly Sunday night radio show, *Pigskin Parade,* on San Francisco station KFRC. The half-hour format of the show included orchestra music and some insider football chatter along with interviews of Bay Area college coaches and players. Leiser's prominence brought him many radio appearances throughout his career, and while appearing on a show on the NBC network in 1941 he was called one of the six top football experts in the country. Meanwhile Leiser continued to improve the sports staff of the *Chronicle,* and in the late 1930s he hired reporter Will Connolly away from the *San Francisco News.* According to Rosenbaum, Leiser admired Connolly's writing talents and hired him to be a sports columnist, and in short order the new writer was authoring the popular and long-running column "Will Connolly Says."

By 1940 Leiser had made the *Chronicle* sports pages stylistically contemporary, while his own long-running column, "As Bill Leiser Sees It," now wandered through a wide range of sports. Harry Smith, who usually wrote on boxing subjects in his "Sports Mirror" column, was still listed as a co-editor, but that practice soon changed. Meanwhile, the stable of writers at the *Chronicle* had benefited from the addition of several more regulars, along with correspondents from each of the major colleges around the Bay Area. Anticipating the general editorial policy at the *Chronicle* that evolved by the end of that decade, Leiser by 1940 had the sports pages filled with a variety of local and syndicated columnists, including such recognizable national names as John Lardner and Grantland Rice. While the *Chronicle* sports pages were now livened up with a substantial amount of artwork in the form of pictures and drawings, more significant to the average reader was the extensive use of Associated Press (AP) and United Press International (UPI) syndicated coverage for such major events as boxing title fights, the Masters golf tournament, major league baseball from spring training through the World Series, and the Wimbledon and United States tennis championships.

While Leiser was still as prolific as ever during the football season, writing both his column and daily bylined articles, the rest of the year his column covered topics that ranged from baseball to women's polo. In 1940 alone his subject material included topics as diverse as advocating the enlargement of the Yacht Harbor in San Francisco and discussing the specifics of the insider politics involved with the possible building of a new race track in the Bay Area. That Leiser was a sportswriter capable of intelligently traversing well beyond the world of college football can be seen in his column of 3 September 1940, as he discusses the possibilities of major league baseball eventually coming to the West Coast. Leiser wrote that "many regard the idea as entirely possible. . . . Many clubs often travel by air now. . . . Big league teams in San Francisco and Los Angeles would pay and would pay well, on a normal basis. Also they would destroy the Coast League as we know it."

The personalities of the sporting world always intrigued Leiser as much as anything. For example, his subjects in 1940 ranged from tennis great Helen Jacobs of Berkeley, who he dubbed as "Little Miss Second Place" as a result of her many finals defeats at Wimbledon and Forest Hills, to the champion racehorse Seabiscuit. In March 1940 he accompanied a party of nearly three hundred racing enthusiasts, sponsored by the *Chronicle,* on a seventeen-car excursion train to Los Angeles for the Santa Anita Handicap race. In his column of 3 March 1940, accompanied by a picture of Seabiscuit giving the cameraman a horse laugh, Leiser wrote with his usual flair and style as he talked of the horse and its performance in the race: "Almost like a horse coming back from the dead, old Seabiscuit stepped out on Santa Anita's race strip today. . . . after losing by a nose in two previous races, and supposedly broken down with a ruptured ligament, he came roaring home at the finish to win a little matter of $86,650. . . . We never saw a victory so popular in any sport."

His columns could also poke humor at sports figures, as on 4 July 1940, when Leiser wrote of former boxing heavyweight champion Jack Dempsey's exhibition tour against wrestlers: "Running around the country knocking out wrestlers at $10,000 per KO doesn't sound like bad business. . . . Now Jack is branching out. Next, he's going to meet a policeman. There are enough wrestlers and policemen in this country to keep Dempsey busy, knocking them out one at a time, every week for the next ten years."

The U.S. entry into World War II brought with it a major impact on the sporting world, and Leiser easily adjusted the coverage in the *Chronicle* to include the major brand of football being played by the service teams. For years he had covered the annual Armistice Day football game that was played in San Francisco between the West Coast Army and Navy teams, and West Coast service teams such as St. Mary's Pre-Flight, March Field, and Del Monte Pre-Flight provided plenty of material. Leiser also found time to cover the biggest of the college games on the West Coast, such as the controversial and now-legendary 1943 showdown in Los Angeles between USC and the College of the Pacific team coached by Stagg.

Further recognition of Leiser's spot among the best of the football writers came in 1942, when he was chosen to replace Los Angeles writer Braven Dyer as the Pacific Coast correspondent for the *Illustrated Football Annual,* an assignment he handled through 1953, when the publication folded. While the format of the preseason reviews for each of the major teams was fairly predictable, and Leiser had been writing a similar preview every year dating back to his days at the *Examiner,* he still brought his colorful and enthusiastic style to bear for national readers, especially when in his opinion particular players stood out, such as Herman Wedemeyer of St. Mary's, Kenny Washington of UCLA, or Ollie Matson of San Francisco. In the 1946 edition of the *Illustrated Football Annual* he called Wedemeyer "the greatest Coast-developed player of all time." Of particular significance to football historians is Leiser's special feature in the 1943 annual, in which he presented a review of the previous ten years of West Coast football and called the 1940 Stanford team the best of the era.

After the war Leiser was ready to handle the major changes that began to evolve on the American sports scene as a by-product of the growing national prosperity. In 1946 San Francisco finally had a big-league professional franchise, when the newly formed All-American Football Conference (AAFC) placed the 49ers team in the city. Recognizing the *Chronicle* sports editor's media influence on the coast, Arch Ward of the *Chicago Tribune,* who was heavily involved in the forming of the AAFC, sent 49ers owner Tony Morabito to see Leiser in the earliest organizational days. According to Rosenbaum the two men became good friends, and from the start Leiser was a vigorous supporter of the new pro football team. His support manifested itself in excellent game coverage and frequent columns urging fans in the city to support the team. After the 1949 season several of the AAFC teams, including the 49ers, were merged into the National Football League as part of the settlement that ended the war between the rival circuits. Leiser had been writing columns since the early 1940s on the possible expansion of professional football to the Bay Area, and when the Chicago Bears came to San Francisco in 1950 for the first time he enthusiastically wrote three brilliant columns on the visit of George Halas and his team.

In 1947 Leiser was honored by his national peers when he was elected to a term as president of the Football Writers of America. During his career Leiser also served three terms as president of the San Francisco Press Club, along with two stints at the head of the Northern California Football Writers Association. In 1948 he was awarded the Helms Foundation Medal for outstanding contributions to sports, as a result of his many civic efforts on behalf of the San Francisco area.

By the early 1950s changes occurred both at the *Chronicle* and in Leiser's personal life. Under its executive editor, Scott Newhall, the *Chronicle* had come to rely primarily on the writing of columnists, which eventually resulted in steadily growing circulation numbers for the newspaper that still billed itself as "The City's Only Home-Owned Newspaper." Leiser had heavily incorporated the use of columnists into the sports section more than a decade previously, and with many of the legendary national writers now in retirement he supplemented his staff with a new batch of prominent names from around the country, including Rube Samuelsen of Los Angeles, Joe King of New York, and Francis Powers of Chicago. By 1950, in keeping with the trends in newspaper sports, Leiser had again converted the style and content of the *Chronicle.* Making expanded use of the AP and UPI wire services, the *Chronicle* sports pages began providing equal amounts of national and local sports coverage, including plenty of attention to major league baseball.

Cover for an issue of the football magazine for which Leiser wrote from 1942 to 1953

By 1951 Leiser was suffering increasing health problems, and that year he underwent the first of several abdominal operations. A chain-smoker for years with incredibly bad eating habits, he was never a particularly healthy individual. Nearly six feet in height, he had always had something of a weaving, ungainly walk, and he eventually became a little stooped in his posture after the onset of his illness. Despite the best efforts of Leiser's wife, he was never known as a neat dresser and certainly did not fit the stereotyped idea of what a sportswriter looked like. According to Rosenbaum, Leiser was often lost in concentration while working on a story or column, and the total package helped to characterize him as somewhat of an eccentric. He had always been a hardworking and prolific newspaperman, however, and was highly respected by the people he worked with. With the onset of Leiser's health problems, which continued throughout the rest of his career, various people on the sports staff began to help him with some of the routine administrative work of the department.

Throughout the 1950s Leiser continued to address a wide range of sporting topics in his columns, as by now he no longer was writing other bylined features. Regularly he supported civic causes that were usually related to amateur athletics, such as promoting a Bay Area television fund-raiser for the U.S. Olympic team, helping to lead a fund-raising drive for a new basketball arena at the University of San Francisco, or helping to promote a high-school all-star baseball game in the city.

Leiser still had his eye on professional sports, however, with major league baseball receiving an increasing amount of his attention. For years he had been an advocate of major league baseball expanding to the West Coast, and throughout the 1950s he monitored the growing national sentiment for the move. When the inevitable finally arrived in late August 1957, with the announcement that the New York Giants and the Brooklyn Dodgers were moving to California, Leiser said in his column of 22 August 1957 that "the move, once it actually becomes official, will be the most tremendous ever made in organized professional sports. Its significance may go beyond sports." Even before opening day in 1958 Leiser was already at work in his column, drumming up support for building a new stadium in San Francisco to replace the old Seals Stadium that the Giants initially called home.

While Leiser had admired boxer Joe Louis throughout his career, once describing the champion as "very much a credit to the game," increasingly throughout the 1950s and into the 1960s he made clear his distaste for the sport of boxing and many of its characters. Topics that came in for his criticism–as being typical of the degeneration of the sport–included Floyd Patterson's title defense against Olympic champion Pete Rademacher, attempts by promoter Jack Hurley to pressure sportswriters into producing favorable publicity, and worst of all, the many questions and unsavory suggestions that followed the pair of Muhammad Ali–Sonny Liston fights.

Leiser had always been a newspaperman capable of looking into the future of sport and discussing the shape of the games to come, a trait that continued until his final days. Typical examples can be found in an April 1958 column, when he forecast the eventual movement of other major league baseball and football teams to new home cities; a May 1952 piece when he wrote that the strongest of football colleges could make fortunes by selling their television rights as they pleased; or his column of 29 March 1964, in which he advocated the U.S. use of professional athletes in the Olympic games, even as he attacked what he believed to be the hypocrisy of the so-called amateur athletics as practiced by American colleges.

Leiser's health continued to deteriorate, however. On 22 November 1964 the *Chronicle* published Leiser's last coverage of a college football game, his beloved Stanford-California showdown. His last column, which appeared on Christmas Day, 1964, dealt with the approaching Shrine Game and the great cause it served.

Leiser died at the Presbyterian Hospital in San Francisco on 16 January 1965 at the age of sixty-six. After services in his adopted hometown of Mill Valley, California, which were attended by many of the sporting personalities of the West Coast, Leiser was laid to rest in the Golden Gate National Cemetery in San Bruno. His full-time sportswriting career had spanned forty years, during which time his enthusiasm for college football and amateur athletics had never flagged, as he pursued a style of reporting that stressed accuracy and insight. On the day of his funeral the *San Francisco Examiner* carried a tribute from the Cable Car Clothiers Association to the longtime sportswriter, "The Legacy of Bill Leiser." The verse describes how "Bill Leiser had a touch of Ernie Pyle in him. . . . He could tell your story and mine. . . . He could tug at your heart with his perception. . . . He told the real San Francisco story as few men could."

Reference:

Art Rosenbaum, "A Farewell to Bill Leiser," *San Francisco Chronicle,* 17 January 1965.

Ed Linn

(14 November 1922 - 7 February 2000)

John Curtis

MAJOR POSITIONS HELD: U.S. Information Service (1951–1952); assistant editor, Macfadden Publications (1952); freelance writer (1953–1963); contributing editor, *The Saturday Evening Post* (1964–1968).

BOOKS: *The Eternal Kid* (New York: Nelson, 1961);
Veeck–As in Wreck: The Autobiography of Bill Veeck, by Linn and Bill Veeck (New York: Putnam, 1962);
The Last Loud Roar, by Linn and Bob Cousy (Englewood Cliffs, N.J.: Prentice-Hall, 1964);
The Hustler's Handbook, by Linn and Veeck (New York: Putnam, 1965);
Koufax, by Linn and Sandy Koufax (New York: Viking, 1966);
Masque of Honor, by Linn and Jack Pearl (New York: Norton, 1969);
Thirty Tons a Day, by Linn and Veeck (New York: Viking, 1972);
The Adversaries (New York: Saturday Review Press, 1973);
Big Julie of Vegas (New York: Walker, 1974);
Nice Guys Finish Last, by Linn and Leo Durocher (New York: Simon & Schuster, 1975);
Out of the Fire, by Linn and Ernst Papanek (New York: Norton, 1975);
Where the Money Was, by Linn and Willie Sutton (New York: Viking, 1976);
Inside the Yankees: The Championship Season (New York: Ballantine, 1978);
Steinbrenner's Yankees (New York: Holt, Rinehart & Winston, 1982);
A Great Connection: J. H. Krehbiel, Sr./Molex (Washington, D.C.: Regnery Gateway, 1988);
The Great Rivalry: The Yankees and the Red Sox, 1901–1990 (New York: Ticknor & Fields, 1991);
Hitter: The Life and Turmoil of Ted Williams (New York: Harcourt Brace Jovanovich, 1993).

OTHER: "'We Conquer,' He Cried, and Fell Dead," in *Best Sports Stories 1955: A Panorama of the 1954 Sports Year,* edited by Irving T. Marsh and Edward Ehre (New York: Dutton, 1955);
"1960: The Kid's Last Game," in *The Third Fireside Book of Baseball,* edited by Charles Einstein (New York: Simon & Schuster, 1958), pp. 272–284.

Ed Linn (photograph © by Jerry Bauer, 1990; from the dust jacket for The Great Rivalry, *1991)*

SELECTED PERIODICAL PUBLICATIONS–UNCOLLECTED: "Casey Stengel," *Sport* (September 1959);
"Don't Call Me Willie," *Sport* (October 1959);
"George P. Marshall: Last of the Small-time Spenders," *True* (October 1961);
"The Meaning of the Game," *Sport* (June 1977).

A top freelance writer since the 1950s, Ed Linn is the co-author of the critically acclaimed autobiographies of Bill Veeck and Leo Durocher. He has written two highly regarded books and several memorable articles on Ted Williams during a career that has produced eleven books on sports and hundreds of magazine stories and essays. Linn's collaborative talents and his wry, forthright style came of age in the 1950s and 1960s, and he was among those who pioneered the new journalism in sportswriting.

Edward Linn was born on 14 November 1922 in Boston. He was the second child of Gertrude and Hyman Linn and younger brother to sister Edith, who was born two years earlier. Hyman Linn worked as a compositor for several local newspapers, including the *Boston American.*

Growing up, young Ed spent as much time on the playground as he did at school. He was an unremarkable student but a tireless baseball player. He liked to play shortstop, and with his cousin Elbie Lafargue at second base, he formed a reputable middle infield combination. In "Warm Breezes from the Past," an article he wrote for *Sport* in 1971, Linn recalled that he and Elbie were known as "the Cousins" around their neighborhood. "We played for three or four teams in Boston's well-organized Park Leagues at the same time," he wrote, "and in between . . .well, we just played."

In an unpublished interview Linn said: "The adult, semi-pro teams in the league played at night, and we played in the afternoon. My mother always made sure that she rented a house near a park." In "Warm Breezes from the Past" he mentions the time he and Elbie attended a baseball clinic at Fenway Park. They had clipped coupons from the newspaper that gave them free entry to the clinic and the Red Sox game afterward. He remembered Boston center fielder Tom Oliver telling the assembled kids how he formed the pocket in his glove by cutting out the center and then sewing it back in. "We always told each other that we were going to do that ourselves," he wrote, "always knowing that we really weren't."

Nothing in Linn's childhood suggested that he would grow up to be a writer. He graduated from high school and took a job as a boilermaker's helper at the Charlestown Navy Yard. "At the time, I had no thought of being much of anything," he recalled. In 1943 he entered the Army Air Corps and served for three years, rising to the rank of sergeant. After receiving an honorable discharge in 1946 Linn returned to civilian life and became a member of what was called the "52–20 Club," a reference to federal assistance to returning veterans of twenty dollars a week for fifty-two weeks. "They gave you a year's worth of unemployment," he said, "and there were some of us who were very good at collecting it."

Although Linn was not overly interested in furthering his education, he took advantage of the free college tuition and monthly subsistence allowance offered through the G.I. Bill to enter the two-year general college program at Boston University. After graduating Linn decided to stay at Boston University, enrolling in the school of journalism. In "Warm Breezes from the Past" Linn wrote that this decision kicked off "a series of accidents that led me into writing about sports." He took a creative-writing course that was being offered by the journalism school for the first time, and thus came under the tutelage of Dorothy Speare, a novelist and screenwriter. Speare taught Linn how to write formula stories for *The Saturday Evening Post* and quality stories for *The New Yorker*. She also showed a story Linn wrote in the *Post* style to her agent, who promptly sold it to the prestigious magazine. Linn recalled that the publication of the story, "My Kind of Music," made him feel like "I'd just gone to the World Series." His writing skills were maturing, but he had little interest in writing about sports. "As a matter of fact," he said, "everyone there wanted to be a sportswriter except me. I'd say to them, why are you going to college to be a sportswriter? You don't have to study to be a sportswriter. You can learn to write a lead in two days."

On 12 June 1949 Linn married Ruth Goldberg, and a year later, after he graduated from Boston University, they both went to work for the U.S. Information Service in Washington, D.C. "My wife and I realized that everyone we were working with had been there for 20 years," Linn said. "They were always talking about leaving and getting into private enterprise. So we got out of there." In 1952 the Linns returned to Boston, where Ruth gave birth to Michael, the first of their three children.

Shortly thereafter, Linn went to New York to look for work, and during his search he contacted his agent (the same one who had sold his first piece to the *Post*) with a story idea on the Boston Marathon, an event that had always fascinated him. His agent got him an interview with the sports editor of *True* magazine, and Linn submitted the article but heard nothing in response. In the meantime, Macfadden Publications hired him as an assistant editor to work on *Saga,* one of its men's magazines.

Linn's article on the Boston Marathon sat on the editor's desk at *True* while the position changed hands. The new editor, formerly an assistant editor at *Sport* (a Macfadden publication), inquired with his old employers about Linn and contacted him. Linn's story, "'We Conquer,' He Cried, and Fell Dead," was published in *True* in 1954. In it he extolled marathoners as

Dust jacket for the 1962 autobiography of the colorful baseball-team owner on which Linn collaborated

"superbly conditioned athletes" and warned that "an untrained entry has about the same chance as a flat-chested cover girl." The story won second prize in the E. P. Dutton anthology *Best Sports Stories 1955: A Panorama of the 1954 Sports Year*.

A short time later Edward Fitzgerald, the editor in chief at Macfadden, asked Linn if he would like to write a story on former Brooklyn Dodgers infielder Don Zimmer, who was then excelling as a minor leaguer at St. Paul in the American Association. "You won't get paid," he remembered Fitzgerald telling him, "but you can write it on company time." Linn responded, "Well, do I fly, take a bus, or walk?" The story, "One Step from the Majors," was the first of a series of assignments from Fitzgerald, sometimes as many as two per month. Linn's success convinced him to leave his job at Macfadden and freelance full-time.

Linn thrived under Fitzgerald's editorial guidance, much as he had under Dorothy Speare's in his college days. "We both had the same idea," he said of his mentor at Macfadden, "that you should use the technique of fiction for non-fiction stories." Fitzgerald also taught Linn that "if the story came out opposite to the way he had assigned it, that's the way you wrote it. He'd even congratulate you for digging up something different. He never second-guessed you, and so I never second-guessed myself." Roger Kahn noticed that, despite a small budget, Fitzgerald had managed to "assemble a stable of splendid writers," which included Linn, Arnold Hano, and John Lardner, Ring Lardner's son.

In 1954 Linn got an important professional break. *Sport* was planning a long article on Boston Red Sox star Ted Williams, who was returning to baseball after serving as a fighter pilot in Korea. Such articles were called "*Sport* Specials," and, as Linn recalled, they "were the last article in the magazine, and they had to be at least 10,000 words. I liked to do them, because I could throw in everything I had researched." For several years Linn and Kahn wrote most of these special features.

The assignment got off to a bad start. On the first day of spring training Williams broke his collarbone–according to Linn he either "dove or slipped going after the first ball hit to him on the first day of training"–and it looked like his rehabilitation would keep him in Florida past Opening Day. Undaunted, Fitzgerald told Linn to go to Boston to write the story, anyway. His instructions, as Linn recalled them, were to "just walk around and interview all the people who know him."

When he spoke with George Susce, who handled publicity for the Red Sox, Linn was surprised to learn that Williams had flown in to Boston that morning from Florida. Susce took Linn into the locker room and told Williams that a writer from *Sport* was waiting to talk to him. "Well, send the sonofabitch in," Williams bellowed. After Linn introduced himself, Williams said, "You look like a pretty good guy, and I think you're entitled to know why I'm not going to talk to you. That magazine of yours–they've been after me for years."

Linn was unaware that Williams's resentment toward *Sport* dated back a few years to 1948, when the magazine ran a story on him that included an interview with his mother. Williams guarded his privacy assiduously, and he considered the story a serious breach. It had infuriated Williams when it first appeared, and, as Linn was discovering, he was still angry about it. When Linn told Williams that Ed Fitzgerald had given him the assignment, Williams slammed his fist down on the trainer's table and roared, "That's the sonofabitch who wrote it." "What if I do this?" Linn asked. "I'll ask you a question, you'll refuse to answer, and I can go back and tell Fitzgerald you wouldn't talk to me because of him and I'll be covered."

Linn asked Williams about a fishing company that he owned, and the tenor of the interview quickly changed. He figured there was a chance Williams would be tempted to say something about his company, and he would have one quote from him. "I do remember, though, how startled I was when he went on to answer the next question, as I was just walking out the door," Linn recalled. The interview proceeded from there, and Williams even agreed to meet him the next day. As Linn was leaving the locker room, Larry Claflin, a columnist with the *Boston Herald,* told him: "You got him going down memory lane. I can't get him to tell me what he did yesterday." He took three days in all to compile the material for the feature. "That piece made me," he recalled later. "It may have been the best piece I ever wrote."

As the assignments continued to come, Linn grew more confident as a writer. He was even beginning to inject himself into his stories. Jack Zanger, an editor at *Sport,* told him that he had a "peculiar style," "like you're writing an article and writing a column at the same time. You're commenting on everything as you go along." Linn did not feel like he was alone with his subjective reporting. "That kind of writing was just coming in," he said. "You had Kahn, Dick Schaap, and Jimmy Breslin, and I think we all fed off each other." Like those and many other sportswriters at the time Linn had also been influenced by the work of W. C. "Bill" Heinz.

"1960: The Kid's Last Game" (*Sport,* September 1960), one of Linn's most memorable articles, displays his maturing style. His subject is again Williams, on the occasion of his retirement. The story was going to be about Williams's final game–which Linn was supposed to cover in New York, where the Red Sox were scheduled to finish the season–but Linn wanted to focus on his last home game at Fenway Park in Boston. At issue that day was Williams's long history of not acknowledging the cheers of the hometown fans. Would he finally tip his cap to them on his last day in Fenway? It became apparent to Linn in the locker room before the game that Williams would not. The forty-two-year-old Red Sox star "seemed resolved to remain true to his own image of himself," Linn wrote in his article, "to permit no sentimentality to crack that mirror through which he looks at the world and allows the world to look upon him."

Even though Williams hit a home run during his last at bat, he "made the trip as always," Linn wrote, "his head down, his stride unbroken." Thirty years later, when Linn was researching *Hitter: The Life and Turmoil of Ted Williams* (1993), Williams confessed that he had thought about tipping his cap as he rounded second base but then decided against it. In the locker room that final day, though, when Linn asked Williams what he had felt out there on the field the slugger said, "I felt nothing. Nothing. Nothing!" As Linn "was toting up the nothings," Williams blew his stack. "'And when you get back there,'" he yelled, "'tell them for me that they're full of . . .' There followed a burst of vituperation which we cannot even begin to approximate, and the old, sad plaint about those twelve years of merciless persecution."

Poking fun at Williams's long-standing feud with *Sport,* Linn refers to himself throughout the article as "the man from *Sport,*" "this reporter," "our man," and "our correspondent." Linn saw Williams for what he was–"sometimes unbearable but never dull." He wrote that "Ted Williams chose his course early, and his course was to turn his face from the world around him. When he walked out of the park, he kept his eyes to the front and he never looked back." "And now," Linn concluded, "Boston knows how England felt when it lost India."

The following year, in 1961, Linn wrote his first book, *The Eternal Kid,* drawing on the articles he had written about Williams. The book was published in paperback by Macfadden. Years later, Linn said, while he was writing a book on the history of the Red Sox–Yankees rivalry, he was told that "all the serious students of Williams" had this book. He was amazed, since he had always thought of it as a "paperback throwaway."

In 1962 Linn collaborated with baseball owner Bill Veeck on his autobiography, *Veeck–As in Wreck.* Veeck had just sold his interest in the Chicago White Sox and was battling a serious illness. To convalesce, Veeck moved with his wife to Easton, Maryland. He began to work on his autobiography as a way to keep himself occupied, and former Detroit Tigers slugger Hank Greenberg, a friend of Veeck's, was responsible for putting him in touch with Linn.

Linn found Veeck to be an excellent writer and an avid reader. He visited him in Easton for three or four days at a time and taped ten or twelve hours of material. He then transcribed the tapes and cross-referenced the transcriptions. He was aided in the process by his wife, Ruth, who at the same time was raising their three children, Michael, David, and Hildy. Linn enjoyed collaborating with Veeck, editing the material over the telephone after Veeck finished reading each chapter and traveling to Easton several times to review the whole manuscript with him. Occasionally they disagreed, however. "When we'd argue," Linn said, "I'd say, 'What you've got to understand, Bill, is that by this time I think I made you up.' And Veeck would say, 'Don't let it worry you, Ed. By this time, I think I wrote the book.'"

When *Veeck–As in Wreck* was published in 1962, Red Smith hailed it in *The New York Times* as "the best

By Edward Linn

The sad end of Big Daddy Lipscomb

His appetites for women, whiskey and sporting life drove him, made him a legend and, in the end, destroyed him before his time.

Opening of Linn's 3 August 1963 Saturday Evening Post *article on the death from a heroin overdose of Baltimore Colts defensive end Gene Lipscomb*

(sports) autobiography ever written." More recently, newspaper columnist Mike Lupica ranked it as "still the best sports book of them all." Though the bulk of the writing was his, Linn had no problem with Veeck being the focus of attention. "It was Veeck's autobiography. The contracts always said the names had to be in the same type-size." Linn confessed that he never liked the phrase *as told to* to describe his collaboration with a subject. He preferred *with* and, later, simply *and*.

Describing his success as a ghostwriter, Linn said, "I have a talent I wish I didn't have. I didn't start out to write other people's books. But it came easy to me. It's like being an actor. You put yourself in somebody else's mind, and that can kind of make it fun." Finding the subject's voice for him was a matter of listening for certain "reference points." In Veeck's case one reference point was William Shakespeare, whom he liked to quote. Linn said, "If an apt Shakespearean quote would fit something, I'd use it. Veeck might not have said it at that particular point, but he easily could have."

Veeck's openness and candor made lasting impressions on Linn, as they did on almost everyone who met him, according to a profile that Linn wrote for *The New York Times:* "To walk the streets of Chicago with Bill Veeck was to encounter a movie gallery of faces lighting up at the sight of him." Linn remembered how Veeck would walk around the ballpark before the gates opened and then be there to greet the fans as they arrived. "What you saw was what you got," he wrote. "The only thing you didn't see was the toughness in him. When people tried to put something over on him, that's when the iron came into his voice."

Linn's next book, *The Last Loud Roar* (1964), united him with one of his childhood idols, Bob Cousy, the all-star guard for the Boston Celtics. The book was the second in a series that brought together a top name in a major sport with a well-known writer, the first, *Run to Daylight!* (1963), pairing the legendary coach of the Green Bay Packers, Vince Lombardi, and Bill Heinz. In "Warm Breezes from the Past" Linn wrote that "we taped the book over the summer, up in his boy's camp in New Hampshire." The collaboration with Cousy turned out to be as enjoyable as the one with Veeck.

In 1963 Linn was named the magazine writer of the year by the National Sportscasters and Sportswriters Association. He was also hired as a contract writer by *The Saturday Evening Post,* where Roger Kahn had just become the sports editor. In "Warm Breezes from the Past" Linn described how he and Kahn "smuggled a triumvirate of Civil Rights articles into the magazine by disguising them as sports stories." One of those articles, "The Sad End of Big Daddy Lipscomb," reported the death of Baltimore Colts defensive end Gene "Big Daddy" Lipscomb. The circumstances were controversial. The cause of death was reported as self-inflicted "acute heroin poisoning," and Linn had to balance the facts of Lipscomb's death against the conviction of the fallen football star's friends, who believed the injection was accidental.

The second story, "I Don't Have to Be Grateful," profiles the star center of the Boston Celtics, Bill Russell. "When I was much younger," Russell said in the article, "I'd get real upset if somebody called me black or nigger. That doesn't bother me anymore." Linn recounted in "Warm Breezes from the Past" how quotable Russell was. He even offered to write the piece under Russell's byline, an offer that could have netted Russell at least five thousand dollars. The controversial basketball star declined, however: "I don't want to get paid for getting a chance to say what I want to say."

Russell and jockey Bill Hartack were two of Linn's favorite subjects. "They were supposed to be tough to get at," he said, "but they were both great talkers." He saw in them two great talents "whose lives had been determined by their size." He also liked their "utter candor and honesty." What impressed Linn about Hartack was his "sense of time and space." During one interview with him Hartack stopped, flipped back three or four pages of Linn's notebook, and said he wanted to "clarify" something Linn had written down. "Not only did he somehow know how far back I had made the notes and where it was on the page," Linn recalled, "he was pointing to writing that was upside-down to him."

After writing another collaboration with Veeck, *The Hustler's Handbook* (1965), Linn's next project, *Koufax* (1966), gave him the opportunity to work with Sandy Koufax, the best pitcher in baseball at the time. Despite reservations about another collaborative project, he began meeting with the Los Angeles Dodgers left-hander soon after the 1963 World Series. When Linn suggested going over the final draft during spring training in 1966, Koufax informed him that he and teammate Don Drysdale were going to stage a joint contract holdout. Linn had just stumbled on one of the biggest sports stories at the time, but he kept it to himself. "I learned something about myself," he said. "I learned that I could keep a secret. I was one of the few people who knew what was going to come off, and I told no one." The two Dodger pitchers took a beating from the local sportswriters, but Linn's association with Koufax, as he recalls in "Warm Breezes from the Past," left him with an appreciation for his "strong sense of integrity. What made Koufax such an admirable person in my eyes was that he absolutely refused to put forth that argument for himself in the book. He wasn't, after all, trying to prove anything to anybody. He was simply being true to himself."

Linn's next book was another collaboration with Veeck, *Thirty Tons a Day* (1972), which focuses on his experience as the owner of the Suffolk Downs racetrack. The book is as much about Boston politics as about sports, and, while it received good reviews, some people who really knew Veeck thought it portrayed him out of context. "Veeck was a baseball guy," Linn said. "They didn't want to hear him talking about racing schedules."

In 1975 Leo Durocher's autobiography, *Nice Guys Finish Last,* for which Linn served as collaborator, was published; like *Veeck–As in Wreck,* it was a critical success. As a writing partner, the fiery former manager of the Dodgers and Giants was the exact opposite of Veeck. "Durocher didn't leave Springfield dreaming of having a book of his on the library shelves," Linn said. "Veeck was the reader, and Durocher was a talker." When the manuscript was finished, Linn recalled, "I would read ten pages aloud, and he would read ten pages aloud. We would take turns, and he would comment as we went along." Linn said that Durocher filled the book with his "best banquet stories"; in one of them he talked about a group of Dodger fans who would shout encouragement at the Brooklyn players as they were coming onto the field and scream insults and spit at them on the way out if they lost. In his version of the story Linn added two words to the final sentence, and when Durocher heard it being read to him, he snapped: "That's wrong. You've got it all wrong." He then repeated, word for word, his original phrasing. "He had absolute pitch for his own voice and rhythms," Linn said.

In his book *The Era: 1947–1957, When the Yankees, the Giants, and the Dodgers Ruled the World* (1993), Roger Kahn ranked *Nice Guys Finished Last* first among his all-time "Golden Dozen" of baseball books. "This book proceeded stormily from a magazine collaboration. Durocher was not comfortable with Linn, an author he could not intimidate. Linn found Durocher difficult and devious. Perhaps that spiky relationship is what gives this book its marvelously pugnacious tone. I've never read a baseball life story, biography, or autobiography, that I enjoyed as much." Kahn describes Linn's predicament with his subject by providing an example of Durocher's penchant for stretching the truth in *Nice Guys Finish Last.* "Durocher boasts that he pursued other Dodger trustees, until finally his 1947 salary was paid in full. On page 269, he swears he was never paid in full. Then on page 270, he gets his money. I do not suggest that *Nice Guys Finish Last* is coherent or accurate, only that it is entertaining (and as accurate as Linn could make it, given his collaborator)." In *The Bill James Historical Abstract* (1985) James, the well-known baseball statistician, calls *Nice Guys Finish Last* "the best baseball autobiography I have ever seen, by far": "The writing is astonishingly good, the pace is right, and all the right details are in place." Baseball writer John Thorn, in *The Armchair Book of Baseball II* (1987), called it a "tough and splendid autobiography."

Linn's next book, *Inside the Yankees: The Championship Season* (1978), was written quickly at his editor's suggestion to cash in on the Yankees' 1977 postseason success. "It sounded like an interesting thing to do," Linn said, and he got to know the Yankee players, as well as some of the front-office personnel of the organization.

These connections served him well in preparing his next book, *Steinbrenner's Yankees* (1982). Reviewer Bill Bell of the *New York Daily News* called it the "best baseball book of the year" and added that "this is the version Steinbrenner hates." Besides exposing the owner's hubris, the book also documents the fortunes of the Yankees from 1977 to 1981, when, according to Linn, "Steinbrenner either beat up or got beat up by an elevator"–a reference to injuries he received allegedly in an altercation after the Yankees lost game 5 of the World Series.

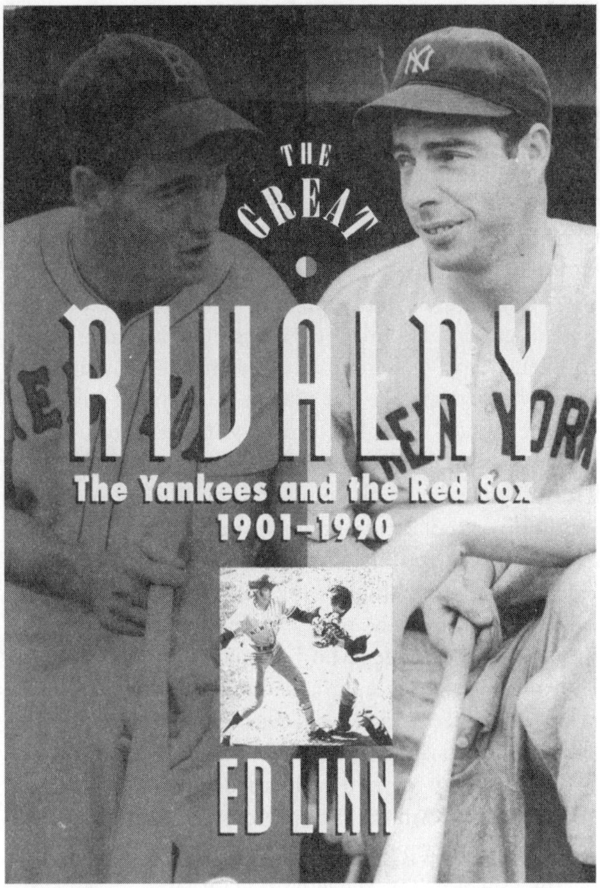

Dust jacket for Linn's 1991 account of the New York and Boston American League teams

Linn's next book, *The Great Rivalry: The Yankees and Red Sox, 1901–1990* (1991), presents the long and colorful history between the Red Sox and the Yankees. "I had always wanted to do that book," Linn said, "but I was always discouraged. 'There's no money in that kind of book,' my agents told me. But I grew up with it, like the Marathon, and it was in my head to do it." Writing in the *San Francisco Examiner* (4 September 1991), Edvins Beitiks praised *The Great Rivalry:* "The whole book is written as if you were in a smoky room with all the men who had something to do with the Red Sox-Yankees matchups over the years."

Linn's portrait of one of those men, Joe DiMaggio, focuses on his cool demeanor. In 1949 DiMaggio missed the first three months of the season after having surgery on his right heel. On 29 June, Linn reports, DiMaggio sat in the dugout and laced up a protective shoe, with not even his manager, Casey Stengel, knowing if he could play. Linn's description of the scene captures the tense relationship between the Yankee star and his first-year manager. "DiMaggio had taken a seat on the far end of the bench alongside Phil Pepe of the *New York Daily News,*" Linn wrote. "He bent down and tightened his shoelaces. Everybody on the bench was looking toward him. 'What about it, Joe?' Pepe asked. 'Yeah,' DiMaggio said, as he straightened himself up. 'I'm going to play.' He didn't tell Stengel he was going to play, you will notice. He allowed Stengel to overhear him telling Pepe."

Linn's 1993 biography of Ted Williams, *Hitter,* was originally intended to coincide with the fiftieth anniversary of Williams's record-setting 1941 season, in which he became the last player to maintain a batting average greater than .400. Linn was resistant to the idea at first, but he produced the volume two years later. "I had researched him all my life," Linn said of Williams, "and I'd written about him every year since he got back from Korea. It was like writing about my brother."

While researching *Hitter* Linn discovered a different Williams from the player he had once known. The surly Red Sox slugger who had played his last game in 1960 was now more approachable, primarily as a result of his improved relationship with his son. Early in the boy's life, according to Linn, Williams was an absent father, often leaving him in the care of former teammate Johnny Pesky. Among the episodes Linn reports in the book is a 1992 trip to San Diego father and son made to see the house where Williams was raised.

Working with him, Linn found out there was still plenty of the old Williams left. He still greeted Linn by saying, "Are you here to psychoanalyze me again?" And he still loved to talk about hitting. Linn said that Williams liked the fact that he wrote about his dedication to it. "He hated to be called a natural hitter," Linn wrote. "He'd say, 'I've swung at more balls than anybody' and 'I practiced more than anybody else.'"

In a 3 May 1993 review of *Hitter* for *The New York Times,* Christopher Lehmann-Haupt acknowledged Linn's mastery as a sports biographer. "He makes what is normally a pedestrian form of writing seem unusual and tells us any number of surprising things about Ted Williams."

Linn died on 7 February 2000. He may have been speaking about Williams and, perhaps, all the sports figures he has encountered during his career when he said, "You have to recognize these people for what they are. They are the best at something everybody wants to do. You can find someone's faults, but you have to recognize that he might be the best in the world." Along the way, he learned something else about them: "People love to talk, and, more than anything else, they love to talk about themselves." Few writers have listened as closely and told their stories as well as Ed Linn.

References:

Bill James, *The Bill James Historical Baseball Abstract* (New York: Villard, 1985);

Roger Kahn, *The Era: 1947–1957, When the Yankees, the Giants, and the Dodgers Ruled the World* (New York: Ticknor & Fields, 1993);

Kahn, *Games We Used to Play: A Lover's Quarrel with the World of Sport* (New York: Ticknor & Fields, 1992);

Kahn, *Memories of Summer: When Baseball Was an Art and Writing about It a Game* (New York: Hyperion Press, 1997);

John Thorn, ed., *The Armchair Book of Baseball II* (New York: Scribners, 1987).

Jack Murphy

(5 February 1923 - 24 September 1980)

David Sanders

MAJOR POSITIONS HELD: Sports reporter, assistant oil editor, police reporter, *Tulsa World,* 1940–1942, 1946–1947; sportswriter, columnist, *Fort Worth Star-Telegram,* 1947–1949; sportswriter, columnist, *Oklahoma City Daily Oklahoman,* 1949–1951; columnist, sports editor, *San Diego Union,* 1951–1980.

BOOKS: *Abe and Me* (San Diego: Joyce, 1977);
Damn You, Al Davis: The Sporting World of Jack Murphy (San Diego: Joyce, 1979).

OTHER: "Roses for the Trojans," in *Best Sports Stories 1953: A Panorama of the 1952 Sports Year,* edited by Irving T. Marsh and Edward Ehre (New York: Dutton, 1953), pp. 103–108;
"The Mongoose," in *Best Sports Stories 1961: A Panorama of the 1960 Sports Year,* edited by Marsh and Ehre (New York: Dutton, 1961), pp. 154–183;
"When the World Stood Still," in *Best Sports Stories 1963: A Panorama of the 1962 Sports Year,* edited by Marsh and Ehre (New York: Dutton, 1963), pp. 17–19;
"The Champ Behind the Mask," in *Best Sports Stories 1964: A Panorama of the 1963 Sports Year,* edited by Marsh and Ehre (New York: Dutton, 1964), pp. 197–203;
"From Arnie's Army to Casper's Crowd," in *Best Sports Stories 1967: A Panorama of the 1966 Sports Year,* edited by Marsh and Ehre (New York: Dutton, 1967), pp. 191–193;
"The No. 2 Hero," in *Best Sports Stories 1969: A Panorama of the 1968 Sports Year,* edited by Marsh and Ehre (New York: Dutton, 1969), pp. 63–65;
"The Drama of Hawking," in *Best Sports Stories 1975: A Panorama of the 1974 Sports Year,* edited by Marsh and Ehre (New York: Dutton, 1975), pp. 284–286.

SELECTED PERIODICAL PUBLICATIONS–UNCOLLECTED: "Battle of the Crippled Champ," *Collier's,* 123 (25 June 1949): 22–23, 73;

Jack Murphy (The San Diego Historical Society Photo Collection)

"Outside the Dugout," *Newsweek,* 47 (18 June 1956): 111;
"The Sporting Scene: Lipstick, Hair Ribbons, Bright-green Shorts," *New Yorker,* 38 (18 August 1962): 76, 78, 80–82, 84, 87;
"The Sporting Scene: Two Ears," *New Yorker,* 38 (15 September 1962): 98, 100, 102, 105;
"It's Only News When He Loses," *New York Times Sunday Magazine,* 8 September 1963, pp. 133–134, 136;
"Ben Casey at the Ballpark," *New York Times Sunday Magazine,* 22 August 1965, pp. 18–19, 32, 35.

Qualcomm Stadium in San Diego is a monument, if no longer a memorial, to Jack Murphy, for twenty-eight years columnist and sports editor of the *San Diego*

Union. As San Diego Stadium, the structure rose in Mission Valley in the 1960s in great part through Murphy's leadership of campaigns to attract major football and baseball franchises, then to win voter approval for construction bonds. In 1980, shortly after his death, the city moved to rename the field Jack Murphy Stadium, making him the only sportswriter ever to be so honored anywhere. The designation remained for almost two decades, until crucial financial support by a local telecommunications firm led to "the Murph" becoming "the Q" in 1997.

The tribute, however ephemeral it proved to be, came about because Murphy had perceived one of the rarest opportunities ever to come by a man of his calling. When he began work at the *Union* in late 1951, the Pacific Coast League Padres were the biggest sports topic in town–except during the racing seasons at Del Mar and Caliente. The San Diego State Aztecs played their state college counterparts under the long shadows of the football programs at the University of Southern California and the University of California at Los Angeles. Distinguished athletes such as Ted Williams and Archie Moore had come from San Diego to find fame elsewhere. At the time, San Diego probably had more golfers, tennis players, surfers, and joggers as a percentage of its citizenry than any other city in the United States, but it seemed to have fewer steady sports fans of any description. As a recent arrival in town, Murphy found that the handful of people who talked about major professional sports coming to San Diego linked their enthusiasm to an even larger vision of the future of the city. A writer and private man who read constantly and walked the Poway hills with his dogs, Murphy became the most successful booster of San Diego for the rest of his busy career.

John Patrick Murphy was born in Tulsa, Oklahoma, on 5 February 1923, the elder son of James and Eula Murphy. Twenty years later he was unimpressed by San Diego when he, among legions of transient servicemen in World War II, paid an obligatory visit in 1943 on a Marine Corps training assignment before proceeding across the Pacific. For the next two years in uniform he remembered nothing about the town to keep him from planning to return to the sports staff of the *Tulsa World.* Already a committed writer at that point, Murphy claimed to have chosen his life's work much earlier, at the age of eleven. He was growing up in Tulsa when the decision "dawned" on him as he read the *World.* It did not follow from any competition in school sports, since Murphy and his brother, Bob (eventually a New York Mets broadcaster), spent their time outdoors hunting and fishing. Their dedication to field and stream was a legacy from their father, a petroleum engineer.

As a seventeen-year-old freshman at the University of Tulsa, Murphy was a stringer for the *World.* Soon he was working full-time on the 4:00 P.M. to 12:00 A.M. shift in the sports department, where he saw the next day's edition taking shape from local prep-school reports, stories about the football fortunes of the University of Tulsa Golden Hurricane in the era of tailback and Heisman Trophy winner Glenn Dobbs, and wire-service accounts from the rest of the world. He enlisted in the Marine Corps in 1943 and qualified for its college training program at Southwestern Louisiana Institute, where he also kept busy as a stringer for the *Houston Post* and the *New Orleans Times-Picayune.* He arrived in Okinawa with the marine infantry–via San Diego and the mandatory basic training for college recruits–and was soon reassigned from an infantry unit to a billet as combat correspondent. He ended up in China after V-J Day, where, just before returning home, he rejected an offer of a position with the Associated Press.

Back in Tulsa in 1946, Murphy reentered civilian life as a reporter for the *World,* where a crowded sports department forced him to take available assignments as assistant oil editor and police reporter. He had no particular affinity for writing about his father's field; the police beat was important for him, though less for its variety than because it introduced him to Patricia Astin, a colleague and former classmate who became his wife on 17 May 1947. Briefly he was sports publicity director at the University of Tulsa, leaving when he came upon his nominal superior opening his mail.

In 1947 he joined the sports staff of the *Fort Worth Star-Telegram,* which was becoming a preeminent newspaper in the Southwest. His experience on the *Star-Telegram* staff "lifted my sights in terms of writing," as he recalled in an interview with Wayne Lockwood, primarily because of his working alongside such other young sportswriters as Dan Jenkins, Blackie Sherrod, and Bud Shrake. He met venerable figures in the profession, including Grantland Rice and O. B. Keeler, while covering major events in the Southwest. His first story in a national publication appeared in the 25 June 1949 issue of *Collier's.* "Battle of the Crippled Champ" deals with Ben Hogan's determination to play tournament golf again despite his critical injuries in an automobile accident the preceding January. Murphy wrote the article while Hogan was just beginning to walk unaided and months before he picked up a club again.

He left the *Star-Telegram* for the *Oklahoma City Daily Oklahoman* because the new position involved mainly writing a column. In his late twenties Murphy was a sportswriter more preoccupied with writing than with sports. For the rest of his life words were his overriding professional concern, no matter what distractions arose from his subjects. He was a writer more than the editor or civic leader that he later became, and he discovered that the way to remain a writer as his career became increasingly complicated was to hang on to his column.

Richard Pourade, then editor of the *San Diego Union,* hired Murphy as sports editor in late 1951. Through extensive research Pourade confirmed the contention he had heard, that Texas and Oklahoma were growing the most promising younger sportswriters in the nation; he then tracked down Murphy at the *Daily Oklahoman* and waited patiently for an answer to his job offer. He also acquiesced to the candidate's insistence on a larger department built on expanded firsthand coverage of out-of-town events. "I decided that I would give it at least a year," Murphy said in the same interview. Despite his initial reluctance to relocate his family, which by this time included a daughter, Robin, and a son, John Patrick Jr., he began the new professional challenge in haste, covering the Oklahoma-Oklahoma A&M football game on Saturday, 1 December, and showing up for his first day of work at the *Union* on the following Monday.

Murphy arrived at the *Union* in time to oversee the coverage of bowl games and the winter golf tour. He began to augment the staff of seven with additions from sports departments throughout the Southwest, including Phil Collier, Jim Trinkle, and Jerry Magee. By all accounts Murphy demonstrated the essential administrative ability of letting capable people do their jobs without discernible interference. Years later some remembered him as a hands-off editor with full-time administrators as assistants, but in the beginning he needed no help nurturing writers by giving them initiative. From the first day he saw his column, "So They Tell Me," as his most important contribution to the work of the department. Murphy's first column, which appeared two weeks after his arrival, underscored the new cosmopolitan thrust of the sports section by considering Coach Lynn "Pappy" Waldorf's determination to keep his California Golden Bears from sustaining a third straight Rose Bowl loss to a Big Ten champion.

"So They Tell Me" ran six times a week for the next twenty years before being cut to five times a week for the remainder of Murphy's career. According to Gene Gregston, an old Oklahoma friend and Fort Worth colleague who eventually became editor of the *Union,* Murphy often expressed a desire to write a political column in the editorial pages. Their discussions inevitably led to the conclusion that for his readers' happiness as well as his own Murphy could not abandon his post on the far left side of the front sports page. Nevertheless, when terrorist violence erupted at the 1972 Munich Olympics, Gregston sent Murphy's first report and all of his follow-up dispatches directly to the front page. They confirmed what readers of his column had long suspected: that Murphy could write understandingly about many subjects other than sports. The question of whether his personal qualities–especially those of humor, grace, and detachment–could have served him as well in a career of political writing as they did in his sports column may rest in a code of behavior Murphy posed years later. A gentleman, he writes in *Abe and Me* (1977), "disagrees without being disagreeable."

Murphy (standing) with colleague and friend Red Smith in Flamingo, Florida, 1976 (from Ira Berkow, Red, *1986)*

"For years I rated him among the five best sports columnists in the country," Gregston wrote in *San Diego Magazine* (November 1980) shortly after Murphy's death, "and a newspaper is very fortunate to have just one of that class in a century of publishing." Never an athlete himself, Murphy wrote about sports with exceptional clarity as an observer. He always insisted that his job gave him a rich opportunity to be a storyteller.

Some of Murphy's colleagues have said that he met Red Smith at a Kentucky Derby in the early 1950s, but Smith insisted in an interview with Michael Grant that "neither of us could remember when or how we first met." Smith, then at the height of his profession with the *New York Herald-Tribune,* became Murphy's close friend and the writer who most influenced his work. Murphy had studied Smith's columns for years, but once they became friends they began to compare their work, including accounts of events they had attended together. "We did not hesitate to steal from one another," Smith said while warming up for the principal speech at a dinner celebrating Murphy's twenty-five years at the *Union.* As Smith's speech, quoted by Wayne Lockwood in the *San Diego Union* (28 November 1976) suggests, the two men shared an affectionate, good-humored relationship: "Jack Murphy is trustworthy, loyal, courteous, kind, helpful, obedient, cheerful, thrifty, brave, clean, and reverent, and a fairly presentable companion if you care for Okies." "He might have been my best friend," Smith told Michael Grant for Murphy's obituary in the *San Deigo Union* (25 September 1980). Jim Murray, writing in the *Los Angeles Times,* could have been describing one of the grounds for Jack Murphy's friendship with Red Smith: "He was a gentleman; he kept the company of gentlemen. . . . He was courtly. He saw all three sides to a story, yours, theirs, and the truth, which he wrote with great wit and insight." Another basis of their relationship, Smith stressed, was their common abhorrence of overwriting and clichés.

Murphy's professional eminence grew along with his place in the civic life of San Diego. Although he could be reserved on many occasions, community groups sought him out as an after-dinner speaker. He had not lived in San Diego a year before he had decided to stay there the rest of his life. He came to call it a "beautiful, shiny, pretty place" and claimed that "every morning I get up and say 'Son of a gun . . . living in San Diego.'" Years after her husband's death, Patricia Murphy explained the affinity between the columnist and San Diego: "He was a stable, conservative fellow at a young age, and he fit in with those people, the establishment," she said to, Robert P. Laurence, a *Union* reporter. "They had the same view of life he did, the same moral values."

Murphy soon began to use the bully pulpit of his "So They Tell Me" column to promote the activities of the Greater San Diego Sports Association, a group he helped form, in attempting to secure major-league sports franchises for the city. When the Dodgers came to Los Angeles in 1958, Murphy had Phil Collier cover the event for the *Union,* not only as part of the broader sports coverage Murphy had made a condition of his accepting the job but also to stress the significance of the expansion of major-league baseball to the West Coast. Of more immediate significance, San Diego writers were on the spot when the American Football League (AFL) organized the Los Angeles Chargers as one of its original franchises. When it became obvious soon thereafter that the Chargers could not compete for attendance with the established Los Angeles Rams of the National Football League, Murphy and his associates were quick to surmise that the talented young team could thrive in San Diego. In 1960, as the Chargers' maiden season was closing with an AFL Western Division championship and disappointing turnouts at the Coliseum in Los Angeles, he arranged meetings between team owner Barron Hilton and San Diego businessmen, during which Hilton challenged them to produce within a week signatures that would guarantee a thousand season-ticket sales. Hilton told S. A. Desick in the *San Diego Union* (25 September 1980), "Jack's tenacity was the motivating factor in convincing me to move the club." Murphy pursued city hall tenaciously, as well, to encourage the renovation and enlargement of the aging Balboa Stadium from twenty-three thousand to thirty-four thousand seats for the 1961 season. The Chargers won another division title their first year in San Diego, and when the team won the AFL championship in 1963, they presented Murphy with a championship ring.

Construction of a larger stadium soon became the subject of feasibility studies, and a political campaign was begun to encourage building in the Mission Valley section of the city. Murphy's columns from the time reflect the work he did behind the scenes in the process. A year before the election in which the bond issue was decided, Murphy had advised his readers that major-league baseball owners were interested in expansion to San Diego: "The pros are just telling us amateurs what we knew from the start–anybody who doesn't live in San Diego is either misinformed or a victim of circumstance"(30 August 1964). The stadium could be a powerful stimulant to the tourist-based economy of the city, he argued, by supporting baseball and adding twenty thousand to the attendance figures for Chargers games. On 31 October 1965, election eve, he wrote: "This is the choice: either the voters drive to the polls on Tuesday or they drive to Los Angeles and Anaheim for the next twenty years to watch major league football and baseball. . . . If Proposition 1 is defeated, San Diego will resume its old role as a suburb of Los Angeles."

Even the forces boosting a stadium may have been surprised when a 73 percent majority voted for the bonds, defying the local conventional wisdom that a third of the electorate could be counted on to vote against any large outlay of money, especially in an off-year election. The city was committed to a fifty-thousand-seat structure that would put San Diego in line for the next expansion of major-league baseball in 1969. "The most important thing that's happened to me on this job is getting the stadium built," Murphy stated in Wayne Lockwood's profile for the *Union* (28 November 1976), which commemorated Murphy's twenty-fifth anniversary with the newspaper.

The *Union* hired Murphy in 1951 because he stood out among many talented young sportswriters in the Southwest. As his work in his first year in San

Diego shows, he continued to build on that early promise. "Roses for the Trojans" (23 November 1952) is an account of one of the most hotly contested games in the bitter sports rivalry between the University of California at Los Angeles and the University of Southern California. Murphy exactly measures the misfortune UCLA suffered in losing its tailback while fully crediting two electrifying plays that brought USC its 14–12 winning margin. He had been in San Diego not quite two years when, as author of "So They Tell Me," he won the Headliner Award of the National Headliners Club for his "consistently outstanding sports column." Murphy considered this recognition, seven years after his earliest column efforts in Tulsa and Fort Worth, a vindication of his efforts to protect his career as a columnist both in going from Fort Worth to Oklahoma City and negotiating for his position in San Diego. As Lockwood reported in an unpublished interview on 23 July 1998, some colleagues have recalled its being said of him that he was "sports editor in charge of his own column." His dedication to his work led to national recognition for his column well before it became a rallying point in the postwar sports history of San Diego.

Murphy's life with his family and dogs in the Poway backcountry just north of San Diego meant more to him than any sports beat or the movers and shakers of San Diego. He was concerned with the major-league teams in San Diego, especially the Chargers, but his columns were less often devoted to football and baseball than his civic accomplishment might suggest. Lockwood, a colleague at the *Union,* ventures that he probably liked writing about boxing and golf more than other sports. Jerry Magee, colleague and fellow Oklahoman, notes that as a football writer he rarely "dealt with x's and o's." Both Lockwood and Magee testify to Murphy's orderly mind and the fact that he was never panicked by a deadline. According to Magee, there was "never a strikeover" in Murphy's copy. Lockwood stated that his writing grew less from his covering sports than it did from the greater time he spent reading books.

In the balmy weather of his new environment Murphy was no more an athlete than he had been as a schoolboy in Tulsa. He avoided golf in San Diego after a brief and awkward exposure to the game. His decision before adolescence to write about sports was not, apparently, any attempt to compensate for being on the sidelines. He considered hunting and fishing to be respites from writing, although he was not often successful in either pursuit, a fact about which Red Smith teased his friend. When Murphy left his study to stroll in the nearby hills, he entered a final, boundless field of subjects for his column. As he wrote in *Abe and Me:*

> I sought an occasional escape from the structured world of sports, especially professional sports, where many cranky voices are heard. In theory, the sports section of a newspaper is a place to browse for entertainment, a refuge from the grim events of the day. But too often it is filled with the arguments of lawyers and agents; it seldom has the grace note of laughter.

In 1961 Smith introduced Murphy to A. J. Liebling, longtime *New Yorker* writer, whose many books include the boxing classic *The Sweet Science* (1956). Murphy told Liebling of his idea for a story about veteran fighter Archie Moore, and in short order Liebling took Murphy to the offices of *The New Yorker* and introduced him to editor William Shawn. The resulting profile of Moore, "The Mongoose," originally published on 11 November 1961, was one of Murphy's most widely praised stories. "The Mongoose" is a bright display of Moore's wit and a quiet insinuation of the author's. Murphy elicited a cascade of extraordinary self-revelation from Moore, and in the essay he skillfully bridges the boxer's wonderful monologues. An initial reference to the haziness surrounding Moore's birth date–he disagreed with his mother about the facts–receives this response: "My mother should know. She was there. But so was I. I have given this a lot of thought, and have decided that I must have been three when I was born."

Moore, at that point in his mid forties, was approaching the end of a long career; yet, Murphy notes, his appearance belied the years he had spent in the profession: "because his build is undistinguished and his countenance unscarred, there is nothing about his appearance that hints at the violent nature of his trade, and he affects a wispy bebop goatee that gives him more the look of a jazz musician than of a fighter." Murphy highlights Moore's loquaciousness and sense of humor, which has a distinctively American quality: "Moore loves to talk. 'I am a great sidewalk talker,' he once said. 'I can talk Mexican-fashion, squatting on my heels, or big-city style, with my spine up against a lamppost or a building, or even garment-center technique, with my backside at the edge of a curb'"; he acknowledges, however, that "there is, I fear, that one chink in my armor. I am inclined to waste words. In fact, I throw them away. It is my only excess."

The writer and his subject are straightforward on Moore's race as an element in his career. "His color was chiefly responsible for his decision" to become a fighter, Murphy states, "because boxing was the only way he could see for a Negro to rise above the kind of poverty he grew up in." "I had to fight," Moore says later in the profile. "For a Negro starting a career, that was the only way. That was the last road." Murphy suggests that it was unlikely "that any fighter has ever put more thought and effort into learning the boxing trade than

Dust jacket for Murphy's 1977 collection of columns about his beloved Labrador retriever

Moore did" and proceeds with a meticulous description of his apprenticeship during the Depression. He relates Moore's evenhanded revelation that a white brakeman almost clubbed Moore to death when he caught him riding a freight, and that years later a white intern–a chance passerby–saved him from bleeding to death in an automobile accident.

Moore's fights throughout the 1950s culminated in the 10 December 1958 bout with Yvon Durelle, "as wild and savage a spectacle as anything that has been seen in the television era of boxing." Moore was knocked down three times in the first round and rallied to batter Durelle unconscious in the eleventh. Yet, the climax of Murphy's account of the bout may come in the dressing-room interview, when the battered heavyweight urbanely states: "I enjoyed the fight very much. I am happy everybody was satisfied with it."

Soon after the Durelle fight, Moore read for the role of Jim in the 1960 movie version of Mark Twain's *The Adventures of Huckleberry Finn* (1884), overcoming competition from professional actors and the perception of some that he was taking an "Uncle Tom role," as well as his own leeriness over "handkerchief-head parts." Moore offers the view that Huck's companion was "really every man trying to be free" and, therefore, a challenge to a boxer who wanted to prove that he "could act without losing any dignity." After Moore's 1960 victory over Giulio Rinaldi at Madison Square Garden, he surprised Murphy and others when he "used the prize-ring as a platform for endorsing both the N.A.A.C.P. and the Freedom Riders," promising the latter a check for a thousand dollars. The article ends with a visit to Moore's home in San Diego, where Murphy asks him how he expects to be remembered by sports historians. Moore's response, which he insists Murphy copy verbatim, is a judgment of impressive length that gives way to a brief dissertation on "breathology" and "escapeology."

A year after this high-spirited collaboration with Moore, Murphy published "The Champ Behind the Mask" in *The New York Times Sunday Magazine* (21 July 1963). No other fighter could have offered a greater contrast to the genial Moore than the remote and fearsome Sonny Liston, in Las Vegas training for his rematch with Floyd Patterson. Murphy had no better luck than most of his colleagues in developing an intimate portrait of the man who "looks mean and menacing" and "seems sleepy-eyed and bored," calling him "a grim, chilling man with frightening appearance." Liston seems to emerge most vividly for Murphy as he watches him sign an autograph:

> Liston signs his name without difficulty, but anything beyond the simple signature is a major effort. I was sitting with him one afternoon when a woman employee of the hotel asked him to autograph a slip of a paper and address it to her son Jeff. It was a slow, almost painful procedure. "How do you spell it?" asked the fighter. The woman spelled her son's name, then repeated the spelling several times. It was embarrassing to watch and I looked the other way until Liston finally completed his little chore.

Murphy does concede to Liston a certain truculent honesty to his estimate of himself and his competition, but his concluding assessment is that the fighter is "the meanest animal in the jungle."

As were "The Mongoose" and "The Champ Behind the Mask," Murphy's account of the 1962 World Series between the Yankees and the Giants, "When the World Stood Still," was included in the *Best Sports Stories* series published by E. P. Dutton. His description of the final out of game 7 evokes the sense of having been present for a pivotal instant of the most memorable sporting event of that year: "a scream died in the throats of a crowd of 43,948 as the ball smashed into the glove of Bobby Richardson and stuck there." To Murphy's credit, he was cited for his account of a particular moment that was also described by many of his professional peers around the country.

Another prizewinning story, "The Drama of Hawking" (reprinted in *Best Sports Stories 1975: A Panorama of the 1974 Sports Year*), relates Murphy's and his wife's first encounter with falconry. Alone with the falconer at one of the coastal lagoons of San Diego, they learn that he has to be subservient to his hawks, to "see that they have an opportunity to kill something to eat every day." One moment the bird rests on the falconer's fist; in an instant, it "was free of all restraints, wheeling high in the clear winter sky. If it chose, it could fly forever, over the horizon, to the ends of the earth." Murphy, an occasional hunter with dogs, concedes that "a man who has hunted with a falcon most likely would sell his shotguns."

In his introduction to *Abe and Me,* a collection of Murphy's columns about his black Labrador retriever, Red Smith observes that his friend was "a peculiar sort of hunter" who "refuses to squeeze the trigger in the deer season because if he shot a deer he couldn't go deerhunting again." Murphy writes of an outing with Abe: "we hunted for hours without firing a shot." The important thing for Murphy was being with his dog. What Murphy and Abe instinctively knew of each other was the subject of occasional columns over most of a decade and may have gained the writer his most devoted local readership in all his tenure in San Diego. Murphy frequently weaves with fresh authenticity the basic scene in his study, when Abe rests against his leg and he reaches down from his keyboard to stroke the dog's head: "Now I am truly at ease in my study when Abe comes to my side, gives my left arm a nudge, and offers his head for caress. Satisfied, he then sprawls in the doorway. He wants me to know of his presence; he is rooting for me, I am not alone, he has faith in me."

Over the years readers learned of Abe's aging, then of the vet's recommendation that he stay home from the hunt. Shortly afterward Abe was hit by an automobile while Murphy was downtown at the *Union,* his column half-written. "The day began like all others," he recalled in his column, starting a fresh page. He wrote a few days later that he would not try to tell anyone how much he missed the dog, then does just that: "Abe is everywhere in the house, but I can't find him."

Inspired partly by the flow of readers' sympathy, *Abe and Me* reprints several of the most poignant columns. Settings for other essays in the collection include ranches in Baja California and the seventy-acre spread the Murphys owned in Montana. In one of the Baja sketches he seeks the "grace note of laughter" that he missed in the business of sports, remarking about a friend: "Dick knows more about cattle than he does women, though that is true of almost everybody, including dudes from the city who are ignorant about cattle."

Damn You, Al Davis: The Sporting World of Jack Murphy (1979) appeared the year before Murphy's death. As though to complement the earlier essays on his private life, he proposes to "share the pleasure I had in the company of some fascinating people I have known on the sports beat." The sections on football and baseball are about not players but owners and coaches such as Sid Gillman, the Chargers' first coach; Paul Brown, who coached in Ohio but owned a home in La Jolla; and Ray Kroc, owner of McDonald's, who bought the Padres in 1984 and kept them in San Diego when they appeared headed for Washington. His stories on fellow San Diegans Moore, Gene Littler, and Billy Casper would seem to confirm his preference for golf and boxing over other sports. As in *Abe and Me,* he also writes about his great recreations, hunting and fishing. Stating that he is "uncomfortable around horses," he indulges old humor about his hunting prowess: "I would not ask you to believe that I am a conservationist by preference. It's just that God, in his infinite wisdom, gave me small skills in the area of finding game and a set of nerves that make my gun waver when an animal blunders into my high-powered scope."

The home park for the San Diego Padres, which was renamed in Murphy's honor shortly after his death in 1980

The title of the book does not come from Murphy's own opinion about the Oakland Raiders head coach, whom he writes about in the chapter "The Genius." It refers instead to the cry, overheard by Murphy, of Chargers coach Harland Svare from deep in the opponents' dressing room at the Oakland Coliseum as the San Diego team was once again frustrated by the Raiders. Davis, a Chargers assistant coach when the team moved to San Diego, was actually a friend of Murphy's, who offered to pay for special nursing care in the writer's last illness.

Murphy's last column appeared on 23 July 1980. "I see they are going to hold the summer of 1980 without me," he wrote. He died of cancer at home in Poway in the morning of 24 September 1980, at age fifty-seven. In the stream of tributes by public figures printed the next day in the *Union,* two from the sports he covered stand out. Davis called him the "one sports writer who was loved whether you agreed with him or not," and Barron Hilton, who hunted with Murphy long after having been major owner of the Chargers, said that "He never let his friendship interfere with viewing the team objectively." *Los Angeles Times* columnist Jim Murray observed: "He was fair. He never raised his voice in print or in person. But he was deft in wounding those who deserved it. He did it so well they never felt a thing." Red Smith, for whom Murphy's death was a grievous personal loss, termed his friend "one of the very best in our business. He had a horror of sloppy writing. . . . If we worked together on the same story, he very often contributed the greater part."

Five months after Murphy died, San Diego Stadium was renamed Jack Murphy Stadium in his honor. The Padres played in "the Murph" for the next sixteen seasons, until the park was renamed again as part of an $18 million expansion project.

References:

S. A. Desick, "Friends, Associates Mourn a 'Journalistic Giant,'" *San Diego Union,* 25 September 1980, pp. A4–5;

Michael Grant, "Jack Murphy Dies at 57," *San Diego Union,* 25 September 1980, p. A1;

Gene Gregston, "Jack Murphy," *San Diego Magazine* (November 1980): 271, 279–282;

Robert P. Laurence, "Jack Murphy Came up Here to Hear the Coyotes Sing," *San Diego Union,* 21 October 1984, p. B2;

Wayne Lockwood, "S.D. Profile: Jack Murphy / Sports Editor Led City into the Majors," *San Diego Union,* 28 November 1976, pp. B1, B5, B7, B9, B13;

Lockwood, "There Are Some Empty Spaces That Remain," *San Diego Union,* 25 September 1980, pp. D1–D2;

Jim Murray

(29 December 1919 – 16 August 1998)

Robert M. Boynton
University of California, San Diego

MAJOR POSITIONS HELD: Reporter, *New Haven Register* (1943); reporter, *Los Angeles Examiner* (1944–1948); reporter, Los Angeles correspondent, *Time* (1948–1961); contributing writer, associate editor, *Sports Illustrated* (1954–1961); sports columnist, *Los Angeles Times* (1961–1998).

BOOKS: *The Best of Jim Murray* (Garden City, N.Y.: Doubleday, 1965);

The Sporting World of Jim Murray (Garden City, N.Y.: Doubleday, 1968);

The Jim Murray Collection (Dallas: Taylor, 1988);

Jim Murray: An Autobiography (New York: Macmillan, 1993);

Jim Murray: The Last of the Best (Los Angeles: Los Angeles Times, 1998).

OTHER: "As If It Weren't Tough Enough," in *Best Sports Stories 1964: A Panorama of the 1963 Sports Year,* edited by Irving T. Marsh and Edward Ehre (New York: Dutton, 1964), pp. 74–80;

"Triumph for Virtue," in *The Third Fireside Book of Baseball,* edited by Charles Einstein (New York: Simon & Schuster, 1968), pp. 326–327;

"Not Just Another Pretty Face," in *Best Sports Stories 1975: A Panorama of the 1974 Sports Year,* edited by Marsh and Ehre (New York: Dutton, 1975), pp. 100–103;

"A Hard Man to Find," in *Best Sports Stories 1976: A Panorama of the 1975 Sports Year,* edited by Marsh and Ehre (New York: Dutton, 1976), pp. 41–43;

"The Irish Haberdasher's Dream," in *Best Sports Stories 1979: A Panorama of the 1978 Sports Year,* edited by Marsh and Ehre (New York: Dutton, 1979), pp. 61–63;

"One Man's Vote: Davey Lopes," in *Best Sports Stories 1982: A Panorama of the 1981 Sports Year,* edited by Marsh and Ehre (New York: Dutton, 1982), pp. 145–147;

Jim Murray (photograph by Jim Cornfield)

"Did Babe Herman Triple into a Triple Play?" in *The Armchair Book of Baseball,* edited by John Thorn (New York: Scribners, 1985), pp. 219–221;

"Ozzie Smith," in *The Fourth Fireside Book of Baseball,* edited by Einstein (New York: Simon & Schuster, 1987), pp. 263–264;

Mike Gallagher and Neil Gallagher, *Mickey Mantle,* introduction by Murray (New York: Chelsea, 1991).

SELECTED PERIODICAL PUBLICATIONS–UNCOLLECTED: "I Hate the Yankees," *Life,* 16 (17 April 1950): 25–36;

"Debacle in the Desert," *Sports Illustrated,* 14 (23 January 1961): 12;
"Track," *Sports Illustrated,* 14 (30 January 1961): 48–49;
"Great Coliseum Murder Mystery," *Sports Illustrated,* 51 (14 August 1961): 16–17;
"The Drubbing," *Sports Illustrated,* 22 (7 June 1965): 53;
"Ronald Reagan to the Rescue!" *Esquire,* 65 (February 1966): 76–84;
"Not Just Another Pretty Face," *Saturday Evening Post,* 246 (November 1974): 42–45;
"Princes of Golf," *Saturday Evening Post,* 246 (July–August 1975): 56–59;
"Wilt Chamberlain," *Sport Magazine,* 77 (December 1986): 49.

On 12 February 1961, forty-one-year-old Jim Murray began the first of his sports columns for the *Los Angeles Times.* A comment in that first column about his own athletic history illustrates the penchant for humor and hyperbole that characterizes his writing: "I have been held up to you as somewhat of a joke athletically but I want you to know I had one superlative as a college freshman baseball player. I was the most nervous right fielder our team ever had. Our coach, Ralph Erickson, had only four fingers on his right hand and the prevailing theory was that he had the regulation five until he saw us and started biting his nails."

The following 1 September, an article in *Time* stated that "sports Columnist Murray has built a reputation and following that, in just six months, qualifies him as one of the best sportswriters in the U.S."

In 1965 Murray was named, for the first of fourteen times, "America's Best Sportswriter" by the National Association of Sportscasters and Sportswriters. That year he also garnered his first National Headliner Award, with two more to follow. Despite having many opportunities, Murray refused to leave Los Angeles, where he lived for more than half a century until his death in 1998. He wrote some ten thousand columns in the *Los Angeles Times* and at one time was syndicated in as many as two hundred newspapers. His career was capped by a Pulitzer Prize for commentary in 1990.

James Patrick Murray was born on 29 December 1919 in Hartford, Connecticut. He was the son of Marry O'Connell Murray and James Murray, a failed pharmacist. James had two sisters, Mary Elizabeth and Eleanor Frances. The family struggled financially during the Great Depression. In common with many who were raised in that era, Murray was left with feelings of financial insecurity that only a steady paycheck could assuage.

When Murray's parents separated in 1929, nine-year-old James was already living with his paternal grandmother who raised him in a household that included uncles Frank and Ed Murray who, along with Murray's father, were sports enthusiasts. Both uncles influenced Murray to become a fan of many sports at an early age and to develop a view of life that might be characterized, despite his fundamentally ambitious nature, as lighthearted and realistically cynical.

Murray received his first eight years of education at Our Lady of Sorrows, a Catholic school in Hartford. At age ten he had a serious bout with rheumatic fever. While bedridden he read prodigiously and precociously in many areas, favoring history most of all. About this time, Murray enjoyed his first success as a writer when he won an essay contest by defending his choice of an American League all-star team.

Murray graduated from West Hartford High School, where he successfully completed the college-preparatory curriculum, which included the study of French, Latin, and math up to calculus. In an unpublished interview he admitted to doing well in English and claimed that he got by in chemistry, which held little interest for him, only because of his excellent memory. Surprisingly, for a nascent journalist, he did not write for the high-school paper.

Murray's grandfather had set some funds aside for Murray to attend college, but these were insufficient to allow him to enroll at Dartmouth, Murray's first choice. Instead, while continuing to live at home, he attended Trinity College, where he did some writing for the *Trinity Tripod* and got his feet wet in the newspaper business as campus correspondent for the *Hartford Times.* He majored in English and minored in history; he was twenty-three years old when he graduated with an A.B. degree in 1943, during the middle of World War II.

After he graduated, Murray walked into the offices of the *New Haven Register* one day, applied for a job, and was hired immediately as a police reporter. He did some impressive work, including a feature article on the Connecticut Company, which controlled public transportation in the state. The *Register* management was too penurious to allow follow-ups on some potentially juicy stories. On those occasions, Murray sometimes provided useful tips to reporters from the Associated Press (AP). When he decided to leave the *Register* later that year, Murray had a letter of recommendation from the AP in his pocket.

Murray was classified 4-F for the draft, which exempted him from military duty because of health reasons. According to Rick Reilly in a profile for *Sports Illustrated* (21 April 1986), Murray was so embarrassed about his inability to serve in the war that he left home and ended up in Los Angeles, where he landed a job as police reporter for the *Los Angeles Examiner.*

While on the police beat, Murray sometimes had trouble satisfying his boss, Jim Richardson, who would demand more pathos and less humor in Murray's routine pieces. In *Jim Murray: An Autobiography* (1993), Murray provides an example of how his writing style sometimes failed to hit the mark. Murray had written, "John Jefferson, 51, was found dead in his room at the Hotel Barclay yesterday. Police dubbed the death as suicide by hanging." When Richardson asked him to get "more oomph" into the story, Murray–on a third try–came back with "John Jefferson, 51, tired of it all, stepped off a chair into eternity." As he dropped Murray's typescript into a wastebasket, Richardson said, "Why don't you just go get a cup of coffee, kid?"

Most of the time, however, Richardson appreciated Murray's gift with words, and before long Murray advanced to become the youngest rewrite man in the entire Hearst chain. In his autobiography Murray recalled this period, the late 1940s, as perhaps the happiest time in his life–both professionally and personally. He had met his future wife, Geraldine Norma Brown (known as Gerry), and they were married on 20 October 1945. "We lived in this tiny, sunwashed apartment. We were living in a dream . . . At the newspaper, I danced every dance. The city was serving up a sensation a day." The older pair of their four children, Theodore James and Anthony Gerald, were born on 22 July 1946 and 4 May 1948, respectively.

Early in 1948 Murray accepted a newly created position as the *Time-Life* correspondent in Los Angeles. Anonymously, he wrote general articles, covered politics, and, as cinema correspondent for *Time,* became involved with the Hollywood movie crowd. He recalled that "the main part of my job was to round up cover stories. The magazine got sick of a steady procession of dour Secretaries of State, Three-Star generals, etc. They wanted pretty women on the cover periodically." His cover stories featured Betty Hutton, Lucille Ball, Ava Gardner, and Katharine Hepburn. He also wrote articles about Mario Lanza, John Wayne, Marlon Brando, and Frank Sinatra. Two of his favorite interview subjects were Marilyn Monroe and Humphrey Bogart. Although he occasionally wrote cover stories on sports figures, including Ben Hogan, Bobby Lane, John Lattner, and Parry O'Brien, he was not yet typecast as a sportswriter.

On 17 April 1950 "I Hate the Yankees" appeared in *Life,* authored by thirty-year-old James (not yet Jim) Murray–his first magazine piece. Like those to follow, it was written by invitation. Referring to a shellacking that the New York Giants had taken fourteen years earlier from the New York Yankees in a World Series game, he began:

> That 18–4 game gave the answer to those who were still fooled by the great Yankee myth, the myth that they were superchampions for the same reason that the Knights of the Round Table were superknights–because of some compelling leadership, some mystical *esprit de* Babe Ruth which had welded them into an all-conquering band of athletes.
>
> Nothing could be more preposterous. For my money the Yankees were and are superchampions for the same reasons General Motors or U.S. Steel are superbusinesses. They have more fans paying more money than any other club in the history of the game.

Here one already finds distinct elements of the Murray style. Rather than discuss Yankee dominance abstractly, he takes a specific game as his takeoff point. Although his first sentence fills an entire paragraph, it nevertheless reads smoothly and grabs the reader's attention. In it he brings forth a metaphorical platoon of straw men, a team whose members supposedly possess the leadership qualities of the Arthurian Knights. Then, after dismissing the importance of any lingering "*esprit de* Babe Ruth," and before offering his own explanation of Yankee dominance, Murray attempts to demolish the Yankee myth.

Later in the article Murray wrote that "a lot of people seem to be picking the Red Sox to win, and if DiMaggio is slow rounding into shape again this year, don't shed any tears over it. The 'poor old New York Yankees' have always managed to get along somehow." Here, after obliquely suggesting that no single player–not even the great DiMaggio–could account for Yankee dominance, he closes the article facetiously, and presciently as well, in what turned out to be Joe DiMaggio's last great season. As the "Yankee Clipper" faded the following year, the "poor old Yankees" came up with Mickey Mantle as his replacement and the team "managed" to dominate the World Series almost every year for the next decade.

From this early piece of sportswriting one learns not to take Murray literally, especially when he gives his opinion of what other people supposedly think. Humor, not accuracy, is the hallmark of Murray's prose. As a master of hyperbole who rarely regarded sport as a grim and serious business, Murray had a tendency to make off-the-cuff attributions while supplying little or no evidence for them. Sometimes an allegation would be so vague or general as to be true by definition. In the foregoing example most informed readers, without being told, would have assumed that Yankee wealth and Yankee dominance were closely related. Moreover, although one could scarcely doubt that "a lot of people" picked the Red Sox to win, it is likely that substantially more people picked the Yankees. In any event, no survey data are supplied because such numbers were neither necessary nor desirable for Murray's purposes.

Murray often sprinkled his free-and-easy prose with outrageous metaphors and deliberate absurdities. In a 21 September 1975 article he wrote, "Tennis is a game in which love counts nothing, deuces are wild, and the scoring system was invented by Lewis Carroll." Although deuces (tied scores) are not necessarily wild occasions in tennis, this familiar expression adds to the levity and cadence of a clever sentence. For the reader familiar with scoring in tennis as well as *Alice in Wonderland,* the double entendres are likely to make the reader laugh as Murray intended.

In 1953, as "one of the few persons in the *TIME-LIFE* company who knew anything about sports," Murray agreed to help launch a new weekly magazine, *Sports Illustrated,* on condition that he be allowed to remain in Los Angeles and continue his work as a *Time* correspondent. He continued for the most part to labor in anonymity until the early 1960s when a few bylines in *Sports Illustrated* identified contributions by the little-known James Murray. One of these (about motorcycle racing) and another (about track and field) appeared shortly before he began his *Times* column in 1961. Later in 1961, on 14 August, *Sports Illustrated* published the second half of a two-part feature called "Feud in the National League," which concerned the rivalry between the Cincinnati Reds and Los Angeles Dodgers. Cincinnati pitcher Jim Brosnan, whose controversial *The Long Season* had just been published, wrote the first part. Murray's second part, subtitled "The Great Coliseum Murder Mystery," is a remarkable parody masquerading as a British drawing-room mystery drama in which the guilty party somehow turns out to be the left-field screen in the Dodgers' temporary home, the Los Angeles Memorial Coliseum.

By the early 1960s Murray had become an associate editor of *Sports Illustrated.* Before he began writing for the *Los Angeles Times* in 1961, however, he had received none of the recognition that was later lavished upon him as a columnist. His increasing affluence, though, permitted him to move his family, now including two more children–Pamela, born 31 July 1950, and Eric, born 28 December 1952–from their urban residence to an acre-and-a-half estate in Malibu. Eventually the Murrays came back to the city, and later they settled comfortably in Brentwood.

After Frank McCulloch, a political correspondent for *Time* who was familiar with Murray's work, became the managing editor of the *Los Angeles Times,* he recruited Murray to write an almost-daily column designed to liven up his sports page. Murray took the position although he knew it would be "like running a railroad. You have to keep the stock rolling . . . If you write a book, a play, a movie, an opera, ballet or poem, you can bask in reflected glory (if it's good) for a while. Write a column, it's around the fish," alluding to the custom of fishmongers using old newspapers to wrap their merchandise.

Murray was a natural for the position. He had already been in Los Angeles for seventeen years. He had the necessary enthusiasm, background, and contacts. Most importantly, he also had abundant talent. Once the column was fairly launched, Murray became enormously popular. His reputation skyrocketed throughout the 1960s, so much so that by 1970 he had been named Sportswriter of the Year five times, and the first of three National Headliner's Awards adorned his trophy case.

Because his efforts to play golf enhanced his appreciation of the skill exhibited by tournament players, Murray especially enjoyed writing columns about that sport. Hockey was his least favorite topic because he found it hard to see what was going on. Without the red light, he wrote, he would have no way of knowing that a goal had been scored. Almost nothing that could be called "sport" escaped his ken. In his writing Murray drew on a wide range of background information, not only about sports but also about many other subjects, dating back to his extensive reading as a youngster and enhanced by his subsequent education and experiences. When combined with the "stand-up comic" aspect of his personality, the resulting prose became uniquely Murray's.

Murray was able to turn out columns six days a week during his early years, meet deadlines as short as half an hour, and still come up with prose in the Murray style–punchy, crisp, and funny. In the beginning Murray used a typewriter, first hunting and pecking and then becoming a skilled touch typist. A word processor later provided less of an advantage for him than for other writers who suffered through many drafts because, once he began to write, the column emerged essentially letter-perfect, without any need for rewriting which, he said, would "take the jazz out of it." Nevertheless, the act of typing must have had an influence on what he produced, because when failing eyesight forced him to use a dictating machine for awhile, he found the adjustment difficult.

Within three years after Murray began his column, Doubleday editor Luther Nichols helped him select a fraction of columns for inclusion in *The Best of Jim Murray* (1965); another collection was published in 1968 as *The Sporting World of Jim Murray.* In the foreword to the first book, Murray began by saying "The only thing I know for sure about sports is that they need dramatizing." To illustrate this point–which he also hammers home in his autobiography–he quotes Walter

Murray interviewing Pittsburgh right fielder Roberto Clemente (photograph by The Tidings Photo)

O'Malley, who said "anyone who thinks he can run baseball without a daily paper, can't run baseball." Murray also commented on his own style of writing, which "leans heavily on what your old English Lit. professor would call 'hyperbole.' This is a two-bit word for 'exaggeration' or 'exaggeration for effect.'" As an example, he offered his description of the diminutive golfer Ben Hogan: "His butt was so non-existent his hip pockets ran together."

In addition to his newspaper work, Murray continued to write occasionally for other publications. Murray's 7 June 1965 *Sports Illustrated* article, "The Drubbing," demonstrates his skillful use of metaphor. The story runs on the page opposite a stunning full-page color photograph of Sonny Liston, just decked by Cassius Clay. Describing the moment, Murray wrote that Liston "hit the floor like a guy slipping on a cake of soap getting out the bathtub." He concluded that Clay "beat Sonny Liston so bad he'll probably need help getting out of bed for a week."

Many of the ideas for Murray's pieces were suggested by other people. In 1966, an editor at *Esquire,* perhaps aware of Murray's conservative leanings, asked him to write an article about Ronald Reagan, then a candidate for governor of California. Murray accepted the assignment and wrote an essay that was as prescient as it was amusing. Murray emphasizes that Reagan "has such a strong, mellifluous delivery that he was once a sports announcer–and a good one at that." The voice, he writes, is one of the attributes that make Reagan a "formidable candidate for public office." Murray metaphorically characterizes another of Reagan's strengths: "Starting off at Governor is like trying to learn how to fly in a crash dive, but if Ronald Reagan has any self-doubts, he's not sharing them with anyone."

Murray began many columns with a colorful description of some individual. A 17 September 1965 column on longtime baseball catcher Smoky Burgess began: "You first look at Forrest C. Burgess out of uniform, and your temptation would be to hand him a transfer, tell him how you wanted your hamburger cooked, or tell him to cut you a piece of Grade A prime, chop off the fat, and keep his thumb off the scale." A 16 November 1978 column starts: "I always thought that if I ever interviewed Richard Petty and he hadn't won a race in a year, it would be because you can't win a race in a hearse." A 15 April 1986 column begins with a blunt observation: "You can see right away what is wrong with Ralph Lee Sampson as a basketball player. He doesn't give a damn."

In other columns Murray tantalizes the reader by referring to his subject anonymously in the opening paragraph. In a 16 August 1967 column on Phillies pitcher Curt Simmons, Murray began with a description of an old accident: "It was a warm day in June of 1953, the front lawn looked a little hairy, and the man of the house had a few hours before he had to show up for work. . . . He hauled out his new gas-driven rotary mower . . . and instead gave himself a pedicure." In a 19 October 1980 column on pitcher Dan Quisenberry, Murray at first identifies his subject only by number: "When No. 28 of the Kansas City Royals comes golf-carting out of the left-field bull pen to take over on the mound in this World Series, you first figure somebody has made a terrible mistake. . . . You figure this is a guy who got lost on his way to the world's softball championships. Either that or he should be wearing a skirt."

In other biographical sketches Murray uses his opening paragraphs to set the stage without directly telling anything at all about the person being described; only later in the column is the subject mentioned and, one way or another, tied in with the opening. For example, Murray's 17 October 1966 column on UCLA quarterback Joseph Beban seems to begin far afield: "The cult of the football hero began quietly enough. See him sitting there on the fence with the blue 'Y' on his white sweater . . . He is for God, for country and for Yale. He is Hinkley and Coy and Dink and Stover and Frank Merriwell."

In a 30 May 1974 column about quarterhorse racing, Murray captures the reader's attention with a humorous fictionalized account of the early life of Frank Vessels, who later became the owner of such an animal. Describing Vessels "flying a patrol bomber in Kwajalein," Murray says that at the time Vessels "thought a 'quarterhorse' was a recipe for French stew." Midway through the column, Murray slips in some information about quarterhorse racing, including the fact that such races take place at the Los Alamitos track a staggering 174 nights during the year. The column concludes with a fusillade of rhyme and rhythm: "The sport has come a long way since Vessels didn't know a quarterhorse from a nickelhorse. The nice thing about it is, if he's a dud as a stud, Frank can always sell his star to the rodeos to rope calves or the studios for John Wayne to win the West."

Although Murray's work was necessarily missing from the first two editions of Charles Einstein's highly regarded *Fireside Book of Baseball,* which were published in the pre-column years 1956 and 1958, samples of Murray's columns appear in the third (1968) and fourth (1987) editions. In volume three, published seven years after Murray began his column in the *Times,* Einstein wrote "Jim Murray . . . is regarded by many, and deservedly so, as the best sports columnist to acquire syndication in the past decade. His delivery might be described, stylistically, as mid-century stand-up comic . . ." In volume four Einstein praises the writer in his introduction of a Murray column about the acrobatic infielder Ozzie Smith: "When Jim Murray, the syndicated columnist of the Los Angeles Times, writes about this shortstop it is a case of the best describing the best." Murray's work has also appeared in John Thorn's *The Armchair Book of Baseball* (1985) and Irving T. Marsh and Edward Ehre's *Best Sports Stories* series (1964, 1975, 1976, 1979, and 1982).

Throughout the 1970s Murray was honored with several awards, including an Alumni Medal from Trinity College in 1972, his second National Headliner Award in 1977, and a niche in the National Sportswriters Hall of Fame, also in 1977. Nearing the age of sixty in 1978, Murray sustained the first of a quartet of serious personal problems when he started to go blind. In his column of 13 February 1979 (included in *The Jim Murray Collection*) Murray maintained his sense of humor even as he wrote about his detached retina. He began "I guess this story should really go to the *Reader's Digest,* you know, one of those 'I Was Joe's Pancreas' stories they run now and then."

During the 1980s Murray's vision had become progressively worse and he became legally blind for almost a year. But laser surgery subsequently restored enough of his sight so that, during his remaining years, he could read, watch sports, and drive safely in familiar territory during the daylight hours. Although he could no longer follow the flight of a golf ball at two hundred yards, such a handicap proved to be minor for a writer whose focus was always on the athlete rather than the ball.

Murray endured three more personal traumas in the first half of the 1980s. In 1982 his son Eric, called Ricky, died at age twenty-nine of a drug overdose. That same year Murray required a heart valve replacement. In spring 1984 his beloved wife, Gerry, succumbed to cancer and died. Writing about these terrible events may have been, at least to some extent, therapeutic for Murray, who told Reilly in 1986 that "I've sat down and attempted humor with every possible facet of my life in utter chaos."

Despite his personal difficulties, Murray continued to produce award-winning work. In 1982 he became the first sportswriter to win the Victor Award, conferred annually by sportswriters, editors, and broadcasters across the country; he also was presented the Red Smith Award for extended meritorious labor in sportswriting. In 1984 Murray won the Associated Press Sports Editors Association Award for best column writing, and in 1987 he was given the J. G. Taylor Spink Award for "meritorious contributions to baseball writing." Murray was inducted into the writers' wing of the Baseball Hall of Fame at Cooperstown, New York, in 1988. The third collection of Murray's columns, *The Jim Murray Collection* (1988), was introduced by long-time Dodger broadcaster Vin Scully, who wrote warmly of Murray: "This is no Halley's Comet that bursts across the sky and is gone in an instant. We're talking permanence right in the middle of the constellation." More honors came Murray's way in the 1990s, starting with the Pulitzer Prize in 1990.

Jim Murray: An Autobiography was dedicated to Linda McCoy, whom Murray married on 3 March 1997. He had originally met her at an Indianapolis 500 race back in 1969 when she had been assigned as his driver. After Gerry's death, McCoy sent a letter of condolence, beginning a friendship that eventually led to their marriage. Murray's autobiography is a curiously mixed work. Wes Lukowsy, writing in *Booklist* (1–15 June 1993), commented: "This is probably the least narcissistic autobiography ever written by anyone with any connection to sports. Murray supplies just enough information about himself to maintain the premise of an autobiography, but the book is actually a series of sketches of the famous people he's known."

Vague about names and dates, Murray does not cite any references. There are serious lacunae where large chunks of his life are barely mentioned, including his college years and his time at *Sports Illustrated.* Some of the material is not autobiographical at all. For example, the penultimate chapter, "Television–the Red Light District," is an essay on how TV has influenced sport and sports commentary. Although it is an excellent piece of writing, television was not Murray's bailiwick, and the text therefore does not relate to him personally.

Murray set aside his typical humor in the autobiography to become serious now and then. In chapter 18, "The Baby of the Family," he tells his son Ricky's story and describes the impact of that tragedy on Gerry. Murray blamed himself as well as the Southern California culture for his son's death. "I had gone chasing my career and, in so doing, had lateraled off the

Murray with tennis star Rod Laver (photograph by Bob Sloan)

main work of raising the kids to my wife while I went after success." Murray also provides the details about how Gerry died following three months in a coma, interrupted only by a brief period of consciousness near the end. In the afterword to the autobiography, Murray writes that "No man should be allowed to own a sports team unless he can first prove he is a fan. . . . Sport should be uplifting, wholesome, inspiring. . . . Whoever would downgrade it, manipulate it, corrupt it, or compromise it should be barred even from watching it."

In 1994 Murray received the Victor XXVIII Hall of Fame Award "in recognition for his remarkable contribution to sports journalism as a literary art form." In 1997 he received the Lincoln Werden Memorial Award for excellence in golf journalism, presented by the New York Metropolitan Golf Writers Association. Even as Murray approached eighty years of age, his columns continued twice a week in the *Los Angeles Times* sports section.

Murray often submitted his columns from the scene of the action, and he wrote his final column from the Del Mar racetrack. The winner of the "Pacific Coast Classic," a horse named Free House ridden by Chris McCarron, was not expected to come in first. Murray puts the race in perspective by comparing it to the Kentucky Derby: "The Pacific Classic is not your Run for the Roses. No bands play Stephen Foster as the horses come on the track. But it's not your basic overnight allowance either. It's a $1-million race, major on the schedule." He goes on to offer a humorous insight into the surprise winner: "What did *Free House* do that turned him into a star? Well, he got older . . . [but] he has one holdover from his misspent youth: he tends to kick out sideways and decelerate in the stretch, almost starts to tap dance. 'He gets to wondering where everybody went and wants to slow down and wait for them,' McCarron explained."

When his final column was transmitted from the Del Mar racetrack there were, typically, no columns in the pipeline. Jim Murray's last written words were "it's nice to know getting older has its flip side." The column appeared the next morning, 16 August 1998, in its usual spot on the front page of the sports section of the Sunday *Los Angeles Times*. Later that day, Murray died of cardiac arrest.

More than three thousand people attended a memorial tribute to Murray at Dodger Stadium in Los Angeles on 26 September 1999. The comments of those who spoke there appear in an epilogue to *Jim Murray: The Last of the Best* (1998), a posthumous selection of his columns published during the last decade of his life. All told, the four collections of Murray's work include about three hundred of his ten thousand columns. It is important to note that Murray's wit and punchy style pervade his writing and are not confined to the relatively few columns that have been brought out as books.

When asked to reflect on his success and prodigious output, Murray replied that he was blessed with an excellent memory that obviated the need for copious note taking. He said that he usually conducted interviews in person because it was his policy not to work by telephone with anyone he did not know. Murray usually traveled to the campus or the locker room to interview a player, engage him in conversation in a natural way without the distraction of a microphone or notebook, and then–with the interview fresh in mind–write a column published the next day. He typically focused on a personality rather than a statistic. Once he had decided on the subject of a column, Murray organized the piece in his head, where his words were bursting to get out. Then he would sit down to write, and "the rest came easy."

References:

Walt Cieplik, "Jim Murray: King of Sports," *Writer's Digest,* 57 (August 1977): 23–24;

Rick Reilly, "King of the Sports Page," *Sports Illustrated,* 64 (21 April 1986): 78–82; reprinted with epilogue in *Sports Illustrated,* 80 (16 May 1994): 18–71.

Jerry Nason

(14 April 1910 - 19 June 1986)

Adam R. Hornbuckle

MAJOR POSITIONS HELD: Sportswriter, *Boston Globe* (1930–1941); sports editor and columnist, *Boston Globe* (1941–1966); executive sports editor, *Boston Globe* (1966–1974).

BOOKS: *Famous American Athletes of Today, Seventh Series,* by Nason and others (Boston: L. C. Page, 1940);
The Story of the Boston Marathon (Boston: Boston Globe, 1966).

OTHER: "Bunion Form Chart," in *Best Sports Stories 1945: A Panorama of the 1944 Sports Year,* edited by Irving T. Marsh and Edward Ehre (New York: Dutton, 1945), pp. 220–223;
"Wrecking Crew at Work," in *Best Sports Stories 1946: A Panorama of the 1945 Sports Year,* edited by Marsh and Ehre (New York: Dutton, 1946), pp. 30–33;
"Wottaman Casey!" in *Best Sports Stories 1947: A Panorama of the 1946 Sports Year,* edited by Marsh and Ehre (New York: Dutton, 1947), pp. 269–271;
"Episode at Heartbreak Hill," in *Best Sports Stories 1948: A Panorama of the 1947 Sports Year,* edited by Marsh and Ehre (New York: Dutton, 1948), pp. 244–249;
"Sain Is Sound," in *Best Sports Stories 1949: A Panorama of the 1948 Sports Year,* edited by Marsh and Ehre (New York: Dutton, 1949), pp. 43–48;
"A Quality of Mercy," in *Best Sports Stories 1950: A Panorama of the 1949 Sports Year,* edited by Marsh and Ehre (New York: Dutton, 1950), pp. 117–121;
"Swift Premium Ham," in *Best Sports Stories 1951: A Panorama of the 1950 Sports Year,* edited by Marsh and Ehre (New York: Dutton, 1951), pp. 279–282;
"Mad Marathon," in *Best Sports Stories 1953: A Panorama of the 1952 Sports Year,* edited by Marsh and Ehre (New York: Dutton, 1953), pp. 260–264;
"A Man from Japan," in *Best Sports Stories 1954: A Panorama of the 1953 Sports Year,* edited by Marsh and Ehre (New York: Dutton, 1954), pp. 260–264;
"Hurricane Rocky," in *Best Sports Stories 1955: A Panorama of the 1954 Sports Year,* edited by Marsh and Ehre (New York: Dutton, 1955), pp. 260–264;

Jerry Nason (from Louis M. Lyons, Newspaper Story, *1971)*

"The Dissection of Harvard," in *Best Sports Stories 1958: A Panorama of the 1957 Sports Year,* edited by Marsh and Ehre (New York: Dutton, 1958), pp. 157–160;
"R-Day at Cambridge," in *Best Sports Stories 1959: A Panorama of the 1958 Sports Year,* edited by Marsh and Ehre (New York: Dutton, 1959), pp. 148–151;
"Joe the Jet," in *Best Sports Stories 1960: A Panorama of the 1959 Sports Year,* edited by Marsh and Ehrc (Ncw York: Dutton, 1960), pp. 124–127;
"Story-Book Finish," in *Best Sports Stories 1961: A Panorama of the 1960 Sports Year,* edited by Marsh and Ehre (New York: Dutton, 1961), pp. 124–127;

"His Name Should Be Job," in *Best Sports Stories 1962: A Panorama of the 1961 Sports Year,* edited by Marsh and Ehre (New York: Dutton, 1962), pp. 231–232;

"The 16-Point Minute," in *Best Sports Stories 1969: A Panorama of the 1968 Sports Year,* edited by Marsh and Ehre (New York: Dutton, 1969).

Paul Edward "Jerry" Nason was born on 14 April 1910 in Newton, Massachusetts, the son of Mabel and Will Nason. His birth five days before the start of the Boston Marathon, at Newton Hospital on the famed marathon course, was prophetic in that the race would become his principal beat as a *Boston Globe* reporter. According to Nason in his *The Story of the Boston Marathon* (1966), he watched the marathoners that year "cradled in the arms of a nurse." As a boy, he and his friends would ride their bikes from Newton to Ashland to watch the start of the marathon and then accompany the runners back to Boston. Nason followed the marathon much as other boys his age would have followed major league baseball, compiling and comparing statistics on the runners. Despite his enthusiasm for long-distance running, he played football at Newton High School. Also attracted to journalism, Nason worked on *The Newtonian,* the school newspaper, as a cartoonist, columnist, and editor.

After graduating from high school in 1927, he went to work for the *Globe* as a copyboy. Nason became an illustrator for the weekly sports and Sunday feature sections in 1929 and, within a year, the high-school sports editor. In 1933 he became the college sports editor and, in 1941, the sports editor. After serving in that post for twenty-five years, the *Globe* named Nason the executive sports editor, a position that he held until his retirement in 1974. Although Nason wrote about most sports in general, he excelled especially in covering college football, track and field, the Olympic Games, and the Boston Marathon. Most track-and-field writers regard him as the leading authority on the Boston Marathon, which he covered routinely from 1932 to 1982. Joe Concannon, who succeeded Nason as the chief Boston Marathon correspondent for the *Globe,* related in an unpublished 1998 interview that he was "as much a part of the marathon as the legends of the race." As another measure of his sportswriting expertise, stories by Nason were included in the *Best Sports Stories* series published by E. P. Dutton fifteen times between 1944 and 1973; three times, in 1945, 1969, and 1972, his contributions won recognition as the top story of the year.

When Nason entered sports journalism in 1930, the "Golden Age" of American sport was on the decline. Since the end of World War I, baseball, boxing, football, golf, tennis, swimming, and track and field had captured the public imagination. Each of these sports had its heroes, and most of the sportswriters of the era described their exploits with hyperbolic, enthusiastic, and overly dramatic prose. Nason grew up in a metropolis with a rich sporting heritage and a cadre of hometown and national sports heroes. As a young marathon enthusiast he witnessed the rise of one of the most indelible local sports heroes, Clarence DeMar, who won the marathon five times in that decade. By 1930, however, the nation had fallen deep in economic depression, and the public had lost much of its zeal for sports and sports superstars. As a reflection of that ebbing interest, sportswriting of that decade acquired a more restrained and pragmatic style. From the outset of his career Nason reflected this change in his sports reporting, writing in a crisp, succinct, and descriptive style. Even his work habits brimmed with efficiency; in the *Globe* (20 June 1986) Neil Sinegelais described him as a "master in making deadlines," typing his stories "with remarkable speed and accuracy."

Nason began his career in sports journalism as the high-school sports illustrator for the *Globe.* He recalled that "he entered the newspaper profession with a bottle of ink in one hand, a No. 3 quill pen in the other, plus a naive belief that the life of newspaper artist was strictly fun and gravy," until realizing that "newspaper artists of his acquaintance lived a perpetually hungry existence in cold, dreary attics." Motivated by a fear of high places and a normal appetite, Nason moved from illustrator to editor in 1930, after a survey of the editorial floor revealed "that members of the sports department were generally more rotund than those found elsewhere." Early in his career Nason demonstrated a penchant for writing attention-grabbing opening paragraphs, such as the following, from a 22 November 1930 article on a come-from-behind victory by Paul Revere High School over Dorchester High School: "A scrappy little Revere High eleven, just chock full of that four-letter word used at times to emphasize courage, came up from behind to wipe out a two-touchdown lead established by Dorchester High in the first period of their clash on the Paul Revere Park this afternoon and win 27–14."

As high-school sports editor Nason embraced an editorial philosophy that accompanied him until retirement. He asserted in the 20 June 1986 *Globe* "that if the *Globe* provided sufficient space for high school sport, the young sports page reader would remain loyal *Globe* readers during their adult years." The *Globe* commemorates Nason's enthusiasm for high-school sports by annually presenting a trophy in his name to the Boston high school with the most accomplished athletic program.

In 1933 Nason became college sports editor. Specializing in college football, he wrote about the games, players, and teams dear to Bostonians and

Cover for Nason's 1966 history of the race he covered for fifty years

New Englanders. The annual gridiron clashes between Boston College and Holy Cross and Harvard and Yale ranked high among his fall repertoire of events. In 1933 Nason covered the first of forty consecutive games between the Boston College Eagles and Holy Cross Crusaders. Played on the Saturday following Thanksgiving, the game probably meant little to anyone except graduates of the two small Catholic colleges. Nason's account of their 1949 meeting, which appeared in *Best Sports Stories 1950: A Panorama of the 1949 Sports Year,* reads as if the national championship hinged on the outcome of the clash. Boston College won the game "by the unparalleled and almost indecent score of 76–0," exacting revenge upon the team that upset them 55–12 in 1942.

At times Nason ventured beyond New England to write about Boston College football. In 1940, for example, he accompanied the Eagles to New Orleans to report their New Year's Day game against the University of Tennessee in the Sugar Bowl. In a front-page story on game day, 1 January 1941, Nason wrote that the Boston College players were "smacking their lips over the underdog role in which they had been cast" against a Tennessee team that had not lost a game in thirty-one starts. In one of the greatest games in the history of Boston College football, the Eagles upset the Volunteers by the score of 19–13. The game belonged to Boston College in the final five minutes of the fourth quarter, when with the scored tied at thirteen, they stopped Tennessee seventeen yards short of a touchdown "with a show of devastating defensive football," as Nason characterized it in his 2 January 1941 account of the game. The Eagles soared to victory on the skillful passing and running of quarterback Charlie O'Rourke, who scored the final touchdown on a twenty-four-yard run into the end zone. "For 55 minutes," Nason concluded, "O'Rourke was destined to be the goat of the game. But in the end it was the thin man with the air-rifle arm and the twinkling shanks who spelled the difference between two mighty football teams."

Although not with the same regularity that he covered the Boston College–Holy Cross game, Nason often wrote about the annual game between Harvard and Yale. Simply known as "The Game" among the alumni and fans of those Ivy League institutions, the contest is one of the oldest rivalries in college football, dating back to 1875. In the late nineteenth and early twentieth centuries, when the Ivy League produced powerhouse football teams, the outcome of the Harvard–Yale game usually carried implications for deciding the national title. Yet, by the early 1930s the importance of "The Game" had diminished along with the caliber of Ivy League football, and the outcome of "The Game" only entitled the winner to New England bragging rights for the year. In 1957, for the fourth time in as many years, Yale had defeated Harvard by a series record score of 54–0. Harvard avenged the loss the following year, defeating Yale by the score of 28–0. Nason's two accounts of these games appeared in the *Best Sports Stories* editions for 1958 and 1959. "R-Day at Cambridge" reflects the sometimes "merciless mood" that had by then characterized the eighty-two-year-old rivalry, as "Harvard flogged a lower-level and limping Yale football team."

In the 1960s Nason's coverage of the Harvard–Yale game won two major prizes. His account of the 1961 game won first place for sportswriting from the New England Associated Press News Executive Association. That year Harvard "stomped Yale 27 to 0 on a brittle day in the Bowl and shared the Ivy League football championship with Columbia," as Nason reported in the *Globe* (26 November 1961). Like his other prize-winning pieces on the Harvard–Yale gridiron clash, Nason's 1961 story captures the animosity that existed between the teams, describing the four fights that broke out during the game as an attempt to "rival the National A.A.U. Amateur Boxing Tournament." As a result of the fisticuffs, officials ejected two players from the game, but according to Nason "every one of the 22 players on the field at the time could have been banished." Nason's report of "The Game" in 1968, in which "Harvard scored 16 points in the final minute of play to bring off an incredible 29–29 deadlock with Yale and a coholder's share of the Ivy Title," was recognized as "Best News-Coverage Story" in *Best Sports Stories 1969: A Panorama of the 1968 Sports Year.*

Besides the Boston College–Holy Cross and the Harvard–Yale games, Nason also covered games played by the U. S. Military and Naval Academies. His account of Army's 48–0 rout of Notre Dame in 1945, "Wrecking Crew at Work," was his second story to appear in Dutton's *Best Sports Stories* series. Recognized by Dutton as the year's "Best News-Coverage Story," the article demonstrates Nason's deft use of metaphor to describe a sporting event played in the new atomic age: he suggested that "Army's set of linesmen have chained atomic power to the degree where it induces immediate and alarming ineptness on the part of the opposition." Nason also warmed New England hearts by highlighting Notre Dame player Frank Dancewicz, of Lynn, Massachusetts, who "made five open field tackles in the first half that either postponed or led to the ultimate denial of Army scores." His accounts of the annual Army–Navy game included in *Best Sports Stories* in 1959 and 1960 emphasize the exceptional play of Joe Bellino, a Navy halfback from Winchester, Massachusetts, who won the Heisman Trophy in 1960. In "Joe the Jet" (republished in *Best Sports Stories 1960: A Panorama of the 1959 Sports Year*) Nason compares his open-field running for two touchdowns against the Cadets in the first ten minutes of the game to that of "a frightened fawn."

In addition to writing about the explosive gridiron plays that highlighted college football, Nason also began writing about running of a different sort–the Boston Athletic Association (BAA) Marathon, a grueling 26.2-mile race from Hopkington to Boston–during his stint as college sports editor. Inspired by the race from Marathon to Athens at the 1896 Olympic Games, the BAA held its first marathon in 1897. In nearly a half century of covering the race for the *Globe,* including eight times after his retirement from the newspaper in 1974, Nason witnessed the marathon evolve from a regional event, attracting runners from the northeast United States and eastern Canada, to one of international scope and significance. Much of his best writing emerged from his marathon coverage, and the *Best Sports Stories* series included five of his race reports, from 1944, 1947, 1950, 1952, and 1953.

Throughout its history the Boston Marathon has furnished its home city with a host of local heroes, including Clarence DeMar, John A. Kelley, John J. Kelley, Bill Rodgers, and Alberto Salazar. As the leading local marathon correspondent Nason contributed stories to the creation of these legends. His 1944 essay "Bunion Form Chart," the first to be included in the *Best Sports Stories* series, helped to construct the John A. Kelley legend. Kelley finished the Boston Marathon fifty-eight times out of sixty-one starts from 1928 to 1991, winning the race in 1935 and 1945. Recognizing the budding reputation of the hometown favorite, Nason noted that "one first (1935) hardly is compensation for the magnificent racing he has done . . . a first, SIX seconds, a third, and a fifth in eleven starts." In 1944 Kelley finished second to Gerard Cote, a Canadian, who won the marathon three additional times. Nason summed up the race as "an epic of endurance and determination" that bestowed "Kelley a greater claim to a lasting legend in the Marathon than the race he WON in 1935."

Since the inception of the race, the course has intrigued correspondents as much as its contestants, often taking center stage in their reporting. The gentle downhill topography of the first half of the course leads most runners to set a fast pace early in the race before they reach several unforgiving hills in the Newton vicinity. Early marathon correspondents referred to this section of the course as the "heart breaking hills" because many front-runners lost the race over these inclines. The sobriquet comes from Nason's description of an encounter between Ellison "Tarzan" Brown and Kelley in the hills in 1936; Kelley caught the front-running Brown in the Newton hills and tapped him on the shoulder before going into the lead. After regaining the lead on the last hill Brown went on to win the race, thereby "breaking Kelley's heart" on the final peak.

Many of Nason's marathon stories revolve around the challenge presented runners by Heartbreak Hill. In his account of the 1947 race, "Episode at Heartbreak Hill," which Dutton included in *Best Sports Stories 1948,* the hill looms significant not only because of its undoing of one runner, but also for another runner's courageous assault up it. Yun Bok Suh of Korea, according to Nason, "tore to shreds this fearsome rise of ground which had broken the hearts of candidates before him" in his pursuit of the front-runner Mikko Hietanen of Finland. "Strong, and sure, and steady," he writes of the Finn, "but he was no match for running over a hill with a mountain man from Korea." Suh won the race in two hours, twenty-five minutes, thirty-nine seconds, then a course record. Korean marathoners proved themselves invincible hill runners again in 1950, as Ki Yong Ham led a Korean sweep of the top three places. In this race the Newton hills only contributed to deciding the finish order of the Korean horde, as Nason noted that Ham "sped away from the [Korean] champion, Yun Chil Choi, who also yielded on the big topographical humps to Kil Yoon Song."

A brilliant noonday sun and unseasonably warm temperatures outweighed the significance of Heartbreak Hill in Nason's account of the 1952 Boston Marathon. Second in the balloting for "Best News-Coverage Story," Nason's story narrowly lost top honors to an article on the world middleweight championship bout between Sugar Ray Robinson and Joey Maxim by Jesse Abramson of the *New York Herald.* Abramson's story also focused on the oppressive heat that dogged Robinson and Maxim that evening in Yankee Stadium. Whereas Abramson vividly describes the physical vulnerability experienced by athletes under such environmental extremes, Nason discusses how others seem to excel under similar conditions. In "Mad Marathon" (reprinted in *Best Sports Stories 1953*) he introduces *Globe* readers to Doroteo Flores, an impoverished Guatemalan mill worker who forged an unprecedented winning margin of four minutes and forty-seven seconds under unseasonably warm conditions. "Flores, in whose veins flows the blood of Indian forebears," writes Nason, "was impervious to the scorching sun, which proved a purgatory to the hopes of domestic favorites." Nason's description of Flores vividly conveys the runner's intensity:

> He is not a picture-book runner–this Doroteo Flores. But he is neat. His stride is short, but it beat the pavement with the regularity of the second hand on the official's stop watches. He looked almost fierce, like some bird of prey about to plummet upon a mid-day meal, as he . . . took complete mastery over the 56th Boston A.A. Marathon race and ruthlessly ran his opposition goofy . . . to the finish. There was a savageness to his performance that has been unequalled on the course since the Indian, Ellison Brown, dedicated his every once of heart and muscle to the task of smashing the record in 1939.

Flores's marathon victory was one of twenty-five, chronicled by Nason in his last thirty-seven years of reporting, by a runner from a nation other than the United States or Canada. The end of World War II marked the end of the provincialism of the Boston Marathon, as runners from Europe, Asia, Central and South America, Oceania, and Scandinavia captured the coveted Patriot Day laurel. As an astute student of the leading marathon competitors from around the world, Nason recognized the increasing international influence upon the marathon and correctly predicted Karl Leandersson of Sweden would win in 1949, as well as the Korean sweep of the first three places in 1950. "A Man from Japan," his account of the 1953 race (included in *Best Sports Stories 1954*), not only describes Keizo Yamada's record-setting victory, but also tells how "the Japanese hit the Tokyo billboards" that afternoon in Boston, by placing fourth, sixth, eighth, and twenty-second. Nason summed the race up as "another rout by the foreign entry."

In addition to reporting the increasingly cosmopolitan character of the Boston Marathon, Nason also commented on two other significant changes: the participation of women in the 1960s and 1970s, and the debate over professionalism in the 1980s. Women

THE BOSTON GLOBE—SATURDAY, APRIL 18, 1936 9

Tarzan Brown to Win Marathon Monday, Says Nason

What a Marathoner's Wife Thinks of Monday's Grind

STRONG INDIAN HAS IMPROVED

Most Favor Either Kelley or Dengis to Triumph

By JERRY NASON

In keeping with our annual custom of not being able to name the winner of the Marathon in advance, your befogged recorder of the doings of the arch excursionists takes great pleasure in picking Ellison Tarzan Brown to go deliberately on the warpath from Hopkinton to Boston on Monday afternoon.

The pleasure is mostly mine . . . certainly Master Brown won't extract any from this stupendous announcement. We ain't, as the boys put it, picked a winner since Pawson in 1933. Naturally none of the lads liked to be picked in this column because they become immediately situated behind the celebrated eight ball.

So we'll take Brown, which means that some other guy will win it, providing the thing progresses the way it has for two years when we picked Steiner, who was third in 1934, and Dengis,

"New Deal" Bees' Infield and Outfield

Boston Celts Play Andover in State Cup Soccer Tomorrow

Tomorrow's Soccer

N. M. AND N. H. STATE CUP, THIRD ROUND

Boston Celts vs Andover F. C. at Lincoln Park.

Scandinavian A. C. vs Swedish Americans at Worcester.

Chicopee Rovers vs Gremio Lusitano at Chicopee.

NATIONAL AMATEUR CUP, SEMIFINAL

Thornton Victorias vs Brooklyn German Americans at Ferri Field, Thornton, R I.

BOSTON AND DISTRICT LEAGUE

Riversides vs Bird and Son at Mel Williams Field, Lynn.

BAY STATE LEAGUE

Peabody C. L. C. vs Riverside Intermediates at Peabody.

OTHER GAMES

Clan MacGregor vs Quincy Point Boys' Club at Quincy.

Highland A. C. vs Victoria Sport Club at Foss Park, Somerville.

Lincoln Park will be the spot tomorrow for soccer fans. Boston Celts, carrying the colors and hopes of all Boston and District League fans, and Andover F. C., lone representative of the Merrimac Valley Leaguers, are due to clash in their important Northern Massachusetts and New Hampshire State Cup game. Kickoff will be at 3 p m. It's a "knockout" in more

Sports page for the Boston Globe, *featuring Nason's accurate prediction of the winner in that year's Boston Marathon*

began participating unofficially in the marathon in 1966, and the BAA added an official women's division in 1972. Describing the first women's participation as a "distaff fad," Nason reacted sarcastically the following year in the 19 April 1967 *Globe:* "Striding along smartly during the first couple of miles was Roberta Gibb of Winchester, a UCLA student who innovated the distaff fad last year. She was fashionably dressed for the inclement weather with leotards and paisley windbreaker."

While permitting women to participate in the once traditionally entirely male affair marked a significant break from custom, the decision to award prize money in 1986 meant an even greater departure from the amateur roots of race. In 29 April 1985 *Globe* Nason joined the debate over the impending professionalization of the marathon, proposing a two-tier race in which the elite would race for prize money and the amateur masses would run for "Boston's traditional gold medal, laurel wreath and beef stew." Noting how the race had evolved from ungainful to profitable sport, he wrote that "for a relatively few runners, the self-acclaimed 'elite,' the job is the Marathon itself. It's a job for which they demand a much more substantial reward."

The *Globe* published *The Story of the Boston Marathon,* a short illustrated history of the race by Nason, in 1966. For those interested in statistics he provided lists of the fastest times recorded at specific checkpoints along the course, various course records, and the ten fastest marathons in history. Nason also briefly summarized each of the races since the inaugural one in 1897, charted the evolution of the course, and noted other significant changes in the conduct of the race. "Probably the most influential decision ever made concerning the event was in 1947," he writes, "when the late Walter A Brown–aghast at the congestion and exhaust fumes on the overcrowded race course–limited the motorcade to the three official buses." Prior to that change, as he indicated to Joe Falls in *The Boston Marathon* (1977), as many as ten to twelve automobiles of writers, photographers, and officials accompanied the runners along the course:

> We'd all be concentrating on the leaders, and we'd be jockeying back and forth to get in position to get the best photos . . . . We kept cutting in and out and back and forth. It was like a race within a race. It was like Indianapolis in slow motion. We'd be yelling at the other cars, "Get out of the way!" and they'd be yelling back at us. All the while, mind you, nobody is thinking of the poor runners, who were being caught up in the fumes from these cars and all but being asphyxiated.

In addition to his coverage of the marathon, Nason also wrote about the Olympic Games for the *Globe* in 1948, 1960, 1964, 1968, and 1972. For much of the early history of the Olympics, American athletes, especially in swimming and track and field, had dominated the games. Although they quickly resumed that trend after World War II, garnering thirty-eight gold medals in 1948, Nason noted in the 15 August 1948 *Globe* that to have "seen the athletes of Belgium, Hungary, and Mexico score their respective nation's first Olympic victories was to appreciate the depth of athletic achievement which Americans so casually accept." In the 25 October 1964 *Globe* he chronicled the decline of American dominance in track and field, as "we failed to pull off sweeps of the hurdles, shot, discus, and pole vault." Noting cracks in American Olympic mettle, he lamented that "the rest of the world was climbing up our backs in the pursuit of the other medals in the other events." For him, as well as other Olympic correspondents, the 1968 Olympic Games marked a low ebb in American participation because of the demonstration by Tommie Smith and John Carlos, the gold and bronze medalists in the two-hundred meters, during the awards ceremony. In the 28 October 1969 *Globe* Nason described their black power salute during the National Anthem as "boorish and misplaced."

Nason's coverage of the 1972 Olympic Games, especially of Dave Wottle's unexpected victory in the eight-hundred meters, received much journalistic praise. Dutton selected his story on Wottle's performance as the best news-coverage piece of the year. The importance of Nason's award-winning story, however, can only be appreciated within the context of his entire Olympic coverage, especially of the events leading up to the eight-hundred meters. Before the eight-hundred meters American track-and-field fortunes looked dim as the top one-hundred meter specialists, Eddie Hart and Rey Robinson, missed the qualifying rounds because of scheduling problems, thereby opening the door for Valery Borzov of the Soviet Union to win the short sprint. "Europe rules the speedway," Nason proclaimed in the 2 September 1972 *Globe,* noting that "only five times since Athens in 1896 has an American ever failed to abscond with the 100-meter gold." "Then along came Dave Wottle," he exclaimed in his award-winning piece the following day, "a bucktoothed honeymooner out of Canton, Ohio, to the 800 meters final with a dramatic drive to the tape and put us back on the gold standard."

About a month before the start of the 1972 Olympic Games, Nason picked Borzov as one of the top three finishers in the one-hundred meters and Wottle as the "sleeper" in the eight-hundred meters. He made these predictions in his "Olympic Outlook" series, in which he analyzed the competition and predicted the top finishers in each track-and-field event. Nason started writing this column before the 1960 Olympic Games, in which he correctly named fifty-five of the sixty medal winners in track and field. One of the five possible gold medalists who fell short of Nason's predictions that year was high jumper John Thomas of Boston. Nason had followed Thomas's rise from high-school star to becoming the first athlete to clear the seven-foot barrier indoors at the Millrose Games in 1959. For the United States, the Olympic high-jump gold medal was "in the bag," as Thomas went into the event undefeated in two years and possessing the indoor world record at seven feet, two-and-one-half inches.) The nineteen-year-old Bostonian, weakened by dysentery, garnered only the bronze medal, however, as Valery Brummel and Robert Shavlakadze of the Soviet Union, respectively, won the gold and silver medals. On the day after the event, 2 September 1960, Nason noted that Thomas "was out of his state of shock, but the Olympic village was not. The entire compound still buzzed with the aftermath of one of the major upsets in all Olympic history."

Although specializing in track and field and college football, Nason often wrote about baseball, basketball, and boxing for the *Globe*. "Sain Is Sound," his story on the first game of the 1948 World Series, in which the Boston Braves defeated the Cleveland Indians 1–0, appeared in *Best Sports Stories 1949*. "Sain Is Sound" focuses on Braves pitcher John Sain, who held the Indians to four singles and no runs in nine innings. Nason describes his final pitch of the day as "a curve which snapped across the corner of the plate with the crack of the whip." His account of Rocky Marciano's knockout of Ezzard Charles for the heavyweight championship in 1954, "Hurricane Rocky," finished third in the Dutton balloting for that year's best story. Marciano defeated Charles with a final flurry of fast and furious punches, prompting Nason to note that "September is the month for hurricanes, and Rocky was one again tonight." His best basketball story, "His Name Should Be Job," published in 1961, was not about the Boston Celtics, but rather their fans' treatment of Wilt Chamberlain, then of the Philadelphia Warriors. Nason observed that "he is pestered, plagued, and pillored by some who watch him perform–all his faults magnified, all his talents mocked." Yet, another of Nason's stories included in the *Best Sports Stories* series, "His Name Should be Job," also received runner-up recognition from the New England Press News Executives Association as the best sports story of the year.

On 19 June 1986 Nason suffered a heart attack and died at his home in Winchester, Massachusetts. In an editorial three days later the *Globe* noted that "his influence on the sports scene in New England from 1942 to 1972, the years of stewardship of the Globe Sports Department, may never be fully appreciated because his way was not to bully or to bellow about this person or that cause, but rather to cajole and to explain." In short, Nason mildly transformed the sports section of the *Globe* from a voice of local to regional if not national significance. He accomplished this transformation through his own writing as well as through the work of "the many young people who came to work, and often to stay, in his department." The *Globe* concluded that "the presence of the by-lines of Nason's students in this newspaper and in newspapers the country over is perhaps his greatest legacy."

Reference:

Hal Higdon, *Boston: A Century of Running* (Emmanus, Pa.: Rodale, 1995), p. 39.

Dan Parker

(1 July 1893 – 20 May 1967)

Lyle Spatz

MAJOR POSITIONS HELD: Court reporter, political reporter, sports reporter, columnist, and sports editor, *Waterbury American* (1910–1924); sports reporter, columnist, sports editor, *New York Daily Mirror* (1924–1963); columnist, *New York Journal-American* (1963–1964).

BOOK: *The ABC of Horse Racing* (New York: Random House, 1947).

OTHER: "Slaughter on Eighth Avenue," in *Best Sports Stories 1945: A Panorama of the 1944 Sports Year,* edited by Irving T. Marsh and Edward Ehre (New York: Dutton, 1945), pp. 154–158;

"Weskit King," in *Collier's Greatest Sports Stories,* edited by Tom Meany (New York: Barnes, 1955), pp. 172–178;

"The Los Angeles Dodgers," in *The National League,* edited by Ed Fitzgerald (New York: Grosset & Dunlap, 1959), pp. 3–49.

SELECTED PERIODICAL PUBLICATIONS–UNCOLLECTED: "Yussel the Muscle," *Collier's,* 104 (1 July 1939): 16+;

"Change for the Bettor," *Collier's,* 105 (15 June 1940): 52–53;

"Hard Luck Champ," *Collier's,* 106 (2 November 1940): 21–22;

"So You Want to be a Sports Editor," *Saturday Evening Post,* 214 (2 May 1942): 30–31;

"Crazy Over Horses," *Collier's,* 109 (13 June 1942): 22+;

"Stutterin' Sam," *Collier's,* 112 (10 July 1943): 19+;

"Bad Boy of Boxing," *Saturday Evening Post,* 218 (11 August 1945): 17+;

"Comes the Baseball Revolution," *Saturday Evening Post,* 218 (6 October 1945): 18–19;

"Mr. Boxing," *Saturday Evening Post,* 218 (16 March 1946): 17+;

"Figurin' Frank," *Collier's,* 121 (5 June 1948): 52+;

"Baseball's Bombshell: The Reserve Clause," *Sport,* 6 (April 1949): 12–13, 80–83;

Dan Parker, 1944

"Horses," *Holiday,* 5 (May 1949);

"Hoyt of the Hambletonian," *Collier's,* 124 (6 August 1949): 22–23+;

"Why Happy Was Sent to the Showers," *Baseball Digest,* 10 (February 1951): 19–20;

"Leo's Golden Left Arm," *Sports Illustrated,* 1 (13 September 1954): 26–30.

Dan Parker occupied a special niche among newspapermen, one that prompted *Newsweek* (13 April 1964) to call him the "conscience of sports columnists." For more than forty years, first in Connecticut and then in New York, Parker exposed corruption and chicanery in the sports world wherever and whenever he saw it. "Dan was always on the side of the angels," said sportswriter Red Smith, then with the *New York Herald Tribune*. "He had no patience at all with sin." Another contemporary, sports columnist W. C. Heinz, said of Parker, "He is the cop on the national sports beat. Let a jockey pull a horse in California, a fighter throw a match in Des Moines, or a Minnesota promoter run off with the profits of a so-called charity show, and Parker will report it." Parker was called "a shy soft-spoken Connecticut Yankee" by *Newsweek,* but there was nothing soft-spoken about his coverage of both the greats and the charlatans of the sports world. Beginning in the "Golden Age" of the 1920s and continuing on through the iconoclastic 1960s, he covered them all, praising when appropriate but never overlooking any incident in which an athlete or any other person connected to that world went astray.

Daniel Francis Parker was born 1 July 1893 at St. Mary's Hospital in Waterbury, Connecticut, to Robert T. and Katherine (Scanlon) Parker. He attended school in Waterbury, graduating at age sixteen from Crosby High School. He was considered an unusually good student and a Latin and Greek scholar; he did not play on any of the school athletic teams, as he recalled in a profile in the *New York Mirror* (9 June 1938): "I was so skinny I would have cracked right in two."

After graduation he worked at a series of jobs at both the *Waterbury Republican* and the *Waterbury American,* where at various times (often simultaneously) he covered court proceedings and Eastern League baseball, served as the sports editor, and wrote a column, "Ben Franklin Says," inspired by a local statue of Franklin. Parker was working as a city hall reporter for the *American* when he tried to join the army in May 1917, a month after the United States entered World War I. While giving him his physical, the army doctor looked at his height and weight–six-feet-four and 160 pounds–and rejected him for being underweight. The army later reversed that decision and drafted him in March 1918. Parker got to be a sergeant in the 345th Infantry, 87th Division, the same outfit as Urban Shocker, a major league pitcher recently traded by the New York Yankees to the St. Louis Browns. Once in the army Parker developed stomach ulcers; but rather than take a medical discharge, he chose to have surgery. In 1949 he again underwent an operation for his ulcers, evidently successfully because they never again bothered him.

When the war ended, Parker came home to Waterbury and resumed his duties with the *American.* He had served in France, and while he saw no combat, he never forgot his wartime service. During World War II he often mentioned how uncomfortable he was writing sports while other men were fighting and dying.

Parker was working as a political and court reporter at the *American* when his boss chose him to replace the sports editor, who was retiring. He was not happy about the change, as he remembered in the *Mirror* profile: "I thought sportswriting was a demotion and argued against it, but he told me that sports was the best field for individual writing."

Four years later, in an interview with *The Sporting News* (30 April 1942), Parker reminisced about those years in Waterbury. "I was made sports editor, and I had to write the whole sports section," he recalled. "In addition, I wrote a column of alleged humor on the editorial page. I was on the Boxing Commission in the town, press-agent for the local burlesque show, contact man for the Chamber of Commerce, and official scorer for the Waterbury Brassos in the Eastern League. I'd say those eight-in-the-morning-to-midnight hours I put in at Waterbury were necessary training for a newspaperman. I've never regretted them. And anybody who learns that way is piling up experience that will repay him." Parker's breakthrough move from small-town Waterbury to New York came as the result of a meeting with fellow journalist Bill Slocum in the summer of 1923. He asked Slocum, who had also left Connecticut to work in New York, to put in a good word for him if an opening ever appeared in the city. A year later Slocum recommended Parker as a good all-around reporter to Gene Fowler, sports editor for the newly formed *New York Daily Mirror.* At Fowler's invitation Parker hurried the one hundred miles down to New York City for an interview one Friday, got the job, and reported to work Monday. He then returned to Waterbury, finished his Saturday workload for the *American,* and resigned. Parker recalled in *The Sporting News* that he regretted having to leave the *American* under such hurried circumstances, but he was unwilling to let pass his opportunity to work in New York: "I actually took less money to come down here."

The *New York Daily Mirror* was the latest addition to William Randolph Hearst's journalistic empire and the most recent entry into the crowded daily New York newspaper wars. Parker worked for the *Mirror* from the first day of the paper, 23 June 1924, to its last, 15 October 1963. His first assignment was as a beat writer for the Yankees, a role he filled for two years. During that time he also took his turn with other members of the staff to write a sports column under the alias of "Jack Conway." When Fowler left in 1926 to return to the *New York American* as its manag-

Present from a friend. Contractor Ben Collings gave Happy this pool, the Truman committee found. *Left foreground, sunning herself,* daughter Mimi Chandler. *Left to right,* sons Dan and Ben, the Senator, and Mrs. Chandler.

Comes the Baseball Revolution

By DAN PARKER

The inside story of the game's most sensational triple play—Chandler to Gottlieb to MacPhail to Chandler—and what it may mean for the future of the game.

WHEN the sports pages announced last winter that Loud Larry MacPhail was bidding for the New York Yankees, Ed Barrow, stern, septuagenarian dictator of this vast baseball empire, snorted, "Only over my dead body will MacPhail buy the Yankees."

The tides of eight or nine moons have stirred the turgid Harlem since Barrow told Loud Larry where to get off, and Ed is still on this side of the Styx. But somewhere along the route his prediction went

cumbed to the lure of this fan philter may suffer th same fate.

The astonishing contrast between strait-lace stern Judge Landis and his ebullient, sophomor successor, Senator Chandler, has been as producti of goose pimples to baseball as a midnight spri through a graveyard. Some of the major-leagu club owners who voted Happy Chandler into offi a few hours after they met in Cleveland last Ap twenty-fourth to hear a report from the committ of four on eligible candidates—and with no inte tion whatsoever of naming a commissioner—ha

First page of Parker's profile of newly appointed commissioner of baseball Albert B. "Happy" Chandler, from the 6 October 1945 issue of The Saturday Evening Post *(Reprinted with permission of* The Saturday Evening Post *© 1945 [Renewed] BFL & MUS, Inc.)*

ing editor, Ray Hegelson succeeded him as sports editor for the *Mirror* and took over the "Jack Conway" column full time. Shortly thereafter Walter Howey, the managing editor, decided he preferred Parker's style to Hegelson's. He called Parker in from St. Louis, where he was traveling with the Yankees that summer, and made him sports editor for the *Mirror*.

Parker's use of wit and humor in his column so impressed Hearst that he sent Parker to Washington with the idea of making him a political columnist. When Joe Conley, one of Hearst's executives at the *Mirror,* protested that Parker's leaving would do severe damage to the sports pages of the paper, however, Hearst acquiesced. In the 1940s Hearst did make Parker a kind of national sports editor, sending him to Chicago and California to evaluate the sports pages in his newspapers there. Yet, shortly after assuming this duty Parker informed Hearst that he did not care much for the assignment, and he was soon back at his desk in New York.

After becoming sports editor Parker continued to write his column under the name "Jack Conway," but he soon ended the practice. "I was blasting the fighters," he wrote in the 9 June 1938 *Mirror,* "and pretty soon, the fellows in the fight racket were saying I was afraid to do it under my own name. That got me mad so I changed to Dan Parker. Next day I got violent letters saying Dan Parker couldn't write." He had another, more substantial reason for switching from the pseudonym to his real name. A feud had quickly developed between the sports departments of the *Mirror* and its major morning competitor, the *New York Daily News.* Paul Gallico, then the sports editor of the *News,* referred to the *Mirror* as the "*New York Looking Glass*" and accused Parker of being a straw man hiding behind an alias.

Parker had engaged in some journalistic battles in Waterbury, but this challenge was his first in New York. He responded with an article about the egotistical editor of "*The Daily Snooze,*" whom he called "All Callico." Years later both men laughed about the incident, but at the time it was a serious feud. Parker felt strongly enough about it to ask Vic Watson, who had replaced Howey as managing editor, to allow him to write the column under his own name. Although Watson thought the name "Jack Conway" on the column was responsible for a significant part of the circulation success of the *Mirror,* he agreed to the change. Parker's feuding days with the *Daily News* were not over, however. He maintained a long-running battle with one of Gallico's successors, Jimmy Powers, although most readers felt that the battle was exceedingly one-sided, with Powers being no match for the wittier and more knowledgeable Parker.

Parker engaged in other battles with sportswriters, including a memorable one in May 1949. For several weeks Parker and Bill Mardo, a columnist for the *Daily Worker,* the American voice of the Communist Party, exchanged vitriolic columns over the "Fred Boysen affair." Boysen was a fan who had been physically beaten by New York Giants manager Leo Durocher at the Polo Grounds following a game in which he had taunted Durocher. The Parker-Mardo exchange had more to do with political ideology than with baseball. For Mardo the crux of the story was the fact that Boysen was black; thus, when baseball commissioner Albert B. "Happy" Chandler exonerated Durocher, he attributed the "whitewashing" of the case to the prevailing Jim Crow attitudes in baseball and all other facets of American life. Parker responded by condemning Mardo for using the incident to stir racial unrest, and the two traded charges and countercharges involving Jackie Robinson, the breaking of the color line in baseball, and the relative attributes of capitalism and communism.

As was his custom, Parker used humor and sarcasm in his response to Mardo. Calling the *Worker* "the Union Square *Pravda*" in the 8 May 1949 *Mirror,* he wrote that the communist paper was treating Robinson and the other black players in baseball as "Negroes" while the *Mirror* and other members of the "capitalist press" treated them as ballplayers. Parker accused Mardo, who did not write about the Boysen affair as being racially motivated until several days after it happened, of doing so under orders from Communist Party bosses.

> As for morbid Mr. Mardo, Moscow's maladroit minion, I would suggest, as a means of getting back in the Kremlin's good graces again after his colossal capitalistic blunder in writing a column from the standpoint of fair play instead of making it "politically correct," that he expose the racial prejudice inherent in the Brooklyn Dodgers' nefarious practice of making Robinson work overtime in extra inning games without compensation. Or, better still, he might dash off another deathless essay, correcting the common capitalistic misconception that Baseball was invented by Gen. Abner Doubleday, a Yankee Doodler. It has been known for years by Pravda that a Russian named Pakudnyak Tsibiliskoff was the actual founder of this game and that the Cincinnati Reds, the first American pro team, were sent over here after the Civil War (Ah, comes the Revolution, Ivan!) to demonstrate Russia's national pastime to the slaves of capitalism.

Mardo was correct, however, in claiming that Parker, like most every other mainstream sportswriter of his time, had never paid much attention to segregation in sports. Unlike some of his journalistic colleagues, however, he had supported and defended Brooklyn Dodgers manager Branch Rickey's signing of Robinson. In the first series of the 1947 season–Robinson's rookie year–between Brooklyn and the Philadelphia Phillies, the Phillies, led by manager Ben Chapman, had been unremitting in their verbal and physical abuse of Robinson. Parker attacked Chapman in his column, recalling his bigoted behavior when he played for the Yankees in the 1930s and calling Robinson "the only gentleman among those involved in the incident."

Much of the Parker humor that had caught Hearst's attention came from his descriptions of the many offbeat personalities that populated the sports world, particularly those in boxing. "All the screwy guys gravitate to me," Parker said in the 9 June 1938 *Mirror,* "and I'd rather write about the characters you run into in sports than the games they play." Parker often rendered his depictions of these characters in dialect, utilizing his ear for English as it was spoken with a Yiddish, Greek, Italian, or other immigrant accent. A particular Parker favorite was Ben "Evil Eye" Finkle, a boxing hanger-on whom he described as the master of the "Slobodka Stare" and the "Warsaw Whammy." Parker said of Finkle that "He's hired by fight managers to put the old whammy on their opponents so they'll lose the fight." Another colorful character on the boxing beat was Mushky Jackson, who, according to Parker in the 9 June 1938 *Mirror,* "was one of the fight racket guys who spoke English you don't find in any other league." While Parker's ethnic references were generally considered acceptable in those days, occasionally the practice backfired. One such incident resulted from his account of Joe DiMaggio's poor performance in the 1936 All-Star Game. Describing the Yankee rookie sensation's difficulties, Parker wrote in the *New York Mirror* (8 July 1936): "Poor Guiseppe DiMaggio found himself in the same predicament as Primo Carnera breaking in a new pair of shoes." The proud DiMaggio never forgot what he felt was the anti-Italian manner in which Parker had criticized him.

Parker often used humor as a weapon, but not in his tireless campaign against what he saw as the increasing commercialism and shady doings of professional sports, particularly boxing. It was a lifelong crusade. Shortly before he retired, in the 13 April 1964 issue of *Newsweek,* he said: "I saw my first fight when I was seventeen, and it was a barney (fixed). There's always been larceny in boxing, and when I've seen it I've written it. But it's worse now than ever before. I've been at its bedside waiting forty years for boxing to die and I think it's about time to make room for someone else."

Writing in the *American Mercury* in September 1955, Howard Rushmore said: "The list of crooks, grafters and mobsters who hate Parker is a long one and increases almost daily with the publication of another column under Dan's by-line." Chief among those mobsters was the group that controlled Primo Carnera and engineered his rise to the world heavyweight championship. More than once they threatened to kill Parker for his columns ridiculing Carnera and the many thrown fights that littered his path to the title. If these threats worried Parker, he did not show it. As one who greatly enjoyed music and other forms of theatrical entertainment, he was often the star of the annual show sponsored by the New York Baseball Writers. One year, Carnera informed the audience from onstage that he "could lick anybody in the house." When he said it he was obviously looking at Parker, who had so often used his column to decry the fact that Carnera's mobster backers were arranging for his opponents to lose. Parker jumped up and began to pantomime someone taking a dive.

Despite the repeated threats from organized crime, Parker continued to devote columns to exposing the underworld influence on boxing. His efforts led to official investigations and sometimes convictions. He was so effective that in 1942 Governor Thomas Dewey, his summer neighbor in Pawling, New York, asked him to become chairman of the New York State Boxing Commission. Parker refused, saying he did not want to become a part of something that for so long had been one of his most treasured targets. "I would have been like a boxer with his right arm cut off," he told *Newsweek.* "Besides, what would I use for a punching bag if I were on the boxing commission myself?"

Instead, he stayed at his typewriter and continued to attack the mob's influence on boxing. Parker is recognized for having played a major role in sending gangster Frankie Carbo to prison and with helping to destroy the notorious International Boxing Club (IBC). Under the leadership of James Norris, the IBC had established a monopoly on boxing in the 1950s by using strong-arm methods to gain control of most of the champions and major venues of the sport. Parker argued that the combination of IBC control and television were killing boxing.

Even before television and the IBC, Parker had tried to alert his readers to the things that were wrong with boxing, however. In the 1930s he used his columns to assail Madison Square Garden boxing promoter and matchmaker Jimmy Johnston, whom he accused of giving preferential treatment to his own stable of fighters. Once, after Parker wrote that Johnston's bouts were "lousy," Johnston removed him from the free-ticket list. After a while he recognized that this tactic was futile as a way to silence Parker and again started sending free tickets, but Parker sent them all back.

The persistent criticism led to Johnston being replaced at the Garden by Mike Jacobs, who helped eliminate some of the graft at the higher levels of the sport. Parker continued to point out the remaining skullduggery when he saw it, but overall he credited Jacobs for making boxing a bit more honest. "The big fights are getting cleaned up because Mike Jacobs found it's good business to have them on the level," he said in the 9 June 1938 *Mirror.* In *The Sporting News* in 1942 he added: "I don't always approve of everything Jacobs does, but I think he and Joe Louis have lifted the game a great deal." Despite his attacks on boxing, or maybe because of them, Parker was the most avidly read writer by those in the fight business.

Typical of his humorous skewering of the fight racket was a column reviewing the 1938 heavyweight bout between "Two Ton" Tony Galento, a "contender," and Charley Massera in Galento's hometown of Orange, New Jersey. Galento knocked out Massera in the third round with a phantom punch, a curiosity that Parker addressed in several pointed rhymes:

They say a left hook
To the chops closed the book
On the prize fighter, Charley Massera.
Though it may not have landed
It left Charley stranded
(And how is your dear old Aunt Sarah?)

After describing the early "battling," Parker wrote: "Two rounds of this and Tony decided the customers had had enough. Did I say Tony? I meant Charley. One of Tony's left hooks landed somewhere–no one is quite sure–and Charley landed on his haunches. He's up. He's down. He's out. It all happened in 45 seconds."

In the same piece Parker quoted Yussel (Joe) Jacobs, Galento's colorful manager and a man whose legendary misuse of the English language often found its way into his columns. Speaking to his victorious warrior after Massera was vanquished, Jacobs said, "He certainly stood down the second time when you left him have that left." Parker is also responsible for Jacobs's unlikely inclusion in *Bartlett's Quotations,* by quoting the fight manager's remark that "I should have stood in bed," uttered in a freezing press box in Detroit during the 1934 Tigers-Cardinals World Series.

Although most often remembered for attacking corruption in boxing, Parker also devoted many columns to exposing the roguery in horse racing and professional wrestling. During one of his campaigns against fixed wrestling matches, he exasperated the promoters by naming the winners before they held the bouts. With a little detective work Parker had found the printer who had the job of making up the cards for the program the following week. By looking at the matchups he was able to extrapolate the likely winners and losers of the current week's bouts. "Anyone who says wrestling is on the level is a wrestler, a promoter, or an imbecile," he told *The Sporting News.* Parker said wrestlers and wrestling promoters had sued him five times, but none of the lawsuits ever reached a courtroom.

Parker never actually criticized those sportswriters who did not take on what he called the bad guys, but it was no secret how he felt about them. "It must be a pleasant existence if a sportswriter sees only the nice side of life," he said in *American Mercury* (September 1958). While referring to sportswriting as a profession composed of men who "remain perpetually juvenile," he wrote in *Newsweek* (14 February 1944) that "A facetious sort of cynicism is a favorite pose of the profession. Crusades aren't popular. Anyone who undertakes them is likely to find himself looked upon with distrust."

In retrospect Parker's most telling comment about the many crusades he undertook appeared in a 30 September 1942 interview with J. G. Taylor Spink of *The Sporting News.* He told Spink that "It makes the job fun. If I can feel I've done a bit of good, helped the fans, exposed a bit of thievery, why, I feel the job's worthwhile. If there wasn't a scrap now and then for me, I'd feel life was getting a little dull." He even went beyond traditional sports to take on the Indianapolis 500 auto race. After the deaths at the 1955 race, he wrote in *American Mercury* (September 1955): "Nothing is proved by these annual flirtations with death except that, even in the most skillful hands, a speeding automobile, whether outside or inside the fence, is one of the most dangerous weapons."

Parker's concern about the ever-increasing influence of television on sports extended even to baseball, which he observed in the same *American Mercury* piece was "gradually being taken over by TV." Still, he believed that game to be the least corruptible of all the sports. "Baseball is the most lily white of the professional sports. Probably because of all the scandals they've had," the onetime Yankee beat writer said in 1938. Parker claimed that he personally broke the news of one baseball scandal, the alleged attempted bribe of two Philadelphia players by Giants' coach Cozy Dolan in October 1924. For that exposé Giants manager John McGraw banned him from the Polo Grounds.

Parker's most memorable crusade in baseball was the relentless one he waged against Commissioner "Happy" Chandler. He believed that Chandler, whom the owners elected in 1945 to succeed Judge Kenesaw Mountain Landis, was unqualified to be commissioner, and he argued the point for the six years that Chandler occupied that office. In a 1947 open letter to Chandler published in *Sport* magazine Parker accused him of many things, including some that happened when Chandler was still a U. S. senator from Kentucky. For example, Parker claimed that Chandler had interceded with President Harry Truman in 1945 to obtain the release of Indiana gambler James J. Gavin from the federal prison in Terre Haute. His most serious accusation concerned Chandler's friend Ben Collins, a Louisville contractor, however. Parker said that Chandler's Committee on Military Affairs had shown blatant favoritism and disregard for the legal bidding process in

Parker (back row, far left) with sportswriting colleagues in St. Petersburg, Florida, March 1957 (photo by Bill Mark)

awarding war contracts to Collins's company, prompting a response by Chandler in the 2 April 1947 edition of *The Sporting News.*

Parker launched his first attack on Chandler's qualifications in a 6 October 1945 *Saturday Evening Post* article, "Comes the Baseball Revolution," which appeared shortly after Chandler became commissioner. The revolution that Parker was referring to was one by a group of so-called Young Turks, a clique of major league executives led by Yankee co-owner Larry MacPhail, against the "Old Guard" of the sport. MacPhail, he said, had defied such old-timers as longtime Yankee executive Ed Barrow in becoming part owner of that club and had used his influence to handpick Chandler for the job as commissioner. Parker claimed that Chandler was therefore beholden to MacPhail, citing as one example the baffling midseason waiver deal in which the Yankees were able to obtain waivers on Hank Borowy, their best pitcher, and then sell him to the Chicago Cubs. Parker suggested that MacPhail was repaying the Cubs for selling him Billy Herman in 1941, a deal that helped MacPhail's Dodgers win their first pennant in twenty-one years. He was even more outraged when in response to demands to know why the Yankees and the seven other American League teams, none of whom were out of the pennant race at the time, had passed on Borowy, Chandler decided there would be no investigation.

While Chandler was a new target for Parker, he had begun chronicling MacPhail's excesses and influence when MacPhail ran the Brooklyn club and continued to do so during his tenure with the Yankees. When asked why he wrote so critically of MacPhail, he told *The Sporting News* (30 April 1942): "I am neither pal nor enemy to the Great Man. I regard him as a great source of readable copy."

Beginning in 1926, when he became the sports editor and columnist for the *Mirror,* until 1963, when the paper ceased publication, Parker wrote seven columns a week. His work extended beyond the confines of New York, since his columns also appeared in eleven other Hearst newspapers via their King Features Syndicate. His one day off was Sunday, when he would retreat to his farm in Pawling (and in later years to his home in Bronxville, New York) to fish for brook trout and smallmouth bass and to relax. Parker was an ardent fisherman and usually spent the month of August, his vacation time, fly-fishing at his summer home in New Milford, Connecticut. His other favorite form of relaxation was reading–his favorite author was Marcel Proust, and Thomas Gray's *An Elegy Written in a Country Churchyard* (1750) was his idea of good poetry.

He was able to relax on Sundays because he wrote his Monday column in advance. "The Broadway Bugle" was constructed in the dot-and-dash format, made up of short statements and news items (many contributed by newsmen on other papers) and often accompanied by amusing sketches done by cartoonist Fred Weatherly. For many of his faithful readers "The Broadway Bugle" was their favorite Parker column.

From time to time he wrote another column, "Around the Clock With . . . ," in which he traced how a particular sports personality spent his typical day. Most often the columns were done in a humorous, ironic style and were less than flattering to their subjects. As was the style for many sportswriters of that time, Parker often used bits of poetry in his columns. Unlike the sentimental fluff that most others wrote, he constructed his verse to censure someone he believed had behaved badly. For example:

Here lies a guy to whom an early grave his greed has sped him
He died from overeating when he bit the hand that fed him.

Parker's most long-lived poem is one in which he good-naturedly paid tribute to the faithful fans of the Brooklyn Dodgers. Written in 1945, it has since appeared in many literary baseball anthologies.

Murgatroyd Darcy, the belle of Canarsie,
Went 'round with a fellow named Rodge.
At dancing the rhumba, or jitterbug number,
You couldn't beat Rodge at this dodge.
Throughout the cold weather, the pair danced together,
But when the trees blossomed again,
Miss Murgatroyd Darcy, the belle of Canarsie,
To Rodgers would sing this refrain:
Leave us go root for the Dodgers, Rodgers,
That's the team for me.
Leave us make noise for the boisterous boys
On the B. M. T.
Summer or winter or any season,
Flatbush fanatics don't need no reason.
Leave us go root for the Dodgers, Rodgers,
That's the team for me.

The bitter strike by the International Typographic Union in 1962–1963 led to the death of several New York newspapers, including the *Mirror.* When the *Mirror* shut down, Parker transferred his column, although not his desk, to the other Hearst paper in New York, the afternoon *New York Journal-American.* He continued to write from the old *Mirror* newsroom at 235 East Forty-fifth Street, as did his close friend, gossip columnist Walter Winchell, who also moved to the *Journal-American* after the *Mirror* folded. The Hearst Syndicate leased the room in which Parker and Winchell worked to a television company that was producing a series on the newspaper business. So as the two real newspapermen, among the best-known in the country, worked on their columns, they were surrounded by television cameras filming actors pretending to be newspapermen.

Parker's stay with the *Journal-American* lasted just six months. He retired on 1 April 1964, the same day that his longtime colleague and rival, John Drebinger of *The New York Times,* chose to step down. An article in the 13 April 1964 issue of *Newsweek,* "Drebby and Dan," lauded the two retiring giants of sports journalism by designating Drebinger the "dean of baseball writers" and Parker the "conscience of sports columnists." In contrasting their styles and personalities, *Newsweek* called Drebinger "a short, fun-loving character," while Parker was "a tall and quiet crusader who has devoted his career to exposing corruption for the flamboyant Hearst chain." Drebinger's "reputation and popularity among his peers was based more on his popularity than his prose," the article said. By contrast, "Parker is a loner, admired more for what he stands and for what he has written than for personal color."

Parker had helped raise millions of dollars for the Damon Runyon Cancer Fund during the last two decades of his life, serving many years as its president and chairman of the board. After he retired he spent even more time at the Fifty-sixth Street office of the Runyon Fund, laboring long hours in its behalf. After retiring, he had several heart attacks that required hospitalization, but cancer eventually claimed his life. Parker, the author of *The ABC of Horse Racing* (1947), died of the disease on 20 May 1967, the same day the great Willie Shoemaker rode Damascus to victory in the Preakness. He died in St. Mary's Hospital in Waterbury, the same hospital in which he was born nearly seventy-four years earlier. He left behind his third wife, the former Alice McGloughlin, a son, Donald T. Parker (Parker's younger son, Barry, had died three months earlier), and an adopted daughter, Norma. His first marriage had ended in divorce and his second wife, Norma Murray, who wrote "Joan's Shopper Column" for the *Mirror,* died.

Representatives from baseball, boxing, the Damon Runyon Cancer Fund, and the city of Waterbury attended his funeral. Among the baseball people present were New York Mets promotions director Arthur Richman and Ken Smith, director of the Baseball Hall of Fame, who served as a pallbearer. Both men had worked as sportswriters under Parker during his tenure as sports editor at the *Mirror.*

Parker once claimed in the *Mirror* (9 June 1938) that "a sports editor is a fellow who spends his day giving out passes to printers, reporters, and pressmen for ball games and fights"; yet, his contributions to the profession were honored throughout his career. He received the Connecticut Sports Writers Alliance Gold Key in 1945; the National Headliners Club Award for Sports Writing in 1949; three Page One Awards of the New York Newspaper Guild; the National Sportscaster and Sportswriter Association Award; the George Polk Award of Long Island University in 1955; and the Schaeffer Award of the New York Newspaper Reporters Association. His hometown of Waterbury also named a street for him, Dan Parker Drive.

In his obituary of Parker for *The New York Times* (23 May 1967) Arthur Daley recalled that he "was a shy, gentle and kindly man with a quick sense of humor and a sharp eye for the incongruous" and that "he spiced his columns with some of the wittiest recitals of malapropisms and of marvelously clever dialect pieces." Daley wrote that Parker "was not an easy man to know" but "was a solid friend to those who could work their way past the shield he always kept in front of him. . . . He deserved better of life than he ever received." The obituary in *The Sporting News* (3 June 1967) truly captured Parker's essence, calling him "a hard-hitting crusader in his columns, fighting against shoddy practices in sports," while "personally, he was a genial, witty man with compassion for athletes who were the victims of misfortune."

Reference:

Howard Rushmore, "Dan Parker, Conscience of the Sports World," in *American Mercury* (September 1955): 57–59.

George Plimpton

(18 March 1927 -   )

Richard Orodenker
Penn State Abington

See also the Plimpton entry in *DLB 185: American Literary Journalists, 1945–1995, First Series.*

George Plimpton

BOOKS: *The Rabbit's Umbrella* (New York: Viking, 1955);

Out of My League (New York: Harper, 1961);

Paper Lion (New York: Harper & Row, 1966);

The Bogey Man (New York: Harper & Row, 1968);

Mad Ducks and Bears (New York: Random House, 1973);

One for the Record: The Inside Story of Hank Aaron's Chase for the Home-Run Record (New York: Harper & Row, 1974);

One More July: A Football Dialogue with Bill Curry (New York: Harper & Row, 1977);

Shadow Box (New York: Putnam, 1977);

Sports! text by Plimpton, photographs by Neil Leifer (New York: Abrams, 1978);

A Sports Bestiary, by Plimpton and Arnold Roth (New York: McGraw-Hill, 1982);

Fireworks: A History and Celebration (Garden City, N.Y.: Doubleday, 1984);

Open Net (New York & London: Norton, 1985);

The Curious Case of Sidd Finch (New York: Macmillan / London: Collier-Macmillan, 1987);

The Official Olympics Triplecast Viewer's Guide, by Plimpton and others (New York: Pindar, 1992);

The X Factor (Knoxville, Tenn.: Whittle Direct Books, 1990; revised, New York: Norton, 1995);

Truman Capote: In Which Various Friends, Enemies, Acquaintances and Detractors Recall His Turbulent Career (New York: Nan A. Talese / Doubleday, 1997);

Pet Peeves; or, Whatever Happened to Dr. Rawff? (New York: Atlantic Monthly Press, 2000).

Collection: *The Best of Plimpton* (New York: Atlantic Monthly Press, 1990).

OTHER: *Writers at Work: The Paris Review Interviews,* 9 volumes, edited by Plimpton (New York: Viking, 1958–1992);

The American Literary Anthology, nos. 1–3, edited by Plimpton and Peter Ardery (New York: Random House, 1968, 1969, 1970);

Jean Stein, *American Journey: The Times of Robert F. Kennedy,* edited by Plimpton (New York: Harcourt Brace Jovanovich, 1970);

Pierre Etchebaster, *Pierre's Book: The Game of Court Tennis,* edited by Plimpton (Barre, Mass.: Barre, 1971);

Bernard Oldsey, ed., *Ernest Hemingway, The Papers of a Writer,* includes a chapter by Plimpton (New York: Garland, 1981);

Edie: An American Biography, edited by Plimpton and Jean Stein (New York: Knopf, 1982);

Diana Vreeland, *D. V.,* edited by Plimpton and Christopher Hemphill (New York: Random House, 1984);

Poets at Work: The Paris Review Interviews, edited by Plimpton (New York: Viking, 1989);

Women Writers at Work, edited by Plimpton (New York: Viking, 1989);

The Best of Bad Hemingway: Choice Entries from the Harry's Bar & American Grill Imitation Hemingway Competition, 2 volumes, edited by Plimpton (San Diego: Harcourt Brace Jovanovich, 1989-1991);

The Paris Review Anthology, edited by Plimpton (New York: Norton, 1990);

The Writer's Chapbook: A Compendium of Fact, Opinion, Wit, and Advice from the 20th-Century's Preeminent Writers, edited by Plimpton (New York: Viking, 1990);

The Norton Book of Sports, edited by Plimpton (New York: Norton, 1992);

Best American Sports Writing, 1997, edited by Plimpton (Boston: Houghton Mifflin, 1997);

Home Run, edited by Plimpton (San Diego: Harcourt, 2000);

Playwrights at Work, edited by Plimpton (New York: Modern Library, 2000).

SELECTED PERIODICAL PUBLICATIONS–UNCOLLECTED: "Dreams of Glory on the Mound," *Sports Illustrated,* 14 (10 April 1961): 112–114, 116, 118, 120, 122, 125–126, 128, 131–132, 134;

"Newport Notes: The Kennedys and Other Salts," *Harper's,* 226 (March 1963): 39–47;

"Miami Notebook: Cassius Clay and Malcolm X," *Harper's,* 228 (June 1964): 54–61;

"World Series with Marianne Moore," *Harper's,* 229 (October 1964): 50–58;

"World Champion Is Refused a Meal," *Sports Illustrated,* 22 (17 May 1965): 24–27;

"Celestial Hell of the Superfan," *Sports Illustrated,* 23 (13 September 1965): 104–106;

"But Why Me, Coach?" *Sports Illustrated,* 23 (13 December 1965): 18–21;

"Observations of a Rookie," *Saturday Review,* 49 (10 December 1966): 60–61;

"What the Deuce Is Going On?" *Sports Illustrated,* 27 (18 September 1967): 34–36;

"Strange Case of the Balls That Go Poof!" *Sports Illustrated,* 28 (22 January 1968): 28–31;

"Man, I'm Dropping Your Bag Right Here," *Sports Illustrated,* 29 (28 October 1968): 34–36;

"Stuff of Dreams," *Sports Illustrated,* 29 (4 November 1968): 36–38;

"Visions of Eight," *Sports Illustrated,* 39 (27 August 1973): 30–35;

"Pony Wars of Bloomfield Hills," *Harper's,* 247 (September 1973): 78–80, 82–84;

"Sportsman of the Year," *Sports Illustrated,* 41 (23 December 1974): 84–89, 93, 97, 98, 101;

"But the Ivies Do Fight Fiercely," *Sports Illustrated,* 43 (8 September 1975): 29–39;

"World Series 1975, in Relief: Agony, Ecstasy, and Comedy," *Sports Illustrated,* 43 (3 November 1975): 28–30, 33–34, 36–37;

"Baseball Stories," *Harper's,* 252 (May 1976): 66–68, 70, 72;

"zzZZZZBOOMMM!! Aaaaaaahhhhhh!" *New York Times,* 30 June 1976, p. 37;

"Golden Fish Out of Water," *Sports Illustrated,* 45 (5 July 1976): 57–58;

"Final Season: Elegy for an Athlete Getting Old," *Harper's,* 254 (January 1977): 61–63, 66–67;

"These Sporting Poets," *Harper's,* 254 (May 1977): 76–79, 82;

"Bozo the Bruin," *Sports Illustrated,* 48 (30 January 1978): 54–60, 62, 64;

"A Frisbee over Moscow," *Time* (11 August 1980): 28–29;

"Birds Thou Never Wert," *Sports Illustrated* (4 January 1982): 82–86, 88, 90, 93, 94, 96;

"More Than Just a Token Effort," *Sports Illustrated* (23 September 1985): 30–32, 37;

"A Sportsman Born and Bred," *Sports Illustrated* (26 December 1988): 140–144, 146–148, 152, 154, 157–158, 160;

"The Wild Blue Yonder," *Sports Illustrated* (3 April 1989): 64–66, 71–72, 74;

"The Smaller the Ball, the Better the Book: A Game Theory of Literature," *New York Times,* 31 May 1992, VII: 16;

"1970: The First Marathon," *New York,* 26 (19 April 1993): 122;

"Final Twist of the Drama," *Sports Illustrated,* 80 (11 April 1994): 86–88, 92, 94, 96, 98–99, 100, 102;

"On the 19th Hole," *New York Times,* 24 April 1994, VI: 30;

"My Last Cobra: Stalking the Wild Prevarication," *Harper's,* 289 (September 1994): 73–77;

"Golfing–In the Swing," *Gourmet,* 55 (May 1995): 70, 247–248;

"Smashing Game, But Not What It Used to Be," *Wall Street Journal,* 5 May 1995, p. A10;

"Playgrounds of Privilege," *Golf Digest,* 46 (June 1995): 108.

George Plimpton is one of America's most respected literary journalists, but he is perhaps best

Plimpton with light-heavyweight champion Archie Moore after a sparring match in 1959, which is the subject of Shadow Box *(1977)*

known for his sports books and essays. No other writer has taken more to heart sportswriter Paul Gallico's advice in "The Feel": "I do not insist that a curiosity and capacity for feeling sports is necessary to be a successful writer, but it is fairly obvious that a man who has been tapped on the chin with five fingers wrapped in a leather boxing glove and propelled by the arm of an expert knows more about that particular sensation than one who has not, always provided he has the gift of expressing himself." As a result of wondering what it would be like, as he put it in his introduction to *The Best of Plimpton* (1990), "to undertake the same kind of research . . . and expand it somewhat–to find out not only about athletic skills at their best, but also something about the society of athletes, to join a team as a kind of 'amateur professional,'" Plimpton quarterbacked for the Detroit Lions, pitched in a postseason all-star exhibition game, served as goalie for the Boston Bruins, and squared off with Archie Moore in the boxing ring, all of which he described–carrying participatory journalism to its limits–in articles and book-length accounts. Furthermore, he has been an editor of sports books, from anthologies to coffee-table varieties, including one on the sport of court tennis. Finally, Plimpton has brought a literary touch to sportswriting, from introducing now well-established "theories" (such as his "Small Ball Theory," which, according to his description in the introduction to *The Best American Sports Writing, 1997,* "states that the quality of the writing seems to depend on the size of the ball. The smaller the ball, the more distinguished the writing") to writing personal essays, not only on sports but also on literature, travel, and nature.

Sportswriting has been but one facet of Plimpton's long career as a distinguished literary editor, essayist, humorist, and, more recently, novelist. His nine volumes of *Paris Review* interviews, *Writers at Work* (1958–1992), remain a lasting contribution to American letters; Plimpton has interviewed authors spanning generations, from Ernest Hemingway to Hunter S. Thompson. He has written witty, elegant profiles (mostly of celebrities, artists, and famous places), which, because of Plimpton's own celebrity status, form a new kind of personal essay that makes the author an integral part of his subject, whether that subject is the Audubon Christmas Bird Count, fireworks, or the actor Warren Beatty. Among his satires are two classics: a *Harper's Magazine* parody of Truman Capote as Hemingway writing a version of "The Snows of Kilimanjaro" and a *Sports Illustrated* spoof about a mysterious pitcher who had learned through Zen-like mastery to throw a ball as fast as 168 miles per hour. When he turned the latter into a full-length work, *The Curious Case of Sidd Finch* (1987), Plimpton had come full circle to baseball, the game that helped launch his sportswriting career almost a quarter-century earlier.

A New Yorker most of his life, George Ames Plimpton was born on 18 March 1927 to Pauline (Ames) Plimpton and Francis T. P. Plimpton, a lawyer, who was appointed ambassador to the United Nations in the Kennedy administration. Plimpton attended St. Bernard's School and Phillips Exeter Academy, where he wrote for the student newspaper, the *Exonian.* At Harvard University, which he entered in 1944 and left to serve in the United States Army from 1945 to 1948, he became editor of *The Lampoon* (the college's humor magazine) before graduating with an A.B. in 1950. He earned an additional B.A. and M.A. from King's College, Cambridge University, which he attended from 1952 to 1954. Viking published his first book, *The Rabbit's Umbrella,* a juvenile, in 1955, written in Paris in the early days of the *Paris Review,* which Plimpton, along with several other Americans, including Peter Matthiessen and Donald Hall, helped found in 1953. The magazine established itself almost immediately as an influential American literary journal. Plimpton has been its editor ever since. The literary quarterly is best known for its probing interviews with contemporary novelists, poets, and dramatists, many of which Plimpton conducted in the early days of the journal. The *Paris Review* interview has been described by *The New York Times* as "a new kind of extended and articulate interview that combined the Boswellian aim with an exploration of the ideas of contemporary writers on the art of fiction and poetry."

Plimpton's actual sportswriting career began after a chance meeting with a friend, Whitney Tower, a writer for the fledgling *Sports Illustrated* when Plimpton was in his early twenties and teaching at Barnard College. He was asked to write a piece on Harold S. Vanderbilt, whose J-Boats helped defend the America's Cup titles in the 1930s. Vanderbilt had proved to be an unforthcoming subject for other writers, but Plimpton relied on his Harvard ties to get an interview with the elder alumnus. As he recalled in *The Best American Sports Writing, 1977,* "The story ran through four issues of *Sports Illustrated.* The fact that my words–a bit stiff and pedantic as I look back on them–had appeared in a national magazine gave me enough courage to quit teaching and to start writing about sports part-time."

An early piece, "Dreams of Glory on the Mound" (*Sports Illustrated,* 10 April 1961), later expanded to book form that same year in *Out of My League,* began Plimpton's longtime relationship with *Sports Illustrated.* "Miami Notebook: Cassius Clay and Malcolm X," published a few years later in the June 1964 issue of *Harper's,* was the first of many pieces Plimpton has written on the great heavyweight champion. Relying on quotes scribbled on a "paper tablecloth, then in a notebook" at a luncheonette, Plimpton hoped to show the major spiritual influence the black Muslim leader had on the young Clay (later Muhammad Ali).

With *Out of My League* Plimpton ventured into participatory sports journalism. "There's been a lot of almanac-type sportswriting," he told a *Time* interviewer in 1967, "with emphasis on records, score cards, statistics. Sportswriters have never given the reader a sense of what it's like to be part of a team, of the mystique, ritual, frights and fears of the game." In *Out of My League* Plimpton tries to enter the closed society of professional baseball players to see "what it was like to be, even if briefly, a member of a team and thus privy to what ballplayers chat about in the dugout or on the team bus; or being party to the exchange, for example, that takes place when a pitcher is lifted." Plimpton sees himself as a sort of *espantaneo,* the man who hurls himself impulsively into the bullring to win the crowd's applause, rather than a Walter Mitty–type. (Hemingway, who provided a blurb for the dust jacket of the book, referred to the result of the experience as "the dark side of the moon of Walter Mitty," and several reviewers have borrowed the Walter Mitty allusion to describe Plimpton's other exploits.) The idea for the piece came from something James Thurber (the creator of Walter Mitty) once wrote: "The majority of American males put themselves to sleep by striking out the batting order of the New York Yankees."

While *Out of My League* deals with some of the arrangements, details, and technicalities involved in getting Plimpton actually on the mound to face American and National League all-stars in a postseason exhibition game, the book recounts no Walter Mittyesque triumphs but rather Plimpton's total humiliation, failure, and disappointment. When he is inevitably removed from the game, Plimpton wears a countenance that Marianne Moore, in the *New York Herald Tribune* (23 April 1961), described as having "a tincture of Charlie Chaplin's smile of agonized gratitude in acknowledgment of rebuffs." He cannot question the players about certain topics or ask to borrow equipment from them or even get someone to warm him up. In the clubhouse "the sense of being an imposter is strong," he reports. Throughout his ordeal on the mound Plimpton's role is reduced to that of "a minor functionary whose sole duty was to serve up a fat pitch"–in other words, he is exactly what pitchers are hoped to be in the eye of most hitters.

One of the great strengths of the book is Plimpton's analysis of the persona of the total ballplayer (Moore praised the book's "verisimilitude"), from his manner of speech and gait to his use of a tobacco chaw (although Plimpton himself never chewed). Trying to emulate the ballplayers occasionally inhibits Plimpton's main function as a writer and hence reveals one of the limitations of participatory journalism. His one saving moment occurs during practice when he surprises (and annoys) a catcher with a curveball ("Hey, kid, dammit, when y'all throw the hook, lemme know, hey?"). Plimpton is proud to have finally thrown something that "had been recognized for what it was supposed to be." Yet, as Plimpton heads for the locker room (and eventually to the stands as a spectator), "driven to the showers before that game had even started," he meditates on the way it feels "hungry when it was all over, and the sluice of shower water on your arms, and before that, on the field, the warmth of the sun and smell of the leather."

He was more at ease attending a 1963 World Series game with Moore (and Robert Lowell in tow), his first encounter with the septuagenarian poet, reveling in her eccentric insights: "she talked about Sandy Koufax, who had pitched his fine game the day before, which she had seen on television. She said 'Koufax' a number of times, working on the name, repeating it often that day, as if what she as a poet would finally sort out of what she had seen of his artistry, and would write about, was somehow locked up in the name itself. Ballplayers' names did intrigue her. 'Vinegar Bend Mizelle,' she said suddenly, in reference to the ex-Mets pitcher. 'A wonderful name.'"

The mid 1960s were a prolific period for Plimpton at *Sports Illustrated.* In "World Champion Is Refused a Meal" (17 May 1965), he covered Cassius Clay (or more precisely Clay's trainer, Bundini Brown) on a private bus trip to Clay's Chicopee Falls, Massachusetts, training camp. In Yulee, Florida, the heavyweight champion of the world and his mostly Muslim entourage are refused a meal at a segregated restaurant, but later in Georgia they receive a warm welcome at a Howard Johnson's, where "a sheriff, if he had been sitting there, might well have stepped up and arrested the whole troupe on suspicion."

In "Celestial Hell of the Superfan" (*Sports Illustrated,* 13 September 1965), Plimpton offers a study of professional football's superfans. "The range is infinite," Plimpton writes, "from the very wealthy–Jerry Wolman, for example, who (it has often been said) bought the Philadelphia Eagles so he could shag footballs with his players on the sidelines–to the crowds in the long overcoats outside the locker room corridors stamping their feet in the cold, waiting for the players so they can crowd forward to aim an affectionate swipe at their shoulder blades as they pass and call out, 'Hey, great game, baby!'"

Plimpton's own "emotional concern" is for the Detroit Lions, with whom he played quarterback during the training period in 1963 (recounted in a series of articles for *Sports Illustrated* and eventually the book *Paper Lion* in 1966). After the success of *Paper Lion* "the Lions were able to get me to do anything for them," so Plimpton was asked to represent the team at the upcoming National Football League (NFL) football draft. "Nothing much to it, they told me–sit at a phone and give the Detroit office the names of the players drafted by the other teams, and announce the Lions' choice (which they phoned me from Detroit) when their turn came up." Like any superfan, he is "terribly grateful to be asked to do this," but in this dimension of football, nearly thirty hours of activity "stretched on endlessly," and his "enthusiasm for all things Detroit began to flag." Soon, though, he is "returned . . . irretrievably to the Detroit fold" when the line coach calls to tell Plimpton that the Lions have decided to select Plimpton himself on the twentieth round of the draft. "What a great gesture, the epitome of the superfan's dream–his allegiance recognized by being picked in the draft, even if it was the last round." It is a prank, of course, and the Lions select instead the head coach's son, an act that Plimpton identifies as "Rank nepotism!" Nonetheless, he remains the long-suffering superfan: "the disease had me thoroughly in its throes. Absolutely hooked."

In contrast to the superfan piece, Plimpton wrote "But Why Me, Coach?" (*Sports Illustrated,* 13 December 1965), about the waiving of New York Giant defensive tackle Mike Bundra: "It was an experience all players went through as rookies–cutdown time, often called the Night of the Turk, or on some teams the Night of the Squeaking Shoes, to signify the emissaries coming along the corridors to fetch the players over to the office to be officially let go." Having bounced around with several clubs before losing his job again, Bundra sees his own woes mirrored by his relatives who call to console him: "They joshed him

Dust jacket for Plimpton's first book-length venture into participatory sports journalism, published in 1961

gently. They were ex-Giant fans now. In just over a year they had been ex-Lion, ex-Viking, ex-Brown and now ex-Giant fans."

In 1966 Plimpton had expanded his *Sports Illustrated* articles (as well as two other sections that appeared in *New York* and *Harper's*) on his experiences as a quarterback with the Detroit Lions into the best-seller (twenty-four weeks) *Paper Lion,* which was later made into a movie. After learning about five plays of the Lions during a three-week training session, Plimpton got to play a series of downs during a preseason intersquad scrimmage. A reviewer for the *Nation* (30 January 1967) admired the way Plimpton had captured "the sight and sound of the real pros," especially "the highly technical lingo of their business, its bruises, its heartaches, its laughs, its tribulations." The Englishman Alan Pryce-Jones, writing in *Commonweal* (2 December 1966), suggested that as a nonfiction novel, Plimpton's book "may stand as a model of its kind." In *Book Week* (23 October 1966) sportswriter Myron Cope felt that although Plimpton might have been "pushing the 'out-of-my league idea' much too far," he nonetheless had "written what is possibly the most arresting and delightful narrative in all of sports literature. For the account of his gimmick soon gives way to solid reportage, in which he captures the sights and sounds of pro football with uncommon fidelity." The reviewer for *Time* (6 January 1966) was impressed by the way in which Plimpton had gotten the players to like him and confide in him, partly because he took their skills as seriously as they did. Again, using the skills of the literary interviewer, Plimpton renders the players' "descriptions of the intricacies of the various positions and their special moments of triumph . . . as authentic as only shop talk can be."

The climactic moment of *Paper Lion* occurs when Plimpton plays in the game: "I *felt* myself a football quarterback, not an interloper," Plimpton notes. Yet, on the first play, despite his brief feelings of contentment and empowerment at the quarterback position, he realizes how out of his depth he is (a seasoned quarterback cannot take "the extra second" it takes Plimpton "to control the ball"). He finds himself in the path of one of his own blockers, like "coming around a corner in a high speed car to find a moose ambling across the center line." On the second play he falls down, and on the third play he is stripped of the ball by defensive tackle Roger Brown, who "tackled me high, and straightened me with his power, so that I churned against his 300-pound girth like a comic bicyclist." On the next play (he has lost twenty yards without having run a complete play), Plimpton throws an incomplete pass, having forgotten to tell his players the signal. He fares no better on the last play of the series. All of these events lead Plimpton to an epiphany as he hears applause upon leaving the field, which he believes was because he had played so poorly. Had he performed spectacularly, their cheers would have been disingenuous. "Their concept of things would have been upset. The outsider did not belong, and there was comfort in that being proved."

Plimpton's reputation was growing quickly by the late 1960s. In 1967 he earned a distinguished achievement award from the University of Southern California and also was named contributing editor to *Sports Illustrated.* In the article "A Swinging Walter Mitty," the reviewer for *Time* (7 April 1967) observed: "He exhibits the genuine journalist's compulsive curiosity about everything that comes to his attention. Nor is he content to be a mere observer; he participates." On 28 March 1968, at age forty-one, Plimpton married photography studio assistant

Freddy Medora Espy. They had two children: Medora Ames and Taylor Ames.

His next book, *The Bogey Man,* appeared in 1968. With the financial backing of *Sports Illustrated,* Plimpton spent a month touring with the Professional Golfers' Association. As he describes the book in his introduction, "The original material was quite skimpy–kept on the run on old score cards, small notebooks scribbled in during car rides and plane trips, in the rain out on the golf course, and especially on driving ranges." He seems to affirm his own Small Ball Theory, for *The Bogey Man,* with its punning title, is one of Plimpton's best books. It covers his participation in the Bing Crosby National Pro-Amateur, the San Francisco Lucky, and the Bob Hope Desert Classic. The narrative has less of a freewheeling style about it than a loosely structured and unpredictable approach, much like an eighteen-hole round of golf. The book includes various talks with and profiles of characters such as Plimpton's caddy, Abe, and other caddies ("they rock back and forth and compare yarns and gossip and talk of their rounds, and particularly about money and how their pros let them down") and professionals, including Jack Nicklaus and Arnold Palmer; critiques of golf books; observations of the idiosyncrasies of the game, such as the *yips* ("a nervous affliction that settled in the wrist and hands, finally, after the years of pressure and the bets and the strain" and "ultimately drove the pros out of the game to teaching jobs at the country clubs") and golfer's rage; and golf tales and golf talk.

Plimpton is at his best in describing the passion, thrill, or frustration of the game itself: "I started by topping my drive badly. It skittered forward a short way. I too rushed forward–as if in an effort to hit my second shot before the enormity of my muffed drive attracted the attention of the distant crowd. The second shot hooked to the left, hitting on top of the sea wall and fortunately kicking back in toward the fairway. It took one high, long bounce and landed in the sand next to the wall. I could hear a faint sigh go up from the gallery as it watched the sand spurt into the air." Portions of the book appeared in several issues of *Sports Illustrated.* The book was reviewed favorably generally, but several critics, Dick Schapp among them, felt that it did not measure up to *Paper Lion.* As Christopher Lehmann-Haupt noted in *Life,* however, "Golf is a lonely and private game lacking the natural drama of football, but Plimpton, by substituting improvisation for plot, has caught its mad comedy and bizarre effects on people in a book just as charming, in its own way, as *Paper Lion.*"

Plimpton published several non-sports-related books, including several collections of *Paris Review* interviews; three volumes of *The American Literary Anthology* (1968, 1969, 1970) with Peter Ardery, and *American Journey: The Times of Robert F. Kennedy* (1970) with Jean Stein. He served as associate editor of *Harper's* and contributing editor at *Food and Wine.* Several Plimpton books on sports were published during the 1970s. First came *Pierre's Book: The Game of Court Tennis* (1971) by Pierre Etchebaster, which Plimpton edited and for which he wrote the introduction. "Court tennis," Plimpton later explained to Clark Whelton in a January 1976 *Esquire* interview, "was an ancestor of modern tennis, a game first played by medieval French kings, who called it *jeu de paume.*"

Mad Ducks and Bears (1973) addresses two unrelated subjects: the first is NFL linemen, in particular the Lions' offensive guard John Gordy (the "Bear" of the title) and defensive lineman Alex Karras (the "Mad Duck"); the second was Plimpton's diary as he prepared to play quarterback again, this time for the Baltimore Colts against the Detroit Lions, for a 1971 television special, *Plimpton! The Great Quarterback Sneak. Mad Ducks and Bears* developed into, in Plimpton's own words, "an irreverent, roguish account of the . . . lives of football players, full of anecdote, reminiscence, and story, often tempered by grievance, but always with an underlying attitude of humor." The two linemen are central to the book, with Plimpton, as Alan Nadel observed in "'My Mind Is Weak but My Body Is Strong': George Plimpton and the Boswellian Tradition" (1989), "play[ing] Boswell to Alex Karras's Johnson."

The two-pronged approach weakens the book considerably, and critics were quick to pick up on the problem. Barbara Grizzuti Harrison, in an otherwise tendentious review in *The New York Times Book Review* (6 January 1974) noted: "There is no cohesive statement, nor is there any attempt to generalize from the rather parochial set of particulars." (Plimpton deleted the television diary for a revised edition of the book published in 1993.) Plimpton's only solace was that he played that day "with considerably more effect than my performance with the Lions. . . . As the Baltimore Colt quarterback darned if we didn't make eighteen yards in four downs–fifteen of them, I must admit, on a roughing-the-passer penalty!"

Henry Aaron's record-breaking 715th home run was the occasion for "Final Twist of the Drama" (*Sports Illustrated,* 11 April 1974), which Plimpton later expanded into book form as *One for the Record: The Inside Story of Hank Aaron's Chase for the Home-Run Record* (1974). Writing in *The New York Times Book Review,* Robert W. Creamer called *One for the Record* "much the best thing that has been done on Bad Henry" and one of the best long essays of what

Dust jacket for Plimpton's 1966 account of his brief time as a quarterback for the Detroit Lions

might be called total reportage: completely immersed in a game or an event and writing in a tone set against the prevailing media hype, the writer reflects on the origins and aftermath of the event while rendering it through a multiplicity of points of view. Thus, the perspectives of the event's two key participants, "the Observer" (Plimpton) and "the Hitter" (Aaron), alternate with those of "the Pitcher," "the Ball," "the Retriever" (of the ball), and others. Al Downing ("the Pitcher"), who throws the home-run pitch to Aaron, reminds Plimpton of baseball's "major sinners" whose "reputations were stamped irrevocably with their misfortune–as if a debt to society had been incurred which could never, under any circumstances, be absolved."

The portrait of Aaron builds steadily, formed by what Plimpton hears about him, reads about him, and learns from Aaron himself. He discovers that Aaron's 1957 pennant-winning homer was far more important to him than number 715, about which "he remembered only his relief that it was over with, and the vague happiness, that a weight 'like a stove' had been lifted from his back, and that his legs seemed rubbery as he took the tour of the bases." Aaron is less a central figure than are those individuals touched by the event: the Cincinnati pitchers, who are "involved in a sort of cosmic game of Russian roulette"; the man broadcasting the game; Aaron's father; a neighborhood fan who plans to erect a statue of Aaron in his backyard. The home run itself is almost anticlimactic: people waiting in concession lines miss the moment entirely, while the pitcher and hitter see the event simply as being over.

Plimpton continued to contribute sports essays to *Harper's.* "Baseball Stories" (May 1976), which also appeared in *The Game and the Glory: The Commissioner's Official Bicentennial Volume* (1976), ruminated on the bullpen, "largely because of its function–it sends out people in moments of crisis to try to put things right, to repair a damaged inning." Weaving anecdotes and personalities, Plimpton remarks on the starkness of the (now antiquated in most ballparks) bullpen as a "place set apart–a wooden bench just at the edge of the uncut meadow of grass, a lane worn smooth in a corner of a sandlot, a tin-roof shelter with the needles of the loblolly pines on the dirt floor."

One More July: A Football Dialogue with Bill Curry (1977) utilizes Plimpton's great interviewing skills (although Plimpton, as Dave Anderson remarked in the 31 July 1977 *New York Times Book Review,* "seldom interrupts. Wisely he lets Curry tell his stories") and seems to wrap up his decadelong infatuation with the game of football. The dialogues with Curry, who played professional football from 1965 to 1975, helped put a coda on a football era that was coming to an end just as a new one was beginning.

One More July was notable for its "good taste," as Anderson observed. The events in the book are recalled during a long car trip Plimpton took with Curry, whom he met during his brief foray with the Colts, as the two men travel from Lexington, Kentucky, to Green Bay, Wisconsin, where Curry, a former all-pro center, was hoping for one last shot with the Packers. The book focuses solely on various football experiences as seen through the eyes of one of its participants, including Curry's acceptance by his black teammates at Georgia Tech; his seasons with legendary coaches Vince Lombardi (about whom Plimpton elicits an extraordinary portrait from Curry), Sid Gilman, Don Shula, and Don McCafferty; his reflections as president of the NFL Players' Association; and his recollections of the "terrifying presence" of defensive linemen. For Curry, football is about neither money nor glory; for all its egocentrism, it is really about teamwork, the extra effort it takes to get "those last 35 yards" to win the game. The book is also something of an elegy for an aging athlete, "a closing out, a frightening sense of cessation" reminiscent of Dylan Thomas's line "After the first death there is no other," which Curry agrees "was an appropriate enough sentiment." While *Library Journal* (August 1977), which had praised Plimpton's earlier books, found this one "lack[ing] the sparkle of first-hand experience," *The New Yorker* (22 August 1977) singled out Plimpton's excellent choice of subject: it "makes one wonder why so many sports books are ghostwritten when a good talker like Bill Curry can fill out a volume in a few days' ramble."

Shadow Box was also published in 1977; like Plimpton's other sports books, participatory or otherwise, it is an attempt by the author to understand a sport he really "never understood." The admission is not merely to feign ignorance but to acknowledge that one can never really get to know a sport or any subject–Plimpton has also tried his hand at stand-up comedy in Las Vegas, acting with John Wayne in the 1970 movie *Rio Lobo,* and guest conducting with the Cincinnati Symphony–unless one gets inside his material either by taking part in it or by studying it thoroughly.

Thus, in *Shadow Box* Plimpton returns to 1959 and his three-round exhibition bout with light heavyweight champion Archie Moore (in which he was assisted by an Ernest Hemingway-recommended trainer, who "could have been a champion if he had been able to accept the idea that he was going to be hit once in a while") and moves forward to a detailed account of the Muhammad Ali–George Foreman match in Kinshasa, Zaire, in 1974, in which the aging Ali reclaimed the heavyweight title. In between events Plimpton recounts boxing-related observations and anecdotes with literary figures and aristocrats spanning several generations. Ali is the central figure, though, and Plimpton, as Joe Flaherty wrote in *The New York Times Book Review* (6 November 1977), "reminds us of the champ's early fun-laden days when the bombast was a minor adjunct to the bravery." Plimpton recalls the Ali he had profiled in an earlier essay for *Sports Illustrated,* "Return of the Big Bopper" (23 December 1974), just after the 1974 fight, when the magazine named Ali "Sportsman of the Year": "He can become a fixation with someone who writes, perhaps because he may be the most astonishing athlete of our time. Charismatic. Talented. Outspoken. Possibly of tragic stature. Unpredictable–both in the ring and out. You never know whether he's going to come in fat or lean, or what sort of fight he has in mind. The only sure bet is that you're going to be surprised."

By the end of the 1970s and early 1980s, during which Plimpton received the Mark Twain Award from the International Platform Association and a few honorary degrees, he published a coffee-table book, *Sports!* (1978), with photographs by Neil Leifer, and *A Sports Bestiary* (1982), with cartoons by Arnold Roth, in which Plimpton lampooned such sports clichés as "the Cliffhanger": "A flightless ducklike bird that hangs from precipices by its beak–a sight that tends to produce consternation and hand-wringing in those who happen to come around a bend to see it. . . . This bird's odd habit causes finger-biting and head-clutching, and can produce ulcers, especially when one sees four or five in a row."

When Plimpton was in his fifties, he turned one last time to participatory journalism to experience the only major sport he had yet to attempt: ice hockey. *Open Net* (1985) tells the story of his playing goaltender for the Boston Bruins. The narrative follows the familiar pattern of Plimpton's other books, providing, for example, a lengthy dissertation on how a goalie puts on his cumbersome uniform: "however graceful he may be once out on the ice, he moves from the locker room across the rubber mattings for the rink with the ponderous gait of a dowager coming down a church aisle." Plimpton himself manages to pass among the

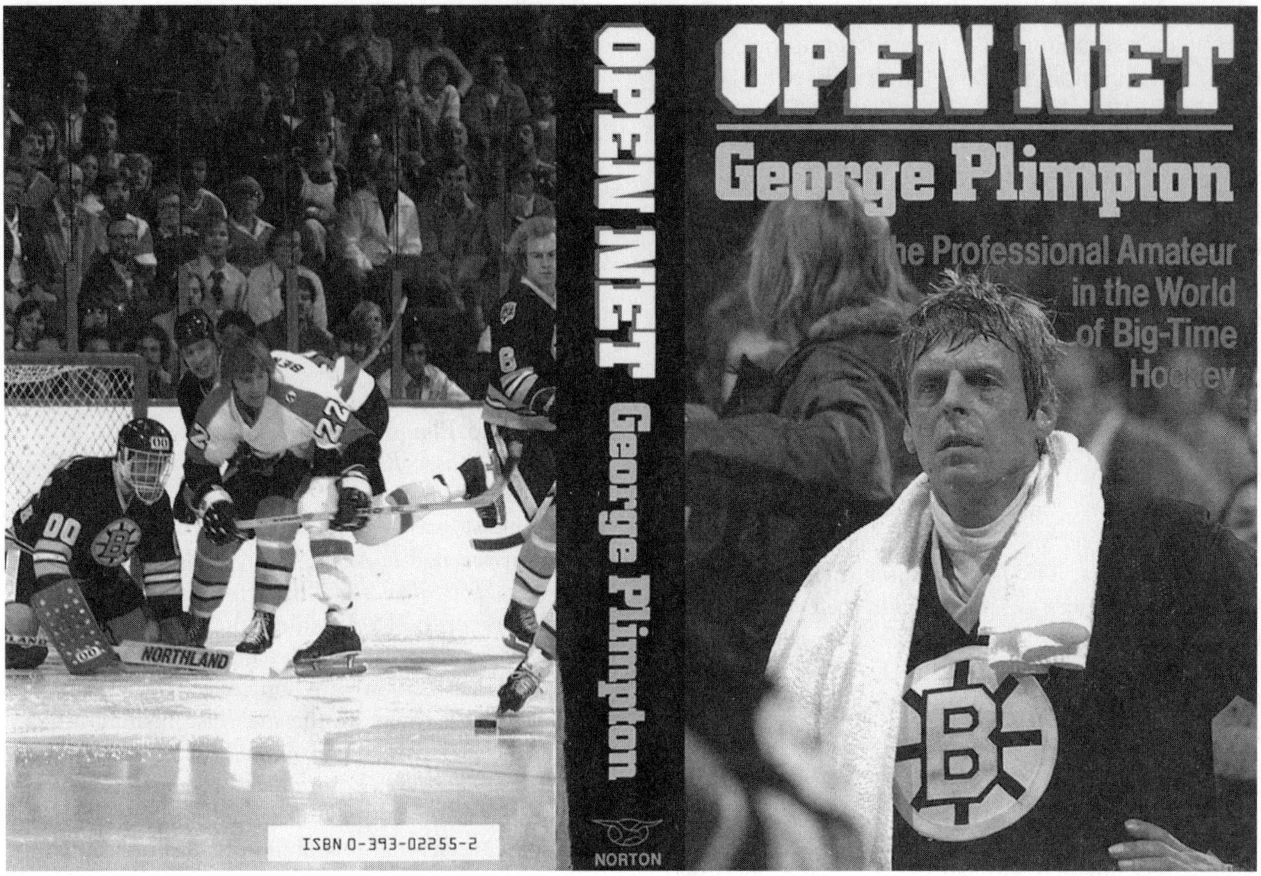

Dust jacket for Plimpton's 1985 account of his short stint as a goalie with the Boston Bruins

other players "leisurely, teetering and bobbing like a child's model of a houseboat launched onto a pond." There are colorful descriptions of hockey stars, from the infamous Broad Street Bullies of Philadelphia to Plimpton's fellow goaltender and roommate, Jim "Seaweed" Pettie, named "for the wild, stringy look of his hair after a game–apparently a hereditary condition because his father's nickname turned out to be 'Kelp.'"

Coming at last to hockey allowed Plimpton to put the other sports in which he had participated in perspective and to appreciate the intensity and uniqueness of the only game played on ice: "The sport had so many different aspects: an implement (the stick) to manipulate, and a projectile (the puck) to hit and pass and shoot, and everyone got a chance to be involved with it, quite unlike football where very few players actually handle the object everyone is tussling over." In gauging the accuracy it takes for one hockey player intentionally to hit the far post of the goal with the puck three times out of ten from sixty feet away, Plimpton remarks: "Could a baseball pitcher maintain such an average against an inch-wide target from that distance? Or a quarterback? Certainly a tennis player would have his difficulties at that range. Or a golfer with a putter. Perhaps only the archer with his bow could compare." Plimpton does manage to save the day in *Open Net,* when on a penalty shot–one of the most dangerous in all of hockey–the puck ricochets away from his skate after he had fallen on the ice–"like the collapse of an ancient sofa."

Plimpton next published his first novel, *The Curious Case of Sidd Finch.* The novel was the outgrowth (urged on by a six-figure advance from Plimpton's publisher) of an April Fool's piece he had written for *Sports Illustrated* in 1985, which claimed that "a converted cricket-bowler from Pakistan" who could throw the ball 168 miles per hour had signed with the New York Mets. (The book was originally titled "Fireballer: The Curious Case of Sidd Finch.") The article was part of an elaborate hoax (with the cooperation of the Mets organization and players), but it read like a straightforward work of investigative journalism, with interviews and biographical information on Finch's Harvard days and later life as an aspirant Buddhist monk. The story managed to fool the media for a short time and caused a minor controversy. The novel version grew out of Plimpton's curiosity, as he told Bruce Weber in *Esquire* (November 1985), "of what would happen if someone like Sidd did come along. How would that affect the game?" In discussing the development of the novel, in which Finch pitches a perfect game by striking out all twenty-seven St. Louis Cardinals, Plimpton told Weber: "The book begins with Mets coaches dropping baseballs from a dirigible at Ronn Reynolds, the catcher. I arranged to go up in a blimp so I can write realistically about what that's like. And I'm trying to get an interview with Peter Ueberroth (then baseball commissioner) to ask him what he would do, what would baseball do, if Sidd Finch came along." In reviewing the novel, future baseball commissioner A. Bartlett Giamatti wrote in *The New York Times Book Review* (5 July 1987) how "Finch's brief, astonishing passage through big-league baseball is at once a parody of every player's as-told-to biography, a satire on professional sports," and "an extended (and intriguing) meditation on our national pastime."

Plimpton continued to edit and write nonsports books throughout the 1980s, including *Edie: An American Biography* (1982), about model and actress Edie Sedgwick, with Jean Stein; *D. V.* (1984), the memoir of Diana Vreeland, edited by Plimpton and Christopher Hemphill; and *Fireworks: A History and Celebration* (1984), as well as several additional *Paris Review Interviews* anthologies. He also published a 26 December 1988 *Sports Illustrated* piece, "A Sportsman Born and Bred," on president-elect George Bush as an all-around American sportsman with perhaps the greatest sporting pedigree of any U.S. president since Theodore Roosevelt. Bush partook in baseball, tennis, golf, fishing, jogging, basketball, and even horseshoes. Plimpton deftly describes Bush's winning toss: "We watched the red horseshoe leave his hand, turn over once in flight, drop toward the pit with its prongs forward and, with a dreadful clang, collect itself around the stake. A ringer! Sixteen points and the victory for the president-elect. He flung his arms straight up in triumph, a tremendous smile on his face." "The Wild Blue Yonder" (*Sports Illustrated,* 3 April 1989) tells the story of "the upper reaches" of Madison Square Garden, "an area known as the blues, for the color of the seats there," from which "most of the obscenities–usually chanted in unison–pour out." For Plimpton, who "was raised in a family in which profanity simply didn't exist . . . (If someone was full of something, it was applesauce)," the experience is jolting, especially when he decides to visit the blue seats. "Venturing down an aisle in the blues was like walking into a Third Avenue saloon on St. Patrick's Day. The steps were slick with beer; popcorn crunched underfoot." When he unveils a Boston Bruin pennant, the blues "unleash . . . a brutal chorus" and Plimpton is "identified as a personal part of the human anatomy." The piece contrasts Plimpton's well-mannered sensibilities against the coarse, spontaneous actions of working-class hockey fans.

Plimpton, who was divorced from his first wife after twenty years of marriage, married Sarah Whitehead Dudley in 1991; they have twin daughters, Olivia Hartley and Laura Dudley. He also published more books in the 1990s: *The Best of Plimpton,* a collection of various material, including several sports pieces, led Malcolm M. Jones Jr. to comment in *Newsweek* (14 January 1991): "Inevitably, Plimpton's most durable role has been as an amateur gamely contending against professionals"; *The Norton Book of Sports* (1992), for which he selected the pieces and wrote the introduction, allowed him to reintroduce his literary theories of sports (the Small Ball Theory and The Uh-Oh Theory, which claims the more dangerous the sport, the more memorable the literature); and *The Official Olympics Triplecast Viewer's Guide* (1992), a commemorative edition of the Barcelona Summer Olympics, which gave him the opportunity to comment upon a sporting event he had not written about before. In 1990 *The X-Factor* appeared, in which Plimpton attempts to define the qualities and character of the pure champion. His last sports book, for which he served as guest editor and wrote an introduction, was *The Best American Sports Writing, 1997.*

The Best of Plimpton collects some of Plimpton's finest and most representative work from his many books and from magazines such as *Esquire, Smart, New York,* and *Audubon.* Plimpton writes about Muhammad Ali in his dressing room, "moving around the room, snapping out jabs and staring at himself in the mirror" as he prepares to fight Jerry Quarry; about nine- and ten-year-old Pony League football players, coached by Alex Karras; and about Marianne Moore and Ali writing a poem together at Toots Shor's restaurant, the champ wondering why such "a distinguished poet was having such a hard time holding up her side: speed of delivery was very much a qualification of a professional poet in his mind." There are other gems and oddities, such as profiles of Paul Tavilla, who catches in his mouth grapes tossed from tall buildings; a very young Caroline Kennedy playing on Bailey's Beach in Newport, Rhode Island; and Plimpton himself, "thinking of managing a wrestler" as his next participatory feat.

Near the end of the century Plimpton continued to write about sportsmen, always searching for the new subject and the new adventure that would stretch his curiosity. In 1998 he profiled Larry Waters, "The Man in the Flying Lawn Chair" (*The New Yorker,* 1 June 1998), who in 1982 had soared to 16,000 feet in a "Sears, Roebuck lawn chair to which were attached four clusters of helium-filled weather balloons, forty-two of them in all." Admitting to having been "always fascinated by balloons," Plimpton seeks out Waters to learn the details of what had been a lifelong dream, one that helped get him through his tour of duty in Vietnam. ("His intent was to drift northeast in the prevailing winds over the San Gabriel Mountains to the Mojave Desert. With him he carried an air pistol, with which to pop the balloons and thus regulate his altitude.") Waters describes the flight, alternately terrifying and exhilarating and nearly, in the end, tragic. Although Plimpton reluctantly agreed not to write about his flight (so that Waters could take advantage of lecturing before aviation clubs), Waters's suicide at a campsite near Mt. Wilson occasioned Plimpton to return to his subject, whose lonely death seemed to explain both his one great flight and Waters's appreciation for the movie *Somewhere in Time* (1980), in the final scene of which "heaven turns out to be the surface of a lake that stretches to the horizon."

Whether playing tennis against Pancho Gonzales or swimming against Don Schollander or playing for two minutes in a Boston Celtics game, Plimpton has undertaken his journalistic exploits, wrote Jones, "with an almost religious sense of purpose." As Plimpton told Jones: "I write these things with enormous care and attention, scared half to death."

What Lehmann-Haupt wrote about Plimpton in his review of *Mad Ducks and Bears* for *The New York Times* (12 November 1973) can still be said to sum up his contributions to sportswriting at the twilight of his career and to serve as sound advice for aspiring sportswriters: "He has a wonderful flair for comic descriptive writing. He has the patience to listen carefully to what others tell him; the imagination to visualize and ask interesting questions; and the persistence to cross reference the best stories he is told, no matter how much time or travel may be involved. Best of all, he never patronizes, and thus has the power to draw intelligence from a stone."

References:

Marianne Moore, *A Marianne Moore Reader* (New York: Viking, 1965), p. 244;

Alan Nadel, "'My Mind Is Weak but My Body Is Strong': George Plimpton and the Boswellian Tradition," *Midwest Quarterly,* 30 (Spring 1989): 372–386;

Richard Orodenker, *The Writers' Game: Baseball Writing in America* (New York: Twayne , 1996), pp. 113–199, 132–134, 159–160;

"A Swinging Walter Mitty," *Time* (7 April 1967): 40;

Clark Whelton, "Paper Plimpton," *Esquire* (January 1976): 115–117, 142, 144, 146.

Jimmy Powers

(9 February 1903 - 11 February 1995)

Rob Edelman

MAJOR POSITIONS HELD: Sportswriter, columnist, sports editor, *New York Daily News* (1928–1963); television commentator (1949–1960).

BOOK: *Baseball Personalities: The Most Colorful Figures of All Time* (New York: Field, 1949).

OTHER: "Tiger Triumph," in *Best Sports Stories 1946: A Panorama of the 1945 Sports Year,* edited by Irving T. Marsh and Edward Ehre (New York: Dutton, 1946).

Jimmy Powers

For more than two decades Jimmy Powers was sports editor of the *New York Daily News,* one of the most widely read newspapers in the United States. During his years as editor, a post he assumed in 1935, Powers presided over an illustrious staff that included Dick Young, Joe Trimble, Gene Ward, Jim McCulley, and cartoonists Leo "the Lion" O'Mealia and Bill Gallo. Additionally, Powers supplanted Paul Gallico as the top sports columnist on his paper. He was the highly opinionated and endlessly controversial author of "The Powerhouse," a popular column that ran in the paper six times per week for decades (and which he continued authoring after his 1957 retirement as sports editor of the *Daily News*). Like Young, who succeeded him as the foremost columnist of the paper, Powers wielded much authority and influence on the New York sports scene. As his colleague Gallo observed in an unpublished interview in 1998: "He was a real big guy in this town in the late 1930s, 1940s, and early 1950s."

Powers went on to earn a national recognition that transcended the readership of his paper, however, when he became the chief announcer and commentator on the *Gillette Cavalcade of Sports* from 1948 to 1960. The television show, which aired nationally Friday evenings on the NBC network and was more popularly known as the "Friday Night Fights," consisted of boxing matches broadcast live from Madison Square Garden. It was the longest-running boxing program in television history, and its longevity allowed Powers to become one of the initial sports scribes to cross over successfully into the television broadcast booth.

He was born James Joseph Aloysius Powers in Cleveland, Ohio, on 9 February 1903, and was the eldest of ten siblings. He spent his youth in Enid, Oklahoma, and eventually attended Marquette University, where he lettered in football, baseball, and track. Indeed, throughout his life Powers participated in sports. He was a consistent winner of the New York sportswriters' golf tournament and was also a diligent tennis player, horseback rider, sailor, and deep-sea fisherman and would pass his vacations aboard his 42-foot cruiser, the *We're Here.*

Powers first worked on newspapers in Muskogee, Oklahoma, Milwaukee, and Cleveland prior to coming to New York in 1928 and signing on as a sportswriter at the *Daily News.* Except for a four-and-a-half-year stint in the navy, from which he was discharged a commander, he remained with the paper for the rest of his journalistic career. "He had a great rise," Gallo recalled. "It didn't take him long to become a popular writer, then a popular columnist, and then a popular sports editor." Regarding the sports Powers most preferred covering, Gallo noted that his favorites were baseball and boxing–"not necessarily in that order."

While Powers never developed into a wordsmith of the rank of Dick Young, his protégé, he still was a talented writer. According to Harold Rosenthal, as quoted in an article by Dave Kaplan, a sportswriter at the *New York Herald Tribune,* "He got the column at an early age, but you never knew how good a writer he could be because he spread himself out so much" (14 February 1995).

Powers's best years as a sports journalist lasted from the Depression through the years just after World War II. During this era he was at his pithiest, most combative, and most confrontational. In a column dated 19 May 1940, for example, he lambasted baseball commissioner Kenesaw Mountain Landis for the hypocrisy of calling Joe DiMaggio on the carpet for his alleged friendships with gamblers. Powers wrote: "Why, there have been baseball owners and their friends mixed up in bucketshop and tax frauds. One Western owner was once a croupier in a notorious gambling house. Other baseball executives have been linked with race track mobs, mortgage jugglers and other border-line businesses." He noted that Ty Cobb and Tris Speaker were "heavy gamblers" and added that professional betters often congregate in the same after-game environs as ballplayers. "What do you expect the ballplayers to do," Powers asked, "jump into a taxi and run home when they bump into them in a bar or grill?" He added: "You can walk down Times Square any night during the summer and see DiMaggio and many another star [*sic*], in the company of men who bet 'em high, wide and handsome. This doesn't mean professional baseball is crooked. It merely means that certain types of professional ballplayers, boxers, bookies, managers, public enemies and public bores all tend to travel in the same orbit." In the same piece Powers labeled DiMaggio "a bit on the Joe Dope order anyway, but certainly far from stupid" and declared "Landis is a judge. He certainly should know you cannot LEGISLATE honesty into the human soul."

Powers also was capable of authoring solid, colorful descriptions of sporting events. In an 11 October 1945 column, "Tiger Triumph," which received the E. P. Dutton award for best sports story of the year and was included in *Best Sports Stories 1946,* he offered a recap of the final game of that year's just-concluded "madcap" World Series. Powers described star Detroit Tigers hurler Hal Newhouser as "a left-handed bowler with the general contour of a mop handle" and a "skinny stand-in for a Japanese prisoner of war." Newhouser's curve ball was "hooking so sharply" that it befuddled the Chicago Cubs batters, "who stared hypnotized with their sticks reposing on their shoulders." Catcher Paul Richards "rammed a double so hard and so deep into left that it caromed off two brick walls and eluded Peanuts Lowery, who was stabbing desperately at it like a man trying to snatch a rabbit by the ears." Powers further offered pithy anecdotes and pointed commentary relating to the series.

As a columnist and editor Powers's influence transcended the sports pages. His appeals resulted in the introduction of "hit" and "error" designations on ballpark scoreboards. After a spate of skull fractures incurred by ballplayers being hit by pitches, he successfully lobbied for the introduction of plastic batting helmets. Powers also was capable of wry humor in his crusades: he advocated, for example, that sports venues install wider seats for the comfort of their fans. In this regard he established a coalition fondly called the "Order of Corrugated Bottoms," the motto of which was "Rear up! We'll put an end to this!"

Powers was portrayed in the *Daily News* as a crusader, one of the good guys. A 2 January 1953 promotional blurb described him as a "genial devil-may-care Irishman . . . whose crusading column is the favorite of more than two million rabid readers every day" and a "scrapper who specializes in spotlighting phony promoters, ticket gyps and the no-good-niks among the gambling hierarchy." In a 12 May 1957 profile of him in the *Daily News,* Bob Lardine described Powers as a "colorful personality at all times" who "has known lots of success in his life but his ambition continues to be the same: 'To be a happy, healthy man and a good father.'" (He and his wife, the former Winona Smyser, were the parents of three children: Patricia, Michael, and Mary Ann.) Powers's obituary in the *Daily News* (14 February 1995) noted that he "also is believed to be the first sports columnist who urged that blacks be admitted to the major leagues." (This assertion is inaccurate, however; two journalists who predate Powers in this regard are African American sportswriters Wendell Smith and Sam Lacy.)

Powers's status as sports editor and columnist with a high-circulation, mass-market daily cannot be discounted in relation to whatever contribution he may have made regarding the integration of baseball. In 1938, for example, Powers lobbied the New York Giants to sign Homestead Grays hurler Ray Brown, who then had a perfect 10–0 Negro League record. If only the Giants had Brown on their roster, according to Powers, the team would roll to a pennant. "Ray Brown is the greatest pitcher in baseball today," he wrote. Powers reacted quite differently when the reality of major-league integration was at hand, however. Negro League historian Larry Lester has quoted him as writing, in the spring of 1947, when Jackie Robinson was about to join the Brooklyn Dodgers, "Robinson will not make the major leagues. He is a thousand-to-one shot at best. The Negro players simply don't have the brains or the skill."

In Robinson's autobiography, *I Never Had It Made* (1972), the Hall of Famer tersely notes that Powers "wrote that I would not make the grade in the big leagues 'next year or the next.' I was, according to him, a thousand-to-one shot." Sports historian Harvey Frommer, in his *New York City Baseball: The Golden Age, 1947–1957* (1980), and Robinson biographer Arnold Rampersad qualify Powers's remarks by placing them in context. Frommer has Powers opining, "we would like to see him make good, but it is unfair to build high hopes and then dash them down . . . he is a thousand to one shot to make the grade." Rampersad, in *Jackie Robinson: A Biography* (1997), notes that Powers was one of the "whites who opposed the ban but saw Jack as the wrong choice" to integrate baseball.

When asked if Powers was pro- or anti-Robinson, Gallo responded: "I think he was pro, but let me tell you. Jimmy Powers was a guy that would write a newspaper or magazine article. And they'd ask him to write it and he'd say, 'Which side do you want me to take?' But I think he was pro-Jackie. . . . I don't remember any bigotry in him."

Between 1943 and 1949 Powers waged a vocal campaign to destroy the career of Brooklyn Dodgers executive Branch Rickey. The writer's main complaint was that Rickey would manipulate his players and pay them the puniest possible wages. He nicknamed Rickey "El Cheapo" and wrote that he was a "tight-fisted man who paid his players coolie salaries." He lobbied for the Dodgers to fire Rickey and even sponsored a contest, quoted in Murray Polner's biography of Rickey, in which he queried his readers: "Shall we send him over Niagara Falls in a barrel? Shall we maroon him on a Bikini atoll?"

In his 1983 biography of Rickey, Polner reported that during this period Powers lambasted Rickey in no less than eighty columns and included negative references in seventy-four others. In 1946 Rickey even circulated a thirty-seven page memo among Dodgers executives, which was "designed to confront him [Powers] with the truth." Rickey noted in the memo that "Powers' smear campaign was deleteriously affecting the operations of the Dodger organization. Players were disturbed; business personnel wondered if matters were as they seemed or as Powers described them. Potential recruits veered away from Dodger scouts to sign contracts with other, supposedly more trustworthy, clubs. Fans, other sports writers, picked up Powers' phrases and used them in conversation and in print." Rickey closed with a declaration that Powers's complaints against him were "poisonous smokescreens, personal vilifications, innuendoes, colored exaggerations, half-truths, untruths, flat lies, a disgrace to the sports writing profession." He never confronted Powers with this memo, however.

The sportswriter's attacks on Rickey suddenly ceased in 1949. According to Polner, the matter was settled after "an anonymous correspondent sent Rickey a copy of a letter Powers had written," which Polner prints:

> I talked to the captain last night and he told me not to worry over latrine gossip picked up by the FBI. That if Winchell and the rest of the Jews had their way America would be a vast concentration camp from Maine to California. There wouldn't be enough barbed wire to hold back all the decent Christians maligned by the Jews and those who run with them. In short, I was in pretty good company with him, Col. McCormick, Joe Kennedy and several other decent family men. . . . How in hell can I be termed 'pro-Nazi' simply because I don't happen to like certain crackpot politicians and Jews?

According to Polner, Rickey might have released the letter to the press and thus destroyed Powers's career. A representative from the Dodgers' front office called Powers, however, and informed him that Rickey was in possession of the letter. "Immediately, without a word of explanation ever, Powers stopped writing negatively about Rickey," Polner wrote.

Powers also was at the epicenter of other controversies. In 1938, according to Dave Kaplan he incurred the wrath of the boxing establishment by characterizing promoter Mike Jacobs and the New York boxing commission as "Snow Mike and the Seven Dwarfs." The following year Lou Gehrig had taken himself out of the New York Yankees lineup because he was ill, his malady then undiagnosed. Gallo recalled that Powers (using the fictitious byline "Jack Smith") attributed the Yankees' subsequent slump to Gehrig's "contagious" disease. The columnist eventually had to offer a public apology for his allegation that Gehrig's teammates were

Dust jacket for Powers's 1949 collection of baseball profiles

the victims of a "mass polio epidemic" after Gehrig's attorneys filed a $1-million libel suit against Powers and the *Daily News.* "Hurting his feelings was far from my mind," the writer observed to Kaplan.

Powers also had a running feud with Dan Parker, sports columnist of the *New York Mirror,* the rival tabloid of the *Daily News.* Parker alleged that Powers often would place his byline on pieces authored by other members of his staff. Bill Gallo admitted as much in his account of Dick Young's debut in the sports pages of the *Daily News.* "During Powers' sports editorship," he recalled, "a young man from the commercial department would deliver columns to sports . . . stories about sports in New York, stories about the Giants and Dodgers, anything the young man found interesting. On one occasion, Powers looked at a piece the kid wrote that dealt with stickball. Powers was so amused by it that he ran it, without changing a word, in his column. The next day, people were calling the sports department praising Powers for 'his' stickball column. . . . Powers saw this young man as a future star and had him transferred to sports."

As Parker lit into Powers, friends and colleagues urged him to confront his rival. Powers insisted that he already was fighting back "by not mentioning his name. I have never used the name Dan Parker in my column."

Despite these controversies Powers remained extremely popular among his readership. During his heyday there were eight daily newspapers in New York City, and each had its star scribe. Yet, as Gallo wrote in the *Daily News* (14 February 1995) upon Powers's death, "if popularity was the yardstick, Powers was perhaps the brightest star of all." Indeed, during the early 1950s he received upward of thirty thousand letters each year from readers commenting on his columns.

Powers's fame as a media personality transcended the printed word. He hosted a show on NBC radio six nights a week, on which he interviewed sports celebrities and media types. In 1948 his fellow *Daily News* columnist, Ed Sullivan, began hosting *Toast of the Town,* which became *The Ed Sullivan Show* in 1955 and was a Sunday night institution on CBS until 1971. In 1949 Powers joined Sullivan as one of the first journalists to become a television personality. His fame may never have matched that of Sullivan, but his impact on the medium in general and the evolution of the manner in which announcers describe sporting events is profound.

Powers wet his feet in the emerging medium in 1949 as an announcer on *Bowling Headliners,* which was broadcast live on ABC from the Rego Park Lanes in the New York City borough of Queens. That same year he became the principal announcer on *Gillette Cavalcade of Sports* shortly after the show began its national broadcasts of Friday night fights from Madison Square Garden. When he signed on for the job, the broadcasting of boxing on television was having a major impact on the burgeoning popularity of the medium. During the broadcasts Powers sat in the Madison Square Garden mezzanine, approximately seventy-five feet from the ring. He occasionally used opera glasses while watching a fight, which allowed him to observe closely the drama inside the ring. At his side was Arthur Susskind, a boxing expert who offered Powers tidbits regarding the fighters to help him embellish his accounts and cued him in if he was being too verbose. Susskind also typed data on index cards, which he handed to Powers at the appropriate time.

Powers described each match with what Val Adams dubbed a "restrained showmanship" in *The New York Times* (8 June 1952). He professed that such an approach was in fact more important than a knowledge of his subject: "The duller the fight, the more showmanship required by the commentator," he told Adams. "No matter how dull the fight is, you just can't come out and say it's dull. If you do it's the same thing as saying 'Listen folks, both of these guys are a couple of bums, so why don't you tune in to a better program.' Naturally, you can't expect a commentator to say that."

Powers realized that his role in promoting boxing on *Gillette Cavalcade of Sports* differed from his role as editor and columnist for the *Daily News.* As controversial as his columns could be, he was always cautious to avoid alienating his television audience. His association with television resulted in further criticism from his print rival Dan Parker, who dubbed Powers "Jimmy the Shill." Parker, as well as other columnists such as Jimmy Cannon, felt that Powers's announcing fights on television while fulfilling his duties on his paper was a conflict of interest. The fact that Powers did voice-overs for Gillette razor commercials further provoked his colleagues in the press. As Gallo noted, when Powers became involved on the *Gillette Cavalcade of Sports* his column appeared less frequently, which seemed to corroborate Parker's and Cannon's allegations.

Powers clearly enjoyed his role on *Gillette Cavalcade of Sports.* He was pleased to be able to educate his viewers about boxing. "Take a fight where there's little action but a lot of clinching," he told Val Adams. "I might say, 'You know folks, the reason there is so much clinching going on here is because these two fighters have the same style. Boxing styles are like gears on an automobile. If two boxers have the same style, they mesh and fall into a clinch. If they have contrasting styles, they wouldn't clinch so much.'" Powers employed other tricks to entertain and illuminate his viewers, including offering anecdotes about the fighters and quizzes between rounds. He verbally painted a portrait of his subjects by commenting not only on their records but their hobbies, marital status, educational background, or non-sports careers. According to Gallo in the 28 October 1984 *New York Daily News,* he once declared: "Believe it or not, I get a ton of mail wanting this type of information." Powers also understood the importance of letting the action speak for itself, however, a lesson derived from his newspaper career: "I learned from my tabloid training to be concise. When I do have something to say, I make sure that it's pertinent."

Powers was associated with other television programs, as well. In 1951 he was a commentator on *Sports Newsreel* on NBC (also known as *Gillette Summer Sports Reel*), the summer replacement show for *Gillette Cavalcade of Sports. Sports Newsreel* consisted of newsreel clips of sporting events from across the globe, with Powers introducing the sequences and critiquing their content. The following year he was a commentator on *Famous Fights,* which aired on the DuMont Network and consisted of filmed highlights of Madison Square Garden boxing matches. Across the years Powers also worked as a sportscaster and sports celebrity interviewer for WPIX, the New York station owned by the *Daily News,* and hosted a pair of syndicated shows, *The Big Playback* and *The Grantland Rice Story.* As a sports announcer he covered everything from hockey and basketball games to tennis matches and dog shows. During the 1950s he also taught a class in journalism, advertising copy writing, and television technique at Marymount College in Tarrytown, New York, where he and his family resided in an eight-room, white, Cape Cod–style house.

As Powers aged, his *Daily News* columns often were more nostalgic than controversial. At his best he still could be an elegant wordsmith, however. In "The Powerhouse" for 2 March 1954–near the beginning of spring training for the baseball season–he lamented the passing of time and the inevitable replacement of aging athletes by hungry up-and-comers. He began the column by observing: "This is the season when old heroes, like Injuns in the horse operas, bite the dust. Why so many typographical tears are shed is a mystery to any realist, or a fan with a reasonable memory. We all hate to see a Vic Raschi go, or a DiMaggio or Henrich, but the sports world of keen competition belongs to youth." He went on to describe Babe Ruth's appearance in 1935, when the New York Yankees gave him his unconditional release: "The Babe was 40, out of shape, with a tummy like a Bavarian hofmeister." After offering a detailed account of how Ruth was let go by Colonel Jacob Ruppert, the Yankees owner, and how he went on to be a "tragic bust" in a short-lived career with the Boston Braves, Powers concluded: "Yes, it can truly be said–more than the clouds wept, that cold wintry morning in 1935, the day Babe Ruth left New York. It is one thing to admit the inroads of Father Time. It is another to reconcile oneself to it."

During the 1957 baseball season there were rumblings that the Brooklyn Dodgers and New York Giants were about to announce their relocation to Los Angeles and San Francisco, respectively. This event signaled the end of an era of baseball in New York–and in a way foreshadowed the passing of Powers from the New York sports scene. In his 6 June 1957 column he mused on the manner in which baseball was considered by some to be a dying sport by quoting Hall of Fame center fielder Tris Speaker. "In the old days," Speaker told Powers, "you lived and suffered with your heroes. You rooted for the home team. Today we have hams in the stands who root openly for the visitors, hoping to attract attention." Additionally, according to Speaker, "What's hurt baseball is the competition. I walked home the other night, and as I went down the street I could see in the houses on either side big television screens all lit up. In front of each set was a group of viewers. This went on house after house. They were prisoners of the new electronic miracle. They were enjoying themselves. It would take a bomb to blow them out of their comfortable chairs and into a ball park 10 or 30 miles away." By quoting Speaker in such a manner, Powers again was aligning himself with the past, so-called good old days of sport. As his role on *Gillette Cavalcade of Sports* made clear, however, he was also part of the "new electronic miracle" that Speaker deplored.

Powers left the *Gillette Cavalcade of Sports* in 1960, when its format changed and matches were aired from across the country rather than Madison Square Garden. The show was canceled two years later. Meanwhile, some reports, such as Kaplan's obituary for Powers, have Powers departing the *Daily News* in 1959, at age fifty-six. He continued writing his column into the 1960s, however, announcing his retirement on 13 July 1963. According to the notice in the *Daily News* that day, his final piece "appeared in the News before the 114-day strike of New York newspapers which ended last April 1."

Gallo observed that Powers "retired to Florida and never wrote another stick of type for any newspaper. I remember that day when Jimmy, without fanfare, . . . left our office for the last time. He was smiling, but to me, I saw a lonely figure walking out on a long, brilliant career." Gallo recalled that he was surprised by Powers's total disassociation from his professional past. "He was such a complete newspaperman and then, when he quit, he didn't go near a typewriter. He also could still be good on the air. But he dropped all his professional tools, and picked up the fishing pole and tennis racquet." In his retirement Powers cultivated a friendship with Eleanor Holm, the former Olympic swimmer, who became his favorite tennis partner. "They got old together, kind of, playing tennis," Gallo added. "All he did was just go to Mexico, go deep-sea fishing. He believed in living a full kind of life, but without doing anything. The only thing he wrote was letters."

Upon his death at his home in Bal Harbour, Florida, on 11 February 1995–thirty-two years after his retirement–Powers was lauded by Dave Kaplan in the *Daily News* (14 February 1995) as a "pioneering sports columnist and sports editor" and "genial and colorful personality." His wife, Winona, had predeceased him by fourteen years, and he was survived by his three children and six granddaughters.

References:

Val Adams, "A Commentator's Views on Boxing," *New York Times,* 8 June 1952;

Red Barber, *1947, When All Hell Broke Loose in Baseball* (New York: Doubleday, 1982);

Harvey Frommer, *New York City Baseball: The Last Golden Age, 1947–1957* (New York: Macmillan, 1980);

Bill Gallo, "Announcer Powers Was Simple and Simply Superb," *New York Daily News,* 28 October 1984;

Gallo, "He Had Inkling I'd Make It," *New York Daily News,* 14 February 1995;

"Jimmy Powers, Columnist for N.Y. News, Retires," *New York Daily News,* 13 July 1963;

Dave Kaplan, "Powerhouse of a Writer: As a Columnist, Powers Made News & Reported It," *New York Daily News,* 14 February 1995;

Bob Lardine, "The Powers of Observation: As Sports Columnist of THE NEWS or as Top Sportscaster, Jimmy Keeps It Short and Sweet," *New York Sunday News,* 12 May 1957;

Murray Polner, *Branch Rickey: A Biography* (New York: Atheneum, 1982), pp. 129–132;

Arnold Rampersad, *Jackie Robinson: A Biography* (New York: Knopf, 1997), pp. 120, 130, 286.

Frank Queen

(12 May 1822 – 18 October 1882)

Dennis Gildea
Springfield College

MAJOR POSITIONS HELD: Editor (1853–1855), publisher and editor, *New York Clipper* (1855–1882).

In the economically uncertain and often morally seamy world of sporting journalism in nineteenth-century America, Frank Queen and his weekly *New York Clipper* occupied a place that was both in step and oddly out of step with his sportswriting contemporaries. Queen's philosophy and practice of sports and entertainment journalism fell somewhere between the more agrarian and aristocratic approach of William Trotter Porter and his *Spirit of the Times* and the gritty, sexually exploitative approach of Richard Kyle Fox and his *National Police Gazette*. Although it was an eclectic blend of sports reporting, fiction, verse, and stage news, Queen's *Clipper,* especially in its sports coverage, was more clearly a precursor of the early-twentieth-century daily sports section than was any other publication of the nineteenth century.

With Harrison Trent, whose primary role was to provide the financial backing, Queen founded the *New York Clipper* in 1853. Unlike the majority of the sporting papers established in the antebellum period, the *Clipper* continued publication up to and beyond Queen's death in 1882. It began as a four-page paper, and during the 1870s and 1880s it typically ran sixteen or twenty pages. Although exact circulation figures are not available, the paper itself claimed that by the 1870s circulation reached a high of fifty thousand. By all accounts Queen was a good businessman, and, following his death, the story became popular that he never left the Clipper Building in New York City for a weekend at his home in Philadelphia without at least $1,000 in cash. Whether that story is apocryphal or not, the sporting and theatrical paper flourished under Queen and continued publishing until 1924, although it was bought in 1923 by Sime Silverman, who published *Variety*. After a year of trying to make the *Clipper* financially viable, Silverman absorbed a $120,000 loss and suspended publication. Except for the infamous *National Police Gazette,* which published under various owners and editors from 1845 to 1932, the run of the *Clipper* was the longest of any of the nineteenth-century sporting papers.

In a retrospective piece on sports and entertainment trade papers, *Variety* praised Queen as a journalistic innovator. "Queen . . . was groping many years ahead of his times in view of the great development of sports and the theatre in this country." Queen was, the story maintained, a brilliant editor "whose ideas . . . have been more latterly adopted in the modern way by the dailies." In his weekly column Queen often argued for the physical and social benefits of leisure and sport, including bare-knuckle prizefighting, which was illegal. John R. Betts, in his article "Sporting Journalism in Nineteenth-Century America" (1953), calls the *Clipper* "the most important of the publications" of its kind in the middle of the century. "The *Clipper* became the prime popularizer of the diamond, employed the pioneer baseball writer and statistician Henry Chadwick, and encouraged most athletic activities. It was one of the few journals which strove to defend the prize ring, and by the 1870's it was considered one of the three leading journals of the 'Sporting Press.'"

Virtually all media historians dealing with pioneering sports papers in the United States regard the *Spirit of the Times,* which was published from 1831 to 1862, and the *National Police Gazette* when it was published and edited by Fox from 1877 to 1919 as the most important and most influential in different ways. Porter, a fine editor and poor businessman who edited various embodiments of the *Spirit of the Times* from 1831 until his death in 1858, is noted as a pioneer in the area of sports journalism and an editor who favored field sports and horse racing and who produced a relatively high-priced paper aimed at a gentlemanly, more rural audience. In 1839, for example, the *Spirit of the Times* sold by subscription for ten dollars per year. Fox's *Police Gazette,* by way of contrast, made its mark by mixing sensationalistic coverage of sex, crime, and sports. Queen and the *Clipper* occupied a journalistic middle ground between the extremes, and in the breadth of its coverage of leisure

NEW YORK CLIPPER.
VOL. I.—No. 1 NEW YORK, MAY 14, 1853. PRICE 2 CENTS.

Flag of the first issue of the weekly sports and theatrical newspaper founded by Frank Queen

activities truly could be regarded as a forerunner of the dailies later in the nineteenth century.

Queen was born on 12 May 1822 to working-class parents in the First Ward of the old district of Southwark by the docks of the Delaware River in Philadelphia. Southwark and neighboring Moyamensing were the roughest, most crime-ridden, and poorest areas in Philadelphia. As a young man Queen became affiliated with the predominantly working-class fire companies of the district. These fire companies were social and quasi-athletic clubs that were organized along ethnic and religious lines. Queen belonged to Weccacoe Engine, a Protestant fire company whose president, Charles Hortz, later became Queen's father-in-law. On at least one occasion Weccacoe Engine fought violently with the Irish-Catholic Weccacoe Hose Company. Significantly, Queen overcame the taint of ethnic and religious animosity, at least as evidenced by his coverage of events later in his life.

Queen's working-class background is noteworthy given the aim of his paper. In his column, "The Skipper's Cabin" (later titled "City Summary" and then "Introductory"), in the second issue of the *Clipper* (14 May 1853) he wrote: "Our principles . . . may always be the principles of the people, the hard working mechanic, and the feeble and careworn poor, whose honesty is ever superior to those who are ranked in the higher walks of society." In a column in the first issue, a week earlier, Queen made it a point to stress his lack of a formal education, indicating that such a lack would not prevent him from writing with intelligence and working hard to provide readers with "full reports of every sporting affair of interest in this or the old country."

To a great extent Queen was self-educated. Orphaned at an early age, he began his career in the publishing business at age fourteen when he became an apprentice to Willis Gaylord Clarke, the editor of the *Philadelphia Gazette.* Clarke, impressed with the boy's dedication and ability, took him under his wing and promised to travel with him to New York City to introduce him to the world of journalism there and in particular to his brother, Lewis Gaylord Clarke, the editor of *The Knickerbocker Magazine.* Willis Clarke died before he could fulfill his promise to Queen, however. Eventually, Queen operated a newsstand and a small bookstore in Southwark and read voraciously from his inventory, providing him with a type of self-education that proved invaluable later in his editorship of the *Clipper,* particularly since his reading schooled him in the form and content of an emerging mass-mediated popular culture.

In 1850 Queen moved to New York City, where he was financially backed by George Adriance, a pioneer in the cheap-book trade. Adriance helped establish Queen as an operator of newsstands in the Bowery and imbued him with a shrewd business sense that aided him during his time as publisher of the *Clipper.* From his newsstand experience Queen soon became aware of "the material most in popular demand," and this knowledge "suggested an opportunity for venturing upon his long-cherished project of starting a newspaper of his own," according to a story headlined "Frank Queen and His Contemporaries" that ran in the *Clipper* on 4 November 1882, shortly after his death. Queen saw a demand for a weekly paper that covered news of athletic contests and the theater, both of which were popular with the urban working class. Prizefighting was of particular interest to a large number of people. "Frank Queen and His Contemporaries" noted: "At the time there was existing in New York what was justly termed the pugilistic craze, consequent upon the arrival in America of Ben Caunt, Yankee Sullivan and other magnates of the prize ring." The prize ring became popular in England in the late eighteenth and early nineteenth centuries in no small part through the writing of Pierce Egan in the periodical *Bell's Life in London.* Egan and *Bell's Life* were clear journalistic models for Queen and his publication.

Historian Melvin L. Adelman, in his *A Sporting Time: New York City and the Rise of Modern Athletics, 1820–70* (1990), notes that the nineteenth-century sporting press articulated three major justifications of modern sport: the promotion of health, the promotion of morality, and the instilling of character values, all of which were interrelated. Time and again Queen relied on those justifications in arguing for sport and leisure activities. Moreover, he philosophically aligned himself with the fledgling labor movement in America when he wrote on 25 February 1860 that while work dignifies man, work should not be an end to itself. Rather, the "end of work is to enjoy leisure." Adelman also notes that the sporting press, the *Clipper* included, was not original in formulating its arguments for sport. Rather, he argues, the chief contribution of the press to the ideology of modern sport lay in its role as "synthesizers and popularizers of others' ideas." Journalistically, though, Queen's publication was different from Porter's and later Fox's sporting papers and certainly different from the occasional sports coverage that appeared in mainstream dailies. If nothing else, the *Clipper* looked different. Queen used many woodcuts, especially on his front page, and the masthead of the paper was a busy mélange of various sporting scenes running together in a style to suggest that sport was the coming rage in America. Consistent with the debt it owed to Egan and to the oral culture of the street and saloon, the *Clipper* frequently published verse or ballads that celebrated an athletic accomplishment and that were meant to be read aloud or even sung. On its front page immediately following John Morrissey's win over John C. Heenan for the bare-knuckle prizefighting championship of America in 1858, the *Clipper* ran two pieces of verse, "The Champion Mill" and "Science versus Size: A Sad Story in Rhyme Dedicated to Heavy Weights Generally." The latter was illustrated with five woodcuts, and both pieces of verse spoke directly to the context of the fight. Because it was a weekly, the *Clipper* seldom could scoop a daily such as the *New York Tribune* or the *New York Herald,* both of which reported the results of the Heenan–Morrissey fight the day after it occurred. Rather, like a contemporary print medium competing with television, the *Clipper* offered its readers more analysis, more in-depth reporting, and more of an insider's view of the happenings. The examples of verse cited above, for instance, were meant more to celebrate the excitement and joy of a successful athletic competition than they were simply to provide information.

In addition to arguing for the health, morality, and character-building aspect of athletic activity, Queen's paper functioned as an educational source for a nation beginning to become interested in sport. Queen ran articles that promoted sport, certainly, but he also featured stories that dealt with its historical background. The *Clipper* regularly reprinted accounts of prominent prizefights, especially those that occurred in England in the halcyon days of the ring. Queen fought a losing cause in an effort to popularize cricket in America. While he favored cricket, he was enough of a newspaperman and a businessman to cover extensively the emerging baseball culture. Significantly, Queen's approach to cricket was decidedly democratic. On 7 January 1860 he criticized the patrician St. George Cricket Club of New York City for allowing "the prejudices and partiality of the few, to control the opinions of many," thereby, in Queen's opinion, stunting the growth of the sport.

When Queen and Trent launched the *Clipper* in 1853, they had to be aware that they were entering a branch of the newspaper business that, in the eyes of polite society and even mainstream journalists, was regarded as less than respectable. Queen characterized his *Clipper* (named after the "speedy and saucy American clipper-ships" that sailed the Atlantic at the time) as "A Weekly Sporting Paper." In antebellum America the term *sporting* carried several meanings, most of which were derogatory; in casting his journal as a "sporting paper" Queen certainly knew that he was engaged in a somewhat revolutionary undertaking.

Within the predominantly oral subculture of the city street and saloon, the "sporting men"–also known as "the boys," the "sporting fraternity," the "fancy," and "flash characters"–were, according to historian Steven A. Riess in *City Games: The Evolution of American Urban Society and the Rise of Sports* (1989), "an informal brotherhood of pleasure seekers who sponsored, participated in, and attended traditional sporting contests." United though they were in their pursuit of pleasure, the members of the informal brotherhood came from a variety of urban backgrounds, including younger members of the social elite, machine politicians, artisans, butchers, seasonal workers, criminals, and Irish immigrants, none of which were mutually exclusive categories. "All part of the male bachelor subculture," Riess writes, "these sportsmen measured manliness by skill at wenching, drinking, gambling, and fighting." The lives and values of sporting men stood in sharp contrast to those of upper-class and middle-class men who lived a productive business and social life and whose primary associations were with the family and the church. While Queen often objected editorially to excesses of wenching, drinking, and gambling, he recognized and argued for the value of the sporting man's interest in and pursuit of leisure activities, whether they be athletic or theatrical. In fact, his espousal of the inherent value of leisure activities formed the philosophical core of his newspaper. In a column from the edition of 7 January 1854, "Our Platform: The Sporting Community of the New World," Queen wrote:

> we have men who would gladly embrace the opportunity of joining in any sport having for its object inno-

> cent recreation and a full development of the muscular powers; but they are deterred by the attacks so frequently heaped upon those who participate in sporting matters. We believe, however, a change is about to take place. . . . there is a growing disposition to uphold and countenance every sport having for its object a vigorous exercise of the body as well as the mind. . . . Altogether, we are but in our infancy as regards sporting affairs; but the word is, Onward!

In his column of 14 May 1859 Queen surmised that the domesticating influence of middle-class women attending sporting events would diminish potentially raucous behavior and thereby improve the cultural image of sport in general. "Let our American ladies visit the cricket grounds, the regattas, the baseball matches, and the most rough or rude among the spectators would acknowledge their magic sway. . . . When ladies are present . . . no class of our population can be found so debased as not to change their external behavior immediately, and that change is always for the better." Queen always favored anything that would improve and popularize sport, but his publication seldom advocated or covered women's sports, although it frequently profiled famous actresses and singers of the day. When anything related to women and sports was covered in the *Clipper,* it was written tongue in cheek, as if to work the incongruity of the event for its humorous value. On 27 November 1858, for example, under the headline "The Ring," the paper covered a "scene of pugilism" in Philadelphia that pitted "two daughters of the Green Isle" who, fortified with a "koort of Maloney's best," fought over a man. The paper satirically reported a round-by-round and blow-by-blow account, as it would with a recognized fight between men, but concluded with the women "sent below by Alderman Femington, in default of bail, to be of future good behavior." To a great extent the satirical coverage of the fight reflects the demeaning of athletic women on the one hand and the immigrant Irish on the other, both characteristic of antebellum media. Both were easy targets, and even Queen's *Clipper* took occasional potshots.

In addition to trying to overcome the cultural meanings conveyed in the expression *sporting* when applied to the men who engaged in or watched the event, Queen had to overcome the negative connotations of the term *sporting paper.* Although his chief competition for readership, at least initially, came from the *Spirit of the Times,* Queen's position as editor and publisher of a new sporting paper was complicated by the existence, in most cases fleeting, of other papers that styled themselves as members of the sporting press. In the 1840s in New York City nine newspapers emerged and prospered briefly, usually before encountering legal difficulties that forced them out of business. These included papers such as *The Flash,* which evolved into *The True Flash; The Rake,* which became *The Weekly Rake; The Sporting Whip,* later known simply as *The Whip; The Libertine; Life in New York;* and, of a less-offensive nature, the original *National Police Gazette,* published first by George Wilkes and later by George Washington Matsell, a former New York City police chief. The editor and publisher of *The Whip,* George B. Woolridge, wrote that his publication was "devoted to the Sports of the Ring, the turf, and city life–such as sprees, larks, criminal conspiracy, seductions, rapes." In the mind of polite society and, obviously, in Woolridge's mind, pugilism in particular and sport in general were equated with criminality and social disorder. In *The Sporting Whip* a weekly column headlined "The Ring" ran along with one that all but extolled the subjects in its headline, "Vice and Immorality." When the *Clipper* appeared with its emphasis on coverage of sport, consequently, it was quickly numbered by Junius Henri Browne in his *The Great Metropolis: A Mirror of New York* (1869), a guidebook to life in the city, as being among "the worst class of weeklies" that are "abominably written, and illustrated with hideous cuts"; the *Clipper,* along with the whole of the sporting press, could only be appreciated by depraved men, who considered them "the most entertaining and instructive journals in the World."

Not surprisingly, Queen never thought of his paper as being at all similar to the more-lurid sheets. When the *Clipper* was launched in 1853, "but one sporting paper was then being published in the entire American Union–*The Spirit of the Times,* edited by William T. Porter with Thomas Picton as his associate," the retrospective "Frank Queen and His Contemporaries" observed. Socially and physically, Porter and Queen were opposites. Porter was a Vermont gentleman born to a family of some wealth and social standing that had been in America for eight generations. He received a formal classical education at a secondary school in Hanover, New Hampshire. Moreover, he was a tall, handsome man. Queen was working class, had no formal education, and was overweight and nearsighted, a condition that worsened as his years in the newspaper business increased. His poor vision may have improved his ability as a careful proofreader, however, as "Frank Queen and His Contemporaries" suggested. "Almost to the end of his life it was his habit to read in manuscript every line designed to appear in this paper . . . and every line of what he had not rejected in manuscript he read in 'proof' after it had been placed in type. Thus he exercised a double supervision over all that went into his columns."

Queen's and Porter's differences extended into the journalistic philosophies of their respective papers. Porter aimed his publication at "sportsmen"

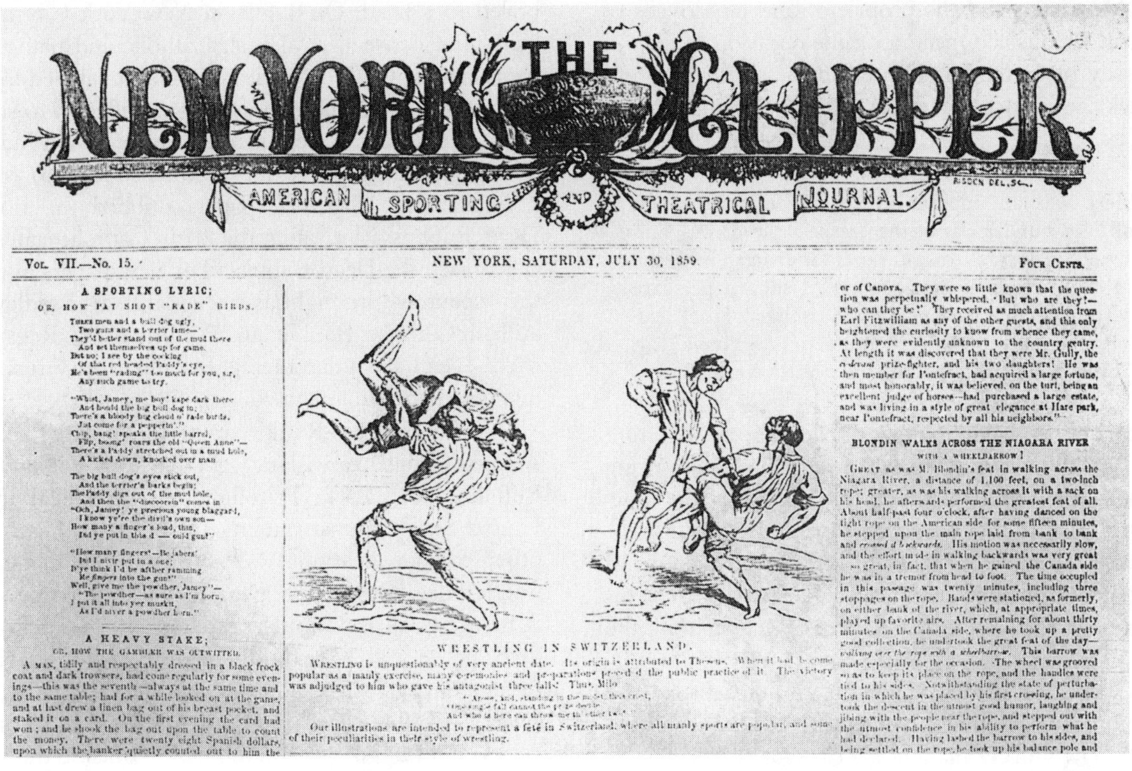

THE NEW YORK CLIPPER
AMERICAN SPORTING AND THEATRICAL JOURNAL.

VOL. VII.—No. 15. NEW YORK, SATURDAY, JULY 30, 1859. FOUR CENTS.

A SPORTING LYRIC;
OR, HOW PAT SHOT "RADE" BIRDS.

Thare men and a bull dog ugly,
Two guns and a terrier lame—
They'd better stand out of the mud there
And set themselves up for game.
But no; I see by the cocking
Of that red headed Paddy's eye,
He's been "rading" too much for you, sir,
Any such game to try.

"Whist, Jamey, me boy! kape dark there
And hould the big bull dog in;
There's a bloody big cloud o' rade birds,
Jist come for a pepperin'."
Chip, bang! speaks the little barrel,
Flip, boong! roars the old "Queen Anne"—
There's a Paddy stretched out in a mud hole,
A kicked down, knocked over man.

The big bull dog's eyes stick out,
And the terrier's barks begin;
The Paddy digs out of the mud hole,
And then the "discoorsin" comes in
"Och, Jamey! ye precious young blaggard,
I know ye're the divil's own son—
How many a finger's load, thin,
Did ye put in this d — ould gun!"

"How many fingers!—Be jabers!
Did I niver put in a one;
D'ye think I'd be afther ramming
Me fingers into the gun!"
Well, give me the powdher, Jamey"—
"The powdher—as sure as I'm born,
I put it all into yer muskit,
As I'd niver a powdher horn."

A HEAVY STAKE;
OR, HOW THE GAMBLER WAS OUTWITTED.

A MAN, tidily and respectably dressed in a black frock coat and dark trowsers, had come regularly for some evenings—this was the seventh—always at the same time and to the same table; had for a while looked on at the game, and at last drew a linen bag out of his breast pocket, and staked it on a card. On the first evening the card had won; and he shook the bag out upon the table to count the money. There were twenty eight Spanish dollars, upon which the banker quietly counted out to him the

WRESTLING IN SWITZERLAND.

WRESTLING is unquestionably of very ancient date. Its origin is attributed to Theseus. When it had become popular as a manly exercise, many ceremonies and preparations preceded the public practice of it. The victory was adjudged to him who gave his antagonist three falls. Thus, Milo

Our illustrations are intended to represent a fête in Switzerland, where all manly sports are popular, and some of their peculiarities in their style of wrestling.

or of Canova. They were so little known that the question was perpetually whispered, 'But who are they?—who can they be?' They received as much attention from Earl Fitzwilliam as any of the other guests, and this only heightened the curiosity to know from whence they came, as they were evidently unknown to the country gentry. At length it was discovered that they were Mr. Gully, the *ci-devant* prize-fighter, and his two daughters! He was then member for Pontefract, had acquired a large fortune, and most honorably, it was believed, on the turf, being an excellent judge of horses—had purchased a large estate, and was living in a style of great elegance at Hare park, near Pontefract, respected by all his neighbors."

BLONDIN WALKS ACROSS THE NIAGARA RIVER
WITH A WHEELBARROW!

GREAT as was M. Blondin's feat in walking across the Niagara River, a distance of 1,100 feet, on a two-inch rope; greater, as was his walking across it with a sack on his head, he afterwards performed the greatest feat of all. About half-past four o'clock, after having danced on the tight rope on the American side for some fifteen minutes, he stepped upon the main rope laid from bank to bank and *crossed it backwards.* His motion was necessarily slow, and the effort made in walking backwards was very great so great, in fact, that when he gained the Canada side he was in a tremor from head to foot. The time occupied in this passage was twenty minutes, including three stoppages on the rope. Bands were stationed, as formerly, on either bank of the river, which, at appropriate times, played up favorite airs. After remaining for about thirty minutes on the Canada side, where he took up a pretty good collection, he undertook the great feat of the day—*walking over the rope with a wheelbarrow.* This barrow was made especially for the occasion. The wheel was grooved so as to keep its place on the rope, and the handles were tied to his sides. Notwithstanding the state of perturbation in which he was placed by his first crossing, he undertook the descent in the utmost good humor, laughing and jibing with the people near the rope, and stepped out with the utmost confidence in his ability to perform what he had declared. Having lashed the barrow to his sides, and being settled on the rope, he took up his balance pole and

Top of the front page of an 1859 issue of Queen's paper

more so than at "sporting men," and in so doing he geared the material in his papers for readers from a background similar to his. In his *Sportsmen and Gamesmen* (1981) historian John Dizikes wrote that Porter "assumed that farmers would be molded in the tradition of English country life, with people like himself as the leading lights. And so the general social tone of the early *Spirit of the Times* was a trifle superior, with a muted but unmistakable English accent." In the 11 May 1835 edition of the *Spirit,* Porter wrote, "we are addressing ourselves to gentlemen of standing, wealth and intelligence, the very corinthian columns of the community."

Another major difference in the papers was that the *Spirit* was sold primarily through mail subscriptions, most of which came from residents of southern states. The *Clipper* sold primarily at city newsstands similar to the ones Queen ran as a younger man and consistent with the sales practices established by the successful penny-press papers in the 1830s and 1840s. In 1853 the *Clipper* sold for two cents per copy; the *Spirit,* if available at a newsstand, sold for six cents per copy. Even the type of individual buying the papers differed, if Browne's account can be believed. In a chapter on the ubiquitous newsdealers of New York City, Browne wrote that the "neatly-dressed, jockey-looking individual seizes on the *Spirit of the Times,*" while the "low brow and hard, cruel eye are in search of the *Clipper.*"

While Queen would object to that characterization of his audience, the different journalistic approaches he and Porter employed were manifested in their treatment of sporting and social events in 1857. For New York City and much of the United States 1857 was a tumultuous year marked by financial panic, continuing debate over slavery, and ethnic animosity involving Irish Catholic immigrants and American-born Protestants. In the summer of that year the New York state legislature declared that New York City "was too corrupt to govern itself" and turned over control of the police force from Mayor Fernando Wood to the state militia. Perhaps one of the events that led the state legislature to that conclusion was that John Morrissey, the reigning American prizefighting champion, attempted to murder three men in a city saloon in May. In fact, throughout 1857 Morrissey was charged on three separate occasions with assault with attempt to kill, but because of his political connections with Mayor Wood and Tammany Hall, all charges were dismissed.

In its edition of 16 May 1857 the *Clipper* ran a story covering the "difficulty" that took place between

"John Morrissey and the proprietor and employees of the Girard House." Queen took the occasion to defend Morrissey for defending himself in the altercation and to attack the mainstream daily press for sensationalizing the story.

> Here was an opportunity for a "sensation paragraph" for our friends of the "respectable press," and forthwith seduction cases, rapes, murders, and the usual "light reading" that readers of such papers are daily regaled with, gave place to the doings of the "brutal pugilist." Well, well, let them rail on: the "boys" can stand the fire, if the gun don't burst with overloading.

Queen's approach to the story is telling, because it minimizes Morrissey's role as a violent brute while accusing the mainstream press of pandering to the public's appetite for stories about "seduction cases, rapes, murders." In effect Queen argues that not only is the account of the incident in his paper more factual, but also that his sporting paper is, in practice, more respectable than the dailies.

Queen concluded the story by chastising the champion for becoming involved in yet another brush with the law and by making his case for the principles of the sporting men.

> We do not wish to be considered as apologists for the conduct of Morrissey, for we detest these bar-room squabbles, no matter where, when, or with whom they originate; but we refer to the matter more, because, when a member of the sporting fraternity is detected in such "entangling alliances," every effort is made to misrepresent the facts, and to place members of the sporting world even lower than the combatants of the church.

As the passage reveals, Queen was acutely aware of the perception and persecution of sporting men in polite society and willing to deal with the issue directly and uncompromisingly in his columns. Despite the fact that Morrissey's latest altercation was covered in the *Clipper* and the New York City dailies, Porter's *Spirit* makes no mention of it. Rather, the *Spirit* pages are filled with its usual fare, stories dealing with hunting, fishing, and horse racing. Unlike the *Clipper,* Porter's paper used bylines, and a "C. E. Whitehead, Esq." is credited with writing "A Winter's Hunting Trip from the Suwanee River to the Florida Keys" (11 July 1857), an article that reflects Porter's interest in the South and Southwest.

The most anticipated sports event of the summer of 1857 was a prizefight, scheduled for 1 August, between two Philadelphians, Dominick Bradley and S. S. Rankin. Interest in the fight was high because not only might it produce a likely challenger for Morrissey's title, but it also reflected religious and ethnic animosity that boiled to a head. On 4 July in New York City a fight broke out between rival Irish Catholic and native-born Protestant gangs. The battle continued unabated for two days before the National Guard was called in to stop it. Eight young men were killed and more than a hundred others suffered injuries, fifty severe enough to require hospitalization. The newspapers dubbed the riot the Dead Rabbits Riot, after the Irish Catholic gang that called itself the Dead Rabbits. The newspapers also cast the impending prizefight as a religious war: Bradley was an Irish Catholic; Rankin, an Irish Protestant. Regardless of the eventual winner, the fight would incite further rioting, newspapers maintained.

The Bradley-Rankin bout took place at Point Albino, Canada, an island in Lake Erie not far from Buffalo, New York. Prizefighting was illegal in the United States, and arranging for bouts in Canada or other remote locations was a way of eluding police interference. Despite its geographical remoteness, the fight drew six thousand spectators, who watched for three hours and 152 rounds before Bradley prevailed. In its coverage of the fight on 3 August the *Philadelphia Bulletin* reported that "there was a great deal of drunkenness, and fights were innumerable outside the ring." Moreover, "Not the least disgusting feature of the disgusting business is the fact that religion . . . has been mixed up in it."

In his "City Summary" column of 15 August, Queen painted a different picture of the fight and its religious overtones. He acknowledged that the potential for a religious riot existed, and not just any riot but "one of the most sanguinary and bloody contests between the friends of the two parties ever witnessed in America." Queen also noted that any existing religious animosity was fanned by "remarks of the press at large concerning the battle." Nevertheless, Queen was quick to contend that according to the report in his publication, the fight was "one of the most peaceable ever fought in this country, and the utmost good humor prevailed among all who witnessed it." So placid was the scene, Queen observed, "Papists and Orangemen mingled together in friendly discussion. . . . The subject of religion was not broached on either side, and the 'bloody conflict between the Papists and the Orangemen' did not come off, much to the disappointment and chagrin of 'the respectable press.'" The entire affair, he concluded, was a victory for "manly spirit" and the "rules governing the prize ring." By contrast, the *Spirit* covered the fight in just eleven lines, confining itself to the outcome and little else.

Queen's column in this instance is consistent with the body of his writing in the *Clipper,* which argued for the uplifting character of "sports for all the people," as its masthead proclaimed with every issue. Queen was

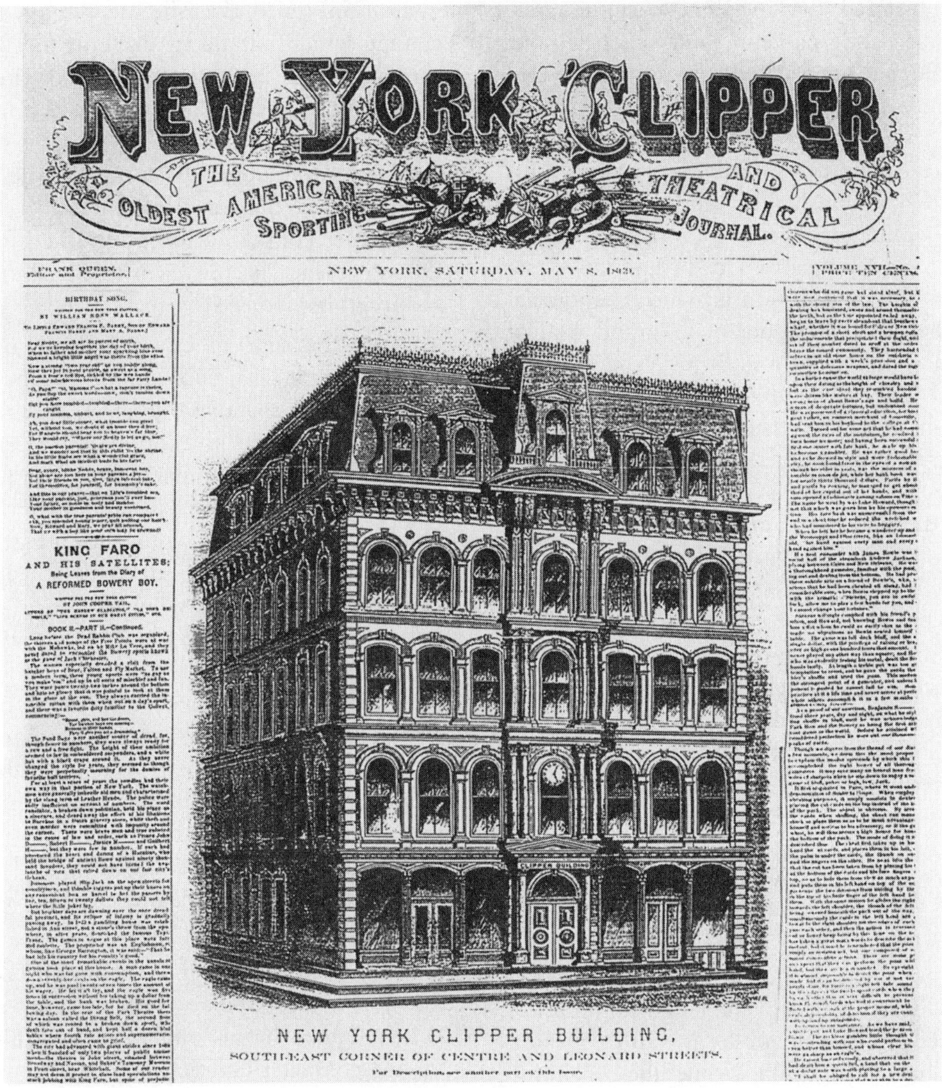

NEW YORK CLIPPER

THE OLDEST AMERICAN SPORTING AND THEATRICAL JOURNAL.

FRANK QUEEN, Editor and Proprietor.

NEW YORK, SATURDAY, MAY 8, 1869.

BIRTHDAY SONG.

BY WILLIAM ROSS WALLACE.

KING FARO AND HIS SATELLITES; Being Leaves from the Diary of A REFORMED BOWERY BOY.

BOOK II.—PART II.—Continued.

NEW YORK CLIPPER BUILDING,

SOUTHEAST CORNER OF CENTRE AND LEONARD STREETS.

Front page of the issue in which the Clipper *announced the completion of its new headquarters*

an ardent promoter of sports, but when a sport failed to live up to his ideals he was an honest enough newsman to turn against it. Such was the case with prizefighting. Interest in pugilism increased until 17 April 1860, when American John C. Heenan and Englishman Tom Sayers fought to a disputed draw in the first major international bout held in England. Following the Civil War the ring was plagued with fixed fights and disorder so great that some bouts were stopped before a true victor could emerge. On 4 December 1869 Queen wrote in his column: "Exponents of the manly art can no longer find the influential backers and patrons who formerly took an interest in this sport, for they have become disgusted with mob rule, and leave the pugs to get along as best they can; and until the mob spirit is eradicated root and branch, 'manly artists' can expect to meet with little encouragement or favor." Within a decade Queen had gone from arguing in favor of the code of honor that governed the behavior of the sporting fraternity to lamenting its absence. Where once he saw a positive value system operating in a subculture, he now saw anarchy. His transformation, which arose from a balanced assessment of the scene, says more about his integrity as a newspaper editor than it does about his seeming disloyalty to a sport he once helped popularize.

While turning away from the ring, Queen devoted his attention and promotion to baseball. On 25 April 1868 the paper began its baseball coverage for the season by patting itself on the back. "The Clipper, as the leading organ of all legitimate sports, was the first to recognize the game of base ball as a recreation that was destined to be the National Game of

America. We fostered the incipient pastime, gave advice to clubs and players, and exerted our wide-spread influence to perpetuate it as a healthy and harmless amusement." The same article announced that the paper would offer "a gold ball, of regulation weight and size, to be contended for by the Clubs aspiring to the Championship." In addition the *Clipper* proclaimed it would give nine gold medals to the members of the winning team. This promotion was a follow-up to an 1861 promotion in which the journal gave a silver ball to the winner of a "grand trial of skill" between the New York and Brooklyn clubs "that came off on the 28th of October, 1861, at the Elysian Fields, Hoboken, in the presence of thousands of spectators." The paper neglects to say who won the game. Typical of its eclectic journalistic style, the stories and box scores of the opening games of the 1868 season run alongside a column on "Cruelty to Animals" and just a page removed from the weekly "Theatrical Record" and a humorous tale, "Cupid's Foibles."

By 1869 the *Clipper* regularly published columns on baseball, cricket, horse racing, prizefighting, pedestrianism, billiards on occasion, card games, and chess, as well as the happenings of the theater, a feature for which it achieved justifiable fame because it provided a record and tracking service for actors on the road. Another weekly feature that provided a service to readers was a column of answers to questions ostensibly mailed in by readers. The column, appearing under the standing headline "To Correspondents," typically ran the full length of a newspaper column and from a quarter to a half of the length of another. The paper never printed the questions; rather, it ran a questioner's initials or nickname, sometimes his home city, and then the answer to the query, as, for example, on 1 November 1873: "INQUIRER–The weight of a 'regulation baseball' is 5¼ ounces." Often it seems that the answer is meant to settle a bet: "J.H.–You must pay the money to B, who, according to your statement, fairly won it" (1 November 1873). It is impossible to determine if all of the answers are in response to readers' questions or if at least some of them are made up. Nevertheless, the column illustrates one of the primary functions of the *Clipper,* that is, to serve as an educational tool for a nation just beginning to immerse itself in a sporting culture.

One of the journalistic and business triumphs of Queen's career occurred in May 1869, when the paper proved profitable enough that its publisher and editor built and moved the operation into a five-story building on the corner of Center and Leonard Streets in lower Manhattan. In announcing the completion of the new Clipper Building, Queen writes: "None who have watched the rapid growth of metropolitan institutions can have failed to remark the wonderful change which has taken place in the news business, for the sale of periodicals is one of the most important branches of internal industry." So great had this industry become for Queen that he could proudly point to his Clipper Building as one of "the most prominent architectural ornaments" of the city. The newspaper continued to occupy the building beyond Queen's death in 1882, up to the time when it was absorbed by *Variety.*

By the time of Queen's death on 18 October 1882, though, his publication was being overshadowed by Fox's *National Police Gazette.* Following his acquisition of the weekly in 1877, Fox turned the *Gazette,* which was printed on pink-tinted paper, into the "Barbershop Bible," a tabloid the likes of which Queen could not and would not attempt to emulate. Sports news ran alongside pages "featuring buxom showgirls, scandals, hangings . . . and spicy stories," Betts noted in his "Sporting Journalism in Nineteenth-Century America." In 1880, in its edition covering the Paddy Ryan–Joe Goss fight, the *Gazette* printed 400,000 papers, an extraordinary total for the time and one that helped strike a death knell for the *Clipper* as the most prominent and widely read sports publication in the nation. Increasingly, and especially after Queen's death, the *Clipper* expanded its coverage of the theater and reduced its coverage of sports.

In the 1860s and 1870s, however, no sporting publication was more influential and no sporting editor was more popular than the *Clipper* and Queen. When Queen began publication in 1853, he argued for the character-building nature of sport and against the lurid immorality of some of the sporting publications that preceded and coexisted with the *Clipper;* by 1882, however, a publication at least as obscene as those earlier ones had supplanted his paper as the leading sporting journal of the United States. Queen's journalistic career covered a thirty-year period of tremendous cultural change, a period that saw public perception of his paper range from being too pernicious to being too prudish to compete with the *Gazette.* Nevertheless, he played a genuinely pioneering role in American sports journalism, and it was not until the early decades of the twentieth century that his more reasoned approach to sportswriting came into vogue again. Of his pioneering role, the historian Elliott J. Gorn wrote in *The Manly Art: Bare-Knuckle Prize Fighting in America* (1986): "Perhaps Frank Queen's greatest sin was inverting the Victorian belief that man played so that he might work. For the *Clipper* editor, sports gave not only strength and health, but pleasure too, a value in its own right."

References:

Melvin L. Adelman, *A Sporting Time: New York City and the Rise of Modern Athletics, 1820–70* (Urbana: University of Illinois Press, 1990), pp. 159, 238–240, 269–286;

Robert C. Allen, *Horrible Prettiness: Burlesque and American Culture* (Chapel Hill: University of North Carolina Press, 1991), pp. 8–15;

Jack W. Berryman, "The Tenuous Attempts of Americans to 'Catch-Up with John Bull': Specialty Magazines and Sporting Journalism, 1800–1835," *Canadian Journal of the History of Sport and Physical Education,* 10 (May 1979): 33–61;

John R. Betts, *America's Sporting Heritage: 1850–1950* (Reading, Mass.: Addison-Wesley, 1974), pp. 55–57;

Betts, "Sporting Journalism in Nineteenth-Century America," *American Quarterly,* 5 (Spring 1953): 39–56;

Betts, "The Technological Revolution and the Rise of Sport, 1850–1900," *Mississippi Valley Historical Review,* 40 (September 1953): 231–256;

Junius Henri Browne, *The Great Metropolis: A Mirror of New York* (Hartford, Conn.: American Publishing, 1869), pp. 69–72;

Virginia Christ-Jahner, "The 'Cyclopedic Dimensions' of the *New York Clipper,*" *Bulletin of the New York Public Library,* 70 (June 1966): 347–355;

"Frank Queen and His Contemporaries," *New York Clipper,* 4 November 1882, p. 533;

Dennis Gildea, "Cross-Counter: The Heenan–Morrissey Fight of 1858 and Frank Queen's Attack on the 'Respectable Press,'" *Colby Quarterly,* 32 (March 1996): 11–22;

Gildea, "Science Versus Size: 'Science' as a Keyword in the Newspaper Debate over Bare-Knuckle Prize Fighting," *American Journalism,* 10 (Winter–Spring 1993): 102–118;

Elliott J. Gorn, *The Manly Art: Bare-Knuckle Prize Fighting in America* (Ithaca, N.Y.: Cornell University Press, 1986), pp. 100–103, 106, 125, 171, 176, 226;

George B. Kirsch, *The Creation of American Team Sports: Baseball and Cricket, 1838–72* (Urbana: University of Illinois Press, 1989), pp. 12–13, 15, 26–27, 36–39, 190, 214–215, 217, 234;

Frank Luther Mott, *A History of American Magazines, 1850–1865* (Cambridge, Mass.: Harvard University Press, 1957), pp. 201–204;

Stephen M. Vallillo, "Popular Entertainment in the Trades: A Case Study of the *New York Clipper* and the *New York Dramatic Mirror,*" in *Performing Arts Resources,* edited by Barbara Naomi Cohen-Stratyner (New York: Theatre Library Association, 1989), pp. 59–68.

Lester Rodney

(17 April 1911 -   )

Robert Klein

MAJOR POSITIONS HELD: Sports reporter, sports columnist, sports editor, *Daily Worker* (1936–1942, 1946–1957); feature writer, religion editor, special sections editor, *Santa Monica Evening Outlook* (1958–1959); publicity director and copywriter, Stiller-Hunt Advertising Agency (1960–1963); feature writer, copyeditor, religion editor, *Long Beach Independent Press-Telegram* (1964–1974).

BOOKS: *The First Book of Baseball,* as Benjamin Brewster (New York: Watts, 1950);
The Real Book about Baseball, as Lyman Hopkins (Garden City, N.Y.: Doubleday, 1951).

SELECTED PERIODICAL PUBLICATIONS–UNCOLLECTED: "The Long Hard Road to Mediocrity," *Negro Digest,* 13 (June 1964): 10–15;
"Managers Play Musical Chairs," *In These Times,* 4–19 April 1979, p. 19;
"Here's a Lonely Vote Against Boycotting the Olympics," *Long Beach Independent Press-Telegram,* 18 February 1980;
"Race-ball: The Front-Office Shuffle," *In These Times,* 29 April–5 May 1987, p. 19.

Lester Rodney (Daily Worker *photo by ART*)

Writing from the often reviled podium of the *Daily Worker,* the newspaper of the American Communist Party, Lester Rodney played an important part in ending racial segregation in professional and amateur baseball in the United States. In the process he changed the focus of the daily newspaper sports section, which tended to be removed from life beyond the stadium turnstiles, making it an advocate for change in what at the time was the American "National Pastime." As a reporter, columnist, and the founding sports editor of the *Worker,* a position he held for seventeen years, Rodney insistently appealed to major-league owners and Americans at large to allow black players to play professionally alongside white players. His career, perhaps like that of no other sportswriter, was inextricably connected to the fortunes and impact of his newspaper. During his tenure, his efforts and those of the sports section of the *Worker* were synonymous.

Always keen to illuminate the alleged capitalist constraints on minorities and the working class, the *Worker* was already decrying the injustice of racial segregation in baseball prior to Rodney's arrival in August 1936. His aggressive advocacy ultimately found expression, albeit in less-radical form, on both the editorial and sports pages of the establishment newspapers around the nation.

A second-generation American, Lester Rodney was born on 17 April 1911, the third of four children born to New Yorkers Isabelle Cotton and Max Rodney. His father, a staunch Republican, peddled automotive parts after losing his job as a silk salesman at the beginning of the Depression. "We were the first house on the block," Rodney told Paul Buhle and Michael Fermanowsky in 1984, "with a black-bordered picture in the window: 'We mourn our loss, Warren Gamaliel Harding.'" When Rodney was six years old, he and his family moved from Manhattan to the Bensonhurst section of Brooklyn, where he graduated from New Utrecht High School in 1929. That same year, within a matter of weeks, Rodney's eleven-year-old younger brother, Ira, was struck and killed by a truck while roller-skating with friends in the street, and Rodney's father's firm closed.

With income at a low ebb, Isabelle Rodney was forced to resume her millinery work, opening a shop in Newark, New Jersey, and commuting daily from her apartment in Brooklyn. The resulting decline in family finances prevented young Rodney from matriculating at Syracuse University, where he had been offered a partial track scholarship. Other than several night courses in journalism, sociology, and political science in 1930 and 1931 at New York University, he never re-enrolled in college. During the day he worked at different times as a chauffeur and shipping clerk.

Typical for an urban youngster, Rodney played a fair amount of street ball while growing up. While in high school, he told Buhle and Fermanowsky, he "ran on the best track team in the city" and in his senior year played basketball. He also did occasional assignments for the *Brooklyn Daily Eagle,* covering school sports. His greatest thrill as a youth, he said, came in the form of a surprise gift from his parents on his thirteenth birthday–a coveted Opening Day, reserved-seat ticket for a lower box at Ebbets Field, home of his beloved Dodgers. "I was the first kid there. I was there before they came out for batting practice."

In 1935, having taken a look at the *Daily Worker* "out of curiosity" and increasingly interested in the social issues of the day, Rodney wrote a letter to the editors of the paper "just modestly suggesting how to improve their sports section and the importance of it, and I made the mistake of having a return address. I immediately was summoned in," he told Buhle and Fermanowsky. The management of the *Daily Worker* worried at first about the political appropriateness of regular sports reporting in a paper with limited space and an emphasis on ideology. It also rigorously questioned the attraction it would have for the readers. Despite their misgivings, the editors agreed to run weekly sports reports by Rodney on a trial basis. When Rodney's reports resulted in an immediate boost in interest and circulation, they offered him a full-time position.

Shortly before Rodney started full-time with the *Daily Worker* in autumn 1936, the paper ran a poll to determine whether its readership even wanted a daily sports section. The recognition of the impact sports was having on the masses was already measurable nationally in newspaper column inches. By the 1920s sports sections had become a standard part of the major dailies, doubling the page allotment typical thirty years earlier, with baseball, according to Benjamin Rader, occupying much of that space. The poll results–"to the astonishment of many people," Rodney told Buhle and Fermanowsky, were six-to-one in favor of a column.

Still, there were those who professed skepticism. Heywood Broun, a former sportswriter and popular Scripps-Howard daily columnist at the time, was one. "The *Daily Worker* has begun a sports section," he advised, according to Rodney in his interview with Buhle and Fermanowsky. "It will be interesting to observe what happens, because, so far as I know, you can't class-angle a box score."

Rodney, who at first was paid $12 a week, early on understood both the opportunity and challenge his paper and its readership presented. Composed to a large extent of Europeans, many of them recent Scandinavian and Jewish immigrants, they found at least one American passion–competitive sports–as bewildering as the language. At first inadvertently, then with conscious effort, the sports stories in the *Worker,* through the filter of such decidedly American activities as baseball, boxing, and college basketball, became daily guideposts to assimilation for many of its readers. The owner of the Workers Book Shop on Thirteenth Street in Manhattan, Rose Barron, once told Rodney: "You know, I don't know from baseball, I don't know from football, but I know this is a wonderful thing you're making. . . . You're helping us to be American."

The *Worker* sports section was in fact something of a misnomer. In the early years especially, and later during the politically constricting times of the Korean War, it often consisted of the back page only. At its height it never exceeded three pages, and even that largesse was infrequent. Under Rodney's leadership, however, those pages provided a service both more enduring and less sectarian for its readers, many of whom were still perplexed by or openly antagonistic to certain national customs. At first emphasizing industrial and union league play–the leagues in which his readers directly participated–Rodney soon shifted focus when it became clear that his readership also craved information about mainstream sports and ballplayers.

Rodney in the dugout with New York Yankees third baseman Red Rolfe in September 1938, discussing Rodney's idea to have Rolfe write about the upcoming World Series against the Chicago Cubs for the Daily Worker

Rodney saw to it that stories about the major leagues began to share space with reporting on the recreational, but competitive, athletic activities of unions, fraternal organizations, and similar labor-oriented groups. The continuing advocacy in the paper of trade-union sports included daily coverage of, among other things, the Trade Union Athletic Association sponsorship of soccer, baseball, and basketball leagues throughout the city. In short, Rodney's *Worker* was steadfast in its parallel coverage of both participant and spectator sports, offering a calibrated balance based on the perceived needs and interests of its readers.

Rodney's sports section and columns were knowledgeable and reader-friendly, and he went out of his way to develop an easy familiarity with his constituents. In 1938 he was able to get popular Yankee third baseman Red Rolfe to write an article after each World Series game in which he played that October. It was a coup of sorts, the first time a New York City daily had turned over space to a professional athlete. At the time sports figures generally were considered semiliterate louts, able to communicate only through the intermediary of a sportswriter, if at all. "The idea of giving a ball player the stature of presenting his own ideas, that was the real root of it," Rodney told Buhle and Fermanowsky. Rolfe, an independent-thinking, "tough New England democrat with a small *d*" and a Dartmouth College graduate, was an immediate success as a correspondent.

By the simple expedient of exposing its hypocrisy and inherent unfairness, Rodney underscored the incoherence and inconsistency of not allowing black ballplayers onto major-league baseball fields. He noted in an early report on African American football standouts that other major sports had already been integrated. At the end of the impassioned piece–published 2 October 1936, two months after Rodney joined the *Worker* full-time–he pleaded: "Boxing, track and field, and now football. When will the ridiculous discrimination against Negro baseball stars be lifted?"

In late 1937 Rodney printed a challenge from Leroy "Satchel" Paige, the great and colorful Negro

League pitcher, who was essentially ignored by the white press. Less than a month before the Yankees overwhelmed the New York Giants four games to one in the World Series, Paige attempted through Rodney to arrange a one-game meeting between the powerhouse Yankees, led by Lou Gehrig and Joe DiMaggio, and Paige's Negro All-Stars at Yankee Stadium. If the major leaguers won, Paige and his teammates would not have to be paid. The effrontery of Paige's dare diminished considerably in Rodney's mind, he said in the *Daily Worker* (16 September 1937), when compared to "the unwritten Jim Crow restriction that keeps him and other Negro ballplayers from their rightful place in America's National Pastime." The offer was never taken up. The challenge, Rodney explained, "was made with a quiet confidence backed by the records."

Rodney's reporting and regular column, "On the Score Board," were eclectic and informed. He gained recognition for his consistent attention to the harsh environment of professional boxing, college football violence, and basketball betting scandals, in addition to baseball integration. He was known for researching the facts before printing them. Nor did he neglect his primary obligation to the everyday fan. New York manager Leo Durocher once told Rodney in the Giants dugout, "For a . . . communist, you know your baseball."

"There were sports fans whose antipathy to the Communist party was as fervid as their devotion to the Brooklyn Dodgers, their beloved Bums," wrote Rodney's former *Daily Worker* colleague Bernard Burton in the introduction to the Buhle and Fermanowsky interview. "But in my neighborhood, during the baseball season, they would wait with three pennies in hand, and later a nickel, to purchase a copy of the *Daily* as soon as it hit the stands. Brooklyn could be up in flames on the front page, but the only thing that mattered to the sports nuts was Rodney's choices on the other side of the paper."

In May 1942 Rodney formally joined the fight against fascism, eventually serving with the Army's Fifty-second Field Hospital for thirty-two months in the South Pacific. He attained the rank of sergeant. Upon his return in 1946 he was joined on the *Worker* sports page by Nat Low and Bill Mardo. Both Low, who edited the sports section while Rodney was overseas, and Mardo shared the same crusading intensity against injustice and discrimination in sports as did Rodney. Their presence briefly enabled Rodney to turn his attentions elsewhere, including a stint in Washington, D.C., where he covered U.S. Senate hearings on returning black veterans. "In fact, I got a little tired of doing sports," he told Buhle and Fermanowsky. "You know, the big fight"–meaning the integration of baseball–"was won."

In his 1947 New Year's column, his first after returning from the war–written a little more than three months before Jackie Robinson's historic first game at Ebbets Field–Rodney offered his readers the wish that the coming year would see "a few more good, hard body blows to lingering un-American discrimination on the sports field–and, of course, a pennant for the Dodgers." Rodney, in his soft, unpretentious prose, never let injustice go unchallenged, but he always remained a fan.

Rodney's position on segregation in baseball was clearly and uncompromisingly articulated. Because of the comparatively low circulation and unpopular politics of the *Worker,* however, his role as one of the first to excoriate in print the sixteen club owners for their racial intransigence was only belatedly recognized. "His finest effort was his pioneering work to break the Jim Crow barriers in major league baseball," wrote Burton. "His unremitting and gratifying crusade to win a berth on the Dodgers for Jackie Robinson, the first black player to be accepted in the big leagues, is now part of baseball and civil rights lore."

Historian Jules Tygiel, who wrote *Baseball's Great Experiment: Jackie Robinson and His Legacy* (1983), perhaps the definitive account of Robinson's entry into organized baseball in 1946 and the major leagues in 1947, documents Rodney's tenacious efforts to publicize (and unabashedly politicize) Robinson's difficulties as well as his progress. Rodney and the *Worker,* Tygiel argues, have been unfairly overlooked regarding the beneficial effects their reportorial and political coverage had on the integration of baseball, especially during the decade or so leading up to Robinson's barrier-breaking season. His contribution was recognized by at least some of his peers at the time, however, if surreptitiously. The day the announcement was made that Robinson would join the Dodgers for the 1947 season, two veteran sportswriters, Dick Young of the *Daily News* and Jim Becker of the Associated Press, quietly approached Rodney and confided: "You can be proud of this."

Still, unwarranted restrictions to full participation in any athletic venue, whether based on race or economic status, continued to draw his ire, and in short order Rodney was back on the sports beat. Echoing his earlier reportorial and personal concerns, he now decried the loss of opportunity for the amateur participant, viewing him as yet another in a long line of disenfranchised American citizens. The measure of his dismay is clear in a 28 March 1949 column, published just prior to the opening of the major-league baseball season. "Outside of a few sections in Queens, the empty lot usable as a ball field is a thing of the past":

First Magnate Adds Voice to Managers, Players

Benswanger, in Answer to 'Daily' Says, 'I Would Be Heartily in favor of It'—Long Campaign Coming to Head

By Lester Rodney

The first big league magnate has spoken out in favor of admitting Negro baseball players to the game!

The President of the Pittsburgh Pirates of the National League, William E. Benswanger, in response to a query from the Daily Worker, says:

"If the question of admitting colored baseball players into organized baseball becomes an issue I would be heartily in favor of it.

"I think the Negro people should have an opportunity in baseball just as they have an opportunity in music or anything else."

This simple statement by a big league owner, the first of its kind, follows the rapidly mounting flood tide of similar statements by big league managers and players themselves, a tide which threatens to rip away the last flimsy excuses for continuing the shameful discrimination against Negro players in our National Pastime.

Already Managers Bill McKechnie, Leo Durocher and Doc Prothro of the National League have named Negro players with the ability to star in the big leagues, and have said bluntly that they would be glad to sign some of them if given permission by the magnates.

In the American League, Managers Haney and Baker have vouched for the fact that there are many Negro stars qualified for big league play, and that the situation is entirely up to the owners.

Players too numerous to mention have expressed their admiration for the Negro players. Most of the big leaguers have played with Negro stars in after the season exhibition games, and know their calibre.

And now, as the campaign ...

... the Negro stars and there was an unwritten agreement between the individual club owners.

With sensational statement by Bill McKechnie that he "knew at least 25 Negro stars good enough," and would "hire some if given permission," the campaign caught fire last month, and was followed rapidly by other clean cut statements by managers and players.

Benswanger's statement is another step forward. "If it becomes and issue . . ." says the Pittsburgh owner. It's becoming the livest issue in the American sports world today and Benswanger has put himself on the side of the overwhelming majority who want an end to an un-American relic of discrimination in our National Pastime.

SPORTS DAILY WORKER

NEW YORK, MONDAY, AUGUST 7, 1939

TWU Upsets Cobblers in TUAA Baseball

Cleaners Continue Title Defense with Win; IWO Trumphs

Freed from worries about the weather, the Trade Union Athletic Association's city championship baseball tournament sailed through the quarter-final round over the weekend with one upset marking the goings on.

The Transport Workers Union, in the quarter-finals after replaying their protested contest with the Red Caps, came through with a surprise victory over the highly touted United Shoe Workers nine by an 8-4 margin.

Last year's titlists, the Cleaners and Dyers, knocked over their strongest rival to continue towards what may be their second successive championship when they defeated the United Wholesale Employees, 4-1.

In the other encounter yesterday, the International Workers Order Blue Sox soundly trounced the Textile Workers Organizing Committee, 10-4. The American Communications Association entered the semi-finals with a quarter-final victory last week.

Fite Schedule For Week

MONDAY

Dexter Park—Yucatan Kid vs. Maurice Arnault, Jack Tolson vs. Vincent Pimpi-...

Buddy's Back in Brooklyn

BUDDY HASSETT, the Bronx Thrush, returns to Brooklyn tonight when the Boston Bees face the Dodgers under the arc lights. Buddy was traded to the Beantowners last winter, and has been holding down first base at National League Park in grand style.

Dodgers Beat Reds, 5-0, Drop 2nd, 8-6

Score Five Times Off Derringer in Last Frame of Opener

CINCINNATI, Aug. 6. — After pouncing on Paul Derringer in the ninth inning of the first game of today's double-header to break up a scoreless pitcher's battle, the Brooklyn Dodgers almost, but not quite, won the nightcap, losing out to the league-leading Reds in the closing innings by an 8-6 count.

The split gives them an even break for the four game series with the Reds and eight victories in fifteen games on the road, their most successful trip West this year.

Luke Hamlin and Derringer toiled away on the mound in the first game, Luke winning out for his twelfth victory in twenty-one decisions while Derringer became the owner of his sixth loss as against fourteen wins.

Until the ninth, Hamlin had given up three hits and Derringer five, both flingers getting themselves out of tight spots with remarkable ease.

But in the final frame Derringer met his Waterloo. Camilli opened the inning with a single, and Phelps and Koy immediately followed suit for one run. Durocher forced Koy at second and Hamlin fouled to Werber, but Hudson doubled off the center-field wall, Lavagetto lined a single to center and Walker tripled ...

Page from the Communist Party newspaper, with Rodney article

On some Saturday or Sunday afternoons and on an occasional week night, these guys who love to play ball and now never get around to it and can't find a place and a group to play with, will pay a buck twenty five apiece and from the grandstands of Ebbets Field, the Polo Grounds and the Yankee Stadium will fade back wistfully and vicariously with Joe DiMaggio for a long fly, make the deep throw from the hole between short and third with Peewee Reese, lay into a fast ball shoulder high with Whitey Lockman.

"It's a wonderful game, big-league baseball," he finishes, "the best money's worth professional sports has to offer." Rodney was keenly aware, though, that sports were slowly becoming less for participants and more for spectators and consumers.

Not all of Rodney's attention was directed to the ball field or other sports arenas, however. During the 1950s United States and Soviet antagonism had spawned a pervasive anticommunist sentiment in the United States. Those formerly associated with the *Daily Worker,* and many others, felt the pressure in the form of lost jobs and curtailed liberties. In 1950, unable to get a contract using his own name and with the interceding of a friend in the publishing business, Rodney published *The First Book of Baseball* under the pseudonym "Benjamin Brewster." In 1951, buoyed by the success of his first book, he discreetly inquired about writing a book on baseball for the popular Doubleday/Franklin Watts series, "The Real Book About . . . ," well-researched, authoritative volumes designed to expose young people to a wide range of fields of interest. Using the name "Lyman Hopkins," Rodney wrote *The Real Book about Baseball.*

Affecting a familiar, conversational style laced with basic facts about the sport, Rodney introduces the reader to the rules of batting, base-running, and each defensive position. He also cleverly weaves in pieces of Americana not normally found in sports books of the time, but which adult readers of the seasoned *Worker* sports columnist had by now come to expect from him:

> Americans of all kinds become big league stars, playing side by side in harmony and with team work. Here are some examples: Frank Malzone and Yogi Berra are of Italian descent. Stan Musial and Ray Narleski are of Polish descent. Sandy Koufax and Saul Rogovin are Jewish. Brooks Lawrence and Hank Aaron are Negroes. Ed Mathews and Johnny O'Brien are of Irish descent. Billy Loes and Lou Skizas are of Greek descent.

He also points out that Bobby Thompson was born in Scotland, Minnie Minoso in Cuba, and Chico Carresquel in Venezuela. "A game with this kind of democracy at its heart has something to teach, something to give to the country," he concludes. Years later, Rodney remarks with a touch of irony, "America being what it is, it [the book] outsold the others [in the series] 3-to-1." It was successful enough to be republished in 1958, with a revised edition in 1962.

Baseball was not the only sport where fair play and equal opportunity were an issue at the time, however. Basketball, long an accessible venue for many first-generation East European city-dwellers, was quietly outstripping its small-time status and suffering from growing pains. In the late 1940s college basketball was increasingly played in major sports arenas such as Madison Square Garden in New York instead of the small gyms of public and private colleges. Gambling money was also becoming a factor in the sport, and Rodney was one of the first to address its corrosive influence.

Three years before a major betting scandal devastated some of the best basketball (and academic) schools in the country, Rodney used his 14 January 1948 column to write an open letter to the editors of *Campus,* the student paper of the City College of New York. He points out that, aside from the four years he was away at war, he had been watching and reporting basketball from the Garden ever since it opened in 1925. "I think I have a good idea of what's going on," he writes. "What I know is that the kids who play the game are overwhelmingly honest and detest this stuff just as much as you and I." Combining, as always, advocacy and reportage, Rodney advises the students to "make some demands for guaranteed student priority on all tickets, including the ones that now go to the big time operators." "Fight the thing," he admonishes, "don't run from it." In a subsequent piece, "The Scandal gets worse," Rodney condemns the "hypocritical official morality that breeds and complacently accepts the crass commercialization of our sports life, because it is profitable, [and] now comes down like a ton of bricks on these young culprits. They are finished, through."

In a 31 August 1950 *Daily Worker* piece on the barrier-breaking efforts of tennis player Althea Gibson, Rodney weaves together an informed narrative of the obstacles this young and talented newcomer had to confront in the summer of 1950 as the first African American in history to compete in the National Tennis Championships. Present in the article are his characteristically gentle, unerring reminders of the damaging effects of wrongs only recently righted and the inevitable restraints on human achievement they represent, as well as his sure grasp of the sport he is examining. Despite the "rapidity of her maturity toward greatness," Rodney tells his readers, Gibson's first major tournament appearance revealed certain weaknesses, flaws "she could undoubtedly get away with against non-top-notch competition." Deftly, Rodney reminds readers of the reality that was and its pernicious, lingering effects.

Rodney's vigilance sometimes led him to come to the defense of those who, once at the apex of their profession, had fallen out of favor with the general public, especially when he suspected racism was involved. When Jack Dempsey's credentials were exalted by some over those of African American heavyweight boxing champion Joe Louis, Rodney defended the "Brown Bomber" and in the process succinctly summed up the careers of a half-dozen of Louis's opponents, some members of the so-called Bum-of-the-Month Club and some champions. The busy Louis, he offers on 26 February 1952,

> guaranteed exposing himself to more styles than Dempsey ever had to solve. The back-pedalling Pastor, the jumping left hooker Galento, the rock-chinned Farr, the hammer-hitting Baer, the man mountain Simon, and, after the war, the clever and unorthodox Walcott. Characterize them as you will, they were the best there were and Louis took them on. And in the speedy, resourceful Billy Conn of 1941, Louis surely met at least as masterful a boxer as any Dempsey ever ran into, and knocked him out.

Nor, when it came to injustice, was Rodney reluctant to take on his fellow sportswriters, many of whom he saw as beholden to club owners and reluctant to write anything even remotely critical of them. In one memorable outburst he blasts sports columnist Milton Gross of the *New York Post,* the leading liberal paper in the city at the time. Gross "has a curious habit. Whenever he deals with the age of baseball players, he always picks out Negro players" while never speculating on the age of white players. He continued: "a player's age is one of the many factors holding down salaries. In the case of Negro players . . . , this is doubly harmful stuff to be writing."

Similarly, in a 7 February 1952 column Rodney excoriates the veteran *New York Times* Brooklyn Dodger beat reporter, Roscoe McGowen, for writing of Dodger pitching ace Don Newcombe "failing in the supreme

Head for Rodney's column in the Daily Worker *in 1947*

test" in the deciding game of the National League playoffs against the Giants in 1951. Why, Rodney asks, did McGowen ignore the "heroic" contributions a tired Newcombe made to his struggling team, while not being similarly critical of his white teammate, left-handed pitcher Preacher Roe? Brimming with indignation, Rodney takes the *Times* reporter to task. "The events of the final hectic week of the 1951 season are not so far in the past that the *Times* writer could possibly have forgotten. Which makes that sentence something less than fair to Newcombe. And that's certainly the best that can be said for it. The *Times* writer knows better. He was there."

In 1956 Rodney traveled to Italy to cover the seventh Winter Olympic Games in Cortina D'Ampezzo, the first winter Olympics in which athletes from the Soviet Union participated. His dispatches back to New York, marked "By Mail" in the dateline at the top of each story, are filled with interviews with American competitors "walking through the streets of this fairyland town." He made it clear that he saw the friendly competition among athletes from the thirty-three participating nations as a microcosm of the hoped-for relations internationally. He often placed the interviews in the context of peace and harmony among the participating nations. "I made a big point of covering it as an American sportswriter," he told Buhle and Fermanowsky about his personal pieces on such American champions as skier Art Devlin and figure skaters Tenley Albright and Dick Button.

In his final years at the *Worker* Rodney was sent on special assignments, occasionally taking him away from his editor's desk at the East Twelfth Street offices of the *Worker* in Manhattan. Increasingly he wrote about venues other than playing fields and athletic arenas. He remained dedicated to covering efforts at racial integration around the nation. In early December 1956, he traveled by bus to Clinton, Tennessee, to file two emotional stories on the turmoil surrounding the desegregation of the local high school under federal order. His next dispatch, a few days later, was from Montgomery, Alabama, where he reported on the observation of the first anniversary of the Montgomery bus boycott.

Rodney resigned from the *Daily Worker* and the Communist Party in 1957. On giving up sportswriting he was voted a lifetime honorary Baseball Writers Association of America member by his peers, "which is usual," he told Mark Naison in 1977, "but not automatic." In the spring of 1958 he and his wife, Clare, whom he had married in 1946 after leaving the service, and their two children, Amy and Ray, left their native New York City for California. By October he found a job as feature writer, religion editor, and editor of special sections for the *Santa Monica Evening Outlook*. No one bothered to check his credentials. "I said I worked for the Brooklyn *Eagle,* and they didn't even know that the Brooklyn *Eagle* had gone out of business." He also changed his name from Lester Rodney to Les Rodney–"which didn't fool the Red Squad attorney."

Rodney quickly established himself as a writer of merit, but left after fourteen months when he went to work for a Beverly Hills advertising agency. He stayed until 1963. For the next ten years, from 1964 until his retirement on the last day of 1974, Rodney wrote features for the *Long Beach Independent Press-Telegram*. During his stint there he garnered Pacific Coast Press Club awards in 1971 and 1973 for daily columns on religion and in 1972 for an op-ed piece on the Vietnam War. Also in 1973, Rodney was given the Bill Hunter Memorial Award for Excellence. A tennis devotee, Rodney also gained recognition as California's number-one player in the eighty-five-years-and-older division.

In the spring of 1997 Rodney was invited to attend a three-day gathering at Long Island University in Brooklyn honoring the fiftieth anniversary of Robinson's entry into major-league baseball. Reunited with Mardo, his sportswriting colleague at the *Worker,* and accorded a measure of recognition for his efforts ultimately enabling Robinson to break the color barrier, Rodney spoke forcefully of the baseball pioneer's impact beyond the ball field. Robinson's legacy "is not, 'Hooray, we did it!' but rather, 'Buddy, there is unfinished business out there.'" Considering the full sweep of Robinson's contribution, the black pioneer demonstrated that baseball "had an overriding importance in American life."

Mardo, in an unpublished letter (1 December 1997), calls his colleague "a consummate professional, sophisticated in style, committed in content. His major contribution will always be his significant role in the fight against Jim Crow in baseball." "I think Lester Rodney is one of the unsung heroes of the effort to integrate baseball," observes Robinson biographer David Falkner in the *Village Voice.* He notes that veteran black sportswriters such as Wendell Smith and Sam Lacy "are often cited, and justifiably so. But Lester Rodney and the *Worker* were at this all the way through the 1930s, and they never really let up." Longtime sportswriter Stan Isaacs adds, in the November 1977 *Silurian News,* the publication of the oldest press club in the United States, "It is always heartwarming to see a somewhat unsung figure get the credit that long has been due him."

"Rodney was more interested in seeing justice done for African-Americans than in just seeing better baseball," contends sports historian Kelly E. Rusinack. He "helped to further legitimize sports as a social concern, and purposely gave a voice to the opinions of athletes formerly considered to be stupid and shallow. . . . Rodney's efforts, sincerity and fair reporting earned him the respect of athletes he interviewed, as well as of other journalists, black and white." His output can thus be measured in impact, not column inches–though his writing filled many of those.

Lester Rodney's recipe for sports reporting is inclusive and straightforward:

> Don't talk down to fans, don't be afraid or ashamed to thrill to the excitement of a classic double play in a close game or an 80-yard run from scrimmage helped by a perfect downfield block. There is not the slightest contradiction in being a sports fan and in being angry at whatever and whoever distorts sports and sportsmanship. On the contrary.

Taken in total, Rodney's writing humanized the athletes, neither overstating their accomplishments nor patronizing them for their public acclaim. Serving up a kind of commonsense advocacy journalism, he operated on the basis that the ills of the sports world were part and parcel of the myriad indecencies and hurts perpetrated beyond the ball field. And, he insisted, neither those ills nor the athletes themselves were larger than life or unmanageable.

Interview:

Paul Buhle and Michael Fermanowsky, "Baseball and Social Conscience," Oral History Program, University of California at Los Angeles, 1984.

References:

Peter Duffy, "Red Rodney–The American Communist Who Helped Liberate Baseball," *Village Voice,* 10 June 1997, p. 122;

Mark Naison, "Sports for the (Daily) Worker," *In These Times,* 12–18 October 1977, pp. 12–14;

Benjamin Rader, *Baseball: A History of America's Game* (Urbana & Chicago: University of Illinois Press, 1992);

Kelly E. Rusinack, "Baseball on the Radical Agenda: The *Daily* and *Sunday Worker* Journalistic Campaign to Desegregate Major League Baseball, 1933 to 1947," in *Jackie Robinson: Race, Sports, and the American Dream,* edited by Joseph Dorinson and Joram Warmund (Armonk, N.Y.: M. E. Sharpe, 1998);

Jules Tygiel, *Baseball's Great Experiment: Jackie Robinson and His Legacy* (New York: Vintage, 1983), pp. 36–37;

D. Q. Voigt, "Reflections on Diamonds: American Baseball and American Culture," *Journal of Sports History,* 1 (Spring 1974): 3–25.

Harold Rosenthal

(11 March 1914 - 29 June 1999)

Richard Orodenker
Penn State Abington

MAJOR POSITIONS HELD: Reporter, columnist, *New York Herald Tribune* (1945–1966); managing editor, *Weekend Sports* (1976–1977); columnist, *New York City Tribune* (1978–1990); columnist, *College and Pro Football Newsweekly* (1978–1998).

BOOKS: *Baseball's Best Managers* (New York: Thomas Nelson, 1961);

The Big Play: Exciting and Dramatic Plays from the Big Games of the NFL That Made or Broke Champions (New York: Random House, 1965);

Playing Pro Football to Win, by Rosenthal and Johnny Unitas (Garden City, N.Y.: Doubleday, 1968; revised edition, New York: Signet, 1971);

Training the High School Athlete, by Rosenthal, Allan Levy, and Allen Webb (Chicago: Contemporary, 1975);

505 Football Questions Your Friends Can't Answer (New York: Walker, 1978);

505 Baseball Questions Your Friends Can't Answer (New York: Walker, 1979);

The Ten Best Years of Baseball: An Informal History of the Fifties (Chicago: Contemporary, 1979);

The Yankees: The Four Fabulous Eras of Baseball's Most Famous Team, by Rosenthal, Dave Anderson, Bob Creamer, and Murray Chass (New York: Random House, 1979);

Fifty Faces of Football (New York: Atheneum, 1981);

Sportsquiz: For Diehard Baseball and Football Fans (New York: Van Nostrand Reinhold, 1983).

OTHER: "Return of the 'Verce,'" in *Best Sports Stories 1945: A Panorama of the 1944 Sports Year,* edited by Irving T. Marsh and Edward Ehre (New York: Dutton, 1945), pp. 189–190;

"A Grim Fairy Tale," in *Best Sports Stories 1947: A Panorama of the 1946 Sports Year,* edited by Marsh and Ehre (New York: Dutton, 1947), pp. 266–268;

"One World Champion," in *Best Sports Stories 1948: A Panorama of the 1947 Sports Year,* edited by Marsh and Ehre (New York: Dutton, 1948), pp. 164–166;

Harold Rosenthal

Baseball Is Their Business, edited by Rosenthal (New York: Random House, 1952);

"The Ten Months That Shook the Boxing World," in *Best Sports Stories 1953: A Panorama of the 1952 Sports Year,* edited by Marsh and Ehre (New York: Dutton, 1953), pp. 194–201;

"Athletic Revolution," in *Best Sports Stories 1954: A Panorama of the 1953 Sports Year,* edited by Marsh and Ehre (New York: Dutton, 1954), pp. 117–120;

"End for the Yankees," in *Best Sports Stories 1955: A Panorama of the 1954 Sports Year,* edited by Marsh and Ehre (New York: Dutton, 1955), pp. 56–58;

"Farm Boss with a Green Thumb," in *Best Sports Stories 1956: A Panorama of the 1955 Sports Year,* edited by

Marsh and Ehre (New York: Dutton, 1956), pp. 86–95;

"An Important Occasion," in *Wake up the Echoes, from the Sports Pages of the New York Herald Tribune,* by Bob Cooke (Garden City, N.Y.: Hanover House, 1956), pp. 161–163;

"The Uniquest Job," in *Best Sports Stories 1957: A Panorama of the 1956 Sports Year,* edited by Marsh and Ehre (New York: Dutton, 1957), pp. 277–280;

"Old Case," in *Best Sports Stories 1958: A Panorama of the 1957 Sports Year,* edited by Marsh and Ehre (New York: Dutton, 1958), pp. 100–102;

"Locker Room," in *Best Sports Stories 1959: A Panorama of the 1958 Sports Year,* edited by Marsh and Ehre (New York: Dutton, 1959), pp. 88–97;

"Hail, and Farewell, Henry," in *Best Sports Stories 1962: A Panorama of the 1961 Sports Year,* edited by Marsh and Ehre (New York: Dutton, 1962), pp. 104–105;

"The Last Bell," in *Best Sports Stories 1964: A Panorama of the 1963 Sports Year,* edited by Marsh and Ehre (New York: Dutton, 1964), pp. 165–167;

"The Colts Are Corraled," in *Best Sports Stories 1965: A Panorama of the 1964 Sports Year,* edited by Marsh and Ehre (New York: Dutton, 1965), pp. 142–143;

Sports All Stars 1966, Baseball, edited by Rosenthal (New York: Maco Magazine, 1966);

"Casey Stegel, The Successful Manger," in *The Realm of Sport,* edited by Herbert Warren Wind (New York: Simon & Schuster, 1966), pp. 80–89;

"Poppa Bear," in *Best Sports Stories 1966: A Panorama of the 1965 Sports Year,* edited by Marsh and Ehre (New York: Dutton, 1966), pp. 86–88;

"Sunny Jim Bottomley," in *The Third Fireside Book of Baseball,* by Charles Einstein (New York: Simon & Schuster, 1968), pp. 396–397;

American Football League Official History, 1960–1969, compiled by the Elias Sports Bureau edited by Rosenthal (St. Louis: Sporting News, 1970);

William B. Mead, *10 Worst Years of Baseball: The Zany, True Story of Baseball in the Forties,* conclusion by Rosenthal (New York: Van Nostrand Reinhold, 1982).

The golden age of sports was perhaps the only event Harold Rosenthal missed in the twentieth century. He was there for just about everything else. He started writing when Jack Kramer and Bobby Riggs were on the tennis circuit in the early 1930s, and he was there in 1997 to write the Super Bowl XXXII essay for the official program booklet (had Super Bowl I failed, Rosenthal mused, "January might as well be missing one Sunday"). Rosenthal was at the top of the sportswriting game during its own golden age in the period just after World War II, and he was for years one of the stalwart figures in Stanley Woodward's sports department at the *New York Herald Tribune.* Although television and computers changed the way fans absorbed their sports entertainment, as well as the way sportswriters wrote their prose, Rosenthal never parted ways with the written word, or his manual typewriter, on which he continued to write letters and articles until shortly before his death in 1999.

Born in Harlem on 11 March 1914 to Jonas and Charlotte Morris Rosenthal, Harold Rosenthal grew up in the South Bronx. His paternal grandfather, Herschel Rosendale, had immigrated to America from Alsace-Lorraine, just in time to go into the Union Army. He returned from the war to settle in the largely German American settlement of Yorkville and changed the family name to Rosenthal, "causing me," quipped Rosenthal in an unpublished interview shortly before his death, "to be sent around to the freight entrance at the Racquet and Tennis Club and some of the better scum-holes of the thirties." Both his grandfather and father were newspaper printers, or "pressmen," and strong union men from whom Rosenthal picked up his liberal bent, which, he said, he "carried alternately as a burden and a prop." Jonas Rosenthal, who died at age forty-eight, was a heavy drinker, a fact that helped Rosenthal avoid alcoholism.

Rosenthal cared little for academics and spent more time in the public library than at school. Throughout his life Rosenthal remained proud of the fact that he was a self-educated man. "Early I learned the value of the printed word, not so much from teachers as from my own burrowing indiscriminately on shelf after shelf of all kinds of offerings–humor, fiction, science, travel biography. . . . I never made college. Instead I read as much as a college instructor and his pupil combined."

As a boy he was not particulary good at sports and followed them only casually. He lived within walking distance of Yankee Stadium, where he watched Red Grange play football. He attended Morris High School in the Bronx and helped support his family by often furnishing several New York newspapers with results from Morris High baseball games, although he had no idea how to keep a box score. He did try out to play high-school football (at age fifteen he weighed nearly 155 pounds) but was cut from the team. When the coach asked him to try playing again as a senior, Rosenthal had to refuse so he could continue working as a correspondent to help his family. He earned five dollars a week at the time. Among his early associations in the field of sportswriting were Arthur E. (Red) Patterson, who was then covering school sports for the *Herald Tri-*

Rosenthal interviewing Brooklyn Dodgers manager Leo Durocher in 1947 (photograph by James Kavallines, New York Herald Tribune*)*

bune; Shirley Povich, columnist and sports editor for the *Washington Post;* and Henry Super of United Press International (UPI).

Rosenthal finally graduated high school well behind his old class, but in his last semester he won a gold medal for a citywide essay competition on what the opening of the George Washington Bridge would mean to people on both sides of the Hudson River. Rosenthal's father was less than supportive of his son's writing award. "It took my father one year to sneak it out of the house and have it melted down," Rosenthal recalled.

Throughout the 1930s Rosenthal worked as a space writer, mostly at the *Herald Tribune* and UPI, which had its headquarters in New York. Working "on space" meant one was paid for what one wrote, provided the paper used it. Rosenthal first covered such small sporting events as public-park tennis championships and swim meets. He hung on in that fashion for almost ten years, marrying Alice, from Poughkeepsie, New York, on 25 December 1941. They had two children, Jonas and Jane Ann.

Rosenthal went into the United States Army Air Force on 3 October 1942 and was honorably discharged on 5 December 1945 at a sergeant's rank. He saw limited service because of poor circulation in his legs and bad vision and worked mainly in supply, including the Office of the Air Communications Officer in the Pentagon. In his last six months of service he was detached to serve as assistant managing editor of the weekly *Bolling Field Beam,* across from the Pentagon, although he worked most of the time as a clerk-typist.

Rosenthal seriously considered staying in Washington, D.C., to work on one of the four newspapers there. But Woodward offered him a half-desk, half-reporter job at the *New York Herald Tribune,* which also paid an extra twenty dollars a week. "He could always spring me from the desk," Rosenthal later said, "for an assignment like the time Happy Chandler suspended Leo Durocher for a year or a blow-by-blow on one of the Joe Louis title defenses." Rosenthal remained indebted to Woodward. "Highly overqualified for the job of sports editor, he should have been *running* a newspaper," Rosenthal told Timothy Quinlan in a 1987 interview. "But he was a great newspaper man."

Rosenthal covered basketball and football in his long career as a sportswriter and occasionally reported on fencing as well as the national handball playoffs, having played that sport as a boy. Mostly he gravitated toward baseball, however. "At the time," Rosenthal told Bob Kurkland in a 12 December 1970 interview in *The Sporting News,* "myself, Dick Young, and Jack Lang were looked on as the rebels of sportswriters by the old-timers." He first covered the New York Giants baseball club and then became the beat writer for the Dodgers in the late 1940s. Rosenthal did not always enjoy traveling with the Dodgers, whom he covered for five years. The "assignment . . . should have come right out of St. Peter's roll-call book, but there were the exacerbations that went with taking a couple of infant kids to a strange environment," he later said.

Rosenthal believed in a sportswriter's ability to cover a variety of events by tailoring his presentation of them to fit their format. "The main thing in covering athletics," he told Quinlan, "is that you have to adjust to the philosophies of the different sports you are writing about. When a person plays golf, he's playing against himself. When you play baseball you're part of a unit trying to beat another unit. So, a writer has got to bring an understanding to all the different sports of the *philosophies* of each and how they are different." His own philosophy of sportswriting enabled him to cover such events as the 1946 Boston A. A. Marathon, won by a "Greek who starved all through the German occupation in Athens and who flies over here two weeks before the race. . . . Then, to the vast mortification of assorted experts who had written him off merely as another fellow named Stylianos Kyriakides, the hero of the piece goes out and runs the field of more than 100 starters bandy-legged in 2 hours 29 minutes 27 seconds, not a Boston record, but a Greek national record."

In the mid 1940s Rosenthal began to write for major magazines, explaining later to Roger Kahn, "the *Herald Tribune* doesn't pay much." *The Saturday Evening Post* and *Pageant* ran his 1945 piece on prizefight announcer Harry Balogh, "The Return of the 'Verce.'" "The secret," Rosenthal wrote, "of the 'Verce's' charm lies in his ability to say the right thing at least twice, and if he's feeling good, three times." In 1947 Rosenthal became a correspondent for *The Sporting News,* for which he wrote for the next twenty years. During this time, according to Robert W. Creamer in *Stengel: His Life and Times* (1984), Rosenthal in May 1949 became the first baseball writer to appropriate the football term "platooning." Borrowing the notion of "two-platoon football" (football teams with defensive and offensive specialists), Rosenthal applied it to baseball to describe Yankee manager Casey Stengel moving his outfielders in and out of the lineup, depending upon the pitcher.

Rosenthal was never completely happy as a sportswriter. A lifelong philatelist, he "couldn't wait for the paper's stamp editor to take his annual two weeks so I could jump in and do the column and get first shot at the pretty new issues and maybe pilfer a few." He once conflated occupation with avocation, writing in *Sport,* "The imprint of baseball greatness is upon Mickey Mantle just as surely as the portrait of Thomas Jefferson graces the current three-cent stamp." He found himself humiliated by Casey Stengel on one occasion and by Leo Durocher on another, in which Durocher insulted him in front of other sportswriters for making too big a deal about Willie Mays's famous catch in the 1954 World Series. He experienced anti-Semitism from Burt Shotton, who called him "Rosenbloom" or "Rosenberg." "After that," Rosenthal told Kahn, "I never mentioned Shotton's name in the *Herald Tribune*. I'd write 'the Dodger manager' but not his name. A disservice to readers, perhaps, but that was how I felt." He thoroughly enjoyed filling in for Red Smith in June 1950 when the latter went on vacation, and Rosenthal wrote a "Views of Sport" column about a "seedy-looking bum" who followed the Dodgers into the Schenley Hotel in Pittsburgh and exclaimed, "'I got a dandy little drop and a great little upshot. I can strike out Kiner.'"

The early 1950s were professionally productive times for Rosenthal. He published major articles on Gil Hodges, Preacher Roe, and Don Newcombe in *The Saturday Evening Post.* In December 1952 *Boxing Life* published his feature piece on the rapid rise and fall of champion Hammerin' Henry Armstrong, who for a brief time in the 1930s held the world titles in the featherweight, welterweight, and lightweight divisions at once. He wrote: "if you're talking about fighters and sheer ability to destroy a foe within a rope-enclosed area and within the limitations imposed by society, it would be difficult indeed to name a man, past or present, better than Henry Armstrong at his peak during those ten months that rocked the boxing world." Rosenthal also wrote the cover story on baseball commissioner Happy Chandler for *True* in 1952. He covered sports for *Variety, The Saturday Review of Literature* from 1951 to 1957, and the *National Catholic Monthly* from 1956 to 1962. His first book, *Baseball Is Their Business* (1952), is a collection of essays he edited "to focus the spotlight on the jobs done by experts in each of ten fields of operation." These jobs included scouting, broadcasting, front-office administration, publicity, statistics, playing, umpiring, televising, reporting, and managing. As he wrote in his introduction to the book, Rosenthal "hoped this book will furnish renewed heart and determination to youngsters who haven't the requirements to rise to the top as players; for it shows them nine avenues that are open." The chapter "The Publicity Man" was written by his former mentor, Red Patterson. Rosenthal wrote end-

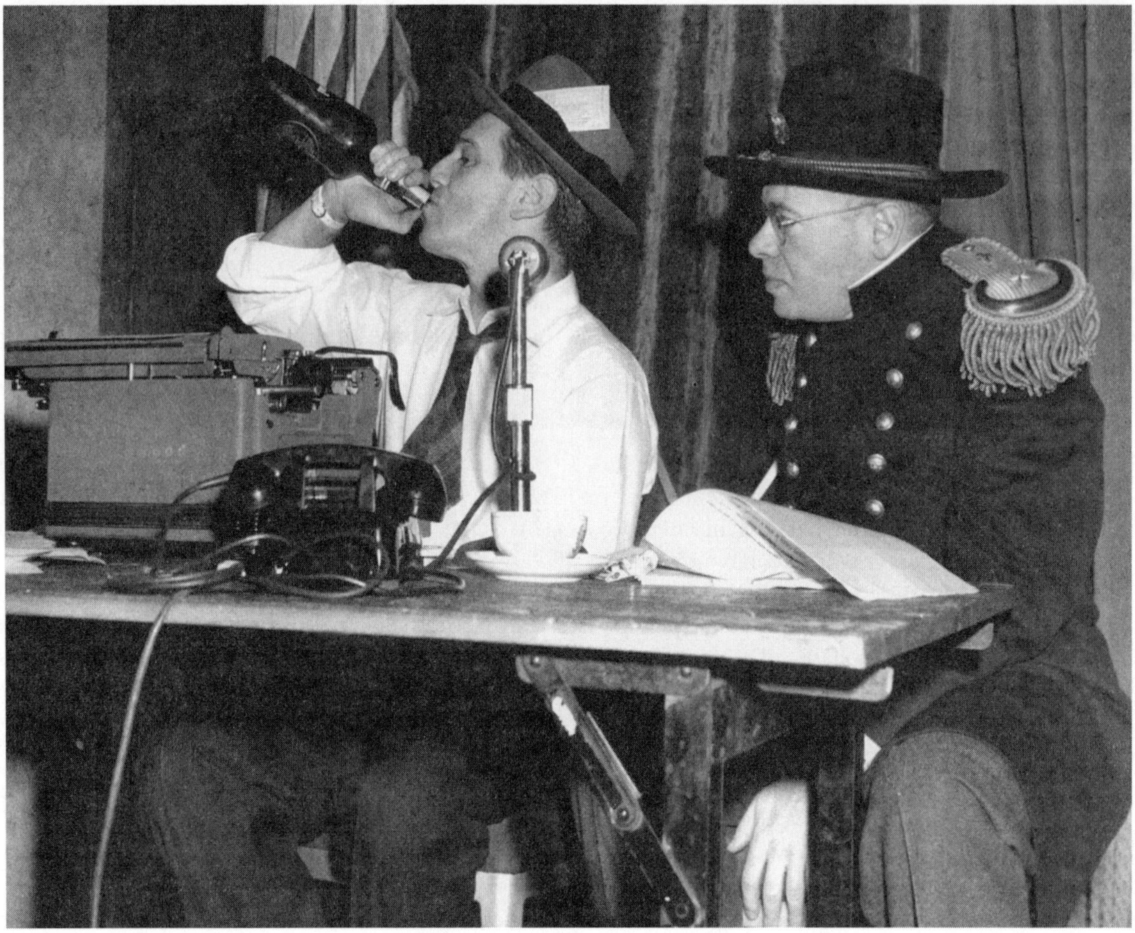

Rosenthal and Dick Young performing at the 1955 New York Baseball Writers Show (photograph by Jack Frank, New York Herald Tribune*)*

notes to each chapter, including an acute observation of Gil Hodges:

> One of the strongest men in baseball, Hodges has astounded people with his mild-manner, his affability, his easy-going attitude, and the fact that the strongest word he ever uses is 'gosh.' He doesn't fool those close to him, however. They know that underneath all this is a man of steel and whipcord, a man who has missed only one game in four years of playing first base for the Dodgers regularly.

By 1952 Rosenthal had tired of covering the Dodgers and walked away, he told Roger Kahn in *The Boys of Summer* (1972), "from the best sportswriting job in New York." Kahn, who assumed Rosenthal's old position as the Dodgers beat writer, remembered him as "a round, stooped man of thirty-eight, with crinkly brown hair and eyeglasses, respected at the Tribune for deft writing." At the *Herald Tribune* Rosenthal settled in as a "swing-man," covering the New York Yankees mostly at home while continuing to write for slick magazines that paid good money. In "Athletic Revolution," a 1953 piece he wrote for *The Sporting News* (reprinted in *Best Sports Stories 1954: A Panorama of the 1953 Sports Year*), he identified the emergence of African Americans as nothing short of "a revolution of No. 1 importance in baseball." Noting the tremendous number of successes of black players from "the upper echelons of organized Negro ball" to the same sandlots where white ballplayers had been discovered, Rosenthal mused on the trajectory that organized baseball had taken since Jackie Robinson broke the color barrier in 1947: "From open rebellion to universal acceptance in seven seasons is a staggering thought." He eschewed "any starry-eyed idealism on the part of some owners or the gate shenanigans of others," however. The black player represented "the only conceivable source of still-untapped talent . . . and talent is still the game's No. 1 concern."

Rosenthal credited senior sportswriters with influencing his variety of subject matter and style. "I paid attention to the older baseball writers like Fred Lieb and John Drebinger and Garry Schumacher, and Dan

Daniel," he noted in an unpublished interview, "and, of course, I automatically switched into cerebral 'record' when Casey Stengel would begin, 'Well, you'd hafta say . . .' so I was never at a loss for colorful material." Indeed, in a 31 August 1957 article for the *Herald Tribune,* Rosenthal wrote, "Substitute the word 'baseball' and you have Casey." Red Smith said of Rosenthal: "He never forgot a thing he heard."

Bob Cooke, who succeeded Woodward as sports editor of the *Herald Tribune,* included "An Important Occasion," a July 1955 Rosenthal piece on Joe DiMaggio's induction into the Baseball Hall of Fame, in his anthology of *Herald Tribune* articles, *Wake Up the Echoes* (1956). Rosenthal wrote in that particular piece that "DiMaggio also looked as though he could shed his severe black suit, the French cuffs with their gold links, fit carefully the black cap with the white 'NY' lettering in front on his gray flecked head, and step up to the plate. Probably could take a pretty good riffle, too." When the Cleveland Indians swept the Yankees in a doubleheader on 13 September 1954 and all but "swept the Yankee pennant hopes into the dustbin," Rosenthal focused on the staggering crowd of more than eighty-six thousand fans:

> And what a crowd it was! It consumed mountains of hot dogs, a lake of beer, tons of pop corn. It sprawled along the runways, where the best views furnished a glimpse of the infield and nothing else. It choked the runways in left and right field, where the patrons were rewarded with nothing more than a view of two or three outfielders. They never knew who was up at the plate. They merely stood, listened, and sweated . . . Sweating along with them were the Yankees, desperate in their knowledge that this was the end.

Cooke offered Rosenthal the assistant sports editor position, but Rosenthal told him, "I'm stupid but not crazy; no thanks." Despite his frequent weariness at work and the hours he put in, Rosenthal could write fondly of his job and looked back on it with much nostalgia throughout his life. In "The 'Uniquest Job,'" published in *Editor & Publisher* (4 August 1956) and collected in *Best Sports Stories 1957: A Panorama of the 1956 Sports Year,* Rosenthal wrote about what it meant to be a sportswriter:

> The job is certainly unique on a daily metropolitan paper. Seldom is a newspaperman required to develop a specialty to such a degree, and seldom is he rewarded with commensurate latitude in his writing. Seldom is he required to travel as much, seldom is he the target of an almost daily shower of incredibly hoary and envious barbs like, 'You mean they PAY you to watch baseball games?'

He was also, he recalled to Kurland, "a fixture in the annual New York Baseball Writers' show," where he did a deadpan imitation of Dodgers owner Walter O'Malley. "One year O'Malley was at the show," Rosenthal reminisced, "and he enjoyed the portrayal so much that he sent me some of his special cigar-holders to use the following year."

During the late 1950s and early 1960s Rosenthal and his family lived in Milford, New Jersey. He continued to write magazine pieces on the behind-the-scenes individuals who worked in major-league baseball, such as the trainer, who "could be, on any given day, the most important man on a ball club." For his *Herald Tribune* articles Rosenthal sought the human-interest angle, mixed with the traditional clubhouse quote. When Henry Bauer decided no longer to be the player-manager of Kansas City and opted to run the club solely from the dugout, Rosenthal observed: "They took the glove away from Hank Bauer last night, or rather Hank handed it over in no-fuss fashion. No one ever took much away from Hank when he didn't want to let it go." In counterpoint fashion, Rosenthal added: "Henry was a Marine who made four invasions in the Pacific, New Georgia, Emirau, Guam, Okinawa. He came out with a couple of souvenirs. One is still in the back of his left thigh." On the death of legendary boxing manager Doc Kearns ("Klondiker and boulevardier, con man and plunger") Rosenthal remarked, "In his late years Kearns was a spare man with a knobby bald dome and a chest made to look sunken by his excessive round-shoulderedness. In his youth he was a dashing figure with a full head of hair, and even that part of his anatomy got into larceny." wrote of the Kearns story, "For a piece that obviously had to be done in a hurry and hence could hit only the highlights of a life story, [it] succeeds admirably–with proper respect, and sentiment too, for the old con man's place in boxing history. It's hard to imagine a ring fan over 50 who won't enjoy it, or a younger one who won't learn something about the Golden Days."

Rosenthal's writing was widely admired. Hutchins wrote that Rosenthal's stories were "properly craftsmanlike in detail, and with that extra touch of style that raises a story above the merely workmanlike." Cooke thought Rosenthal capable of producing "drama, poignancy, and humor." "'Jazzy writing,' his readers have been known to call it," noted Quinlan. "They also use descriptive terms such as 'lively,' 'easy-flowing,' and 'bouncy' to characterize the Rosenthal prose."

In 1961 Rosenthal finished his second book, *Baseball's Best Managers.* Rosenthal wrote brief "unauthorized biographies" of contemporary baseball managers Stengel, Charley Dressen, Leo Durocher, Danny Murtaugh, Paul Richards, and Al Lopez. Each chapter records a particular aspect of the individual and how he used that quality to achieve success in the big leagues, particularly the effect each manager had on individual ballplayers as well as their teams. Rosenthal mixes anecdotal material, personal reminisces, and clubhouse quotes while also reviewing the playing days of each great manager. Stengel's great success, for example, was the result of his tenacity: "If ever a man managed in the big leagues with the attitude of 'win 'em all,' it was Stengel. The law of averages meant nothing to him. He was being paid to win 154 games and he meant to win every one. Woe unto the hired hand who was stupid enough to say out loud, 'Oh, well, you can't win 'em all.'"

He commends Dressen's knowledge of the game, which extended to the interviews he gave to reporters: "Ask a comparatively simple question and stand back or be drowned in the ensuing flood." He writes of Durocher's controversial personal problems that left him without a job in baseball: "It seems almost incredible that with baseball in such desperate need of personalities in its mortal battles with TV, traffic problems and do-it-yourself activities by former fans, Leo was left on the sidelines for five years." Murtaugh's reserve allowed him to "run . . . an easy ship . . . Danny's humor is of the my-feet-hurt type. There's a streak of the working philosopher in him and he comes up with things like, 'Keep your mouth shut and people won't know whether you're a fool or not,' and 'Back in Chester we say don't rap the fellow until he's been given a chance to fail.'" Paul Richards, "Master of the Young Ballplayer," succeeded through some of the most "cogent observations in baseball," and Al Lopez, "the Gentle," succeeded through his adaptability while keeping "his working relationships . . . steadfast. He praised rather than knocked, suggested rather than ordered."

Baseball's Best Managers provides Rosenthal an opportunity to settle a score with Stengel. He recalls an incident he had with the manager that described the often tenuous relationship between sportswriters and the men they covered. After Stengel commented favorably on the improved fielding of infielder Billy Hunter and Rosenthal disagreed, Stengel upbraided the writer in the middle of a press conference. "Before the writer could beat an embarrassed, bewildered retreat a flood of rhetoric descended upon his head. The visiting delegation of Chicago writers laughed embarrassedly. This was no trouble-maker Stengel had reprimanded, but a respected representative of a paper which didn't demand the sensational story. The writer never forgave Stengel. Every one of Casey's subsequent successes had a 'lucky-bum' tarnish, a patina of bitterness for him." Rosenthal understood that "the public didn't give a darn whether Casey read a book or not," however, and in the end, despite personally never forgiving Stengel, he gave the manager his professional due. "Stengel," Rosenthal told Quinlan more than twenty-five years later, "was a remarkable person" who "took the time to learn everything about the newspapermen covering his club. In addition to helping you learn everything about the ball club through him, also–through him–you learned the game, the nuances, the subtleties. He had a half-century of experience, and he had an explanation for everything that happened."

In 1957, about the same time the Brooklyn and New York National League teams moved to Los Angeles and San Francisco, respectively, Rosenthal, tired of traveling again, gave up the Yankees beat. The *Herald Tribune* assigned him to cover the two teams on the West Coast. "The paper decided that the Dodgers and Giants still belonged to the New York readers. . . . So, instead of short road trips I'd spend a month at a clip in California," he told Kurkland.

When the *Herald Tribune* finally severed ties with the old New York teams, Rosenthal turned his attention to the new National League baseball team, the New York Mets. Rosenthal was in the room when owner Joan Payson and other team officials were deciding what to name the new ball club. One of his most memorable Mets pieces concerned their 31 May 1964 doubleheader loss to the San Francisco Giants; together the games took nine hours and fifty-two mintues to play, the second game lasting twenty-three innings. "The Mets took time by the forelock yesterday," Rosenthal wrote, "and wound up with someone's unclaimed toupee."

Rosenthal had been on the baseball beat too long, so he began turning his attention to professional football, although at one time he was convinced that the pro game would never become widely popular. Regarding his years of covering baseball, he told Kurkland, "By that time one game started looking like the other so the challenge of covering a different sport interested me." The paper offered him the opportunity to cover the New York Giants in 1963, and Rosenthal jumped at the chance. He had covered his first football game in 1934 as a stringer and had written some filler material during the 1956 National Football League championship game between New York and Chicago. He relished covering the game and soon, in fact, became president of the Football Writers Association of New York. He brought color and action to his reportage, having picked up a feel for football coverage from Woodward. For a 1964 playoff game between the underdog Cleveland Browns and the Baltimore Colts, which the Browns won 27–0, Rosenthal described the crucial play:

> [Jim] Brown warmed up with a three-yard plunge. Then he turned the corner for 46 yards in demonstra-

> tion of the skill and ferocity that has earned him the accolade of the game's all-time rusher. Cutting back to the middle and shedding tacklers, he ran into Jerry Logan on the 40 just as Logan was getting set to try to bring him down. Logan picked himself up, joined the pursuit, and finally collared Brown on the 18. Here Ryan hit Collins with a payoff pitch into the end zone, placing the ball so that Collins made an unmolested catch right between Boyd and Welch.

"The Colts Are Corraled," a 1965 piece on George Halas, was included in *Best Sports Stories of 1966,* the fourteenth and final time a Rosenthal article appeared in that series. Wrote Rosenthal of the legendary Chicago Bears coach, "Popa George is the unquestioned Mount Rushmore of the pro game, a septuagenarian freak (he'll really love that) in a setup where 40-year-old commissioners are fashionable with matching owners. Halas didn't come with a lease; he wrote it, after lugging a hod to help build the joint." That year Rosenthal also published his first football book, *The Big Play: Exciting and Dramatic Plays from the Big Games of the NFL That Made or Broke Champions,* part of the "Punt, Pass and Kick Library" series geared toward juvenile audiences.

In April 1966 the *New York Herald Tribune* shut down after 150 years in the business. Rosenthal decided not to join the other veteran sportswriters who agreed to write for the doomed new newspaper that had merged with the *Journal-American* and *World-Telegram.* Instead he signed on as the public-relations director and assistant to the commissioner of the fledgling Continental Football League. The league floundered, however, and Rosenthal was out of a job in 1968. He worked for a short time on the public-relations staff of the New York Giants and then turned his attention to freelance writing. He authored, with Baltimore Colts quarterback Johnny Unitas, *Playing Pro Football to Win* (1968), one of the several "inside books" on the modern game that proliferated in the late 1960s. He revised and updated the book for a Signet paperback edition in 1971.

In 1968 Rosenthal became the public-relations director for the American Football League. Following the league merger, he was the director of information for the American Football Conference, a job he held from 1971 to 1976. During this time he continued to freelance. Charles Einstein included Rosenthal's essay on "Sunny" Jim Bottomley in *The Third Fireside Book of Baseball* (1968). Part of the description of Bottomley read:

> There was never mistaking Jim Bottomley, however, numbered or otherwise. The rangy Cardinal first baseman wore his working clothes with a special insouciance. He turned an ordinary baseball cap into a figurative plumed hat, and his flannel shirt and pants made it appear as though his teammates were running around in gunny sacks. And in 1924, on a midweek September afternoon, he tailored for himself a remarkable record which still stands–a dozen runs batted in during a single nine-inning game.

Rosenthal's work continued to appear regularly in *The Sporting News,* mostly reminiscences of the old days: "You may think of a stern-visaged rifleman and Indian fighter when the name Chuck Conners is dropped at a diplomatic cocktail party," he wrote on 17 August 1974, "but I think of his playing first base and stopping a bad hopper with his lower lip in an exhibition game the Dodgers played in Atlanta." When Red Smith won the Pulitzer Prize on 3 May 1976, Rosenthal (revealing how Stanley Woodward had cut a few years off Smith's age when Smith first came to work at the *Herald Tribune* in 1945) observed in the 22 May 1976 issue of *The Sporting News:* "Red Smith had a semi-owl-eyed college prof look which made it a bit difficult to guess his age. He still has that look and we're not going to reveal the numbers here except to say he can ride half-fare on the bus and in a year or two he'll be able to collect both his full Social Security check and his paycheck as well."

Throughout the late 1970s and early 1980s, Rosenthal wrote several sports trivia books, as well as *Fifty Faces of Football* (1981), which looked at the question of what made football the new "American game." In 1979 he published his best book, *The Ten Best Years of Baseball: An Informal History of the Fifties.* The book is an exhaustive retelling of familiar anecdotes and personal recollections of baseball and its stars in the mid twentieth century, when "the lunatic owner had not yet appeared" and the "ball player was celebrity because of his actions on the field, not because of his corporate activities or his ability to smirk through a commercial."

The Ten Best Years of Baseball is not organized chronologically, but rather by certain themes, such as club ownership, team travel, no-hitters, and sports coverage. When not covering old ground, Rosenthal mines the "hot-stove league" for telling stories. In recalling Rogers Hornsby's last managerial job with the Reds in the early 1950s, Rosenthal writes:

> Hornsby's attitudes hardened to the point where he wouldn't even bother going to the mound to take the pitcher out. He'd simply climb to the top step of the dugout and beckon the unfortunate one with one finger, leaving him to cringe his way off the field. How many grievances would be filed by today's crop of millionaire pitchers against this treatment? Nor was this the ultimate. Hornsby would never let the shelled pitcher depart for the merciful isolation of the clubhouse. No sir, sit right down here alongside me and watch the rest of this game. Not that Hornsby would say a word to him, or even indicate he was aware of his being there.

rosenthal (2)

newspaper job at the Post, moved through baseball writing into a column spot when Stanley Frank left after the war for "serious" writing.

First time I encountered Jimmy Cannon was as a reader of his column on radio (pre-TV papers carried radio news-and-gossip columns which were big box office). He was so good I remember clipping him. Next he moved tothe American, then to the Posts, then to PM, then to the Post after the War, then to the Journal then to the Post as a once-a-week invalid. He was a smallish man, intense and ego ridden, and gould write like a striped-ass ape, even though he tended to repeat (I must have read his line about punch-drunk fighters having a private Chinese orchestra playing in their heads at least fifty times). Also, I never saw him carrying a book, much less reading one.

Ditto for Gross, who spent twenty years digging up things under rocks (he was at his finest during the basketball scandals which rocked New York periodically). Milt died of a heart condition about the same time Cannon did. Helping him along was the fact that he recognized a new generation of writers were pulling the same journalistic tricks he had to get ahead....ahead of him.

Cannon's ego was incredible. He had been a big drinker as a youth but once he quit he never touched the stuff again. He stayed away from marriage too although he'd occasionally give a series of plugs to some actress sufficinetly strong to make you wonder whether he was finally going to take the jump.

He was on a show with Mike Wallace in Wallace's early days and Wallace, who couldn't change the typewriter ribbon in Jimmy's portable, thought he'd have a little fun. "How come you never got married, Jimmy?" he asked.

Cannon wasn't having any of THAT. "For the same reason, Mike," he said, "that you've been married two times. Or is it three?"

For someone who could write as well as Cannon, he was remarkably insecure. He'd seek you out and say, "Present company excepted, who do you think is writing the best sports column in town?" And he wasn't including YOU in his "present company."

Corrected typescript page from an unpublished article by Rosenthal, "Jimmy, Red, and Others" (Collection of Richard Orodenker)

Dust jacket for Rosenthal's 1981 book

In writing *The Ten Best Years of Baseball* Rosenthal took the opportunity to reveal his private, and sometimes cynical, opinions. In his chapter on the Hall of Fame, he writes:

> There are a number of items laid out for voting guidance but most go by performance and contribution to the game. There's something in there about character or setting an example to the youth of the nation, but all that tends to become a wry gag. Some of the men in the Hall of Fame would have humped a wolverine in their day before going to the ball park, given the opportunity. Others followed the precept that whiskey will spoil once it's uncorked so you'd better not leave any. Another group specialized in staying up all night trying to cheat a little at stud or gin.

Rosenthal also used the 1950s ("a time of high excitement in baseball") as a context to contrast and compare contemporary baseball: "The game, like some mighty body of water, is calm and stormy by turns. It can engulf completely such nit-witticisms as designated hitters, six o'clock World Series starts, cold hot dogs, and warm beer. Everything soon becomes part of the whole, and the ripples disappear quickly."

In 1976–1977 Rosenthal was the managing editor of *Weekend Sports,* a television supplement insert for various newspapers. In addition to continued freelance work, he wrote sports and commentary for the *New York City Tribune* (a daily published by the Unification Church), from 1978 until its closing in 1990. He was also contributing sports editor of *American Way,* the in-flight magazine of American Airlines, from 1979 to 1984. From 1982 to 1989 he helped select and publicize the All-America Teams and Outland Trophy winners for Mercedes-Benz of North America, and he also was interviewed for Peter Golenbock's *Bums–An Oral History of the Brooklyn Dodgers* (1984).

Throughout his career Rosenthal never lost his sense of humor or his light touch. In the 14 March 1980 issue of *The News World,* responding to a woman who had called the paper to see if she could get an obituary from 1923, Rosenthal mused:

> It's axiomatic that if the question is sufficiently weird it usually filters through the newspaper's switchboard into the sports department. The assumption apparently is that anyone who can make sense out of the Yankees' relations with Billy Martin will be able to advise on all matters ranging from what to do for a wasp sting (apply a packing of moist meat-tenderizer) to what round Dempsey knocked out Firpo (the second).

In 1994 he contributed a chapter on two-position players, such as Sammy Baugh, Ernie Nevers, and Pete Pihos, for the coffee-table book *75 Seasons: The Complete Story of the National Football League, 1920–1995.* Selecting "The All-Two-Way Team" of these players, Rosenthal noted, "None of the dictionary descriptions of the adjective 'two-way' focus on those unforgettable football heroes who played when 'two-way' meant only one thing: playing two ways. You played on offense, gulped a breath or two and a dipper of water, and switched to defense. Then back to offense. Then to kicking off. Then to receiving."

Rosenthal's last columns appeared in *College & Pro Football Weekly,* for which he had written retrospectives and current articles since 1978. In the 23 October 1997 article "Let's Go, Light Blue," he recalled the time in 1947 when "a ticket for the annual clash with Notre Dame, No. 2 in the nation, Army draft or no Army draft, was hotter on the New York scalper market than ration stamps for ten pounds of unsalted butter." In "It Wasn't Always 'Banner' Day at the Park" (2 October 1997) Rosenthal reflected on the days when "they *didn't* play the Star-Spangled Banner, or anything else, to start a ball game." "Football had the two teams line up, the referee yelled, 'Let's go,' and blew his starting whistle," he wrote. "Delaying the game by three minutes or so would only provide an opportunity for some guy looking to serve a summons to find the joint and slap it on a beleaguered owner."

Rosenthal and his wife lived a few years in Boca Raton, Florida, and then moved to Colorado Springs, where they resided for two years before he died on 29 June 1999, following a stroke. He was still writing just five days or so before he went into the hospital for the last time, reminding his wife from his hospital bed to look for any checks that were due him. His greatest accomplishment, in baseball at least, he once said, was having written leads on seventeen World Series.

Just a few years before his death, Rosenthal had given what may well have been his own epitaph:

> I've outlived most of my contemporaries, ninety percent of this being correct genes rather than anything else, though staying away from booze and cigarettes probably helped. There will always be people around bemoaning the passing of the 'good old days,' but sports coverage has changed. There'll always be newspapers, though definitely not in the profusion of the 50s and 60s, and there'll always be a couple of young people coming along to whom words are precious beyond anything else. Tie them in with daily sports writing and you provide them with a gold lifetime pass. And they'll be so caught up in it they won't realize what's happened until someone asks that they put it down on paper (or in readable type, anyway) a half-century later.

References:

Bob Kurkland, "Rosenthal Fumbled As Seer: 'Pro Grid Hasn't a Chance,'" *Sporting News,* 12 December 1970, pp. 35, 37;

Timothy Quinlan, "Hal Rosenthal: A Reminiscence on Sports Reporting Past and Present," *New York City Tribune,* 13 November 1987, pp. 1, 5–6.

Fred Russell

(27 August 1906 -)

William J. Plott
The Birmingham News

MAJOR POSITIONS HELD: Sports editor, *Nashville Banner* (1930–1969); sports director, *Nashville Banner* (1969–1987).

BOOKS: *I'll Go Quietly* (Nashville: McQuiddy, 1944);
I'll Try Anything Twice (Nashville: McQuiddy, 1945);
Funny Thing about Sports (Nashville: McQuiddy, 1948);
Vol Feats, by Russell and George Leonard (Nashville: Nashville Banner, 1950);
Bury Me in an Old Press Box: Good Times and Life of a Sportswriter (New York: Barnes, 1957);
Big Bowl Football: The Great Postseason Classics, by Russell and Leonard (New York: Ronald, 1963);
The Libel Case of Wally Butts vs. The Saturday Evening Post (Nashville: Nashville Banner, 1963).

OTHER: *Fifty Years of Vanderbilt Football,* edited by Russell and Maxwell Benson (Nashville: Privately printed, 1938).

SELECTED PERIODICAL PUBLICATIONS–UNCOLLECTED: "Touchdown Engineer," *Saturday Evening Post,* 212 (30 December 1939): 14–15;
"They're Simply Wild about Larry," *Saturday Evening Post,* 214 (30 May 1942): 11;
"Gay Deceiver of Georgia Tech," *Saturday Evening Post,* 221 (27 November 1948): 26–27;
"Pigskin Preview," *Saturday Evening Post,* 222 (17 September 1949): 30–31;
"Georgia Plays for Keeps," *Saturday Evening Post,* 222 (5 November 1949): 28–29;
"Pigskin Preview," *Saturday Evening Post,* 223 (9 September 1950): 26–27;
"They're All Rooting for Red," by Russell and Guy Tiller, *Saturday Evening Post,* 223 (11 November 1950): 34;
"Greatest Test in Golf," *Saturday Evening Post,* 223 (7 April 1951): 28–29;
"Pigskin Preview," *Saturday Evening Post,* 224 (15 September 1951): 32–33;

Fred Russell

"Pigskin Preview," *Saturday Evening Post,* 225 (6 September 1952): 26–27;
"Football's Weirdest Rivalry," *Saturday Evening Post,* 225 (22 November 1952): 31;
"Pigskin Preview," *Saturday Evening Post,* 226 (12 September 1953): 24–25;
"Pigskin Preview," *Saturday Evening Post,* 227 (11 September 1954): 26–27;
"New Wonder Day of Notre Dame," *Saturday Evening Post,* 227 (25 September 1954): 28–29;
"Pigskin Preview," *Saturday Evening Post,* 228 (10 September 1955): 32–33;

Heads for Russell's column in the Nashville Banner: *(top) the first column, which appeared on 5 November 1931; (bottom) the column for 2 September 1975, showing the title change that occurred in 1941*

"Ballplayer and the Lady," *Saturday Evening Post,* 228 (24 March 1956): 32;

"Pigskin Preview," *Saturday Evening Post,* 229 (8 September 1956): 32–33;

"Winningest Basketball Court," by Russell and George Leonard, *Saturday Evening Post,* 229 (19 January 1957): 36;

"Pigskin Preview," *Saturday Evening Post,* 230 (7 September 1957): 32–33;

"Something's Got to Give at Texas," by Russell and Jack Gallagher, *Saturday Evening Post,* 230 (9 November 1957): 38–39;

"Visit with Bobby Jones," by Russell and Harry T. Paxton, *Saturday Evening Post,* 230 (5 September 1958): 27–30;

"Pigskin Preview," *Saturday Evening Post,* 231 (6 September 1958): 26–27;

"What Price Auburn's Football Glory," *Saturday Evening Post,* 231 (15 November 1958): 37;

"Pigskin Preview," *Saturday Evening Post,* 232 (12 September 1959): 31–33;

"Pigskin Preview," *Saturday Evening Post,* 233 (10 September 1960): 32–33;

"Can Arkansas Keep Her Coach?" *Saturday Evening Post,* 233 (15 October 1960): 31;

"Pigskin Preview," *Saturday Evening Post,* 234 (9 September 1961): 11–13;

"Pigskin Preview," *Saturday Evening Post,* 235 (8 September 1962): 20–25;

"Nothing Left to Chance," *American City,* 77 (December 1962): 768.

Fred Russell was one of the best-known and most-popular sportswriters in the South, as well as one of the wittiest and certainly the most enduring. In 1998, at the age of ninety-two, he was still turning out regular columns, a practice that Randy Horick, a writer for *Nashville Scene* magazine, found awe inspiring. In a 1998 profile of Russell, Horick called Russell a transcendent figure "who has been a sportswriter longer than most people have been alive," writing more than 12,250 columns and befriending four generations of sportswriters and athletes over eight decades.

Frederick McFerrin Russell was born in Nashville, Tennessee, on 27 August 1906 to John E. and Mabel McFerrin Russell. John Russell was a journalist for a brief period of time, having started a weekly newspaper. When it failed, he moved to Nashville, where he worked as an assistant to a hotel and restaurant operator, developing "a fondness for the horse racing sports avid theater atmosphere," all of which were peripheral to journalism at the time. The elder Russell eventually decided that a small town was the best place to rear children, moving his family back to the small town where he had tried his hand at editing.

Russell grew up in Wartrace, while his father traveled across middle Tennessee, bringing home the family income and collecting funny stories that he shared at the dinner table. In 1920 the family moved back to Nashville, where Russell attended Duncan Preparatory School. Upon graduation in 1920 he took a job as a soda jerk at the United Cigar Store, working to save enough money to carry out his mother's wish that he attend Vanderbilt University. One of his friends, and a likely influence on Russell's sense of humor, was a young budding musician, Phil Harris.

Although he came close to earning a law degree from Vanderbilt, Russell wrote that his "finest classroom experience was the freshman English course under Dr. Edwin Mimes. He aroused one's appreciation for stirring passages of poetry–and for the precisely fitting word. . . . He pleaded that the liberally educated man should have deep respect for clarity and directness of expression." Those characteristics were reflected in Russell's own writing.

In 1927 Russell left school and took a job with a Nashville title company, processing a variety of real estate and legal documents. Soon afterward he passed the bar exam, thus increasing opportunities in his new profession, but his first love remained sports. The following year the title company was sold, leaving Russell unemployed. He decided he wanted to get into the newspaper business. Jimmy Stahlman, the owner and publisher of the *Nashville Banner,* gave him the choice of either a job on the classified ad desk at $25 a week or a cub reporter's position at $6 a week. Russell took the reporting job without hesitation.

He covered the police beat for a few weeks, then moved into sports, assigned to cover Vanderbilt football. A year later, at the age of twenty-four, he became sports editor, a position from which he enjoyed the closing years of the so-called Golden Age of sports, an era populated by such legends as Red Grange and Knute Rockne in football, Bobby Jones in golf, Jack Dempsey in boxing, Babe Ruth in baseball, Johnny Weismueller and Gertrude Ederly in swimming, and Bill Tilden in tennis.

The era was populated not only by extraordinary personalities in sports but also by an unparalleled group of sportswriters–literate, bright, and witty masters of verse and bon mots. To Russell they were craftsmen who were just as gifted in their work as the athletes were in their games. He read and savored the work of Grantland Rice, Ring Lardner, Westbrook Pegler, Damon Runyon, H. G. Salsinger, John Kieran, W. O. McGeehan, Paul Gallico, Bill Cunningham, Ed Danforth, Ralph McGill, Morgan Blake, and Blinkey Horn.

Russell rushed with unbounded enthusiasm into the profession of sportswriter for a major metropolitan daily. In the fall of 1931 he was in South Bend, Indiana, when Southern California staged a dramatic upset over the Fighting Irish of Notre Dame on their home field. Russell's enthusiastic coverage of the game and the setting included not only a report on the heroics of the athletes but also a look at the social aspects of the occasion. He took notes of the presence of many celebrities, including film star Joan Crawford:

> Before I start this, will you please reach over there on the shelf and pass me the smelling salts, the bromo, the aromatic spirits and any other sweet essence of revival that you find handy.
>
> It's absolutely necessary, which you would agree had you seen Southern California score 16 points in the last quarter here Saturday afternoon and win from Notre Dame, 16 to 14 before 52,000 gasping fans.
>
> No more thrilling awe-inspiring battle has been staged in the history of the great college game of football. Oh, boy! Oh, boy, was it a burner!
>
> Miss Crawford has much lighter hair than you would think. For the benefit of the ladies, she wore a green hat, green cloak suit–but I give up, that's as far as I know.

The exuberant report from South Bend came just slightly more than two weeks after his first bylined column, "Sideline Sidelights," appeared on 5 November 1931. The column continued under that name several times each week until 2 June 1947, when, without comment or explanation, it became simply "Sidelines."

Russell married Katherine Wyche Early on 2 November 1933. They had four children, and Katherine Russell became as prominent in charitable, artistic, and historical affairs in Nashville as her husband was in sports. She was regent of the Ladies Hermitage Association when that organization

Harold "Red" Grange, Bobby Jones, Russell, and Jack Dempsey at the banquet commemorating Russell's twenty-fifth year with the Banner *in 1953*

undertook with the University of Tennessee-Nashville the preparation and publication of the complete papers of President Andrew Jackson.

Humor permeated Russell's writing and his speech. Occasionally he interviewed and profiled sports figures. While attending the major league baseball annual meeting in Miami in 1947, he happened across a former Nashville Vols catcher named Charles "Greek" George. The entire column was devoted to George's discoursing on his curious eating habits, such as having nothing but grapes for days at a time to lose weight. But most of Russell's daily "Sidelines" pieces were "notes" columns, a trade expression for columns that are a smorgasbord of short news items, jokes, and humorous anecdotes. Russell also loved carefully crafting practical jokes, some of which required elaborate preparation.

A typical notes column might be like the 1975 piece that began with three short items on Vanderbilt football coach Fred Pancoast and his team's upcoming opener with Tennessee-Chattanooga. The column also included, under the heading of "This and That," an assortment of brief miscellaneous sports news items and under "Quoteboard" a series of the sort of humorous quips so readily identified with Russell:

> COACH ALEX AGASE, addressing Purdue alumni: "If you really want to advise me, do it on Saturday between 1 and 4 o'clock, and you get 25 seconds to do it between plays. Not on Monday. I don't need it then. I know the right thing to do by Monday."
>
> * * *

Russell with fellow sportswriters Red Smith and Bill Corum

ANONYMOUS: "A bore is a person who deprives you of your privacy without providing you with company."

* * *

BUD MOORE, Kansas head football coach and former Alabama assistant, on the reason for Bear Bryant's success: "He's a good listener. It never mattered how wild an idea was, he always listened to what an assistant had to say. Sometimes you might think he really wasn't paying much attention, then a month or so later he would say, 'We ought to use what you suggested.'"

Items from such geographically diverse institutions as Vanderbilt, Purdue, and Kansas reflect the national scope of Russell's interest and writing. He served as chairman of the honors committee of the National Football Foundation and Hall of Fame for twenty-five years, from 1967 to 1992, and was southern chairman of the Heisman Trophy Committee from 1946 until 1992. He was also president of the Football Writers Association in 1960–1961.

Former *Birmingham Post-Herald* sports editor Bill Lumpkin suggested that Russell got exclusives on stories because of his national influence. Russell and Tom Siler, sports editor of the *Knoxville News-Sentinel,* were probably in their heyday the most recognizable writers in the South. They were charter members of the Football Writers Association. They covered most major national events, and both often wrote for national general circulation magazines, Russell in *The Saturday Evening Post* and Siler in both *Collier's* and the Street and Smith yearbooks. In 1949 the *Post* hired Russell to do a preseason college football All-American team. He accepted the assignment with zest and professionalism, continuing the annual article until the magazine folded in the 1960s.

When the *Post* was sued by former University of Georgia football coach Wally Butts over an article alleging that he and University of Alabama coach Paul "Bear" Bryant had conspired to fix a football game, the *Banner* sent Russell to Atlanta to cover the trial. Blackie Sherrod, sports editor of the *Dallas Morning News,* said Russell covered the libel trial much like Damon Runyon covered murder trials. The idea of a sportswriter being sent to cover a judicial event of national interest was a source of pride for other sportswriters. When the trial was over, the *Banner* collected Russell's pieces and published them in a pamphlet, *The Libel Case of Wally Butts vs. The Saturday Evening Post* (1963). His prose indicated that he had little problem switching from the world of sports to that of law. Indeed, his attention to details and perceptions of human nature were often evident in his coverage. One day Butts broke down and sobbed on the witness stand, forcing Federal District Judge Lewis Morgan to declare a five-minute recess. Russell described the scene in the courtroom during the recess: "The people in the crowded courtroom showed what they thought through their impressively respectful silence during the five-minute recess. Usually at these periods there is moving and chattering. This time everybody stayed where he was, quiet, some crying, many misty-eyed."

Previously, in 1936, Russell had worked outside his usual sports beat on another case of national significance, the kidnapping of Alice Speed Stoll, a prominent Louisville, Kentucky, resident, by Thomas H. Robinson Jr. of Nashville. During Robinson's time as a fugitive he was listed on the "Most Wanted List" of the Federal Bureau of Investigation. Russell, who had attended school with Robinson at Vanderbilt, was able to obtain an exclusive interview with the kidnapper shortly after his conviction for the crime.

Russell was a figure of such national prominence that a veritable who's who of the Golden Age of sports paraded to Nashville in 1954 to celebrate his twenty-fifth anniversary at the *Nashville Banner,* his only journalistic employer until the paper folded in 1998. Among those who came to Nashville for the event were Dempsey, Grange, and Jones, who made the trip despite being in poor health.

Russell's other colleagues have expressed similar affection and respect for him. Edgar Allen, originally hired by Russell during World War II, said that his gentlemanly demeanor and unabashed, sometimes outrageous sense of humor were reflected in both his personality and his writing, which always portrayed the positive. Russell told Allen that he espoused Rice's philosophy that "if you can't write anything nice about a person, then don't write it." When the Grantland Rice Award for outstanding sportswriting was created in 1955, Russell was the first recipient.

The notes-column style carried over into most of his books, which were largely collections of jokes and anecdotes about sports figures. The exceptions were histories of Vanderbilt University football and Nashville Vols baseball teams and the autobiographical *Bury Me in an Old Press Box: Good Times and Life of a Sportswriter* (1957). Russell rarely displayed verse or high metaphor, but his stories and columns usually captured the essence of the subject in clear, easily digested language. Allen said Russell "was just a slave to timing in his writing, both his column and his speeches. The timing seemed to be everything. I've known him to make a note and put something up for eight or nine months" before using it.

Furman Bisher described Russell's writing style as "purely Southern, purely Russell," rarely resorting to hyperbole or shock tactics to get the reader's attention. "He wrote pretty true to the line. He was s stickler for what he wrote being right. I think he was an entertaining writer, but he didn't try to impress you with flowery language and lofty terms." Joe Biddle, who, along with Russell, was offered a position with the *Tennesseean* when the *Banner* folded in February 1998, has always been amazed by Russell's endurance: at the time of Biddle's arrival in Nashville, Russell "was officially retired, yet still in the office every day. He wrote a column every week that was fresh and lively. It was unbelievable for anyone his age."

Russell's love of practical jokes began when he was a student at Vanderbilt, where his partner and sometimes competitor in mischief was Red Sanders, later head football coach at Vanderbilt and the University of California at Los Angeles. Blackie Sherrod and Joe Biddle also took note of Russell's love of pranks, which he would play on strangers as well as friends and colleagues and sometimes took weeks to pull off.

Russell's basic philosophy of looking for the good in all people sometimes led him to write with compassion about the failings of sports personalities. After tennis great "Big" Bill Tilden was scandalized by charges of molestation, which led to a trial, conviction, and incarceration, Russell reflected in *Bury Me in an Old Press Box:*

> That such a brilliant career should have terminated in shame was one of the saddest tragedies in American sports. What struck me as inexcusably cruel was the handling of his case and his virtual abandonment by his acquaintances. I realize that Tilden had few friends. But here was an individual who, while he was winning tennis glory for the

Magazine cover featuring Russell's annual preview of the college football season

> United States, was acceptable despite wide knowledge of his aberrations brought on by Nature's having dealt him a sorry hand. Then when he became involved in serious difficulties, ill and probably in need of quarantine, he was sentenced to the county road.

Russell has won many awards throughout his career, including the College Football Centennial Award in 1969; a Golf Writers Association of America writing award in 1972; the U.S. Olympic Committee award for distinguished journalism in 1976; the National Football Foundation and Hall of Fame Distinguished American Award in 1980; the American Football Coaches Association Amos Alonzo Stagg Award in 1981; the National Turf Writers Association Award in 1983; and the Associated Press Sports Editors' Red Smith award in 1984. Russell was inducted into the Tennessee Sports Hall of Fame in 1974 and the National Sportscasters and Sportswriters Hall of Fame in 1988.

The fact that Russell was not only still alive but also actively writing long after so many of his contemporaries had passed away led *Nashville Scene* writer Randy Horick to observe:

> He witnessed the reshaping of the entire sports landscape, from college football teams that didn't offer scholarships to athletic departments that are run like corporations; from an era of unpretentious baseball players to a time of millionaire media stars; from the days of cold type and Western Union to real-time, all-the-time information. He is a living link to a world that no longer exists.

References:

Nelson Bryan, "70 Years in the Making," *Vanderbilt Magazine* (Spring 1995): 6–9;

Randy Horick, "The Time of His Life: How Fred Russell Got the Story," *Nashville Scene* (26 March 1998): 22–32.

Jack Ryder

(16 November 1871 – 5 June 1936)

James B. Dworkin
Purdue University

and

Sarah Geis
Indiana University

Jack Ryder

MAJOR POSITIONS HELD: Columnist, *Cincinnati Commercial-Tribune* (1904); baseball editor and columnist, *Cincinnati Enquirer* (1904–1936).

WORK: Edward Michael Ashenback, *Humor among the Minors: True Tales from the Baseball Bush,* edited by Jack Ryder (Chicago: Donohue, 1911).

As baseball historian Lee Allen wrote in his *The Cincinnati Reds: An Informal History* (1948), "in the isolationist cocoon of the Midwest, breakfast wasn't ten minutes on a drugstore stool and a dash to punch the time clock. . . . Breakfast in Cincinnati was plump sausage and barnyard-fresh eggs, strong, fragrant coffee, and Jack Ryder's column." As a chronicler of the Cincinnati Reds for more than three decades, Allen wrote, Ryder "always spiced up his columns with gentle sarcasm, sly digs, and subtle quips about life in general."

Frederick Bushnell Ryder was born on 16 November 1871, in Oberlin, Ohio. Shortly after his birth the family moved to New England, where his father served as a Congregational minister and as a professor of theology at Andover Academy in Massachusetts. Ryder graduated in 1889 from Phillips Exeter Academy in Exeter, New Hampshire, where he learned Greek and Latin, and from Williams College in 1892. Ryder and his brother, Robert, were instrumental in the founding and running of a preparatory school for boys in Columbus, Ohio, an association they maintained until 1898. Ryder then served on a cattle boat bound for England in order to receive passage to visit Europe. Later he returned to the United States to enlist as an army private during the Spanish American War, "with never a sight of a Cuban or a Spaniard," as his Baseball Writers Association of America (BBWAA) biography wryly reported. Ryder spent several summers while in the army in Lakeland, Florida, and Huntsville, Alabama.

After his stint in the army Ryder served for one season as a salaried football coach at Ohio State University. He had learned the game of football at Williams College, where he played guard. Both Ryder brothers were more interested in newspaper work than anything else, however, and soon began their careers. Robert Ryder began his career as an editorial writer for the *Ohio State Journal,* while Jack ventured to Cincinnati in July 1904 to join the staff of the *Commercial-Tribune,* for which he wrote a column, "Ginger Jar."

Jack Ryder joined the *Cincinnati Enquirer* on 1 December 1904. He succeeded Ren Mulford as a baseball reporter and editor and soon was recognized as an expert of the game. His stories took up about two-and-a-half columns, followed by two more columns of notes. He covered the game in Cincinnati from 1904 until his death in 1936. Ryder followed the Reds at League Park (also called the Palace of Fans) during those early years and recorded the exploits of local stars, including John Ganzel, Hans Lobert, and Miller Huggins, the latter the future great New York Yankees manager, whom Ryder once praised for his deft fielding. He recorded the exploits of many National League players, recalling once to Edward Konetchy of the St. Louis Cardinals that he had seen him hit a home run that he thought was "the longest drive of many years in the Cincinnati ball yard." He was also on hand for the opening of Redlands Field in 1909 and its rechristening as Crosley Field in 1934. The Reds, however, were a weak team in the early part of the century, finishing below .500 for eleven seasons until their role in the infamous 1919 World Series.

Nonetheless, Ryder was an unabashed supporter of the Reds, and he always looked for something good to say about his team, even when he was poking light fun at them or his audience. The Reds were always "our boys" or "our noble athletes," or, if he needed to find something particularly kind to say about them, a "team which usually drives southpaws to the tall and uncut"–that is, they usually beat a left-handed pitcher. Ryder frequently chalked up losses to fate or other unfortunate circumstances, as for example when he rationalized that "the national game is an uncertain affair" or reported that the players "were suddenly seized with an attack of the wobbles." The other team was invariably portrayed as "the enemy," and their successes were "lucky." At other times he displays a sense of irony, as when the Reds were beaten by Giants veteran Joe "Iron Man" McGinnity the day after their management turned down an offer to buy his contract. "Isn't baseball a funny proposition?" Ryder asks. McGinnity gets by with "nerve, control, and a dinky curve ball" and only because "necessity forces his use" just hours after he has been offered to the opposing team. "According to immemorial custom, the batter never hits at the first one, so old Joe has him in the hole right off the reel. Then a little nerve, perfect control, and the queer little curve, calculated to an inch, cause a pop-up or a small-sized fanning bee."

His early florid style of writing was typical of the era, as in his description of three runs being scored: "the tender footsies of Kane, Lobert, and Mitchell pressed the pan in rapid succession." His writing was filled with the droll words and catch-phrases of early baseball: *foozle* for an error, *bingles* for hits. Ryder strove for color and irony as well as a clever introduction. Reporting on a game in which the Reds forced the removal of New York Giants pitching great Christy Mathewson in the second inning, Ryder began: "Christopher Mathewson had plenty of time to play his favorite game of checkers yesterday," adding that he "had left the yard without saying 'Thank you,' and did not seem highly delighted at the hospitality of our boys." When Mathewson faced the Reds again two days later, he was again "knocked sky-high and forced to retire" early. Ryder again played on the checker theme, observing that Mathewson would no doubt "whale the everlasting tar" out of Bob Spade, the Reds pitcher that day. "But checkers is too tough a rough a game to be allowed in the refined atmosphere of League Park, where baseball has the call. So Spade confined his attention to the national sport yesterday and made the great Matty look like a sucker."

In addition to writing about the colorful Mathewson, who in 1916 joined the Reds as player-manager, Ryder liked poking fun at the irascible manager of the Giants, John J. McGraw. McGraw had demanded that the Reds and Giants play a 7 August 1908 game on a rain-soaked field although "there was every legitimate reason for a postponement." McGraw was sure that the Reds "would be easy picking." The Reds won 5–0, however, denying the Giants first place in the National League standings. Ryder's lead the next day asserted that "Mr. John J. McGraw thought he was cutting into a fine, ripe cantaloupe this afternoon and was much surprised to find a lemon of the sourest variety." Once in a while he was able to get both Mathewson and McGraw in a column, especially after Mathewson joined the Reds. On 19 August 1917, the Reds and Giants, against the law, played the first Sunday game in the history of the Polo Grounds. As Ryder observed in the *Enquirer* the next day:

> After the game Matty and McGraw had to appear in Washington Heights Police Court to answer the terrible charge of instigating a game of baseball on Sunday. The summons was issued by the so-called Sabbath Society. Magistrate Frothingham dismissed the case and complimented the managers for providing enjoyment for soldiers who were in the stands. As a comment on the hypocrisy of human nature, however, it was necessary for him to announce that he let them off because the money taken in at the gate was paid by the fans to hear the alleged sacred concert which preceded the game, and not to see the contest. It's a queer world!

He wrote periodically for the annual *Spalding's Official Base Ball Guide,* including a 1908 entry about Chicago Cubs pitcher Ed Reulbach, whose success in the 1907 season Ryder, unfairly, credited largely to manager Frank Chance, "who seldom let a man stay in the box too long when he was proving ineffective." Reulbach, an "effective at times but extremely wild and unreliable" pitcher, "was allowed to lose only four games, being yanked out invariably at the first sign of weakness."

Ryder brought into his pieces pithy observations about the game or the crowd that helped to embellish routine game-day stories. As Allen notes, "He wrote about the team as if he were describing the gallant battle of titans, but still gave the impression that his tongue was in his cheek." Though he later eschewed this style, it made enjoyable reading in the heyday of American journalism. For example, he once wrote: "A man who can crack out such a hit, with the bases full, is entitled to all the candy, cigars, booze, household goods, and other paraphernalia that comes to the four-base hitter on the home lot." Noting that men often had a difficult time seeing a ball game when a woman sat in front of them, Ryder remarked, "At a ball game you can tell whether a woman is a real lady or just a plain female by noting whether she has her hat on or not."

According to Bill James, Ryder was also responsible for hiring a young Allen as "an unofficial, unpaid pitch counter." Allen went on to a career as a writer, historian, and baseball researcher. In *The Cincinnati Reds* he cites all the Cincinnati baseball scribes. "But Ryder was the king," he wrote. Noting that Ryder usually referred to baseball players by their last names or nicknames, Allen relates a story about Reds pitcher Harry Gaspar, whom Ryder always called "Mr. Gaspar." Responding to a fan who wondered about this practice, Ryder wrote with characteristic repartee: "Pitcher Gaspar is referred to by the

The offices of the Cincinnati Enquirer, *for which Ryder worked from 1904 until his death in 1936*

title of Mr. because of his dignity as a merchant prince at his home in Kingsley, Iowa. It seems proper to refer to the ordinary player by some nickname, such as Old Wapak, Long Bob, Big Jeff, French Johnny, etc., but in speaking of a man who owns the largest store in his county, and is recognized as a leader in the financial world of his section, the respectful title of Mr. is naturally applied."

One of Ryder's major accomplishments within the profession was his role in the establishment of the BBWAA, formed on 14 October 1908. He helped craft the constitution of the organization, which laid out three primary goals: the encouragement of a "square deal" in baseball; the promotion of uniform scoring and simplified rules; and the creation of better facilities for reporters and the regulation of box scores during postseason play. He also served on the rules committee and wrote several changes in the scoring code. At the first meeting of the new association at the Waldorf-Astoria Hotel in New York in 1908, Ryder was appointed to head a committee, according to Philadelphia sporting editor William H. Weart, "to notify the two major leagues then in session that an organization had been perfected and to explain the objects of the association. Mr. Ryder acted as spokesman for the committee, which was given a very cordial reception."

Ryder was involved in at least one major controversy involving BBWAA members during voting for the National League Most Valuable Player after the 1924 season. Arguably, Rogers Hornsby of St. Louis, who hit .424, should have won; but Brooklyn pitcher Dazzy Vance, who finished with a record of 28–6 and 262 strikeouts, beat out Hornsby seventy-four to sixty-two. Yet, Ryder had left Hornsby's name entirely off his ballot of ten nominees, which caused uproar in the league and made it virtually impossible for Hornsby to win. According to Charles C. Alexander in *Rogers Hornsby: A Biography* (1995), Ryder told Fred Lieb, BBWAA selection committee chairman: "This contest supposedly is for a player who is most valuable to his team. I will concede Hornsby is a most valuable player to himself, but not to his team. On that basis I couldn't give him a solitary vote." The next year Ryder was replaced by Tom Swope, his friend and rival at the *Cincinnati Post,* as the representative of the Cincinnati Baseball Writers Association. As Alexander notes, in 1962 the New York BBWAA awarded Hornsby "a silver bat, . . . retroactively recognizing him as the National League's Most Valuable Player for 1924 and finally undoing Jack Ryder's dirty work."

The Hornsby incident is one of the few things for which Ryder has been remembered. Nonetheless, he had a long and distinguished career as a sportswriter covering the Cincinnati Reds as well as many of the important baseball events in the early part of the twentieth century. When, for example, nineteen-year-old Giants first baseman Fred Merkle made a baserunning error that cost the Giants the National League pennant in 1908–the infamous "Merkle boner"–Ryder, like most baseball writers, teased him mercilessly after the incident. On 26 September 1908 he wrote: "No plays came up in which Merkle had to think, so he got by."

Ryder was a strong proponent of upholding the rules of the game, which were being "cast aside in favor of baseball by affidavit" in light of the Merkle incident. His editorial of 6 October 1908 attacks the board of the directors of the National League for "hemming, hawing, delaying and pondering on the affidavits of partisans." He was disdainful of the use of affidavits, especially Merkle's belated one, and its willingness to "hand a decisive game to a club which threw it away through a stupid performance on the part of one of its players." Ryder was also critical of the way in which the umpires were treated at these hearings. "They could not be shaken on these important points, though every effort was made to muddle them by severe cross-questioning on unimportant details." Ryder eventually applauded the decision of the board to uphold the umpires' ruling and require the two teams to play a makeup game at the end of the season. Despite Ryder's concern for rules, he seemed willing to "stretch . . . the league constitution slightly, by extending the season beyond the date set by the regular schedule." He felt that "it was not more than fair to both clubs that this important contest be played off, and in this decision they have the baseball public with them." In 1924, however, when Branch Rickey postponed three straight games against the Reds in sunny St. Louis due to "threatening water," Ryder, noting an injury to Cardinals second baseman Hornsby, wrote: "Three successive games have now been called off due to cold feet. Umpires and not club owners should decide such matters."

Ryder was a baseball purist who rarely hesitated to let his readers know what he thought. After Pittsburgh player-manager Fred Clarke had contested three games during the 1911 season, Ryder called him "a fancy protestor." Giants pitcher Ken Greenfield hailed "from the vast Methodist wilderness of Guthrie, Kentucky." Of the often-inebriated Reds pitcher Rube Benton, Ryder wrote: "Rube Benton will pitch for the Reds if he puts in an appearance by game time." In 1913 Ryder caused a controversy when he interviewed Joe Tinker, the new Reds player-manager, who lambasted Reds owner August Herrmann for the misfortunes of the team. Herrmann, according to Allen, angrily responded that Tinker "had violated baseball law by his statement." As good a reporter as he was a columnist, Ryder let Tinker respond through his column: "I don't know what law I have violated. If there is a law requiring nothing but pleasant compliments to be handed out about the officials of the club, perhaps I am a lawbreaker."

On 19 June 1909 Ryder was on hand at League Park for the first night game–a semipro contest–ever played at a major-league park. Though he "considered the announcement of a night game of ball as in the nature of a joke," he was duly impressed, calling the event "a revelation" and suggesting the future possibilities of night baseball. "To walk into the park out of darkness," he wrote, "one would think they [*sic*] were seated directly under the sun's rays, the lights having wonderful lighting power."

Shaken by the aftereffects of the 1919 Black Sox scandal, which clouded the only world championship for the Reds he ever witnessed, Ryder nonetheless vouched for two Cincinnati players in front of National League President John Heydler when a potential gambling scandal rocked the Reds organization in August 1923.

He continued to write for the *Cincinnati Enquirer* for the rest of his life. When Leo Durocher joined the Reds in 1930, Ryder tagged him "Undeniably a memorable defensive player although a light hitter," further noting how Durocher had "caught the fancy of the crowd by his rapid maneuvering around second." Ryder wrote what is perhaps one of the best assessments of Durocher, one of the all-time great defensive shortstops, as a player: he possessed "a keen eye and a quick pair of hands, and his throwing arm is always right to the mark. He gets the ball away very rapidly. He is, also, quite clever at going back for short fly ball." Ryder concluded with an observation about Durocher's indifference to setting any personal fielding records:

> But the best thing about Leo's work is . . . that he was never known to shirk a play.
>
> In many years of observation, [this] writer has seen a good many players who, under such conditions, would be careful not to take a chance on a very difficult play for fear of breaking the [streak]. Not so with the Reds' shortstop. Leo goes after everything regardless of his record. . . . He lets his fielding average take care of itself, which is the sign of a good, game ball player.

When Durocher departed the team for St. Louis in 1933, Ryder saluted his "fire and pepper on the field" and noted that he would "be missed by both fans and players, with all of whom he is a popular member."

August Herrmann, chairman of the National Baseball Commission, to whom Ryder wrote the letter that is the source of most of the information about his life

By the mid 1930s Ryder, along with Joe Vila of the *New York Sun* and Irving Vaughan of the *Chicago Tribune,* was the most veteran of sportswriters covering the national pastime. The 1934 season–which G. H. Fleming chronicled in his *The Dizziest Season: The Gashouse Gang Chases the Pennant* (1984), a reference to St. Louis Cardinals pitcher "Dizzy" Dean–was one of the last Ryder covered. In early May he covered what he called "a purely second-division contest" between the Reds and the St. Louis Cardinals, whose "only pleasing feature from the Red standpoint was the sincere walloping administered to Dizzy." The eccentric Dean trumpeted that he and his brother, Paul, would combine to win forty-five games that year and lead manager Frankie Frisch's Cardinals to a pennant, a prediction that nearly came true (the Deans won forty games). Ryder countered: "If the Dean brothers are going to win the pennant for the Cardinals, the Frisch outfit may as well resign itself to defeat."

The Reds finished last in 1934, and Ryder, ever the apologist, offered excuses for them. His team was often "the tottering Reds" or "those surprising Reds." He clung to archaic terms, noting that a pitcher's "unlucky . . . shoot"–or pitch–"grazed a batter's shirt, entitling him to first base." Fate continued to be responsible for the misfortunes of the Reds: "As is almost invariably the case with a tail-end club, nothing clicks at the right time. When the team is hitting, the other side is hitting harder, and when a well-pitched game is delivered the trailers fall into a slump to offset it."

When the Reds won, especially when they beat a better team such as the Cardinals, Ryder's enthusiasm poured over into his prose: "Red stood out all over the place during the super-heated matinee yesterday on the sun-baked turf of Crosley Field. The countenances of the athletes glistened under the violent rays of Old Sol, an umpire had to be removed in a parboiled condition, and our boys climaxed an afternoon of brilliant hue by soaking the Cardinals, their first victory over the Frisch faction this season." For Ryder, runs were still "tallies"; hits, "hard blows"; and innings, "frames" or "rounds." For readers of sports pages, however, Ryder's style of writing was beginning to grow tiresome, and a new generation of sports editors, led by the influential Stanley Woodward of the *New York Herald Tribune,* frequently criticized it. Ryder's baseball lingo soon disappeared from the sports pages altogether, as did pretentious lead paragraphs that failed even to mention the score of the game, a Woodward pet peeve.

Ryder remained unfazed. He may have been a dinosaur, but he was still popular and respected by his readers and by most of his peers. If Damon Runyon, Westbrook Pegler, Paul Gallico, and other "Golden Age" writers were stretching the genre, while still others like John Lardner and Frank Graham were giving it a new respectability, Ryder seemed willing to "stand the gaff," as he might have put it. A player did not merely make a great catch; he "cut back toward the scoreboard like a startled hare, leaped high, and came down with the ball tightly encased in his glove." If he had begun the 1934 season critical of the Dean brothers, he ended it with sheer admiration. The Deans, "the Cardinals mainstay," would pitch in both games of a doubleheader in Cincinnati in the thick of the pennant race, with Dizzy Dean finishing both games: "so the afternoon was quite full of Deans, a condition which was perfectly satisfactory to the fans."

What little is known about Ryder's life comes from a letter he wrote to August Herrmann, chairman of the National Baseball Commission, which is held in the August Herrmann papers at the National Baseball Hall of Fame and Museum in Cooperstown, New York. It suggests that he was beset with financial difficulties:

> Dear Garry:
>
> Yours received with regard to the $500 loan, which you so kindly made me last year. I have delayed answering, hoping that the team would have cinched fourth place by this time. I have made a rather large bet on this proposition, and, in case I lose, have signed over my check for the official scoring to Joe Nolan. The instant the team cinches fourth place, I will turn over that check to you, but I cannot leave Joe in the hole while it is uncertain. If I do lose that bet, I will make some arrangement to settle the debt as soon as I reach home, which will be next Wednesday. I have been rather hard up this year, on account of losing all my savings in the failure of the Cincinnati Trust Co., or I should have repaid you long ago. The team looked so bad yesterday that I am in doubt as to our sticking in fourth place. But, if the matter should be settled favorably before I get home, you may use my scoring check. Otherwise I shall have to dig up the coin in some other way as soon as I get back.

Ryder also loved minor-league ball and, in fact, edited and ghostwrote a delightful book, *Humor among the Minors: True Tales from the Baseball Bush* (1911), credited to Edward Michael Ashenback, the manager of the Syracuse club of the New York State League at the time. As Ryder asserts in the introduction to the volume, "Every tale in the book is authentic and the history of an actual experience. . . . The volume is dedicated to the players of the United States and the fans of the hundreds of minor league cities in the commonwealth." Ryder relates fantastic baseball fables, from a humorous tale of a somnambulist player to those of penurious or balding players. He also offers interesting baseball conundrums, such as the following description of a play that occurred during an American Association game: "There are three men on the bases with one man out. Batter hits the ball to fair territory. There is no hit, no error, two assists, one put out, yet three runs score." The answer: "Batter hits the ball to the right field fence, but fails to touch first base. Right-fielder relays the ball to second base, and he relays to first base. The batter does not get a hit, but all three runs score!"

Humor among the Minors also offers a list of "Twenty Don'ts for Young Players," including "Don't imagine you are going to a picnic when entering the profession"; "Don't when you are up against a streak of misfortune, whine and hang your head"; "Don't eat with your knife. The day of the sword-swallower is past"; and "Don't make yourself a petty larceny or doormat thief, by carrying home the club's uniforms and sweaters at the end of the season."

Ryder made his last road trip with the club in 1936. He died of a heart attack on 5 June of that year. The most fitting tribute of those published at the time came from his own newspaper, the *Enquirer,* shortly after his death:

> Ryder worked as hard at each game as did the players, rejoicing when the Reds won and sorrowing when they lost, but always looking forward to the next day after a loss or slump. He always foresaw the Reds doing better on the road, if they had a losing streak at home, or visa versa. The brightest year in his career was 1919, when the Reds won the world's championship. Humorous to the point where he always was good company, Ryder made little effort to inject his humor into his accounts of baseball games. As a news getter, he had no peer. His convictions were strong and he did not hesitate to state them by mouth or in print.

References:

Lee Allen, *The Cincinnati Reds: An Informal History* (New York: Putnam, 1948), pp. 241–243;

Gerald Eskenazi, *The Lip: A Biography of Leo Durocher* (New York: Morrow, 1993), pp. 54–59, 65;

G. H. Fleming, *The Dizziest Season: The Gashouse Gang Chases the Pennant* (New York: Morrow, 1984), pp. 8, 76, 102, 134–135, 196, 260–261;

Fleming, *The Unforgettable Season* (New York: Holt, Rinehart & Winston, 1981), pp. 68, 69, 71, 95, 118, 158, 177–178, 180, 257, 290, 296;

Bill James, *The Bill James Historical Baseball Abstract* (New York: Villard, 1985), pp. 73–74;

James, *Whatever Happened to the Hall of Fame?: Baseball, Cooperstown, and the Politics of Glory* (New York: Simon & Schuster, 1995), p. 143;

David Pietrusza, *Judge and Jury: The Life and Times of Judge Kenesaw Mountain Landis* (South Bend, Ind.: Diamond Communications, 1998), p. 258;

Alfred H. Spink, *The National Game* (Carbondale: Southern Illinois University Press, 2000), pp. 350–351;

Edward G. White, *Creating the National Pastime: Baseball Transforms Itself, 1903–1953* (Princeton: Princeton University Press, 1996), p. 161.

Blackie Sherrod

(9 November 1919 -   )

Kevin Kerrane
University of Delaware

MAJOR POSITIONS HELD: Reporter, *Temple Daily Telegram* (1941–1942, 1946); reporter, sportswriter, sports editor, *Fort Worth Press* (1946–1958); sports editor, sports columnist, assistant managing editor, *Dallas Times Herald* (1958–1985); sports columnist and general columnist, *Dallas Morning News* (1985-   ).

BOOKS: *Darrell Royal Talks Football,* by Sherrod and Darrell Royal (Englewood Cliffs, N.J.: Prentice-Hall, 1963);

I Play to Win, by Sherrod and Freddie Steinmark (Boston: Little, Brown, 1971);

Scattershooting (Huntsville, Ala.: Strode, 1975);

The Blackie Sherrod Collection (Dallas: Taylor, 1988).

Blackie Sherrod at the Fort Worth Press *sports desk, circa 1955*

OTHER: "Keep It Honest," in *Best Sports Stories 1953: A Panorama of the 1952 Sports Year,* edited by Irving T. Marsh and Edward Ehre (New York: Dutton, 1953), pp. 274–276;

"The Fourth Escape," in *Best Sports Stories 1954: A Panorama of the 1953 Sports Year,* edited by Marsh and Ehre (New York: Dutton, 1954), pp. 280–281;

"The Raving," in *Best Sports Stories 1955: A Panorama of the 1954 Sports Year,* edited by Marsh and Ehre (New York: Dutton, 1955), pp. 147–148;

"He Needs Rubbers Bands?" in *Best Sports Stories 1957: A Panorama of the 1956 Sports Year,* edited by Marsh and Ehre (New York: Dutton, 1957), pp. 201–203;

"The Sad Story of Silky Sullivan," in *Best Sports Stories 1958: A Panorama of the 1957 Sports Year,* edited by Marsh and Ehre (New York: Dutton, 1958), pp. 177–179;

"Open Rebellion on the Links," in *Best Sports Stories 1959: A Panorama of the 1958 Sports Year,* edited by Marsh and Ehre (New York: Dutton, 1959), pp. 188–189;

"Old Buster in Ivyland," in *Best Sports Stories 1960: A Panorama of the 1959 Sports Year,* edited by Marsh and Ehre (New York: Dutton, 1960), pp. 130–132;

"Anybody, Si! Yankee, No!" in *Best Sports Stories 1963: A Panorama of the 1962 Sports Year,* edited by Marsh and Ehre (New York: Dutton, 1963), pp. 96–97;

"A Tragic Case of Mistaken Identity," in *Best Sports Stories 1964: A Panorama of the 1963 Sports Year,* edited by Marsh and Ehre (New York: Dutton, 1964), pp. 191–193;

"The Varied Reception," in *Best Sports Stories 1965: A Panorama of the 1964 Sports Year,* edited by Marsh and Ehre (New York: Dutton, 1965), pp. 186–187;

"The Name of the Game Is Autograph," in *Best Sports Stories 1966: A Panorama of the 1965 Sports Year,* edited by Marsh and Ehre (New York: Dutton, 1966), pp. 87–89;

"Sad Start, Sad End," in *Best Sports Stories 1967: A Panorama of the 1966 Sports Year,* edited by Marsh and Ehre (New York: Dutton, 1967), pp. 137–139;

"The Eyes Had It," in *Best Sports Stories 1968: A Panorama of the 1967 Sports Year,* edited by Marsh and Ehre (New York: Dutton, 1968), pp. 261–263;

"Calling the Old Shots," in *Best Sports Stories 1969: A Panorama of the 1968 Sports Year,* edited by Marsh and Ehre (New York: Dutton, 1969), pp. 216–218;

"Through History with the American League," in *Best Sports Stories 1970: A Panorama of the 1969 Sports Year,* edited by Marsh and Ehre (New York: Dutton, 1970), pp. 257–259;

"Frankenstein's Monster Rebels," in *Best Sports Stories 1971: A Panorama of the 1970 Sports Year,* edited by Marsh and Ehre (New York: Dutton, 1971), pp. 129–132;

"Nightmare for the Longhorns," in *Best Sports Stories 1973: A Panorama of the 1972 Sports Year,* edited by Marsh and Ehre (New York: Dutton, 1973), pp. 93–96;

"His Final Bow," in *Best Sports Stories 1974: A Panorama of the 1973 Sports Year,* edited by Marsh and Ehre (New York: Dutton, 1974), pp. 117–120;

"Randle's Big Explosion," in *Best Sports Stories 1977: A Panorama of the 1976 Sports Year,* edited by Marsh and Ehre (New York: Dutton, 1977), pp. 34–36;

"Grant Teaff and His Amazing Worm Act," in *Best Sports Stories 1978: A Panorama of the 1977 Sports Year,* edited by Marsh and Ehre (New York: Dutton, 1978), pp. 109–110;

"The Ump Bump Has Gone a Little Too Far," in *Best Sports Stories 1981: A Panorama of the 1980 Sports Year,* edited by Marsh and Ehre (New York: Dutton, 1981), pp. 60–62;

Jon Holmes, *Texas Sport: The Illustrated History,* introduction by Sherrod (Austin: Texas Monthly Press, 1984);

Carlton Stowers, *The Cotton Bowl Classic: The First Fifty Years,* foreword by Sherrod (San Antonio, Tex.: Host Communications, 1986);

"Blackie's Texas," "On Awe, the Babe, and Making Money Playing Golf," and "Preston Trail: Last Bastion of Male Chauvinism," in *Under the Lone Star Flagstick: A Collection of Writings on Texas Golf and Golfers,* edited by Melanie Hauser (New York: Simon & Schuster, 1997), pp. 29–33, 193–197, 284–287.

As Blackie Sherrod marked his eightieth birthday, shortly before the new millennium, he was still writing two columns a week for the *Dallas Morning News* and still entertaining readers with funny stories and sharp observations. Sherrod's comic style is reminiscent of Mark Twain and Damon Runyon (two of his favorite writers), but his voice is distinctively Texan. He was born, raised, and educated in the Lone Star State and has spent his entire journalistic career there. Sherrod has been named Texas Sports Writer of the Year sixteen times and has had immense influence as a sports editor in Fort Worth and Dallas, where he assembled and coached veritable all-star teams of writers. Sherrod's public admirers include many of the athletes and coaches he has covered, such as golfer Don January, former University of Texas coach Darrell Royal, and former Dallas Cowboys linebacker Lee Roy Jordan. "To me," Jordan once said, "Dallas has three institutions: the Cowboys, Neiman-Marcus, and Blackie."

William Forrest Sherrod was born on 9 November 1919 and grew up in Belton, Texas, the only child of Marvin Sherrod, a barber, and Leola Forrest Sherrod, a music teacher. He was an all-around athlete in high school, winning seven letters in basketball, track (as a pole vaulter and middle-distance runner), and football (as starting quarterback). He developed an early love of good sportswriting, keeping a collection of favorite stories and columns, and also read widely in literature and history. He won an academic scholarship to Baylor University but soon transferred to Howard Payne College in Brownwood, Texas, on a football scholarship. Because of Sherrod's deep tan and dark, wavy hair, assistant coach Clarence McCarver nicknamed him "Blackie."

Sherrod wrote for the Howard Payne weekly newspaper, *The Yellow Jacket,* and became its editor in his senior year. After graduating in 1941 with a degree in English, he worked as a reporter for the *Daily Telegram* in Temple, Texas. His editor, Walter Humphrey, became a journalistic mentor.

On the day after Pearl Harbor was attacked Sherrod enlisted in the Navy and served four years in the Pacific as a torpedo plane gunner. He saw action all across the Pacific, from Guadalcanal to the Indian Ocean, and at the end of the war rode on an unauthorized flight over the recently bombed city of Hiroshima. Forty years later he recalled a "dead, depressing blanket" of debris that seemed like ferric oxide–"not the deep color of iron rust, but a faded shade . . . a harsh color, harsh and pale at the same time."

During the war Sherrod contributed frequently to *Our Navy,* an independent magazine, but later said that his growth as a journalist resulted less from writing than from reading. When he served on the carrier USS *Saratoga,* he says, "I devoured the ship's library, especially the humorists: James Thurber, S. J. Perelman, Max Shulman, Will Cuppy." Sherrod later came to see how humor could illuminate the world of sports, citing as models John Lardner, Red Smith, and Jim Murray–"excellent writers who just happen to use sports as a vehicle." None of these writers, Sherrod notes, is a self-important analyst or a soapbox orator: "None takes his subject or himself seriously, only his craft."

After the war, in 1946, Humphrey, now with the *Fort Worth Press,* hired him as an all-purpose reporter. After a brief stint on the police beat Sherrod was soon specializing in sports. He displayed a special knack for baseball writing and in 1949 was dispatched to the Brooklyn Dodgers' spring training camp at Vero Beach, Florida. (The Fort Worth Cats were a Dodgers minor league affiliate.) As one of the few journalists with a car, the young Texan was befriended by a covey of New York sportswriters–including Roscoe McGowan, Dan Daniel, Harold Rosenthal, Jack Lang, and Dick Young–and Sherrod haunted the Western Union office at the camp, open twenty-four hours a day, to read the copy of veteran writers and study their techniques.

Sherrod's recollections of Dodgertown evoke memorable players in moments of relaxation: Roy Campanella talking baseball with impressionable minor-leaguers, Gil Hodges shooting pool, Rocky Bridges slapping ping-pong balls, Pee Wee Reese and Duke Snider playing cards, Carl Erskine strumming a guitar and singing "Up a Lazy River." As Sherrod reminds readers, however, the setting of this idyll was a tightly organized talent factory, and hovering over everything was Dodgers general manager Branch Rickey: "He lived in his jeep, floppy sun hat, batwing bow tie, sunshades, everywhere at once–at the four diamonds, the batting cages, sliding pits and pitching strings. He knew the name and history of every minion in his production line. Henry Ford could have learned."

Sherrod covered the Fort Worth Cats for eight years, traveling by train with them on road trips and filing a story and column every day. Team manager Bobby Bragan became a tutor as well as a friend, providing fresh angles on the games and suggesting things that the journalist might look for. "In writing baseball," Sherrod said, "you try to isolate the key play of the game and make it a key to the story, too. But you don't have to start off with a blank. During each game, you can play around with four or five themes, and then wait for one to develop." In the sports pages of the *Fort Worth Press* such tactical analysis was always leavened by humor. When a Cats pitcher named Bob Austin pitched a no-hitter, Sherrod–now the sports editor–responded with the headline "Why Don't We Name the State Capital after Him?" "It was hard to take sports quite so seriously after the war," Sherrod said, "especially for those of us who had been overseas. After what we'd seen, and what the country had been through, no athletic contest seemed like a matter of life and death. It seemed like *play*. So there wasn't the grim tone you find in so much sportswriting today, maybe because there still wasn't all that much money in sports."

Sherrod defined the tone of the *Fort Worth Press* sports coverage–playful and bold–in opposition to the sedate style of its wealthy rival, the *Star-Telegram.* Because of the smaller circulation of the *Press* (rarely more than sixty thousand), its sportswriters were encouraged to take chances: "You could write the TCU game story in iambic pentameter if you wanted," Sherrod once said.

In fact, Sherrod's own game stories often use verse epigraphs in the form of rhyming couplets that identify the key play or players, in a style familiar to readers of Grantland Rice or Shirley Povich. He occasionally wrote whole poems, or parodies of poems, as offbeat commentaries on the world of sport; in 1955, for example, he recast Edgar Allan Poe's "The Raven" as "The Raving," recounting in seven stanzas an imaginary interview with a football coach who, instead of spouting the clichés of false modesty and pregame caution, says what he really thinks:

> Yes, distinctly I remember, it was in the cold November
> When the coach brought honesty to the fore.
> "Why yes, I know we'll beat them, we'll cook them and we'll eat them,
> And if we have to cheat them, well, we'll cheat them," he swore.
> "To hell with building character, that's something I ignore.
> You've got to win, and nothing more."

Because the *Fort Worth Press* was an afternoon paper, its editors assumed that fans who cared about the previous day's games already knew the results. Thus, the stories in the *Press* tended to be features, written with more of an emphasis on fresh and engaging narrative rather than factual detail. Sherrod was consciously trying to attract women readers, particularly those with little sports experience who might have been watching games on television with their husbands: "We started 'writing' instead of just 'reporting' about what they'd seen the night before–we used allusions and other literary techniques that had never been tried in this part of the country. I didn't want textbook sportswriting. I wanted writing that amused and interested all of the readers, and we happened to have some damned good talent to do it."

At the *Press,* Sherrod built a team of young and irreverent writers–including Dan Jenkins, Bud Shrake, and Gary Cartwright–and led them by stern example and practical instruction in the arts of journalism. In covering football, for example, Sherrod taught the writers to cultivate assistant coaches as tipsters. "Those guys will talk to you," he says, "because they're always

Dust jacket for the second collection of Sherrod's articles, published in 1988

ambitious. And our writers understood that, when you're doing an interview, you never ever say: 'I already knew that.'"

According to Cartwright, having Sherrod as an editor was as enlightening, and intimidating, as having Bear Bryant or Vince Lombardi as a coach: "I'd take a story that I was really proud of, and he'd immediately ask me twenty questions that I couldn't answer and that should have been answered in the story." Jenkins remembers the office bulletin board where Sherrod posted the worst of what his staff wrote: "Rotten stories, lazy efforts, failed scoops, precious prose, dopey similes, they all wound up on the bulletin board for Blackie and other staff members to ridicule with whoops, cackling, and falling about. It was the best training ground in the world."

Sherrod left Fort Worth in 1958 to become sports editor of the *Dallas Times Herald.* For the next twenty-five years he ran a stellar sports section (temporarily reuniting Shrake, Cartwright, and Jenkins), introduced new layout and graphic designs for the whole paper, and wrote prizewinning stories and columns. *Times Herald* editor Felix McKnight (himself a former Associated Press sportswriter) considered Sherrod "the best newspaperman on the staff" and often gave him general assignments. In 1960 Sherrod reported on the Democratic convention in Los Angeles. In 1963, in the aftermath of President John F. Kennedy's assassination in Dallas, he was the rewrite coordinator at the news desk as the *Times Herald* staff worked feverishly for two days to keep up with unfolding events. In 1969 Sherrod won the annual award for science writing presented by the Texas Headliners Club for his coverage of the *Apollo 11* moon flight.

Starting in 1953 Sherrod's work was represented in almost every yearly volume of the *Best Sports Stories* series published by E. P. Dutton, and he found a wide audience outside Texas. His reportage has extended to the 1976 Summer Olympics in Montreal and World Cup matches in Germany, as well as all major sporting events in the United States–including the World Series, the Super Bowl, the NCAA Final Four, the Kentucky Derby, and the Indianapolis 500. Sherrod reported on Billie Jean King's triumph in a 20 September 1973 tennis exhibition against Bobby Riggs, the "No mas" surrender of fighter Roberto Duran to Sugar Ray Leonard on 25 November 1980, and the massive earthquake that hit the Bay Area before a World Series game on 17 October 1989.

Sherrod says that he has found boxing the easiest sport to write about because its action is so concentrated. He avoids romanticizing the ring–"At the most, boxing is as esthetically pleasing as a wart hog, even when it is clean and courageous"–but he is attuned to its primal elements. Reporting on the 1976 Olympics, when American heavyweight "Big John" Tate was knocked out in the first round by Teofilo Stevenson of Cuba, Sherrod described the short, straight right hand that felled him: "Tate stumbled backward across the ring as if pulled by invisible wire, his eyes suddenly coated with gauze. His back hit the corner ropes, the first friendly touch he had felt, and he slid down them gratefully, as a man falling from Pike's Peak finds a stray bush in his grasp. The referee counted as a regulatory gesture, but the big sleepy-eyed Tate was off somewhere in the infinite, counting clouds."

Sherrod's boxing stories are informed by a strong sense of ring history, using fighters of the past such as Archie Moore and Willie Pastrano to put more contemporary fighters in perspective. When Larry Holmes barely defeated young Carl Williams on 20 May 1985, Sherrod devoted less attention to the laborious action than to an old television clip of Rocky Marciano knocking out Jersey Joe Walcott to win the heavyweight title in 1952. Sherrod's story describes "Marciano leaning forward, off-balance as usual, chin jutting like a dreadnought bearing down on a U-boat," and Walcott, after frustrating Marciano for twelve rounds, ducking a left hook only to meet an explosive right uppercut: "Rocky might have been the only boxer ever to start a swing with one hand before the other glove landed. . . . Walcott bent slowly to the floor, head down, as a Hindu on a prayer rug. His knees touched and then his brow and there he remained, like an upended slice of cantaloupe." Marciano, tired as he was, ran to the neutral corner. By contrast, Sherrod says, Larry Holmes at age thirty-five "couldn't have knocked anybody out or *run* to a corner if bloodhounds nipped his heels." Yet, Holmes wished to put his then-undefeated record next to Marciano's, to claim a comparable niche in boxing history. Sherrod concludes: "Forget it, Larry, please."

Horse racing is another sport that Sherrod describes as relatively easy to write about, primarily because of the Runyonesque characters who frequent the track. His writing also personalizes the horses themselves: the "matinee idol" Silky Sullivan, who floundered in the 1958 Kentucky Derby; the upstart Canonero II, who came from Venezuela to post shocking wins in the 1971 Derby and Preakness; and the rivals Alydar, ridden by Jorge Velasquez, and Affirmed, ridden by Steve Cauthen, whose furious stretch drive in the 1978 Belmont Stakes remains one of Sherrod's favorite moments in sports: "At the head of the stretch, there wasn't a windowpane difference and they stayed that way to the wire, Cauthen and Velasquez flailing and rolling and hunching, the animals with wild eyes and sure, slashing hooves that *clawed* at the dirt. Never a yield, never an *inch!* Watching transfixed, I remember wondering insanely if a horse's heart had ever burst. Surely one would explode; it was beyond human concept that the battle could go on at such a mad pace for so long."

Sherrod has also excelled as a golf writer. Early in his career he wrote profiles of Texas giants Ben Hogan and Babe Didrikson Zaharias, and over the decades he has charted the golfing careers of such players as Lee Trevino and Johnny Miller. In a charming essay, "Blackie's Texas," reprinted in *Under the Lone Star Flagstick: A Collection of Writings on Texas Golf and Golfers* (1997), Sherrod claims that his native state, from the beginning, was remarkably hospitable to golf: "There were abundant prairie-dog holes, and gutta percha abounded in every stream. The weather was conducive to year-round participation with only an occasional day off to let a tornado play through. . . . Besides, the hardy defenders of the Alamo discovered that a mashie niblick came in rather handy for close infighting and drawing lines in the dirt. Brassies were frequently used for stirring chili and fending off the pesky Commanche."

Of all sports, football lies deepest in the hearts of Texans, and Sherrod has explored the game at every level. One Saturday in 1960, he reported from Boston on the Harvard-Yale game, describing it as the epitome of amateur sport, a "holiday" defined less by the players than the fans: "denizens of a corduroy world–a brown pageantry of parkas and suede boots, of teeth braces and horn-rim glasses, of fuzzy little hats with shaving brushes on the bands and, yet, of heavy raccoon coats calculated to give Big Daddy Lipscomb a hernia."

One week later Sherrod reported from New York on a National Football League game that epitomized the other side of football: the often brutal action on the field. In the waning moments of that game Frank Gifford, the New York Giants halfback, was in full stride when he was blindsided by the toughest player in the league, linebacker Chuck Bednarik of the Philadelphia Eagles. Sherrod's short sentences convey the stark violence of that collision: "Gifford gave a perfect imitation of a sprinter caught in the throat by a backyard clothesline. His feet flew up while his head remained stationary. When his body was parallel to the ground, it fell sickeningly. And he didn't even twitch. Not a muscle moved. The ball popped loose and other people chased it downfield. Above Gifford's body, Bednarik clenched his fists and jumped up and down. Like a Tarzan who has just slain his foremost enemy."

Sherrod has covered most of the biggest games of the Dallas Cowboys, as well as the sharp rivalries, national prominence, and eventual dissolution of the old NCAA Southwest Conference. When Darrell Royal was the University of Texas football coach, he came to appreciate Sherrod's persistence and professionalism: "At press conferences after games, he was always the one who asked the astute questions." In 1963 Sherrod conducted a series of in-depth interviews with Royal and edited them into a book, *Darrell Royal Talks Football.*

Sherrod's next book project, *I Play to Win* (1971), is another collaborative effort. Freddie Steinmark, a defensive back on Royal's 1969 national championship team, was diagnosed at the end of that season with osteogenic sarcoma, necessitating the amputation of his left leg. He continued to battle cancer for another seventeen months before his death, a struggle chronicled in *I Play to Win.* Sherrod edited Steinmark's words so that the young man's virtues shine without affectation. An outstanding high-school athlete, he became a first-string safety at the University of Texas and the team's leading punt returner as a sophomore.

Even after his traumatic surgery Steinmark returned to his classes, took up golf (balancing on one leg as he swung the club) and water skiing, and served as an assistant coach for Royal's defensive backs–even while undergoing rigorous chemotherapy. Steinmark was also deeply religious, and Sherrod's editing allows readers to appreciate a piety that is vigorous and wholesome, not preachy or cloying.

A few days after Steinmark's death in 1971, Sherrod's "Requiem for an All-American" appeared in the *Dallas Times Herald*. This tribute was subsequently nominated for a Pulitzer Prize and was reprinted in *Scattershooting* (1975), the first anthology of Sherrod's newspaper writing. The title of the book comes from the heading on his column of occasional notes, in which he offered a sequence of short, disjointed items. The idea for such a column may have originated with sportswriter Joe Williams–"I unabashedly stole that from him," Sherrod once admitted–but the *Times Herald* version has always had its own singular voice. Sometimes the sports observations give way to general one-liners, such as "That argument the husband thinks he won at dinner ain't over yet" and "No politician ever listened himself out of office, nor reporter out of a story." A recurring character is "Our neighbor Jones," who serves both as a wry observer (like Finley Peter Dunne's Mr. Dooley) and as a universal comic loser: "Our neighbor Jones made a New Year's resolution to go on the wagon and sure enough, the cops brought him home in one."

Just as often, Sherrod's columns include pointed judgments on the current sporting scene. After the NCAA banned athletic dormitories in 1996, Sherrod quoted Arkansas football coach Danny Ford–"What are these players going to do for the first time without supervision?"–and then offered a sharp riposte: "Well, for one thing, Coach Ford, they can do the same thing as math majors will do, or chemistry or engineering students. Unless, of course, a coach recruits players who require constant supervision. In which case, it's his fault."

For all his distrust of press-box moralizing, Sherrod draws on a code of old-fashioned decency and professionalism that applies to athletes as well as journalists. He reacts viscerally to showboating and taunting, for example, whether in the prancing celebration of pro football players or in some of the ring antics of Muhammad Ali and Sugar Ray Leonard. "Now and then," he writes, "us old goats get nostalgic for the quiet work of champions like Joe Louis and Rocky Marciano, who pulled their shift, toweled off, shook hands all around and went down the street for a beer with the boys. Louis was the most serious and stolid and hardest of workers; he treated opponents with respect and they loved him for it."

Showcasing the same values, Sherrod's style is modest, even self-deprecating. His prose, though elegant, conveys the persona of a common man: folksy, weathered (with such identifying tags as "old buster" or "our aging hero"), and street-smart rather than book-smart. In a column about hockey violence, Sherrod begins by lamenting his difficulties with math. As a schoolboy, he says, "I was always getting the hypotenuse mixed up with the oxymoron, and goodness knows what else. . . . I could never understand why, if one ship could cross the Atlantic in seven days, that seven ships couldn't cross in one day." This comic opening allows Sherrod to write as a satirist rather than a crusader. Observing that fights among hockey fans in the stands or the parking lot are prosecuted aggressively, while worse mayhem on the ice is ignored, Sherrod suggests that he is not the only one who has trouble with the concept of distance.

His style is also marked by precise images and fresh metaphors, guided by a reportorial style that can break a moment of sports action into a striking series of still scenes. Sherrod described the scene at the Indy 500 in 1971, for example, when Rick Muther and David Hobbs collided at nearly 180 miles per hour:

> It was as though you found a cricket that had been dead for two years, dry and brittle, and dashed it on the sidewalk. Muther's car turned broadside and tilted up on its right wheels and, in that ridiculous position, skidded a hundred yards down the asphalt. . . . Behind it came Hobbs' car, front end smashed and twisted as tinfoil off a gum package, and it was whirling around and around, like when you used to play spin-the-bottle with a vinegar bottle on a linoleum floor. . . . Bits of aluminum tubing flew through the dust like wasps. A squatty wide tire, blown and twisted loose by Muther's long skid, rolled crazily down the track as if it were wounded and dazed and trying to escape.

Sherrod's narrative skill is matched by his gift for characterization. He has a keen ear for dialogue and dialect, and his profiles are usually enlivened by his subjects' special turns of phrase. His tribute to Texas Christian University football coach Abe Martin, for example, enshrines a moment from Martin's weekly television show when public-relations man Jim Brock showed a film clip of a good block by a player for the Horned Frogs: "Eye dogies, you're right, Jimbo! Ah'm gonna hafta buy that peckerwood a cream cone!"

Sherrod has also had great success in profiling such taciturn figures as Hogan, Ivan Lendl, Chuck Noll, and especially Tom Landry. These sketches rely on sequences of anecdotes rather than strings of quotes, and they carefully balance conflicting views. Sherrod often referred to the impassive Dallas coach as "Mount Landry," or "the well-known marble bust who supervises the Cowboys." Landry's humorlessness–"Nothing funny ever happens on a football field," the coach once said–stood in direct contrast to Sherrod's celebration of the comic: "We choose to think something funny may happen at any time, on a football field or in a war or even at a funeral." Yet, when Landry was replaced as the Dallas coach in 1989, Sherrod's column characterized him as a strong and decent man, with particular appreciation for "his constant courtesy and utter lack of individual resentment toward his media critics."

In some profiles Sherrod draws on his formidable knowledge of sports to think his way into his subject's mind, conveying or imagining an interior point of view. A 1981 story describes the "football world" of Randy White, the Cowboys' star defensive tackle, as "limited to a few square yards, what he can see between the iron bars of his helmet cage." During the game, Sherrod writes, White explodes mightily with each play and then focuses on the next snap. "A half hour after the game it's still a blur to him, a disjointed cacophony of crashes and collisions and thudding forearms and clutching hands and awkward falls and groans and gasps and grunts normally associated with a Kenya waterhole at dusk."

Sherrod is particularly adept at defining two sports figures by considering them relative to each other. Covering a tennis match between Rod Laver and Ken Rosewall, or a basketball game featuring Larry Bird and Magic Johnson, Sherrod dwells on contrasts of appearance, demeanor, or athletic style to sketch each opponent more sharply. Sometimes he exploits the humorous possibilities of dual portraiture. A column preceding the 1986 Super Bowl, for example, describes the opposing coaches in extravagant detail: Mike Ditka of the Chicago Bears, with his "bowling ball face" and "thick stern mustache," glares belligerently and strides "as though he is stomping out cinders"; Raymond Berry of the New England Patriots "has a drawn, long face with practically no expression . . . and he walks as though he doesn't want to wake up the baby." Sherrod then mines the contrasts for comic potential: "If they were tobacco, Ditka would be a chaw, Berry a pipe. If they were material, Ditka would be canvas, Berry tweed. If they were transportation, Ditka would be a locomotive, Berry a glider. A weapon: Ditka a blackjack, Berry a snare. If they went to a current movie, Mike would choose *Rambo,* while Raymond might opt for *101 Dalmatians.*"

When the *Dallas Morning News* hired Sherrod away from the *Times Herald* in 1985, one of the provisions was that he would write stories on topics beyond the world of sports. He began writing one general-interest column a week, commenting on a personal experience, a memorable character, a book or movie, a local issue, or a national controversy. The Sunday sports section has remained anchored by Sherrod's "Scattershooting," however.

His second anthology, *The Blackie Sherrod Collection,* was published in 1988 as part of the "Sportswriter's Eye" series published by Taylor, which includes volumes by Jim Murray, Edwin Pope, and Bob Verdi. Like Murray, who was a longtime friend, Sherrod is a member of the National Sportscaster-Sportswriter Hall of Fame, and a recipient of the Red Smith Award, recognizing lifetime achievement in sportswriting.

Looking back over his career, Sherrod cites several favorite sports figures, distinguished mainly by their courtesy and wit. Davy O'Brien, the gritty little quarterback of Texas Christian University in the late 1930s, went on to become an FBI agent and a valued friend. Baseball manager and executive Paul Richards, renowned as a high-level strategist, remained for Sherrod a hometown boy from Waxahachie, Texas. Zaharias, another Texan with a down-home style, impressed Sherrod with her utter naturalness and "freewheeling ease in interviews," as well as her brilliance in every sport she tried.

Sherrod saw similar qualities in Doak Walker, an all-around athlete at Southern Methodist University in the late 1940s. His career at the *Fort Worth Press* was just taking off when Walker led SMU to national football prominence, won the Heisman Trophy, lettered in basketball and baseball, and excelled as a swimmer, bowler, and tennis player. For Sherrod, Walker's brightest attribute was his unaffected humility: "To my knowledge, no one ever caught Doak Walker in an immodest utterance." Walker became a backfield star for the Detroit Lions but played only six seasons in the NFL, which led some members of the selection committee for the Pro Football Hall of Fame to overlook him. As a voting member of that committee Sherrod lobbied on Walker's behalf for many years, finally resigning in protest in 1985. (Walker was elected the following year.)

Of all his accomplishments, Sherrod may be proudest of his 1969 award for science writing. He also takes pride in the success of his protégés from the *Fort Worth Press.* Early in 2000 he tried to tally how much writing had sprung from the trio of Jenkins, Shrake, and Cartwright: eighteen novels and seventeen nonfiction books, as well as "a dozen movies and television plays and approximately two million and three magazine pieces." Jenkins and Shrake left Dallas in the 1960s to write for *Sports Illustrated.* In the Time-Life Building, where the offices of the magazine are located, Shrake recalls, "we'd see guys who'd be gone for a week on assignment and would come back and say, 'There's no story.' Jenkins and I would just look at each other and say, 'What would Blackie say to those guys?'"

However great the influence of Sherrod the editor, Sherrod won fans for three generations with his writing. His range as a reporter, his storytelling skill, his evocation of character, and his writing voice–regional and yet universal–all have made an enduring mark on American sportswriting. When Sherrod left the *Times Herald* in 1985 his career was put into clear perspective by a colleague, sportswriter Frank Luksa: "Once past the fact that Blackie ranks high on any list of all-time Top Ten sports columnists, you come to another fact: Everything he ever wrote, or will write, is a pleasure to read."

References:

Gary Cartwright, *Confessions of a Washed-Up Sportswriter* (Austin: Texas Monthly Press, 1983), pp. 9–34;

Bob Drury, "The Sportswriter's Apocalypse," *Men's Journal,* 7 (February 1998): 69–71, 102;

David Gaines, "Blackie Sherrod," *Continental* (November 1985): 42–43;

Jim Haughton, "The Richest Sportswriter in the Business," *Editor & Publisher* (15 June 1985): 20–21;

Mark MacCambridge, *The Franchise: A History of Sports Illustrated Magazine* (New York: Hyperion Press, 1998);

"A Philosopher in Newsprint," *Southern Living* (April 1978): 142, 145;

Kevin Sherrington, "Still a Prose Pro," *Dallas Morning News,* 11 November 1999, pp. D1, D5;

Bill Shirley, "Sports Columnists Have Their Own Little Corner, So to Speak," *Los Angeles Times,* 27 July 1981, pp. 1, 7–8;

Chris Thomas, "Blackie Sherrod: Sportswriter, Artist, and Part American Indian," *Dallas Free Press,* November 1991, pp. 15, 18.

J. G. Taylor Spink

(6 November 1888 – 7 December 1962)

Steven P. Gietschier
The Sporting News

MAJOR POSITION HELD: Publisher, *The Sporting News* (1914–1962).

BOOK: *Judge Landis and 25 Years of Baseball* (New York: Crowell, 1947).

OTHER: "Sports Writing and Editing: An address, 43rd Annual Journalism Week, School of Journalism, University of Missouri," *University of Missouri Bulletin,* 52 (Columbia: University of Missouri, 3 May 1951);
Daguerreotypes: Hall of Fame Members and Other Immortals, complied by Spink with Paul A. Rickart and Ray J. Naymer (St. Louis: C. C. Spink, 1961).

J. G. Taylor Spink

For nearly half a century Taylor Spink occupied a command post in the business of American journalism. As publisher of *The Sporting News* from 1914 until his death, he produced a weekly newspaper so indispensable to the baseball fraternity that it was venerated for decades as the "Bible of Baseball." Players, managers, umpires, executives, broadcasters, sportswriters, and fans felt compelled to read *The Sporting News* each week for its mixture of news, features, statistics, opinions, and "inside dope." At the head of this enterprise stood the diminutive and indefatigable Spink. Addicted to long hours of hard work, married to the telephone, and obsessed with accuracy and perfection, he achieved the status of a legend for both himself and his publication.

John George Taylor Spink was born in St. Louis, Missouri, to Charles Claude and Marie Taylor Spink on 6 November 1888. Spink's paternal grandparents, William, a former legislator in Quebec, and Frances Woodbury Spink, had immigrated to the United States from Canada during the American Civil War. Together with their eight children, they eventually settled on Chicago's West Side. The older boys (later Taylor Spinks's uncles) had played cricket in Canada, but in their new home they soon developed an enthusiasm for baseball, the game already dubbed "the national pastime." They played on several of Chicago's prominent amateur teams, including the Mutuals, named for a famous New York club. Taylor Spink's father Charles as well as his uncles Billy and Al made their livelihood in baseball and newspapers.

Two years before Taylor was born, his uncle Al launched *The Sporting News* on 17 March 1886. Taylor's father abandoned a South Dakota homestead and became the business manager of this embryonic venture. He met and married Marie, daughter of a local businessman who made a substantial investment in his new son-in-law's enterprise. The Spinks, assisted by nephew and future baseball statistician Ernest J. Lanigan, made *The Sporting News* an editorial and financial success. Charles Spink negotiated to publish the statistics of several minor leagues, which positioned the paper to be an intimate and essential part of the baseball establishment.

While still in grammar school, Taylor Spink was commissioned by his father to sell four copies of the family paper a week. The boy soon doubled this total and hawked *The Saturday Evening Post* as well. School itself was another matter. Taylor hustled to finish eighth grade and encountered further difficulties in high school. He later joked that his academic undoing came in part from a "narrow-minded English teacher" who insisted that words be spelled "only one way." Eager to drop out after tenth grade, he asked his mother to intercede with his father, who gave his consent. "My father decided that I would never be a Rhodes scholar," he recalled in the 21 May 1936 issue of *The Sporting News,* "and might as well go into business. Not wishing to take a chance himself on breaking me in, he farmed me out, so to speak." Spink worked as a stock boy for the Rawlings Sporting Goods Company for five months and then as a copyboy in the sports department of the *St. Louis Post-Dispatch* for another six months.

Al Spink was wiped out financially by an unsuccessful theatrical tour of his play, *The Derby Winner,* and sold his stock in *The Sporting News* to his brother. Charles Spink redoubled his efforts to make his business prosperous. In 1899 he began publishing *The Sporting Goods Dealer,* a monthly trade magazine that quickly became enormously profitable. Early in the century he added *Toys and Novelties,* a monthly, and *The Toy Buyer's Guide,* an annual, both of which were later sold to a Chicago publisher.

When young Taylor was brought back into the family business as an office boy, his main job, he wrote, "was keeping out of my father's way. Whatever schooling I received in writing was obtained from Joe Flanner, who told me, among other things, never to use the word 'got' and that whenever 'neither' was used, it was always followed by 'nor.' He also impressed upon me that 99 times out of 100, a comma came before the word 'but.'" Spink's job was no sinecure. He was expected to be at the office seven days a week. "One of the reasons I have worked as hard as I have," he later admitted, "is that my father got me into the habit of going to the office on Saturday and Sunday." He did some editorial work on both *The Sporting News* and the *Dealer* and helped to launch the other publications of the company. His pet project, begun in 1909, was *The Sporting News Record Book,* still published after several metamorphoses.

As a sideline, Spink became the St. Louis correspondent for the *New York Morning Telegraph,* a theatrical publication edited by Bat Masterson, the former western peace officer. Spink covered touring stage productions when they played St. Louis, but his burning ambition was to serve as an official scorer for the World Series. Not yet twenty-one and unqualified for the position, he nevertheless began to bombard the office of American League president Byron (Ban) Johnson with telegrams pleading for an appointment. Johnson, keenly aware that Charles Spink's editorial support had played a crucial role in the birth of the American League, finally relented. Spink held this position for a decade, but the lesson he learned in acquiring it remained with him far longer. "Persistence," he often said, "is the last key on the ring of success."

With little time for a social life, Spink still managed to meet and woo Blanche Keene. They were married at St. Peter's Episcopal Church in St. Louis on 15 April 1914 and later had two children. Their Chicago honeymoon was interrupted by the unexpected death of Charles Spink. Thus, at the age of twenty-five, Taylor Spink found himself at the head of a rather substantial business.

Spink initiated two major changes once he took over the family periodical. He damned the writing in *The Sporting News* as "steady, run-of-the-mine stuff" and laid the blame on his father for employing only two full-time correspondents, W. H. Rankin, who wrote major-league news from New York, and H. G. Merrill, who covered the minor leagues from Wilkes-Barre, Pennsylvania. Taylor Spink set up a network of correspondents, one for each major-league team, and thereby made the paper livelier, more current, and more authoritative.

Spink also changed the editorial policy of *The Sporting News,* which, under Charles Spink's direction, had given the outlaw Federal League thorough news coverage and constructive editorial criticism. Taylor Spink did not support this approach. In the first issue of *The Sporting News* published after his father's death (23 April 1914) Spink took sarcastic note of the Federals' opening day attendance in an editorial:

> Since it has been shown that a frame grand stand and a strip of bleacher erected at an outside cost for material and labor of $40,000, can be made to hold from 20,000 upwards, and the fanbody seems to be willing to pay the price and take a look, there is absolutely no reason why we should not have a "major league" in every nook and cranny of the land.

Spink (right) in 1910, scoring his first World Series, with Francis C. Ritcher

A few months later, after the Federal League had filed suit to have organized baseball declared an illegal monopoly under the Sherman Antitrust Act, Spink took sides even more forthrightly. In the 14 January 1915 issue he declared:

> The motto at the head of the editorial page of *The Sporting News*–"DEVOTED TO ORGANIZED BASE BALL"–was placed there by Charles C. Spink. . . . When the Great Umpire called Charles C. Spink . . . , the editor of this paper renewed his pledge to that motto and returned from the burial of his dead leader resolved to hew one course.
>
> That has been and will be the course of *The Sporting News*. It will continue devoted to Organized Base Ball.

One of the by-products of the Federal League's collapse after the 1915 season was the demise two years later of *The Sporting Life,* the only other national baseball weekly. Despite its new monopoly position, *The Sporting News* found itself in difficulty once the United States entered World War I. Ballplayers and readers joined the armed forces and headed for Europe, and circulation plummeted. Attending a meeting of major-league owners in New York, Spink heard Tillinghast Huston, co-owner of the New York Yankees, say that he had seen American troops in France passing around copies of *The Sporting News*. Spink soon convinced Ban Johnson to purchase 150,000 copies of each issue for distribution overseas. Club owners bought a total of 25,000 copies for the same purpose, and Spink sent an additional 5,000 copies of the 1917 Christmas issue with one page titled "A Message of Good Cheer and Remembrance." Wartime shortages caused *The Sporting News* to raise its prices twice, but the company survived, even handing out free copies to soldiers and sailors on their way home after the Armistice.

When the Cincinnati Reds upset the Chicago White Sox to win the 1919 World Series, *The Sporting News* dismissed rumors that the competition had been tainted. "Reds Won Fair and Square and Well Deserve Honors" was the headline over a post-Series analysis. Spink, like almost every other sports journalist, expressed blind faith

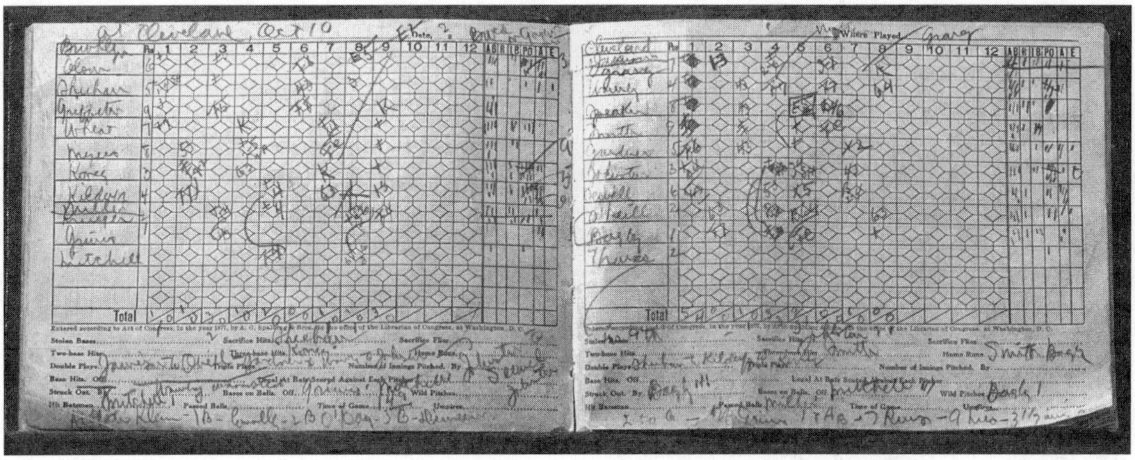

*Spink's scorebook for game 5 of the 1920 World Series between the Brooklyn Dodgers and Cleveland Indians (*The Sporting News *Archives)*

in the integrity of baseball. When the rumblings of a fix refused to die and a Cook County, Illinois, grand jury returned indictments against eight members of the White Sox plus five other defendants, Spink helped Johnson begin his own investigation. Spink provided many leads, including the names of St. Louis gamblers who possessed inside information. The eight "Black Sox" were acquitted, but Kenesaw Mountain Landis, baseball's first and newly appointed commissioner, banned them for life anyway. Spink called the scandal "baseball's blackest hour." In a way, though, *The Sporting News* profited from this travail as the sport emerged chastened and cleansed, elevated to the stature that Spink thought it merited.

In 1921 Landis, who viewed Spink as one of the "boys" of his antagonist, Ban Johnson, removed Spink as official scorer for the World Series. The paper remained cordial to the commissioner until the 1923 World Series, when an editorial questioned Landis's decision to award to charity the gate receipts of a controversial tie game. Landis blasted Spink publicly at baseball's winter meetings, and the paper responded in kind.

As baseball became more popular than ever before, mainly because of the effects of a phenomenon named Babe Ruth, Landis scowled as Spink prospered. *The Sporting News* lavished praise upon itself as "the intermediary by which fans, players and officials of the game throughout the country keep in touch with the affairs of the game." Nor did the commissioner cede to Spink any role in the protection of baseball's morals. Landis bristled in 1924 when the paper editorialized, "*The Sporting News,* first and last, is for Organized Baseball. . . . It has criticized and it has praised and it has praised vastly more than it has criticized."

Spink's roster of correspondents grew in size and strength. He recruited most of the best baseball writers in the country to file for him, generally after they had completed their assignments for their daily newspapers. That stories appearing in *The Sporting News* might be not much more than warmed-over versions of news already published elsewhere did not bother Spink or his staff. Even as late as 1975, the managing editor of the paper, Lowell Reidenbaugh, explained the rationale for republication: "Our readership is national, so 95 percent of our audience is seeing most writers' stuff for the first time. We don't mind getting material they've used before, as long as they're not just sending us their carbons." In 1925 the lineup of writers included, among others, Joe Vila in New York, Thomas S. Rice in Brooklyn, Ralph Davis in Pittsburgh, Tom Swope in Cincinnati, Irving Vaughn in Chicago, and James Isaminger in Philadelphia. These men undoubtedly appreciated the extra money Spink sent their way, but they also valued the prestige that writing for a national publication brought.

In 1925 Spink decided that his paper should name a postseason all-star team. Members of the Base Ball Writers' Association of American (BBWAA) got ballots, and the result, a first team and a second team for both leagues combined, was announced in November. In 1929, when the leagues abandoned their most valuable player awards, Spink stepped into the breach and had *The Sporting News* create its own awards with the voting done, again, by members of the BBWAA. Spink later campaigned for separate awards for rookies, pitchers, and relief pitchers.

In a *Sporting News* editorial (22 December 1962), Spink recalled the first time he heard his publication called the "Bible of Baseball." During a European vacation in the 1920s, the Spinks were preparing to board an ocean liner in Le Havre, France, when a voice hailed them from the bridge. "I had no idea who was calling me," Spink said, "but when I looked up, I recognized Jack Potter [son of a former co-owner of the Philadelphia Phillies], and, believe it or not, there was a copy of *The Sporting News* in his

Dust jacket for Spink's 1947 biography of the first baseball commissioner, Kenesaw Mountain Landis

pocket." Potter turned to the captain of the ship and said, "There is the man who wrote the Bible." The captain asked, "Who is he, Matthew, Mark, Luke or John?" Potter said, "That's Taylor Spink, and he writes the Baseball Bible." Spink knew a good thing when he heard it, and the alliterative nickname stuck as a handy synonym.

The Great Depression sent the circulation of *The Sporting News* into a tailspin. Spink tried various gimmicks and innovations to hold on, including a series of reader polls and contests (such as "My Favorite Radio Announcer," once won by Ronald Reagan, and the "Major Star Crossword Puzzle") and a variety of new editorial columns. Frederick G. Lieb moved from semiretirement in St. Petersburg, Florida, to St. Louis to become one of two national correspondents and to write two columns, "Cutting the Plate" and "Casual Comment." Westbrook Pegler contributed "Peggin' Em," and Daniel M. Daniel of the *New York World-Telegram* signed on to cover the Yankees and write a humor column, "Rambling Round the Circuit with Pitcher Snorter Casey." *The Sporting News* also added a letter-to-the-editor column, "The Voice of the Fan," and "Daguerreotypes," a series of biographical and statistical sketches of old players that became the basis of a book with the same title (1961). These changes, taken as a whole, were made to cement the relationship between the paper and its readers, particularly ordinary baseball fans, by suggesting to them that they were reading inside information, or "dope," that was available nowhere else.

Spink traveled widely, promoting the game and becoming a trusted confidant of baseball's decision makers. "Never break a confidence, just for the sake of a four-hour scoop," he wrote in the 9 May 1951 issue, and the record suggests that he never did. He put his name on two columns, "Three and One–Looking Them Over with J. G. Taylor Spink," and "Looping the Loops," but it is unclear how much of these columns he actually wrote, for throughout his career he exercised the publisher's privilege of signing his name to others' work. He was, however, the de facto editor of *The Sporting News,* as he pored over every story in detail and rewrote passages, sometimes extensively, before each issue went to press. "Taylor Spink lived and breathed every line that appeared under his name, even if he had not personally written it," said columnist Harold Parrot.

When *The Sporting News* did take an editorial stand in the 1930s, the text was usually written by Edgar G. Brands, a veteran newspaperman who served as editor from 1931 until his retirement in 1954. Brands spent a good deal of time traipsing around the country handing out minor awards to individuals and groups, with photographs of these presentations often appearing in the paper. He also helped set a conservative editorial tone that helped to solidify the position of *The Sporting News* as the guardian voice of the baseball establishment. Brands's style was to advocate change reluctantly and to embrace it enthusiastically once it had occurred. In 1931, for example, the editor expressed grave doubts that major-league teams would ever play night baseball. When the Cincinnati Reds inaugurated night ball in 1935, however, *The Sporting News* gave the event full coverage and editorial approval. Spink and Brands were no crusaders, especially if circulation was at stake. Instead, they often used their editorial space to pick at frivolous matters, such as asking fans to return home-run balls hit into the stands because "baseballs cost money" or suggesting that scorecard printers should put the name of the home team at the bottom on the scorecard instead of at the top.

Commissioner Landis remained the paper's most persistent target, but even these criticisms were muted after a while. In 1941 when the A. G. Spalding and Brothers Company decided to discontinue publication of its baseball guide, an annual statistical compilation to the previous season, Spink prevailed upon Landis to award him the contract. His staff, which since 1940 had been publishing the annual *Baseball Register* featuring the statistical records of current players, completed production of the 1942 guide in less than three months, and Landis called the result "a damn fine book."

Baseball struggled during World War II, as it had during World War I, and so did *The Sporting News.* Editorially, Spink campaigned for baseball's continuation and was more than grateful when President Franklin Delano Roosevelt wrote his famous "green light" letter. He then convinced the two major leagues and various club owners to renew the arrangements of twenty-five years before, to ship copies of *The Sporting News*–in this case, a special Overseas Edition–to servicemen in Europe and the Pacific. The print run began at less than 20,000 and escalated to more than 880,000 during the World Series. Spink augmented this effort with another special edition, sponsored by Chesterfield cigarettes, designed for soldiers and sailors serving stateside, and he was not bashful about printing letters of appreciation from GIs around the globe. He also added coverage of army and navy baseball to the paper's pages.

The war brought two more profound changes. In the fall of 1942 *The Sporting News* abandoned its thirty-six-year-old baseball-only policy and began covering college and professional football; the paper then added hockey in November and basketball in December. Spink made the changes to widen his audience to include both sports fans who did not give their complete allegiance to baseball and military personnel who might not be baseball fans at all. In addition, since the overseas edition made such a hit as a tabloid, Spink, at the urging of stateside newsdealers, decided to try the tabloid form for the regular edition. Starting on 1 July 1943, the change in format was an immediate hit, even though sportswriter Tom Meany called the change "as startling as though the ball players suddenly started running the bases clockwise, instead of counter-clockwise."

On 20 June 1942 *The Saturday Evening Post,* then one of the leading weekly magazines, published a tribute to Spink by Stanley Frank titled "Bible of Baseball." The article amounted to free advertising, as Frank told the company anecdotes, lauded the hard work of the publisher, and wrote not a word of criticism. Spink commissioned Daniel to review the article in *The Sporting News,* and even got permission from the *Post* to reprint Frank's essay as a pamphlet.

The article and Spink's self-promotion made Landis furious. He objected strenuously to Frank's calling Spink "the game's unofficial conscience" and dubbing him "Mr. Baseball." More importantly, Landis blamed Spink for these supposed transgressions. When the publisher visited the commissioner in August 1942 to renew the contract for the baseball guide, permission was denied. The commissioner's office would publish the official guide, Landis said. Spink went ahead with an unofficial guide that made its debut a month before the 1943 season began and sold out by May. The commissioner's guide, by contrast, did not appear until midsummer and was a bust. In 1944 Spink got his unofficial guide out again, and Landis failed to produce a book at all. Landis died in November 1944, and his staff published a book in early 1945 that included the statistics for both 1943 and 1944, but the new commissioner, Albert B. "Happy" Chandler, returned the contract to Spink.

Spink brought his uneven relationship with Landis to closure by putting his name on a biography of the late commissioner, *Judge Landis and 25 Years of Baseball* (1947). Even though Fred Lieb may have written most of the text, Spink's name was on the title page and he autographed copies during a packed book signing hosted by a downtown St. Louis department store. *The Sporting News* covered this event and supplemented its story with a favorable review of the book by Daniel and excerpts from other reviews, all of them positive. A few weeks later *The Sporting News* printed still another review by the associate dean of Columbia University's Graduate School of Journalism, Roscoe Ellard. He called the book "a singularly dramatic as well as valuably factual biography." It remained the only biographical treatment of Landis until David Pietrusza's *Judge and Jury: The Life and Times of Judge Kenesaw Mountain Landis* appeared in 1998.

Baseball enjoyed a renaissance after World War II. Players returned from military service to reassume their positions on the diamond. Attendance rose dramatically and so did the circulation of *The Sporting News,* abetted no doubt by purchases by veterans who had read it overseas. Nevertheless, as baseball confronted several potentially disruptive challenges, the paper reacted, as it always had, with a combination of thorough, objective news coverage and cautious editorials. "I am an opinionated man," wrote Spink in *The Sporting News* of 22 December 1962, "but if the other fellow has a story, I am willing to listen to it–and give it full coverage." *The Sporting News* took the side of organized baseball in 1946 when Jorge Pasquel and his brothers attempted to lure players to Mexico and create a third major league. Spink backed the owners, too, when a Boston labor activist, Robert Murphy, tried to organize players into a union called the American Baseball Guild. Still, the paper admitted that both insurgencies exposed genuine grievances that needed to be addressed.

More complicated was the stance *The Sporting News* adopted when the Brooklyn Dodgers organization signed Jackie Robinson in November 1945 to play for its Montreal farm club. As early as 1942 *The Sporting News* had editorialized against the integration of the major leagues. The argument was basically two pronged: integration would not be good for African American players, for whom the road would not be easy, and it would harm Negro League baseball. When Robinson signed his contract, the paper in its 1 November 1945 issue declared its belief that he would

Spink giving Jackie Robinson The Sporting News *Rookie of the Year Award in 1947*

be confronted by a difficult situation: "placed in competition with a vast number of younger, more skilled and more experienced players. . . . six years too old. . . . confronted with the . . . social rebuffs and the competitive heartaches which are inevitable for a Negro trail-blazer . . . [and] expected to demonstrate skills far beyond those he is reported to possess, or to be able to develop." While the paper stated further that Robinson's signing had gotten more attention in the press than it deserved, it also lambasted those white players who had criticized the event. "'It's all right with me, just so long as Robinson isn't on our club'–the standard reply–is unsportsmanlike, and, above all else, un-American."

The Sporting News followed Robinson closely as he went to spring training with the Royals in 1946, made the club, and became an International League star. An August headline proclaimed, "Robinson, Topping Int Hitters, Rated Ready for Dodgers in '47." Spink's paper covered Robinson's second spring training thoroughly. As Dodgers president Branch Rickey cagily concealed his intentions, correspondents weighed in with various judgments on Robinson's abilities and on how other players might receive him. Robinson's debut with the Dodgers earned a full-page story and an approving editorial. "Jackie Robinson's presence among the Brooklyn personnel marks a vast forward stride for Organized Baseball in the social revolution that had gained a tremendous impetus through the world war." In September Robinson won *The Sporting News* Rookie of the Year Award.

As Spink approached his fortieth anniversary as publisher of *The Sporting News,* both he and his paper enjoyed celebrity status unparalleled in American sports journalism. He had never been adverse to self-promotion–photos of him traveling across the country and around the world and receiving one award after another were staples of the editorial pages of the paper–but by the 1950s, other sportswriters began to write about Spink in a host of other publications on a fairly regular basis. Spink's personality and work habits fairly begged for such treatment. He was regarded as a character, the living embodiment of the stereotypical publisher: gruff, demanding, competitive, impatient, and dedicated to getting the story.

Most of those who exalted Spink had weathered his personal and professional demeanor firsthand when they had been asked to write for *The Sporting News*. Taking an assignment from Spink and then completing it to his specifications and on his deadline was often an exasperating, exhausting, and frustrating ordeal. Writers did not shy away, though, perhaps because Spink, for all his bluster, demanded of them their best work.

For Spink and the writers he employed, the first goal for each issue of *The Sporting News* and every story in it was accuracy. "He insisted always that his publications be as perfect as mind, ingenuity and hard work could make them," wrote Carl T. Felker, Spink's longtime assistant, in *Taylor Spink: The Legend and the Man* (1973). Spink concurred with this view. "We . . . check, double-check and triple-check on copy and proofs," he wrote in the 9 May 1951 issue of his paper. "Even then, some reader out in the sticks will discover where we made a mistake and write to us with fiendish glee in pointing it out."

Spink's quest for editorial and typographical perfection knew no bounds. A visitor to his office often found him reviewing and editing copy, throwing each page over his shoulder onto the floor when he was finished. As he worked, recalled a longtime baseball broadcaster, "Spink was constantly grabbing the telephone to talk to one of the paper's contributors. He would harshly criticize the copy content, the writer's style, lack of perception and preparation, question his ancestry, suggest an impossible disposition of the story and then turn and say, 'There's a wonderful man, trustworthy, loyal, has a nose for news and is a damn good writer.'"

Spink often picked up the telephone at any hour of the day or night to get what he needed. Frank estimated in 1942 that his annual telephone bill amounted to $6,500 and his telegraph bill to $10,000. Western Union, in fact, installed a branch office at *The Sporting News* "in order to have some messenger boys available for other duties in Greater St. Louis," Frank wrote. Spink had a long list of contacts and a knack for tracking people down, wherever they might be. As is reported in *Taylor Spink: The Legend and the Man,* Spink could not abide people being away from their desks, out of their offices or, worst of all, on vacation, but if they were, he would find them anyway. Robert Burnes, executive sports editor of *St. Louis Globe-Democrat* and a contributor to *The Sporting News,* recalled finishing a long assignment for Spink on the eve of the 1955 World Series and then taking refuge in a New York restaurant he had never visited before. Less than ten minutes after Burnes sat down, the maître d' brought him a telephone with Spink's voice on the other end. "I just wanted to prove I could find you," he said.

Sketch by Karl Hubenthal that accompanied Carl T. Felker's obituary for Spink in the 22 December 1962 issue of The Sporting News

Spink worked long hours throughout his life and was contemptuous of the clock and the calendar. By 1961 ill health supposedly had slowed him down. A chauffeur drove him to his office by 11:00 A.M. and was supposed to pick him up at 4:00 P.M. Spink, though, still rose at 6:30 A.M., had his mail delivered to his home, and spent several hours on the telephone before his car arrived. He invariably found something to keep him at the office until after 5:00 P.M. and then take work home, where he would make still more calls.

Spink knew everyone in the baseball establishment and used these connections to make stories better. When

Gerald Holland was assigned to write a Spink profile for *Sports Illustrated,* a competitor, Spink called sports artist Willard Mullin, writers Bob Addie and Shirley Povich, and baseball executives Larry MacPhail and Branch Rickey to make sure they would consent to interviews.

Spink's work ethic regularly resulted in what journalists used to call scoops. Even though *The Sporting News* was a weekly publication with each issue delivered to subscribers and most newsstands several days after it came off the presses, Spink lived for the thrill of a scoop. In 1953, perhaps climaxing his career, he got three of them: the sale of the St. Louis Cardinals from Fred Saigh to Anheuser-Busch in February, the shift of the Boston Braves to Milwaukee in March, and the first hint that Kansas City would become the home of a major-league franchise in July. On at least two other occasions, Spink's knowledge of inside information prevented events from transpiring. When Spink told Stan Musial in 1958 that the St. Louis Cardinals planned to trade him, Musial threatened to retire, and the trade was canceled. A year later Spink's revelation that the Washington Senators planned to move to Minnesota delayed that franchise shift.

Spink's lifetime of accomplishments led many writers to entertain the unprecedented notion that he be inducted into the Baseball Hall of Fame. Journalists were not eligible for induction, but advocates of this cause simply suggested that the rules be changed. Hugh Bradley of the *New York Journal-American* argued that "strictly on his merit he deserves to be in Baseball's Hall of Fame." "Baseball," wrote Bob Burnes in the 22 September 1962 issue of *The Sporting News,* should "cut whatever red tape must be severed and give a deserving man his due." Since the Hall of Fame did not change its rules, the New York chapter of the BBWAA honored Spink the best way it could. At its annual dinner in January 1962 Spink received the prestigious Bill Slocum Memorial Award, given for "long and meritorious service to baseball." At the World Series that fall, after consulting with the directors of the Hall of Fame, the national BBWAA unanimously adopted a resolution establishing the J. G. Taylor Spink Award for outstanding baseball writing. This award is presented annually at the Hall of Fame induction ceremony and is often confused with the induction itself. Spink, of course, was its first recipient.

Suffering from emphysema, Spink was too ill to receive the Slocum Award in person. Spending the winter in the dry air of Phoenix, Arizona, he sent his son, Charles Claude Johnson Spink, to New York for the presentation. Back in St. Louis, when the weather got warmer, Spink seldom visited the office. In October he assumed the title of chairman of the board with his son, Johnson, taking over as president, treasurer, and publisher. On 7 December 1962 Spink telephoned the press room to check on the progress on the 15 December issue. He died a short while later of a heart attack. With the presses already rolling, there was time only to insert a short announcement on page one. The full obituary written by Carl T. Felker appeared the following week.

Because Taylor Spink worked entirely in sports journalism, heading a weekly periodical, his place in American newspaper history has never been clearly defined or appreciated. Those looking to assess his life and work might with profit turn to the editorial that accompanied Felker's obituary. It said in part: "By any standard of measurement, Taylor Spink was a great personality. In whatever field of action he had been placed, he would have been a leader by the sheer force of his character, his ability and his extraordinary energy. Circumstances made him a publisher, with baseball as his chief arena. And in that field, he was unique, without a peer."

References:

Carl T. Felker, "J. G. Taylor Spink, 1882–1962," *Sporting News,* 22 December 1962, pp. 13–16, 20;

Felker, *Taylor Spink: The Legend and the Man* (St. Louis: *Sporting News,* 1973);

Roy D. Franke, "*The Sporting News* from 1936 to 1966," M.A. thesis, University of Missouri, 1968;

C. W. Hardin, "*The Sporting News:* Its First Fifty Years, 1886–1936," M.A. thesis, University of Missouri, 1966;

Gerald Holland, "'Taylor Spink Is First-Class,'" *Sports Illustrated* (27 February 1961): 58–66;

Ernest J. Lanigan, "*The Sporting News* Spans Half a Century With Baseball," *Sporting News,* 21 May 1936, pp. 1A, 6A;

Frederick G. Lieb, "80 Candles Dot *The Sporting News* Cake," *Sporting News,* 19 March 1966, pp. 21–24;

Lowell Reidenbaugh, *The Sporting News First Hundred Years, 1886–1986* (St. Louis: *Sporting News,* 1985).

Papers:

Some of J. G. Taylor Spink's correspondence can be found in the collection of the Branch Rickey papers in the Library of Congress.

J. Roy Stockton

(16 December 1892 - 24 August 1972)

James A. Vlasich
Southern Utah University

MAJOR POSITIONS HELD: Reporter, *St. Louis Republic* (1912–1915); sportswriter, *St. Louis Globe-Democrat* (1915–1917); copyeditor (1917–1920), sportswriter (1920–1946), sports editor, *St. Louis Post-Dispatch* (1946–1958).

BOOKS: *The Gashouse Gang and a Couple of Other Guys* (New York: Barnes, 1945);

Frank Frisch: The Fordham Flash, by Stockton and Frank Frisch (Garden City, N.Y.: Doubleday, 1962).

OTHER: "Touring the Foxhole Circuit," in *Best Sports Stories of 1945,* edited by Irving T. Marsh and Edward Ehre (New York: Dutton, 1946), pp. 277–285;

Rogers Hornsby, *My Kind of Baseball,* edited by Stockton (New York: McKay, 1953).

SELECTED PERIODICAL PUBLICATIONS–UNCOLLECTED: "Singing Sam, the Cut-Rate Man," *Saturday Evening Post,* 219 (22 February 1947): 17, 132, 134, 137, 138, 140;

"Baseball's Amazing Amateur," *Saturday Evening Post,* 222 (27 May 1950): 38–39, 136, 138, 140, 142;

"Can the Rajah Rejuvenate the Browns?" *Saturday Evening Post,* 224 (9 February 1952): 30, 111–114;

"How to Get Fired," *Look,* 17 (14 July 1953): 76–78, 80–81;

"What to Watch for in Big League Baseball," *Look,* 17 (28 July 1953): 56, 59.

J. Roy Stockton (The Sporting News *Archive)*

One of America's finest sportswriters of the first half of the twentieth century, James Roy Stockton was a clever writer whose sarcastic humor, written or spoken, often stung his targets. His irreverence made him the enemy of the pompous and the delight of his readers. Bob Broeg, who worked for and succeeded Stockton as the sports editor of the *St. Louis Globe-Democrat,* described him in an obituary as a master of rapier wit who "could thrust so cleanly that he didn't even draw blood." With his pipe clenched in his teeth, Stockton would put the second finger of each hand over the first and pound away at his typewriter. According to Broeg, Stockton "didn't always bear down," but when he did do his best work, such as the articles he wrote for *The Saturday Evening Post,* he was as good as any sportswriter of his time. He was especially noted as the chronicler of the Gashouse Gang, the colorful St. Louis Cardinal baseball clubs of the 1930s.

Born in St. Louis, Missouri, on 16 December 1892, Stockton went to McKinley High School and attended Washington University beginning in 1910.

Although these institutions provided him an educational background, they did not provide him with any newspaper experience. During his junior year in college Stockton learned that classmate Wilbur Wood had quit his part-time job with the *St. Louis Republic.* Despite his lack of experience, Stockton acquired a position with the paper as a reporter.

Starting in the sports department, he gradually moved over to covering local news and general assignments. When the job began to conflict with his studies, Stockton quit school in 1913, during his junior year, when the job began to conflict with his studies. In 1915 he left to join the staff of the *St. Louis Globe-Democrat* when he was offered the assignment of covering the St. Louis Federal League baseball team in Cuba. While on the island he also reported on the Jack Johnson–Jess Willard fight. Stockton briefly dropped out of the newspaper business in 1916 to work as an advance man for travelogue lecturer Frank R. Robinson. After Robinson died on tour in Canada, Stockton returned to his previous employer. He left the *Globe-Democrat* in July 1917 to join what became his permanent professional home–the *St. Louis Post-Dispatch.*

The advent of the United States into World War I interrupted Stockton's job at the copydesk. After fifteen months in uniform, he returned to the paper in 1919, moving to the sports department the next year, where he stayed until his retirement. To his new position as sportswriter he brought a copyreader's mentality for straightening up another writer's work and a familiarity with various forms of writing. In 1921 Stockton married Charlotte Burton, who later became recognized in St. Louis musical circles as a concert violinist, head of a women's research organization dedicated to the study and performance of music, and member of a national honorary musical sorority. The couple had one son, Richard Burton Stockton. Charlotte Stockton died of a heart ailment in 1953. The next year Stockton married the former Mrs. Josephine Knox Rassieur.

Stockton matured professionally as a sportswriter under the dignified sports editor for the *Post-Dispatch,* John Edward Wray, who, Stockton said, had the "quaint idea that sports should be written in good, sound English." Wray gave Stockton the name that became his byline when one day he could not remember the reporter's first name and used the initial *J* instead. When he later became an editor, in 1946, Stockton maintained that his staff should have an excellent education, know the language, read for the sake of writing, and "practice writing for the wastebasket."

Stockton had been an active athlete as a youth. In addition to sandlot baseball, he also participated in cinder-lot football and basketball. Tall and trim, he continued his participation in physical activity as an adult and was an avid duck hunter, golfer, and horseshoe pitcher into his old age. His varied interest in sports prepared him for a wide variety of assignments in his early years. Although he was largely identified with major league baseball, Stockton also covered boxing, tennis, football, basketball, rowing, horse racing, and golf.

His interest in golf proved valuable in one important assignment in September 1921. Stockton got his first big break that year when the United States Amateur golf tournament came to the St. Louis Country Club. O. K. Bovard, the managing editor of the newspaper, was so impressed by the rookie sportswriter's prose that he made no changes to Stockton's story. Stockton was sent to the World Series that year as a reward.

The golf tournament also marked the beginning of Stockton's experience with radio. On 18 September 1921 the *Post-Dispatch* ran an article explaining how their reporter had transmitted "hole-by-hole" descriptions of the tournament by wireless radiophone to the newspaper offices. The paper reported that "Boy Scouts in East St. Louis" listened in to the bulletins and heard them clearly. Working as a radio announcer eventually became a lucrative second career for Stockton. For fifteen years, from the early 1930s to the late 1940s, he conducted an evening sports news and commentary show on KSD radio in St. Louis. Rather than scripting his show, Stockton worked informally, conducting interviews in the style of a newspaper reporter. His approach opened the door for the kind of sports talk shows that later swept the nation. Stockton also became involved in early baseball television broadcasts following the first telecast of a St. Louis Cardinals game when KSD-TV went on the air in 1947.

Stockton began to cover the St. Louis Browns in 1922, the year they nearly won the pennant. In 1926 he moved over to cover the Cardinals. In nearly twenty years on the beat Stockton attended almost every game. Around 1935 he also spent a year as a ghostwriter for Jay Hanna "Dizzy" Dean, producing a short syndicated column, "Popping Off," that contained Dean's daily observations on sports. More important to local readers was Stockton's signature column, "Extra Innings," which became an established feature of the *Post-Dispatch* from the mid 1930s until he became sports editor in 1946, when he continued the column on an infrequent basis. Generally, Stockton's column concerned the pennant races, but the writer was never shy about speaking his mind on other sports when the occasion arose. His peers in the profession recognized his skills as a writer on the national pastime when they elected him president of the Baseball Writers Association of America in 1932.

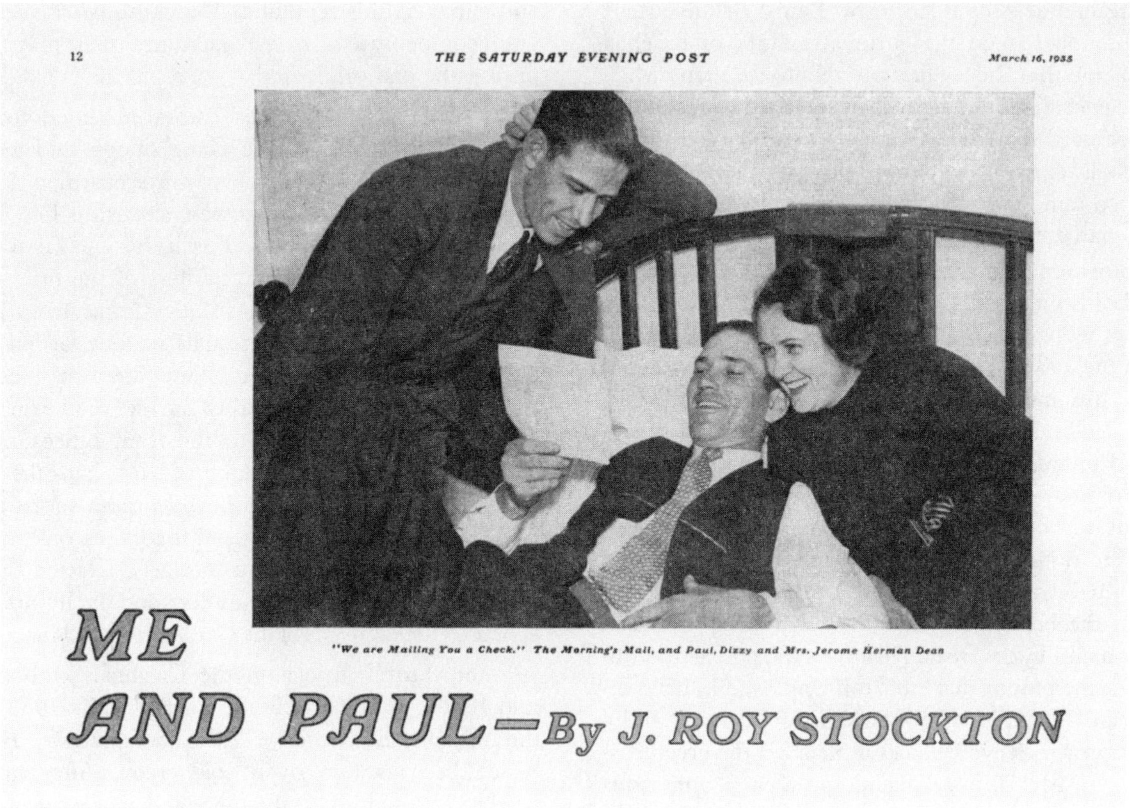
12 THE SATURDAY EVENING POST March 16, 1935

"We are Mailing You a Check." The Morning's Mail, and Paul, Dizzy and Mrs. Jerome Herman Dean

ME AND PAUL—By J. ROY STOCKTON

Opening of the article that began Stockton's association with St. Louis Cardinals pitcher Jay Hanna "Dizzy" Dean (reprinted with permission of The Saturday Evening Post *© 1935 [Renewed] BFL & MUS, Inc.)*

Stockton opted for straightforward description rather than merely colorful phrasing in his reportage. Typical of his style is his description of the success of Cardinals slugger Joe Medwick in the 31 May 1934 issue of the *St. Louis Post-Dispatch:* "Hostile pitchers have tried every trick in the bag. They have pitched inside, and Joe has whacked the ball against the left field fence. They have pitched outside, and he has banged extra base hits down the right field line. They have pitched high and low, fast and slow, and they haven't found a weakness." His columns generally relied on his own insights, as well as on "insider stuff" and the clubhouse quote, for which Stockton had a keen ear.

Like all good writers, Stockton knew what angles made good leads. In a 30 July 1934 article on a recent 9–5 St. Louis victory in Pittsburgh, Stockton began with the Cardinals slugger with Pennsylvania roots:

> James 'Ripper' Collins is a happy young man today, and the good people of Nant-y-glo, a little Pennsylvania mining community, are happy, too, and they are proud. Collins–'Lefty' to the folks back home–hit a home run for the old home town yesterday afternoon, and today his picture is in the Nant-y-glo paper–if they have a paper–and it's too bad that there isn't more of this small town sentiment in major league baseball.

While "Extra Innings" made his regional reputation, Stockton gained national recognition through the articles published in *The Saturday Evening Post* from 1935 to 1952. He was able to sell the magazine on a story about Branch Rickey, the general manager of the Cardinals, and Sam Breadon, the club owner, who worked together to turn the organization around in the 1920s. "From Rags to Riches" (9 March 1935) detailed Rickey's initiation of the farm system, which eventually allowed the club to dominate the National League for nearly a generation. Stockton also focused on the famous trade of Rogers Hornsby to the Giants for Frankie Frisch in 1926, which still stands as one of the most dynamic exchanges of superstars in baseball history. Stockton emphasized the indignation of Cardinals fans over the trade by stating, "Pro Bono Publico, Vox Populi and Beowulf Q. Phan vowed never to make another turnstile click."

Eight years later, in "A Brain Comes to Brooklyn" (13 February 1943), Stockton again wrote on Rickey, who had moved over to do for the Dodgers what he had accomplished in St. Louis. In this article Stockton focused on the curious mixture of baseball and religion that Rickey first brought to the game when it was "considered an adjunct of the beer garden." He also discussed the general manager's convoluted syntax that left listeners in a daze of polysyllables. Stockton described him "as a man who can do more tricks with words than a monkey can do with another monkey."

Stockton capitalized on the fame and popularity of St. Louis pitchers Dizzy and Paul "Daffy" Dean, the brothers who won two victories apiece for the Cardinals in the 1934 World Series, with the famously titled article "Me and Paul" in *The Saturday Evening Post* (16 March 1935). Realizing the importance of a good lead to a story, Stockton awoke in the middle of the night with the idea of telling the humorous story of Dizzy's claiming to be born in three places on three different dates. He rattled off the yarn in quick order, and the *Post* printed it with hardly any changes. This piece also marked the beginning of a long relationship between Stockton and Dizzy Dean. Dean was the perfect mouthpiece for the humor that Stockton employed in his writing because "he'd give you the shirt off his back, and a laugh up each sleeve." Stockton detailed the eccentricities of the backcountry pitcher in such a humorous fashion that Dean became, in part, a folkloric figure in the eyes of his adoring public. Dean did not always endear himself to managers, however, and once, one of them, Gabby Street, became so infuriated with Dean that Stockton found Dizzy "down like a Scotchman's razor blade." Years after the article was published, *The Saturday Evening Post* paid Stockton a great compliment when it informed him that a reader-interest survey rated "Me and Paul" higher than any article the magazine had ever printed.

Stockton wrote another article for *The Saturday Evening Post* on Dean the next year, "Me and My Public" (12 September 1936), which traced Dean's misadventures with money, including attempts to exploit the star and Dizzy's demands for a higher salary from the fiscally conservative Rickey. Flushed by his own success, Dean, according to Stockton, became arrogant, refusing to appear in exhibition games and disobeying direct orders from Rickey, and "tumbled from the sumptuous lap of Grandma Public." At one point Stockton, serving as a mediator, had to write a letter to Rickey on Dean's behalf before a contract could be signed. While Dean had become contrite about his role in the dispute, Stockton warned the general manager "that a parrot might learn to recite the Lord's Prayer, but that wouldn't make the bird a good Christian." Although Dean needed little help with colorful phrases, Stockton clearly at times embellished the pitcher's ability to embroider the English language and enhanced his reputation. Stockton twice sued and won compensation from magazines that plagiarized phrases he had originated.

While all of America embraced the riotous St. Louis Cardinals Gashouse Gang of the mid 1930s–including the Dean brothers, third baseman Pepper Martin, outfielder Joe Medwick, shortstop Leo Durocher, and manager Frankie Frisch–no one knew them better than Stockton. Many writers of the time wrote about the Gashousers, whose name came from Durocher's remark that the Cardinals were regarded as "a bunch of gas house players," but Stockton lived and traveled with them on trains during road trips. His close relationship with both the front office and the clubhouse gained him the kind of trust that other writers could not garner. Lloyd Lewis, former sports editor of the *Chicago Daily News,* stated that Stockton "was the right man to have collected the facts, ferreted out the secrets, filed the anecdotes, understood the humors and appraised the deeds . . . of the Cardinal baseball machine."

Stockton's article on the Cardinals club of the mid 1930s, "The Gas House Gang" (4 July 1936), was the only one he wrote for *The Saturday Evening Post* for which he was not given sole credit. After he had worked up the bulk of the piece and sent it off, the editors of the magazine decided that they wanted to list Frisch as the writer in an "as-told-to" format. Reluctantly, Stockton agreed to the arrangement that also called for a split of the remuneration, although the writer argued his way to a bonus check. When the story later appeared in *The Gashouse Gang and a Couple of Other Guys* (1945), Stockton wrote a disclaimer in which he explained that ghostwriting had become unfashionable and claimed that he would not engage in it again. He asserted that the publisher used the byline of an athlete only to make the work seem more authoritative. Still, Stockton took a jab at the manager when the article was published. He included a collaborator's note about how an umpire once told Dean that he could not remember anyone "who could compare, even remotely, with Frisch when it came to making swearing one of the elegant arts."

The Gashouse Gang story, allegedly written by Frisch in the first person, became a classic in its own time. The focus of the piece was the club clowns–Pepper Martin and Dizzy Dean. It follows them through escapades that focus on midget racing cars, rodeos, musical interludes, and pregame juggling acts to entertain fans. Stockton's acerbic wit did not come through as usual in this piece because it was not written in his voice. He instead allowed the actors to carry the show, believing that hyperbole would only detract from the material.

Stockton did not always focus on the Cardinals in his stories. By 1937 *The Saturday Evening Post* was contacting him with story suggestions, and that year they asked him to travel to Van Meter, Iowa, to do a story on Bob Feller. Feller's Des Moines ball club protested to the commissioner's office that Cleveland had illegally acquired his services. Commissioner Kenesaw Mountain Landis, however, declared Feller a free agent, and the Indians signed him to a contract worth $100,000. The author concluded: "no patch of ground ten times the size of the Oak View Baseball Park ever yielded an Iowa crop like that." This piece, "Bob Feller, Storybook Ball Player" (20 February 1937), however, did not flow as nicely as the Dean pieces and Stockton had to rewrite the article several times.

That same year Stockton wrote "Bill Likes Terry's Judgment" (27 March 1937), a story for *The Saturday Evening Post* on manager and first baseman Bill Terry, who had led the New York Giants to pennants in the years after he replaced John McGraw in 1933. Needing a catcher, Terry contacted Branch Rickey of the Cardinals, who had gained a reputation "as an astute dealer in baseball flesh." Upon seeing a general manager trade with the Mahatma (as Rickey was called), others would "ask him if he still has his shirt; the implication being that when you swap haberdashery with Rickey, you're likely to wind up a nudist," wrote Stockton. Still, Terry managed to acquire a more than adequate catcher, while the Cardinals eventually wound up with nothing.

In "Them Phillies," published in the 4 October 1941 issue of *The Saturday Evening Post,* Stockton wrote on the perennially cellar-dwelling team from Philadelphia. He wrote that their archaic ballpark, known as Baker Bowl, produced "showers of grimy rust falling in our thinning hair each time a foul hit the roof above." The 1938 club finished so poorly, Stockton wrote, that "fans were suggesting that all the Phillies wear the same number, No. 8, with a big black ball in front of the numeral"–a reference to their last-place finishes in an eight-team league, for many years.

Stockton took a personal and sometimes offbeat look at the national pastime in some of his writing. In "Baseball's Famous Tightwads" (11 July 1942), he wrote about many players' inability to part with their money. He accused them of being tightwads who always bought wholesale, stole newspapers from the hotel lobbies, and escaped restaurants behind waiters' backs rather than leave a tip. In spite of their shortcomings, however, he remained an ardent supporter of "a fellow who would be siding Old Bess down the corn row if it weren't for his peculiar ability to hit baseballs against faraway fences." In a chapter from *The Gashouse Gang and a Couple of Other Guys* on umpires, "You're Out!," Stockton emphasized their kinder, gentler side so as to balance the disrespect typically shown by "Fanaticus Baseballicus Americanus." He demonstrated his bias for the National League in "The People's Choice: National League" (*The Saturday Evening Post,* 16 July 1938), which he wrote in response to two articles in *The Saturday Evening Post* that had championed the Americans. He cited the Yankees as the cause for the apparent superiority of the American League and specifically the acquisition of Babe Ruth, which, he lamented, changed the style of baseball from one of finesse to one of power. To Stockton, this resulted in the junior circuit becoming New York and "a seven-team second division."

Stockton in the press box at Sportsman's Park in St. Louis, circa 1945 (photograph by Rud Rennie)

In "The Brown's Secret Weapon" (30 September 1944) he affectionately profiled his friend Jimmy Conzelman, citing the influence the new assistant to the president had brought in helping the St. Louis Browns win their only league title. Actually, the piece had more to do with Stockton's good friend and radio partner than with the club. The former player, manager, public speaker, Washington University football coach, radio commentator, and piano player was the master of so many trades, Stockton wrote, "that many persons probably don't know how good he is in his favorite lifework–or what that work really is if he has one." The author had such intimate knowledge of his subject that he was able to produce one of his most humorous works for the *Post.*

Most of Stockton's writing, though, naturally focused on the Cardinals. In "Born for the Gashouse" (22 May 1937) he stressed catcher Mickey Owen's "engaging screwiness that should be clothed in Cardinal livery." In "Lord Medwick of Cartaret" (1938) he emphasized Medwick's prowess in the 1934 Series, in which he proved that the only way Detroit could get the St. Louis hitter out was by throwing an assortment of produce at him. Other players who became subjects for his writing ranged from "Two-Game Johnny," a chapter for *The Gashouse Gang* on Johnny Beazley, a minor hero of the 1942 World Series victory over the Yankees, to "Stan Musial, The Donora Greyhound" (*The Saturday Evening Post,* 12 September 1942), in which he argued that the outfielder's performance in the previous year's pennant drive was worthy of "Rookie of the Year" honors.

Stockton, however, was not content with just writing about players. He also profiled coach Mike Gonzalez, trainer Harrison J. "Doc" Weaver, and manager Billy Southworth. Southworth, a former player and manager for the St. Louis team in the 1920s, who had lost his job in the last year of the decade because "when Redbirds, July and a lowly place in the league are in juxtaposition, that's a bad omen for a manager." As chronicled in "The Redbirds Fly Again" (9 August 1941), he returned, in 1941 to bring the Cardinals back to prominence. The difference was so noteworthy that Stockton wrote, "If you couldn't give all you had for a man like that–well, the heel was in your shoes." Weaver was highlighted in "Double-Whammy Doc" (31 July 1943) for the finger pointing "whammy" he employed in the 1942 World Series that supposedly jinxed the opposition. Gonzalez was the subject of a piece titled "Mike, Maybe She Know Something" (20 May 1939), in which Stockton failed to Anglicize the coach's English. Thus the coach, "who had an especially tough time in the pronoun department" mentioned that "if (Mickey) Owen take care of himself, she be a great star." To Stockton, "Mike never bothered to replace the divots as he sliced and pulled our language." Still, Gonzalez was a tremendous aid to his manager during a pennant race as he helped "to brush away the cobwebs of discontent and iron the pretzels out of the Frisch forehead."

All of Stockton's *Saturday Evening Post* articles up to 1945 were published with minor changes as *The Gashouse Gang and a Couple of Other Guys.* The book went through six printings in three years and became the author's signature work. It sold well because sports books had become important for servicemen at that time and it included a variety of photographs of his subjects. Critics considered it a work of Americana whose contents contained the ideal subjects for the nation's success saga. The Gashouse boys were the Horatio Algers of baseball who came from rural backgrounds to scale the heights of major league glory–and J. Roy Stockton was their classic storyteller.

About the time the book came out, a World War II incident made a lasting impression on Stockton and his readers. In spite of his fifteen-month service in World War I, he had never seen action up front. In 1944–1945 he went on a USO-sponsored trip with Frank Frisch, Bucky Walters, Mel Ott, and Dutch Leonard to the European theater that nearly got them caught in the Battle of the Bulge. Traveling through France, Belgium, Luxembourg, and Holland and into Germany, the group heard buzz bombs overhead and artillery fire uncomfortably close as they journeyed to give baseball shows to homesick troops. When the major battle broke out, their itinerary was altered to keep the civilian entertainers out of harm's way. Carrying identification cards giving each of them a captain's rank in case of capture, the group was overwhelmed by the bravery they encountered in hospitals and in their audiences when they appeared on makeshift stages. Escaping in the middle of the night, they managed to avoid German attacks. In the initial stages of the tour, Stockton wondered if the trip was worth it, but by the end he was deeply moved by the strength they had been giving troops through the power of baseball. After he wrote about this harrowing war experience for the 28 January and 9 February 1945 editions of the *St. Louis Post-Dispatch,* Stockton did not want his writers to use the word "courage" when referring to ballplayers because he had witnessed the finest example of what that word meant.

In April 1946 Stockton became the sports editor of the *Post-Dispatch,* but his work for *The Saturday Evening Post* continued and contained some of his finest writing. From 1947 to 1952 he produced three more pieces for the magazine–all of which dealt with the Cardinals. The subject of the first, "Singing Sam, the Cut-Rate Man" (22 February 1947), was club president Sam Breadon, who managed to rearrange the Cardinal roster, keep the club competitive, and make a tidy profit in the smallest market in the big leagues. Assuming the club leadership by 1920, he gradually became the slyest of businessmen: Stockton wrote that "no enterprising delicatessen maestro ever sliced his salami finer than Breadon . . . in squeezing out the maximum cash-register return." When Stockton criticized the president for his tactics in a speech, "Breadon put his chin on his vest and snubbed all Stocktons for a month." Three years later in "Baseball's Amazing Ama-

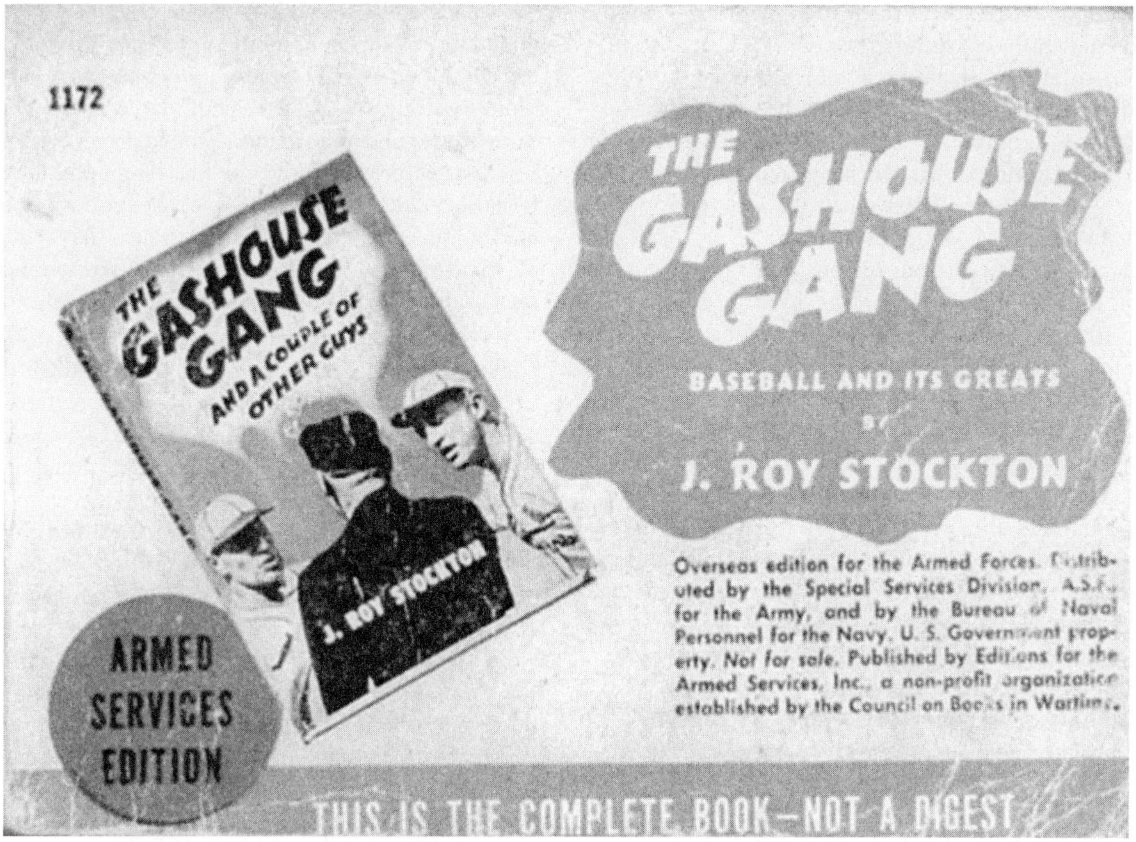

Cover for the Armed Forces Edition (1946) of Stockton's 1945 collection of his articles about the Cardinals that first appeared in The Saturday Evening Post *(Bruccoli Collection, Thomas Cooper Library, University of South Carolina)*

teur" (27 May 1950) he examined the new Cardinals owner Fred Saigh, a corporate tax wizard, who purchased the team from an ailing Breadon. Stockton described this deal with intimate financial knowledge and revealed how Saigh revolutionized the business side of the pastime so that, in term of seats for postseason games, "Beowulf Q. Phan . . . gets a fair shake."

Stockton's last article for *The Saturday Evening Post,* "Can the Rajah Rejuvenate the Browns?" (9 February 1952) treated Browns owner Bill Veeck's naming of the controversial Rogers Hornsby as manager. Having already worked in this position for four clubs, the famous Hall of Fame second baseman and manager of the 1926 Cardinals had once been angered that Breadon insisted on exhibition games being scheduled during a late season pennant drive in order to beef up the club's revenues. Stockton eliminated the profanity that followed in the confrontation between the two by writing that Hornsby "suggested a vulgar disposition of the exhibition games." Twenty-six years later Hornsby claimed to have mellowed, but Stockton insisted, "He still swears at the drop of an adjective."

In 1953 Stockton wrote two more articles on Hornsby for *Look* magazine, "How to Get Fired" (14 July) and "What to Watch for in Big League Baseball" (28 July), which served as advertisement for a biographical book on the tempestuous player/manager, *My Kind of Baseball* (1953). Both *Look* articles listed Hornsby as author, with the real writer given "as-told-to" status, despite Stockton's earlier vow that he would not participate in such an arrangement again. Neither article offered any fresh writing, since both were made up of snippets from the book.

My Kind of Baseball, written partly in third person, represented a departure in Stockton's style that set the pattern for his subsequent writing. Strewn throughout the foreword are references to "we are convinced," "we can't find," and "we saw." Stockton found Hornsby's memory to be something less than precise and therefore had to rely on his own knowledge of the baseball great and the recollection of contemporary writers, who were listed in footnotes. Thus, while Stockton did conduct interviews with Hornsby, the book is only loosely based on those sessions and is mostly in Stockton's own words. The result is a rather mediocre book. Still, in his lengthy foreword, Stockton does demonstrate his stylistic humor in a classic statement on an alleged weakness of Hornsby's game. The second baseman, he wrote, "was to be excused, if he was not too familiar with pop flies–he hit so few of them." He also noted that Hornsby could still swing a bat later in his career "even when the legs were gone and the avoirdupois was excessive."

Stockton retired from his position as sports editor for the *St. Louis Post-Dispatch* in July 1958. He moved to St. Petersburg, Florida, but still occasionally wrote for the *Post-Dispatch* and other publications. In November 1959 he wrote a significant piece for *The Quill* about the changing sports scene he had experienced during his days with the paper. On the light side, Stockton lamented the rise of night baseball, which extended the writer's hours to the late night. More seriously, though, he wrote about ownership changes that had turned the reins of control of the game from baseball people to business types. In a more-positive vein he noted that the sheer size of the sports department had tripled during his tenure and that almost everyone was now considered a well-rounded newspaper person. He observed that the wire services paid much greater attention to sports than in the past. In sum, Stockton argued that sportswriting was better and that good English had replaced the slang of the ballparks. He believed that the sports pages had become "a newspaper within a newspaper."

In 1962 Stockton produced his second biography and his final book, *Frank Frisch: The Fordham Flash,* which dealt with the other second baseman in the Cardinal-Giants switch of 1926. Once again, the player was listed as author and Stockton received "as-told-to" status. One particular picture in the book demonstrates that the author may have been tiring of his second-class position, for it shows Frisch holding a copy of Stockton's *Gashouse Gang,* noting that he liked to relax with a good book. Like his first biography on Hornsby, Stockton's book on Frisch includes parts borrowed from previous writing combined with interviews, personal knowledge, and information gained from others. The Frisch book is a cut above the first biography, however, because Stockton knew his subject better, having associated with him during the Gashouse days and the World War II tour. Also, it had been written in retirement, allowing the author more time to craft his prose.

Stockton took over the job as president of the Class A Florida State League in January 1963 at the age of seventy, but he found the job too arduous and resigned nine months later. He died from leukemia on 24 August 1972. Stockton posthumously earned national recognition in December when he was chosen as a winner of the annual J. G. Taylor Spink Award. Johnson Spink of *The Sporting News* called him "one of the last of a vanishing breed" of journalistic giants. Broeg asserted that Stockton was "the cleverest fast writer or fastest clever writer" he had ever seen. Through his character, his emphasis on tight and clear writing, and his ability to teach others, J. Roy Stockton helped to elevate sportswriting into its modern professional status.

References:

Bob Broeg, "Broeg on Baseball," *Sporting News,* 174 (9 September 1972): 4;

Broeg, "Daniel, Lieb and Stockton Win Spink Award," *Sporting News,* 174 (9 December 1972): 41;

Broeg, "Fearless, Funny Stockton Master of Rapier Wit," *St. Louis Post-Dispatch,* 25 August 1972, p. B5;

"Sports Editor Stockton Retires After 41 Years; Bob Broeg is Successor," *St. Louis Post-Dispatch,* 29 June 1958.

Al Stump

(20 October 1916 – 21 December 1995)

Nate Stone
University of California at Berkeley

and

James C. Kaufman
Yale University

BOOKS: *Champions against Odds* (Philadelphia: Macrae Smith, 1952);

My Life in Baseball: The True Record, by Stump and Ty Cobb (Garden City, N.Y.: Doubleday, 1961);

The Education of a Golfer, by Stump and Sam Snead (New York: Simon & Schuster, 1962);

Cobb: A Biography (Chapel Hill, N.C.: Algonquin, 1994).

Edition: *My Life in Baseball: The True Record,* by Stump and Ty Cobb, introduction by Charles C. Alexander (Lincoln: University of Nebraska Press, 1993).

Al Stump (photograph by K. C. Andersen)

OTHER: "Football's Biggest Bargain," in *Best Sports Stories 1949: A Panorama of the 1948 Sports Year,* edited by Irving T. Marsh and Edward Ehre (New York: Dutton, 1949), pp. 135–146;

"The Amazing Nobodies," in *Best Sports Stories 1950: A Panorama of the 1949 Sports Year,* edited by Marsh and Ehre (New York: Dutton, 1950), pp. 169–180;

"Fancy Diving Only Looks Like Fun," in *Best Sports Stories 1952: A Panorama of the 1951 Sports Year,* edited by Marsh and Ehre (New York: Dutton, 1952), pp. 255–266;

"Football's Private Eyes," in *Best Sports Stories 1953: A Panorama of the 1952 Sports Year,* edited by Marsh and Ehre (New York: Dutton, 1953), pp. 118–123;

"All Jeff Had Was His Fists," in *Sportswriters' Choice,* edited by Richard P. Goldman (New York: Barnes, 1958), pp. 281–296;

"Jackpot Jockey," in *Best Sports Stories 1958: A Panorama of the 1957 Sports Year,* edited by Marsh and Ehre (New York: Dutton, 1958), pp. 183–195;

"Baseball's Biggest Headaches–Dames," in *Best Sports Stories 1960: A Panorama of the 1959 Sports Year,* edited by Marsh and Ehre (New York: Dutton, 1960), pp. 65–78;

"Headhunter with a Horsehide," in *Best Sports Stories 1961: A Panorama of the 1960 Sports Year,* edited by Marsh and Ehre (New York: Dutton, 1961), pp. 74–87;

"The Fight to Live," in *Best Sports Stories 1962: A Panorama of the 1961 Sports Year,* edited by Marsh and Ehre (New York: Dutton, 1962), pp. 35–55; republished as "Ty Cobb's Wild Ten-Month Fight to Live," in *The Third Fireside Book of Baseball,* edited by Charles Einstein (New York: Simon & Schuster, 1968), pp. 441–452;

"Baseball Is Inviting Tragedy," in *Best Sports Stories 1963: A Panorama of the 1962 Sports Year,* edited by Marsh and Ehre (New York: Dutton, 1963), pp. 86–99;

"The Angels' Tiny Terror," in *Best Sports Stories 1964: A Panorama of the 1963 Sports Year,* edited by Marsh and Ehre (New York: Dutton, 1964), pp. 84–95;

"The Last Triumphant Ride of Johnny Longden," in *Best Sports Stories 1967: A Panorama of the 1966 Sports Year,* edited by Marsh and Ehre (New York: Dutton, 1967), pp. 216–226;

"Always They Want More, More, More," in *Best Sports Stories 1968: A Panorama of the 1967 Sports Year,* edited by Marsh and Ehre (New York: Dutton, 1968), pp. 83–91;

"No Rams Like Old Rams," in *Best Sports Stories 1969: A Panorama of the 1968 Sports Year,* edited by Marsh and Ehre (New York: Dutton, 1969), pp. 113–124;

"High-Scoring Catastrophe," in *Best Sports Stories 1970: A Panorama of the 1969 Sports Year,* edited by Marsh and Ehre (New York: Dutton, 1970), pp. 155–165;

"Joe Kapp–Football's Fury," in *Best Sports Stories 1971: A Panorama of the 1970 Sports Year,* edited by Marsh and Ehre (New York: Dutton, 1971), pp. 92–99.

Sportswriters are often remembered as being intricately linked with a particular city or a particular team. Rarely, however, has a sportswriter been so associated with an individual athlete as Al Stump was with the baseball player Ty Cobb. Stump co-authored Cobb's autobiography in 1961, and he capped his career in 1994 by telling the true story of the baseball legend in his biography of Cobb. Like the Hall of Famer with whom he is always paired, Stump had a long career marked by both greatness and controversy. Using his gift for narrative and his insight into the athlete's psyche, Stump helped create myths and then broke them down.

Alvin J. Stump was born in Colorado Springs, Colorado, on 20 October 1916. As a teenager he covered the 1934 Columbia-Stanford Rose Bowl game for his hometown newspaper. After graduating from Vancouver High School in 1935 he attended the University of Washington, where he became the sports editor of the school newspaper, *The Columbian.* In those days "sports editor" meant reporter, layout designer, and editor rolled into one. This post helped prepare him for work at the *Portland Oregonian* upon graduation.

In 1939, soon after joining the *Oregonian,* Stump published his first magazine article in *The Saturday Evening Post.* During World War II he served in the U.S. Navy on the aircraft carrier U.S.S. *Hancock* while also working as a war correspondent. After the war Stump left the *Oregonian* and became a freelance writer, contributing articles to the *Los Angeles Herald-Examiner,* the *Los Angeles Times, The Saturday Evening Post, True, American Heritage, Esquire,* and *Sport.* He interviewed luminaries such as writer Ernest Hemingway; athlete Jim Thorpe; actors John Wayne, Alan Ladd, and Humphrey Bogart; and gangster Benjamin "Bugsy" Siegel. Stump covered the Charles Manson murder trial in 1970–1971, reported from Vietnam with Vice President Spiro Agnew, and was evicted from the M-G-M lot by director John Ford. Nevertheless, Stump always considered himself a sportswriter.

Perhaps the most often repeated theme in Stump's writing is the intimate link between the athlete and his or her fans. Sports are for the fans, Stump believed, and he sought out the common ground between his readers and their idols. When he could find no such connection, he went on the offensive, found the dirt, and pounced on the person or sport that had betrayed the fans.

In a 1948 essay for *The Saturday Evening Post,* "Football's Biggest Bargain," Stump describes small-college football and the fans who devour it. Stump points out that seven million fans attend small-college games, but this "phase of football" is "blithely overlooked by the rating bureaus, syndicated columnists, national radio networks and most metropolitan fans." The small-college fans, however, "proved that you don't have to pay scalpers' prices of $5.50 for a Rose Bowl seat to enjoy the pastime to a hilt." Stump notes that a ninety-eight-yard touchdown run by Spec Sanders of the New York Yankees against the Los Angeles Dons (both teams were in the old All-America Football Conference) was generally accepted as the most exciting play of the 1948 professional football season; while in college in Lawton, Oklahoma, however, Sanders had exploded for many such plays for a ticket price that would have astounded Yankees fans. "Things like that happen all the time in football's bargain basement."

For the 12 February 1949 issue of *The Saturday Evening Post* Stump wrote about "one of the best shows in America": the University of Utah basketball team, the Utes. The sport had an unusually rich history in the Mormon state: "On nearly every farm a hoop is nailed to a barn wall. Even in summertime, kids are out shooting. Sprouts of five and six show an amazing ability to fake, dribble, pass and shoot–the latter, of course, in the Western one-handed style that was developed in Utah fifteen years before the East saw and tried it."

In a 1951 article for *The Saturday Evening Post,* "Fancy Diving Only Looks Like Fun," Stump delved into the darker side of female platform diving. In a sport where grace and beauty are the standards for judgment, Stump finds bumps, cuts, bruises, and competitive fury that are usually associated with boxing. "Behind all that poetry-in-motion you see in the newsreels, there is enough

You haven't seen anything until you've been to institutions like Willamette, where play may halt while the ball is fished from the creek.

Football's Biggest Bargain

By AL STUMP

Where does a fan get the most for his money? Notre Dame vs. Northwestern? Bears vs. Cardinals? No, says the writer, and proves his point with the inside story of small-college competition. Prize example: Oregon's Willamette.

LATE in the 1940 football season, the suburban community of Parkland, Washington, found itself torn between two crises. A windstorm sweeping through Puget Sound had ripped away the center span of "Galloping Gertie"—the $7,000,000 Tacoma Narrows bridge—and dumped the tons of steel into the channel, leaving the whole area without a connecting link between the mainland and the Olympic Peninsula. Engineers termed it one of the worst structural catastrophes in West Coast history.

Gloomy as was this outlook, even more depressing from Parkland's viewpoint was Saturday night's game involving the local Pacific Lutheran College team. The little Lutes, who only recently had become affluent enough to afford a football and an air pump, were unbeaten and untied in two straight seasons. Dopesters had it that the winning streak was about to be snapped by Gonzaga, of Spokane, a long-time spoiler among small colleges. While civic leaders cried out at the paralyzing blow wrought by loss of the bridge, 15,000 aroused Parklanders and Tacomans rallied to the gridiron emergency.

Gonzaga opened with a dazzling ground attack led by Tony Canadeo, later a star with the Green Bay Packers. When the Zags easily grabbed a 13–0 second-period lead, a deep groan came from the packed bowl.

But despair shortly turned to bedlam when Marv Tommervik, the Lutheran Little-All-American back, threw two hair-raising touchdown passes, missing one conversion, but tying the score. With only seconds left to play in the game, the Lutherans butted their way to the Gonzaga thirty-two-yard line.

"Kick!" screamed the throng.

The angle was bad and a stiff wind off the sound blew in his face, but Marvel Harshman, the Lute fullback, gamely dug his toe into the ball. Harshman had never before tried a field goal. The ball tumbled high and far, wavering in the wind—and then the referee suddenly flung his hands upward.

The riot was on. For hours after the 16–13 upset, bonfires glared and citizens danced in the streets. The tragedy of Galloping Gertie was temporarily forgotten.

28

Opening of Stump's 20 November 1948 article in The Saturday Evening Post *about small-college football (reprinted with permission of* The Saturday Evening Post © *1948 [Renewed] BFL & MUS, Inc.)*

feuding and fussing and nerve-and-body strain to make the diving stars the heaviest consumers of sleeping tablets in sports." Stump introduces his reader to a platform-circuit professional, Pat Keller McCormick, describing her grueling four-hour-a-day training schedule and a visit to the doctor: "Mrs. McCormick had: a six-inch, healed-over scalp wound, all of her front teeth chipped, several mysterious scars above the base of her spine, fresh lacerations of the feet and elbows, a once-cracked rib and broken finger, and a loose jaw that threatened to pop from its hinges. In addition, spread across her collarbones were a number of ugly blood welts that puzzled the doctor." Describing the haggling over the liveliness of the diving board, Stump writes of a "meet at which three boards were installed and torn down and a nose punched before a majority decision was reached."

In a 1953 *Esquire* piece on the Rose Bowl game Stump noted:

> The Bowl has long been final examinations for gate-crashers. Fans have attacked the fence with shears, formed human pyramids, and even dug elaborate tunnels during the night. The senior master of these zanies, "One-Eyed" Connolly, boasted in 1941 that he would attend the Nebraska-Stanford game without a ticket ("probably," he said loftily, "as a guest of the governor of Nebraska"), then showed up disguised as a Pasadena sanitation inspector, badge and all. He was thrown out. Tackling the fence, the great crasher suffered the worst indignity of his career: he was snagged on the wire, caught and jailed for the afternoon.

Not all of Stump's pieces have aged well. A 1959 article for the men's magazine *True,* "Baseball's Biggest Headaches–Dames," would not be published today: "The typical baseball frau is pretty, 23 years old, wasn't able to hold a job after a year of business college and overcooks the pot roast. Nonetheless, she no sooner joins the wives' box in the stands than she's an expert on tactics." Citing several examples of interfering spouses, he continues: "What can be done about purging man's favorite pastime of women? If you have an idea don't throw it away. . . ."

Stump tried to set the historical record straight in regard to the long-forgotten pugilist James J. Jeffries in a December 1954 profile for *Argosy:* "The trouble was, Jeff could only fight. Fans could adore [John L.] Sullivan for his drinking and boasting, admire [James J.] Corbett's elegance, become outraged at Jack Johnson's affairs with white women. Beside them Jeffries was a clod." Stump finds Jeffries in his last years a humanitarian and a man of character, despite many dark chapters in his life and boxing career. Yet, "as pure fist-slinger, the unbeatable ring animal, he remains . . . an object of authentic wonder. Quite possibly he was the greatest heavyweight of all time."

Stump profiled the UCLA football coach Red Sanders–"The small man with guts enough to defy the big fellows and the brains to improvise ways to make up for his lack of size"–for *Sport* magazine (December 1956) and the extraordinarily wealthy jockey Johnny "Pumper" Longden for *True* in 1958: "But the big talent–the one that made him a millionaire–is his gift for lifting a thoroughbred at the finish, of throwing his head across the wire with a pumping action of legs, thighs, arms, and hands. Thus Longden's nickname."

In 1959 Stump received a life-changing assignment: to ghostwrite the autobiography of a living legend. Cobb had been persuaded by acquaintances, including the sportswriter Grantland Rice, to tell his life story. The Hall of Famer had already angered or frightened off six other writers; the biographer Gene Fowler recommended Stump, and Cobb offered him the job. Stump and Cobb committed to the project in January 1960, agreeing to split $6,000 from Doubleday. "We met with Cobb in a hotel in Manhattan," Stump's agent, Sterling Lord, told Richard Sandomir. "He had no agent. He represented himself. Boy, was he tough and irascible. When I explained that we had to let Al in on some of the subsidiary rights, Cobb said, 'I understand what you're saying, but I only know this man for 10 minutes.'"

Stump and Cobb spent the winter of 1960–1961 at Cobb's lodge at Lake Tahoe. Cobb needed a wide variety of medications to fight his cancer, high blood pressure, heart disease, and diabetes. A heavy drinker, he could neither sort the pills properly nor manage a useful insulin injection; since he had no servants or nurses, despite his multimillion-dollar fortune–their absence was a testament to Cobb's demeanor: he had a short temper and was known to blow up for the most inconsequential actions–Stump took over caretaking details. Cobb's fierce desire to finish the book–and Stump's care–may have been the only things that kept him alive during the ten months he spent with the sportswriter.

Late in the winter Cobb decided that he and Stump should go to Reno, Nevada. When Stump protested that Cobb belonged in a hospital, not a casino, Cobb brandished the Luger handgun that was always at his side and informed Stump that the trip would occur with or without the sportswriter's presence. In a blizzard so fierce that the windshield wipers had no effect, Stump followed Cobb down the mountain. Racing ahead, Cobb crashed his car into a snowdrift. Stump rescued the baseball star, who had only suffered a bump on the head. In Reno, Cobb shot craps until he got into a scuffle with a casino worker, and he and Stump were thrown out of the establishment.

A few weeks later Stump found Cobb unconscious on the floor of the lodge. He tried to call for a doctor but found the line dead: Cobb had had the telephone disconnected because he feared that people were eavesdropping on him. Stump ran to a neighboring home and phoned a doctor, but on his return to the lodge Cobb had recovered and was brushing off the experience as just a dizzy spell. Cobb then decided that they would travel to his home in Atherton, California. When they arrived, Stump found no electric power or gas in the eleven-room villa: Cobb was having a dispute with Pacific Gas and Electric and had refused to pay his bill. For the duration of their time in Atherton, Stump took cold showers and cooked meals over a Coleman camp stove.

In late December, Cobb and Stump flew to Georgia so that Cobb could see his hometown, Royston, once more. Their visit to the cemetery that contained the graves of Cobb's mother and father and the mausoleum that Cobb had built for himself and his family was one of their closest moments. Cobb's mother had killed his father in a shooting accident just before Cobb reached the major leagues. As they prayed at the grave site, Cobb told Stump that he had spent his entire life trying to please the ghost of his father.

In March 1961 Stump and Cobb spent a few weeks at the major league spring training camps in Scottsdale, Arizona. Players, managers, and writers came to Cobb's hotel to get his opinions on the state of baseball and the quality of the players. Stump then invited Cobb to his home in Santa Barbara, California, where they worked together until Cobb returned to Atherton in May. Cobb died on 17 July 1961, as Stump was completing work on the autobiography.

My Life in Baseball: The True Record (1961) sold well because of Cobb's death, and it remained in print until 1965. In 1993 the University of Nebraska press republished the book with a new introduction by Charles C. Alexander, who had written a popular 1984 biography of Cobb. The publication of the book "was the end of it for me," Stump told reporters. "I thought I had seen the last of Cobb's story. I didn't attend his funeral, and few other people did. I was fed up with him. I thought he was a monster who had no love for his fellow man." In fact, however, soon after the release of the autobiography Stump recounted his experiences with Cobb for *True* magazine in "Ty Cobb's Wild Ten-Month Fight to Live." Stump thought that Cobb had whitewashed his image in the autobiography and that it was important to set the record straight. He concludes that Cobb was a great baseball player but "a badly disturbed personality."

Bob Considine praised "Ty Cobb's Wild Ten-Month Fight to Live" as "perhaps the best sports piece I have ever read." The article won the E. P. Dutton Best Magazine Sports Story award and the Associated Press Best Sports Story of the Year Award in 1962 and was widely anthologized. The accuracy of the piece, however, was called into question. In his foreword to the 1993 edition of *My Life in Baseball* Alexander said that Stump's article "reads like a gothic horror story," calling it "at best an exercise in poor taste, at worst a severe injustice to a man who had done much for his hometown and substantial good otherwise." Alexander also accuses Stump of only seeing Cobb a handful of times during the ten-month period he was writing the book. Cobb's son, Jimmy, told Mark Reese, "The last two years of his life, my father suffered tremendously healthwise. . . . The book that was written by Al Stump was good. But then there was a very brutal article in *True* magazine. It was very brutal, and it was a time when my dad was going through a lot of hell." Nonetheless, John Chamberlain called the article "a reportorial triumph," and Charles Einstein, anthologizing it in *The Third Fireside Book of Baseball* (1968), characterized it as "a stark characterization of an all-time baseball immortal in the last year of his life."

Stump went on to collaborate with golfing legend Sam Snead on *The Education of a Golfer* (1962) and to write profiles of such greats as boxers Joe Louis and Jack Dempsey, basketball player Earvin "Magic" Johnson, and baseball manager Billy Martin. The five-foot, four and seven-eighths-inch, 150-pound Los Angeles Angels outfielder Albie Pearson was the focus of a 1964 *True* essay in which Stump marveled at Pearson's unusual power: "It is almost Holy Writ that a lightweight can succeed only by . . . poking the ball through defensive holes, seeking the base-on-balls–but Albie digs in and cockily goes for the long ball with a bat as heavy (up to 36 ounces) as Willie Mays'." In 1970, also for *True,* he wrote on the Minnesota Vikings' Joe Kapp, "Football's Fury"–"a rare sight in sports, a quarterback who is a practicing cynic and a socially conscious, hard-fisted activist. He doesn't talk fancy; he barks at crowds as if they were in a huddle with him." Of Los Angeles Lakers coach Butch van Breda Kolff, Stump wrote: "The bibulous, night-walking, fun-loving Butch, the only coach whose athletes have to call a curfew on him, also has the richest Pier Six vocabulary in basketball and the largest hate for the whistle tooters: last season he led the NBA in technical fouls with 30, at the cost of $24 each." Stump wrote for the top magazines of the day, including *TV Guide, Sports Illustrated, Golf,* and *Golf Journal.* He wrote a piece for *Los Angeles* magazine on Pancho Villa that was optioned for a motion picture but has not been filmed. By the end of his active writing days Stump had won ten Greater Los Angeles Press Club Awards and two Dutton Best American Sports Story Awards. But his definitive final work was yet to come.

Stump had always been upset about the Cobb autobiography. His contract had stated that Cobb had final editorial approval, and when the book was sent to the publisher it had been exactly as Cobb wanted it. "The first book was a cover-up," he told reporters. "I felt very bad about it. I felt I wasn't being a good newspaperman." His *True* article had evened the score to an extent, but only

Dust jacket for Stump's 1994 biography of the former Detroit Tigers star

when plans were under way to film the motion picture *Cobb* did Stump get his chance to tell his side of the story in a book. Ron Shelton, who had written and directed the 1988 baseball movie *Bull Durham,* was set to take on the same chores on the movie version of Cobb's life. "Growing up, I had heard of one sportswriter," Shelton told reporters. "There was only one I could name on the planet, and it was Al Stump." Stump felt the same way about Shelton. "Al was more thrilled that Ron Shelton did the movie than the fact that there is a movie," his wife, Jo Mosher, told reporters. "Ron and Robert [Wuhl, who portrayed Stump in the movie] came here and spent a lot of time with us."

Stump had trouble visualizing what actor would play the Hall of Famer. "Who do you get to play the dyspeptic, villainous Tiger as hero of a drama depicting his life?" he asked reporters. "You need a Boris Karloff, at least. Or Bela Lugosi. Face it–who could possibly play someone so bilious, hostile to humankind and so driven to win . . . ? With T. R. Cobb, what we have is an anti-hero to surpass Edward G. Robinson as Scarface Capone." (Tommy Lee Jones played the role.)

After submitting the *True* article and another chapter to Algonquin Books of Chapel Hill, North Carolina, Stump received a contract to tell his version of the story. He originally wanted to title the biography "Blood on His Spikes," after Cobb's famous cleats-high slides, but he settled for *Cobb* (1994). This time Stump held nothing back, recording a scathing portrayal of a man driven by a competitiveness that went beyond obsession. In the introduction Stump admits that his

> feelings for Ty Cobb were often in flux. My respect for his greatness, my contempt for his vile temper and mistreatment of others, my pity for his deteriorating health, and my admiration for his stubbornness and persistence produced a frustrating mix of emotions. As far as I could see . . . he wasn't merely erratic and trigger tempered, but suffering from megalomania, or acute self-worship, delusions of persecution, and more than a touch of dipsomania. . . . He scared the hell out of me most of the time I was around him.

Stump makes it clear that "the greatest ballplayer who ever lived" had few, if any, other redeeming qualities.

Publication of *Cobb* brought much praise and much anger. Naming it a Notable Book of the Year, *The New York Times* said that it was "an excellent job of plumbing the character of a sports legend." Roger Kahn dubbed it "The most powerful baseball biography I have ever read," while Jim Murray crowed that "The pen was mightier than the curveball. . . . Cobb finally found a pitch–and a pitcher–he couldn't hit. Stump popped him up." Jules Tygiel wrote in the *Washington Post* that "Stump has resurrected Cobb in all his terrifying malevolence" and called the book an "engrossing horror tale." The *Los Angeles Times Book Review* called the work "the definitive book on Cobb." Harry Kisor said in the *Chicago Sun-Times:* "Stump is no stylist. His prose is as euphonious as his names. In too many places it plods like a tired old catcher on the basepaths. . . . A few of his sentences never should have been allowed out of the minors. All the same, *Cobb* is absolutely riveting. Stump . . . forges connections many of today's more stylish but also self-absorbed sportswriters often seem incapable of making."

Many, however, were upset by Stump's denigration of a legend. Los Angeles Dodgers manager Tommy Lasorda told Terry Frei that he thought Stump was a traitor, not just to Cobb but to baseball. "The book shouldn't be the story," wrote journalist John O'Rourke in the *Albuquerque Tribune* (28 June 1995) of the movie. "Cobb should be. . . . It takes more eyes, more views than just Al Stump's to capture all the dimensions of Ty Cobb."

Not surprisingly, the surviving members of Cobb's family were furious with Stump. "Why don't they leave the private life alone and stay with Daddy's records and give him his due?" Beverly McLaren, Cobb's daughter, asked Lowell Cohn. "People want to know the dirt." While McLaren did not question Stump's accuracy, she objected to his invasion of her father's privacy. "I met Al Stump, and I'm not very fond of him," she said. "I think he had no consideration for family, the fact that there are a lot of grandchildren and great grandchildren. I didn't extol my father, but I also didn't have a lot of unpleasant input for my children. Why should I?" McLaren's sister-in-law, Shirley, told Cohn, "None of us have any respect for Stump. He's just a money grubber. . . . This is aging us fast."

More troubling than the issue of the appropriateness of the book were questions that arose about its accuracy. Steve Gietschier, in his review in *The Sporting News* (28 November 1994), pointed out "that the careful reader has no way to judge its accuracy. There are no footnotes, and so the question must be asked: Where did all this material come from?" Gietschier pointed out that there was little evidence of new research on Stump's part. Errors appear, such as Stump's mentioning the New York Mets to Cobb, who died before their debut, and unrecorded conversations are remembered too well. Stump's editor, Louis D. Rubin Jr., confirmed that the accuracy of the book was a problem. "Al was not quite as sharp as he might have been earlier on," Rubin said. "It was a very difficult editing job. He just wasn't in control at that stage. He'd write a chapter and we'd have to edit it very carefully because it would be full of errors." In addition, Rubin said, Stump's sources may have been questionable. "I don't know exactly where he was finding all the historical material. By the time he interviewed Cobb, he [Cobb] was a pretty unreliable source. I knew that if Al's book came out and didn't take into account the facts that Alexander had, he would be severely criticized." But this consideration led to another problem for Rubin: "Exactly what he was basing his information on, I didn't know. At one point, I got worried that he might be using Alexander and I wrote him and said, 'You can't do that. You've got to give credit.' He thought I was accusing him of plagiarizing and he was upset." In the end, however, Rubin said he believed that *Cobb* was an outstanding book by an outstanding man: "I admire very much his struggles. He was in and out of the hospital; it took a lot of guts. I think it was a great finale for a very good sportswriter. Al's book is the scope of life–Alexander's book is pretty dull."

Stump died of congestive heart failure on 21 December 1995 in Newport Beach, California. Working until the end, he was planning to write a new book about horse racing. He was survived by his wife, Jo, a journalist who wrote travel and feature articles for the *Los Angeles Herald Examiner* and was a past president of the Los Angeles Press Club; four children; two stepdaughters; and many grandchildren. His ashes were scattered at sea with military honors, and Shelton delivered the eulogy. "There are only a couple of things I would want to learn from Ty Cobb," the director said. "How to hit a baseball or steal a base. But if you want to learn to seek the truth your whole life, if you want to be an artist and a man, look to Al Stump." He could have been speaking for the many fans, writers, and critics who saw the best and the worst of sports through Stump's eyes.

References:

Geoff Boucher, "This Raconteur Was Simply the Best of the Best," *Los Angeles Times,* 26 January 1996, p. E10;

Lowell Cohn, "Ty's Dirty Laundry: Daughter Angered by Cobb Movie, Book," *San Francisco Chronicle,* 9 January 1995, p. E1;

Richard Sandomir, "The Search for the Real Cobb: Writer Al Stump Gets His Second Swing at the Truth," *Houston Chronicle,* 4 December 1994, Sports Section, p. 1.

William Howland Taylor

(31 May 1901 - 6 January 1966)

Robert Cole
University of Missouri at Kansas City

MAJOR POSITIONS HELD: Reporter, *New Bedford Standard, Fall River News, Boston Herald* (1923–1927); yachting editor, *New York Herald Tribune* (1927–1942); associate editor, *Yachting* (1945–1952); managing editor, *Yachting* (1952–1964).

BOOKS: *Yachting in North America along the Atlantic and Pacific and Gulf Coasts and on the Great Lakes and on the Western and Canadian Lakes and Rivers,* by Taylor and others, edited by Eugene V. Connett (New York: Van Nostrand, 1948);

Outboards at Work (Nassau, Bahamas: Outboard Marine International, 1958);

The America's Cup Races, by Taylor and Herbert L. Stone (New York: Van Nostrand, 1958);

The Story of American Yachting, Told in Pictures, photographs by Morris Rosenfeld, text by Taylor and Stanley Rosenfeld (New York: Appleton-Century-Crofts, 1958).

OTHER: *Just Cruising,* edited by Taylor (New York: Van Nostrand, 1949);

On & Off Soundings, edited by Taylor (New York: Van Nostrand, 1951);

"Lively Old Lady," in *Best Sports Stories 1951: A Panorama of the 1950 Sports Year,* edited by Irving T. Marsh and Edward Ehre (New York: Dutton, 1951), pp. 239–253;

Frank G. Menke, ed., *The Encyclopedia of Sports,* third revised edition, includes articles by Taylor (New York: Barnes, 1963), pp. 1023–1031;

"Just Cruisin,'" "The Day We Thought the Cup Was Lost," and "The America's Cup Stays Here," in *The Best from Yachting* (New York: Scribners, 1967), pp. 26–30, 155–160, 175–188.

SELECTED PERIODICAL PUBLICATIONS–UNCOLLECTED: "Cruising for Swordfish," *Yachting* (January 1923);

"Old Salt Returns," *New York Herald Tribune,* 27 July 1944;

William Howland Taylor

"There Is Nothing Like a Boat," *House & Garden,* 96 (August 1949): 46–47;

"Yachting Books and How to Sell Them," *Publishers Weekly,* 158 (15 July 1950): 191–195;

"End of a Great Old Ship," *Yachting,* 113 (May 1963): 198;

"Key West to Cedar Keys," *Yachting,* 114 (November 1963): 46–48;

"Long Islands Sounding," *Yachting* (March 1964).

William Howland Taylor was a widely known and respected writer on yachting and yachting subjects and the first writer to win the Pulitzer Prize for sportswriting. A newspaperman and magazine editor, Taylor devoted much of his working life to yachting. He was the author and editor of five books on the subject, knowledge derived from the salty background and small boats of his native Massachusetts. He wrote about the finest yachtsmen of his day and of history–Sir Thomas Lipton, Tom Sopwith, Captain Charlier Barr–as well as famous boat builders and designers such as W. Starling Burgess and Nathanael Greene Herreshoff. He also wrote about the great boats, with names such as *Yankee, Rainbow, Endeavour,* and *America,* as though they were racehorses.

While working on the staff of the *New York Herald Tribune* Taylor won the Pulitzer Prize for his coverage of the America's Cup races of 1934 between *Rainbow,* the American defender, and Britain's *Endeavour* off Newport, Rhode Island. The citation of the prestigious award, given in 1935, read: "A distinguished example of a reporter's work during the year, the test being strict accuracy, terseness, the preference being given to articles that acknowledged the accomplishment of some public good commanding attention and respect." Although he had been firmly established in the field prior to winning the award, the recognition brought Taylor even more renown outside the realm of yachting reporting.

Taylor was born on 31 May 1901 in New Bedford, Massachusetts, a product of New England stock. His ancestors had been seamen, manning whaling ships and other vessels. As soon as he was big enough to climb over a gunwale, Taylor learned to row. Throughout his life he learned to sail all kinds of boats, including schooners and catboats, during summer stays at his family's place at Salters Point in South Dartmouth, Massachusetts. He loved sailing out to his favorite haunts at Cuttyhunk Island, Menemsha, Hadley, and Tarpaulin Cove. Taylor relished his time on the water and gradually accumulated knowledge of a variety of distinctive boats.

Following his graduation from Dartmouth College in 1923, Taylor's first job was covering the waterfront for his hometown paper, the *New Bedford Standard.* Before coming to New York, Taylor also served with the *Fall River News* and the *Boston Herald.* In 1927 Taylor joined the staff of the *New York Herald Tribune* as yachting editor, a position he held for fifteen years.

In 1942, nearly twenty years after his graduation from Dartmouth, Taylor joined the U.S. Navy as a lieutenant. He was executive officer and commanding officer of the USS *PC 598* in 1943 and 1944. Taylor also commanded a PC 173–foot subchaser in the Pacific and served aboard a tanker. He eventually became a lieutenant commander and executive officer of the USS *Kennebec.*

During the 1920s and 1930s Taylor was a contributor of articles and special coverage for *Yachting* magazine and joined the magazine full-time as an associate editor in November 1945. His first contribution to *Yachting,* "Cruising for Swordfish," was published in January 1923, and in January 1952 he was named managing editor, a position he held until illness forced him to relinquish his responsibilities. While managing editor, Taylor also served as a vice president of Yachting Publishing Corporation. His last bylines for the magazine, published in March 1964, were a "Long Islands Soundings" column, a progress report on the America's Cup, and a piece on the boat steerer of the *Gam.*

The 1930s marked the advent of a new era in the America's Cup, most of which Taylor chronicled. In 1929 leaders in American and European racing agreed to adopt the American Universal Measurement Rule for boats rated higher than 46 feet. The adoption created the J Class of boats, vessels that were rated all the same and provided no handicaps. The design of the J Class boats was distinctive: all rated 76 feet, they ranged in size from 119 feet overall and 81 feet on the water, to 136 feet overall and 87 feet on the water. The sail area was approximately 7,540 square feet.

In addition to the new J Class, the America's Cup changed in other ways during the 1930s. In 1930 the race moved to a new location for better sailing conditions: Newport, Rhode Island. The competition now consisted of the best of seven races rather than the best of five, and new "Marconi rigs" were used for the first time. The rigs, often labeled "Bermudan," consisted of one tall triangular mainsail rather than a gaff mainsail and topsail. The stays that held the masts were reminiscent of Marconi radio antennas. The life of the J Class boats in the America's Cup, however, was relatively brief–only eight years, from 1930, the fourteenth defense of the cup, to 1937, the sixteenth defense.

Endeavour, a J Class challenger from England in 1934, came as close to winning the America's Cup as any boat for the next fifty years. The boat was owned by T. O. M. (Thomas Octave Murdock) Sopwith, known as "Tom." Designed by Charles Nicholson, *Endeavour* was beautiful in design and stylish in new technology. It came equipped with rowing winches, which allowed two men seated on deck, facing opposite directions, to push on four-foot-long horizontal bars. The masthead of the ship included the first electric apparent-wind direction indicator and a wind-speed indicator, with readouts in the cockpit. Both *Endeavour* and *Rainbow,* the American challenger, sported rod rigging, a first in sailing technology. Despite the *Endeavour's* attributes, however, Sopwith was hampered in the 1934 race by a lack of professional sailors: he was forced to use gentleman sailors with no big-boat experience.

Taylor's account of the last race in the series appeared in the *New York Herald Tribune* on 25 Septem-

THE WEATHER

NEW YORK Herald Tribune

LATE CITY EDITION

Vol. XCIV No. 32,083 TUESDAY, SEPTEMBER 18, 1934

Endeavour Wins First Of America's Cup Series By 2 Minutes 9 Seconds

Challenger Scores Over Rainbow in 15-Mile Sail for Home After Trailing Rival on Windward Leg

Winner Concludes Her Run in 3:38:44

Victory Off Newport Is 4th for a British Cup Aspirant in 81 Years of Yacht Series History

By William H. Taylor

Winner of First Decision in America's Cup Series

Skipper T. O. M. Sopwith at the wheel of Endeavour

Pratt, Whitney Air Profit Is Placed at 1,143,725%

Senate Investigators Are Told of $11,437,250 Gains Since 1925 on $1,000 Capital; Huge Sales of Plane Engines to Hitler Revealed

Mills Leads Constitution Day Attacks on Roosevelt Policies

Income and Trade Tax With City Run Lottery Agreed Upon for Relief

Morro Castle Crew Tells of Second Fire

Ventilators Said to Have Sucked Flames Into Hold; Warms Suspended for Laxity in 1926

Tells of Panic on Ship

Robert J. Smith, Cruise Director

38 More Closed Banks to Open, O'Connor Says

Substitute Program Calls for One-tenth Per Cent Levy on Business; Aldermen to Adopt It Today

Payments of Cash To Needy Resumed

15 P. C. Impost on Federal Income Tax Provides Deductions for Those Who Pay Twice

Front page with the opening of one of the articles in Taylor's Pulitzer Prize–winning series on the 1934 America's Cup race

ber 1934. The piece is exceptional as an example of Taylor's prose: clear, straightforward explanations of a different and technical sport. For Taylor the America's Cup races were the epitome of the sport. He was less concerned about the millions spent in earning or defending it than in the goodwill it generated. As he wrote elsewhere,

> the history that has woven itself around this trophy in the century-plus of competition for it . . . is the history of the whole sport. It is the history of naval architecture, as applied to sailing craft throughout the yachting world. It is the history of the sport's outstanding men down through the years. It is the history of the development of sportsmanship and the ethics of competition, from the days when some people said that "a match should be won when its terms are made" to today's ideal of starting the contestants off with an even break.

The first paragraphs of Taylor's 1934 piece show the writer at his best, simply describing for the reader what, when, where, and how things happened:

> Rainbow, ably sailed by Harold S. Vanderbilt and his crew, completed her defense of the America's cup with a 55-second victory over the fifteenth challenger for the trophy, T.O.M. Sopwith's *Endeavour,* off here today. The trophy, which the New York Yacht Club has held for eighty-three years, will stay in this country for a while longer, at least, and the Royal Yacht Squadron, which was represented here by *Endeavour* and which originally put up the historic trophy eighty-three years ago returns empty-handed again. The race today, sixth of the series, went to a better-sailed boat over a probably faster boat, but it was not until long after the race was finished that the decision was affirmed. Both Vanderbilt and Sopwith went over the starting line of today's race with protest flags flying, and finished the same way. At 8:30 tonight the second of the two protests was withdrawn.

The races came at a time when diplomatic relations between the United States and England were strained because of incidents during the America's Cup. The series, Taylor writes, was "to set a new high on international squabbles over the racing rules"; but protests and challenges notwithstanding, "the majority of even the British yachtsmen here will admit that their challenger didn't by any stretch of the imagination prove title to the America's Cup."

Taylor reflected on the race again in "The Day We Thought the Cup Was Lost," a piece originally published in *Yachting* in 1962. Early in the best of seven series the hopes of America's Cup returning to America appeared dim. Writes Taylor, "It looked as if, after 83 years, the cup the schooner America has so proudly sent home from her British adventure was going back to where it came from. Those who had watched the two boats, and understood what they saw, felt that Charles Nicholson had produced so much faster a boat, in *Endeavour,* that only a miracle could keep the Cup here."

In a credited entry in Frank G. Menke's *The Encyclopedia of Sports* (1963) Taylor clearly describes what makes yachting so different from other competitive sports: "Yacht racing is peculiar in that it has hundreds of championships but no one overall champion. All classes have their own champions, but they rarely meet each other since each sails only his kind of boat and there is no final way of deciding that one kind of skipper or one group of sailors is at the top of the entire sport, even in a limited area, let alone the world."

A September 1950 feature-length piece Taylor wrote for *True* magazine, "Lively Old Lady," was included in *Best Sports Stories 1951: A Panorama of the 1950 Sports Year.* The article, about "a little, light-blue, fifty-nine-foot long schooner called the Nina" on the verge of the Bermuda race of 1950, serves as a fine example of writing in which a boat becomes something of a character in a narrative: "Because she differed in appearance from the typical schooner in 1928, she was often called an ugly boat. But handsome is as handsome does, and today Nina stands out in most yachtsmen's eyes as a handsome vessel with a distinctive air of her own." Though the *Nina* had won three major races, it went through a period of abandonment in its prime: "Now a yacht on the beach too long, like a sailor in port, generally comes to no good. A couple of years lying neglected in a shipyard exposed to broiling summer suns and winter dampness can do a ship more damage than many years in service with proper care. Nina, though still a new vessel, was on the skids and going downhill at a rate that, apparently, nobody realized until it was perilously near too late."

In addition to writing about yachting races, Taylor also sailed in them. He worked frequently as a crewman in the Bermuda Races, the leading American offshore competition. In a *New York Times Magazine* article Taylor describes his experience as a crewman as being "ideal days in the event while the yacht was gliding, swiftly under sunny skies and moonlit night." In the same piece he writes: "There are such days–well hours, anyway. There are also endless night watches when the rain sluices down under the collar of your oilskin jacket while the ship rolls and her sails slant futily in a flat calm. There are screeching Gulf Stream squalls in which, if you don't get the canvas down and furled quickly enough, the wind will dispose of it for you–and maybe the mast along with it." The example is typical of Taylor's easy-flowing writing style: lucid, uncluttered, and often spiked with humor.

While working in New York, Taylor was one of a small group of men that originated frostbite dinghy racing, a winter activity that subsequently became a thriving sport at area yacht clubs. The first regatta was arranged in the living room of Taylor's home in December 1932 and the first race was held the following 2 January on Manhasset Bay. Later, Taylor was named a commodore of the Frostbite Yacht Club.

Several of Taylor's magazine pieces are included in *The Best from Yachting* (1967), a collection of articles published on the sixtieth anniversary of the founding of the magazine. "Just Cruisin'" is a short, charming essay that reveals Taylor's love for sailing while meandering and discoursing about boat liquor lockers and "unorthodox little cruising boats." He also makes clear the basic distinction among sailors: they are either cruising men or racing men. Sailing small boats, Taylor writes, gives one the chance to get to know the country intimately: "You know just how close you can skin the beach and where you can dodge in among the boulders." The cruising man keeps a mental file of shortcuts and channels away from well-marked harbors. Learning these unmarked passages is difficult but rewarding: "You can puzzle your way into all sorts of snug little unmarked anchorages–the kind of places you sort of crawl into and pull the hole in after you. You won't be bothered by weekend merrymakers in 'em and the few other boats you do find there are apt to be manned by kindred spirits."

"Old Salt Returns," with a dateline of Larchmont, New York, was written by Taylor during his navy tenure as a lieutenant commander. The piece, published in the *New York Herald Tribune* on 27 July 1944, was the first newspaper article Taylor had written since July 1942, when he began his naval career. The article describes the opening of Larchmont Race Week and the variety of International and S Class boats in the fleet. Taylor writes: "Of course the boats run smaller, with Internationals and S boats topping the fleet, because some of the bigger boats are still fighting the war in the offshore patrol and others are laid up for lack of crews. But by and large, things looked delightfully familiar, except the breeze, which was abnormally fine." The article ends on a personal note, with Taylor observing the "kids sailing little boats of all kinds, and that more than anything else is what gives an old ex-sailor, bogged down in a mess of diesel oil and Navy Regs., a cheering assurance that some time, when we get the current job cleaned up, there will be more and better sailing than ever on the sound–and everything else."

In all of his writing Taylor strove for clarity and accuracy, utilizing concise phrasing that lent credibility to his coverage of a sport new to most readers. Whether he was covering the arduous details of an America's Cup race or the rigorous adventures of a Bermuda fleet, he was dedicated in his devotion to his craft. Overall, his work gained a following even among nonsailors.

At *Yachting* magazine Taylor was the expert on nautical accuracy. He was revered for his subtle humor and dedicated mastery with the blue pencil as he worked over a piece of copy. He was the first to scrap timeworn phrases such as "sleek sloop" and "coveted trophy" if they came across his desk.

Apart from his naval service, his newspaper and magazine articles, and his work as editor at *Yachting,* Taylor also edited and wrote books. His works include *Just Cruising* (1949) and *The Story of American Yachting, Told in Pictures* (1958). *The Story of American Yachting,* authored in collaboration with Stanley Rosenfeld, features hundreds of photographs from the collection of Rosenfeld's father, Morris Rosenfeld. Written in a narrative fashion similar to that of an ocean adventure, Taylor and Rosenfeld examine the workaday and social lives of American yachtsmen, from the races to yacht-club life from the mid nineteenth century to the twentieth century. The book attempts to answer the question of the appeal of yachting, which has in its own way as long and rich a lore as baseball.

Taylor saw two reasons for the attraction of the sport: first was "the sense of power and authority that comes from command" felt by young and old alike, experienced and inexperienced. The other reason, less personal and stronger, was the sense of oneness felt by all those on the boat:

> It is the feeling, particularly sharp when the going is rough, that between them they have the power of mastery over the elements. Straining shrouds, taut sheets and sails, and driving hull seem an extension of the bodies of the crew. The will to go seems to be in the boat as well as them. . . . When wind and wave are high, since the boat is bigger than the people in it, the communion between them so close and the mastery of the elements so real, the sailor immediately knows a strength greater than his own.

Taylor was co-author with Herbert L. Stone, also a *Yachting* editor, of *The America's Cup Races* (1958), a compilation of the history of the foremost international sailing competition. In the chapter on "Cowes, 1851: *America* Carries the Day," Taylor and Stone recount the victory of the lone American entry, which set the stage, in fact, for the many British challenges that followed through the decades.

Describing one of the first tests Commodore John C. Stevens's *America* faced, when the English cutter *Laverock* challenged her "into a trial of speed," Taylor demonstrates technical expertise as well as a strong dramatic sense. Though Stevens was reluctant "to show too much speed just then," hoping to land bigger and better contests and not lose the psychological advantage, he took the *Laverock* on: "It was a beat back to Cowes, and in those few miles the *America* worked out to windward surprisingly fast, finishing well ahead of the Englishmen. Not many hours afterward it was known throughout the yachting community that no English yacht was the *America*'s equal in going to windward. That little brush proved unfortunate for the American hopes of putting their venture 'in the black' by winning substantial bets on match races." Taylor goes on to describe the extraordinary influence the *America,* with its "sharp, lean, concave bow," had on yacht design in the United States and around the world.

In an article published in *The New York Times* (8 January 1966), Taylor was described as a big, easygoing, quiet-spoken pipe smoker whose relish for the life of the sea came to him naturally. Throughout his life he developed an intimate knowledge of seamanship. Stanley Rosenfeld, Taylor's co-author on *The Story of American Yachting, Told in Pictures,* agreed, calling Taylor "a man of wholesome good humor and unstinting energy, tempered with the benefit of his wealth of yachting lore and experience."

Following an illness of two years brought on by a series of severe strokes, Taylor died at age sixty-four on 6 January 1966 at the Sands Point Nursing Home on Port Washington, Long Island. At the time of his death Taylor was survived by his wife, the former Anne Kay Hocking, and two sons, Stephen Howland and William Hocking Taylor.

Reference:

Dennis Connor and Michael Levitt, *The America's Cup* (New York: St. Martin's Press, 1998).

Wells Twombly

(24 October 1935 - 30 May 1977)

Ron Briley

MAJOR POSITIONS HELD: Sports columnist and sports editor, *Willimantic* (Conn.) *Daily Chronicle* (1956–1958); sports columnist, *Pasadena Star-News* (1958–1959); *Hollywood Citizen News* (1959–1962); *San Fernando Valley Times Today* (1959–1962); *The Sporting News* (1961–1977); *Houston Chronicle* (1962–1968); sports director, KXYZ-TV (Houston) (1964–1966); sports columnist, *Detroit Free Press* (1968–1969); *San Francisco Examiner* (1969–1977).

*Wells Twombly (*The Sporting News *Archives)*

BOOKS: *Blanda, Alive and Kicking: The Exclusive Authorized Biography* (Los Angeles: Nash, 1972);

Oakland's Raiders: Fireworks and Fury (Englewood Cliffs, N.J.: Prentice-Hall, 1973);

Shake Down the Thunder! The Official Biography of Notre Dame's Frank Leahy (Radnor, Pa.: Chilton, 1974);

200 Years of Sport in America: A Pageant of a Nation at Play, edited by Jeremy Friedlander and John Wiebusch (New York: McGraw-Hill, 1976).

OTHER: "From Riches to Rags," in *Best Sports Stories 1961: A Panorama of the Year 1960,* edited by Irving T. Marsh and Edward Ehre (New York: Dutton, 1961), pp. 127–129;

"Baby Ray," in *Best Sports Stories 1963: A Panorama of the Year 1962,* edited by Marsh and Ehre (New York: Dutton, 1963), pp. 156–158;

"Win Some, Lose Some," in *Best Sports Stories 1964: A Panorama of the Year 1963,* edited by Marsh and Ehre (New York: Dutton, 1964), pp. 280–281;

"A Little More Bull," in *Best Sports Stories 1967: A Panorama of the Year 1966,* edited by Marsh and Ehre (New York: Dutton, 1967), pp. 278–280;

"You Shouldn't Go Home Again," in *Best Sports Stories 1968: A Panorama of the Year 1967,* edited by Marsh and Ehre (New York: Dutton, 1968), pp. 287–289;

"La Corrida Lays un Huevo Grande," in *Best Sports Stories 1969: A Panorama of the Year 1968,* edited by Marsh and Ehre (New York: Dutton, 1969), p. 241–243;

"The Impossible Dream," in *Best Sports Stories 1970: A Panorama of the Year 1969,* edited by Marsh and Ehre (New York: Dutton, 1970), pp. 23–26;

"The Hero Sandwich of Sports," in *Best Sports Stories 1971: A Panorama of the Year 1970,* edited by Marsh and Ehre (New York: Dutton, 1971), pp. 268–270;

"Fallen Angel," in *Best Sports Stories 1972: A Panorama of the Year 1971,* edited by Marsh and Ehre (New York: Dutton, 1972), pp. 255–257;

"Gallery of Goats," in *Best Sports Stories 1973: A Panorama of the Year 1972,* edited by Marsh and Ehre (New York: Dutton, 1973), pp. 264–266;

"Super Hero," in *Best Sports Stories 1974: A Panorama of the Year 1973,* edited by Marsh and Ehre (New York: Dutton, 1974), pp. 87–89;

"Globetrotters: A Racist Anachronism," in *Best Sports Stories 1975: A Panorama of the Year 1974,* edited by Marsh and Ehre (New York: Dutton, 1975), pp. 156–158;

"There Was Only One Casey," in *Best Sports Stories 1976: A Panorama of the Year 1975,* edited by Marsh and Ehre (New York: Dutton, 1976), pp. 37–40.

In an October 1974 *Esquire* article Randall Poe called Wells Twombly one of six journalists who were transforming the nature of sportswriting and reporting. Rather than engaging in hero worship of athletes or extolling the virtues of the home team, the college-educated Twombly raised questions about the role of athletics in American society. While some readers found his consciously literary prose enigmatic and confusing, Twombly defended his style, asserting:

> I try to be as literate as I can be. Anybody who writes down to a reader in this age of higher education is living in the past. . . . I don't want anybody skimming through anything I write. I've been battling the Who-What-Where-Why-When and KISS (Keep it Simple Stupid) crowd ever since I started. Lord, we're in a war with television. I try to recreate scenes for readers, take them places where even the damned camera can't go.

The son of Albert F. and Dale Wells Twombly, Wells A. Twombly was born in St. Johnsburg, Vermont, on 24 October 1935. On 9 December 1955, while attending the University of Connecticut, he married Margaret (Peggy) Zera, with whom he eventually had four children: Wells Jr., Jason, Scott, and Dale Helen. After earning a B.A. in English and history in 1957, Twombly became sports editor at the *Willimantic* (Conn.) *Daily Chronicle,* for which he had been writing since the previous year. In 1958 he moved to California, where he worked for the *Pasadena Star-News* (1958–1959), the *Hollywood Citizen News* (1959–1962), and the *San Fernando Valley Times Today* (1959–1962).

Twombly's attempt at creating a literary style is evident throughout his early work. His 1960 *Valley Times Today* story "From Rags to Riches," on the debut of former Cleveland Browns quarterback Otto Graham as coach at the Coast Guard Academy, for example, begins with a metaphor-laden statement: "High above the thrashing patch of foam, where the plodding River Thames says a sudden hello to Long Island Sound, stands a trim row of white colonial mansions that house the United States Coast Guard Academy." Twombly's early work in California is also notable for focusing on the less glamorous aspects of sport, as in his 1962 feature article "Baby Ray," on the release of Los Angeles Laker reserve Ray Felix, whom Twombly described as "a gangling titan whose appealing cocker spaniel eyes seemed to be always filled with soul-churning hurt. Here was a body that was merely tall and not talented." Twombly's story points to a troubling situation that is prevalent among professional athletes: the seven-foot-tall basketball player, who had been with the team for nine years, had failed to earn a degree during his brief tenure at Long Island University and was apprehensive about a future outside of professional basketball. Laker officials seemed unconcerned, assuring Twombly that Felix would probably be able to obtain employment as a youth-center director, basketball referee, or "some such thing."

In 1962 Twombly gravitated to Texas, where he became a sports columnist for the *Houston Chronicle.* While in Texas he also worked as sports director for Houston television station KXYZ (1964–1966) and earned an M.A. (1966) at the University of Houston. His irreverent side is evident in some of his columns for the *Houston Chronicle.* For example, in his 1966 article "A Little More Bull" he lampooned the efforts of Houston entrepreneur Roy Hofheinz to fill the seats of the Astrodome by featuring bloodless bullfighting. After describing a matador as "the most awesome sight anyone in these parts had seen since Santa Anna marched north from the Alamo," the irrepressible Twombly proceeded to concoct a traditional sports interview with the bulls, who reportedly could not comment until they had screened the "game" footage.

Twombly inserted himself into some of his columns. In the 1967 piece "You Shouldn't Go Home Again," on attending homecoming at the University of Connecticut, he commented that football was treated less reverently there than in Texas. Referring to himself as a "lost sheep," Twombly proclaimed his alma mater a "massive brain factory" that viewed "any game that is played with a ball that isn't round and can't be dribbled as no sport at all." Twombly and a companion retreated to a student "watering hole," where "a lot of skinny people in beards" were discussing subjects that could not be "mentioned in a family newspaper."

In 1968 Twombly accepted a position as a columnist for the *Detroit Free Press,* for which his reporting was often more traditional than his earlier stories. His straightforward account of the 1969 Super Bowl triumph of the New York Jets, which became the fifth of his pieces selected for *Best Sports Stories,* extols the emergence of the American Football League as a genuine equal for the older National Football League (NFL). The article begins:

> Play soft music and send flowers to the relatives. Let's have a little reverence. An era passed into oblivion in the third annual Super Bowl and professional football will never quite be the same. For the first time since it was founded 49 years ago, the National Football League no longer dominates its universe.

According to Twombly, the man who had turned the football world upside down was no other than the "brassy, sleepy-eyed" Joe Namath, "the hippie quarterback" for the Jets.

Despite his admiration for Namath and his reputation for expressing antiestablishment views, Twombly was not ready to embrace the counterculture. In a 1969 column for the *Detroit Free Press* (republished on 31 May in *The Sporting News,* for which he wrote for sixteen years) Twombly defended baseball as the national pastime in a "society where rioting has replaced beer-drinking as an undergraduate pursuit." Extolling baseball as the soul of the nation, Twombly concluded that, while some considered it old-fashioned, the sport was "nostalgia, sweet and thick, warm and everlasting."

In 1969 Twombly went to work at the *San Francisco Examiner,* where his nationwide reputation was established in large part by his idiosyncratic columns, which ran six times a week. The three books on football that he wrote during the early 1970s also increased his national exposure. He dedicated his 1972 authorized biography of the aging Oakland Raiders quarterback George Blanda to his late father, whom he described as a victim of the Great Depression who nonetheless taught his son how to compete, "who brought the *Sporting News* home every Monday night, who knew all there was to know about the infield fly rule, the buck lateral series and the two-handed push-shot, and who died one awful night in 1953, erroneously thinking he was a failure."

Twombly's biography of Blanda is marred by his attempts to be literary. Characterizing the twenty-season veteran as a cunning "wolf," for example, Twombly asserted:

> The pack follows the quarterback with a singular obedience, because the quarterback is the only sensible alternative to starvation. The quarterback is an Alpha Male, taller, tougher, stronger, more determined than the other members of the species. He will survive. He will find a way.

The following year Twombly wrote a heavily illustrated tribute to the Oakland Raiders, whom he called the "towering epitome of a non-frivolous organi-

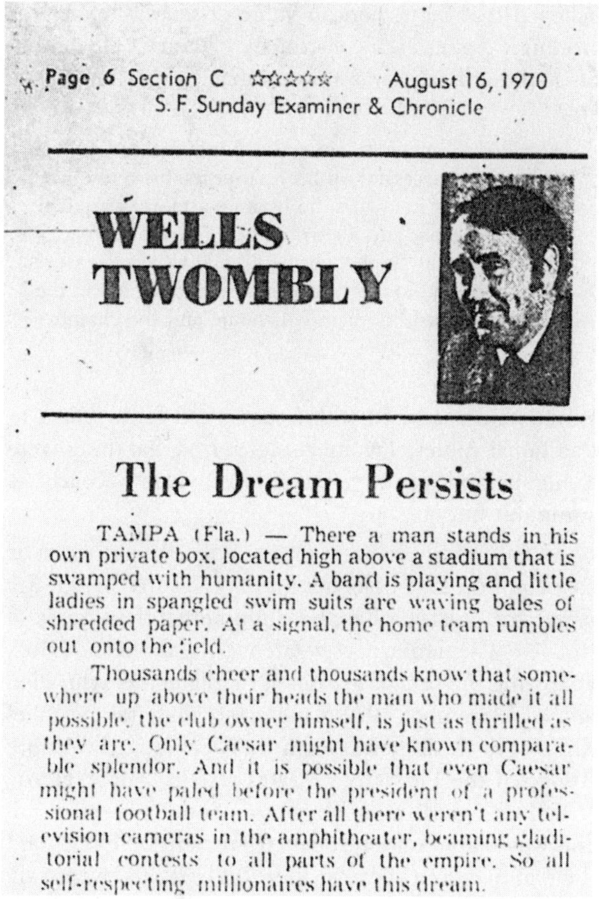
Page 6 Section C ☆☆☆☆☆ August 16, 1970
S. F. Sunday Examiner & Chronicle

WELLS TWOMBLY

The Dream Persists

TAMPA (Fla.) — There a man stands in his own private box, located high above a stadium that is swamped with humanity. A band is playing and little ladies in spangled swim suits are waving bales of shredded paper. At a signal, the home team rumbles out onto the field.

Thousands cheer and thousands know that somewhere up above their heads the man who made it all possible, the club owner himself, is just as thrilled as they are. Only Caesar might have known comparable splendor. And it is possible that even Caesar might have paled before the president of a professional football team. After all there weren't any television cameras in the amphitheater, beaming gladitorial contests to all parts of the empire. So all self-respecting millionaires have this dream.

Opening of one of Twombly's columns

zation, the model of efficiency." He had formed a lasting friendship with Al Davis, the controversial Raiders owner whom many in the NFL establishment accused of running an "outlaw" organization. Twombly, however, found Davis to be a sort of renaissance man. Employing a simpler style than in his previous book, the San Francisco sportswriter concluded: "Al Davis is a skilled football man, a person with a remarkably eclectic mind who reads great books and is fascinated by the study of history. He has a healthy interest in the arts and sciences." Twombly also had little critical to say about the Raider defensive star Jack Tatum, who had earned a reputation for rough tackling and dirty play. Twombly lauded Tatum, claiming: "There are folks who insist that Tatum is not very big. These are folks who never have had the exquisite pleasure of being hit by Jack. Here is a man who can straighten a spine so fast you'll think you always walked with perfect posture."

Twombly's 1974 authorized biography of Notre Dame coaching legend Frank Leahy lionizes a man who believed that the American value of self-discipline was eroding. Again self-consciously literary, Twombly insisted that Leahy was a proud man,

> erect, stern, righteous, shrewd, resourceful, tough, tremendously successful. In his final years, his body literally betraying its owner, he became a moral crusader, wobbling to podium after podium to caution America about the decay he thought he saw. His speeches were filled with Babbitt-esque sophistries, warning about the dangers to God, motherhood, home and the chamber of commerce.

While he empathized with Leahy's call for a return to traditional values, Twombly recognized that times were changing and portrayed the Notre Dame coach as admirable but quixotic.

Twombly's reputation as a sports journalist is based not on his books but on his columns for the *San Francisco Examiner,* where he championed the virtues of Roberto Clemente, Casey Stengel, and the hot dog. Following the premature death of Clemente, who died in a 31 December 1972 plane crash while taking relief supplies to earthquake victims in Nicaragua, Twombly eulogized the Pittsburgh Pirates star in "Super Hero" (1973) as a great man whose tremendous baseball talent was often underestimated by fans: "They paid their money and they sat there as baseballs went sailing off toward a glove that never made a mistake. It was far too easy, far too sweet. Roberto just couldn't make the game of baseball look hard enough." Beyond admiring the exquisite, effortless talent he displayed on the playing field, Twombly praised Clemente for his honesty in challenging the racial assumptions of many in the baseball establishment. Clemente, who was born in Puerto Rico, believed that Latin blacks were "nobody's children," assigned to the bottom of a sort of racial pecking order. Twombly admired Clemente's sense of community and desire to help others: "He had this wild notion about a sports city in his native Puerto Rico where indigent children could live. They could grow to manhood with the high ideals of competitive athletics to guide them. Their whole lives would be changed by the opportunity to play games, to get a decent meal, to wear clean clothes." Twombly championed Clemente's dreams and his challenge to discrimination in American sport.

Twombly also displayed a soft spot for legendary manager Stengel, who died on 29 September 1975. Describing the crusty Stengel as beautiful, but not necessarily in a physical sense, Twombly wrote in "There Was Only One Casey" (1975): "It was the beauty of a rare antique, tenderly rendered and gracefully aged. It was the beauty of a three-hundred-year-old handcrafted pipe, rubbed by a thousand hands and redolent of a thousand aromatic tobaccos." Twombly loved Stengel's manipulation of the English language, insisting:

> The man was a clever and articulate comic who spoke two languages. When he was unguarded he would talk in this straightforward, highly lucid English, which nobody paid any attention to. When there were reporters and other assorted individuals present he spoke in tongues. It was a tangled rat's nest of verbiage that bore only a scanty resemblance to the Mother Tongue so heartily endorsed by the queen of England. Even the mightiest of journalists cowed when he turned on the juice.

Nevertheless, Twombly warned that those who focused on the baseball legend's syntax might miss the essential fact that Stengel was a masterful teacher of baseball fundamentals.

Twombly also became known for his humor. He extolled ball-park hot dogs as a "whole lot more nutritious than a wisp of cotton candy and nowhere near as good for you as a spoonful of wheat germ (brrrrk!)." He contended that American sport would not be the same without the hot dog and lavished praise on the concessionaire as a "strategical genius who goes into a game with a plan that makes Vince Lombardi look like an improviser in comparison. Have you, the spectator, ever noticed how a kid comes along and sells you peanuts and just when you have finished the last salty little item in the bag, along comes a man peddling beer? Hmmmmm!"

Twombly could also be critical. In "Gallery of Goats" (1972) he attacked Olympic track coach Stanley Wright, whose failure to read the schedule properly led to the disqualification of sprinters Reynaud Robinson and Ed Hart. Revisiting the exploits of individuals such as Roy Reigels, the University of California player whose long fumble return in the wrong direction led to a game-deciding safety for Georgia Tech in the 1929 Rose Bowl; Brooklyn Dodger Ralph Branca, whose home-run pitch to Bobby Thomson gave the 1951 National League pennant to the New York Giants; and jockey legend Willie Shoemaker, who reined in Gallant Man at the sixteenth pole and blew the 1957 Kentucky Derby; Twombly concluded that Wright was the greatest "goat" of them all:

> Silently, the other goats stood up. These were the greatest nincompoops in all of athletic history. Without bothering to take a vote they shifted one space to the left, leaving Stanley Wright a place right next to the door. The keeper arched his ancient neck and let out a roar so terrible it stopped the blood in mid-vein. Then he slammed the door shut, leaving Stanley Wright there with his tears for all eternity.

Twombly was also critical of the Harlem Globetrotters, writing in "Globetrotters: A Racist Anachronism" (1974) that "They belong to an era when black people had no pride, no dignity, no sense of purpose. They were simply planted in this country to handle menial chores, to tug their forelocks when it seemed proper and to pretend that they lacked even the most modest amount of intelligence." Twombly acknowledged that the Globetrotters might have served a purpose when professional basketball was closed to African American athletes. Yet, in the 1970s, he charged, their minstrel-show antics played to American racism. Twombly suggested that, if Americans wanted to perpetuate bigotry, they should make "the Harlem Globetrotters the central point of a carnival that gives the public what it really wants, shuffling Spades, drunken Micks, greasy Dagos, passionate Spicks, dumb Polacks, cheap Scotsmen, inscrutable Chinks, scheming Hebes, aggressive Krauts, and brutal Redskins." Maintaining that the antics of athlete-comedians such as Meadowlark Lemon were no longer funny, Twombly announced that he was returning his complimentary tickets to the Globetrotters.

Twombly was not always so well attuned to the changing climate of race relations in America. When Native American activist Russell Means suggested that the Cleveland Indians mascot Chief Wahoo was a racist caricature, Twombly insisted that the Cleveland franchise was championing the heroic fighting ability of the Native American. In a 5 February 1972 article for *The Sporting News* Twombly asserted that "Means ought to investigate other, more responsible ways to help his people. Most Indians aren't as narrow minded as he appears to be. Otherwise, they would have asked for their country back a long time ago."

It was impossible for any journalist covering the Bay Area during the early 1970s to avoid the antics of the Oakland Athletics and their owner Charles Finley. While disapproving of Finley and calling him a tyrant, Twombly, who embraced controversy, described the A's in "Finley's Rascals in Midseason Form" (*The Sporting News,* 23 March 1974) as "outrageous, candid, cantankerous, uncompromising and irrepressible." In the emerging labor wars between management and players, the columnist sided with the ballplayers, observing that in challenging the reserve clause, which bound a player to one team, Marvin Miller, head of the Major League Baseball Players Association, was dragging the owners into the twentieth century.

In a 1973 column for *The Sporting News* Twombly acknowledged that reporters were traditionally little more than spokespersons for team owners. Twombly, however, considered himself above being a lackey for the home team, and he had no problem confronting athletes when they refused to treat him with respect. It has been alleged that after Oakland star Reggie Jackson shunned Twombly, the reporter remarked that he was as good a writer as Jackson was a ballplayer, and if Jackson wanted any further coverage, he would have to contact Twombly–a demand to which the recalcitrant player yielded.

Twombly often expressed cynicism. Following the shootings at Kent State University in May 1970, Twombly lamented in an *Examiner* column, "There are days when you don't feel like writing about children's games, especially when children are lying on the street." In a 26 June 1971 article for *The Sporting News,* Twombly sounded disillusioned when he charged that the pursuit of money was destroying the fun of sport. It was a chore, he said, to listen to a wealthy athlete complaining about job benefits. He concluded that professional sports "began to change" in the mid 1960s: "The toy universe started getting shabby. The catalyst was television. When big money came pouring in, sports lost its fragile beauty. It became less heroic, more plastic. It was Hollywood-ized."

While Twombly had begun to feel ambivalent about the nature of American sports, his genuine appreciation for his subject was most apparent in his final book, *200 Years of Sport in America.* A *New York Times* reviewer liked the attractive illustrations but asserted that "Wells Twombly's text is even more vivid, a splendid impressionistic rendering of the major sports entertainments. Spare, unsentimental, yet stylish, Twombly's prose could easily stand alone." Twombly celebrated the triumph and defeat of pure sport and accepted modern athletes who questioned the sporting establishment and its racial policies. Yet, his history also expresses his concern with the growing commercialization of American games. He was unimpressed with the conspicuous consumption displayed by Houston entrepreneur Roy Hofheinz in the construction of the Astrodome, commenting: "When the fan reached the stadium, he could spend his beer money in a Bavarian garden beneath the bleachers. Perhaps the prices were a bit high and the food less than delectable, but a ballpark paradise, even one with plastic trees and synthetic leaves, can't do everything." Twombly concluded his book on a pessimistic note: "American sport had become grandiose. Big money, big attendance, big attractions, big television audiences. From 1959 to 1976, $5.3 billion was spent on athletic facilities; nearly every major city constructed either a multipurpose stadium or an arena or both." Twombly was perceptive in his description of the growing commercialization of sport.

Twombly died of liver disease in San Francisco on 30 May 1977. He was survived by his wife and four children. While often inserting himself into his columns, Twombly had kept his family life private. In his introduction to his final book, however, he had acknowledged the toll that his meandering career had taken on his family. He dedicated the volume to his wife, "The freshman girl who married the sports editor of the campus daily, who bore four children in different parts of the nation and who endured the cross-country journey like pioneer women of the nineteenth century–with tears, but not complaints."

Twombly's last column for the *San Francisco Examiner* had appeared on 4 May. In it he displayed his love for football but continued to assert his somewhat jaundiced view of the role of big money in sports. Writing of the college football draft, Twombly commented:

> Through the mercy of some judge who probably never had the decency to go out and pay to see some defensive tackle gnaw on a quarterback's leg like some prehistoric beast discovering some raw roots, they actually managed to get the annual selection of collegiate flesh started yesterday. . . . That certainly gladdened the hearts of saloon keepers everywhere because nothing stimulates the sale of beer like continuous arguments and nothing touches off more disputes than the annual professional football league draft which was almost postponed forever because of various law suits and legal decisions. Thanks to judicial wisdom, halfback Tony Dorsett can either sign with the Dallas Cowboys or the Toronto Argonauts or pump gas for a year and then pledge his sacred honor to whomever he pleases.

Following the appearance of this column the *Examiner* ran the statement "Wells Twombly is ill" in place of his column, until the journalist's demise.

The *Examiner* offered a moving tribute to its effusive columnist. Acknowledging that the verbose Twombly was often an editor's nightmare, the paper remembered him as "an essayist, an artist who happened to write about sports. Most good writers address themselves to the human condition. Twombly took the human condition he found in the locker room, in the private lives, in the joys of winning and the sorrows of defeat, and turned those events into the stuff of his columns." Attempting to capture the Twombly style, the salute to Twombly concluded, "So vital and alert and intelligent a man still had much to say. But there was no escaping the severity of his illness. Finally the winter that he had predicted arrived. It was as chilling and bleak as a New England winter, and it was sad as a Welshman's heart."

Colleagues and contemporaries were generous in their praise for Twombly. *Examiner* sports editor Larry Beaumont extolled Twombly as an "inspiration to us, a standard we all tried to meet. He would not settle for second best either as a reporter, writer, or thinker." Edwin Pope, sports editor of the *Miami Herald,* asserted that Twombly's prose "just lived and breathed. It would go straight from his heart and head into the typewriter." David Nightingale of the *Chicago Daily News* proclaimed, "If there was one writing contemporary in the country of whom I was genuinely envious, it was Wells. He spoke for my generation, saying what I wished I was saying in a way I wished I was saying it." Spec Richardson, general manager of the San Francisco Giants, who had also worked with the Houston Astros when Twombly was a columnist in Texas, expressed disbelief at the reporter's death, asserting, "He was an outstanding writer and his column will be missed by everyone." Al Michaels of ABC Television noted, "It leaves you with a empty feeling. He was a major, major talent. To say journalism lost a great man is an understatement." A distraught Al Davis had worked until the end attempting to find a suitable liver transplant for Twombly, who finally resigned himself to leaving life with the "liver God gave me."

Colleague and rival Art Spander of the *San Francisco Chronicle* addressed Twombly's legacy from a more critical perspective, questioning Twombly's journalistic ethics in an infamous 1973 telephone interview in which Twombly had pretended to be Oakland A's pitcher Ken Holtzman. Spander reported Twombly's death as the result of weight problems and excessive drinking, which had led to jaundice, mononucleosis, and finally cirrhosis of the liver. According to Spander, Twombly's habits made him appear more like sixty than forty-one.

Spander was also critical of Twombly's reporting style, calling his writing "verbose, pretentious, bewildering and sometimes untruthful"–and "not the work of a man attempting to communicate with mankind." Nevertheless, Spander eulogized Twombly as an idealist who became a cynic and who never surrendered to the established tenets of sports journalism.

Embracing the purity and possibility of sport, Twombly was repelled by the crass commercialization of professional athletics. Wells Twombly left behind a body of writing that suggests the literary possibilities of sports reporting and the enigmatic quality of American sports, which is both a business and a game.

References:

Randall Poe, "The Writing of Sports," *Esquire,* 74 (October 1974): 173–176, 373–379;

Art Spander, "What Drove Wells Twombly?" *Sporting News,* 30 July 1977, pp. 43–44.

Richards Vidmer

(7 October 1898 - 23 July 1978)

Bernard J. Crowley

MAJOR POSITIONS HELD: Reporter, *Washington Herald* (1921–1922); sports editor, *Washington Daily News* (1922–1924); sports reporter, *New York Times* (1924–1929); sports reporter, *New York Morning Telegraph* (1929); sports reporter/columnist, *New York Herald Tribune* (1929–1942); foreign correspondent, *New York Herald Tribune* (1946–1951).

SELECTED PERIODICAL PUBLICATIONS–UNCOLLECTED: "The Swell Head," *Saturday Evening Post* (4 November 1933): 29–30, 38, 40; "Batter Up," *Current History* (May 1940): 40–41, 62.

Richards Vidmer elevated the craft of sportswriting with the simple approach of amusing and entertaining his readers. His colorful prose enhanced the story but never overstated the message he was attempting to convey. Vidmer never took himself, or sports, too seriously. In the twenty years he reported sports he maintained a crisp, innovative approach, endowing almost every story he wrote with a fresh angle.

Richards Vidmer was born on 7 October 1898 in Washington, D.C. He was the second child of George Vidmer and Carol Richards Vidmer. George Vidmer was a captain of cavalry in the U.S. Army at the time of Richards's birth. A poised career officer, George reached the rank of general and served as superintendent of West Point. Richards grew up on horseback and played polo. This familiarity with horses later enhanced his sportswriting when he reported on polo matches for *The New York Times.*

Reared in the nomadic style of the military, Vidmer did not suffer from a parochial outlook on life. Before he reached his teens he had lived in Washington, D.C., Cuba, Japan, West Point, the Philippines, and Texas. As a result, he brought polish and worldliness to his later work as a sportswriter. Star athletes did not impress him as much as they did some of his peers.

In 1917 Vidmer graduated from St. Luke's School in Wayne, Pennsylvania. Although he had been accepted at West Point as the United States entered World War I, Vidmer was eager to join the war effort. He passed on West Point and enlisted in the U.S. Army Air Corps, eventually earning his wings as a pursuit pilot. To his disappointment, however, he never experienced combat overseas. While attempting to land on a field in Hicksville, Long Island, following a routine training flight, his plane collided with another aircraft in an overcast sky. Of the four people aboard the two aircraft, Vidmer was the lone survivor. Nine months of surgery and rehabilitation in Walter Reed Hospital followed.

Richards Vidmer

After his release from the Air Corps, Vidmer enrolled at George Washington University. He had recovered from his wartime injuries sufficiently enough to play football and baseball in college. While still in high school he had played professional baseball in El Paso, Texas, but in order to protect his eventual college eligibility he had played under the name of "Widmeyer." Vidmer's experience as an athlete prepared him to report sports with insight. He knew that an errant bounce of the ball or a momentary lapse of concentration endowed even the greatest with feet of clay. He never hesitated to criticize a ballplayer for doing something foolish or irresponsible.

In June 1921 a casual meeting on a street in Washington initiated Vidmer's newspaper career. Just out of George Washington University, he met the managing editor of the *Washington Herald,* who offered Vidmer a job at $25 a week. He did general assignment work and on occasion wrote a feature story. His first feature was about the fiftieth anniversary of the Chicago fire.

In June 1922 Vidmer married Miriam Miller in Washington, D.C. They had three children: two sons and a daughter. It was the first of three marriages for Vidmer. When Vidmer's managing editor at the *Herald* left to join the *Washington Daily News* in 1922, he took along Vidmer as sports editor. At the same time, Vidmer was the football coach at St. John's College, a military prep school in Washington. Knowledgeable of sports but unsure what an editor did, he accepted the position at the *Daily News,* covering the Washington Senators as well as football and boxing.

While in New York in 1924 to cover a heavyweight bout Vidmer visited the offices of *The New York Times* and spoke with managing editor Carr Van Anda, who introduced Vidmer to sports editor Bernard Thomson. Two weeks later Thomson offered Vidmer a job.

Vidmer, unsure of his ability to compete in the New York market, hesitated to accept the offer. He recalled to Jerome Holtzman, the *Chicago Tribune* writer, that he asked his friend Washington Senators pitcher Walter Johnson for advice. Johnson encouraged him to take the job, saying that it had always been his dream to pitch in New York.

Vidmer reveled in the "gee whiz" style that dominated sportswriting in the 1920s, with its "jargon, florid phraseology and mixed figures," as Stanley Woodward characterized it in his *Sports Page* (1949). Vidmer preferred to begin his stories with an angle. A story he wrote for *The New York Times* while covering the 1925 World Series between the Pittsburgh Pirates and Washington Senators, for example, leads by focusing on a former Pittsburgh player now relegated to obscurity:

> Just after noon a big broad merchant emerged from his little shop on Wood Street. . . . His gnarled fingers fumbled with a key, turned a rusty lock and with curtains drawn the store was closed to customers for the rest of the day. Bowlegs rolled the big body up the street and boarded a surface car. . . .
>
> Just sixteen years ago the same bow-legged, hook-nosed Buccaneer entered the park to the clamor of the multitude in the World Series of that year. He flitted around shortstop in the Pirate's infield, occupied today by a younger member of the crew. Hans Wagner was just a name to most who gathered here today.

Every fall Vidmer made the transition to football coverage, drawing on his own experience as a player at George Washington University. His favorite game to report on was always baseball, however, and his sport of choice as a player was golf. He played the game at par or below for most of his life and was also a master bridge player. He reported with equal skill on polo, horse shows, boxing, tennis, track and field, rowing, and golf. While at *The New York Times* he was a regular contributor to the column "This Week in Sports," for which he recorded the off-season baseball news, noting matter-of-factly the winter injuries and deals.

Vidmer's primary goal as a sportswriter was always to entertain the fans. In his account of a 31 October 1925 Michigan Wolverines game, for example, he demonstrates his penchant for the lively metaphor, reporting that "A hungry pack of Wolverines set upon the Navy eleven from Annapolis on Ferry Field today, chewed and clawed and finally buried the Easterners under a 54–0 score." Vidmer made full metaphorical use of the fact that the game was played on Halloween, writing that "The Wolverines played many and sundry tricks on this day when the spirits came to haunt the world" and that "the pack started charging through the line, crashing as though it were just a huge tissue-paper Jack o' Lantern. . . ."

Vidmer delighted in the fast life of New York City. Novelist Katharine Brush based Toby McLean, the protagonist of her best-selling novel *Young Man of Manhattan* (1930), on him. McLean is a playboy sportswriter on a New York City newspaper, gifted but with a bent for dawdling. When he is beset by misfortune he responds with a flourish. Set in the speakeasies and city rooms of New York City newspapers during the Roaring Twenties, the novel added to Vidmer's dashing reputation. Bob Cooke, later sports editor of the *New York Herald Tribune,* observed, "Young writers . . . wanted to be debonair like Dick Vidmer."

Vidmer's "gee whiz" approach to sportswriting was fully in evidence in his report on the 10 October 1926 World Series game, in which the St. Louis Cardinals beat the New York Yankees for their first championship. In the seventh inning of game 7, the Cardinals' manager made the surprising decision to send in pitcher

THE SATURDAY EVENING POST 29

The Next Afternoon the Field Was Attacked by a Regiment of Photographers

THE SWELL HEAD

By

RICHARDS VIDMER

ILLUSTRATED BY CHARLES LA SALLE

ANYONE who has strolled across a college campus between late September and early June knows what Johnny Scott was like when he came back in the fall of his senior year, shouting greetings from the swaying taxicab that carried him from the station, drinking in familiar scenes with enthusiastic eyes, bounding up the steps of the Thete house and hurling two suitcases into the hall by way of announcing his arrival.

There was nothing you could put your finger on to distinguish Johnny from other seniors. He wasn't an all-American halfback, but he had played two years on the varsity; he wasn't a Phi Beta Kappa, but he never had been threatened with a condition; he wasn't president of his class, or even vice president, but when serious problems crept into undergraduate life they never were completely settled until someone suggested: "Let's see what Johnny Scott thinks about it."

Everyone liked Johnny. Older men called him "a splendid youngster," mothers spoke of him as "such a fine young man," girls thought him a "perfect dear," and his classmates declared he was "a great kid." He listened more than he talked, and smiled oftener than he laughed aloud.

This was the Johnny Scott that Phant Cotter rescued from the back-slapping, hand-pumping crowd in the Thete house and dragged upstairs, two freshmen following with a suitcase each.

Phant Cotter was Johnny's roommate. He also was captain of the football team. He was the most famous man in college, including Professor Mortimer, head of the department of philosophy. Phant was short for Phantom. You may remember having seen his name in the headlines.

"Why, you handsome old son of a gun!"

"Why, you broken-down wreck!"

"Have a good summer?"

"Swell! How did you make out?"

"Gained eight pounds and grew half an inch. You look heavier yourself." Phant ran an eye of estimation over Johnny's long, lean frame.

"I am, a little." Johnny had started unpacking, taking double handfuls of shirts, ties, shorts and socks from the opened suitcases and dumping them into a dresser drawer. "Say, it's good to get back, isn't it?" he added, with a glance out of the window where the elms were heavy with green branches and the sidewalks were dotted with silver dollars where the afternoon sun shone through the leaves.

"It's good to get you back! The squad has been out a week. Sorry you couldn't be here for early practice."

"How does the team look?" Johnny knew the subject closest to his roommate's heart.

"Not bad. Not bad at all. Pomeroy isn't returning, but we got a pretty fair bunch of linemen from last year's freshmen. McPherson is down in his studies and can't play. Biggs is figuring on shifting one of the second-string backs out to take his place at end, but we'll have to dig up a drop-kicker some place. You used to do some of that at St. Luke's, didn't you?"

Phant prattled on about football. It was his team. Johnny was just a take-out back; the spearhead of the interference. He cleared the way for Phant to make long sweeps around the opposing flanks. He helped to open holes in the line for Bullet Joe Benton to come plowing through. He protected Chick Painter when the little quarterback faded back to make long, sensational forward passes. He always was near the man who gained the glory, but he never was that man. Everybody knew of Phant Cotter and Bullet Benton and Chick Painter. Theirs were names that had been spread across the sports pages for two seasons, but everybody had to stop and think when it came to the fourth member of that backfield that had played together since freshman year. Oh, yes—Scott—that was the other fellow. He didn't do much.

Only Biggs, the coach, and Johnny's running mates realized how important he was in that machine. Even Johnny considered himself lucky to be part of it.

"Anybody would fit in with those three," he had told his father back home. "They only need three men in the backfield as long as they are Phant and Bullet and Chick. They can do everything! I just happened to be with them on the freshman team, and I guess the coach keeps me in there for luck or something."

So, to Johnny, football wasn't of paramount importance, as it was with Phant, for instance. Phant was building up a national reputation through the game. He was a cinch to make the all-American, and already he had received a couple of offers of jobs when he graduated. But football wasn't leading to any vast riches or undying fame where Johnny was concerned. It just was a lot of fun. Besides, he was thinking of other things as Phant talked on about timed shifts, shuttle passes, unbalanced lines and the heavy schedule.

The other things included a pair of wide gray eyes, fringed by black lashes; a slender, graceful body that swayed to dance music like a moonbeam on the

Opening of a short story by Vidmer that appeared on 4 November 1933 (reprinted with permission of The Saturday Evening Post *© 1933 [Renewed] BFL & MUS, Inc.)*

Grover Cleveland Alexander in relief, despite the fact that the thirty-nine-year-old veteran had just pitched a complete game to beat the Yankees the previous day.

> A ghostly figure walked through the dull gray haze that shrouded Yankee Stadium. As a blotch of red showed against the leaden background in far left-field, a thrill-swept throng peered forth into the mist, eager to see who it was that strode forth to face the fire of a Yankee uprising that threatened to wipe out the Cardinals' one-run lead and sweep the western warriors down to defeat in the seventh, last and deciding game of the World Series. . . . As he emerged from the bull pen his blazing Cardinal sweater showed brilliant against the sodden background. Over the long stretch of left field he lumbered, his shoulders bent, his crooked legs wobbling, his shoulders drooping. Not an imposing figure or fearful man. He looked more like an old man, bent with age. But as he drew nearer it was seen that his little gray cap was tipped sideways and slanting at a disdainful, cocky, devil-may-care angle. And the crowd roared one word as it recognized him: "Alexander!"

In 1929 sports editor Harry Cross asked Vidmer to consider joining the *New York Herald Tribune*. Arthur Draper, a special assistant to publisher Ogden Reid, wanted him on the staff. Vidmer was considering another offer at the same time, however.

Gene Fowler, managing editor of the *New York Morning Telegraph,* had also approached him with a job offer. A group of investors had purchased the *Morning Telegraph,* hoping to mold it into the dominant journal of arts, sports, and politics in New York City. They planned to hire only the most talented writers and paid top wages. Vidmer could not refuse Fowler's job offer and joined Walter Winchell, Ben Hecht, Ring Lardner, and Westbrook Pegler on the staff of the *Morning Telegraph.* The paper quickly failed, however, primarily because of its large payroll. Sensing the end, Vidmer moved over to the city room of the *Herald Tribune* in 1929.

By the 1930s sportswriters were beginning to shift away from the "gee whiz" approach to covering events. Vidmer, as one of the leading practitioners of that style, came under some criticism. *New York Herald Tribune* city editor Stanley Walker, in his book *City Editor* (1934), singled out Vidmer and Heywood Broun as examples of "otherwise fairly sensible writers" who depended on a melodramatic lead to their stories. Walker offered Vidmer's *Herald Tribune* coverage of the heavyweight championship bout between Primo Carnera and challenger Max Baer as an example of his tendency to use a suspended, or "Fabian," lead:

> The Baer went over the mountain and brought the heavyweight championship of the world back to the United States in his right hand.
>
> With audacious confidence, smiling surety and a sledgehammer punch developed slaughtering cattle, Max Baer whittled Primo Carnera, the man, down to the size of a Singer midget in the Madison Square Garden Bowl last night, toyed with him like a mongoose teasing a cobra, and made his final strike in 2:16 of the eleventh round scoring his eleventh knockdown.

Walker held that the reader was forced to wade through half a column to discover the pertinent details of the fight: "this sort of thing, even when it is understandable and apt, soon becomes meaningless, even obnoxious."

Vidmer believed in respecting the privacy of the athletes he covered. A he told Holtzman, "I never could see blowing the whistle on somebody." On the road he was a golfing partner to various players, including Babe Ruth, who also drank and played bridge with Vidmer. Vidmer only reported on his on-field performance. He afforded a similar measure of privacy to another player he respected, Lou Gehrig, after he pulled himself from the Yankee lineup in 1939. Vidmer spoke with Gehrig's doctors in the Yankee clubhouse but declined to report that he was suffering from an untreatable creeping paralysis out of consideration for the player.

When Bill McGeehan, who wrote the popular column "Down the Line" for the *New York Herald Tribune,* died in 1933, Vidmer was asked to replace him. Although there were, in his opinion, two or three better writers on the staff, he credited his ability to report on a variety of sports, not just football and baseball, for the offer. The column was renamed "Down in Front" and was nationally syndicated in more than one hundred newspapers.

The "Down in Front" column gave Vidmer a wider creative latitude. He eschewed rewrites, believing that his first draft was the best, and he employed a variety of styles, including sometimes verse:

> The Golden Bears from the Golden West
> Beat Alabama in New Year's test,
> Which causes the East at large to wonder
> if Fordham wouldn't have snowed them under. . . .

In 1936 he wrote a column, "Girl at the Game," dedicated to female football fans:

> You've seen her.
>
> You've seen her trudging along the road on her way to the Yale Bowl, her sturdy little boots scuffing up the dust.
>
> You've seen her sauntering beneath the brown, bare-limbed trees at Princeton.
>
> You've seen her walking with decisive strides across the bridge at Cambridge, her steps turned to Soldiers Field. . . .
>
> She's the All-American Girl.

DOWN IN FRONT

By Richards Vidmer

Copyright, 1938, New York Tribune Inc.

Iron Horses

I THINK it was the late Tex Rickard who first made the claim that it never rains in Madison Square Garden and his statement certainly has been substantiated during the current week.

It has rained in the Polo Grounds and as a result the Pirates practically are floating into the National League championships on a tidal wave.

It has rained in the West Side Stadium so long and so hard that the semi-finalists in the national championships may have to switch their entries to the veterans' division before they get a chance to play for any titles.

Richards Vidmer

And it has rained in Belmont Park so insistently that the Racing Commission is considering making boat races perfectly legal, if not preferable.

But it hasn't rained in Madison Square Garden. Not a drop has seeped through the roof and the wheels go round and round, like the music of another year. Day and night the six-day bike race goes on and the crowds come in to seek shelter and remain to sit fascinated at the closest thing in perpetual motion that the sphere of sports has been able to produce.

They sit and watch the teams Harry Mendel has paired—Letourner and Guimbretiere, the Peden brothers, Walthour and Crossley, Georgetti and Moretti and all the rest. But strangely they have to look all the way back to the end of the parade to find the favorite, for Gerard Debaets, the Belgian, is riding last.

Debaets may not have been the favorite in the betting when the race started and he certainly isn't the favorite to win now. But he's the crowd's favorite every day and every night, as he has been through the years, spring and fall.

Vidmer's New York Herald Tribune *column for 22 September 1938*

The close of the piece states: "They always look better when they're with the other guy."

Vidmer also used his column to highlight some of the customs, legends, and traditional rivalries of sports. In a column surveying many Saturday afternoon football rituals, for example, Vidmer wrote: "On the last day of practice at North Central College the varsity squad gathers around and burns a pair of football pants, silently going over past mistakes and vowing not to repeat them in the final game."

Vidmer sometimes used humor to convey scorn, as well. During the 1941 World Series, when Brooklyn Dodgers catcher Mickey Owen dropped a third strike that would have won the game against crosstown rivals the Yankees–a game in which the Yankees rallied and then won–Vidmer created "Baseball's Gallery of Goats," with Owen the newest member: "'Move over Merkle. Out of the way Zimmerman. Back to the shadows, Gowdy and Wilson, Snodgrass and Miljus. Make room for a new member–ya bums!"

When the United States entered World War II Vidmer received a commission as a major in the Army Air Corps. He was assigned as an intelligence staff officer in Washington, D.C. In 1943 he joined the Eighth Air Force in England, finally realizing his opportunity to be an active part of the war effort. He landed in France with the Eighty-fourth Fighter Wing as the air-ground control officer. Vidmer became one of the few pilots who flew in both World War I and World War II. In June 1994, outside Cherbourg, France, Vidmer was wounded while on a reconnaissance mission to locate a site for an advanced airfield. After the war, he remained in England as a foreign correspondent for the *New York Herald Tribune*. He never wrote about sports again. Vidmer recalled that Grantland Rice had told him: "When athletes are not heroes to you anymore it's time to stop writing sports." After all the action Vidmer had seen in Europe, sports were no longer glamorous.

Vidmer's twenty-year marriage to Miriam was also a casualty of war. Their years of wartime separation led to divorce. While a foreign correspondent in England he met Elizabeth Brooke, the daughter of the rajah of Sarawak, a British protectorate located in northwest Borneo. She became his second wife. Vidmer left the *Herald Tribune* in 1951 and with Elizabeth relocated to Barbados, where he worked as a golf pro. He also helped his friend, golfer Bobby Jones, design golf courses. After nearly a decade of life on Barbados, however, Vidmer became homesick for the United States.

Vidmer's second marriage ended with his decision to resume working in New York. He worked as an editor for Dun and Bradstreet and married again, to Mary Field. The couple retired to Murray, Kentucky, in the mid 1970s.

Respected as both a sportswriter and military officer, Vidmer counted among his friends such notables as Babe Ruth, Grantland Rice, Gene Fowler, Dwight D. Eisenhower, Elliot Roosevelt, and George S. Patton. Another friend of Vidmer's, sportswriter Bill Corum, recalling the 1913 West Point football team in his book *Off and Running* (1959), wrote: "it included a fellow with a twisted knee named Eisenhower, . . . and a skinny mascot named Richards Vidmer, who later sank to the level of sportswriting," a sardonic observation that Vidmer likely appreciated.

Richards Vidmer died in the Murray-Calloway County Hospital in Murray, Kentucky, on 23 July 1978. The cause of death was heart failure brought on by complications from emphysema.

Interview:

Jerome Holtzman, *No Cheering in the Press Box* (New York: Holt, Rinehart & Winston, 1974), pp. 98–113.

References:

Ira Berkow, *Red: A Biography of Red Smith* (New York: Times Press, 1986);

Jimmy Breslin, *Damon Runyon–A Life* (New York: Ticknor & Fields, 1991);

Bob Cooke, ed., *Wake Up the Echoes, from the Sports Pages of the New York Herald Tribune* (Garden City, N.Y.: Hanover House, 1956), pp. 5–18, 144;

Bill Corum, *Off and Running,* edited by Arthur Mann (New York: Holt, 1959), p. 11;

Gene Fowler, *Skyline: A Reporter's Reminiscence of the 1920s* (New York: Viking, 1961);

Stanley Frank, ed., *Sports Extra: Classics of Sports Reporting* (New York: Barnes, 1944), p. 185;

Richard Kluger, *The Paper: The Life and Death of The New York Herald Tribune* (New York: Knopf, 1986);

Stanley Walker, *City Editor* (New York: Stokes, 1934), pp. 115, 124–125;

Stanley Woodward, *Paper Tiger* (New York: Atheneum, 1964);

Woodward, *Sports Page* (New York: Simon & Schuster, 1949), p. 49;

Jonathan Yardley, *Ring: A Biography of Ring Lardner* (New York: Random House, 1977).

Joe Williams

(12 December 1889 - 14 February 1972)

Bill Knight
Western Illinois University

MAJOR POSITIONS HELD: Reporter, *Memphis Commercial Appeal* (1910–1914); assistant sports editor and cartoonist, *Memphis Commercial Appeal* (1914–1916); sportswriter, *Cleveland News* (1916–1919); sports and drama editor, *Memphis Commercial Appeal* (1919–1920); assistant sports editor, *Cleveland News* (1920–1923); assistant sports editor, Newspaper Enterprise Association (1923–1925); sports editor, *Cleveland Press* (1925–1927); sports editor and columnist, *New York Telegram* (1927-1931); sports director, Scripps-Howard Newspapers (1927–1964); sports editor and columnist, *New York World-Telegram* (1931–1950); sports editor and columnist, *New York World-Telegram and Sun* (1950–1964); weekly columnist, *New York Morning Telegraph* (1965).

Joe Williams

BOOKS: *Joe Williams' TV-Boxing Book* (New York: Van Nostrand, 1954);

The Joe Williams Baseball Reader: The Glorious Game from Ty Cobb and Babe Ruth to the Amazing Mets: 50 Years of Baseball Writing by the Celebrated Newspaper Columnist, edited by Peter Williams (Chapel Hill, N.C.: Algonquin, 1989).

OTHER: "Boos for the President," in *Sports Extra,* edited by Stanley Frank (New York: Barnes, 1944), pp. 171–174;

"TV or Not TV," in *Best Sports Stories 1951: A Panorama of the 1950 Sports Year,* edited by Irving T. Marsh and Edward Ehre (New York: Dutton, 1951), pp. 82–84;

"Adventure on the Waterfront," in *Best Sports Stories 1953: A Panorama of the 1952 Sports Year,* edited by Marsh and Ehre (New York: Dutton, 1953), pp. 278–283;

"What They Think about Ford Frick," in *Best Sports Stories 1957: A Panorama of the 1956 Sports Year,* edited by Marsh and Ehre (New York: Dutton, 1957), pp. 75–89;

"Managers Are a Dime a Dozen," in *The Second Fireside Book of Baseball,* edited by Charles Einstein (New York: Simon & Schuster, 1958), pp. 371–375;

"Abe Attell Takes the Stand," in *The Fireside Book of Boxing,* edited by W. C. Heinz (New York: Simon & Schuster, 1961), pp. 393–394;

"Great Day for the Irish . . . But at Notre Dame?" in *A Treasury of Notre Dame Football,* edited by Gene Schoor (New York: Funk & Wagnalls, 1962), pp. 281–282;

"Game Two, 1950," in *The Phillies Reader,* edited by Richard Orodenker (Philadelphia: Temple University Press, 1996), pp. 85–88.

One of the first writers to cover sports in a frank, critical way, Joe Williams broke legendary stories and new ground in his decades-long career. His scoops included Babe Ruth's "called shot" home run, American League Most Valuable Player George Sisler's disabling eye problem, and an apparent conflict of interest between other well-known sportswriters and a boxing promoter. His innovations ranged from the College Football Coach of the Year to the adoption of mutuels on New York racetracks. Williams built a large following as an outspoken, provocative advocate for fans. In addition to sportswriting, including many articles for such sports magazines as *Judge, Sport,* and *The Sporting News,* Williams was also a member of the National Sports Committee, the Dutch Treat, Silurians, Players, and Artists and Writers clubs of New York. He was most at home where sports took place or where newspapers were assembled, however. He liked to think of himself as a "sporting writer." William N. Wallace in the *New York Times* wrote, "Williams was no gee whiz worshipper. With a pithy, trenchant style, he was one of the first to view sports in a realistic, cynical fashion." His credo, Wallace added, "was 'inform and then entertain,'" and "Time and again, he supported 'Gus H. Fan' against dubious promotions and deftly lanced the pompous traditionalists."

Joseph Peter Williams was born in Memphis, Tennessee, on 12 December 1889, his family says, although at times he claimed 1890, 1891, and 1893 as a birth date. His parents were cotton broker Edward Metcalfe and Anne Elizabeth (Connolly) Williams. Young Williams attended the Market Street and Mosby Street schools in Memphis and Christian Brothers College, also in Memphis. According to his son Peter Williams in *The Joe Williams Baseball Reader* (1989), Joe spent his boyhood with his brother Bill swimming in the Wolf River and vending at the Red Elm Park, until their grandmother forced the boys to quit because she thought ballplayers to be "drunkards or worse." The sharp-tongued, witty Williams loved sports. After an attempt at boxing at the Phoenix Athletic Club in Memphis, he began to prefer covering athletics to participating in them. "I was allergic to a punch in the snout," he recalled.

In the 1910s Memphis was a center of boxing, college football, and minor-league baseball, where major leaguers frequently barnstormed through town. There Williams met Ty Cobb, Joe Jackson, Frank Chance, Burleigh Grimes, Casey Stengel, and Tris Speaker, whom Williams later nicknamed the "Gray Eagle" while covering the Indians in Cleveland. "I used to hang around the prize fights and the baseball park most of my waking hours," Williams said. "I got to know the players, the fighters, the managers and what have you. I was just bound to become a sports writer with that background." He got a job at space rates for the *Memphis Commercial Appeal,* writing school and amateur sports, although to boost his income he admittedly fabricated stories. Once he even invented a baseball league, complete with players and game accounts.

Earning $3.00 per column of type, Williams took a sizeable pay cut when editor C. P. J. Mooney hired him as a full-time reporter in 1910. One of his first stories was a Minneapolis Millers–Memphis Turtles minor-league practice game held outside nearby Hickman, Kentucky, where Williams, having paid his own way, watched the great former major-league southpaw Rube Waddell in one of his final performances. Williams was more than a sportswriter early in his newspaper career. He drew an occasional cartoon at the *Commercial Appeal* and reviewed drama in Memphis and movies in Cleveland. His duties as a critic included a question-answer column written under the byline of "Lottie Lee."

A case of mistaken identity indirectly led to Williams's leaving Memphis. Hoping to score an interview with Cleveland infielder Terry Turner, he grabbed Turner–he thought–at the hotel where the team was staying. The man gave Williams plenty of information, but only later did Williams discover that he was actually *Cleveland News* reporter Tom Terrell, who apologized for the hoax and offered Williams a job in 1916. Actual scoops followed as Williams exploited chances, emboldened his own status, and embellished his observations.

On 17 October 1914 Williams married Helen Schauman. They had two children, Charles Edward and Louise Adelaide.

While covering the Indians in the spring of 1923, Williams traveled to New Orleans for an exhibition game with the St. Louis Browns. A mix-up in accommodations placed Williams in the room his friend Lee Fohl, the Browns manager, was to have occupied. While there, Williams took a phone call meant for Fohl and learned that the Browns' first baseman, George Sisler, needed season-ending (and possibly career-ending) eye surgery. Williams called sports editor Ed Bang in Cleveland who "rushed out with a copyrighted scoop that shook the baseball world for at least 24 hours."

Within a few years Williams came to the attention of Roy Howard, and the Cleveland sportswriter and editor became sports director for Scripps-Howard Newspapers, a position in which he served from 1927 to 1931, and sports editor and columnist

Newspaper delivery truck with promotional sign for Williams

at the *New York Telegram,* where he was employed from 1927 to 1964.

Williams did not limit himself to newsbreaking scoops. He also delved into what may be called "sports-features," giving readers in-depth views of some of the influential persons of sports. For instance, in 1929 Williams profiled baseball commissioner Judge Kenesaw Mountain Landis:

> It takes courage to interview the Judge. He drives his points home with a swishing hand and a roughhouse windup. Whack! That is the Judge telling you tricky baseball deals must end. Whack! That is the Judge telling you the chain-store system of baseball ownership is an evil. Whack! That is the Judge telling you that his cold is worse, that the weather is bad, that you can't get good tarpon steaks in the East; in short, that is the Judge telling you 'most anything.

With light, precise prose, Williams brought home the figures his readers otherwise likely would not have ever known.

Writing for the *Telegram* through two successive mergers with other newspapers (first with the *New York World* in 1931 and then with the *New York Sun* in 1950), Williams developed a national standing covering many of the famous athletes of his day. Writing about Rogers Hornsby, for instance, Williams revealed his simultaneous admiration for athletes and his reluctance to anoint them as heroes: "There is nothing strange about a man having enemies. Only in sports is the emotional situation different, and this is due, I suppose, to the indiscriminate eagerness of the sports follower to make gods of anyone that can hit a ball or land a knockout." Nevertheless, through the decades Williams conceded that he appreciated, even idolized, a few athletes: Mordecai "Three-Finger" Brown, Shoeless Joe Jackson, and Babe Ruth, his favorite sports figure. "The Bam," Nashville sportswriter Fred Russell quoted Williams as saying, "had the precious gift of being himself at all times. He rolled through a long and gripping career, almost constantly in the glare of the white lights, and at the finish he was essentially the same gangling kid . . . unchanged and unspoiled."

Williams's long relationship with Ruth may have been cemented in the circumstances surrounding Ruth's "called shot" during the 1 October 1932 World Series game against the Cubs in Chicago. Williams's game story in afternoon editions that day was the only account that specifically said Ruth, with two strikes on him, pointed at the fence before hitting a home run to deep center field off pitcher Charlie Root, according to Ruth biographer Robert Creamer. Under a *World-Telegram* headline announcing, "Ruth Calls Shot as He Puts Homer No. 2 in Side Pocket," Williams wrote:

> The Bambino hit two homers during the day, each of them a record breaker, and on the occasion of his second round-tripper even went so far as to call his shot. . . . In the fifth, with the Cubs riding him unmercifully from the bench, Ruth pointed to center and punched a screaming liner to a spot where no ball had ever been hit before.

In the next few days New York sportswriters Bill Corum, Paul Gallico, and Tom Meany all mentioned Ruth's pointing beforehand, although Ruth himself generally gave some other explanation of the event until he came to accept the legend built on the momentum Williams launched. By 1950 Williams conceded that Ruth probably was just indicating that he still had one strike left. "Even if Ruth didn't mean it," Williams later said, "the thunderous drama still lives in my memory. And no amount of testimony to the contrary is ever going to change it in the slightest. I always was a pushover for wonderful fairy tale, anyway."

Though Williams lauded Ruth, he did not paint every aspect of baseball in glowing terms. In fact, Roger Kahn commented that Williams could write with satiric "acid," which he did whenever something struck his ire. A 1932 piece bemoans "pansy reformers" who replaced bottles with paper containers in ballparks:

> It probably is true that the country began to come loose at the seems at about the same time the sport of bottle heaving was stripped of its masculine virility. Where is there a Teddy Roosevelt (rah) to lead us out of the chaos and confusion? Or a John L. Sullivan? Or a Pop Anson? Or a Lilllian Russell? What does a guy do today at the Stadium or the Polo Grounds or at Ebbets Field when he is moved to display the beast in him? He seizes his scorecard, tears it into little pieces, takes a sissy windup, throws a ball of paper snow at the umps and chirps, "There now, you old dirty-dirty." I ask you, would Lincoln stand for that?

Chicago Cubs slugger Hack Wilson also came under fire from Williams's acerbic pen in the 1930s: "a short, stumpy geezer, built close to the ground like a toadstool, Mr. Wilson is a field hand at heart. . . . There are a lot of people who would rather watch Babe Ruth hit a long fly than see Hack Wilson smack the ball over the garden wall. One is an artist, the other a plumber."

During the initial years of the Great Depression, Williams used his baseball connections to help the unemployed. In 1931 he organized a round-robin baseball tournament among the Giants, Yankees, and Dodgers that benefited New York's jobless. In 1932 Williams hired the then-unknown cartoonist Willard Mullins, basing his assessment of Mullins's work on mailed-in art samples. Longtime newspaperman Stanley Walker noted in a backhanded compliment in his 1934 autobiography *City Editor* that Williams had become "somewhat more editorial, and battles for reforms. His ideas, even when they make dull reading, still show the workings of a mind that is alive and inquiring." Williams was opinionated and throughout his career championed specific causes and ideals of sportsmanship.

On 23 June 1934 Williams married Emma Herbers. He had two children by his second marriage, Joseph Peter and Curtis Michael.

In 1935 a hunch helped Williams land an exclusive on Ruth's resignation from the Yankees. "In the newspaper game," Williams once said, "hunches are of tremendous importance." He learned that Ruth had given Yankee owner Colonel Jacob Ruppert the ultimatum of choosing either him or Joe McCarthy as team manager. "Colonel Jacob Ruppert will pay off Joe McCarthy and appoint Babe Ruth as a manager of the Yankees for the next year or the Babe's career with the New York club has come to an end. You may accept that from Ruth himself." Not even Bill Slocum, Ruth's ghostwriter, knew of his intentions. Williams's exclusive was one of the biggest scoops of his career. Later, in August 1948, while on vacation, Williams received a telegram asking him to be a pallbearer at Ruth's funeral. He was reluctant to participate in such a public, emotional event, however, and pretended he had not been notified in time to go.

Williams helped develop the first major-league all-star game in the Deep South–a Tampa, Florida, exhibition that benefited the Finland War Relief program, launched in 1939 by former President Herbert Hoover. He persuaded several colleagues to help, including Bob Considine, who ghostwrote a speech for Hoover at a rally for the event. For Williams's efforts he was made a knight, first class, of the Order of the White Rose of Finland.

Williams (right) with sportswriter Harry Grayson and Stan Musial

In the newspaper industry at the time "leg men" commonly developed sources, visited the scenes of stories, soaked in details, and sometimes phoned in material to rewrite desks that actually wrote the story; Williams, however, experienced for himself the games and interviews he conveyed to his readers. A trained observer with reporting skills and writing talent, he appreciated the minutiae of sports and the nostalgia and trivia its followers sought. For instance, he wrote on 14 August 1941: "There is an unwritten law in the press box that no piece having to do with the beanball shall be written without reference to the death of Ray Chapman." Williams composed several articles over the years alluding to the 1920 event in which Chapman was hit with Carl Mays's pitch "with such force" that the ball "bounded clear over Wally Pipp's head at first base." Williams got the eyewitness accounts of Jack McAllister and Tris Speaker, assistant manager and manager, respectively, of the Cleveland Indians. In 1964 he commented that "if Mays was haunted by brooding memories the record book doesn't show it."

Williams enjoyed beating others to stories, using his insider access, and expressing insight on behalf of fans. No matter the subject or deadline, he could write with precision and pacing, as a 1949 piece on Army football coach Red Blaik shows:

> A number of ingredients go into the success of the 51-year old Red Blaik, who isn't a redhead at all but sandy gray, an articulate country gentleman of soft voice, pleasant of manner, and, while not exactly gregarious, there is surely nothing anti-social about him. He's a profound football scholar with a definitely modern outlook, an unremitting enthusiasm, and a limitless capacity for work.

Sometimes Williams showed uncommon insight–or foresight. In a 1949 column disagreeing with the *Wall Street Journal,* which questioned the profitability of baseball as a business venture, Williams cited several examples of moneymaking clubs and sales of franchises for millions of dollars. "I think the editors," Williams wrote, "will concede this shows it is quite possible to make a fast buck in baseball. It's a lush field for a smart operator. Whether this . . . serves the game's stability over the long haul may be open to question."

On 30 September 1950 Williams was injured in a plane crash, in which the pilot was killed. Hospitalized for two days, Williams received dozens of telegrams from athletes, newsmen, celebrities, and other well-wishers. Concerned, however, that he would miss his first World Series in thirty years, Williams covered some of the action from his bed, via television:

> Such is TV's distrust of audience discernment, or perhaps so boundless its solicitude, that we were repeatedly reminded it was a great pitcher's battle. Any medium which presents a picture of the obvious and then explains it is not likely ever to be faulted as too subtle or esoteric. We of the TV audience simply can't get enough useless information, a fact which our hosts, very sensibly, do not dispute.

In his coverage of the 1950 Series, Williams wrote with good-natured sarcasm about the Philadelphia Phillies team, known as the "Whiz Kids," and their star pitcher showing too little respect for their New York elders: "Sooner or later, the brat in them shows, like this Robin Roberts." When Phillies shortstop Granny Hamner ("who must be no less than an Eagle scout") hit a triple, Williams remarked:

> Those of us in the TV audience could only imagine the great wave of boyish joy which must have swept over the Philly bench and the happy shrieks of, 'Oh, you Superman!' . . . 'Just like Capt. Marvel.' . . . 'Wait 'til Hopalong hears about this.' All against a staccato background of bubble gum explosions and a shower of torn comic books.

Before a slumping Joe DiMaggio–who had not hit a ball past the infield–hit a home run to win game 2 in the tenth inning, Williams continued: "The malevolent moppets in the Philly nursery pen no doubt were laughing like crazy at the big man's feeble effort to solve Master Roberts' magic. It was funnier than Howdy Doody."

Novelist and essayist Wilfred Sheed, the author of *Baseball and Lesser Sports,* admired Williams's "rich voice," which is on display in another 1950 column, on the "taciturn general," Bob Neyland, head coach of the Tennessee football Volunteers. "His young men tackle with terrifying violence, and once a ballcarrier gets running, his blockers form quickly and proceed to upend everybody in sight," Williams wrote. "In a few seconds a chaotic scramble becomes a pattern of disciplined destruction–the mark and result of long hours of patient and knowing coaching."

One two-part column, published just before Christmas Eve and on New Year's Eve 1952, was a departure from straight-up sports reporting. "Adventure on the Waterfront" is reminiscent of both Heywood Broun's sentimental Christmas columns and Damon Runyon's colorful character studies. "A group of evil-looking characters had a little redfaced round man with enormous white whiskers against a wall in the dismal old pier and there was menace in their manner," the dreamy fable begins. "Tic and Trigger Mike, Tiny the Cheese, Three Fingered Brown and Meatball Moody, Mike the Bite, Slim Lucy, John the Beefer" all strongarm the little old man until he offers seasons' greetings. The column resumes in a mysterious airport, where "a group of men, sullen morose, stood nearby, clearly waiting for someone. To anyone in sports the men were easily identifiable, Jersey Joe Walcott, Ben Hogan, Leo Durocher, Paul Brown, Branch Rickey, Spikee Briggs, Russell Kingman, Chuck Taylor and Warren Giles." As the figure of Old Man Time "came hobbling through the entrance gate . . . there was the mournful hint of a dirge." The group is not waiting for a second chance, for new hope, to redeem themselves after having a miserable, losing 1952, but to ensure that the past year leaves, never to return.

A complimentary 1953 column about Yankees infielder Billy Martin, who had a great World Series against the Dodgers, carries the same sort of whimsy, though it is more grounded in description than the fantastic: "There is nothing about Billy Martin that is remindful of Yankee heroes of the past. Gehrig could have put him in his hip pocket. Ruth would have mistaken him for the bat boy. DiMaggio, in a whimsical mood, might have let him carry his glove."

Williams experimented with various stylistic effects, with varying degrees of success. Sometimes his effective use of quotes enlivens interviews and reads similarly to literary dialogue. At other times he intrudes into his own material, letting himself become a character in the column, or writes in the first person in such an undisciplined way that readers could be distracted from the topic by the obstacle the author becomes. In an August 1956 piece for *Sport,* "What They Think about Ford Frick," Williams lays out all the particulars in a thoroughly analytical essay format while also including implied references to himself:

> This was the assignment: "Let's see what gives with Ford Frick, the baseball boss. Has he been a good commissioner? What have been his accomplishments? Has he left anything undone that should be done in the interests of a better game? What do the club owners, the players, the sportswriters think of him? Happy Chandler got knocked off trying to win a second term. What are Frick's prospects?"

Although Williams cranked out six columns a week, Monday pieces usually were an unrelated

Williams with baseball manager Casey Stengel

assortment of notes and short items that Williams made "look easy," Fred Russell recalled in his 1957 autobiography, *Bury Me in an Old Press Box.* Russell thought Williams was "a genius at weaving the fragments together smoothly, injecting wise-cracks and barbs."

Another piece, "Great Day for the Irish . . . But at Notre Dame?" (*New York World Telegram and Sun,* 9 November 1960), tied together the recent election of the first Irish Catholic president, John F. Kennedy, in November 1960 and a six-game losing streak for Notre Dame, "the first time in history such a calamity has occurred." Wrote Williams: "The result of the race was declared hours ago, yet Our New Leader, who had described himself to the electorate as a man of positive, instant action, has done nothing about the harrowing situation at Notre Dame. Hasn't even appointed a committee." Williams could not underestimate the importance of football to Notre Dame: "Whether the good fathers like it or not, a winning team is a necessary adjunct to Notre Dame, a school that literally attained national prestige by means of the sport. Few people are aware that the basic formulae for synthetic rubber were the work of Notre Dame scientists. Millions still remember Knute Rockne and the Four Horsemen."

Williams wrote about baseball, golf, college football, and horseracing in addition to sports features and Monday sports tidbits. He also relieved Heywood Broun when the "It Seems To Me" columnist of the *World-Telegram* was absent, writing about topics other than sports.

As the *World-Telegram* sports editor and Scipps-Howard sports director, Williams was influential in and out of sports and journalism. He assembled a talented writing staff, which included Dan Daniel and Tom Meany. He helped found a charity hole-in-one golf tournament sponsored by the *World-Telegram,* as well as the contest to establish the most valuable high-school baseball player in New York, and Scripps-Howard's college football coach of the year award. He also advocated the no-foul rule in New York boxing.

Williams often gave free rein to his caustic wit in describing various sports figures. "When Mr. Doyle chuckles the effect is startling," he wrote. "It is a cross between a barnyard cackle and a mailman's whistle." He wrote about Dodgers pitcher Don Drysdale that he "throws more strikes than Hoffa." Describing the rotund Detroit Tiger Bob Fothergill in a 1929 column, Williams noted:

> Fothergill has supplanted Mr. Ruth as baseball's widest girth. His barrier to greatness is a Graf Zeppelin belt line. He is a living example to what confirmed Republicanism and full dinner pails will do for you. Warming the bench this year he will look like the Four Horseman, the Volga Boatman and two other fellows all in one.

Baseball and its subjects always seemed to encourage Williams to more elaborate descriptions in his prose. He wrote about fastball pitcher Walter Johnson: "If you ever saw him walk to the box you could never forget that gangling, awkward stride. For a man who threw the ball with such an easy, rhythmic motion, he was unbelievably gawky. He had a slovenly walk, he was slew-footed and his arms dangled at his side like two cuts of flabby fire hose." Former pitcher and Senators owner Clark Griffith was "a hustling, articulate, cantankerous remnant of a thinning old guard who has seen the game come over from the other side of the tracks and take its place with the freshly scrubbed aristocrats of sport." Ty Cobb was "an egoist with a brain" and John McGraw "a black-haired, pasty-faced Irishman to whom roughhouse tactics were merely a part of the trade." Garry Herrmann of the Cincinnati Reds–bankrupted by "conviviality"–"was a cross between Bacchus and Falstaff."

Next to baseball, boxing was Williams's favorite sport. In his interviews with Abe Attell, an eleven-year featherweight champion, Williams reflected on the lost art of boxers carrying their opponents:

> It takes superlative skills to make a bad fighter look good. Attell made 'em look great. And there'd always be a demand for a return bout–which was the main idea from the start. Then if the return was a betting fight Attell would send it in and go to work on the startled young man in front of him. "The trick was to let the yokel hold you even," Attell said. "In those days the newspapers gave the decisions. I always felt I'd turned in a bad job when they gave me a shade."

His 1954 book, *Joe Williams' TV-Boxing Book,* with a foreword by Bob Hope, sold well enough to go into a second printing, according to *The Sporting News* (17 November 1954), which praised the book as being "rich in dramatic incident, incredible scandal, historical episode and humorous anecdotes."

After Roy Howard's death in 1964, Williams was forced out of the Scripps-Howard organization by its management. Although Williams was lauded in the announcement of his retirement, he felt betrayed. The next year Lester Bromberg and Bob Sullivan helped him put out a subscription-only newsletter, *By Joe Williams,* focusing mostly on the racetrack, and he wrote a weekly notes column for the *Morning Telegraph.*

Williams died on 14 February 1972 in Pine Brook, New Jersey, reportedly because of intestinal cancer, after a series of strokes. *Newsweek* cited his "caustic humor and hard-hitting criticism" and called him "one of the best-known sportswriters of an era."

Williams's legacy as a sportswriter has been the occasion for controversy, with authors Robert Smith, Jack Orr, Murray Polner, and Peter Golenbock alleging that he had unfairly criticized Jackie Robinson and had been opposed to integrating Major League Baseball. Williams's son, Peter, refuted the allegations in a 1995 article in the journal *Nine,* quoting his father as saying that "if only one Negro player were denied the right to play big league baseball because of his race, that would be evil."

In his day Williams was respected and admired by his peers. Edward R. Murrow called him "a soft-spoken, peace-loving man" who "somehow manages to be always in a fight, a fight against abuses and corruption in the sports world." In Jerome Holtzman's 1973 book, *No Cheering in the Press Box,* sportswriter Red Smith counted Williams among the "many writing heroes, writers who have influenced me. . . . At the top of his game, I thought Joe Williams was pretty good." Jim Murray said Williams "belongs with the legendary figures like Ring Lardner, Damon Runyon, Grantland Rice and the rest," while Considine, in his *It's All News to Me: A Reporter's Deposition* (1967), described Williams as "one of the most trenchant sportswriters of my time" and listed him with the best of the era. Robert W. Creamer, in *Babe: The Legend Comes to Life* (1974), added: "Williams was a positive, opinionated observer and a vigorous journalist, always probing."

Sports for Williams was not merely a subject for his writing; he tried to live by the principles that he believed athletic competition represented. "I've often wondered how it would be," he once wrote, "how it would affect the lives of our people if we all kept a daily box score on ourselves. As a matter of fact, I believe in sports as a way of life. The principles of decent citizenship are born on the sand lots of Bass River, Massachusetts; Peoria, Illinois; and Southgate, California: fair play, sportsmanship, and working together in a common cause."

Interviews:

J. G. Taylor Spink, "Three and One," *Sporting News* (22 August 1940);

John Rogers, "Joe Williams, Back Home, Tells Stories of Past, Discusses Sports of Present," *Memphis Press-Scimitar,* 20 August 1949.

References:

Happy Chandler, *Heroes, Plain Folks, and Skunks* (Chicago: Bonus Books, 1989), pp. 179, 186;

Bob Considine, *It's All News to Me: A Reporter's Deposition* (New York: Meredith Press, 1967), pp. 8, 71, 271;

Robert Creamer, *Babe: The Legend Comes to Life* (New York: Simon & Schuster, 1974), pp. 363–365, 376–377;

Allison Danzig, *The History of American Football* (Englewood Cliffs, N.J.: Prentice-Hall, 1956), pp. 99–100, 382, 438;

Louis I. Gelfand and Harry E. Heath, *Modern Sportswriting* (Ames: Iowa State University Press, 1969), pp. 116–117;

W. C. Handy, *Father of the Blues* (New York: Macmillan, 1941), p. 233;

Jerome Holtzman, *No Cheering in the Press Box* (New York: Holt, Rinehart & Winston, 1973), p. 248;

Chris Mead, *Champion: Joe Louis, Black Hero in White America* (New York: Scribners, 1985), pp. 132–133, 161, 205;

Edward R. Murrow, *This I Believe* (New York: Simon & Schuster, 1952), pp. 189–190;

Jackie Robinson, *My Own Story* (New York: Greenberg, 1948), pp. 56–57, 60–61, 171;

Fred Russell, *Bury Me in an Old Press Box* (New York: Barnes, 1957), pp. 17–18, 224;

J. G. Taylor Spink, "TV-Boxing Rich in Drama, Humor," *Sporting News* (17 November 1954);

Stanley Walker, *City Editor* (New York: Stokes, 1934), p. 130;

Peter Williams, "Did the Babe Call His Shot?" in *The Perfect Game,* edited by Mark Alvarez (Dallas: Taylor, 1993), pp. 234–240;

Williams, "When Chipmunks Become Wolves: The Scapegoating of Sportswriter Joe Williams by His Peers," *Nine: A Journal of Baseball History and Social Policy Perspectives* (Fall 1995): 51–61.

Papers:

Some of Joe Williams's papers are at the Department of English, Community College of Morris, Randolph, New Jersey.

A. S. "Doc" Young

(29 October 1919 - 6 September 1996)

Michael Marsh

MAJOR POSITIONS HELD: Sports reporter, sports editor, columnist, managing editor, executive editor, *Los Angeles Sentinel* (1943–1946, 1949–1951, 1958–1961, 1963–1966, 1985–1986); sports reporter, sports editor, sports columnist, *Cleveland Call and Post* (1946–1948); sports editor, *Chicago Defender* (1951); associate editor, Johnson Publishing Company (1951–1958); sports editor, *New York Amsterdam News* (1965–1966).

BOOKS: *Great Negro Baseball Stars, and How They Made the Major Leagues* (New York: A. S. Barnes, 1953);
Negro Firsts in Sports (Chicago: Johnson Publishing, 1963);
Sonny Liston: The Champ Nobody Wanted (Chicago: Johnson Publishing, 1963);
Black Champions of the Gridiron: Leroy Keyes & O. J. Simpson (New York: Harcourt, Brace & World, 1969);
The Mets From Mobile: Tommie Agee and Cleon Jones (New York: Harcourt, Brace & World, 1970).

OTHER: *The Incomparable Nat King Cole,* edited by Young (Fort Worth, Tex.: Sepia Publishing, 1965).

SELECTED PERIODICAL PUBLICATIONS–UNCOLLECTED: "Home Run King of the Giants," *Ebony,* 17 (July 1962): 47–53;
"The Storm in Adam's Eden, Part 111," *Sepia,* 16 (May 1967): 8–12, 14;
"New Job for an Old Ball Player," *Sepia,* 16 (May 1967): 32–37;
"Nancy Wilson Goes Back to School," *Sepia,* 16 (May 1967): 42–46;
"Frank Robinson: The Challenge of '67," *Sepia,* 16 (May 1967): 55–58;
"The Black Athlete in the Golden Age of Sports: The Black Sportswriter," *Ebony,* 25 (October 1970): 56–64;
"Why Ali Can Never Beat Frazier," *Sepia,* 20 (July 1971): 28–33;
"Is Baseball Ready for a Black Manager?" *Sepia,* 20 (September 1971): 50–58.

A. S. "Doc" Young

A. S. "Doc" Young, who never held a full-time job at a mainstream daily newspaper, established a legacy in sports journalism through his extensive contributions to black weekly newspapers and weekly and monthly magazines and his several books about sports. One of the first African American members of the Baseball Writers Association of America, he combined strong powers of observation with an encyclopedic knowledge of sports. He was an advocate for African American athletes, but he criticized those who, in his eyes, were not good representatives of the black community. Although Young often wrote about social issues, business, politics, and entertainment as well as sports, he remained a sportswriter at heart. According to an unpublished interview with his son, Norman Gregory Young, the elder Young claimed sportswriters were more individualistic–and therefore more effective–in the way they saw and reported events than other journalists. As his son added, "He felt that the most stirring writing was that of sportswriters."

Andrew Spurgeon Nash Young was born on 29 October 1919 to Andrew and Gertrude Young in Dunbrooke, Virginia. He was the elder of two children; his sister was named Ruth. The family later moved to Bowling Green, Virginia. Young's father was a high-school teacher with postgraduate training in divinity. His mother, who had graduated from Hampton Institute (now Hampton University) and earned a graduate degree in music at Barnard College of Columbia University, was a homemaker and taught piano in the family's home. Andrew played piano, clarinet, and saxophone and grew up loving jazz. (As an adult, he established friendships with Nat King Cole and Lionel Hampton.) According to an unpublished 1971 interview with Henry LaBrie (available at the Columbia University Oral History Research Office), Young enjoyed reading books, and he memorized stock information and sports statistics from newspapers. These statistics helped him keep up with a local high-school teacher who often chatted with Young about baseball. According to Norman Gregory Young, his father's childhood friends nicknamed him "Doc" because they considered him exceptionally bright. Because Young did not like his given name, he used the byline A. S. "Doc" Young throughout his career.

Baseball became Young's favorite sport while he was growing up. He confirmed his lifelong passion for the art of hitting–as well as revealing something about his own personality–in a recording he made on 31 December 1991 for the Moorland-Spingarn Research Center at Howard University: "Hitting is my favorite thing in all of sports. I have never gotten tired of hitting, of being at bat." He went on to praise Boston Red Sox player Ted Williams as "a thinking man's hitter. He wrote the best book that I have ever read on hitting. . . . He was an independent person. He was not a person who believed in kissing behinds, as some people do, to get ahead. He was his own man." Young's interest in hitting is also evident in "Home Run King of the Giants" (*Ebony,* July 1962), in which he described the batting stroke of San Francisco slugger Orlando Cepeda: "Just before the pitcher starts his motion, Cepeda draws his bat back, far behind his right shoulder. As the pitcher hurls the ball toward home plate, Cepeda fuses remarkably the titanic power of his body with incredible timing, whips the bat around with the speed of light to meet the ball at precisely the proper fractional second, at precisely the right angle, and . . . by by baby! *Home run!*"

During his junior year of high school, Young dislocated his left hip while playing football. Unable to walk for more than a year, he spent part of his recovery in bed and later used a wheelchair. Because his left leg became slightly shorter than his right, he walked with a slight limp for the rest of his life. Young completed high school with the help of a tutor, graduating among the top students in his class at Union High School in Bowling Green in 1937. That fall Young enrolled in Hampton Institute, planning to prepare for a career in business. According to a 1942 letter in the Hampton University archives, accounting, business, and economics classes represented more than half of Young's credits. He failed English 101 during his first year in school, but he passed the course during his second year. He had only four hours in journalism because the school did not offer a major in the subject.

Nonetheless, Young began preparing for a career in journalism during college. At the suggestion of an English teacher he joined the staff of the campus newspaper, the *Hampton Script,* becoming a reporter and business manager. Years later, he sent a letter to a school official listing several Hampton alumni, including *Chicago Defender* publisher John Sengstacke, who succeeded in journalism. "Certainly, if Hampton could make such production without a full-fledged Journalism course there is no telling what it could do if its attention were put to this field," he wrote in his letter, which is in the Hampton archives.

After he earned a bachelor's degree in business administration with honors in May 1941, Young spent the next year as a student accounting clerk in the school comptroller's office. In 1943 he moved to Los Angeles, where he found work as an assistant manager of a grocery store and as a sportswriter with the *Los Angeles Sentinel,* a black weekly newspaper. While working at the store in 1944, Young met his future wife, Hazel Jackson. They married the following year on 28 October 1945 and eventually had two children, Norman Gregory and Brenda, both of whom eventually earned law degrees.

In 1946 Young went to work for the *Cleveland Call and Post,* a black weekly, as a sportswriter and advanced to sports editor and columnist in September of the following year. He covered baseball, football, and boxing and started a column called "Sportivanting." In his 25 October 1947 column he articulated one of his core beliefs: "Sports are powerful factors for democracy and downright good in these United States. It may not be as intended or as it should be; but, the righteous truth is that the doings of a Joe Louis or a Jackie Robinson have more gripping and moving effects on the thinking of the majority people than all of the long-studied and wise words of a W. E. B. Du Bois, a Walter White or an A. Phillip Randolph. (Candidly, I'm not sure that is the way it should be!)"

While in Cleveland, Young covered outfielder Larry Doby, the first black in the American League, and Satchel Paige, the first black American League pitcher, when they joined the Cleveland Indians in 1947 and 1948, respectively. Young occasionally defended Doby's play, once arguing that Indians manager Lou Boudreau did not use him properly and rarely communicated with him during his rookie year. Young was also supportive of Paige. After watching Paige work out in Cleveland, Young reported that the pitcher said he did not know he was throwing a slider until an observer told him. Young wrote: "That statement is testimony to a remarkable arm. The slider is an arm-punishing pitch and is, supposedly, one of the causes of Ewell Blackwell's poor showing this year after a sensational 1947. Paige has thrown the thing for 20 years!" Young and his wife often entertained Doby and Paige at their house.

Young became involved in a controversy in June 1948, when he ghostwrote "What's Wrong with Negro Baseball," an *Ebony* cover article by Brooklyn Dodgers great Jackie Robinson. Robinson complained about the manner in which the Negro-leagues baseball teams operated, arguing that the players had to cope with a lack of written contracts, poor umpiring, and bad accommodations. In a 1996 memoir former *Ebony* executive editor Ben Burns wrote that he used such controversial articles to promote the magazine.

In 1949 Young rejoined the *Los Angeles Sentinel* as sports editor and sold "Is Larry Doby the Successor to Tris Speaker?" to *Sport* magazine. Later, in his *Great Negro Baseball Stars, and How They Made the Major Leagues* (1953), he claimed that he was the first black writer to sell an article to a major sports magazine. Two years later he joined Johnson Publishing Company as an associate editor for *Ebony.* During the 1950s he also served as sports editor of the magazine, as well as associate editor, assistant managing editor, managing editor, and sports editor of *Jet,* another Johnson magazine.

A longtime friend, former *Ebony* editor Herbert Nipson, said Young was valuable because he had established relationships with top athletes and considered the needs of readers when he wrote his stories. When the company wanted to run an article about a sports figure, Young was often able to locate the person quickly and write a piece that told readers "what he thought they wanted to know. When you read Doc Young, you came away with a better understanding of why the athlete was the way he was."

Another of Young's friends was Tommy Hawkins, former Los Angeles Lakers star and vice president of

Dust jacket for Young's first book (1953), which describes the careers of the first thirteen African Americans to play in the major leagues

communications for the Los Angeles Dodgers. Hawkins also admired his writing style. "Doc's articles not only focused on the individual, but the intervening variables that made the individual what he was and the circumstances in which that individual existed," he said. After Young died, Hawkins conducted a memorial service for him.

In 1953 Young completed his first book, *Great Negro Baseball Stars,* which describes the careers of the blacks who entered the major leagues from 1947 up to the time the book was completed. It also includes an appendix with extensive facts about blacks in organized baseball, including lists of blacks who played in the World Series and honors won by black major leaguers.

In the book Young compared the conduct of Robinson and Doby:

> In many ways, Doby had been the perfect choice for the pioneering job in the American League. In others, as in his tendency to tighten up, he was a puzzler, a lad who not infrequently confused his closest friends. It

> might be said that the major difference between Jackie and Larry was this: Jackie, as time was to prove, dressed himself in the cloak of humility and made it into a perfect fit through one of the greatest acting jobs in baseball history; Doby wore the cloak as a gift of nature.

While covering the Cleveland Indians, Young often interviewed William Veeck, who owned the team during the late 1940s. In a 1962 memoir Veeck claimed that Young aided his 1942 effort to buy the Philadelphia Phillies and stock the team with black players from the Negro leagues. Young mentioned the alleged attempt in *Great Negro Baseball Stars,* but he said that he had nothing to do with it.

In 1963 Young solidified his status as an historian of black athletes with *Negro Firsts in Sports.* The book includes brief profiles of athletes ranging from early black boxers and jockeys to black baseball players entering the major leagues. Pioneers mentioned in the book included Tom Molineaux, a slave who earned his freedom by winning a fist fight and then traveled to England as a professional boxer, and Isaac Murphy, the first jockey to win the Kentucky Derby three times.

A staunch supporter of integration, Young wrote the book during the civil rights era. He was proud that blacks were assimilating in sports, commenting in his introduction: "The fact is that, while perfection in this aspect of sports cannot be honestly attested to here, Negroes approach closer to the democratic ideal in the world of sports than in any other facet of American life." To emphasize his point Young described an encounter with a woman newspaper vendor who was angry because the black newspaper she read had several stories about racial injustice. She challenged Young to find news stories that showed blacks as achievers rather than victims. Young found them by turning to the sports pages of the black paper and a mainstream daily.

Negro Firsts in Sports is among Young's top achievements. The American Library Association named it one of the top reference books of 1963. Furthermore, *Negro Firsts in Sports* established him as a successor to Edwin Henderson, who wrote many articles about black sports figures and *The Negro in Sports* (1939), the first comprehensive history of black athletes. Young, who paid tribute to Henderson in *Negro Firsts in Sports,* may in turn be viewed as a predecessor of tennis great Arthur Ashe, who interviewed Young for *Hard Road to Glory* (1988), his three-volume study of black athletes, and used *Great Negro Baseball Stars* and *Negro Firsts in Sports* as sources.

Young wrote another book in 1963. *Sonny Liston: The Champ Nobody Wanted* traces the heavyweight boxer's life from his impoverished childhood in Arkansas to his quick knockout of champion Floyd Patterson in 1962. Countering negative perceptions of Liston, a former convict who projected a mean image and was rumored to be tied to organized crime, Young described Liston's performance during a press conference following the fight: "Liston's display of a fine, subtle wit softened up critical reporters considerably. He had at no time resorted to overt braggadocio over his triumph." Young also criticized the spectators who booed Liston before the fight:

> The booing was also unmistakable evidence of considerable hypocrisy among the fans themselves. For they, the fans, had established Liston as a solid betting favorite to win the fight and, of course, the title. They had, in other words, bet their money on *Evil.* Now, they were paying lip-service to *Good.*

The book provided background for the 1995 Home Box Office (HBO) documentary *Sonny Liston: The Mysterious Life and Death of a Champion.* Yet, HBO producer Kirby Bradley commented in an unpublished interview that some of the stories in the book were not substantiated, while others proved to be accurate.

Willie Mays was one of Young's all-time favorite athletes. When Mays announced his retirement from baseball, Young wrote in his 27 September 1973 column for the *Sentinel,* "No one ever played that game with a finer combination of color and flair, enthusiasm, and superior ability. He was one of a kind, an original, a once-in-a-lifetime saga." Twelve years later, Young was upset when Mays's former teammate John Milner accused him of using a stimulant, which turned out to be cough syrup. Young reacted strongly in his 19 September 1985 *Sentinel* column, saying that Milner was not "worth remembering" as a player or a person.

Young admired black athletes who succeeded at jobs after retiring from competition and served the black community. He appreciated Jackie Robinson's well-spoken manner, civil rights activism, and business career. Other athletes Young admired included Joe Black, a former Brooklyn Dodgers pitcher who became an executive with Greyhound, and Ashe, who was a social activist.

Young also admired retired Dodgers pitcher Don Newcombe and Baltimore Orioles outfielder Frank Robinson, writing about both men for the May 1967 issue of *Sepia* magazine. Newcombe was working as a public-information officer for the Opportunities Industrialization Center, a job-training organization, and had earned the admiration of other staff members for his fund-raising abilities. Robinson had rebounded after a controversial trade from the Cincinnati Reds to the Ori-

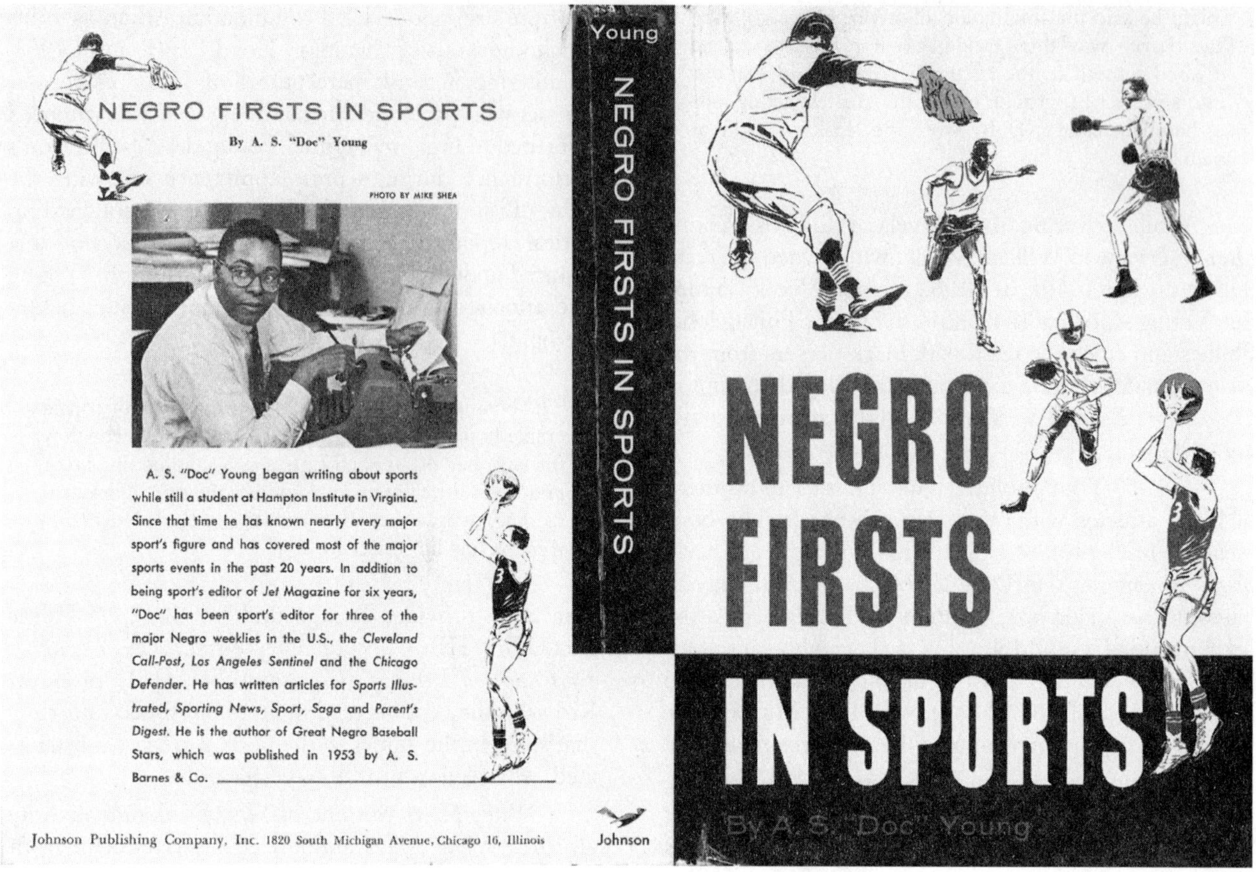

Dust jacket for Young's history of African American athletes, which the American Library Association named one of the top reference books of 1963

oles after the 1965 season. Reds president Bill DeWitt had publicly called Robinson "an old 30" following the deal, but in 1966 the outfielder won the Triple Crown and the American League Most Valuable Player award while helping Baltimore win the World Series. Young described Robinson sympathetically, calling him "an inspirational leader" and ranking him with Maury Wills as "among the greatest since Jackie Robinson."

Several years later, Young wrote about Robinson and Wills in "Is Baseball Ready for a Black Manager?" (*Sepia,* September 1971). In this article Young claimed that Robinson and Wills, a former star for the Los Angeles Dodgers, were the blacks most likely to be major-league managers:

> The fact of the matter is that both Robinson and Wills have gained the high regard of white and black players alike in their winter league managerial posts (Wills won a pennant in his very first outing last winter as manager of the Hermosillo, Mexico, team). Robinson has been praised by white players for his understanding managerial style and Wills is one of the best teachers in baseball.

Robinson, in fact, became the first major-league black manager when the Cleveland Indians named him player-manager in 1974. Wills was the third, managing the Seattle Mariners for eighty-three games in the 1980 and 1981 seasons.

While Young praised African American sports figures who were solid citizens, he was tough on those he felt were poor representatives of the black community. In a 30 January 1989 column for the *Chicago Defender,* he reacted strongly to news about boxer Mike Tyson's troubled marriage with Robin Givens and his bad partnership with promoter Don King: "Please, Heavenly Father, deliver us as soon as possible from these soap opera stars." In his 9 February 1989 *Defender* column, Young blasted college basketball coaches John Thompson and John Chaney for opposing Proposition 42, a National Collegiate Athletic Association rule that set stricter admissions standards for athletes. Thompson and Chaney claimed the rule discriminated against black athletes, causing Young to retort: "until the Thompsons and the Chaneys came along, I never thought I'd live to see the day when Afro-American

Dust jacket for Young's 1963 biography of the heavyweight champion, who had won the title from Floyd Patterson the previous year

coaches would say the Afro-Americans were too dumb to learn!" Young was also critical of black athletes who did not speak well. In his 31 January 1985 *Sentinel* column, for example, he wrote: "Moses Malone, the Philadelphia 76ers' great center, earns more than $2 million annually. But, Malone and proper English are total strangers."

Young was once complimentary of football star O. J. Simpson. In his 1969 book *Black Champions of the Gridiron: Leroy Keyes & O. J. Simpson,* Young profiled the two when they were senior backfield stars at the University of Southern California and Purdue, respectively. A slim, heavily illustrated volume intended for younger readers, the book presents both men as hardworking, honest, and articulate people who planned to compete in the National Football League and then work with young people. Young changed his view of Simpson in 1994, when he was charged with killing his wife, Nicole Brown Simpson, and a waiter, Ronald Goldman. Young was bothered that people cheered for Simpson as he and a friend fled from police in his Ford Bronco and by allegations that Simpson had beaten his wife during their marriage. In a 30 June 1994 column for the *Sentinel,* he wrote: "O. J. Simpson's case proves the folly of worshipping athletes and entertainers and trying to make role models out of them." Comparing Simpson to Keyes, Young added that Keyes "works in the Office of Desegregation in the Philadelphia school system" and "works hard in an effort to keep kids in school"; yet, "he rarely (if ever) is mentioned by the major media these days." "In sports," Young concluded, "priorities are so screwed up they cannot be sorted out. Leroy Keyes is fortunate in that he never was Hollywoodized."

Young could also criticize himself. In his 29 November 1973 *Sentinel* column he acknowledged he made a mistake by picking the University of California, Los Angeles, football team to beat its main rival, the University of Southern California. He had originally picked USC, which was the underdog, but changed his mind: "There is nothing more disgusting than second-guessing one's self on a sporting event, especially after one originally has picked the underdog to win and the underdog wins."

Another of his predictions had also proved wrong. After heavyweight boxing champion Joe Frazier defeated Muhammad Ali in a 1971 bout, Young wrote "Why Ali Can Never Beat Frazier," which was published as a cover story in the July 1971 issue of *Sepia.* He argued Ali lacked the skills to defeat Frazier in a rematch. In a letter to the editor, one reader claimed the article was "the most ludicrous piece of editorial writing I have read in some time and could only have been penned by a biased buffoon." Ali beat Frazier in 1974 and 1975.

Young's empathy for other black sportswriters, especially those who toiled at black weeklies, is evident in the series of articles about black sports figures he wrote for *Ebony* in 1969 and 1970. In one of the pieces, "The Black Athlete in the Golden Age of Sports: The Black Sportswriter" (October 1970), he complained that black sportswriters campaigned on behalf of black athletes and ably covered sports but did not advance:

> The black sportswriter today is a professional man. He is often talented. He knows his field. He loves sports. He is dedicated. He is always a crusader for the rights of his people. . . . He wears the callouses of numerous battles, rebuffs and insults. For, you see, in all the glory and all the glamour of sports, the black sportswriter, on the average, is the guy holding the short end of the very, very dirty stick.

One black sportswriter Young befriended was Dan Burley, who worked with Young at *Ebony.* In a 3 January 1985 *Sentinel* column Young wrote that Burley helped him ~~and~~ Jackie Robinson patch up their friendship, which had been damaged when Robinson denied making a statement Young had attributed to him.

While Young was essentially a sportswriter, he often wrote on other topics. The May 1967 issue of *Sepia* provides proof of his versatility. Along with the pieces about Newcombe and Robinson, he contributed articles about politician Adam Clayton Powell Jr. and singer Nancy Wilson. In an article published in the 21 December 1969 issue of *The New York Times,* Young defended *The Bill Cosby Show* after a critic claimed it did not properly represent blacks.

Young often wrote about issues relating to the black community. In a 6 December 1973 *Sentinel* column he commented on violence in black neighborhoods: "Teachers don't feel safe anymore in their classrooms. Bus drivers are frightened when they enter certain 'ghetto' areas and the passengers can never be sure of their safety either. Some kids are carrying guns to class to protect themselves from other kids. Gang activity is expanding faster than Watergate rumors. . . . One sure thing: This is no time for the professional excuse makers who always contrive to 'blame it all on Whitey.'"

In his 24 November 1994 *Sentinel* column, Young recommended the civil rights activist Andrew Young's *A Way Out Of No Way* (1994), which argues that nonviolence and spirituality helped the cause. A. S. "Doc" Young agreed with him: "Long ago, I learned that anger and hatred derange the mind. I now believe that anger, hatred, and jealousy should be added to The Four Horsemen of the Apocalypse. Conquest, war, famine, and death."

Young believed blacks could help themselves by owning businesses. He bought the weekly *California Eagle* with two partners in 1964. At the time it was the oldest continuing black paper in the country. According to Clint Wilson, Young, who served as executive editor, hired a strong staff, which wrote its own stories about Los Angeles instead of relying on wire-service copy. He also persuaded KGFJ, a black-owned radio station, to air a news show from the *Eagle* offices in order to promote both operations. Despite such efforts, however, the paper folded in 1966.

Young had a multifaceted career. One of the first black publicists hired by a Hollywood studio, he helped market movies such as *The Defiant Ones* (1958) and *Uptown Saturday Night* (1974). In 1972–1973 he was director of the public-relations office for the Los Angeles branch of Pepperdine University. While holding that job, he arranged boxer Ken Norton's visit to the campus and taught a class in advanced reporting. According to Hawkins, Young was also a contributor to Dodger publications, including *The Big Blue Review* and *Dodger Magazine*. He often spoke on radio shows in Chicago, Cleveland, and Los Angeles. According to Young's résumé, which was located in Burns's personal papers, his work was published in *The Sporting News, The Saturday Evening Post,* the *New York Post, Parent's Digest, Saga, Negro Digest,* the *Las Vegas Sun,* the *Los Angeles Mirror-News,* and the *Chicago American.* He held managerial positions at several publications and supervised the production of special issues of the *Sentinel,* the *Chicago Defender,* and the *New York Amsterdam News.* During the early 1950s he briefly served as managing editor for the West Coast edition of the *Defender.*

Dust jacket for Young's 1969 book about two black college football stars

At times Young could be hard on his friends. After learning that his full name had been included in Wilson's 1991 book *Black Journalists in Paradox,* Young berated Wilson for fifteen minutes. Young had never given that information to Wilson, who had found it in a reference book. Young later called back and said all was forgiven. Young also had a penchant for calling friends to chat regardless of the hour. Yet, his friends admired his usually gregarious and outgoing nature, as well as his strong work ethic. (He was even known to jot down notes at stoplights while driving.) He was also willing to lend his voluminous collection of papers, books, and documents to colleagues; as a friend recalled to Norman Gregory Young at the memorial service for his father, Young used his clippings file to teach him the basics of hockey when he received a magazine assignment and knew nothing about the sport. A friend and former coworker, Libby Clark, summed up Young's complex nature in a tribute that ran in the 7 November 1996 issue of the *Sentinel:* "He was a deep thinker, argumentative, a visionary, a great writer, profoundly loyal to those he liked, a master with the printed word, and a 'loner.' One never knew really what made Doc tick. He could be warm and engaging at times and as 'cold' as last year's mashed potatoes at other times. Cross him and you had hell on your hands."

Young's typing ability was legendary. He typed 125 words a minute using one finger from each hand. According to *Black Journalists in Paradox,* Young often impressed observers in the press box by typing as many as eight columns during baseball games. "Once he started doing a piece, it just flowed," Wilson recalled in 1998. "It would go like a stream. He would go into a zone. Once the idea was there, you knew not to bother him."

Young received several honors during his career. In addition to his 1963 American Library Association award for *Negro Firsts in Sports,* he was presented the National Newspaper Publishers Association (NNPA) President's Anniversary Sports Award (1970) as well as "Best Sports Column" and "Best Sports Section" honors from the NNPA. He also received the *Los Angeles Sentinel* National Service Award (1993). After retiring in 1986, he continued to work as a freelance writer. He died of pneumonia on 6 September 1996. In a tribute to Young published in the 31 October 1996 issue of the *Sentinel,* Jim Cleaver wrote: "Although there was a humorous side to Doc, there was also a very sincere side that dealt with politics, government, business, et al. Without question however, his main forte was sports."

References:

Ben Burns, *Nitty Gritty: A White Editor in Black Journalism* (Jackson: University Press of Mississippi, 1996);

James P. Murray, *To Find an Image: Black Films from Uncle Tom to Super Fly* (Indianapolis & New York: Bobbs-Merrill, 1973);

William Veeck, with Ed Linn, *Veeck–As in Wreck* (New York: Putnam, 1962);

Clint Wilson, *Black Journalists in Paradox: Historical Perspectives and Current Dilemmas,* Contributions in Afro-American and African Studies, no. 145 (New York: Greenwood Press, 1991).

Frank A. "Fay" Young

(2 October 1884 - 27 October 1957)

Joel Sternberg
Saint Xavier University

MAJOR POSITIONS HELD: Managing editor, sports editor, *Chicago Defender* (1916–1934); managing editor, *Abbott's Monthly* (ca. 1930–1931); managing editor, *Kansas City Call* (1934–1937); reporter-columnist, *Chicago Defender* (1937–1949); weekly columnist, *Chicago Defender* (1949–1957).

SELECTED PERIODICAL PUBLICATIONS–UNCOLLECTED: "Change the Umpires," *Chicago Defender,* 19 August 1922, I:10;
"Rube Foster–The Master Mind of Baseball," *Abbott's Monthly,* 1 (November 1930): 42–45, 47–49, 93;
"Bill Buckner–Greatest Trainer of Baseball Players," *Abbott's Monthly,* 2 (January 1931): 16–19, 65;
"The Man Who Came Back," *Abbott's Monthly,* 2 (June 1931): 42–46, 69, 81;
"He Made Records–H. Binga Dismond–Athlete, Scholar, Gentleman," *Abbott's Monthly,* 3 (July 1931): 52–57;
"Was the Johnson-Willard Fight a Fake?" *Abbott's Monthly,* 3 (August 1931): 16–20, 64;
"Judge Landis' Decision–Bosh," *Chicago Defender,* 25 July 1942, II:20;
"Challenge to the Big Leagues: Barring of Negro Players in Major Leagues Flouts Democratic Ideals of War," *Chicago Defender,* 26 September 1942, IV:18;
"Back on the Job," *Chicago Defender,* 9 July 1949, II:14;
"Memories," *Chicago Defender,* 7 May 1955, p. 26;
"Anniversary Year!" *Chicago Defender,* 14 May 1955, p. 27;
"Trotters on Parade," *Chicago Defender,* 2 November 1957, p. 23.

Frank A. "Fay" Young (photo courtesy of the Chicago Daily Defender*)*

Frank A. "Fay" Young was considered the dean of black sportswriters in a career that spanned fifty years. Working in virtual anonymity relative to the mainstream white press in the United States, Young evinced a love of athletics, and his eagerness and courage to speak out against racial injustice helped level American playing fields and provided opportunities for black men and women. Acknowledged as the first full-time black sportswriter in the country and the first sportswriter to report on black college athletics, Young has been described as gruff, caustic, and highly independent in his managerial style. He was also considered generous to a fault, and his pioneering spirit and restless energy provided hope for black athletes and *Chicago Defender* readers during the difficult days of racial segregation.

Not much is known about Young's early days. Born in Williamsport, Pennsylvania, on 2 October 1884, he was orphaned at the age of eight. He attended Medford High School for one year in Massachusetts and South Division High School for an additional year in Chicago. Reminiscing in his *Chicago Defender* column of 4 July 1942, he recalled selling newspapers as early as 1900 on the South Side of Chicago and thinking that he was "doing something." Seven years later, by some accounts, he was doing occasional work for the

Defender, which had been established in 1905 by publisher Robert S. Abbott on a friend's kitchen table.

In his master's degree thesis, "The Evolution of the *Chicago Defender,*" Curtis J. Morris relates that Young began his association with the newspaper by bringing incorrect sports facts published in the paper to Abbott's attention. The *Defender* had no sportswriter on staff and the publisher was impressed with the young man's knowledge. Working as a dining-car waiter for the Chicago and Northwestern Railroad, Young also had gained experience writing for the *Indianapolis Recorder,* and Abbott, sensing his value to the *Defender,* quickly put Young to work during his spare time.

As was common with black newspapers in those days, black barbers, railroad porters, and waiters were a great source of news and gossip, and Young's activities at the newspaper, therefore, are not surprising. He solved much of his problem of holding two jobs by collecting all the newspapers he encountered during his train runs to and from Chicago. He clipped all news pertaining to Negro athletes and, in the process, became a one-man exchange editor or, as Morris wrote, "a human wire service."

Young's railroad schedule allowed him to spend a great deal of time at the *Defender.* Five days a week he reported to the railway station at six o'clock in the evening. Thirty minutes later, the train left on its regular run for Minneapolis. The diner only traveled as far as Milwaukee, where it was "cut off." Early the following morning Young made the return trip to Chicago, arriving at nine o'clock. As Young was quoted in Roi Ottley's *The Lonely Warrior: The Life and Times of Robert S. Abbott,* "That gave me five days all day at the *Defender* office, plus the days and nights I was off. I received no salary. I expected none. I paid car fares to cover assignments out of my own pocket, sometimes even paying Mr. Abbott's."

Influenced by Abbott and by the publisher's belief that there was a place in the United States for a first-class Negro newspaper, Young worked his early years at the *Defender* without compensation. In 1912 he asked to join the newspaper as a paid employee but was told by J. Hockley Smiley, the newspaper's managing editor and first salaried employee, there was no money for Young's position, though any contributions he could make would be gladly accepted. In 1912 Young supervised the first full page of black sports in a black newspaper. When on the road with the railroad, he continued to clip newspaper stories and mail them back to Abbott or directly to Smiley. For his efforts, in 1914, he received his first "pay"–three one-dollar bills from Abbott as a token of the publisher's appreciation.

By 1915, as the *Defender* expanded and increased its circulation to 230,000, there was a need for quality personnel. Morris implies that in June 1915 Young began receiving three dollars a week, which was increased slightly over the ensuing months. Despite the salary and the raises, he maintained his position with the railroad. Realizing that an unpaid volunteer staff was not dependable for the newspaper, Abbott asked Young to resign his railroad job and work solely for the *Defender.* Young was reluctant because Abbott's offer, fifteen dollars a week, was less than what he was earning as a waiter. As Ottley points out, taking the job also would have meant a reduction in social status "as railroad men were among the sought-after figures in Negro society, and newspapermen were considered merely hustlers." The railroad offered black men well-paying jobs, and Abbott's standard reflected salaries blacks earned as post-office employees. "Even so," said Ottley, "the staff regarded themselves as adequately paid, as no one then thought of Negro journalism as professional work."

Young was finally persuaded to leave his railroad job and join the *Defender* full-time. When financial pressures became difficult and he was unable to make ends meet, however, he sought out extra work, as did most of his colleagues. He worked at the post office during Christmas, as a waiter at the prestigious Palmer House in Chicago and Edgewater Beach Hotels, and in 1915 managed the Lincoln Athletic club–a semipro football team from Chicago. Despite these extra activities, he soon fell behind in his payments for a typewriter he had purchased on an installment plan. He offered the machine to Abbott with the understanding that the publisher would pay off the balance. *Defender* copy previously had been written in longhand, and when Abbott agreed to Young's terms, the newspaper acquired its first typewriter.

Young's value at the *Defender* grew consistently in all areas of the operation, from cooking meals on nights when galley proofs needed correcting to assuming layout and news handling responsibilities when a *Defender* editor became ill. When Booker T. Washington passed away on 14 November 1915 Young and Abbott made the rounds of black churches, supplying ministers single sheets of a *Defender* "extra"–acknowledged as a first among black weeklies. The extra promoted the 20 November 1915 regular edition, which provided full details of Washington's life. In that issue also, the second full page of black sports coverage in the history of black journalism appeared, and from that day sports became a prominent feature in all *Defender* editions.

In June 1916, as the managing editor of the newspaper, Young received twenty-five dollars a week. He ultimately dropped this position to work as city editor and then again as sports editor. Notwithstanding his success, Young continued to stay busy on

Offices of the African American newspaper, the Chicago Defender, *where Fay began his sportswriting career*

weekends as a referee for several college circuits and a timekeeper for boxing matches as an official of the Illinois Athletic Commission.

A one-man sports department, the medium-sized, bespectacled, immaculately dressed, abrasive Young was proud of his position but was characterized as somewhat selfish when it came to operating his department. Reported A. S. Young in "Black Athlete in Golden Age of Sports: Part IX–The Black Sportswriter," an October 1970 *Ebony* magazine feature, "Fay Young worked himself to a frazzle in an individual capacity when, I'm sure, he could have had it much easier, and increased his influence even more, by hiring a staff."

As sports editor for both the local weekly *Defender* and the national edition of the paper, Young produced the local section, traveled into the South to cover black college sports, then traveled back to Chicago to prepare the national edition. This procedure often meant arriving by train in Chicago on Sunday morning and heading to the office to spend a full day at work on the local sports section. As Young was quick to point out, the task was made more difficult by bad travel accommodations and slow trains. Quoted by his *Defender* colleague, Russ J. Cowans, in "Fabulous 'Fay': Defender's Frank Young Has Long Well-Rounded and Colorful Career" (*Chicago Defender,* 9 November 1957), Young said: "You can now go further in two hours than I could go in a day."

Typical of Young's style was his crusading spirit in matters pertaining to racial equality. During his fifty years as a columnist-reporter-editor, he reacted quickly and angrily to racial slights, abuses, and indignities. Along with other notable black journalists such as Wendell Smith of the *Pittsburgh Courier,* Sam Lacy of the *Baltimore Afro-American,* and Joe Bostic of the *Harlem People's Voice,* Young's reputation was that of a man who fought consistently against segregation. Present at the formation of the Negro National League in Kansas City, Missouri, in 1920 and the official scorer-statistician of the league until its disorganization in 1931, Young agitated continually in his *Defender* columns for the inclusion of blacks in major league baseball. He estimated that gate receipts for clubs hiring one black player would increase by $100,000 and repeatedly voiced the opinion that there were players who could have won a berth on any major-league team of the time.

In one of his early battles Young took on incompetent baseball umpires, calling for changes in no uncertain terms. Criticizing the Baseball Umpires Association that assigned umpires to the Chicago American Giants' games, on 19 August 1922 Young's lead in the *Defender* read: "Umpires bad, umpires rotten, fine game but bad umpiring." Claiming that the umpires often made their decisions and were ready to call them before the plays were completed, he cited an instance in which the plate umpire had called a ball on a pitch at which the batter had swung. Reiterating a *Defender* position demanding men of color be utilized as umpires, he reminded his readers that many baseball authorities had said the time was not right. He noted that the black league had bided its time since its formation in 1920, however: "The pot has been boiling and in the language of the street, 'The darn pot is about to boil over.'" Young told his readers: "It isn't necessary for us to sit by the thousands watching 18 men perform in the national pastime, using every bit of strategy and brain work, to have it all spoiled by thinking it is impossible to have any other men officiating but pale faces. Give us a change. The sooner it comes the better we will like it."

Working to build his career and his reputation, Young occasionally promoted his own editorship on the *Defender* sports pages with banner headlines proclaiming "Sports by Frank Young" in the early to mid 1920s. In addition, throughout the decade he contributed columns under the titles "It's All in the Game," "Just Confidential," and "Fay Says"–*Fay* being a nickname created by combining the initials of his full name. In time, Young came to know virtually every major black athlete, coach, and athletic director in the United States. While he reported nearly every mainstream American sporting event, including world heavyweight boxing championships, World Series, and national track meets, he was also the first black sportswriter to cover black college football games and is noted for playing a significant role in the building of sports activities on black college campuses. In 1923 he helped to establish the Alabama State–Tuskegee game as an annual Thanksgiving Day event. Three years later he worked with Tuskegee Institute coach Cleve Abbott to establish the annual Tuskegee track-and-field relays. He then served as one of the relays' officials and ultimately agreed to supply the trophy to each year's winner in the 880-yard race. In 1929 Young was also one of the founders of the annual Prairie View Bowl football game in Houston, Texas–the second oldest postseason bowl game in America and the first black postseason bowl game in history.

Between 1929 and 1934 Young served again as the managing editor for the *Defender,* and for a brief time he concurrently held the same position for *Abbott's Monthly,* a short-lived magazine of fact, fiction, editorials, and romance published for blacks by the Abbott Publishing Company. During his tenure with the magazine Young wrote lengthy feature articles focusing on notable black athletes, including one of his all-time favorites, Rube Foster, the former pitching star, team owner, Negro National League president, and financial wizard whom Young touted as the "Master Mind" of baseball. Writing in *Abbott's Monthly* in November 1930 Young declared the pitcher-manager to be in a class with John McGraw and Connie Mack and comparable to Babe Ruth in terms of the daily newspaper space he received. But, noted Young, the legendary Foster had fallen on hard times, having developed a severe case of dementia at the age of forty-nine. Sympathetic to Foster's debilitating illness and appreciative of his efforts to put Negro League baseball on a par with the white major leagues, Young scolded National Negro League club owners and officials:

> The man who gave his time, money and health for the upbuilding of the national game among his own people today is a sick man and not one of the club owners, nor has anyone of the league owners, to my knowledge and I am pretty familiar with the workings of the league, set aside one sunny day in their home town and played for a benefit game in Foster's home.

Shortly after these words were published, on 9 December 1930, Foster passed away. Following the 1931 season the Negro National League, on hard times without Foster's leadership, also passed away, unable to survive the Great Depression.

Experiencing financial pressures because of a decline in circulation, the *Defender* instituted a series of personnel cutbacks, and in December 1934 Young was asked to leave the newspaper. He assumed the role of managing editor for the *Kansas City Call* but, within three years Abbott brought him back to the *Defender* in the familiar role of sports editor. At this time, he also began a new sports column, "The Stuff Is Here . . . ," which debuted on 14 August 1937 under the byline "Fay Young." For his game reportorial pieces, he often used "Frank A. Young," but he switched to "Fay" or "Fay Young" for his columns, opinion pieces, and denunciations of racial intolerance.

In one particularly ugly incident in early August 1938, Jake Powell, outfielder for the New York Yankees

Head for Young's Chicago Defender *column for 14 August 1937*

and a police officer in Ohio during the offseason, told Chicago's WGN radio sports commentator Bob Elson "that he kept in trim during the winter months 'by hitting n– over the head with my blackjack while on my beat.'" Elson reacted quickly by taking Powell off the air but, reported Young on 6 August 1938, the damage had already been done. Also of concern to Young was baseball commissioner Judge Kenesaw Mountain Landis's punishment for Powell–a ten-day suspension. Though aware that Powell's act was not directly concerned with the play of a game or actions within a game and that Landis might have acted to the extent of his powers, Young was not pacified. He went on to warn the commissioner that trouble was brewing for Powell. In fact, the only cities that might be safe for him would be St. Louis and Washington, but even then police escorts would be needed to and from the field. Young encouraged a New York boycott of the brewery operated by Yankee owner Colonel Jacob Ruppert and noted that nothing in recent years had aroused the black population, plus thousands of whites, as had Powell's remarks:

> Jake Powell has no business in organized baseball. Let's get him out of it. He has no business traveling a beat as a member of the Dayton, Ohio, police force. Dayton is 17 miles from Wilberforce. The Wilberforce students aren't safe on the streets of Dayton with such a man traveling a beat during the winter months.
>
> Jake Powell is the type that causes race riots. It is easier to get rid of a skunk like him than to spend hundreds of thousands of dollars to put an end to the trouble he will start.

Landis, who received thousands of letters from outraged blacks, maintained his position on the ten-day suspension. The Yankees added to the punishment by making Powell visit bars in Harlem to personally apologize to black fans. As Young had predicted, Powell was subject to verbal abuse by black fans at white games and physical abuse in the form of thrown bottles. A petition circulated to extend Powell's suspension to one year, but Landis let the matter slide. Powell also visited the New York offices of the *Chicago Defender* and formally apologized with a front-page statement. The *Defender* noted that Harlem was not satisfied and a movement was underway to declare a "year's holiday" against drinking any of Colonel Ruppert's beer if the owner kept Powell on the team. Powell stayed with the Yankees through the 1940 season, although his playing time was reduced substantially.

Young's return to Chicago from Kansas City provided him with ample opportunity to be involved with baseball and its players. In 1937 a new Negro American League had been established with headquarters in Chicago, and from 1939 to 1948 Young served as its secretary and, for a period of time, as director of publicity.

In promoting the Negro American League, in August 1938 the East-West All-Star Game was played in Chicago's Comiskey Park. Young invited Lloyd Lewis, a white sports editor at the *Chicago Daily News,* to be his guest. Young wanted the experienced baseball reporter to give his professional opinion of the caliber of play by the Negro League athletes. Lewis was treated to an exciting game won by the East team, 5 to 4, and Young's strategy paid off, as Lewis wrote a positive report. True, said Lewis, the players exhibited somewhat lackluster batting skills, but the speed of both teams was impressive. In his *Defender* column on 27 August 1938 Young reported that Lewis also agreed there was no rule in the major leagues or in the constitution or bylaws of the National and American Leagues that prohibited blacks from playing.

Excited about the game and Lewis's enthusiasm, Young went on to point out that the one blot in the picture was that the Negro Leagues needed a park of its own. Said Young, the All-Star Game at Comiskey Park attracted thirty thousand fans and put six thousand dollars into the coffers of the Chicago White Sox. "The day isn't far off," he continued, "when some of our business men in Chicago will 'get hip to themselves' and build a baseball and amusement park. If you don't think it will pay–then something is the matter with your noodle."

In the 1940s, with America at war, Young remained active as a reporter and columnist and worked hard to publicize the efforts of black athletes in the military. On 17 January 1942 the title of his column–"The Stuff Is Here . . ."–was changed to "Through the Years Past Present Future." While Young meant that his readers could find the "real stuff" in his columns, some people interpreted the title as nothing more than "gutter slang," thus effecting the change. The new title remained in effect until 9 October 1948, when Young reverted to his "Fay Says" column title of the 1920s.

Regardless of the title, Young's columns never lost their vitriolic edge. In May 1942 an all-star game for the Navy Relief Fund brought Dizzy Dean's All-Stars together with the Kansas City Monarchs at Wrigley Field–reportedly the first time a black team had played in the National League park. The Monarchs won 3–1 behind the pitching of Satchel Paige. Young reported on 30 May 1942 that the large, integrated crowd "proved once and for all that America's baseball fandom want to see a ball game regardless to the race, color or creed of the performers." Concurrent with the Monarch benefit game, Young noted, the Chicago White Sox were being beaten 14–0 in one game of a doubleheader at Comiskey Park on the South Side. Yet, Paige and other Monarch players "performing in big league style" on the north side were "denied the right to play in the big leagues because of their color." He continued:

> Maybe the front office at Wrigley Field will sit up and take notice. The best part of the crowd of near 30,000 was not white. These brown American fans are baseball hungry but they are sick and tired of paying their hard-earned money to see second rate performers because the performers must necessarily be white according to Judge Landis, high mogul of organized baseball and the various prejudiced owners.

On 25 July 1942, under the subtitle "Judge Landis' Decision–Bosh," Young took exception to the commissioner's statement that "Negroes are not barred from organized baseball by the commissioner and never have been during the 21 years I have served as a commissioner." This column had followed on the heels of Brooklyn Dodgers manager Leo Durocher's comment that he would like to hire Negro players but was barred from doing so.

After a closed-door meeting with the commissioner, Durocher denied his statement, saying he was misquoted; but Young pointed out emphatically that there was no law or rule prohibiting players based on race, creed, or color. There did seem to be an unwritten law, however, that had been passed from owner to manager and manager to owner. Young saw the banning of blacks as a money issue–the owners not wanting to pay major-league salaries to blacks. "In the meantime," wrote Young, "Negro fans argue, fight, and go to see baseball as played by men who do not want you in the game–AND WON'T HAVE YOU."

Continuing to apply pressure on major-league baseball, on 1 August 1942 Young again reacted to Commissioner Landis's comment that there were no rules barring Negroes from major league baseball. "Since no Negroes are barred," asked Young, "what keeps them out? That's a question that Landis ought to answer. They are out–and they are not in." Young went on to contrast Landis with George S. Mays, who had permitted blacks to play in the $15,000 Tam O'Shanter Open golf tournament and "saw to it that they did":

> Landis isn't going to take the "hell" Mays took because there aren't many George Mayses in the world. Mays stood pat in face of a threat that the Professional Golfers association would withdraw if Negroes played.
>
> I remind you of the old man who said, "Man, I'm coming." We are coming but we "ain't there yet."

Young's philosophy, said Morris, coincided with the philosophy of the *Defender*–"show what the Negro can do and show him at his best." Consequently, pictures showing the black man excelling in sports were given space, as were stories highlighting the successful interaction of blacks and whites, such as the 1942 Col-

Head for Fay's 23 April 1949 column in the Chicago Defender

lege All-Star football game. As Young pointed out, no major-league baseball team has had more southern white men on it than the *Chicago Tribune's* All-Star football squad, and blacks and whites proved they could live and train together.

In the vernacular of the day, the sports pages of the *Defender* identified black victors as "Race" men and women and covered athletes in every category–from the professional ranks to the amateur. No one, though, matched Joe Louis and the coverage he received in the late 1930s and 1940s. Promoting Louis and his accomplishments, the *Defender* published a twelve-page paper on Wednesday every time he fought, and staff members took to the streets to sell copies at five cents apiece. Loudspeakers in office windows reputedly lured four to five thousand people to the *Defender* on Louis fight nights to hear the fights, and copies of the paper sold rapidly on the spot.

In "Victory through Unity," a special World War II edition of the *Defender* on 26 September 1942, Young's full-page feature on black athletes focused on a familiar theme–major-league segregation. "If baseball is to be all America's national pastime," he pointed out, "the door which has been closed to the Negro ball player must be opened." In a strong and clear voice Young went on to say that "any man or set of men who deny American citizens the right to earn a decent livelihood because of color must be jotted down in this day and time as enemies of fullfledged loyal American citizens." Countering arguments against the inclusion of black ballplayers in the major leagues, he wrote:

> In big time circles, I often hear the remark "the time isn't quite ripe now–besides we are in a war."
>
> For 30 years, I have been hearing that remark. In 1918, I was apprised that things would be different after peace was declared. I never was so much fooled in my life. I had really believed it. I will now believe the Negro ball player will get his chance in the major and the minor leagues when I see it happen.

While baseball remained preeminent in his writing, during the mid 1940s Young's columns also took a strong stand against perceived improprieties in a variety of settings. He spoke out against overly sexy cheerleaders, ignorant public-address football announcers attempting to emulate popular radio announcers such as Bill Stern, and black athletes of prominence who ridiculed themselves or behaved badly in public, including Paige, who was portrayed as being too much of a playboy.

In a highly publicized event, Jesse Owens was booked to run a race against a horse as a promotion at a baseball game in Louisville, Kentucky. Totally opposed to the stunt, Young declared in his 16 June 1945 column that to be impartial on this matter meant he was siding with the event, which he did not want to do. "Columnists," wrote Young, "find it hard sometimes to speak out because when they battle for this or that cause or question or problem, there are too many who are quick to draw the conclusion that they do so in order to profit by it or to create a sensation, or to satisfy a secret ambition, or to draw attention to themselves." Cognizant of his obligations as a columnist, in his criticism of Owens he felt he was being "faithful to the Negro baseball fans, the public in general, and to the great number of athletes who are record holders." The tone of his column implied that Owens, a world-record holder in track, a university graduate, and an example to children, would be acting improperly and would be demeaning his athletic accomplishments by participating in the event.

Perhaps Young's most biting and noteworthy criticism was saved for the Brooklyn Dodgers executive Branch Rickey in the days prior to Jackie Robinson joining the major leagues. Rickey had announced at one point that he would create a Brooklyn Brown Dodgers team that would play in Ebbets Field when the white Dodgers were away. Many blacks resented these remarks, including Young, who denounced Rickey in his *Defender* column on 26 May 1945 saying that he was "trying to assume the role of an Abraham Lincoln in Negro baseball"–a charge, says Arnold Rampersad in his book, *Jackie Robinson: A Biography,* that Rickey would hear "with increasing frequency and perhaps some satisfaction." To Rampersad, the Brown Dodgers team was a myth that freed Rickey to scout black players more openly.

Noting that Rickey had refused to discuss the role of Negroes in a recent press conference, Young said, "We want Negroes in the major leagues if they have to crawl to get there but we won't have the major league owners running any segregated league for us. We have enough 'Black' this and 'Brown' that in tagging ball clubs in various cities now and we don't need any more." Young concluded by saying: "Rickey is no Abraham Lincoln or Franklin D. Roosevelt, and we won't accept him as a dictator of Negro baseball. Hitler and Mussolini are dead! We need no American dictator!!"

With the signing of Robinson in October 1945 to a minor-league contract with Montreal in the Dodger organization, Young and Dr. J. B. Martin, Negro American League president, issued a joint statement announcing that it was "an elevation of Negro baseball." Yet, the victory was not complete. Young continued his vigilance, and two years after Robinson broke the major-league color line, in a 23 April 1949 "Fay Says" column subtitled "Kidding Whom?" he brought his hometown Chicago Cubs and White Sox to task for not signing black players. He also suggested that major-league teams use Negro League teams as possible farm clubs to avoid sending black players into the South, and he rallied on behalf of those star Negro League players thought to be too old to play on white teams. Touting Lorenzo "Piper" Davis, infielder for the Birmingham Black Barons, as a player who could make an immediate difference for either of the major league teams in Chicago, Young wrote:

> We've heard that "age" business for so long that it ceases to be funny. Smart men don't go on ages any more. Some men play out early. Others, 20 to 30 years their senior, are still going strong. Employers of men soon will determine physical qualifications from a physician's report and not by the date of birth. The Army and the Navy found that out. No youngster handles the throttle of a Presidential train.

Maintaining a busy schedule including charitable activities, a series of weekly afternoon radio broadcasts on Chicago's WSBC-AM, and his columns, on 7 August 1948 Young began a ten-month series of forty feature articles focusing on notable black athletes under the title "Through the Years"–the first article highlighting his old friend Rube Foster. In May 1949 Young was stricken with a ruptured appendix and peritonitis. His column continued to appear under his byline but was written by other writers, university coaches, and physical education specialists of his acquaintance while he went through a series of operations and a twenty-day period of daily blood transfusions. In two months Young resumed his work.

Technically, at this point in time, Young was retired, but, as Morris relates, in most matters concerning the *Defender,* he was given carte blanche. While not spending much time at the office, he continued to contribute columns and remained busy as an official in three Negro conferences in football, boxing, and track, and in 1951 he was ringside as a timekeeper at the Jake LaMotta–Sugar Ray Robinson middleweight championship boxing match. Beyond his love of athletics, throughout his life Young was also noted as a philanthropist, horticulturist, stockbreeder, and poultry fancier. When Tennessee A and I State University dedicated its new poultry building on Thanksgiving Day, 1953, the president of the university, Dr. Walter S. Davis, named it the Frank A. Young Poultry Plant in honor of the man who had helped to establish it. As his *Defender* colleague Cowans said, Young was interested in young men and women who were trying to get an education. In Cowan's *Defender* obituary of Young he wrote: "Oh, he would grumble and one would believe he was the meanest fellow in the world, but deep down in his heart there was a soft spot, and it could be reached by anyone with a heart-touching story."

Brad Pye Jr., sports editor for the Los Angeles Sentinel; *Jackie Robinson; and Young in Los Angeles in 1962 (photograph by Harry Adams)*

Young died on Sunday afternoon, 27 October 1957. The official cause of death was reported as an intestinal obstruction brought on by shock caused by the death of his sister in New York on 25 October. On that same date Young had submitted his last column, personally bringing it to the *Defender* office. He was survived by his wife, Cora; his daughter, Louise; his son, Frank Jr.; and a stepbrother and stepsister. Young's funeral services were held in the Everybody's Church, which he helped found in 1952. Among the pallbearers were athletes Owens and Ralph Metcalfe, reporter Wendell Smith, *Defender* publisher John Sengstacke, and Cowans, whom he had hired in 1929 and had recommended as his replacement. His final column, highlighting the history and success of the Harlem Globetrotters basketball team, was published posthumously on 2 November 1957.

In more than fifty years Young lived through what he acknowledged as the glorious years. He had witnessed major sporting events, black athletes taking their places as champions in the sporting arenas of the world, and the democratization of American sports. Celebrating the fiftieth anniversary of the *Defender* in his 14 May 1955 column, he noted with satisfaction that he had come to see the national pastime now signing "men of ability rather than on a basis of color."

In his October 1970 *Ebony* magazine feature, A. S. Young noted that Frank Young, as father of the Negro newspaper sports section, created weekly *Defender* sports sections that "compare favorably with modern sports sections in coverage, writing, format and imagination." Labeling Young the "patron saint of black college athletics," from the *Ebony* reporter's perspective, "Other black newspapers around the nation followed Fay Young's and the *Defender's* lead." The mainstream press, however, provided minimum recognition for the man who had covered sports so diligently, eloquently, and passionately for half a century.

References:

Ocania Chalk, *Pioneers of Black Sport* (New York: Dodd, Mead, 1975), pp. 63, 76–77;

Russ J. Cowans, "The End of a Great Career," *Chicago Defender,* 9 November 1957, p. 24;

Cowans, "Fabulous 'Fay': Defender's Frank Young Has Long Well-Rounded and Colorful Career," *Chicago Defender,* 9 November 1957, p. 11;

Cowans, "Frank 'Fay' Young, Ex-Sports Editor, Dies," *Chicago Defender,* 2 November 1957, pp. 1–2;

Cowans, "He's Worthy of Tribute," *Chicago Defender,* 28 November 1953, p. 24;

Edwin Bancroft Henderson, *The Negro in Sports* (Washington, D.C.: Associated Publishers, 1939), pp. 259, 291–292;

Kyle P. McNary, *Ted "Double Duty" Radcliffe: 36 Years of Pitching & Catching in Baseball's Negro Leagues* (Minneapolis: McNary, 1994), pp. 26, 146–149;

Curtis J. Morris, "The Evolution of the *Chicago Defender,*" M.A. thesis, Indiana University, June 1951;

Clotye Murdock, "Robert Abbott: Defender of His Race," *Ebony,* 10 (June 1955): 69–75;

Ron Ottley, *The Lonely Warrior: The Life and Times of Robert S. Abbott* (Chicago: Regnery, 1955), pp. 4, 114, 116, 118, 129, 196, 199, 252, 293, 300, 301, 335;

Robert Peterson, *Only the Ball Was White: A History of Legendary Black Players and All-Black Professional Teams* (New York: Oxford University Press, 1970), pp. 113, 185, 187;

Arnold Rampersad, *Jackie Robinson: A Biography* (New York: Knopf, 1997), pp. 120, 123;

Jim Reisler, *Black Writers/Black Baseball: An Anthology of Articles from Black Sportswriters Who Covered the Negro Leagues* (Jefferson, N.C.: McFarland, 1994), pp. 1, 3, 6, 12, 57–59, 113, 118;

Mark Ribowsky, *A Complete History of the Negro Leagues 1884 to 1955* (Secaucus, N.J.: Citadel, 1995), pp. 128, 136, 137, 216, 247–248, 255, 270;

"Tenn U. Honors Fay Young," *Chicago Defender,* 5 December 1953, p. 1;

Jules Tygiel, *Baseball's Great Experiment: Jackie Robinson and His Legacy* (New York: Oxford University Press, 1997), pp. 234, 238;

Enoch P. Waters, *American Diary: A Personal History of the Black Press* (Chicago: Path, 1987), pp. 125, 178–179, 188, 235;

"West Virginia State Quits Mid-West Conference: Fay Young is Given Award," *Chicago Defender,* 20 December 1941, p. 23;

A. S. Young, "Black Athletes in Golden Age of Sports: The Black Sportswriter," *Ebony,* 25 (October 1970): 56–58, 60–62, 64.

Notable Twentieth-Century Books about Sports, Selected by the Editor

A. J. Liebling, *The Sweet Science* (New York: Viking, 1956);

Roger Kahn, *The Boys of Summer* (New York: Harper & Row, 1972);

W. C. Heinz, *American Mirror* (Garden City, N.Y.: Doubleday, 1982);

John Lardner, *White Hopes and Other Tigers* (Philadelphia: Lippincott, 1951);

Arnold Hano, *A Day in the Bleachers* (New York: Crowell, 1955);

Joe H. Palmer, *This Was Racing,* edited by Red Smith (New York: Barnes, 1953);

Robert T. Jones Jr. and O. B. Keeler, *Down the Fairway: The Golf Life and Play of Robert T. Jones, Jr.* (New York: Minton, Balch, 1927);

Roger Angell, *The Summer Game* (New York: Viking, 1972);

Red Smith, *Strawberries in the Wintertime: The Sporting World of Red Smith* (New York: Quadrangle/New York Times, 1974);

John A. McPhee, *The Levels of the Game* (New York: Farrar, Straus & Giroux, 1969);

George Plimpton, *Paper Lion* (New York: Harper & Row, 1966);

Norman Mailer, *The Fight* (Boston: Little, Brown, 1975);

Lawrence S. Ritter, comp., *The Glory of Their Times: The Story of the Early Days of Baseball Told by the Men Who Played It* (New York: Macmillan, 1966);

Jim Bouton, *Ball Four: My Life and Hard Times Throwing the Knuckleball in the Major Leagues,* edited by Leonard Shecter (New York: World, 1970);

Jimmy Breslin, *Can't Anybody Here Play This Game?* (New York: Viking, 1963);

Thomas Boswell, *How Life Imitates the World Series: An Inquiry into the Game* (Garden City, N.Y.: Doubleday, 1982);

Grantland Rice, *The Tumult and the Shouting: My Life in Sport* (New York: Barnes, 1954);

Chris Mead, *Champion: Joe Louis, Black Hero in White America* (New York: Scribners, 1985);

Robert W. Creamer, *Stengel: His Life and Times* (New York: Simon & Schuster, 1984);

Michael Novak, *The Joy of Sports: End Zones, Bases, Baskets, Balls, and the Consecration of the American Spirit* (New York: Basic Books, 1976);

Paul Gallico, *Farewell to Sport* (New York: Knopf, 1938);

George Will, *Men at Work: The Craft of Baseball* (New York: Macmillan, 1990);

George V. Higgins, *The Progress of the Seasons: Forty Years of Baseball in Our Town* (New York: Holt, 1989);

Jake La Motta, Joseph Carter, and Peter Savage, *Raging Bull: My Story* (Englewood Cliffs, N.J.: Prentice-Hall, 1970);

Sugar Ray Robinson and Dave Anderson, *Sugar Ray* (New York: Viking, 1970);

Jimmy Cannon, *Who Struck John?* (New York: Dial, 1956);

David Halberstam, *The Breaks of the Game* (New York: Knopf, 1981);

Frank Fitzpatrick, *And the Walls Came Tumbling Down: Kentucky, Texas Western, and the Game That Changed American Sports* (New York: Simon & Schuster, 1999);

Eliot Asinoff, *Eight Men Out* (New York: Holt, Rinehart & Winston, 1963);

Wells Twombly, *Blanda, Alive and Kicking: The Exclusive, Authorized Biography* (Los Angeles: Nash, 1972);

William Howland Taylor and Herbert L. Stone, *The America's Cup Races* (New York: Van Nostrand, 1958);

Nick Tosches, *The Devil and Sonny Liston* (Boston: Little, Brown, 2000);

Jerry Kramer, *Instant Replay: The Green Bay Diary of Jerry Kramer,* edited by Dick Shaap (New York: World, 1968);

John Feinstein, *A Season on the Brink: A Year with Bob Knight and the Indian Hoosiers* (New York: Macmillan, 1986);

Herbert Warren Wind, *Following Through* (New York: Ticknor & Fields, 1985);

Pat Jordan, *A False Spring* (New York: Dodd, Mead, 1975);

Ed Linn and Bill Veeck, *Veeck–As in Wreck: The Autobiography of Bill Veeck* (New York: Putnam, 1962);

Ray Robinson, *Matty: An American Hero* (New York: Oxford University Press, 1993);

Gary Paulsen, *Winterdance: The Fine Madness of Running the Iditarod* (New York: Harcourt Brace, 1994);

Ty Cobb and Al Stump, *My Life in Baseball: The True Record* (Garden City, N.Y.: Doubleday, 1961);

Furman Bisher, *The Furman Bisher Collection* (Dallas: Taylor, 1989);

Satchel Paige, *Maybe I'll Pitch Forever: A Great Baseball Player Tells the Hilarious Story Behind the Legend,* as told to David Lipman (Garden City, N.Y.: Doubleday, 1962);

A. J. McClane, *The Compleat McClane: A Treasury of A. J. McClane's Great Angling Adventures,* edited, with an introduction, by John Merwin (New York: Dutton, 1968);

John J. McGraw and Boseman Bulger, *My Thirty Years in Baseball* (New York: Boni & Liveright, 1923);

Gerald Early, ed., *The Muhammad Ali Reader* (Hopewell, N.J.: Ecco Press, 1998);

Donald Hall, *Fathers Playing Catch with Sons: Essays on Sport, Mostly Baseball* (San Francisco: North Point, 1985);

David Wolf, *Foul! The Connie Hawkins Story* (New York: Holt, Rinehart & Winston, 1972);

Christy Mathewson, *Pitching in a Pinch; or, Baseball from the Inside* (New York & London: Putnam, 1912);

Jim Brosnan, *The Long Season* (New York: Harper, 1960);

H. G. Bissinger, *Friday Night Lights: A Town, a Team, and a Dream* (Reading, Mass.: Addison-Wesley, 1990).

Books for Further Reading

Early, Gerald, ed. *The Muhammad Ali Reader.* Hopewell, N.J.: Ecco Press, 1998.

Einstein, Charles, ed. *The Fireside Book of Baseball,* fourth edition. New York: Simon & Schuster, 1987.

Einstein, ed. *The Second Fireside Book of Baseball.* New York: Simon & Schuster, 1958.

Einstein, ed. *The Third Fireside Book of Baseball.* New York: Simon & Schuster, 1968.

Goldman, Richard P., ed. *Sportswriters' Choice: Their Best Stories.* New York: Barnes, 1958.

Graber, Ralph S., ed. *The Baseball Reader.* New York: Barnes, 1951.

Halberstam, David, ed. *The Best American Sports Writing of the Century.* Boston: Houghton Mifflin, 1999.

Heinz, W. C., ed. *The Fireside Book of Boxing.* New York: Simon & Schuster, 1961.

Kahn, Roger. *Memories of Summer: When Baseball Was an Art, and Writing about It a Game.* New York: Hyperion Press, 1997.

McDonough, Will, Peter King, Paul Zimmerman, and others. *The NFL Century: The Complete Story of the National Football League, 1920–2000.* New York: Smithmark, 1999.

Meany, Tom, ed. *Collier's Greatest Sports Stories.* New York: Barnes, 1955.

Newcombe, Jack, ed. *The Fireside Book of Football.* New York: Simon & Schuster, 1964.

Novak, Michael. *The Joy of Sports: End Zones, Bases, Baskets, Balls, and the Consecration of the American Spirit,* revised edition. Lanham, Md.: Madison, 1994.

Orodenker, Richard. *The Writers' Game: Baseball Writing in America.* New York: Twayne / London: Prentice Hall International, 1996.

Schoor, Gene, ed. *A Treasury of Notre Dame Football.* New York: Funk & Wagnalls, 1962.

Schwed, Peter, and Allison Danzig, eds. *The Fireside Book of Tennis.* New York: Simon & Schuster, 1972.

Schwed and Herbert Warren Wind, eds. *Great Stories from the World of Sport,* 3 volumes. New York: Simon & Schuster, 1958.

Smith, Red, ed. *Press Box: Red Smith's Favorite Sports Stories.* New York: Norton, 1976.

Thorn, John, ed. *The Armchair Book of Baseball.* New York: Collier / Toronto: Maxwell Macmillan Canada / New York: Maxwell Macmillan International, 1992.

Thorn and David Reuther, eds. *The Armchair Quarterback.* New York: Scribners, 1982.

Trudell, Dennis, ed. *Full Court: A Literary Anthology of Basketball.* New York: Breakaway Books, 1996.

Tygiel, Jules, ed. *The Jackie Robinson Reader: Perspectives on an American Hero.* New York: Dutton, 1997.

Wind, Herbert Warren, ed. *The Complete Golfer.* New York: Simon & Schuster, 1954.

Wind, ed. *The Realm of Sport: A Classic Collection of the World's Great Sporting Events and Personalities as Recorded by the Most Distinguished Writers.* New York: Simon & Schuster, 1966.

Contributors

David Ball	*Cincinnati, Ohio*
Robert M. Boynton	*University of California, San Diego*
Ron Briley	*Albuquerque, New Mexico*
Robert Cole	*University of Missouri at Kansas City*
Scott A. G. M. Crawford	*Eastern Illinois University*
Bernard J. Crowley	*Bridgeport, Connecticut*
John Curtis	*San Diego, California*
James B. Dworkin	*Purdue University*
Rob Edelman	*Amsterdam, New York*
Sarah Geis	*Indiana University*
Steven P. Gietschier	*The Sporting News*
Dennis Gildea	*Springfield College*
Adam R. Hornbuckle	*Alexandria, Virginia*
James C. Kaufman	*Yale University*
Kevin Kerrane	*University of Delaware*
Robert Klein	*Editorial Board,* Nine
Bill Knight	*Western Illinois University*
Martin J. Manning	*United States Information Agency*
Joe Marren	*Business First of Buffalo*
Michael Marsh	Chicago Reader
Jack Morris	*West Chester, Pennsylvania*
Richard Orodenker	*Penn State Abington*
William J. Plott	The Birmingham News
Kelly E. Rusinack	*Dunbar, Pennsylvania*
David Sanders	*Carlsbad, California*
Raymond Schmidt	*College Football Historical Society*
Leverett T. Smith Jr.	*North Carolina Wesleyan College*
Lyle Spatz	*Edgewater, Maryland*
Joel Sternberg	*Saint Xavier University*
Nate Stone	*University of California at Berkeley*
Edward J. Tassinari	*Scarsdale, New York*
Stew Thornley	*Roseville, Minnesota*
George Tuttle	*Library of Hattiesburg, Petal, and Forrest County*
James A. Vlasich	*Southern Utah University*
Jerry J. Wright	*Penn State University*
Jack Ziegler	*Cochise College*

Cumulative Index

Dictionary of Literary Biography, Volumes 1-241
Dictionary of Literary Biography Yearbook, 1980-2000
Dictionary of Literary Biography Documentary Series, Volumes 1-19
Concise Dictionary of American Literary Biography, Volumes 1-7
Concise Dictionary of British Literary Biography, Volumes 1-8
Concise Dictionary of World Literary Biography, Volumes 1-4

Cumulative Index

DLB before number: *Dictionary of Literary Biography,* Volumes 1-241
Y before number: *Dictionary of Literary Biography Yearbook,* 1980-2000
DS before number: *Dictionary of Literary Biography Documentary Series,* Volumes 1-19
CDALB before number: *Concise Dictionary of American Literary Biography,* Volumes 1-7
CDBLB before number: *Concise Dictionary of British Literary Biography,* Volumes 1-8
CDWLB before number: *Concise Dictionary of World Literary Biography,* Volumes 1-4

A

C

D

E

F

H

I

J

K

L

N

O

P

Q

R

S

U

V

W

X

Y

Z

ISBN 0-7876-4658-X
90000
9 780787 646585